The Franco-Prussian War Volume 1
H.M. Hozier

THE Franco-Prussian War

PART I. INTRODUCTORY.

CHAPTER I.

Perception of Cause and Effect in History—Prussia and German Unity—France and Revolution—The Treaty of Vienna—Its inefficiency—France under Louis Philippe—The revolutionary spirit in Italy and Spain—Russia and Turkey—Austria and Prussia—Congress of Laybach—Congress of Verona—French Interference in Spain—English Recognition of South American Free States—Temporary Suppression of Revolts—Rise and Independence of Greece—Russian Influence—The Czar Alexander I. and the Holy Alliance—Capture of Missolonghi—Battle of Navarino—War of Czar Nicholas with Turkey—Treaty of Adrianople—Erection of Belgium into an Independent Kingdom, Prince Leopold of Saxe Coburg king—General Recognition by Treaty of 1839—Reforms in England in Taxation, Criminal Law, Religious Disabilities, Parliamentary Representation, Municipal Corporations, Poor-law, Charities, Free Trade, Irish Land Tenure, Education of the People—Constitutions given to British Colonies—Wars, Colonial, Indian, and Crimean—Revolution in Europe in 1848—Action and Reaction of Opinion—Radicalism, Chartism, Socialism, Republicanism—10th April in London—Lord Palmerston—Switzerland—Cracow—Metternich—Italy—Pope Pius IX., his Amnesty, Reforms, Dangers—Rome a Revolutionary Centre—Leopold Grand Duke of Tuscany—Charles Albert King of Piedmont and Sardinia—Austrian influence—Occupation of Ferrara—Ferment among Italians—The Cry of 'Independence of Italy'—Guizot's Policy—English Policy—Lord Minto's Mission—Demonstrations at Turin, Lucca, Rome, Naples—Concession of a Liberal Constitution by the King of Naples—Increased Excitement—Prevalence of the Revolution throughout Italy—Parliamentary Government in France—Charges of Corruption—Foreign Policy—Electoral Reform—Banquets—King's Speech, December, 1847—Stubbornness of Louis Philippe—24th February, 1848—Republican Manoeuvres—Soldiers and National Guard—King's Unwillingness to shed Blood—Guizot's Resignation—Thiers—Odillon Barrot—Abdication of Louis Philippe—His Flight to England—Another Exile in London buys a Newspaper—French Republic—Lamartine—National Assembly—Organization of Labour—Insurrection of June—Four Days' Battle—Four Thousand Barricades—General Cavaignac Dictator—French Intervention at Rome—Assassination of Rossi—Roman Republic—Flight of the Pope—War in Lombardy—Radetzky—Battle of Novara—Abdication of Charles Albert—Restoration of Austrian Supremacy—War in Hungary—All Germany in Revolt—National Unity—King Frederic William at Berlin—The 'Vor-Parlament' at Frankfort—General Collapse of Revolutionary Projects.

POSTERITY will judge far more easily and accurately than the present generation possibly can, the relation of cause and effect, in the series of events culminating this year, 1870, in the tremendous struggle of nations on the banks of the Rhine. After the lapse of ages, the occurrences of a century are narrated in a few pregnant sentences, stating what was the germ, growth, and culmination of one or two fecund ideas, one or two national aspirations. The present decade, so memorable in Prussian history, commenced a hundred years after the triumphs of Frederic the Great in the Seven Years' War (1756-63). That far-off indication of Prussia's military power marked her as the leader of Germany, and the humiliations she endured at the hands of the first Napoleon served only to intensify in her a disposition to restore the German race to the honour and dignity which is its due. On the other hand, the revolutionary ideas which in France and neighbouring states produced astounding results, both for good and evil, eighty years ago, re-appeared in great force in the European uprisings of 1848. Again the French people, after a vain effort at self-government and liberty of action, yielded to the despotic sway of personal government, while the Germans strove for national unity with a national Parliament, also in vain. Yet the patient Germanic spirit, abiding its time, looked forward hopefully and eagerly to the day when unity should endow the nation with commanding strength. To accomplish this great end many sacrifices were necessary, and much boldness, both civil and political, in the leaders. Above all, the elimination of foreign and heterogeneous elements from the national life was essential. France under the second Empire, as the child of Revolution, had raised the cry of "nationalities," and by a rude stroke at Austrian and papal power had brought about the unity of Italy. Germany, the seat of learning and of the highest civilisation, sighed at its own confederated impotence. There it lay, rich in all the elements of political greatness, but unable to combine them by reason of its division into petty principalities and dukedoms. The national aspirations pointed to the welding of these parts into one solid whole; but a great leader was wanting to give form and vitality to these aspirations. At length came the hour and the man. Count von Bismarck was made prime minister and minister for foreign affairs to the king of Prussia. He had deeply pondered all the intricate problems which the state of Germany presented. With profound insight he saw the causes of national weakness and laboured assiduously to remove them. With his one object in view, and with little tenderness for other courts or other princes, he began his great task at the easiest end, by despoiling the Danish crown of its German appanages. After a brief pause, he proceeded to get rid, as far as possible, of the non-German elements existing in the Austrian empire, and by a reconstruction of the German Confederation excluded that Slavonic and Hungarian compound of peoples from Germany proper. His wonderful success in these great achievements waited but the crowning step of a close federal union with the states of South Germany, when the emperor of the French, goaded by the jealous murmurs of his people, who can bear no rival near the throne of their supremacy, rushed into a war that seems destined to complete all Count Bismarck's designs, and make Germany the chief military power of Europe.

Of this general outline a few explanatory details will be necessary. The grand product of the Revolutionary and Napoleonic wars which ended in 1814 was that celebrated instrument, the Treaty of Vienna. Such at least it seemed in the eyes of men who do not observe the under-currents of history. It has been the vain boast of the admirers of this document that it preserved the peace of Europe for forty years; it had in truth very little to do with preserving the peace of Europe, and unquestionably it failed to secure the observance of its own provisions for even half that time. Even while the plenipotentiaries were seated round the Congress table, an ominous interruption compelled them to throw down their protocols and provisos, and hasten to their respective courts. The great disturber of the equilibrium which the Congress was attempting to restore had broken loose from Elba. His name once more inflamed the martial ardour of France, and he cast his last bloody die for empire on the field of Waterloo, forfeiting for ever his liberty and crown. The Congress was resumed—the Treaty solemnly signed and ratified. Its leading provision, in accordance with the ostensible purpose of the allied powers in making war against the usurper, was that the elder branch of the Bourbons should reign over France. This arrangement made no allowance for the vast change wrought in the French people, morally, intellectually, and socially, by the Revolution; and after a painful duration of fifteen years it crumbled into dust before the three July days of revolution in 1830.

Louis Philippe, the elected citizen king, with all his merits and accomplishments, did not suit the excitable nation over which he reigned for eighteen years. His government by party, in regular constitutional form, with a Right and a Left, a Centre, Right Centre, and Left Centre, was not adapted to the genius of Frenchmen. "La Gloire" seemed wanting in this system, and Beranger was still trumpeting forth in his songs the renown of their famous Corsican soldier. The name of Napoleon Bonaparte was a name of power when, in a feverish fit which seized them in February, 1848, the populace of Paris drove away the able and respectable family of Orleans, and prepared a way to the throne for Louis Napoleon Bonaparte. The French, endowed with so much keen common sense in the transactions of private life, are lamentably under the sway of their imagination in matters of public concern. Thus came about another grievous infraction of the Treaty of Vienna, which had decreed in the most stringent manner that no Bonaparte should again reign in Europe.

The revolutionary spirit that wrought these changes in France, and rent in twain the artificial instrument elaborated by the Congress, had been for years fermenting in all the countries of Europe. Organized by the Carbonari and other secret societies, it broke out in Italy and Spain with great violence in 1821, and virtually reduced King Ferdinand to a nonentity. At the same time Greece rose against her Turkish rulers, and sought to establish her independence. These events excited lively apprehensions at all the courts of Europe. France, in defence of royalty, would suppress the revolution in Spain, and put down the *communeros* (communists) and *descamisados* (shirtless) at all cost. Russia was not sorry to see Turkey embarrassed by the Greek insurrection, and England was favourable to the cause of liberty in both countries. Austria, in the person of her foreign minister, represented the principle of pure absolutism, and Prussia held a somewhat neutral position, siding now with Austria, anon with Russia. Austria with a strong hand suppressed the rising liberties of Italy, and at the Congress of Laybach (January, 1821) concluded arrangements which gave her virtual possession of the fairest parts of that peninsula. Another congress was erelong proposed to settle the difficulties of the hour, and in 1822 representatives of the various powers met at Verona. Divergence of opinion soon made itself apparent at this assembly. France, with her traditional jealousy of any foreign influence in Spain, would interfere in the Spanish question, and would allow no one else to do so. England deprecated interference, but the French views were supported by Russia, Austria, and Prussia. England desired the recognition as independent states of the revolted Spanish colonies in South America, which none of the other powers would agree to without the consent of the king of Spain. The result was that the duke of Wellington, the English plenipotentiary, refused to sign the *proces verbaux* of the conference, and the French government gained its point. The hero of Waterloo, on his way home, had an interview with Louis XVIII., and well nigh persuaded that monarch to abandon the line of policy marked out by the Verona Congress. But the current of public opinion setting the other way, the Duc d'Angoulême, at the head of a hundred thousand men, entered Spain on April 5, 1823, for the purpose of defending its Bourbon king against his own subjects. French soldiers once more marched along roads which they had disputed mile by mile with the soldiers of Wellington ten years before, between the Bidassoa and Madrid. This event excited not only lively scenes in the French Chamber, from which Manuel, an opposition member, was forcibly dragged by the gend'armes, but called forth expressions of loud indignation in the English House of Commons, where Mr. Brougham, in allusion to the help proffered to France by Russia and the German Powers, uttered the following prognostication:— "I say that if the king of France calls in the modern Teutones, or the modern Scythians, to assist him in this unholy war, judgment will that moment go forth against him and his family, and the dynasty of Gaul will be changed at once and for ever."

For all this, however, the French were successful in suppressing the revolution, and restoring Ferdinand unshackled to his throne. When the Duc d'Angoulême had returned in triumph to Paris, the English government, considering that they had sustained a defeat, carried out the measure they advocated at the Congress of Verona, and formally recognized the independence of the revolted Spanish colonies in South America. Spain "with the Indies" had been a power formidable to England. By finally separating from her "the Indies" she would be no longer formidable. "I called the new world into existence," said Mr. Canning, melo-dramatically, "to redress the balance of the old." Curiously enough, Châteaubriand, who was then the French minister for foreign affairs, has admitted in his memoirs, that his government had a plan for "breaking through or modifying the Treaty of Vienna, by establishing Bourbon monarchies in South America."

Poor Treaty of Vienna! its power for keeping the peace of Europe for forty years seems to have been but small.

Early in 1821, and not many months after the outbreak of the Spanish revolution, the Greeks, after four centuries of submission, rose against their masters the Turks. This insurrection was fomented by a secret society of "Hetairists," and supported by the friends of Greece in various parts of Europe calling themselves Philhellenes. Capo d'Istria, a Greek, who occupied the post of private secretary to Alexander, emperor of Russia, was a member of the society of Hetairists. The English poet Byron was an eminent Philhellene. Bound together by community of interest, religious and secular, it was supposed that Russia gave secret aid to this movement; but it is on re-cord that the Czar had so great a horror of insurrection, and felt so completely bound by the principles of the Holy Alliance, that he refused altogether to countenance the Greeks in their rebellion against the Sublime Porte. Not until his death and the accession of his more ambitious brother, the Emperor Nicholas, did the Greeks succeed in establishing that independence on behalf of which they had exhibited heroism surpassing the dreams of romance, and had committed atrocities exceeded only by the cruelties of their fierce Moslem oppressors. In 1822 the provisional Greek government had made an earnest application to the Congress at Verona, to be admitted into the European family of nations, and to be taken under the protection of the Western powers; but the members of the Holy Alliance, so powerful in that Congress, rejected the application of rebels, insisting upon the maintenance of sovereign rights even when symbolized by the domination of the crescent over the cross—the figure of Islam trampling upon the church of Christ. Four years' prolongation of the contest however, and the awful scenes which characterized the fall of Missolonghi into the hands of the Turks, fully aroused the sympathies of western Europe. The representatives of the people having signed a solemn act, in virtue of which "the Greek nation placed the sacred deposit of its liberty, independence, and political existence, under the absolute protection of Great Britain," Mr. Canning took steps to make the desired protection effective. Terms of accommodation were arranged at a secret interview held in January, 1826, on an island near Hydra, between Mr. Stratford Canning (the present Lord Stratford de Redcliffe), British envoy at Constantinople, and Prince Mavrocordato, president of the Greek government. The duke of Wellington, on an embassy of congratulation to the Czar Nicholas on his accession, concluded with the Russian government a convention for the protection of Greece, which was signed on the 4th April, 1826. More than a year of negotiation however elapsed before the treaty between England, France, and Russia was signed (6th July, 1827) for the protection of Greece as an independent state. Meanwhile the Greeks had been reduced to a very low condition by Ibrahim Pasha and his Egyptian troops, and the Sultan, naturally indignant at the interference of the three allied powers, made preparations for resistance. A combined fleet of English, French, and Russian men-of-war, in all twenty-six sail, entered the Bay of Navarino, on the 20th October, 1827, and destroyed the Turkish fleet, while Ibrahim Pasha was away doing his best to exterminate the inhabitants of the Morea and render their homes desolate. The independence of Greece was secured by the battle of Navarino, but the pride of the Sultan and his divan was not subdued. Stiff-necked as ever, the indomitable tone of his reply to the allied ministers after his misfortune was worthy of a better cause, "My positive, absolute, definitive, unchangeable, eternal answer is, that the Sublime Porte does not accept any proposition regarding the Greeks, and will persist in its own will regarding them even to the day of the last judgment." That day, so rashly appealed to, seemed about to dawn upon Turkey in the war which shortly ensued between her and Russia. The contest bears little upon the questions agitating Europe in this year, 1870, excepting as showing the direction of Russian ambition, and as giving England a reason for watching the progress of that colossal power in the East. The war broke out in 1828, after the conclusion of a war with Persia, in which the Czar had been triumphant. After a series of brilliant successes, the Moslems were again humbled, and Russian superiority acknowledged in a treaty dictated by Marshal Diebitsch at Adrianople itself, in the closing month of 1829.

When Greece, in 1830, assumed the form of a constitutional monarchy, its throne was offered to Prince Leopold of Saxe-Coburg, the widowed husband of Princess Charlotte of England. He declined the honour, but accepted a similar proposal made in June, 1831, on behalf of the people of Belgium. By the settlement of 1815 this country formed part of the kingdom of the

Netherlands. Dutchmen and Belgians, however, found themselves but ill-mated; and on the 4th October, 1830, another infringement of the great treaty took place by the secession of the Belgians from the kingdom of Holland, and the formation of a provisional government with the sanction of Great Britain and France. The crown was offered to and refused by the Duc de Nemours, second son of Louis Philippe king of the French, and was finally bestowed upon Leopold. Some years elapsed before the recognition of this new and prosperous little kingdom was made by all the great powers. On the 19th April, 1839, a treaty was signed at London which established peaceful relations between King Leopold I. and the sovereign of the Netherlands, and obtained the recognition of the kingdom of Belgium by all the states of Europe. It is by this treaty that Great Britain deems herself morally bound to protect the integrity of the state, and her neutrality when neighbouring kingdoms are at war. The special treaties of 1870 between England on one side, and France and Prussia severally on the other, extend only to the period of one year after the conclusion of peace between those belligerent powers.

The spirit of revolution, it will be seen, was not effectively restrained on the continent of Europe by the virtue of the Holy Alliance. In England that spirit accomplished changes and improvements of great national and social importance, but by gentler and more benignant courses than those employed in France, Italy, Spain, and Greece. The heavy burdens of taxation entailed by a long and costly war were gradually lightened, the abuses of a paper currency were restrained, and trade was developed. A criminal law of Draconian severity was rendered more humane, while a corrupt and inefficient system of police was replaced by one that for more than forty years has fully justified the change. Gross injustice to a large section of the community was removed by the passing, after some violent agitation, of the Roman Catholic Emancipation Bill, and some years later by a law relieving Jews from disabilities laid upon them by theological prejudice. This class of legislation was carried on by the regulation of ecclesiastical incomes in the church of England, by means of a standing commission; by the abolition of tests, and quite recently by the disestablishment of a Protestant state church in Ireland, a Roman Catholic country. In order to achieve most of these beneficent ameliorations of the law, it was essential to improve, first of all, the instrument of legislation itself. The Reform Act of 1832 abolished a large number of pocket boroughs, and gave representatives to large towns and important centres of trade which had been left unrepresented. By the later Act for reforming the representation of the people passed in 1867—68, the constituencies were indefinitely enlarged by the extension of the franchise to every rate-payer, and to lodgers. The Parliaments under the first Reform Act accomplished great things. Besides the measures mentioned above, there were the final abolition of the slave trade, the reform of the municipal corporations, the new poor law, the charity commission, the repeal of the corn laws, and the adoption of free trade with respect to almost every article of export and import. The partial substitution of direct for indirect taxation in the form of an income-tax, is not yet acknowledged as a public benefit with entire unanimity. The abolition of the newspaper stamp, and of the duty on paper, increased in an extraordinary degree the scope and influence of that great educator the press. The first Parliament under the new Reform Act has already performed great tasks:—The disestablishment of the church in Ireland, the adaptation of the law of land tenure in that country to the circumstances of the people, and finally, the education of the people of every parish by rate-supported schools. The adoption of the last-named measure is a remarkable proof of the progress made by public opinion in the direction of religious tolerance, and as an indication of the enlightenment and elevation of mind of the House of Commons, serves to rebut the charge of "Philistinism" so conceitedly brought forward against Englishmen by certain writers of the day.

Legislation has also been most beneficially employed in conferring upon the colonies of Great Britain free constitutions of their own, by which they will be fitted to stand alone when the time shall come for snapping asunder the slender thread that binds them to the mother country. The discovery of gold in many of these distant dependencies gave a vigorous impulse to the tide of emigration from home. As many as seven million emigrants have quitted the United Kingdom since 1815, the greater number directing their steps to the boundless and fertile territories of the United States.

All the wars in which England has engaged since the Congress of Vienna have been, with the exception of Navarino, the China, and the Crimean wars, on behalf of her colonies or her Indian possessions. The Kafirs at the Cape of Good Hope, the Maoris in New Zealand, the Affghans of Northern India, the warriors of Scinde, the inhabitants of Burmah, and most formidable of all, the mutinous Sepoys of Hindostan, have all in turn come into deadly collision with England's military power, and have all been compelled to yield. After the suppression of the Indian mutiny of 1857, the government of that vast dependency, which had been vested in the East Indian Company, under the control of a government board, was formally transferred by Act of Parliament, in 1858, to the crown. The war with China, not highly honourable in its commencement, had the noteworthy effect of giving to Europeans tolerably free access to that jealously guarded country, and of opening up a commerce of yearly increasing magnitude. The Crimean war was a development of the Eastern question, in which England became entangled through a careful jealousy of Russia's power in the East. In 1854 was seen the singular spectacle of a deadly quarrel on account of Turkey, by the three powers who twenty-seven years previously united at Navarino to secure the infant kingdom of Greece against the oppression of Turkey. England and France stood forward as protectors of the quondam oppressor against his powerful and ambitious assailant, Czar Nicholas. All the belligerents suffered severely in this war, which lasted more than two years, the heavy losses sustained by the Russians, and the fatal discovery made by the Czar, that his apparently boundless resources were cankered and eaten away by official corruption, broke the proud sovereign's heart and induced his successor, the Emperor Alexander II., to sue for peace. The main result of the war was the dissipation of an illusive and vague dread that lay like an incubus on the mind of Europe, to the effect that the "Colossus of the North" was irresistible. Germany especially was supposed to be paralyzed by this tremendous overhanging power. The hollowness of these vast pretensions was made manifest in the Crimean war; but the Western Powers had to pay a high price for the dismissal of their vain fears, and for the knowledge that the dreaded Colossus had his weak points. The principal gainer by this war was England's ally, the emperor of the French, who acquired by it that which he so much wanted—prestige.

It will now be necessary to recur to the rise of this prince to power, and to the violent disturbances which shook Europe like an earthquake in 1848, before proceeding to explain the complication of German politics in Holstein, Austria, and Prussia, and the vigorous development of the last-named power, which has excited the jealousy of other nations, and has brought it into such violent collision with military France.

During the thirty years succeeding the peace of 1815 a new generation of men had come into existence in Europe, who felt little of the misery produced by the revolutionary wars, and who yet learned by hearsay and by reading what a glorious struggle had taken place on behalf of the rights of man. By the Treaty of Vienna an attempt was made to restore that balance of power which had kept Europe steady during the greater part of the eighteenth century, and had served to protect small states as well as large, with the notable exception of Silesia, which was annexed by Prussia, and of Poland, which was partitioned. Under the old system nations were too exclusively identified with their nominal rulers, and the interests of the empire, kingdom, or duchy were too liberally presumed to be the same as the interests of the emperor, king, or duke. The revolution of 1789 was a protest against this presumption; but a protest of so violent a kind that reaction was inevitable, and the triumph of the sans culottes at Jemappes led ultimately to the Holy Alliance of the absolute monarchs of Europe. The first great rebound of public opinion from this union of absolutists brought about the revolution of July, 1830, in France. The next swing of the political pendulum produced the tremendous concussion, or rather series of concussions, of 1848.

All Europe was convulsed. Under the several standards of Radicalism, Chartism, Socialism, Communism, Republicanism, the masses of the people, with one consent, rose against their rulers, and demanded a new programme of life. In England the forms of regulated freedom permitted the Chartists to make a harmless show of strength, that evaporated with the display. On occasion of the monster procession (10th April, 1848) which bore the people's charter, in the shape of a huge petition to the House of Commons, a counter demonstration, equally harmless, was made by the easier classes of society, who took the oath and staff of special constables for the maintenance of the peace of London. Among these improvised officials stood, according to authentic report, Lord Palmerston and Louis Napoleon Bonaparte. Anti-chartist as Lord Palmerston showed himself at home, he was radical enough abroad. Only a few months before this, at the close of 1847, he had, as English secretary for foreign affairs, incurred the resentment of the potentates of Europe by his open encouragement of the Radicals of Switzerland, who triumphed over the reactionists in a civil war. Words written at this time by the Vaudois deputy, M. Druey, expressed the thoughts of many thousands of his contemporaries. Addressing a French radical, he said:—"We sympathize with you, and you sympathize with us. The time has now arrived when it is necessary, on both sides the Jura, to transfer from the region of ideas to that of action the great principles of liberty, equality, fraternity, which constitute the happiness of men, as well as the glory of societies." Here was the watchword of the insurgent nations. To the credit of Switzerland it must be said, that she alone, of all competitors in the race for freedom, achieved anything like a realization of the great principles of liberty and equality. Meanwhile the rupture of the *entente cordiale* between England and France, in consequence of the Spanish marriages, gave Austria an opportunity of absorbing the republic of Cracow, the last remnant of independent Poland. Metternich, the Austrian minister, seemed supreme in European affairs, and his country at the height of prosperity and power, when suddenly the absolutist system gave way, and the mighty dominion of the emperor of Austria fell gradually to pieces, only to be reconstructed partially, and after many humiliations.

The revolutionary explosion was first heard in Italy, and the hand that applied the spark to the combustible mass of liberalism, which lay ready to receive it, was that of the pope of Rome—Pius IX—after his election in June, 1846. The particulars of this extensive outbreak, as derived from Alison's History, will serve to explain with tolerable accuracy the course taken by the revolutionary eruptions in the other countries of Europe. "The first important act of the new pontiff," says the conservative historian, "was one eminently popular. An amnesty for the large number of persons convicted of political offences was greatly desired. Yielding alike to his own inclination and the general wish, Pius IX. proclaimed the desired act of oblivion, and the joyous news was early on the morning of the 16th July placarded all over Rome. No words can paint the transports which ensued. The prison doors were opened; their country was restored to 1500 captives or exiles. From morning to night crowds of all ranks and professions hastened to the Quirinal to express to the holy father the unbounded joy which the act of mercy had diffused. Twice in the space of a few hours the pope gave his blessing to successive multitudes which filled the place, and on their knees received the sacred benediction; and as a third crowd arrived from the more distant parts of the city, he came out, contrary to etiquette, after nightfall, and by torchlight again bestowed it amidst tears of joy. A spontaneous illumination lighted up the whole city."

The general hopes thus awakened were not damped by the first administrative acts of the new pope. On the 8th November three commissions were issued, composed of prelates and laymen, to report on the reform required in the criminal procedure, on the amelioration of the municipal system, and on the repression of vagrant mendicity, and various decrees were shortly after published for the establishment of primary schools, agricultural institutions, hospitals for the poor, the reorganization of the army, and that of the ancient and far-famed university of Bologna.

The holy father speedily found himself beset with difficulties inseparable from the new state of affairs—difficulties which were much enhanced by the personal character of the pope, who yielded alternately to the solicitations of opposite parties, and deprived government of all real consideration by taking from it the character of consistency.

The dangers of the situation were much augmented in the close of 1846, by the great confluence of refugees who, taking advantage of the amnesty, flocked to Rome, and brought with them not only the liberalism of their own country, but the concentrated spirit of revolution from all other states. The Eternal City became the headquarters of the movement from all parts of Europe. Liberals from France, Spain, Poland, Germany, the Austrian states—all flocked thither, as at once to an asylum from the persecution of the governments which they had offended, and a central point from which they could renew their machinations for ulterior aggressions. No practical or useful reforms by the Papal government could keep pace with the heated imaginations of this band of enthusiasts. They openly aspired, not merely to reform the Holy See, but to subvert the government in all the adjoining states, and realize the dream of a united Italian Republic, one and indivisible.

Several also of the temporal princes of Italy embarked in a liberal policy. Leopold, grand-duke of Tuscany, was the first to adventure on the inviting but perilous path. That beautiful duchy had long been more lightly and equitably governed than any of the other Italian states, and it embraced a greater number of highly educated and enlightened persons. To them a certain intervention in the affairs of government had long been the subject of desire, and the moderation of their temperament and extent of their information pointed them out as peculiarly fitted for this enjoyment. Their aspirations were now in a great measure realized. Leopold emancipated the press from its shackles, and adopted other reforms which were acceptable to his subjects.

Sardinia also shared in the movement. Charles Albert, who in early youth had fought by the side of the Liberals in 1823, looked to that party alone for the support of his favourite project of turning the Austrians out of Italy. To conciliate them during the general ferment of men's minds in the peninsula consequent on the amnesty and reform of Pius IX., he commenced some changes, and promised more. Seeing that Sardinia was the power which could alone in the peninsula face the Austrian bayonets, and which must necessarily take the lead in any efforts to assert the independence of Italy, these symptoms excited the utmost interest in the inhabitants of the whole country. The hopes that had been excited by the general enthusiasm, and the direction it was taking, were clearly evinced by what occurred in the beginning of winter. On a given night in December bale-fires were simultaneously lighted on the principal heights of the Apennines, which reflected the ruddy glow from the mountains of Bologna to the extreme point of the Calabrian peninsula.

Meanwhile the pope grew alarmed at the storm he had raised, and on the 12th June, 1847, a *Motu Proprio* appeared, which was soon after followed by a more detailed exposition of the views of the Papal government. "The holy father," said this document, "has not beheld without grief the doctrines and the attempts of some excited persons, who aim at introducing into the measures of government maxims subversive of the elevated and pacific character of the vicar of Jesus Christ, and to awaken in the people ideas and hopes inconsistent with the pontifical government." These decided words seemed a mortal stroke to the exalted Liberals; they immediately lost all confidence in the pope, who, they declared, had fallen entirely under the Austrian influence; and to the enthusiastic transports which had signalized his accession a year before succeeded a cold indifference.

Metternich and the cabinet of Vienna made a movement professedly to support the government of the pope, really to terminate the ascendancy of the Liberals in his councils, which threatened to prove so dangerous to Austrian rule in Italy. By the sixty-third article of the Treaty of Vienna the Austrians were authorized to keep a garrison in the citadel of Ferrara; but the custody of the gates of the town was still intrusted to the pontifical troops. Now, however, a more decided demonstration was deemed necessary. On the 10th August a division of Austrian troops crossed the Po, and took entire possession of the fortress, threatening to put to the sword whoever offered any resistance.

The Papal liberal government, assured of the support of France, protested energetically against this occupation, and the general feeling underwent a change attended with important effects. The holy father was no longer regarded as the head of the revolutionary, but of the national party; and to the cry of "Long live reform!" succeeded the still more thrilling one of "Italian independence!" which soon spread beyond the Roman states; animating all the states of the peninsula, and embracing numbers of the higher and educated classes, who, albeit opposed to organic changes in the form of government, were yet passionately desirous of emancipating the country from the degrading state of tutelage in which it had so long been kept to the northern powers.

In Turin especially, at the cry "Independence of Italy!" a general enthusiasm seized all classes, and Charles Albert let drop hints that the time was not far distant when he would draw his sword for the "Sacred cause."

In France M. Guizot's policy at this period was directed to the double object of preventing an explosion of revolutionary violence in Italy, and of taking away all pretext for Austrian interference. We are at peace and on good terms with Austria, he said, and we wish to continue on such; for a war with Austria is a general war and universal revolution.

The English government resolved to send out a confidential diplomatic agent to examine the state of the peninsula, and give such counsel to its various governments as might best tend to bring them in safety through the dangers by which they were surrounded. Lord Minto, who was selected for the mission, was looked upon as the champion of Italian independence; manifestations of popular feeling preceded or followed him wherever he went; Turin, Genoa, Florence, Rome, Naples, Sicily, had no sooner hailed his arrival than they became violently agitated; and at Milan the people broke out into open riot amidst cries of "Down with the Austrians!" which were only repressed after collision and bloodshed.

At Turin the king issued a very liberal programme of the changes which the government were about to introduce into the internal administration of the kingdom. These concessions produced universal transports; the popularity of Charles Albert equalled that which Pius IX. had enjoyed a year before; the whole capital was spontaneously illuminated for several nights; he could not leave his palace without being surrounded by an enthusiastic crowd; and when later in the autumn he set out for Genoa, the greater part of the inhabitants of both cities attended him with joyous acclamations, both on his departure and return. Nor did the acts of the sovereign belie these flattering appearances; for he communicated at this time to the French government his resolution, in the event of the pope requiring his assistance against the Austrians, not to refuse his armed support.

A demonstration in favour of Liberal opinions and Italian independence in Lucca, brought that beautiful little duchy into unison with Tuscany, much to the joy of the inhabitants of both duchies.

It was in the midst of the effervescence caused by these events that Lord Minto arrived at Rome, and at once became the object of a popular ovation. A few days after his arrival a vast crowd, which assembled in the Corso, suddenly entered the *Piazza di Spagna*, and soon filled the inner court of the Hotel Melza, where Lord Minto resided. Cries of "Long live Lord Minto!" "Long live Italian Independence!" were heard on all sides. White handkerchiefs were seen to wave in reply from the windows of the hotel, and augmented the general enthusiasm. The Radical journals in France immediately published an inflated account of the event, accompanied by a statement that England had openly put itself at the head of the league for promoting Italian independence; and the appearance of some leading Liberals in Lord Minto's box at the opera a few nights after, when they were received with thunders' of applause, dispelled all doubt in the minds of the ardent patriots of the truth of the report.

Seriously alarmed at the turn which affairs were taking, which threatened not only a revolutionary convulsion in Italy, but the lighting up of a general conflagration in Europe, M. Rossi, the French ambassador, in several conferences with the pope, endeavoured to convince his Holiness of the necessity of admitting some laymen into his cabinet, and after considerable difficulty succeeded in extorting this concession from the monopolizing ecclesiastics. At the same time he used his utmost endeavours to point out to the Liberals the danger which they were incurring, not only for their country, but for Europe, by rushing headlong into a war with Austria, with the feeble warlike elements which were alone at their disposal.

The times were past, however, when these warnings could produce any effect. The train had been kid, the torch applied, and the explosion was inevitable. Power had changed hands at Rome. It had slipped from the feeble grasp of the pope and the cardinals, and been seized by the hands of violent men, destitute alike of information or prudence. Hardly a day passed without something occurring which demonstrated the deplorable prostration of government, and the entire contempt into which the pope, recently so popular, had fallen.

At Naples, whither Lord Minto proceeded from Rome, the king outstripped all the concessions of the other Italian sovereigns by the publication of a constitution, by a decree which removed nearly all the restrictions on the liberty of the press, and by a large amnesty for political offenders.

It is difficult for a stranger, especially in a free country to the north of the Alps, to form a conception of the sensation which these decrees, following each other in rapid succession, and all breathing so liberal a spirit, produced in Italy. It seemed impossible that the antiquated fabric of superstition and despotism could any longer be maintained in the peninsula, when the most absolute monarch within its bounds had become the first to stretch forth his hand to pull it down.

The cabinets in the centre and northern parts of the country were thunderstruck at the intelligence; but ere long the enthusiasm became so general, the torrent so powerful, that they saw no chance of escape but in yielding to it. Constitutions on the model of that of Naples were speedily published at Turin and Florence. In Rome, even, the extreme difficulty of reconciling the forms and popular powers of a constitutional monarchy with an absolute government based on theocracy, yielded to the same necessity. In a word, Italy, save where kept down by Austrian bayonets, from the base of the Alps to the point of Calabria, was as completely revolutionized, though as yet without the shedding of blood, as France had been by the innovations of the Constituent Assembly.

Meanwhile, in France parliamentary government was undergoing a severe strain. The king as he advanced in years, yielding to the temptations of his position, strove to keep the reins of government more and more in his own hands. His cabinet, which was conservative in politics, seemed a tool in his hands. Rightly or wrongly, it was said that the subserviency of his ministers and the fidelity of the majority in the two Chambers were bought with a price. Charges of peculation and corruption were openly brought against officials, and scandalous trials ensued. The peerage, at the same time, was greatly disgraced in the popular mind on the murder of Marshal Sebastiani's daughter by her own husband, the Duc de Praslin, who had conceived a guilty passion for their children's governess. There was scarcity in the country, also, to stimulate the rising exasperation. The foreign policy of the government, so tender towards Austria, so timid on behalf of the movement in Italy, exposed the king and his ministers to the charge of pusillanimity. "Yes," said Lamartine, "a revolution is approaching, and it is the revolution of contempt."

In this state of things the liberal party then in opposition raised the question of parliamentary reform. The constitutional liberals, with their leader M. Thiers, fondly imagined that the question would be argued within the limits of due parliamentary order, and end in a peaceable party triumph. But the vivacious sections of Communists, Socialists, and Red Republicans had other views, which they resolved audaciously to carry out if opportunity offered. The opportunity was not long in arriving. The approved mode of carrying on a political agitation was by means of banquets in the principal cities, at which leading men delivered orations of more or less power and effect. The speeches, printed in the newspapers, exercised a wide influence. Thus Odillon Barret and Duvergier de Haurane invited the Parisians, at Château Rouge, to return to the pure principles of the July government; while Lamartine, at Macon, set forth in glowing colours the virtues of a beneficent communism. The movement was sufficiently pronounced to require notice in the king's speech at the opening of the Chambers, in December, 1847. "In the midst of the agitation," he said, "which hostile and blind passions have fostered, one conviction has animated and supported me; it is, that we possess in the constitutional monarchy, in the union of the three powers of the state, the most effectual means of surmounting all our difficulties and of providing for all the moral and material interests of our dear country." A long and animated debate on the address ensued. It was moved that the words "hostile and blind," which were repeated in the address, should be left out. The ministry, however, defeated the amendment by a majority of 43, and the Liberals began anew their agitation out of doors. It was determined to hold a great meeting in the capital, at a banquet which had already been forbidden by the police, and the day fixed for it was the 22nd of February. This defiance of the executive gave hopes to the turbulent, which were raised still higher when a monster procession was also agreed upon. The king was firm to obstinacy. "Reform," he said, "meant a change of ministry, and a change of ministry meant war with foreign powers;" that is to say, encouragement of the revolutionary parties in Europe and defiance of the absolute monarchies. The 22nd of February, however, passed with small disturbance, yet enough to induce the government to occupy the streets with soldiers on the 23rd, and to call out the national guard. This force, to which the king was thought to owe his throne, had grown dissatisfied, and some radical leaders persuaded them to take up a position of apparent neutrality between the military and the populace.

That this neutrality was not impartial may be gathered from the following passage in Alison's history:—

"The 23rd February opened upon a city agitated but undecided, ready to obey the strongest impulse, to surrender the direction to whoever had the courage to seize it. The presence of the military in all the principal quarters sufficiently revealed the apprehensions of government—the conduct of the civic force too clearly evinced to which side it would incline. At ten, M. Flocon, a determined revolutionist, entered in haste the office of the *Reforme*, and exclaimed, 'Quick, all clothe yourselves in the uniform of the national guard: never mind whether they are your own or not: intimate to all patriots to do the same. As soon as you are dressed, hasten to the mayor's, calling out, Vive la réforme! Directly you are there, put yourselves at the head of the detachments as they arrive, *and interpose them between the soldiers and the people.* Quick, quick! the Republic is to be had for the taking.' These directions, emanating from the headquarters of the movement, were too faithfully adopted; and the national guard, timid, desirous to avoid a collision and avert the shedding of blood, were in general too happy to follow them. The orders of government being that all the posts should be occupied by the troops of the line and the civic forces jointly, the latter were everywhere on the spot with the soldiers, and, in conformity with their injunction, they constantly interposed between the military and the populace, so as to render any attempt to disperse the assemblages impossible, as no officer would incur the responsibility of engaging in a conflict with the national guard of the capital. Several of the legions openly joined the people, at least in words, and traversed the streets, crying out, 'Vive la réforme!'

The Republic *was* had for the taking. The agitation in the capital became greater every hour, and with it grew the alarm at the Tuileries. The queen having suggested the resignation of M. Guizot, that statesman proudly gave up his office and announced the fact in the Chamber of Deputies. The Liberals and Ultra-liberals received this concession with transports of delight. The former trusted that the battle was over, and that new men and new measures would restore tranquillity. The latter thought there was a chance for establishing their cherished form of government—a republic. The untamed classes of society emerged from their squalid homes and swelled the crowds around the Tuileries, the Palais Bourbon, where the Chambers sat, and the offices of the radical newspapers. Such power as the secret societies possessed was brought into play. The national guard had gone home content and eager to illuminate their houses in honour of victory, when a ragged crowd, armed with sabres and pikes, was led by one Charles Lagrange to the Foreign Office, still occupied by M. Guizot and guarded by a detachment of infantry. Lagrange fired a pistol in the direction of the military, who deeming themselves attacked replied with a volley, which brought down some fifty men. The revolution had begun. All that night Paris continued in a state of frantic excitement. Marshal Bugeand was appointed commander of the forces, and by seven o'clock in the morning of the 24th had taken military possession of the capital. M. Thiers, however, who had succeeded Guizot as prime minister, disapproved of the employment of military force, and requested the withdrawal of the troops. This step, instead of calming, served but to intensify the public excitement. At ten o'clock Thiers resigned office in favour of Odillon Barrot. The king was very unwilling to shed blood. The military, surrounded and pressed upon by the populace, received no orders to fire, and began to fraternize with the mob. A rabble broke into the Palais Royal, and did great damage. Matters grew rapidly worse. In a few hours the reins of government had slipped out of the king's hands. Change of ministers availed nothing. Abdication was mentioned, and the king abdicated; and by one o'clock in the afternoon of that 24th February his discrowned Majesty, with the queen and princesses, quietly escaped from Paris to the sea-coast, on their way to England. Never, perhaps, in the history of the world did so great an event happen so unexpectedly as this sudden fall of Louis Philippe. The news spread like wildfire, and as the newsmen of London were bawling it through the streets of that metropolis it was heard by a lonely refugee there, at the moment he was undergoing the manipulations of his barber. He sprang from his seat to buy the printed message, which Destiny at length had sent to call him to a splendid throne. It was Louis Napoleon Bonaparte, of whom much yet will have to be said. In Paris, after a brave attempt to secure the appointment of the infant Comte de Paris as successor to his grandfather, with his mother, the duchess of Orleans, for regent, a provisional government was formed and the Republic proclaimed.

The republican sentiment, however, as Lamartine, the chief of the provisional government, afterwards admitted, was weak in France. The National Assembly that met on the 4th May, and which was elected by universal suffrage, showed a majority against the socialists and ultra liberals. A vain attempt was made to "organize labour;" but the national workshops established at the public expense developed more idleness than industry in the population. It soon became necessary to abolish these burdensome institutions, which the people were very unwilling to abandon. A most sanguinary struggle in consequence took place in Paris between the populace on the one side, and on the other the executive government, supported by the national guard and the regular soldiery. The contest lasted from the 23rd to the 26th of June, forced the nomination of General Cavaignac to a dictatorship, engaged some fifty thousand men on each side in bloody conflict, and caused the death of about twenty thousand men of all ranks, who had fought for the possession of about four thousand barricades, erected in the different streets of Paris. Never were the fighting qualities of the Parisians more fiercely displayed than in this stubborn effort to destroy each other. The most striking incident of the insurrection was the death of the archbishop of Paris, who was shot while surmounting a barricade, cross in hand, with a view to negotiate an accommodation. General Cavaignac's conduct on this occasion exposed him to blame from both parties. The Red Republicans condemned his resolute suppression of the insurrection, while the moderate party openly accused him of wilful tardiness in attacking the insurgents, when in truth the force at his command was not sufficient to insure victory. He incurred additional unpopularity by acceding to a request, made by the pope, for assistance against his rebellious subjects. The revolution at Rome had been stained by the cruel assassination of M. Rossi as he entered the Chamber of Representatives. He had been ambassador for France at the Papal court, and was induced to accept office as minister of the Interior and of Finance under the pontiff. He meditated many useful reforms, but seeming to be disposed to a compromise with Austria, the national enemy, he was slain by order of the secret societies. The pope fled to Gaeta. A republic was established in Rome, and the assistance of France invoked against it. The conflict between her domestic and foreign policy exhibited by France at this juncture, is to be explained by jealousy of Austria, and the fear lest that power should be beforehand in assuming a protectorate of the pope and his church. Meanwhile Austria had been hotly engaged in strife for the preservation of her power in Lombardy and Venice. The veteran Marshal Radetsky had retreated from Milan before the Italians, under the leadership of Charles Albert, king of Sardinia and Piedmont. But the old soldier after a time avenged this blow by the battle of Novara, at which Charles Albert was humbled to the dust, and the Austrian sway in Lombardy was restored.

On the evening of his defeat, the 23rd March, 1849, the unhappy king of Sardinia abdicated in favour of his son, Victor Emmanuel. "This is my last day," he said; "let me die. I have sacrificed myself to the Italian cause. For it I have exposed my life, that of my children, and my throne. I have failed, and remain the sole obstacle to a peace now necessary to the state." Having said these words, he dismissed his attendants, wrote a farewell letter to his wife, and at one o'clock in the morning went over to the Austrian lines. As Count de Barge, a Piedmontese officer on leave, he was allowed to pass on to Nice, whence he reached Portugal, where he remained until his death. His son has lived to fulfil more than all the hopes and wishes of this patriot king. The democrats of Italy fought hard for their principles, but strove in vain to keep the trophies. Lombardy, Tuscany, and the Two Sicilies, yielded one after the other to the power of Austria, until Rome remained the sole refuge of the Italian republic. The triumvirate which governed her, consisting of Mazzini, Armellini, and Saffi, was greatly strengthened by Garibaldi, who had returned from the war in Sardinia, and by Avezzana, who had been driven from Genoa. But France (now under the government of Prince Louis Napoleon) sent a military force under General Oudinot to take possession of the Eternal City. The Italian patriots, strongly suspecting that their neighbour republicans were not altogether friendly to their cause, resisted and repelled their invasion, only, however, to be again attacked with fatal success. The French possession of Rome dates from 3rd July, 1849. In the following month Venice, and the gallant Daniel Manin, capitulated to the Austrians, and Italy returned once more under the dominion of her ancient rulers, conscious, nevertheless, of having made a great advance morally towards national unity and independence. The fulfilment of her aspirations she was destined to owe in great measure to the ruler of France, who in exile had been a member of her secret societies, and had there learned the art that enabled him to maintain a lofty position in the world for more than twenty years. The Austrian government, however, had to encounter rebellion in other quarters besides Italy. Her

German and Hungarian subjects raised the standard of revolt, and achieved so many important successes, that the house of Hapsburg seemed doomed, when Nicholas, the autocrat of all the Russias, came to the rescue with overwhelming force, and overturned the democratic government established in Hungary under the presidency of the great orator Kossuth. The civil war in Hungary, be it noted, turned upon questions of race and nationality, rather than on the distribution of political power, just as national unity was found ultimately to be a stronger motive to revolution with the Italians and Germans than mere forms of government. In the smaller German states the revolutionary shock which overthrew Louis Philippe acted with extraordinary rapidity and force. The sovereigns taken by surprise offered no resistance, and the conservative element of society, though destined soon to recover its vigour, seemed suddenly dissolved. The grand duke of Baden publicly acknowledged the sovereignty of the people, and established a national guard; the king of Würtemburg abolished feudal rights, and also accepted civic guards; the king of Saxony appointed a liberal ministry, and convoked the Chambers for the purpose of settling a new constitution; the king of Bavaria not only parted for a time with his unworthy favourite Lola Montes, but subsequently abdicated his throne. Belgium and Holland escaped the convulsion by reasonable concessions. King Leopold frankly told the Chamber of Deputies at Brussels, that he only valued his crown because it had been given to him by popular election; and that if they liked to have it back again, it was at their disposal. In Prussia the agitation was very great. The scholarly and amiable king sympathized in many points with the German liberals, and committed himself somewhat too hastily to the popular view. In a proclamation issued by him on the 18th March, 1848, he said: "Above all we demand that Germany shall be transformed from a federation of states into one federal state. We demand a general military system for Germany—a federal army assembled under one federal banner, and we hope to see a federal commander-in-chief at its head." A federal tribunal, a common law of settlement, the abolition of all custom-houses impeding internal commerce, a general Zollverein for the whole of Germany, and uniformity of weights, measures, and money, formed other material points of the royal proclamation. For the execution of this just and liberal programme a firm hand was needed, and a mind thoroughly made up as to the course to be followed. Such was not the case with King Frederick William. In the midst of the joyful demonstration caused by his prompt concessions, a tumult arose, in which several persons were killed by the troops, and more wounded. The sincere regret of the king at what he thought a lamentable accident, emboldened the republican party to push forward their pretensions. The dead bodies of the citizens killed on the 18th March were on the 22nd paraded with great pomp before the royal palace, where his majesty from the balcony bowed his head as the lifeless remains were carried by. A national guard was established in Berlin, and the king announced his intention of putting himself at the head of a restored and united Germany. "His Majesty," said his minister in the assembly of Prussian Estates, "has promised a real constitutional charter, and we are assembled to lay the foundation stone of the enduring edifice. We hope that the work will proceed rapidly, and that it will perfect a great constitutional system for the whole German race." Prussia, however, was not as yet destined to be the instrument of this great work.

The popular party had succeeded in gathering at Frankfort an assembly of three hundred representatives, to which was given the name of the "Vor Parlament." This body decided the form of election to the German National Assembly, which was to meet at Frankfort in May, the members being returned on the radical principle of electoral districts—one deputy for every 7000 voters. The Assembly, when duly constituted, elected a regent of United Germany in the person of Archduke John of Austria. The choice was highly distasteful to the Prussian court, and King Frederick William soon began to show that his ardent liberalism was tempered by events. The counsels of his brother, then Crown Prince, now King William, a conservative in principle, exercised considerable influence over him. Armed force was employed to control the radical members of the Parliament assembled in Berlin, and it was not long before similar treatment was brought to bear upon the national representatives gathered at Frankfort. In September, 1848, a revolt of the democrats in Frankfort against the national government was put down by Prussian and other federal soldiers. A similar insurrection in Baden, under the leadership of Struve, was suppressed with corresponding vigour. Altogether the German National Assembly did not prosper. Its aims were greater than its power to attain them. To Austria, especially, the democratic nature of the constitution propounded was extremely distasteful. So also was the growing importance of Prussia, whom Austria, in Metternich's time, had succeeded in relegating to a subordinate position in German affairs. As the dangers which threatened monarchy in 1848 diminished, the dualism of Austria and Prussia came out in stronger light, to the disadvantage of the National Assembly and its great work—German unification. The men assembled at Frankfort were stigmatized as a body of professors unacquainted with practical politics. While the revolutionary impulse was upon them and behind them, the idea of unity exercised a potency that seemed likely to give it permanence in the heart and mind of the nation. But these worthy gentlemen lost invaluable time in debating over paragraphs of the constitution, and fencing round principles of law and right, until their antagonists, the existing governments, regained strength, and "the ideal fabric of a new Germany dissolved like a castle in the clouds." In March, 1849, when the Assembly voted that the king of Prussia should be requested to become emperor of Germany, that monarch politely declined the honour; the Archduke John immediately resigned the office of regent, and the government at Vienna openly set at nought the Assembly, from which a few days later 121 Austrian members altogether withdrew. The rest of the Assembly split in two—part remaining in Frankfort, part going to Stuttgard. The latter made some noisy attempts to democratize the institutions of the country, and were extinguished by the Würtemburg police. Thus the celebrated Frankfort assembly finally broke up, having sown precious seed in the popular mind, and laid the groundwork of a federal constitution which one day or other should be made compatible with the benefit of the whole country and the rights of single states—no easy task.

It became more and more evident that no unity was possible in Germany while two powers so nearly matched were rival competitors for the leadership. Whatever was undertaken or promoted by Prussia was either secretly or openly opposed by Austria. " Germany," says Dr. Strauss, "fell into the condition of a waggon with one horse before and another of equal strength behind, pulling one against the other, with no hope of moving." In 1850 these powers went so far as to attempt to make two confederacies: Prussia had her union of princes (twenty-two and more) at Erfurth, while Austria collected her royal supporters at Munich, and matters were brought to a crisis by both parties interfering in a dispute which the elector of Cassel had with his Chamber of Representatives. Prussia having sided with the Chamber, and Austria with the sovereign, both sent into his territory troops, which were on the verge of a collision that would have anticipated 1866, when the emperor of Russia interposed his authority, and secured the treaty of Olmutz. Germany resumed for a time its former shape, as settled by the Confederation treaty of 1815, and the old Diet met again at Frankfort in May, 1851. The vexed question of Schleswig and Holstein was also settled upon its ancient basis. After a sharp war, in which the Danes gained the victories of Fredericia and Idstedt, the insurgent German population returned to their allegiance without abandoning their claim to separate constitutions, as parts of the German Confederation. The battle of Idstedt was one of the first occasions on which the needle gun was employed in war. That terrible instrument was destined to play no mean part in the work of "blood and iron," by which alone the "thirty-seven rags" of Central Europe, as Max Midler expresses it, were to be sewed together in one strong garment of German unity. One important bond uniting the separate states had been patiently woven by Prussia in the course of years. It was the Zollverein, or Custom's Union, commenced in 1818, and gradually extended by treaty to an extent of country bounded by the Netherlands and Russia, by the Baltic, Switzerland, and Bohemia. Throughout this wide territory freedom of commerce has now prevailed for years, and a commodity, whether for consumption or transit, that has once passed the frontier of the league, may be conveyed without let or hindrance throughout its whole extent. The trials endured by Austria in the year of revolution, and her war of nationalities between Teuton and Magyar, have been alluded to, and will be again treated of hereafter.

CHAPTER II.

IT is necessary now to give an outline of the career of that remarkable man who exercised so much influence over events in Europe for the following twenty years—Napoleon III.

Born at Paris in 1808, he was but seven years old when he last saw his uncle the emperor, at Malmaison, during the Hundred Days. On the banishment of his family from France the same year, he accompanied his mother Hortense, ex-queen of Holland, to Geneva, thence to Aix in Savoy, to Carlsruhe, and to Augsbourg. In the last-named ancient German city he was a student at the gymnasium, and became an enthusiastic admirer of Schiller, one of whose poems he subsequently translated into French. When of sufficient age he served as an officer in the Swiss federal army. After the French revolution of 1830 he asked permission to re-enter France, which was refused. He and his elder brother then joined the Italians of Romagna in a struggle for independence. The brother died of his wounds, and Louis, after a dangerous illness, escaped with his mother to Paris, which they were ordered forthwith to quit. After a brief visit to England, he returned to his mother's house on Lake Constance, the Château d'Arenenberg. In 1831 the Poles offered him the dangerous distinction of being their leader in insurrection against Russia, but before he could reach Warsaw that city had been captured. The death of the duke of Reichstadt in 1832 left him heir to the first Napoleon; and as Louis Philippe persistently turned a deaf ear to his solicitations for leave to reside in France, thoughts of entering his native country by other means began to press upon his mind. That the prince had reasons for wishing to re-enter France that fully justified the king's prohibition, the sequel will show. He was a diligent student and a busy writer, with a subtle and penetrating brain, subject to the influences of a vague, cloudy imagination, and an indecisive, not to say irresolute will. He paid great attention to artillery and engineering, and though he wrote and published many things of historical and literary interest, his best work is one entitled "Studies on the Past and Future of Artillery." For the memory of his uncle he entertained a feeling nearly allied to worship, and relied upon the magic of his name for doing great things some day. The throne of the citizen king was not very firm. Abominable plots and attempts at regicide were frequently coming to light, and the king, with a shortsighted deference to the national vanity, encouraged the popular worship of Napoleon I. by erecting monuments to his memory, placing his portrait in public buildings, and finally by bringing his remains from the grave in St. Helena to be buried with great pomp in Paris. This was playing into the hands of the sombre watcher on the Castle of Arenenberg. The first attempt made by the young pretender to seize the throne of France was ridiculously inadequate to the occasion. He trusted almost entirely to the magic of the name Napoleon, which he seemed to think would produce as startling an effect as did the emperor's return from Elba in 1815. Leaving his home on the 25th October, 1836, for Strasburg, the wheel of his carriage came off at Lahr, delaying his project for a day, and filling a mind much given to ponderings on destiny with the weight of an evil omen. He reached Strasburg on the 28th, at eleven o'clock at night, and having gained over Colonel Vaudrey and about a dozen officers, he went next morning at six o'clock to the artillery barracks, where he was received with some cheers. Proceeding further with a band of music before him, he tried to impose himself and his cause on General Voirol, but without success. That stouthearted soldier had the prince arrested. The examination which followed throws some light on the Napoleonian ideas of that time:—"What urged you to act as you have done?" "My political opinions and a wish to see my country again, of which foreign invasion had deprived me. In 1830 I asked to be received as a simple citizen, and I was treated as a pretender; very well, I have now behaved like a pretender." "You wanted to set up a military government?" I wished to set up a government founded on popular election." Having declared that he alone assumed all responsibility of the movement, he was removed to Paris, and by the 21st November was on board a frigate bound for America, dismissed from custody with a royal clemency that smacked strongly of contempt.

Here will be seen the force of Mr. Kinglake's estimate of the prince's character:—"He had boldness of the kind which is produced by reflection, rather than that which is the result of temperament. In order to cope with the extraordinary perils into which he now and then thrust himself, and to cope with them dexterously, there was wanted a fiery quality which nature had refused to the great bulk of mankind as well as to him. But it was only in emergencies of a really trying sort, and involving instant physical danger, that his boldness fell short. He had all the courage which would have enabled him in a private station of life to pass through the common trials of the world with honour unquestioned; but he had besides now and then a factitious kind of audacity produced by long dreamy meditation; and when he had wrought himself into that state, he was apt to expose his firmness to trials beyond his strength. His imagination had so great a sway over him as to make him love the idea of enterprises, but it had not strength enough to give him a foreknowledge of what his sensations would be in the hour of trial." There is much justice in this elaborate analysis of character, as events have amply proved. The love of imaginary enterprise, which made the prince a participator in the Eglinton Tournament, was the same ingredient in his character as that which led him to his second descent upon France. This singular transaction, which only escapes the epithet of ludicrous from its having been the cause of an honest man's death, took place at Boulogne on the 6th of August, 1840. After a few months' stay in New York the prince had returned to Europe in the autumn of 1837, to be present at his mother's death, and subsequently, in consequence of representations made by the French government to the government of Switzerland, he had quitted the latter country to reside in England.

The following is a contemporary account of what was characterized as an "insane expedition:" The prince having hired, as for a voyage of pleasure, the *Edinburgh Castle* steamer from the Commercial Steam Navigation Company, embarked from London in August, accompanied by about fifty men, among whom were General Montholon, Colonels Voisin, Laborde, Montauban, and Parquin, and several other officers of inferior rank. At three o'clock on the morning of the sixth they landed at Wimereux, a small port about two leagues from Boulogne, and directed their march to that town, where they arrived about five o'clock. They distributed their proclamations to every body they met, and strewed five franc pieces to a rabble which preceded them. After traversing the lower town, they at length reached the barracks, where they found a company or two of the 42nd regiment of the line just rising from their beds. The soldiers, assured that a revolution had been effected in Paris, and summoned to join the eagle of the Empire, were for some time puzzled as to how they should act. One of their officers, however, hurrying to the barracks, relieved the men from their perplexity, and they recognized his authority. Louis Napoleon drew a pistol, and attempted to shoot the inopportune intruder; the shot took effect upon a soldier, who died in the course of the day. After this fruitless experiment, an attempt was made on the post of St. Nicholas, which was occupied by four men and a sergeant. This post was firm, and would not yield. The prince then directed his march on the Upper Town, but found the gate which opens on the Esplanade shut before he reached it. Forced to make a tour round the town, the prince took the Calais road to the Colonne de Napoleon, which one of his party entered by breaking open the door at the foot, and, mounting to the top, placed their flag upon it. General Montholon and Colonel Parquin went to the port, expecting to have better success with the maritime part of the population, but they were there arrested by the commissary of police.

The town authorities and national guard then went in pursuit of the prince, who, being intercepted on the side of the column, made for the beach, with the view to embark and regain the packet in which he had arrived. He took possession of the life-boat; but scarcely had his followers got into it when the national guard also arrived on the beach, and discharged a volley on the boat, which immediately upset, and the whole company tumbled into the sea. In the meantime, the steam-packet was already taken possession of by the lieutenant of the port. The prince was then made prisoner, and three hours after his attempt on Boulogne he and his followers were in the castle prison.

The prince was removed to the castle of Ham, and placed in the rooms once occupied by Prince Polignac. The most ludicrous feature of the exhibition is omitted by the chronicler; namely, that the pretender bore with him a trained eagle, that was to fly from his arms to Paris, an emblem of his victorious march thither, and a living souvenir of the first empire. Tried before the Chamber of Peers, in September, the prince delivered an able speech, evidently the fruit of much study, and intended to interest his hearers in the Bonapartist claims. His peroration terminated with words that have been often quoted; words that made a profound, if unwholesome impression, on the martial mind of France, while they revealed the secret of a line of conduct that was to lead the utterer to a throne, and of a subsequent policy that was to end in his captivity. "One last word, gentlemen!" he said; "I represent before you a principle, a cause, and a defeat: the principle is the sovereignty of the people; the cause is the empire; the defeat, Waterloo. The principle you have acknowledged; the cause you have served. The defeat you wish to avenge." This appeal to the coarsest national instincts sank into the minds of numberless Frenchmen, and bore fruit after many days. The prince was condemned to perpetual imprisonment, and removed with General Montholon and Dr. Conneau to the castle of Ham, where he employed his enforced leisure in study and literary composition. One of his lucubrations, viewed by the light of recent events, possesses just now a peculiar interest. It was a paper contributed by him on the 7th May, 1843, to a journal called *Progrés du Pas de Calais*, for which he wrote several articles at different times, and it sets forth very clearly the great superiority of the military organization of Prussia over that of France. He describes the four great elements of the Prussian forces, the army, the reserve, the landwehr, and the landsturm, and adds, "Thus Prussia, whose population scarcely amounts to two-fifths of that of France, is enabled for the defence of her territory to call into action 530,000 trained men, and this armed force does not cost her 50,000,000 francs a year, while a few taps of the drum suffice to make these troops assemble or return to their homes." After condemning the conscription as a "white slave trade, briefly defined as the purchase of a man by him who has the means to obtain remission from military service, and thus to send a man of the people to be killed in his stead;" he says, "In Prussia there are no substitutes," and proceeds to develop a plan by which France, if she were to adopt the Prussian system, would possess for the defence of the country an army of a million and a half of men, and costing less to the national exchequer than the then existing army of 344,000 men. Most remarkable is the conclusion of the article:—"Subtracting the 30,000 men required in Algeria, 14,000 gendarmes, the veterans and the garrisons of Paris and of Lyons, France would not be able to bring 200,000 men into line upon the frontiers, while upon the line of the Rhine alone upwards of 500,000 could be collected against her in less than a fortnight." What strange mental blindness and perversity can it have been that hid from the eyes of the emperor of 1870 the momentous facts which were so clearly visible to the meditative prisoner of Ham twenty-seven years before? An authentic anecdote is related of him at this time, which serves to illustrate the strong faith he had in his star or destiny. The leading dentist in Paris, an American, went to see the prince professionally during his incarceration at Ham. At the moment of separating there happened to be a heavy shower of rain. "I have not even an umbrella to lend you," said the captive; "yet, do you know, I am persuaded that I shall one day be emperor of the French!"

In 1846 the prince was invited to undertake the guidance of a project for uniting the Atlantic and Pacific Oceans by a ship canal in Nicaragua. At the same period his father, the ex-king of Holland, fell seriously ill at Florence. Unable to obtain his release from the French government, he took measures for escaping from prison, and with the aid of his physician, Conneau, he walked out of the prison gate in the disguise of a workman on the morning of the 25th May, 1846. "We cannot," said a writer of the time, and a supporter of the government of M. Thiers, "we cannot speak of the escape of the Prince Louis Napoleon as of a political event. The liberty of that singular pretender is no more a danger to public order than his captivity was a guarantee of it." The writer of these contemptuous words shared with many others in the ignorance of a potential element of mischief that was latent in the mass of French society, in the form of worship of Napoleon Bonaparte. M. Thiers himself was one of those who by their writings encouraged this false idolatry, and revived a cruel lust for military glory, by playing upon which Prince Louis at length gained his ends. After his escape, abandoning the Nicaraguan scheme, he resided in England, awaiting and watching events. At length, on the 24th of February, 1848, he learnt in the manner already described, that his hour had come. With characteristic indecision, however, he still waited, and even after being elected a member of the National Assembly by five or six different constituencies he declined, in the face of a very slight opposition, to take his place in the Chamber. After the awful purification which the Republic underwent in the murderous insurrection of June, fresh elections ensued, and Louis Napoleon, returned by five several departments at once, took his seat on the 17th September. He found himself, says one biographer, face to face with three clearly defined conditions; to wit, the hostility of the Executive, the distrust of the Assembly, the confidence of the Electorate. The two first he had to subdue, the last to strengthen and extend. His reception by the Chamber was not encouraging. His impassive countenance, German accent, and slow utterance, gave little promise of intellectual power. "He is a wooden-headed fellow," said M. Thiers. "I will not," said M. Thouret in his presence, "do pretenders the honour to think aught of them individually." Nevertheless, the election of President of the Republic by universal suffrage was at hand, and on the 10th December the prince was raised to that distinction by five and a half million votes. Having thus conquered the "hostility of the Executive," whom he had supplanted, he prepared for his encounter with the mistrustful Assembly, whom he overthrew after three years' struggle by a conspiracy that has been described with highly coloured embellishments in the first volume of Mr. Kinglake's celebrated "History of the Invasion of the Crimea." The actual Assembly called the Constituent, to which Louis Napoleon was first sent as deputy, was dissolved in May, 1849, and a new Assembly—the Legislative—elected. It was in this body, better disposed though it was to the chief of the state, that M. Ledru Rollin and the Mountain proposed an impeachment of the president and his ministers for having violated the constitution by their intervention at Rome. Some tumult ensued (13th June, 1849), and Paris for a while was placed under martial law. The Right or moderate section of the Chamber succeeded, on the other hand, in placing some restriction on the universality of the suffrage, and evinced a determination to control the supplies. The president, on his side, made progresses through the provinces, where he delivered conciliatory speeches. He also caressed the army, granting them indulgences of wine and cigars, and sought popularity in every possible way. Not having obtained the confidence of any leading statesmen or distinguished members of the best class of society, he was resolved to place his reliance on the "confidence of the Electorate" already spoken of; and associating himself with certain adventurous spirits, who had everything to gain by the change, and little to lose in case of failure, he prepared the celebrated coup d'état of 1851. On the Monday night, says Mr. Kinglake, between the 1st and the 2nd of December, the president had his usual assembly at the Elysée. Ministers who were loyally ignorant of what was going on, were mingled with those who were in the plot. Vieyra was present. He was spoken to by the president, and he undertook that the national guard should not beat to arms that night. He went away, and it is said that he fulfilled his humble task by causing the drums to be mutilated. At the usual hour the assembly began to disperse, and by eleven o'clock there were only three guests who remained. These were Morny (who had previously taken care to show himself at one of the theatres), Maupas, and St. Arnaud, formerly Le Roy. There was, besides, an orderly officer of the president, called Colonel Beville, who was initiated in the secret. Persigny, it seems, was not present.

Morny, Maupas, and St. Arnaud went with the president into his cabinet; Colonel Beville followed them. Mocquard, the private secretary of the president, was in the secret, but it does not appear that he was in the room at this time. Fleury too, it seems, was away; he was probably on an errand which tended to put an end to the hesitation of his more elderly comrades, and drive them to make the venture. They were to strike the blow that night.

The president intrusted a packet of letters to Colonel Beville, and despatched him to the state printing office. These papers were the proclamations required for the early morning, and M. St. Georges, the director, gave orders to put them into type. They said that there was something like resistance; but in the end, if not at first, the printers obeyed. Each compositor stood, whilst he worked, between two policemen, and the manuscript being cut into many pieces, no one could make out what he was printing. By these proclamations the president asserted that the Assembly was a hot-bed of plots; declared it dissolved; pronounced for universal suffrage; proposed a new constitution; vowed anew that his duty was to maintain the Republic; and placed Paris and the twelve surrounding departments under martial law.

In one of the proclamations he appealed to the army, and strove to whet its enmity against civilians, by reminding it of the defeats inflicted upon the troops in 1830 and 1848. The president wrote letters dismissing the members of the government who were not in the plot; but he did not cause these letters to be delivered until the following morning. He also signed a paper appointing Morny to the Home Office.

At six o'clock a brigade of infantry, under Forey, occupied the Quai d'Orsay, and other troops in considerable force occupied important points in the capital. Almost at the same time Maupas, chief of the police, who had been instructed to arrest the disaffected, had his orders carefully obeyed. At the appointed minute, and whilst it was still dark, the designated houses were entered. The most famous generals of France were seized. General Changarnier, General Bedeau, General Lamoriciere, General Cavaignac, and General Leflô, were taken from their beds and carried away through the sleeping city, and thrown into prison. In the same minute the like was done with some of the chief officers of the Assembly, and amongst others with Thiers, Miot, Baze, Colonel Charras, Roger du Nord, and several of the democratic leaders. Some men, believed to be the chiefs of secret societies, were also seized. The number of men thus seized in the dark was seventy-eight. Eighteen of these were members of the Assembly. When the fight of the morning dawned, people saw the proclamations on the walls, and slowly came to hear that numbers of the foremost men of France had been seized in the night-time, and that every general to whom the friends of law and order could look for help was lying in one or other of the prisons. The newspapers to which a man might run in order to know, and know truly, what others thought and intended, were all seized and stopped. The gates of the Assembly were closed and guarded. In the course of the morning the president, accompanied by his uncle Jerome Bonaparte and Count Flahault, and attended by many general officers and a numerous staff, rode through some of the streets of Paris. Upon the whole, the reception he met with seems to have been neither friendly nor violently hostile, but chilling, and in a quiet way scornful. Prince Louis rode home, and went in out of sight. Thenceforth, for the most part, he remained close shut up in the Elysée. There, in an inner room, still decked in red trousers, but with his back to the day-light, they say he sat bent over a fireplace for hours and hours together, resting his elbows on his knees, and burying his face in his hands.

The remnant of the Assembly, to the number of 220 deputies, having met at the mayoralty of the tenth arrondissement, was driven out and marched between files of soldiery through the streets to the D'Orsay barracks, where they were held in custody. At a quarter before ten o'clock at night a large number of the windowless vans which are used for the transport of felons were brought into the court of the barracks, and into these 230 members were thrust. They were carried off, some to the fort of Mount Valerian, some to the fortress of Vincennes, and some to the prison of Mazas. Still, there was a remnant of the old insurrectionary forces, which was willing to try the experiment of throwing up a few barricades. Having formed a Committee of Resistance, several members of the Assembly went into the Faubourg St. Antoine, and strove to raise the people. They also caused barricades to be thrown up in that mass of streets between the Hotel de Ville and the Bouvelard, which is the accustomed centre of an insurrection in Paris.

In the afternoon of the 4th, numbers of spectators, including many women, crowded the foot pavement. These gazers had no reason for supposing that they incurred any danger, for they could see no one with whom the army would have to contend. According to some, a shot was fired from a window or a house-top near the Rue du Sentier. Some of the soldiery in reply fired point blank into the mass of spectators who stood gazing upon them from the foot pavement, and the rest of the troops fired up at the gay crowded windows and balconies. Of the people on the foot pavement who were not struck down at first, some rushed away and strove to find a shelter, or even a half shelter, at any spot within reach. Others tried to crawl away on their hands and knees, for they hoped that perhaps the balls might fly over them. The impulse to shoot people had been sudden, but was not momentary. The soldiers loaded and reloaded with a strange industry, and made haste to kill and kill, as though their lives depended upon the quantity of the slaughter they could get through in some given period of time. They broke into many houses, hunted the inmates from floor to floor, caught them at last and slaughtered them. These things, no doubt, they did under a notion that shots had been fired from the house which they entered, but it is certain that in almost all these instances, if not in every one of them, the impression was false. The whole number of people killed by the troops during the forty hours which followed upon the commencement of the massacre of the Boulevards will never be known. The burying of the bodies was done for the most part at night. In the army which did these things, the whole number of killed was twenty-five. Before the morning of the 5th, the armed insurrection had ceased. The fate of the provinces resembled the fate of the capital.

These are the things which Charles Louis Napoleon did. What he had sworn to do was set forth in the oath which he took on the 20th of December, 1848. On that day he stood before the National Assembly, and lifting his right arm towards Heaven thus swore:—"In the presence of God, and before the French people represented by the National Assembly, I swear to remain faithful to the democratic republic, one and indivisible, and to fulfil all the duties which the constitution imposes upon me."

What he had pledged his honour to do was set forth in the promise which of his own free will he addressed to the Assembly. Beading from a paper which he had prepared, he uttered these words:—"The votes of the nation, and the oath which I have just taken, command my future conduct. My duty is clear. I will fulfil it as a man of honour. I shall regard as enemies of the country all those who endeavour to change, by illegal means, that which all France has established."

So little did oaths and declarations avail to secure the constitution, when craft and force united to overturn it. Yet all the guile and violence of the world would not have achieved this sad victory had there not been developed in the French nation principles of division, that form a potent auxiliary to every usurper and every political adventurer that knows but how to use them. There are, says an able publicist, in France two intense political passions—the passion of property among the country peasants, and the passion for socialism among the town *ouvriers*. And, unhappily, these passions are entirely opposed. "Socialism" is an obscure term, and the idea in the minds of those who cleave to it is of the vaguest and wildest kind; still, on the whole, it means a system wishing to amend property—a system incompatible with present property. The passionate part of the Republicans in 1848, the only part of them who were eager and many, meant more or less distinctly what Louis Blanc said distinctly. He aimed avowedly at a system in which wages received should be proportionate, not to work done, but to wants felt. He would have given a man with many children much, and a man with few children little; and he would have taxed without limit existing property for that object. A still more violent reasoner invented the celebrated phrase *La propriéte, c'est le vol,* or "Property is robbery." And this is only a strict deduction from the elementary wish of socialists that all men are to "start fair." In that case all inherited property is unjust, and all gifts among the living by which the children of the rich become better off than the children of the poor are unjust too. Both violate the equality of the start; both make life an adjusted and "handicapped" race—an existence where accidental advantages impair or outweigh intrinsic qualities. Roughly it may be said that the main desire of the city socialists in France, on grounds more or less honest, is to attack property; and that the sole desire of the country peasants is, on grounds more or less selfish, to maintain property. And between the two how can you mediate? or out of the two combined how can you make anything? The antagonism is as perfect as between *plus* and *minus*: you can make up no compound; you can find no intermediate term; you must choose between the two.

The selection can, we fear, only be made by force; hitherto at least it has been so. Paris is France for the purpose of making a government, but it is not France for the purpose of keeping a government. The Parisians put in a Republic by revolution resting more or less on socialism and the artisans. The Republic, as its nature requires, appeals to the people—that is, to the country. In response to the appeal back comes an assembly full of dislike to the socialistic Republic, above all things anxious for property, full of the panic of the proprietary peasantry. And then begins the strife between the conservative Chamber and the innovating mob—a strife which is too keen and internecine to be confined to words only, which soon takes to arms and to the streets, and settles the victory there. If the Republic asks France not for a Chamber, but for a president, the result will be the same in essence. The President Louis Napoleon was the nominee of the country, while the Republic was the choice of the towns.

The proclamation which greeted the waking eyes of the Parisians on that 2nd December, 1851, contained the following five propositions, on which France was required to vote "aye" or "no" by universal suffrage. 1. A responsible chief, elected for ten years. 2. A cabinet appointed by him alone. 3. A council of state, consisting of the most eminent men, who are to prepare the laws which are to be introduced, and support them before the legislative body. 4. A legislative body named by universal suffrage, without any scrutiny of the votes. 5. A second assembly formed of all the eminent men in the country, at once the guardians of the fundamental paction and the public liberties. These proposals, which, to a people in mortal terror of socialism and the red revolution, seemed plausible enough, were voted for by 7,481,231 hands, and practically secured imperial power to Louis Napoleon. The simple issue of *aye* or *no* left the people little choice. A large deportation also of ultra-republicans, to the extent of 30,000 men, helped to paralyze the intellectual and political independence of the country. The voters of no amounted to no more than 684,399. Thus by an overwhelming majority France closed the convulsions of the revolution of 1848 by a military despotism based on universal suffrage. A great crime was committed, but surviving France had peace for a time, and material prosperity returned to her. Again, in the summer of 1852, the president made a progress through the provinces, and at Bordeaux delivered a speech which revealed his intention to make further changes:—"France seems to wish to return to the Empire" he said, "but a certain fear exists which I would dispel. Certain persons say that the Empire means war, but I say the Empire means peace! Peace because France wishes it; and when France is satisfied, the world is tranquil." After this the senate, on the 7th of November, voted there-establishment of the Empire, which decision was confirmed by another plebiscitum, in which there were 7,824,189 affirmative votes; and on the 1st December, 1852, the prince president was solemnly proclaimed at St. Cloud to be "Napoleon III., by the grace of God and the will of the people, Emperor of the French." In the following month (29th January, 1853), the emperor married Eugenie Marie de Guzman, comtesse de Teba, a lady with Scotch blood in her veins, and twenty-seven years of age. Thus enthroned and domesticated the *parvenu*, as his Majesty described himself, in announcing his marriage to the Senate, sought to strengthen his position by occupying his people in a foreign war. England, in the person of Lord Palmerston, had been in haste to recognize his accession to the imperial throne, and England would serve well if she could be drawn into a close alliance, offensive and defensive. The reader who wishes to know how such an alliance was brought about, is referred to Mr. Kinglake's History, which, though exaggerated in tone and bitter in temper, is substantially correct as regards the main facts. English jealousy of Russian power in the East was the moral engine used to draw her into the Crimean war. That England "drifted" into that war without good reason, and at a vain sacrifice of blood and treasure, is now generally admitted. Its history in brief is this:—It had long been the annual practice of Christians of the Latin and of the Greek church to make a pilgrimage to the Church of the Holy Sepulchre at Jerusalem, and when there in numbers sufficient, to show their mutual animosity by a quarrelsome tumult that had to be suppressed by the Mahometan soldiers of the Sultan. The czar of Russia, self-elected protector of the Greek Church, demanded possession of this church, and the emperor of the French, self-elected patron of the Romish church, also demanded the key. The general question of the protection of and influence with the Christian subjects of the Sublime Porte underlay this petty squabble. The Czar, with a covetous eye on Constantinople, revealed to the English ambassador at his court, that in his opinion Turkey was like a sick man, the division of whose inheritance it would be well to anticipate. He hinted pretty plainly that England might take Egypt, if Russia were allowed to take Constantinople. The publication of this imprudent conversation created much ill feeling between the countries. Russia pushed her claims upon Turkey for fresh privileges to the Christians under Ottoman rule. The Porte, learning that France and England would give support, assumed a determined aspect, and resented an affront offered to the Sultan by the Czar's envoy Prince Mentschikoff. Hereupon Russian troops crossing the river Pruth entered Turkish territory, and the English and French fleets approached the Dardanelles. The Turks had a fleet at Sinope in the Black Sea, which the Russians surprised and burnt to the water's edge. Indignation was roused in the West by this act of destruction, and war began in earnest. At Sevastopol in the Crimea the Russians had built at enormous cost a very strong fortress, which, commanding the Black Sea, was a perpetual menace to Turkey. Against this a joint expedition was undertaken in September, 1854, by the naval and military forces of England, France, and Turkey, with the subsequent addition, early in 1855, of a contingent furnished by the king of Sardinia. The victorious battle of the Alma (20th September, 1854), was followed by the tedious siege of Sevastopol, which lasted 330 days, having cost many thousand lives from cold and disease, as much as from the bullet and the sword. The battles of Balaclava, Inkermann, and Tchernaya were brilliant episodes in this siege. Czar Nicholas being dead, his son Alexander II., after the fall of Sevastopol (September 8, 1855), made peace on easy terms with the allied powers at a congress which met at Paris in February, 1856. England gained little in this contest but the honour of having fought. To the Emperor Napoleon such honour was of great value, as it placed him on a level with the ancient sovereigns of Europe, and revived in a faint degree the remembrance of the first Napoleon. Yet a keen-sighted man and profound politician, the late M. de Tocqueville, formed no high opinion of the emperor's capacity for conducting a great war like this. Speaking of it in 1854, he said:—"The real prime minister is, without doubt, Louis Napoleon himself. But he is not a man of business. He does not understand details. He may order certain things to be done; but he will not be able to ascertain whether the proper means have been taken. He does not know, indeed, what these means are. He does not trust those who do. A war which would have tasked all the power of Napoleon, and of Napoleon's ministers and generals, is to be carried on, without any master mind to direct it, or any good instruments to execute it. I fear some great disaster." If these words had been spoken of the Prussian war, in 1870, they would have been more apt and prophetic.

Since the reconquest of Italy by Austria in 1849, the elements of revolt had been fermenting. The secret societies laboured to bring about a republic in obedience to the promptings of their indefatigable leader Mazzini. But the prospects of success seemed to diminish daily, and a rancorous feeling against the man who had driven the triumvirate from Rome, and still held the possession of the Eternal City, urged these impetuous spirits to avenge their wrongs by his death. A plot for the assassination of Napoleon III. was arranged in London, and it fell to the lot of Felice Orsini, an enthusiastic republican of good education, to be the emperor's executioner. Evading the vigilance of the French police, he and three accomplices reached Paris in February, 1858, and on the 14th of that month, as the emperor and empress were going to the opera in state, three bombs were flung at the cortege and exploded with fatal effect. The imperial carriage was broken, and several passers by and soldiers of the escort were killed and wounded, but the emperor and empress remained unhurt. Great was the indignation that this criminal attempt caused throughout France, not only against the conspirators but against the place of their refuge. England was vilified as being a nest of assassins, and certain vapouring French colonels talked of avenging Waterloo there and then. To the surprise of Englishmen a somewhat dictatorial letter of Count Walewski's on the subject, was not answered with the spirit that men expected from Lord Palmerston, the then minister. On the contrary, a bill was brought into Parliament, in compliance with the wish of the French government, in order to strengthen the law against aliens who should plot against sovereigns in friendly alliance with England. The offence, which had previously been a misdemeanour, was to be made a felony, and to be visited with a punishment proportionately condign. Not unfair in itself, this bill by its occasion excited the anger of the English public; and the House of Commons, responsive to the popular feeling, threw out the bill, and with it Lord Palmerston and the ministry. It is not impossible that this sharp rebuff taught the French emperor, that the defeat of which he styled himself the representative, namely, Waterloo, was not just then to be avenged with advantage to himself. The next January revealed other schemes, resulting it may be in part from impressions produced on the mind of the old Carbonaro by Orsini's attack, his language when in prison, and the letter written by him on the eve of execution, in which he called upon the emperor to deliver his country from the yoke of the foreigner. Italy should be freed, and Austria humbled.

Europe had not seen without surprise Sardinian troops taking part in the expedition to the Crimea. The presence of Cavour, the minister of Victor Emmanuel, at the Paris congress, and the language he held there, led sagacious observers to think that more would come of this alliance between Sardinia, France, and England, than then appeared on the surface. At the congress he protested in the name of his government against the new extension of Austrian influence in the Italian peninsula in defiance of treaty stipulations, and averred that if nothing were done to remedy this state of things, grave dangers to the peace of the world might ensue. Count Walewski, president of the congress, taking this protest into consideration, invited the attentive solicitude of the assembled plenipotentiaries to the internal condition of Italy, and in this he was warmly supported by Lord Clarendon, the English envoy. A word or two on Count Cavour will not be misplaced here.

Camillo Benso di Cavour was born at Turin in 1810, five years before the Congress of Vienna had concocted that treaty, the deadly effects of which in Italy he was destined within half a century to counteract. His father held office in Piedmont under Prince Borghese, who married Pauline Bonaparte, the sister of Napoleon I. Young Camillo, being god-child to these high personages, had an early predilection in favour of the Bonaparte family. The revolutionary changes accomplished in Italy under the first Napoleon, in which so many of the divisions of territory disappeared, planted in his mind fruitful ideas favourable to Italian unity. As a boy he served Charles Albert, then known as a liberal, in the capacity of page. While an officer of engineers he was for his free speech on political topics ordered to the fort of Bard for a year, at the expiration of which he resigned his commission, and devoted his mind to the social and political questions of the day. In reply to a letter of condolence at this time (1832), he wrote these prophetic words:—"I thank you for the interest you take in my misfortune; but believe me I shall still accomplish my career in spite of it. I am a very, an enormously ambitious man, and when I am minister I shall justify my ambition; for I tell you, in my dreams I already see myself minister of the kingdom of Italy." On the accession of Charles Albert, the father of Cavour was appointed vicario of Turin, an office involving the charge of the police and the duty of watching the liberal party. The odium connected with this office was partly reflected on the enthusiastic young liberal, who, on the other hand, was disliked by the aristocratic party for his opinions. He went to Geneva, to Paris, to London, and studied the English constitution with great satisfaction and profit. Returning to Italy in 1842, he took part in such social reforms as were feasible, and published many valuable papers on historical subjects and on questions of political economy. As the year 1848 approached, more momentous interests came into view. Cavour, says Signor Botta, in his admirable discourse on this statesman, regarded the projects of Mazzini as utterly powerless to lighten the burden of domestic rule, and to emancipate the country from foreign domination. A practical man by nature, and a statesman of the school which acknowledges Machiavelli as its founder, and Richelieu and Burke as its great representatives, his policy was not engendered in the secret chambers of conspiracy, but was moulded on a comprehensive knowledge of the forces which patriotism could command, and on the just appreciation of the necessity of the time. Accordingly he believed that the conquest of nationality could only be effected through the harmonizing of many antagonistic interests, and the combination of many clashing tendencies, the control of which depended entirely on slow, patient, and steady action. From the first appearance of Mazzini, he had not only refused to take any part in his futile and spasmodic efforts, but he had unreservedly discouraged and condemned his policy as anti-national, and big with calamities. Regarding the growth of public sentiment as the true regenerative force, he now hailed with delight the favour with which the more conservative views of Cesare Balbo, Massimo d'Azeglio, and Vincenzo Gioberti were received.

These writers, however discordant in minor points, all agreed in urging upon their countrymen the necessity of radically changing the method of revolutionary action, of doing away with all secret conspiracies, and of openly labouring for the attainment of national independence. They strove to enlist in the cause the interest and ambition of the Italian princes, and insisted on the possibility of a compact between them and the states, by which the rulers were to grant concessions calculated to infuse new life into the country, and the people to extend to them the tenure of their power. Had the princes followed that course they would have been thrown into the onward current, and, soon separated from Austria, they would have been forced into a confederation in order to protect themselves from the common enemy, who sooner or later would have been expelled from the peninsula. So, while Mazzini struggled for nationality by attempting to establish a republic—an enterprise rendered impossible by the condition of Europe and Italy herself—the chiefs of the new party proposed to accomplish the same object through the existing monarchy, renovated, however, by constitutional liberty.

Prominent among these leaders was Gioberti. A man of lofty patriotism and saintly character, a philosophical writer of great renown, distinguished by depth, breadth, and novelty of thought, as well as by brilliancy of style, his influence was powerful and salutary. Considering the papal and the Austrian governments as the two main stumbling blocks to Italian independence, in his works he aimed at the overthrow of both. The Papacy he did not directly attack, as his predecessors in philosophy had done, but he attempted to flank and turn it into the service of the nation. He sketched an ideal Papacy, youthful and vigorous, which he endeavoured to assimilate to the old and worn-out institution of the Vatican, and to place at the head of the Italian movement. The appearance of Pius IX. in the garb of a reformer seemed for a moment to reduce his theory to fact, though in reality it rendered the discrepancies and incongruities between the ideal and the real Papacy more conspicuous and irreconcilable. When Pius IX. abandoned the Italian cause, which as pope he could not consistently support, Gioberti, leaving at once the Papacy to its own destiny, sought other more substantial bases for national existence, and pointed out the house of Savoy as the only hope of Italy.

The project of an Italian confederacy, under the nominal presidency of the pope, and the actual leadership of Sardinia, being the only form of national existence which at that time appeared practicable, was accepted by Cavour, and he shaped his policy accordingly, giving, however, but little importance to the papal element. When the censorship of the press was somewhat relaxed, he established in Turin, in connection with Cesare Balbo and others, the *Risorgimento*, a daily paper, of which he became the chief editor, and which, owing to his skilful management, exerted a great influence on the course of events. In this paper he advocated the independence of Italy, union between princes and people, progressive reform, and a confederation of the Italian states; he developed also those more general principles of free government which he afterwards carried out in his administration. In the beginning of 1848 Cavour took the still more important step of demanding from Charles Albert a constitution for his native state, till then under absolute sway. Whatever may have been the effect of this communication, it is certain that the constitution was soon after granted, and he who was first to demand it was, within a few years, called to mould it into the corner stone of the liberties of the whole Italian people. Had Charles Albert longer resisted the advancing tide of public opinion, his dynasty would in all probability have been swept away with those of the other Italian rulers. In 1848 he waged war, and issued the famous proclamation by which he placed himself at the head of the revolution, and secured for his state the leadership of the nation. Occupying a commanding position between the Alps and the Mediterranean, inhabited by a people distinguished by their practical sense, vigour of character, and warlike spirit, and ruled by a dynasty whose power in Italy had been gradually augmented during eight centuries, Sardinia seemed peculiarly fitted for the destiny assigned her. From this time she made common cause with the whole nation; and bravely entering into the arena, staked her own existence on the issue. Believing the democratic tendencies of the times utterly ruinous to the national cause, Cavour fearlessly threw himself against the prevailing current of opinion, and thus greatly increased his unpopularity. But this could not deter him from performing what he considered his duty, for he did not belong to that class of politicians whose love of country is subservient to self-interest, and whose object is confined to flattering popular passions and prejudices. It was a striking spectacle to see him at that time, from his seat in the Chamber, defying the storm of hisses and yells with which he was frequently assailed from the galleries. Often he called them to order, or moved that they should be cleared, according to the rules. "I am not to be prevented from speaking," said he on one occasion, "by shouts and hisses. What I believe to be true, that will I speak out. If you compel me to silence, you insult not me alone, but the Chamber; and now I shall proceed:" and with his usual self-possession he resumed his discourse. The disasters of 1848 and 1849 were mainly owing to the want of unity in the pursuit of national independence. As the first campaign had failed through the defection of Pius IX. and other princes, the misfortunes of the second were chiefly due to the attempts of the minority to introduce republican governments into some of the states. So Italy fell; on the plains of Novara, on the lagoons of Venice, within the walls of her ancient capital, she was defeated because she was not united; because while Nice was fighting for the common cause, Naples and Palermo bowed under the iron yoke of the Bourbon, and Rome and Florence allowed themselves to be led astray by the mad hallucinations of Mazzini. With Italy Sardinia was crushed; she saw her king in disguise pass through the camp of the enemy on his way to exile, her standards trailed in the dust, the stronghold of Alessandria garrisoned by the Austrians, her army almost destroyed, her finances ruined, her commerce obstructed, her people distracted, her very existence imperilled. Victor Emmanuel pledged his word to uphold the free institutions of the state, and to retain the leadership of the nation; he intrusted himself and the administration of the country to Massimo d'Azeglio, whose name alone was a symbol of nationality. No man represented the cause more entirely, and none was more fitted to guide the state through that dangerous period. Though born in Turin, he had passed his life chiefly in Rome and Florence, and from the study of Italian history, literature, and art, he had derived that national character by which his career has been so singularly marked.

In 1848 he had laid aside the pencil and the pen for the sword; he had fought gallantly, and had been wounded on the field; and thus prepared both by thought and action, on the accession of Victor Emmanuel he was called to the premiership of the cabinet. His high moral nature, his earnestness, his accomplishments, the simplicity and the refinement of his manners, softened by the influence of literature and the arts, his eloquence, and his devotion to the country, endeared him to the people; while his aristocratic connections, his well known moderation and prudence, and his open opposition to the Mazzini party, rendered him acceptable to the courts of Europe. When reaction menaced the only free state of the peninsula, and the republicans by their futile attempts at revolution seemed bent on precipitating a crisis that would involve the armed intervention of Europe, the constitutional party stood by Azeglio, and opposed the enemies of the constitution both at home and abroad. Thus Sardinia was saved from the dire calamities prepared for her by the conspiracies concocted, at the same time and for the same purpose, in the cabinets of diplomacy and in the secret councils of agitators. The constitutional party found in Cavour its most powerful and devoted supporter; and when the storm had somewhat subsided, he at once urged upon the government more progressive measures. Vastly surpassed by Azeglio in aesthetic attainments, Cavour towered over him in extent of knowledge, comprehensiveness of intellect, quickness of perception, force of character, and energy of action; and while the one in great crises advanced timidly and slowly, feeling his way, the other, with his object clearly in view, and the full consciousness of his power, overleaped all impediments.

These peculiarities in the character of the two statesmen nature had impressed even on their external appearance. The slender form, the delicate features, and the poetical expression of Azeglio, marked him as a man of refined sensibility and romantic sentiments; as the keen eye, the broad brow, and the sturdy figure of Cavour indicated at once the iron will and the power to enforce it. Cavour urged on Azeglio vigorous measures of reform, and advocating a progressive policy, he thus | addressed the administration, "Go on boldly, then, in the path of reform. Do not hesitate because you are told that the time is inexpedient; do not fear lest you should weaken the constitutional monarchy intrusted to your charge. Instead of weakening it; you will cause it to the eyes of posterity by achieving the noble task of 'Italian liberation.' "Garibaldi could not forget the French expedition against Rome ten years before. At this moment the king, who always felt a deep regard for Garibaldi, took him by the hand, assured him that Louis Napoleon had always desired to see Italy free and happy, and added that he (the king) had consented to the marriage of his daughter with Prince Napoleon, because he was certain of the emperor's good intentions towards Italy. The campaign of Garibaldi and his Cacciatori delle Alpi, a corps of volunteers organized by General Cialdini, is not the least interesting part of this war. With scarcely 3000 men in the picturesque and mountainous scenery of Northern Italy, he baffled and defeated the manoeuvres of the Austrian General Urban, who had 10,000 regular soldiers under his command.

It was while the preliminaries of a European congress were under discussion, that Francis Joseph suddenly broke off all negotiations and sent his ultimatum to Turin, requiring the government to disarm immediately, on penalty of an invasion. Ten years had elapsed since Austria, by a prodigious effort, and by help of the skill and courage of her army, had recovered from a state of prostration that to many observers had seemed final and irremediable. In the revolution of 1848 her ancient and despotic government was assailed, not only as other German governments were, by political malcontents seeking reforms in domestic administration, but the animosities of race came in and threatened the heterogeneous dominion of the Kaiser with absolute dissolution.

On the first tumultuous outbreak in Vienna in March, 1848, the universal cry was for the liberty of the press, religious liberty, universal education, a general arming of the people, a constitution, and the unity of Germany. "Long live free and independent Germany!" "Long live the Italians in arms!" "Long live the Magyars!" "Long live the patriots of Prague!" Such were the cries which rose from the crowd, and were no sooner heard than they were frantically cheered. Though the insurgents were for the most part cultured men, students from the university and professors, Prince Metternich was subjected to personal outrage; and having resigned his office, he retreated into England. The insurrection conquered the government at Vienna, at Presburg, and at Prague. The Magyars of Hungary, under the leadership of Kossuth, and the Tchecks of Bohemia, endeavoured to secure the independence of their several countries, retaining the emperor of Austria as their nominal king. The Tchecks, being of Sclavonic race, sought a union of all the Sclaves of Europe, including the inhabitants of Croatia, Sclavonia, Servia, Bohemia, Moravia, Livonia, and Gallicia, and looked ultimately to the czar of Russia as their chief. Panslavism, however, was a doctrine that was not sustained by any practical or vital force. A violent revolt of the people took place at Prague, where the governor's wife, the Princess Windischgrätz, was killed in a cowardly manner as she stood at a window, by a shot fired from the crowd, and soon after the town was bombarded into submission. The proud, aristocratic Magyars, on their side, demanded the elimination of every German element from the administration of Hungary, and the concession of self-government to their race. The emperor yielded so far as to grant a constitution, by which Hungary, Transylvania, and Croatia were erected into a separate kingdom, having its own ministers, legislature, taxes, its own army and civil and municipal government. Other parts of the empire participated in the benefits of like concessions. But a reaction soon commenced. The four or five million Magyars wished to be themselves free from German control, but they grudged the position of equality granted to their ruder neighbours, the Croats. United by the Hungarian constitution with that kingdom, the Croatians, Sclavonians by descent, perceived only a fatal deterioration of their position in the predominance of the Magyar magnates and race in the National Assembly at Pesth. The ancient hatred of Sclavonian to Magyar broke forth with unextinguishable fury at this prospect. Too weak to contend, either in the field or the Assembly, with the Hungarian power, the Croatians saw no prospect of protection but in the German race and the shield of the emperor. "The emperor, and the unity of the empire," became in this manner the warcry of the Croatians, as that of "the unity and independence of Hungary" was of the Magyars. No sooner, accordingly, did it distinctly appear what turn affairs were taking, and the pretensions of the Magyars were openly declared, than a deputation from Croatia set out for Vienna, to lay before the emperor the assurances of their devotion and the expression of their apprehensions. They were willing to spend the last drop of their blood in behalf of the imperial crown, and to preserve the integrity of the empire; but they could not hope for success unless he placed at their head a chief in whom they had confidence. Jellachich alone was this man. The deputation met with the most favourable reception; mutual confidence was at once established from the perception of common danger. Jellachich was immediately elevated to the rank of *Ban*, or governor of Croatia, and shortly afterwards created field-marshal, councillor of the empire, colonel-commandant of two regiments, and commander-in-chief of the provinces of Bannat, Warasdin, and Carlsbadt, in the Illyrian districts.

The emperor now fled from Vienna to the Tyrol, and thence issued a proclamation condemning the violence of his German and Hungarian subjects. The Croats, on their side, publicly declared that they would never consent to the separation of Hungary from the imperial crown, and prepared to support their declaration by force of arms, averring that they would prefer the knout of the Russians to the insolence of the Magyar. The bitterness of feeling between the opposing parties found expression at a conference which took place at Vienna on the 29th of July. M. Bach, the minister of justice, and Baron Jellachich, supported it, on the one side; Count Louis Bathiany and Prince Esterhazy, on the other. It began in a solemn manner, and with measured expressions on both sides; but ere long the intensity of feeling broke through their courtly restraints, and the debate became animated and violent in the highest degree. "Between the cabinets of Pesth and Vienna," said Count Bathiany, "there is now an insurmountable barrier." "Which you have raised up yourselves," replied Bach. Take care, count, there is behind that barrier on your side an abyss, the name of which is Revolution." "And who has dug that abyss?" "You know better than we do; ask Kossuth. Meanwhile, I will tell you what will fill it up, oceans of blood, thousands of corpses; perhaps your own, count." Before separating, Count Bathiany approached Jellachich, and taking him by the hand, said, "For the last time, do you wish peace or war?" "We wish for peace," replied the Ban, "if the Magyars, better inspired than they now are, are willing to render to Caesar what belongs to Caesar, and to Austria what belongs to Austria;

but if they persist in wishing to shiver to pieces the fundamental laws of the empire, then we are for war." "May God protect the right," replied Bathiany; "the sabre must now decide betwixt us. Adieu, baron; I assign a rendezvous on the banks of the Drave." "We shall meet before on those of the Danube," replied Jellachich; and he was as good as his word. With these words they separated, and both sides prepared for war.

Taking advantage of this national animosity, and acting upon their old maxim, *Divide et impera*, the Austrian government set about reducing Hungary to submission by means of Jellachich and his Croats. The ultimatum they sent to Pesth was that the ministries of war, finance, and foreign affairs in Hungary should be united to those of Vienna, and that an entire community of right should be established between all the inhabitants of Austria and Hungary, be they Magyars, Germans, Croats, Slovaks, or Servians. The last clause was especially distasteful to the proud Magyar. Hostilities were precipitated by the barbarous murder of Count Lamberg on the bridge at Pesth, where he was attacked by an infuriated mob as he was on his way to the Diet to present the emperor's rescripts. The fear of being deprived of their newly-recovered nationality, and of being again absorbed in the despotism of Austria, maddened the populace. The war in Hungary had scarce begun when a fresh revolution, aided by a mutiny of the soldiers, broke out in Vienna, resulting in fearful carnage, and the murder of Count Latour, the minister of war. The emperor again fled from his capital (October 7, 1848), which was left in the hands of the insurgents until the arrival of Jellachich from Hungary, and Windischgrätz from Bohemia, each with an army, turned the scale against them. The barricades were stormed, and after a stubborn resistance carried with great slaughter. The town was set on fire in six and twenty different places, and the rebels, with their leader, the Polish General Bern, capitulated. While the terms of capitulation were being carried out, however, an army of Hungarians was seen approaching the city to assist the insurgents; and all the tumultuous excitement began again, to be rigorously and finally suppressed with fire and sword. Though the imperial authority was thus far restored, the burden of government was too heavy for the Emperor Ferdinand to bear. On the 2nd December, at Olmutz, he abdicated the throne in favour of Francis Joseph, then eighteen years of age, and the son of Francis Carl, the emperor's brother, who also renounced his right to the crown. In his first proclamation the young emperor boasted that "Austria had crushed the rebellion in Lombardy, driven back the Piedmontese into their own territory, planted the Austrian flag again in triumph on the walls of Milan, which had for centuries been a fief of the house of Hapsburg." In Hungary, too, he added, "the imperial arms have been uniformly successful, and there is every reason to expect a victorious issue to the campaign." Much had to be done before that expectation was fulfilled. Kossuth, the president of Hungary, Bern, Dembinski, Georgey, Klapka, and other military leaders, with their brave troops, taxed all the energies of the veteran Windischgrätz, who strove manfully to restore imperial authority in the rebellious kingdom. At length General Piickner being in a strait solicited the aid of the Russian General Luders, who at once sent troops across the frontier from Wallachia, where he was stationed. This happened in the month of February, 1849, yet in April the Hungarians recovered possession of their capital Pesth, and threatened the safety of Vienna itself. On the 14th of April

Kossuth issued the proclamation of Hungarian independence, to the great displeasure of Georgey and the Magyar aristocratic party, who desired to maintain the union with Austria. Russian aid was once more invoked by the Kaiser, and the Emperor Nicholas, hating democracy and uneasy about Poland, was only too glad to assist in crushing the independence of such dangerous neighbours as the Magyar republicans, while he laid an onerous obligation upon the emperor of Austria.

Unfortunately for the Hungarian cause, General Georgey had an invincible repugnance to Kossuth and his schemes for independence, and was as a matter of course not trusted by him with the command of all the troops. This division in the camp proved a more potent auxiliary to the Austrians than even the Muscovite bayonets. After several bloody battles, in which prodigies of valour were performed, the cause of the Magyars was by the month of August rendered utterly desperate. Kossuth's eloquent proclamation of that date well expresses the condition into which they had fallen:—

"After several unfortunate battles, in which God, in the latter days, has proved the Hungarian nation, we have no longer any hope of continuing with success our defensive struggles against the considerable forces of the Austrians and Russians. In this state of affairs, the safety of the nation and the security for its future have come to depend entirely on the general who is at the head of the army; and I am profoundly convinced that the prolonged existence of the present government would not only be useless to the nation, but might be attended with serious evils. I make known to the nation, as well in the name of myself as of the entire ministry, that, animated by the same sentiments which have guided all my steps, and induced the sacrifice of my entire existence to the good of our country, I retire from the government, and invest with supreme military and civil power the general, Arthur Georgey, until the nation, in the exercise of its rights, sees fit to dispose of it otherwise. May he love his fatherland as disinterestedly as I have done, and may he be more fortunate than I have been in securing the prosperity of the nation! I can no longer be of use to the country by my actions; if my death can be of any service to it, I willingly give it the sacrifice of my life. May the God of justice and mercy be with the nation!

"KOSSUTH.

"*Dated*, FORTRESS OF ARAD, *August* 11, 1849."

This transfer of authority was effected in the hope that Georgey would obtain better terms from the Russians than the democrat leader was likely to do. On the 13th of August the Hungarian army, 28,000 strong, laid down their arms, and Georgey surrendered to Count Rudiger. Austria once more swayed the country, and glutted her vengeance by the death of many of the brave Magyar officers on the scaffold. They were in some sort avenged by the acrimonious feelings that arose between the conquerors, the Austrians and Russians, each of whom affected to ignore the services of the other during the campaign. The sore feeling that arose from this unlucky alliance engendered a covert enmity that did effective mischief to Russia during the Crimean war, and of which the world may possibly yet see bitter fruit.

Austria had barely passed ten years' breathing time when Russia had the grim satisfaction of seeing her exposed to a violent and unjustifiable attack from France. By the joint action of

French and Italian diplomacy matters were so contrived that Austria was led to take the first warlike step; and in the hope of repeating Radetzky's Novara campaign, her army crossed the Ticino into Piedmontese territory on the 26th of April, 1859. This was made the ostensible ground of French interference, and on the 3rd of May Napoleon III. issued a proclamation declaring war against Austria. It was in this proclamation that he charged the Austrian government with having brought things to that extremity "that either she must rule right up to the Alps, or Italy must be free as far as the Adriatic." "The end of this war," he continued, "is to restore Italy to herself, not to give her a change of masters; and we shall have on our frontiers a friendly people who will owe to us their independence."

The French emperor did feel, nevertheless, the sting of certain expressions in the manifesto of Francis Joseph, that seemed aimed at the Bonapartist policy. "When the shadows of revolution," said the Kaiser, "which imperil the most precious gifts of humanity, threatened the whole of Europe, Providence made use of the sword of Austria to dissipate those shadows. We are again on the eve of one of those epochs, in which doctrines subversive of all order are preached, not only by sectarians, *but are hurled upon the world from the height of thrones.*" This was the voice of a champion of legitimacy challenging the monarch who reigned by the will of the nation, and who represented in some sort the principles of the Revolution of 1789. The emperor quitted the Tuileries on the 10th of May to join his army, which had entered Piedmont by Mont Cenis, the Col de Genevre, and by Genoa, and established his head-quarters at Alessandria. The first engagement took place at Montebello on the 20th of May, and on the 4th of June occurred the general action of Magenta, in which the Austrians were defeated by General MacMahon, who won the title of duke and the baton of a field-marshal. The emperor had directed the previous movements of the army, and in order to signalize his mastery of the art of war had placed the French army in a position that a prompt and skilful enemy might have used to his ruin—a movement not unlike that which has led to the disaster of Sedan. To avoid making a direct attack on Giulay's two strongest positions at Pavia and Piacenza, the Austrian left, Napoleon led the whole of his army against the enemy's right at Buffalora, on the upper Ticino; his object being to make the Austrians abandon their positions and accept battle on ground that was not of their own choice. The danger of this movement, which began on the 28th of May and was not completed till the 2nd of June, was extreme, as it was performed at a very short distance from the enemy, who, with but a small display of alertness, might have attacked the French on their march and destroyed them in detail. The victory of Magenta followed by that of Melegnano dislodged the Austrians from Milanese territory; and on the 9th of June Napoleon and Victor Emmanuel made their solemn entry into Milan. The emperor, in an address to the Milanese, defended himself from the charge of personal ambition. "If there are men," said he, "who do not understand their epoch, I am not of the number. In the enlightened state of public opinion, a man is greater nowadays by the moral influence he exercises than by sterile conquests; and this moral influence I seek, proud to aid in giving liberty to one of the most beautiful parts of Europe." The master of legions was also a great master of phrases. But the war was not over, and the decisive battle of the campaign was fought on ground that had long been consecrated to war. The Austrian General

Giulay having proved his incompetence at Magenta, the young Kaiser himself assumed the command of the army, with General Hess for his right hand. The army of Germans had retired to Mantua and Verona, and the French emperor with Iris marshals, together with Victor Emmanuel and the Sardinian army, went marching on secure in the thought that their antagonists were on the other side the Mincio, when suddenly they found themselves opposed by 140,000 armed men. On the 23rd of June General Hess had caused this vast army to sally out from the Quadrilateral, and re-occupy positions which they had but partially abandoned three days before. Though uninformed as to the exact whereabouts of his enemy, the general had formed a skilful plan to be executed on the battlefield, near Castiglione, where Prince Eugene in Marlborough's day, and Napoleon I. more recently, had severally exhibited their military genius. The Austrians occupied a space of hilly ground almost in the form of a parallelogram about twelve miles long and nine wide, the centre of which was Cavriana, where Francis Joseph established his headquarters. The key of the position was the village of Solferino, which stands on an eminence commanding a most extensive view of the country. From the summit of a tower in this village, named the "watch-tower of Italy," the eye embraces an extent of country reaching from the Alps to the Apennines. Mantua, Verona, Ceresara, Bozzolo, Cremona, and the broad plain beside it are distinctly visible. The Lake of Garda, the bluest and most transparent sheet of water in the Italian peninsula, appears on the edge of the farthest slope of hills stretching away into the heart of the Tyrolese Alps. The battle to which this village has given a name, identified as it is with the liberation of Italy from the Austrian yoke, merits a brief notice. The French troops began their forward movement before dawn on Midsummer day, and by five o'clock had commenced a battle which lasted altogether sixteen hours. When Napoleon arrived at Castiglione, ascending the steeple of St. Peter's church, he surveyed the whole ground, being directed by the smoke of the guns to the movements of the different corps. To the left Baraguay d'Hilliers was encountering a tremendous artillery fire from the enemy, while MacMahon was advancing towards him through the fields bordering the Mantua road. The several French corps had been marching too widely apart, and the Austrians had very nearly succeeded in separating them one from the other. General Niel was in such expectation of being outflanked by the enemy, that he sent word to Canrobert that it was impossible to afford him any support until their respective corps had effected a junction. As the battle proceeded, the hill of Solferino became the object of the severest contest. Regiment after regiment was driven back by the Austrians, under Stadion, with fearful loss to the French as they ascended the slopes, but at length the mount was occupied and the Austrian artillery captured. The Tower Hill, still higher up, continued to be most vigorously defended. At length General Forey gave orders to storm the steep ascent. The drums beat, the trumpets sounded; shouts of "Vive l'Empereur" rent the air; voltigeurs of the imperial guard, chasseurs, and battalions of the line, rushed to the assault with an impetuosity that the Austrians could not withstand. The heights were covered in a moment by thousands of French troops, and the tower of Solferino was won. Leboeuf brought his artillery to bear on the retreating regiments, but the battle still raged furiously along the extensive field. The Sardinians and their king at San Martino had a fierce struggle with his terrible antagonist, Benedek, and

20,000 Austrians. About four o'clock in the afternoon the Algerian sharpshooters and the voltigeurs of the guard, after a hand to hand fight with the prince of Hesse's division, carried Cavriana, the Kaiser's headquarters, and a general retreat of the Austrians became inevitable. Two hours afterwards the house which had been the temporary dwelling of Francis Joseph opened its doors to receive the rival emperor. When the retreat began the scene of battle was visited by a fearful tempest—one of those summer storms which envelope in a whirlwind of rain and fire the region they fall on. Dark clouds hung over, and thunder and lightning rivalled with their elemental horror the glare and clamour of the contending artillery below. When the storm abated, the French resumed the offensive, and Canrobert, who had been inactive all day, came to continue, in the plain below Cavriana, the conflict that had been carried on with so much stubborn valour all day upon the hills. Night came at last to close the dreadful scene, the Austrians retiring in good order, and with a feeling that though they had been defeated, the French had paid dearly for their victory. The Austrians retired beyond the Adige, and after a short week's pause the French army followed them, crossing the Mincio on the 30th of June. Another battle seemed at hand, which, as the Italians hoped, would drive their German masters out of the country, and liberate the peninsula from the Alps to the Adriatic. But the Emperor Napoleon had a surprise in store for them. Two days after the battle of Solferino, Count Cavour and his secretary Nigra had a long interview with the emperor, whom they found very proud of the achievements of his army and its triumphs over the Austrians, but much disgusted with the quarrels of his generals, and deeply impressed with the horrible nature of the scenes he had for the first time witnessed on the battlefield. They were made to understand, however, that the war would proceed, and that his Majesty was lending a favourable ear to the requests of the Hungarian refugees, who demanded help for the liberation of their country from Austrian domination.

But there was work enough yet in Italy if the formidable fortresses of the Quadrilateral were to be taken. On the 7th of May the French were ranged about Valeggio in strong military array in expectation of a general engagement, which it was thought the enemy was not unwilling to commence, when General Floury returned from a secret mission on which he had been sent to Verona. This was no less than a proposal for peace, which Napoleon, in his mysterious, theatrical way, had sent the night before to the Emperor Francis Joseph, without saying a word to his ally Victor Emmanuel, or to any of his marshals save Vaillant. He had soon tired of the war, and probably began to feel that he might do too much for Sardinia, which now showed signs of absorbing all Italy, and that a show of generosity to Austria might secure him a powerful friend in the person of a legitimate emperor, to say nothing of hints and rumours that Prussia might interfere. So, as his biographer says, "by a sudden inspiration, he resolved to propose an armistice in the middle of his victorious army's march. The conqueror asks for peace, what grandeur! moderation in victory is so rare." The Kaiser was taken so much by surprise, that he suspected a snare, and deferred his answer to Napoleon's letter, which he received on the 6th July, till the morrow. An interview was agreed upon, and the two sovereigns met on the 11th at Villafranca, a village half-way between Solferino and Verona. It was arranged with all those accessories that the French know so well how to employ, in order to produce a dramatic effect. Napoleon rode at the head of his troops until he saw Francis Joseph approaching at the head of his escort, when he galloped forward alone to meet him, and the two emperors having shaken hands, dismounted, entered the house of a M. Morelli, in Villafranca, and in a conversation of nearly two hours, settled the preliminaries of the peace of Villafranca, which were ratified subsequently by the treaty of Zurich. These preliminaries consisted of seven clauses:—1. The two sovereigns are favourable to the creation of an Italian confederation. 2. This confederation shall be under the honorary presidency of the Holy Father. 3. The emperor of Austria cedes to the emperor of the French his rights over Lombardy, with the exception of the fortresses of Mantua and Peschiera, in such a manner as that the frontier of the Austrian possessions shall start from the farthest radius of the fortress of Peschiera, and extend in a straight line along the Mincio as far as Grazia; from thence to Scarzarola and Suzana to the Po, whence the existing frontier line shall continue to form the borders of Austria. The emperor of the French will transfer the ceded territory to the king of Sardinia. 4. Venetia shall form part of the Italian confederation while remaining under the crown of the emperor of Austria. 5. The grand duke of Tuscany and the duke of Modena shall re-enter their states on granting a general amnesty. 6. The two emperors will request the Holy Father to introduce the reforms that are indispensable in his states. 7. A full and complete amnesty is granted on both sides to all persons compromised by recent events in the territories of the belligerents.

What a falling off was here from the mighty plan on which the Italians had built their lofty and sanguine hopes! Deep and bitter was the disappointment to them. The people felt that the dignity of their honest king, and of the whole nation, had been lowered, and their most cherished ambitions thwarted. Victor Emmanuel bore himself with the composure of a king, and coldly thanked Louis Napoleon for the service he had rendered to Italy. To Cavour the news of the peace was a crushing blow. He seemed, says Professor Botta, to feel the concentrated bitterness of the nation. The cry of anguish which arose from the Italians fell upon his heart like a reproach, and the blood of those who had fallen on the plains of Lombardy cried to him from the ground. The very darkness in which he was left as to the motives of that sudden interview made him suspect that he and his country had been betrayed. For a time he lost his usual self-control, and in a stormy interview with his royal master, declined to see the emperor, urged the king to reject the terms of peace, to recall his army, and to leave Napoleon to his designs. His advice not being accepted, he resigned office, and retired to his country seat at Leri, feeling that the destinies of Italy had been transferred from the hands of men of action to those of diplomatists with whom he knew himself to be in bad odour. The whole story and its moral are well summed up in a simple poem by Mrs. Barrett Browning, entitled "A Tale of Villafranca:"—

> My little son, my Florentine,
> Sit down beside my knee,
> And I will tell you why the sign
> Of joy which flushed our Italy
> Has faded since but yesternight;

And why your Florence of delight
Is mourning as you see.
A great man (who was crowned one day)
Imagined a great deed:
He shaped it out of cloud and clay;
He touched it finely till the seed
Possessed the flower: from heart and brain
He fed it with large thoughts humane,
To help a people's need.
He brought it out into the sun—
They blessed it to his face:
"Oh, great pure deed, that hast undone
So many bad and base!
O generous deed, heroic deed,
Come forth, be perfected, succeed,
Deliver by God's grace!"
Then sovereigns, statesmen, north and south,
Rose up in wrath and fear,
And cried, protesting by one mouth,
What monster have we here?
A great deed at this hour of day?
A great just deed, and not for pay?
Absurd—or insincere!
"And if sincere, the heavier blow
In that case we shall bear;
For where's our blessed status quo,
Our holy treaties, where
Our rights to sell a race, or buy,
Protect and pillage, occupy,
And civilize despair?"
Some muttered that the great deed meant
A great pretest to sin;
And others, the pretext, so lent,
Was heinous (to begin).
Volcanic terms of *great* and *just?*
Admit such tongues of flame, the crust
Of time and law falls in.
A great deed in this world of ours
Unheard of the pretence is:
It threatens plainly the great powers;

Is fatal in all senses.
A great just deed in the world?—call out
The rifles! be not slack about
The national defences.
And many murmured, "From this source
What red blood must be poured!"
And some rejoined, " 'Tis even worse;
What red tape is ignored!"
All cursed the doer for an evil,
Called here, enlarging on the devil,
There, monkeying the Lord.
Some said, it could not be explained;
Some, could not be excused;
And others, "Leave it unrestrained,
Gehenna's self is loosed."
And all cried, "Crush it, maim it, gag it!
Set dog-toothed lies to tear it ragged,
Truncated, and traduced!"
But he stood sad before the sun:
(The peoples felt their fate).
"The world is many, I am one;
My great deed was too great.
God's fruit of justice ripens slow;
Men's souls are narrow; let them grow.
My brothers, we must wait."
The tale is ended, child of mine,
Turned graver at my knee.
They say your eyes, my Florentine,
Are English: it may be:
And yet I've marked as blue a pair
Following the doves across the square,
At Venice by the sea.
Ah child, ah child! I cannot say
A word more. You conceive
The reason now why just to-day
We see our Florence grieve.
Ah child, look up into the sky!
In this low world, where great deeds die,
What matter if we live?

The most humiliating part of the transaction to Sardinia was the sacrifice it had to make to France, in compliance with a secret treaty, of its ancient possessions, Savoy and Nice, given by vote of the population, be it said, to its powerful friend, as a "compensation and for the rectification of his frontier." On the other hand a secret stipulation made by Napoleon at Villafranca was of immense service to Italy, inaugurating as it did the great principle of popular sovereignty. It was to the effect that no coercion should be employed to enforce the offensive terms of the treaty there agreed upon, a proviso that came to be the keystone of Italian nationality. The provinces which had been freed from their petty tyrants were, said the letter of the treaty, to be restored to them; but the restoration of the runaway dukes and duchesses, and the re-establishment of his Holiness's authority over the Legations, were only to take place with the concurrence of the populations, uninfluenced by the armed force of foreign powers. The Italians, in fact, for the first time since the middle ages, were really left to themselves. Alarmed at the outbreak of the war, and the accompanying manifestations of popular feeling, the smaller sovereigns had fled to the protecting wing of Austria. The government of their states then devolved upon the Constitutional Assemblies, who acted with promptitude and vigour. In Modena and Parma a dictator was appointed in the person of Farini, while the Tuscans conferred similar authority on Baron Ricasoli, a noble of the antique Roman type. The Legations, which had cut themselves free from the papal dominion, acted under the directions of Cipriani. With these men Cavour kept up continual communication, for though no longer minister, he was the recognized leader of the national movement. When he discovered that non-intervention was the principle of the Zurich treaty, he felt that Italy would be able after all to achieve unity and consolidation, spite of Napoleon's schemes for a confederation. The people of the Tuscan and Æmilian provinces positively refused to receive back their princes, notwithstanding the urgent entreaties of the emperor of the French, and declined every plan of adjustment save that of annexation to Sardinia. At this juncture, in the spring of 1860, Cavour was recalled to power, and having previously mapped out the central provinces into electoral districts, he appealed to the inhabitants to elect representatives who should take their seats in the Parliament of Italy. This was done, and the northern part of the peninsula was united under Victor Emmanuel, the constitutional king of Italy. Well might the king, in addressing the new Parliament, congratulate the country that "Italy was no longer the Italy of municipal governments, or that of the middle ages, but the Italy of the Italians." Attended by his minister, he went to visit the new dominions, which not the sword, says Signor Botta, but the hearts of the people, had bestowed upon him. The enthusiasm with which the visitors were received in the new provinces exceeds description. For the first time the sentiment which before had been so long restrained by the boundaries of cities and states overleaped all barriers, and was merged in the deep emotion of patriotism; all traces of ancient feuds vanished; the once rival cities emulated each other in their expressions of mutual affection. Genoa restored to Pisa the chains of her harbour, which seized centuries before, had been retained as a trophy; the sword bequeathed in the fourteenth century by Castruccio Castracani to him who should deliver the country, was presented to Victor Emmanuel, and Niccolini, the venerable poet, carried to the king with tottering steps his master-piece, the

"Arnaldo de Brescia," blessing the "kind fate that had allowed him, before his eyes closed on the sweet air of Italy, to see the aspiration of his life accomplished."

But another act of the great drama now opens, another hero appears on the stage—Guiseppe Garibaldi. We search in vain the archives of history for heroic deeds and marvellous achievements like those which, at the time here spoken of, sent a thrill of admiration and joy through the hearts of all the friends of liberty. For this, says Sig. Botta, we must go back to the legendary ages, when the gods mingled with men, the ages of Hercules and Theseus, of Odin and Thor. When centuries shall have passed, and Italy shall again have reached the summit of her greatness, the memory of the great chieftain will be embellished by popular imagination, and the name of Garibaldi will be invested with a mythical glory surpassing that of the Cid in Spain, and Joan of Arc in France. On the 11th of May, 1860, Garibaldi, at the head of one thousand patriots, landed at Marsala. He came, he saw, he conquered. Within less than four months he had delivered ten millions of Italians from the hated yoke of the Bourbons. For a work like that which Garibaldi had accomplished Cavour had no power. A statesman far removed from revolutionary impulses, his genius consisted rather in directing events than forcing them. Believing in the ultimate union of the nations, his original plan had been the consolidation of northern Italy into one kingdom, which should gradually absorb the entire peninsula. But the peace of Villafranca having defeated that design, his next object became the annexation of central Italy. The instinct of the people, however, outstripped this process of gradual absorption, and hastened to precipitate the immediate union of the whole country. Of this instinct Garibaldi was the great representative. Essentially a man of the masses, sharing their virtues as well as their faults, with the heart of a Hon in the frame of an athlete, trained amidst the tempests of the ocean, and on the battlefields of the old and new worlds, and burning with the fire of liberty and patriotism, the hero of Caprera became the leader of the national movement at the time when it began to assume a more revolutionary character.

This was the most embarrassing period of the political career of Cavour. On one hand it was impossible for Sardinia openly to take part in the expeditions of Garibaldi, directed against the king of the Two Sicilies, still on his throne, and with whom Victor Emmanuel held neutral, if not friendly relations. Such a step would probably have induced Austria again to take the field, and in the face of such a flagrant violation of international law, France would have been unable to protect the country from an armed intervention. On the other hand, that movement could not be prevented without seriously endangering the national cause. The idea of political unity had taken such deep hold on the public mind, that any attempt to check its development would have resulted in revolution. Again, the court of Rome was gathering the papist mercenaries of Europe to its support, and having secured the services of General Lamoriciere, it threatened the new kingdom with an alliance with Francis II., openly supported by Austria and other powers. In this emergency Garibaldi appeared, and organized his expeditions for the deliverance of Southern Italy. Although his success might be doubtful, his bold attempt would spread terror among the enemy, divide the forces of Naples and Rome, and drive them from their threatening attitude. So, without either encouraging or preventing the departure of Garibaldi, Cavour awaited events, ready to avail himself of all the advantages which might result from the daring enterprise, or to avert any danger which it might provoke. This policy evinced scarcely less boldness than the achievements of the dashing leader himself. The principle of national rights over dynastic interests was regarded as so heretical by the cabinets of Europe, that it was mainly due to the skill of Cavour that their opposition on this occasion was confined to protest. By appealing to their conservative tendencies, and by representing that an effort to put down the movement by force of arms would cause a revolution throughout the peninsula, and endanger the existence of monarchical institutions, he saved the expeditions from an armed intervention. But when success appeared certain, Cavour changed his policy of inaction to one of active sympathy, and not only allowed volunteers to depart from the ports of the state, and subscriptions for their aid to be widely circulated, but he himself afforded the enterprise direct assistance. Before the war of 1859, Sardinia had proposed an alliance with the king of Naples on condition of his granting a constitution to his people and joining in the war against Austria. Hitherto he had resisted all advances. But now that Garibaldi, having possessed himself of Sicily, was knocking at the gates of Naples, Francis II. hastened to accede to those terms, and proposed to share with Sardinia the pontifical dominions. But it was too late. Since the war had commenced such changes had occurred in the peninsula, that Cavour in turn declined the proposed alliance; and as England, France, and Russia urged upon him its acceptance, he wisely insisted on delaying all negotiations on the subject until that sovereign should prove himself able to maintain his throne; and in the meantime claimed as a preliminary that he should recognize the independence of Sicily. But Garibaldi left no time for decision; he at once made his triumphant entry into Naples, while the fugitive king took refuge in Gaeta.

Between Cavour and Garibaldi, as has been already said, there existed great differences of character, which are pointed out with admirable discrimination by Signor Botta. The one was endowed with comprehensive genius, with a clear, keen intellect, that neither imagination nor impulse could seduce; affluent, aristocratic, reserved, often satirical and imperious, unyielding in his opinions, with power to bend the convictions of others to his own; too confident in himself to court popular favour, and devoted to labours more calculated to excite the admiration of the thoughtful than to dazzle the multitude. The other, of more limited capacity, but of wider sympathies, was ruled by imagination and impulse; disposed to regard all questions from a single point of view; democratic by birth and principles, of Spartan simplicity of life and manners, despising rank and wealth; kind, straightforward, easily influenced by all who approached him in the name of patriotism, and from his wonderful success as well as from his rare personal qualities, the idol of the masses.

Both true patriots, both equally courageous and energetic, while the one exerted his genius in diplomatic strategy, the other was engaged in irregular warfare. Both equally ambitious to serve their country, while one accepted the honours bestowed on him, the other disclaimed all distinctions, but delighted to appear in public in his worn red shirt. Both of sterling integrity, while the one on entering office disposed of his shares in the public stocks to place himself beyond the reach of suspicion, the other during his dictatorship received but two dollars a day from the public treasury, and after conquering a kingdom, retired, like Cincinnatus of old, to his farm, to live by the labour of his hands. These characteristics, combined with an intense hatred of all diplomacy, produced in Garibaldi a personal antipathy to Cavour, which on the surrender of Nice culminated in open hostility. That his birthplace should have been ceded to Napoleon, whom he disliked still more than Cavour, he regarded almost as a personal insult; and although that surrender had been approved by the Parliament and the king, and voted for by the people, Cavour appeared to him as its sole author. He did not see that had Nice been refused the Italian cause would have been in danger, and that the minister who should have incurred the responsibility of the refusal would have been liable to impeachment as a traitor. He overlooked the fact that his expeditions had found a supporter in Cavour, who had protected them from foreign intervention; and that it was in no small degree due to his efforts that he was enabled to enter Naples alone, and to be received with open arms by the Neapolitan troops, who still held possession of the city. His prejudice was no doubt, in great measure, the effect of the influences by which he was surrounded. He had early in life been connected with Mazzini, and long continued to manifest his sympathy with the republican party. But when Manin, the Venetian patriot, urged the union of all parties under the leadership of the house of Savoy, he renounced his former alliance, and generously gave his adherence to the constitutional monarchy of Victor Emmanuel. Later, on becoming personally acquainted with the king, he found in his character simplicity, straightforwardness, and patriotism, much that was congenial to himself, and he conceived for him a loyal attachment.

This course was at the time bitterly condemned by his former associates, and by Mazzini himself. But now, in the hour of his triumph, those who not long before had been engaged in vilifying his name in Europe and in America flocked to Naples, insinuated themselves again into his confidence, and by playing on his real or fancied grievances, strove to widen the breach between him and Cavour, whom they justly regarded as the great supporter of constitutional monarchy, and the staunch opponent of their schemes. Good, unsophisticated, generous, and new in the art of government, the hero of the battlefield became a child in the hands of those adventurers. Naples and Sicily fell under their control, and exhibited more completely than ever the effects of that disorganization to which they had been previously reduced by a long reign of despotism. From Gaeta, Francis II. now threatened an invasion of his former dominions, whilst Austria from Verona and Mantua, and Lamoriciere from Ancona, were preparing to act in concert with him. In this state of things it was necessary that Southern Italy should at once declare her union with the northern and central provinces, and thus justify the intervention of Sardinia, by which alone regularity could be introduced into the administration, and the invasion repelled. The great majority demanded annexation; but Garibaldi, who had taken possession of the kingdom in the name of Victor Emmanuel, seemed to waver between his former adherence to Mazzini and his fidelity to the king. Pressed by public opinion to consult the vote of the people, he at last consented to open the ballot-box, but only on condition of the dismissal of Cavour from the cabinet. Such a request, destructive of all constitutional liberty, found no favour with the king; and Cavour, receiving new assurances of confidence from the Parliament, decided on a bold movement. The situation was growing every day more alarming; while anarchy threatened Naples, the mercenaries of the pope were pouring in from all quarters, and Garibaldi himself was held in check on the Volturno; the republicans began to speak openly of attacking the French garrison at Rome, and the Austrians in the fortresses of the Quadrilateral. Baffled in their plan of removing Cavour from the government, the same party prevailed on Garibaldi to subordinate the annexation of Southern Italy to the deliverance of Rome and Venice, and he, in fact, proclaimed that he would allow the union to be consummated only when he could crown Victor Emmanuel king of Italy on the Quirinal. Cavour saw that the attempt to carry out this plan would bring certain defeat, involve Sardinia in a war with Austria, break up the French alliance, cause the abandonment of the non-intervention policy, and probably sacrifice the conquests already achieved. Had Garibaldi been able to carry out his dream, to make his triumphal passage across Umbria and the Marches, rout the troops of Lamoriciere, put to flight the French army, expel Austria, and bring aid to Hungary and Poland, his very successes would have provoked an armed intervention. His triumphs as well as his defeats appeared equally fatal to Italy. There was no time to lose; "If we do not reach the Cattolica before Garibaldi, we are lost," said Cavour. By a master stroke of policy, he determined at once to take possession of Umbria and the Marches, push forward the army to Naples and Sicily, and wrest from Garibaldi the leadership of the nation. The deputations from these provinces, demanding immediate annexation, were at once favourably listened to. Cardinal Antonelli was summoned, in the name of Italy, to disband his mercenaries, the Sardinian army crossed the frontier, and the fleet set sail for the Adriatic. By the victory of Castelfidardo and the siege of Ancona the papal army was scattered to the winds, Lamoriciere taken prisoner, Perugia avenged, and the national flag unfurled over the papal dominions.

Victor Emmanuel, at the head of his troops, now entered the Neapolitan territory, and on approaching the camp at Capua was met by Garibaldi, who, amidst the enthusiastic cheers of the two armies, saluted him King of Italy. The wisdom of the policy followed by Cavour on this occasion can only be questioned by those who make the principle of nationality subservient to the interests of dynasties and to the claims of despotism.

By taking possession of Umbria and the Marches, and by occupying Southern Italy, he defeated the rash designs of the Republicans, and put an end to the not less menacing projects of Lamoriciere and Francis II. He showed also a just appreciation of the character of Garibaldi, on whose patriotism, loyalty, and generous instincts he confidently relied; and he was not mistaken; for scarcely had the king announced his intention to proceed to Naples when the great chieftain, listening to the voice of his heart, summoned the people to the ballot box, and the annexation being voted for by a large majority, he at once resigned his dictatorship and retired to his humble home.

On the 18th of February, 1861, the first Italian Parliament representing united Italy was convened in the old capital of Sardinia. The roar of the cannon which celebrated its first meeting mingled with that which announced the fall of Gaeta; the sound echoed throughout the peninsula, and bore to Austria and the papacy a warning of their approaching downfall. Italy at last revived in the unity of her people, her constitution, and monarchy. She rose from beneath the ruins of thrones which crushed her and divided her as by barriers, and now she has taken her place among the nations. Her standard proudly waves from Milan to Palermo; her army marches in triumph from Monte Rosa to Æna; her navy rides joyfully on the Mediterranean and the Adriatic. Another war in later years fought unsuccessfully by Austria against other enemies, bore fruit to Italy in the restoration of Venice and the Quadrilateral; and as these lines are penned, the troops of Victor Emmanuel are taking possession of Rome in the name of the Italian people.

But Cavour did not live to see this wondrous conclusion, which gave so marvellous a completeness to his plans for the regeneration of his country. The ill feeling entertained towards him by Garibaldi was one among several causes to which his last fatal illness has been attributed. The occupation of Naples by Sardinian troops, the yielding to Louis Napoleon on the Roman question, and government measures for disbanding the volunteers when the war was over, were three sources of the increased bitterness which the hero of the volunteers felt toward the statesman. Garibaldi, with his contempt for policy, declined at first to sit in the Italian Parliament, to which he was elected by several constituencies; but at length he consented to represent a district of Naples, and on the 18th April, 1861, he made his first appearance in the Chamber of Deputies for the purpose, as it soon appeared, of making an attack on the prime minister. The debate that arose was upon the subject of the volunteers, concerning whom Baron Ricasoli had moved for papers, with a view to bring about a reconciliation between the two eminent men in question. Garibaldi entered the hall in his worn red shirt, surrounded by his friends, amid the cheers of the house and the galleries, and after hearing Ricasoli and the secretary of war, he rose to address the Chamber. He thanked Ricasoli for introducing a subject of such vital importance to him, as it concerned the interests of his companions in arms; he admitted the disagreement existing between him and Cavour, but declared that he was always ready to yield whenever the welfare of the country demanded it. Then, instigated, it is said, by some of his most reckless adherents, he gave way to a lamentable burst of ill feeling. He repeated an old taunt that Cavour had made him a foreigner in his native land (Nice); reproached him for having blighted his success in Naples by his cold and baneful influence; and rising to a climax of bitterness, he accused him of having instigated civil war and of being the enemy of his country. Wounded to the quick, Cavour rose to protest. But the Chamber protested for him; the members sprang to their feet as one man, and amidst the general confusion and shouts of an indignant assembly, the chairman declared the house adjourned. This protest found an echo through the civilized world; and the press of Europe and America, while they bestowed their tribute of admiration on the great volunteer, were unanimous in the expression of their sorrow, that he who represented the arm of Italy should have indulged in such an attack upon him who represented the national mind. Order being restored in the house, General Bixio, a warm friend of Garibaldi and one of his bravest lieutenants, made an earnest appeal to him not to sacrifice to his feeling the holy cause in which they all with equal patriotism were engaged; he implored Cavour to forgive his chief, and both to unite their efforts in accomplishing the great work which Providence had intrusted to their hands. Cavour was the first to accept the proposed reconciliation, and with his usual urbanity offered not only forgiveness but oblivion of what had just occurred; he had even the magnanimity to justify the attack of his adversary by remarking that "from the grief which he himself felt, when he thought it his duty to advise the king to cede Nice and Savoy, he could well understand the feelings of the general and the resentment he had shown." The house by an overwhelming majority expressed its adhesion to Cavour's policy, but Garibaldi still showed distrust, even after the king had made a personal effort to reconcile him to the great statesman. Cavour, though victorious in Parliament, felt deeply the wound inflicted on him by the misappreciation of his labours proclaimed so loudly and persistently by Garibaldi and the most extreme among his followers. Incessant labour, immense responsibility, and bitter disappointment, began to affect his health, and he had two or three attacks of brain congestion. For the first time he complained of fatigue, of the inability to rest, and confessed to the feeling that "his frame was giving way beneath his mind and will." He wished for time to finish his work. Then he would care little what might happen; "indeed," he said, "I should be glad to die." Still he worked on with redoubled zeal till the last; he was every day at his post in the Parliament, answering questions, initiating the new house into the proceedings of constitutional government, urging forward measures best adapted to accomplish the unity of the nation, and explaining his policy with increased power and earnestness, as if a secret voice told him it was the legacy he was to bequeath to his country. As the head of the executive department, his labours were still greater; the sudden annexation of so many new provinces increased his duties to a prodigious extent. Old abuses were to be done away with, new institutions introduced, clashing interests reconciled, finances systematized, taxes revised, ways and means provided, the codes reformed, railroads marked out and built, telegraphs extended, the army and navy increased, every department re-organized, and, in short, order created out of chaos. As minister of foreign affairs the whole burden of the complicated relations with other countries rested upon him; and he was forced to keep a constant watch over the chess-board of European diplomacy, in order that he might influence the movements of friendly powers, ward off the attacks of enemies, and seize the moment in which he might checkmate the emperor of Austria and the government of Rome. In fact, he had the control of a Titanic revolution, which his position obliged him to direct solely through diplomatic skill and energy.

On Thursday, the 4th of June, alarming symptoms began to appear in the sufferer, and the news of his dangerous condition spreading through Turin, cast a deep gloom over the city. The streets leading to his palace were soon filled with a silent and sorrowful multitude, eagerly awaiting reports from the sick chamber. Those who but the day before had been his bitter opponents, now laying aside all party considerations, mingled with that anxious crowd; eyes which had regarded him with coldness or envy were now wet with tears, and many a one among that throng would willingly have given himself a sacrifice to save the life on which the fate of the nation seemed to hang. And when, toward the last, that deep silence was broken by the sound of the bell of the Viaticum, alternating with the prayers for the dying; and the solemn procession of torch-bearers, led by the good Fra Giacomo bearing the Host, was seen entering the palace—a sob of anguish arose from that multitude, as if the last hope of the country was about to be extinguished for ever.

Within, beneath the roof under which he was born, conscious that his last hour had come, yet calm, confident, and serene, lay the dying statesman, dying at the close of the first festival of the national birthday, thus rendered doubly sacred to posterity; surrounded by his household and friends, in the embrace of the king to whom he had given the crown of Italy; amidst the anxiety of all Europe, expressed by the hourly telegrams received from the various capitals; dying as he lived—an honest man, a true patriot, opposing to the last the papal church, whose sacraments, the symbols of Christianity, he received in spite of her excommunication, thus showing that he could be a Christian without being a Papist. Whether in the full possession of his faculties or in the wanderings of delirium, no bitterness or rancour escaped his lips, but he spake words of cheer and consolation to his friends, assuring them that all was saved, that Italy was secure; and as the morning of the 6th June dawned he gradually sank, still absorbed in the one thought of his country, for whose greatness he had lived, and uttering faintly and at intervals the darling names of Italy, Venice, Rome.

The grandeur of Cavour's character as a statesman must be estimated by the magnitude of his object, the boldness and the prudence with which he executed his designs, and the extraordinary power which he possessed of foreseeing results, and of converting obstacles into means. He combined the originality and depth of a theorist with the practical genius of a true reformer; he understood the character of the age in which he lived, and made it tributary to his great purposes. He made self-government the object of legislation, political economy the source of liberty, and liberty the basis of nationality. Aware that neither revolution nor conservatism alone could produce the regeneration of his country, he opposed them in their separate action, while he grasped them both with a firm hand, yoked them together, and led them on to conquest. He saw that Italian independence could only be attained through the aid of foreign alliance. He recognized in Napoleon III. the personification of organized revolution, and the natural ally of the Italian people; and the work which he foreshadowed in the union of the Sardinian troops with the armies of England and France in the Crimea, and for which he laid the foundation in the Congress of Paris, was achieved with the victories of Magenta and Solferino, and was followed by the recognition of the new kingdom of Italy by all the states of Europe save two—Austria and Spain. The thought of Venice and the Quadrilateral lay heavy on his heart in his last hours. Another and a foreign statesman was destined to accomplish the completion of the new kingdom on that side—a statesman who doubtless pondered deeply over the career of Count Cavour, and who undertook a task of kindred nature to his, of yet larger scope, the task of unifying the German nation. Of that statesman, Count von Bismarck, and of his work for Italy as well as for his own country, much will have to be said in future chapters. It is enough to indicate here the resemblance of the work he had to do with that which was so admirably performed by the long-lamented Cavour.

The Roman question, unsolved at the time of Cavour's death, was taken up by his successor in the ministry, Baron Ricasoli, who, full of respect for the church, endeavoured to reconcile its head with the state and the king. In August, 1861, he wrote a most conciliatory letter to the pope, in which he reminded his Holiness of the events of 1848 and 1849, when "Italy, moved by words of gentleness and pardon which came from your lips, conceived the hope of closing the series of its secular misfortunes, and beginning the era of its regeneration." The pope's resistance, he went on to say, or rather his want of co-operation with the cause of independence, filled the minds of the Italians with bitterness. "But the rights of nationality are imperishable, and the See of Holy Peter, by virtue of a divine promise, is imperishable also. Since neither of the two adversaries can disappear from the field of battle, they must become reconciled, so that the world may not be thrown into terrible and endless perturbations." The good baron proceeds to argue that a free church in a free state would be the very thing to suit both pope and people. "You can," he concluded, "you can, Holy Father, once more change the face of the world; you can raise the Apostolic See to a height unknown to the church in past ages. If you wish to be greater than kings of the earth, free yourself from the miseries of this royalty which makes you only their equal. Italy will give you a secure see, an entire liberty, a new grandeur. She venerates the pontiff, but she cannot arrest her march before the prince; she wishes to remain Catholic, but she wishes to be a nation free and independent. If you listen to the prayer of this favourite daughter, you will gain in souls more power than you have lost as a prince; and from the height of the Vatican, when stretching your hand over Rome and the world to bless them, you will see the nations re-established in their rights, bending before you their defender and protector." Impressive words and true, but the pope was too much a man of the world not to know that his temporalities were worth having as long as he could keep them; and neither the blandishments of Ricasoli nor the abuse of Petrucelli made his Holiness loose his hold on the temporal power, so long as there was protection at hand. The letters were sent through the French government, and all the answer vouchsafed to them was that the pope was "not in a humour "to entertain such proposals. The "most holy Janus," as Petrucelli styled him in the Italian Parliament, relied on French bayonets, and answered every appeal of his fellow-countrymen for friendly alliance by a *non possumus*. A Janus indeed, "with two faces, one that of the pontiff, serene and august; the other, that of the king of Rome, idiotic, ferocious, brutal." Still the French held Rome, and bound over the Italians to keep the peace with the spiritual "head of all the faithful."

Garibaldi, however, was not restrained by the same power, and about a year after the rejection of Ricasoli's proposals, the volunteer chief improvised an expedition that, starting from Genoa, landed in Sicily, passed thence into Calabria, and marched towards Rome, in the hope of planting the flag of Italy on the walls of the Eternal City. He endeavoured to secure the sympathy and assistance of the Hungarians, upon whom the Austrian rule still pressed heavily, and who, as Garibaldi trusted, would rise in thousands at the trumpet call of revolution. But the "sons of Arpad" were deaf to the voice of the charmer, and their feelings were expressed in a very sober, sensible letter, addressed by Klapka from Turin to the Italian chief, and pointing out that neither time nor place were propitious to revolution, and that the Hungarians would do well to wait for a more favourable opportunity. King Victor Emmanuel issued a proclamation condemning the expedition in grave and emphatic terms, and General Cialdini was sent to oppose it with Italian troops. The latter sent forward Major-general Pallavicino from Reggio to overtake Garibaldi. He found him on the morning of the 29th of August encamped at the foot of the plateau of

Aspromonte. An engagement ensued, in which the rebels had no chance. They were surrounded on all sides, and both Garibaldi and his son Menotti were wounded, the former having a bullet in his ankle, which was not extracted without considerable difficulty. A very characteristic letter from Garibaldi bewailing the conflict of Italian against Italian, appeared in the month of September. "They thirsted for blood, and I wished to spare it. I ran to the front of our line crying out to them not to fire, and from the centre to the left where my voice and those of my aides-de-camp could be heard, not a trigger was pulled. It was not thus on the attacking side. . . . If I had not been wounded at the outset, and if my people had not received the order under all circumstances to avoid any collision with the regular troops, the contest between men of the same race would have been terrible. However, far better as it is. Whatever may be the result of my wounds, whatever fate the government prepares for me, I have the consciousness of having done my duty; and the sacrifice of my life is a very little tiling if it has contributed to save that of a great number of my fellow-countrymen." A prisoner so simple-minded, and so illustrious by deeds of heroism, could not be dealt with harshly, and the king with the consent of his ministers granted a slightly qualified amnesty to all the prisoners, and a free pardon to their leader, who again returned to his island home at Caprera. Thus the pope continued to sit on his temporal throne at Rome, or rather upon French bayonets, performing agreeably to his high pretensions what Talleyrand pronounced to be an impossibility. "You can do anything with bayonets but sit upon them," said the witty diplomatist when speaking once of the military occupation of a foreign territory'. The French emperor, to obviate the inconvenience of further expeditions like Garibaldi's, contracted a treaty with the king of Italy, which is generally known as the September Convention. It defined the period within which the Papal States were to be evacuated by the French troops, and contained the following four articles:—1, Italy engages not to attack the present territory of the Holy Father, and to prevent, even by force, every attack upon the said territory coming from without; 2, France will withdraw her troops from the Pontifical States gradually, and in proportion as the army of the Holy Father shall be organized. The evacuation shall nevertheless be accomplished within the space of two years; 3, The Italian government engages to raise no protest against the organization of a Papal army, even if composed of foreign Catholic volunteers, sufficing to maintain the authority of the Holy Father, and tranquillity as well in the interior as upon the frontier of his states, provided that this force should not degenerate into a means of attack against the Italian government; 4, Italy declares herself ready to enter into an arrangement to take under her charge a proportionate part of the debt of the former states of the church. This convention, as its name implies, was dated on the 15th of September, 1864.

At the same time it was determined to remove the capital of Italy from Turin to Florence. Several reasons conspired to make this a desirable change, but the chief was the exposed situation of Turin, in case of war, to attack either by France or Austria. Florence is beneath the shelter of the Apennines; and except Rome, which at that time was unattainable, it is, amongst the principal towns of Italy, the one that lies nearest the centre of the kingdom. But the population of Turin were naturally opposed to a measure which would reduce their fair city from a capital to a provincial town, and the demeanour of the crowd assembled in the square or place opposite the palace was so turbulent, that the soldiers fired upon it and several lives were lost.

A bill brought into the Chamber to authorize the transfer of the capital, gave rise to a long debate at the end of November, in the course of which General Cialdini delivered a speech remarkable for its spirit and eloquence. "Italy," he said, "has two-thirds and more of her frontier washed by the sea. The other third is joined to the continent by the circle of the Alps. In a sublime contrast at the foot of these gigantic and snowy Alps stretch out the vast and fertile plains of Lombardy and Piedmont. The Apennines, as if weary of the Mediterranean, bend back and cross over to the Adriatic, forming a great, curtain, an immense towering curtain, between the two seas, from Genoa to La Cattolica. In front of the Apennines you have the vast and beautiful valley of the Po, in which you find the Austrian encamped in his strong Quadrilateral, and of which—I mean the valley of the Po—we can neither fortify nor defend the principal outlets, because they are not" (this was spoken in 1864) "in our hands. The valley of the Po, therefore, shows us an enemy solidly established in a house which has its door open to whoever chooses to enter. Can it be pretended or desired that the capital of the kingdom should be in this valley of the Po? Let us hasten to remove behind the Apennines, not only the capital, but the arsenals, the depôts, the reserves, all our resources, all our most vital interests; then let the passes of the Apennines be put in a state of defence. From Genoa to La Cattolica the roads across them are only seven or eight. All these roads offer gorges, defiles, which are real Thermopylae, where a few earthworks, a few guns, and a handful of brave men, can arrest a whole army. Let us erect some solid fortifications at La Cattolica to secure the flank, and then multiply as far as possible the permanent and portable means of passing from one bank of the Po to the other, and thus prepare the possibility of useful, rapid, and decisive manoeuvres. Whenever this general system of defence of the state is accepted and carried out, the destinies of Italy can never depend on the uncertain issue of a battle. At our pleasure, and according to circumstances, we can retire behind the Po, and beyond the Apennines to await better days; or, if it suits us, if we are in a position to fight, we may come down and try the fate of arms in the valley of the Po. I too," he continued, in allusion to the grievance of the Turinese, "have a heart which profoundly feels the bitterness of political life, and can understand great affections and great sorrows. Heaven forbid, therefore, that a word, a single syllable, should fall from my lips which should in any degree wound those affections, those sorrows, which I fully comprehend and thoroughly respect. But when the security, the greatness, the future life of Italy are at stake, affection must be silent, the heart must not speak; logic alone, cold and inexorable, must reason. An eye filled with tears does not see. A heart wrung by profound pain has only sad previsions, mournful presentiments. A suffering brain is oppressed by black images, by sorrowful ideas. But are we to pause, dismayed by presentiments, previsions, fears? Oh! if all the prophecies of misfortune had been verified, what would have become of us, what would have become of Italy? Let us take heart, and recognize that a secret force, more quick-sighted, stronger, more enlightened than we, guides Italy on a determined course; let us acknowledge that the Italian revolution pursues its march, slow and pacific, but more irresistible than we could have imagined or desired, beyond the limits which we ourselves had imagined and traced out. I deplore the injury to Turin as much as any one, as on the field of battle I have often wept over fallen soldiers and friends; but, not to lose soldiers and friends, ought we to renounce combats and victories! Not to cause local injuries and sorrows, shall we sacrifice the general interest, shall we sacrifice the public weal? With Turin, seated at the foot of the Alps, at the extremity of the state, but a few miles from the French frontier, in the most eccentric conditions which can be laid down, I dispute with pain, but with entire conviction, the title of a capital. If from this solemn place you tell the cities and provinces whence you come, that the sacrifices asked are indispensable for the safety, the strength, the future of Italy, be sure the people will believe you. If you tell them that liberty, independence, national unity, are blessings for which too high a price can never be paid, the people will believe you. Tell them so, I implore you. The school of sacrifice ennobles great causes, retempers the soul, and magnifies the national character of peoples. Prometheus could transform clay into men. Sacrifice alone changes men into heroes?"

Such noble eloquence, vivid even in a bald translation, was borne, in the gallant general's native tongue, to the inmost hearts of his hearers. The bill was carried by a majority of 134 to 47, and on the 11th of December appeared a royal decree, declaring that the capital of the kingdom should be transferred to Florence within six months, which decree was duly carried into effect in the year 1865. Rome and Venice only were wanting to complete the kingdom of Italy, and already had begun that solemn march of events which was to lead to the fulfilment of the Italian patriot's dream.

CHAPTER III.

THE spirit of Louisa, the heroic queen of Prussia, would have been soothed in the darkest hour of her depression and her country's humiliation had she been able to foresee, that on two of her sons in succession the eyes of all Germany were to be steadfastly fixed as leaders in the great movement for the unification of the Fatherland. The eldest son, King Frederick William IV., trusted to have accomplished the great task by placing himself at the head of the liberalism of Central Europe; but he failed. The second son, King William I., allied himself with the conservatism of his country, and by military prowess succeeds in the great achievement. "Prussia disappears, Germany is called into existence," was one of the significant utterances of Frederick William during the revolutionary epoch of 1848-49. His refined and cultured nature shrank, however, from the excesses committed by the insurgents of that day, and he refused the proffered crown of Germany, on the plea that it was the fruit of revolution. The liberal constitution granted by him to his own subjects, and proclaimed in the first month of the year 1850, was subsequently modified by him on eight different occasions: namely, once in April, 1851; once in May, and again in June, 1852; after that twice in May, 1853; then in June, 1854; and in the following May,

1855; and finally in May, 1857. The result of these numerous modifications by royal decree was a tolerably conservative constitution, vesting considerable power in the executive. The king did not long survive the last change that was made. His health had suffered from the excitement produced by the scenes in which he participated at the time of the national convulsions, and in the autumn of 1858 he was unfitted for the duties of government by an attack of apoplexy. He died in January, 1861, at the age of sixty-six, and was succeeded on the throne by his brother William, who had been regent for more than two years, and who at the time of his coronation was in the sixty-fifth year of his age.

Two political legacies bequeathed to the new king were destined to be fruitful of important consequences: they were the Schleswig and Holstein question, and the humiliation which the late king had received from Prince Schwartzenberg, the Austrian prime minister, in the matter of Hesse-Cassel. As already mentioned, Austria had insisted that Frederick William should withdraw his troops, both from the duchies north of the Elbe and from Hesse. The king was undecided and unhappy. For a moment he thought of resistance, delivered a warlike speech at the opening of the Chambers, and nominated Herr Radowitz to the ministry. The army was put on a war footing, and the landwehr called out. A warlike spirit breathed through the nation, which began to recall the glorious days of the Great Frederick. But Schwartzenberg drew closer his alliance with Bavaria, and gathered a formidable army of 180,000 men on the Hessian frontier with a promptitude that astonished Europe, and revealed for the first time the great change that the use of railways had introduced into strategy. War seemed inevitable. The heir to the Prussian throne and the conservative party wished for it. Already shots had been exchanged by the outposts, when M. Prokesch, the Austrian envoy, summoned Prussia to quit Hesse in four and twenty hours. At the critical moment the king's kindly nature made him shrink from the responsibility of war between German and German. He gave way, dismissed the Radowitz ministry, and sent M. Manteuffel to Olmutz to submit to the dictation of Prince Schwartzenberg. Prussia was obliged to sacrifice her allies, the popular party in Hesse and in Schleswig respectively, and to recognize the authority of that Diet in which her rival reigned supreme.

The day of the treaty of Olmutz sank deep into the heart of Prussia, and was remembered by the army especially as a time of shame and ridicule that called for vengeance—a vengeance that was not slaked until the "crowning mercy" of Sadowa had visited their arms. For a time Austria was triumphant, and endeavoured even to incorporate all her various populations, German, Magyar, and Sclavonic, in the German Confederation, with a view to perpetuate her absolute preponderance in central Europe. But France and other foreign powers were so strongly opposed to this scheme that it was given up. Indeed, every step that had been taken towards national unity seemed to end only in greater disunion. "German unity," said an Austrian pamphleteer of this time, "is like squaring the circle; when you think you have got hold of it you discover that it is impossible. It is like our cathedrals; there is not one that is finished."

The war which Louis Napoleon carried into Italy brought new hope to the German unionists, although it excited the anger of the sovereigns, and almost drove Bavaria into an alliance with Austria. "The Italian war," wrote the democratic socialist Lasalle, "is not only sanctified by every principle of democracy, but it is an enormous advantage for Germany, to whom it brings salvation. Napoleon III., when he invites the Italians to drive the Austrians out of the peninsula, performs a German mission; he overthrows Austria, the eternal obstacle that prevents the unity of our country. If the map of Europe is reconstructed on behalf of the nationalities of the south, let us apply the same principle to the north. Let Prussia act without hesitation. If she does not she will have given a proof that monarchy is incapable of national action." Did this challenge of the socialist and democrat sink into the heart of the trenchant conservative Karl Otto von Bismarck? Unquestionably he pondered deeply on the Italian war, and was himself the author, as it is confidently reported, of a pamphlet entitled, "La Prusse et la Question Italienne." To him the career of Count Cavour must have been profoundly instructive and full of suggestion, as will be seen anon.

It behoves now to speak of that second unpleasant political heritage which had descended to King William from his brother—the Schleswig-Holstein question, the intricacy of which demands some care on the part of the writer to unravel, and on the part of the reader some patience to follow. Lord Palmerston used to say there was only one man besides himself who understood the Schleswig-Holstein question, and that man was dead. It is in perfect keeping with the character of the most learned people of Europe that the first appeal to arms made on behalf of German national unity should rest on historical questions nearly a thousand years old. Was the duchy of Holstein a fief of the empire, and therefore part of the Germanic empire? If it was, could Schleswig be said to exist in the same dependence by virtue of a union with Holstein that had existed from a remote period of time? Schleswig, it was clear, never had, per se, been a fief of the empire, for the northern boundary of Charlemagne's territory was known to be the river Eider, which divides Schleswig from Holstein. Only part of the population of Schleswig, moreover, was of German race, settlers who at various times had straggled across the river from the southern duchy; and no theory of nationality can justly demand the absorption of the Danish population of North Schleswig by the Germanic Confederation. Such were the questions discussed with great heat and learning in all the German universities, but in none more hotly or more learnedly than in the university of Kiel in Holstein; nor did the most accomplished civilians of Europe disdain to attempt an elucidation of a subject so thorny and so obscure. It has been seen on a previous page that, in the year of universal revolution (1848), the Holsteiners, prompted by the men of Kiel, had risen in insurrection against the Danish government, had been assisted by the Prussians armed with the authority of the German Diet, had achieved a temporary independence, and finally had succumbed to the Danes after two pitched battles in which they were grievously defeated. The conquerors, following up their advantage, resolved to deprive the duchies of the separate constitution under which they had been governed, and to incorporate the duchy of Schleswig at least in a common constitution with the kingdom of Denmark. This proceeding was deeply resented by the German population of the duchies, and by their kindred on the continent of Europe. In view of the death of King Frederick VII. without male heirs, the great powers of Europe, "taking into consideration that the maintenance of the integrity of the Danish monarchy, as connected with the general interests of the balance of power in Europe, is of high importance to the preservation of peace, signed a treaty at London on May 8, 1852, by the terms of which the succession to the crown of Denmark was made over to Prince Christian of Schleswig-Holstein-Sonderburg-Glücksburg, and to the direct male descendants of his union with the Princess Louise of Hesse-Cassel, granddaughter of King Christian VIII. of Denmark." This unfortunate treaty, the latest production of the effete "balance of power "doctrine, was soon brought to the test, having to face the new and infinitely more potent principles known by the names of "nationality" and "nonintervention." In the month of November, 1863, King Frederick died, and Prince Christian ascended the throne of Denmark, with the style and title of King Christian IX. The signatories of the treaty of London of 1852 were England, France, Russia, Austria, and Prussia, who all by their governments ratified the provisions of it—provisions made for dynastic purposes, and in complete disregard of the wishes of the German population of the Elbe duchies. The treaty, in fact, ought not to have been made, and as events are sometimes stronger than promises, even the most solemn, so it proved in this case. All the five powers found themselves under the necessity of breaking faith with their brave ally Denmark. Yet, in the nature of things, it was hardly possible to do otherwise. The Germans of Schleswig and Holstein had every right to be freed from the yoke which the Danes were striving to render more galling every day. The common constitution, of which more anon, proved to be, among other things, a means of giving all the offices of the duchies into the hands of Danes, to the exclusion of Germans. Christian IX., when king of Denmark, practically ceased to be duke of Schleswig and Holstein. Yet the treaty and the five powers upheld this anomalous state of things. One political body alone had declined to ratify the treaty, the Diet of the Germanic Confederation, and that body, strong in two of its members, Austria and Prussia, took action in the Schleswig-Holstein matter, and brought about the war with Denmark of 1864. The strange spectacle offered by Austria and Prussia, of two states that individually acknowledged the validity of the treaty of 1852, yet jointly trampled upon it at the bidding of the Diet, was not edifying. Russia was not anxious to see the nationality theory applied in the north of Europe, yet abstained from interference. France had cooled towards England because the latter had declined to share in the support of the Polish insurgents, and had rejected her proposal for a general congress; while the Emperor Napoleon, consistently with the principles of the treaty of Zurich, again practised the doctrine of non-intervention towards a nation shaking off the yoke of a foreign race, and would not second the English cabinet in its endeavours to preserve the integrity of the Danish kingdom. Upon England fell the greatest amount of obloquy in this matter, because the government— wisely, in the interest of the nation, yet not without ignominy—failed to maintain the guarantee inconsiderately given by treaty. That she failed in company with her co-signatories was rightly held to have been no sufficient excuse.

The reasoning on the subject at the time bears upon a somewhat analogous state of things at the present day, and may not unprofitably be briefly reviewed.

"They haven't heart of grace to fight." "Was ever England brought into such a contemptible position?" "No language can describe the degree of ignominious shame and degradation to which we have fallen." "What must Europe think of us?" Such were a few of the mildest phrases current in the social and political circles of Westminster and the surrounding neighbourhood. They expressed feelings that properly belong to the days of Pitt and of Castlereagh. In some instances they were uttered by relics of that age. That was the time of England's greatest glory. Standing for a while alone against the mighty power of Napoleon, she succeeded in forming a vast combination by which the proud Corsican was at length overthrown, and England became the first of the nations of the earth. The cost was great, a heavy debt had to be repaid or to be borne for an indefinite number of years, with an annual charge of twenty-eight millions sterling. What of that? Has not our country prospered ever since? Did not the influence then secured make her voice potent for the settling of many a dispute without recourse to arms, open new regions to our commerce, and make us feel so safe that the council of the nation could settle down to wise and liberal legislation which has borne fruit a thousand-fold? We have surely got our equivalent for the cost of the war; and, taking their own base view of the matter, the peace-at-any-price men ought to consider that trade and industry and the material wealth of the country have been developed to their highest pitch since our great naval and military triumphs in the Napoleonic war. Viewed from higher ground, the truth that a nation cannot live by commerce only is as certain as that man cannot live by bread alone. Look at Holland! With a glorious beginning leading to power that made her respected by the greatest and most ancient nations, having rich dependencies in every quarter of the globe, she has become, by a too exclusive devotion to trade interests—what she is.

Let us save England from sinking like that.

This is a fair statement of the doctrine of "vigorous measures," a doctrine which Lord Palmerston, with his motto "*Civis Romanus sum*" and Lord Russell, with his waving-banner-like inscription of "God defend the right," both had opportunities of applying on behalf of Don Pacifico, the Sultan, his Danubian provinces, &c.

Happily for mankind, however, the opposite political doctrine of non-intervention, which some years ago could hardly hold its ground at all, took deep root in the popular mind, and rapidly spread among all classes of society.

The difficulties of the British government in 1864 sprang from a want of courage in declaring boldly and distinctly at the outset of the Danish quarrel, that England did not mean again to intervene by force of arms in mere European squabbles. The senior members of the cabinet were hampered with the traditions of English policy, as it was half a century earlier. They knew that the country was opposed to intervention, and as representatives of the national will acted rightly in abstaining from warlike demonstrations, but as exponents of that will they failed. They used threatening language and made confident boastings at the beginning of the Schleswig-Holstein dispute, in the hope that Germany would pause before it encountered the phantom terrors of British wrath. But the Polish correspondence had revealed the emptiness of ministerial "tall talk," and the Germans felt safe in pursuing their own course. A truly brave English minister had only to say, "I hold my office by virtue of that public opinion which has intrusted to me the interests of the British nation. Those interests demand a friendly intercourse with all nations, interference in the affairs of none. Our commercial and political relations are so extensive in all the quarters of the globe, in America, in Asia, in Australia, in Africa, that really it is of very little moment what Europe may say or think of us. We can better do without Europe, than Europe can do without us. Therefore if you wish to be friendly with us we shall be happy to reciprocate amity; if not, we shall know how to defend ourselves. In a great cause we will assist our neighbours, but your own dynastic quarrels you must, if you please, settle at home without British interference." Such language would have been fully understood by the youngest generation of our politicians as being quite consistent with the honour and dignity of England on the one hand, and with the peace and welfare of the world on the other. Let the last rags of the old flag of intervention be flung away, and let the principles of non-intervention be openly avowed without fear of the loss of influence. Halting between two opinions, divided by feelings of the past and feelings of the present, our ministers spoke ill and wrote ill, but, thank God, they acted right. Whether to save their own credit or from an abstract love of truth and justice, they obtained a conference, at which all that could be done was done to induce the belligerent powers to come to terms. This was humane and deserving of credit. By what secret schemes and intrigues they were foiled it is impossible to say. The passions of the antagonists alone suffice to account for the resumption of hostilities. Surmises of many kinds were floating in the air. "Cousin Bernadotte" was directed in 1807 by Napoleon I. to occupy Denmark either as friend or foe, according to the circumstances of the hour. The descendant of that French general was from the throne of Sweden a spectator of the dismemberment of Denmark without the smallest loss of *sang froid*. Had he been inspired from the Tuileries with the notion, that if he waited the ripe pear would drop into his mouth? If so, the approval of the German invasion of Holstein and Schleswig by Napoleon III. would become intelligible. By the small sacrifice of King Christian IX. and the annexation of Jutland and the islands to Sweden and Norway, France as she faces Europe would have had on her advanced left a mighty ally in the new Scandinavian kingdom, as she had already on her advanced right a pretty strong friend in the new kingdom of Italy. A formidable neighbour indeed would France, under such circumstances, appear, were English interests in north-eastern Europe of a nature to be endangered by French preponderance! Russia, it is to be hoped, however, will take care of that part of the world. This political surmise must be taken for no more than it is worth. Meanwhile, let England not fail to maintain her ancient alliance with Germany, as long as she can do so with a good conscience.

The conflict had long been inevitable. It was a struggle, not for the uplifting of every different nationality into independence, but for the absorption of the small nations by the great. German literature, science, and art had long before invaded Denmark, and must ultimately conquer it, unless the Scandinavian mind derive new force from a union of Denmark, Sweden, and Norway. The tendency of our age is the destruction, not the restoration, of small separate nationalities; and it is not a tendency to evil.

Since the times shadowed forth in the history of the Tower of Babel, mankind has been striving to recover from that fearful curse of dispersion and division of tongues which constitute the principal element of distinct nationalities. It is not good to attempt to thwart this process of amalgamation. Its success will be the strongest guarantee of the permanency of modern

European civilization. The Roman empire maintained its great power for five centuries under atrocious tyrants and corrupt governors by virtue of the cohesion derived from the amalgamation of the provinces with Rome, that is, by the total destruction of nationalities, accompanied by a large measure of municipal freedom.

What Julius and the other Caesars did for the pagan world eighteen hundred years ago, railways, steamboats, the electric telegraph, and the public press are now doing for Christendom. Puny efforts to arrest the march of events by recurring to old systems, traditionary policies, and the like, will be not only futile, but fatal to those who make the attempt. England has more weighty duties to perform than to defend gallant little nations that run their heads into danger. Private feeling may lament the result of an unequal struggle between Danes and Germans, but public duty teaches that war on merely chivalrous grounds must be avoided. The Prussian monarch believed that his mission was to liberate Schleswig and Holstein from the Danes. England has nothing to fear from Prussian ambition, her advantage lying rather in the formation of a strong, united Germany, that will divide Russia from France.

The future destiny of England is bound up with vaster interests and wider regions than Europe possesses. Animated with a nobler ambition than that which war engenders, the people of these islands are qualified by their freedom, their knowledge, their wealth, and even by their geographical position, to make England the real metropolis of the world, the centre and fountain-head of the civilization of mankind. To peril so great a destiny by engaging in disputes concerning other people's boundaries, on principles that place "honour" (the offspring of lawless ages) above the Christian duty which we profess to follow, is not only impolitic and unpatriotic, but inhuman. Such was the train of reasoning that shaped the conduct of the English government in the Dano-German dispute, with certain qualifying protests made by the foreign secretary, Lord Russell.

To return to the duchies. In March, 1863, a proclamation had been issued from Copenhagen, establishing an administrative separation between Holstein and the rest of the monarchy. The laws of Holstein, the budget of Holstein, even the army of Holstein, were to be under the control of the Holstein Estates, and made entirely independent of the *Rigsraad*, which was only allowed to deliberate on those subjects so far as they regarded Denmark Proper and Schleswig. The object of this arrangement was evidently to cut off Schleswig from the German influence of Holstein, by separating the latter as much as possible from the rest of the state, and thus leaving the Danes unimpeded in their attempts to make Schleswig Danish. On the 14th of July, Frederick VII. being still alive, the Federal Diet protested against the proclamation, and threatened execution unless it was withdrawn. The Danish government, however, disregarding both protest and threat, submitted their scheme, which included the "common constitution" of Schleswig and Denmark Proper, to the *Rigsraad*, by whom it was adopted. On the 14th November, 1863, it was embodied in a charter, and became the ostensible cause of a war that led to the dismemberment of Denmark.

In the diplomatic campaign which preceded and accompanied the military one, the palm for political insight and strategic skill fell to Herr von Bismarck, the king of Prussia's prime minister. It is true that he derived a great advantage over some of his antagonists, by the facility with which he seemed to shift his policy to suit his ends; but underneath this apparent unscrupulousness lay the one grand aim of his life, the healing of the divisions of his country— the welding together of Germany into one grand whole. When Prussian envoy at the Diet, of which Count Rechberg, the Austrian envoy, was president, Bismarck made no secret of his opinion that the policy of Austria should be turned in an eastern direction, and that her intervention in the affairs of Germany was misplaced and unnatural. Count Rechberg doubtless smiled at his colleague's presumption, and abated not one jot of the Kaiser's pretensions to absolute preponderance in the Diet and in Germany. It is believed that the meeting of sovereigns at Frankfort in 1863, on the invitation of Austria, to deliberate on the reform of the Federal Union, was the occasion on which Bismarck resolved to labour with all his energy at the exclusion of Austria from all participation in German affairs. The king of Prussia did not attend that meeting, which when not under the influence of his minister he seemed disposed to favour. Herr von Bismarck's first step on coming to power was to secure the support of Russia while he followed his own bent, by a policy that was strongly condemned by the rest of Europe. In February, 1863, he made a convention with the stern master of Poland, that any Polish insurgents who might take refuge in Posen or other parts of Prussia, should be sent back across the frontier into Russian Poland; that is, into the hands of the enemy from whom they fled. This convention brought much obloquy on its author; but he knew well what the alliance of Russia was worth, and the result proved that he had no cause to fear the hostility of France and England. In the Danish question, his predecessors left him the opportunity of attacking a weak power, and he was not the man to throw away such an opportunity. He began by cautiously feeling his way with some modest expressions of opinion, such as that Denmark was bound in honour to fulfil her engagements towards Germany, and that she was blameable for having resisted the mediation of England. After the proclamation of the 13th of March, he joined in the protests of Austria against the new Danish projects. When execution was threatened by the Federal Diet, Lord Russell in alarm suggested to that body, that it would be "desirable that nothing should occur to augment the already existing dangers and complications of Europe." Upon this all the German governments hastened to calm the fears of his lordship by the allegation that an execution did not mean a war; and Herr von Bismarck went so far as to declare that "if a war did take place, it would be an offensive war on the part of Denmark against the Germanic Confederation."

The situation was, indeed, at that time sufficiently perilous for Prussia to necessitate the greatest caution on the part of her ministers. England, France, and Austria were united on the Polish question, and it almost seemed as if a general crusade was preparing against Russia and her audacious ally. There is now no doubt that the unfortunate declarations made by Lords Russell and Palmerston in July, 1863, which were afterwards appealed to as giving Denmark a claim to the armed assistance of England, were the fruit of the general feeling that, in any European difficulty, the policy of France and England would be identical; and if Prussia had then taken any precipitate step in the Danish affair, it is pretty certain she would at once have received a humiliating check. But Herr von Bismarck was too wary to expose himself to such a danger.

He quietly bided his time, expressing himself to foreign powers in ambiguous terms about the duchies, firmly adhering to the Russian alliance, and rivalizing with Austria for influence in Germany. He had not to wait long. The failure of the Polish negotiations produced a coolness between France and England, and when Lord Russell proposed to the French government, on the 16th of September, a common intervention in favour of Denmark, he was answered with a refusal. Herr von Bismarck now began to assume a more decisive attitude, and proposed to the Diet that Prussian troops only should be employed in the execution which was now imminent. But, towards the end of September, the famous speech of Lord Russell at Blairgowrie seemed to offer a chance of reviving the Anglo-French alliance. The despatch declaring that the Czar had forfeited his rights to Poland was fully agreed to by France; and Herr von Bismarck, with that ready adaptation to circumstances which is so characteristic of him, immediately proposed, much to the disappointment of Germany, a compromise with Denmark. The terms of this compromise—namely, that Denmark should declare herself ready to give satisfaction to the Diet in regard to the claim of Holstein and Lauenburg to control their own legislation and expenditure of all money raised in the duchies, and to accept the mediation of Great Britain for the arrangement of the international or Schleswig question—were agreed to by Denmark; and all seemed to be going well when Herr von Bismarck dropped his plan, and prepared to carry out the "execution." This apparently unaccountable conduct was thus explained by those who were said to be behind the scenes. The "forfeiture" despatch of Lord Russell, which was to have consolidated the Anglo-French alliance, never reached its destination, but at the earnest representation of Herr von Bismarck, who expressed his conviction that Russia would regard it as a *casus belli*, was stopped on its way to St. Petersburg, and a meaningless document, without object or conclusion, was sent in its place. The situation was now completely changed. France and England were isolated, Prussia had the support of Russia and the Confederation, and Austria, though unwillingly, was forced by the break-up of the Western alliance to join Prussia. Bismarck triumphed on every side, and could now give full scope to the audacious policy most in accordance with his character and abilities. The proposal of the congress, which followed close upon the affair of the "forfeiture" despatch, strikingly displayed the changes which a few months had brought about in the relative positions of the European powers. England refused the proposal of France, and these two powers, which in the summer of that very year had rebuked Prussia and Russia for their conduct towards Poland and Denmark, now sought the aid of the cabinets of Berlin and St. Petersburg for carrying out their respective views. After a long negotiation Russia adopted the English view, and talked of the "perfect harmony" with which "the four governments (*i.e.*, Russia, Austria, Prussia, and England) thought and acted." Herr von Bismarck was more difficult to manage. He had his policy to carry out on the Eider, and was in no hurry to put an end to a situation where France and England both strove for his favour; he therefore coquetted with them both, and satisfied neither, until the matter dropped of itself. His "moderate views," as they were called by Prince Gortschakoff, however, soon changed when the publication of the November charter and the death of King Frederick VII. made it necessary for him to assume a more active attitude.

The right of succession established by the treaty of London now came into force, and under the treaty Christian IX. became the new king of Denmark and the duchies; but the Confederation refused to be bound by the treaty which it had not signed, and appointed a committee to inquire into the pretensions of the young duke of Augustenburg, who now claimed the sovereignty in Schleswig and Holstein. No blame could be attached to him for advancing a claim, as he had not joined in his father's renunciation; nor could the Confederation be bound by a treaty to which it had not adhered, and which was in direct opposition to the wishes of the German nation. The fault really lay with Austria and Prussia, who ought not to have signed the treaty of London (a treaty regulating the succession in a German federal state) except as representatives of the Confederation, and with the mediating powers, who did not negotiate in this question with the Confederation, but with Austria and Prussia. These two powers had now determined not to let the matter out of their hands. Count Rechberg, dreading above all things the democratic tendencies of the rest of the minor states of Germany, agreed to the views of Herr von Bismarck, and rashly associated himself with Prussian policy in the duchies. Both Austria and Prussia held firmly to the treaty of London, and both overtly rejected the pretensions of Prince Frederick. After the occupation of Holstein by federal troops on the 21st of December, Bismarck openly declared that Prussia could not bind herself to any particular line of policy in a question, the aspect of which was constantly changing; and proposed to the Diet that the Austrian and Prussian troops should occupy Schleswig as a guarantee for the performance by Denmark of her engagements of 1851-52. The smaller German states meanwhile organized a strong opposition against Prussia, but after fruitless struggles were forced to yield her the ascendancy. Bismarck marched his troops on Holstein, and became master of the situation. On the 16th of January he summoned King Christian to abolish the November constitution in two days, and on a hesitating response sent the Prussian troops into Schleswig. He compelled the recalcitrant middle states to comply with his views, and on the 25th February Prussia and Austria declared to the Diet that they were about to assume the military and civil command in the duchies, which had hitherto been under the authority of the Confederation, an announcement to which no one dared object. Bismarck further strengthened his position by concluding a convention with Austria, binding his government to give her material assistance in case her possessions in Italy should be attacked, and at the same time consolidated the alliance between the three northern courts, by persuading Count Rechberg to proclaim a state of siege in Galicia, and thus give the final blow to the Polish insurrection. Seven days afterwards the troops of Austria and Prussia entered Jutland.

When Denmark was all but overrun, one effort more was made to obtain peace, by the assembly of plenipotentiaries at a conference in London. They met on the 29th of April, and after a session of six weeks broke up without coming to any decision. The only purpose served by this diplomatic assemblage was, that it gave Prussia and Austria an opportunity of formally declaring that the state of war with Denmark absolved them from all engagements entered into before the war began. The conference also brought into view the by-play of the great powers, when the Czar of Russia ceded all his family claims on Holstein to the duke of Oldenburg, who was put forward as a rival to the prince of Augustenburg. The plan for making an independent sovereignty of the united duchies under one of these princes, was quite opposite to Bismarck's scheme of national unification, and he was only ready to accede to it provided that the nominal sovereign gave up the control of the naval and military forces, the principal ports, and the projected sea-canal, to Prussia. These conditions Augustenburg, the popular candidate in the duchies, declined to accept. The course of the history has here been somewhat anticipated in order to bring the military narrative into a consecutive story. The war now to be described began two months before the conference at London, and was ended about two months after that conference, by the severance of Holstein, Schleswig, and Lauenberg from the ancient kingdom of Denmark.

On Tuesday, 2nd February, 1864, hostilities were begun by the Austro-Prussians attacking the Danes at Misunde. Misunde, or Mysunde, is situated on the narrowest part of the Schlei, just before it widens into the large lake which forms the natural protection of the town of Schleswig. It consists of a group of five or six forts, which completes the line of the Dannewerk on the east. The Dannewerk, or as the Danes call it, Dannevirke, is one of the two strongholds of Schleswig; the other being the island of Alsen with its approaches. This line of fortification, which is made up of twenty-seven forts, runs some thirteen miles in a southwesterly direction as far as Hollingsted, a town on the river Freene, midway between Frederickstadt, on the Eider, and Misunde. Besides the defences of the Dannewerk, the Danes had batteries round the north bank of the great pond, or lake, made by the Schlei between Misunde and Schleswig. The Austrians and Prussians, under the command of Field-marshal von Wrangel, marched from Kiel, by way of Eckenforde, and met with some resistance from the Danes, under Lieutenant-general Gerlach, at the outposts of Misunde. The next day the Austrians made an attack at Bustrup, a point in the Dannewerk about three miles from the town of Schleswig. Night prevented the assailants from reaping the benefit of whatever advantage they had over their enemies. It is probable that, had daylight lasted, or had they known the extent of their success, they might have taken the town. Nothing further was done on the one side or the other till the 5th February, when the Danes evacuated the Dannewerk. The abandonment of this stronghold was decided upon by the council of war very suddenly. As late as ten o'clock in the evening of the day that this step was taken, one of the brigadiers, who had placed himself at the head of his columns, with the full understanding that he was to make to the advanced posts at Fredericksburg and Bustrup, received orders to change his march to Flensburg. The news of this resolution created great dissatisfaction among the Danes, both soldiers and people generally. The government at Copenhagen so far gave way to public opinion, as to recall the commander-in-chief, General de Meza, and appoint Lieutenant-general Gerlach in his place, seemingly for no other reason than because, by some accident, the latter happened to be absent from the council that determined on the evacuation. When the strength of their army, the condition of their artillery, and their resources are considered, the wisdom of the decision will remain unchallenged by every one acquainted with the great superiority of the German army in numbers and artillery. To defend thirteen miles of forts, and the unprotected line beyond them to Frederickstadt, the Danes had but 30,000 men. In all the forts there was not one rifled gun; and no gun had more than 100 charges of powder. The question of the expediency of the retreat to Alsen, where their defences presented a far more contracted front, is not doubtful. Alsen, too, was nearer Jutland, and proportionately more inclined to the Danish cause. In Schleswig there was the great disadvantage of the presence of much unsympathetic feeling. In some instances the carelessness of the Schleswigers for their defenders took the more positive form of rendering secret assistance to the Austro-Prussians. With this half hostile population around them the Danes could not make any movement without the enemy's knowledge. The weather, which for five or six days before the 5th had been soft and sloppy, on this day changed. A boisterous north-east wind set in, bringing frost, accompanied with a heavy fall of snow. The roads soon became difficult for locomotion. In this inclement weather the Danish army set out on its march about eleven o'clock at night. No preparation had been made for the slipperiness of the roads by roughing the horses' shoes. Neither horses nor men could keep their feet. The cavalry had to dismount and lead their beasts. The artillery had to be drawn by the men. The progress of the army was soon checked by the fallen horses. Guns, waggons, and ambulance vans had soon to be left with them, encumbering the way still more. The first part of the journey was the most calamitous. In nine hours little more than six miles were made. Flensburg was not reached till four o'clock the next day. They halted here for two hours, and then continued their march to Alsen by way of Krasan and Gravenstein. The difficulties of the preceding night had to be encountered in a more aggravated form. At length, after eight and forty hours of toiling and suffering, they arrived at their destination. That their retreat was not more disastrous was owing to the comparatively short distance they had to traverse. Time was the only element wanting to have made this march rival in horrors the retreat from Moscow. As it was, many died from exposure to the cold and from fatigue. If, however, the loss of life was not very great, that of *matériel* was very serious, and was one that could be ill afforded. Everything they had to abandon fell into the hands of the Austrians. Their retreat did not escape the attention of the Austro-Prussians, who entered Schleswig about five hours after they had left the town, and without any delay set out after them. The inclemency of the weather, which had put such an obstacle in the way of the retreat of the Danes, was no less unfavourable to their enemies' pursuit. Although the Austrians when they started were ten miles only in the rear, they did not come up with the Danes till Saturday afternoon, the 6th. About five miles from Flensburg they came into collision with two regiments, the first and eleventh, under the command of Colonels Müller and Beck. The Austrians greatly overmatched the Danes in numbers. They had, moreover, with them some squadrons of hussars and sixteen cannon; while their opponents had but two field pieces and no horse. The Danes offered a brave resistance, meeting the cavalry with the bayonet. They had to fall back at last, after suffering severe losses, especially among their officers. One of the companies of the first regiment lost its whole staff. This was the only engagement between the Austrians and Danes worthy of mention. The result of this contest is a sample of the fortune that pursued them in every open field. Their very resistance insured their defeat. To make any stand against their enemy was to give him time to gather fresh strength, like another Antaeus. As the whole force of the Danish army was not thought necessary to defend Alsen, 4000 men, chiefly cavalry, received orders from Copenhagen to march to Fredericia in Jutland. Shortly after, the third division, under General Wilster, was directed to embark for the same town. This division consisted of about 10,000 men, including two field batteries and half a regiment of dragoons. Their forces were thus divided into two. Their example was followed by the Austrians and Prussians, who parted company, the former making for Jutland, and the latter proceeding to the reduction of the Danish position at Dybböl.

This siege was the greatest event of the war. In fact, it was the only place in Schleswig at which the Danes made a decided stand. A description of the defences of Dybböl will render more intelligible the plan of attack which was carried out to so successful an issue by the Prussians. The island of Alsen is separated from the continent by a sound about thirteen miles in length, and about two or three miles in width at its entrance. At Sönderborg the width of the sound narrows to about 150 yards. Here the mainland of Söndered is connected with the island by a bridge. On the mainland, beyond the bridge, was the Dybböl stronghold, consisting of four distinct lines. First, there was the *tête du pont* proper, immediately across the water, a narrow gorge or defile winding between two hills of moderate height, flanked on either side by two batteries, and barred by a double range of palisades. Beyond that, after an esplanade of about half a mile, there was the second line, or Dybböl line proper, on Dybböl Hill, consisting of ten forts, disposed on a somewhat circular line from No. 1, close to the water's edge, on the Vemmingbund to No. 10, at a very little distance from the Alsund shore. The Dybböl windmill was nearly in the middle of this arc, somewhat in the rear of forts Nos. 4, 5, 6, and 7, and close to the main road leading from Sönderborg to Nyböl, Graasten, and Flensburg. The third line was made by the broad skirts and summit of the Arnbjerg, by the village of Dybböl, and by the somewhat broken and uncleared ground of Rageböl. The fourth line was drawn across two woods, called Stenterupskov and Boffel Kobbel, lining the above-mentioned road on either side. All these four lines stretched out in concentric arcs, and had their centre at the Sönderborg bridges, from which they were placed at the respective distance of half a mile, one mile, a mile and a half, and two miles. About half a mile from the fourth line, on the north, was Nyböl, and at the southern was the isthmus which joins the little peninsula of Broagerland to the Söndered mainland. The second line extended for about one and a half mile, and its ten forts were mounted with one hundred heavy cannon. The Dybböl position, taken altogether, was very strong by nature. In 1849 the Danes successfully withstood a siege here; and they had great confidence in the result of one in 1864. Little or nothing was done this year toward strengthening their position. They contented themselves with restoring their old works and batteries of 1849. In fifteen years, however, a revolution had taken place in the art of war, to which they had paid no heed. The little peninsula of Broagerland was left unprotected, and became the key by which the Prussians opened the stronghold. Before the days of rifled guns Dybböl was quite safe on this side; but the case was different in 1864. The Danes manned the first and second lines only, using the third and fourth as outposts. Flensburg was the headquarters of the Prussian army; but their outposts extended as far as Nyböl on the south, and Sattrup on the north. At the southern extremity of the Danes' fourth line was the neck of the Broager peninsula, which was covered with the woods of Stenterup and Boffel above mentioned. These woods were, by an unpardonable supineness of the Danes, occupied by pickets only. The importance of the position was seen by the Prussians, who during the whole campaign showed themselves superior to the Danes in foresight. The Danish outposts were driven back, and the peninsula seized by the Prussians. The same want of providence on the part of the Danes in the case of the village of Dybböl, which they had not fortified, stood the Prussians in good stead on the 22nd February. On this day, coming up by the woods of Stenterup Skov and Boffel Kobbel, which they now held, they attacked the Danes in great force and drove them from Dybböl village. Although at the end of the day the Danes succeeded in recovering their position, it was only at a great sacrifice of life. For some time after this reconnaissance of the Prussians there was almost a complete cessation of arms. Indeed, the whole war evinced such a listlessness on the part of invaders and defenders, that it is difficult at times to believe that either one side or the other was in earnest. It was the custom of the pickets, when being changed, to send a parting shot to the enemy, and this for a long time was the extent of the firing on both sides. On one occasion, even, the Danes and Prussians were seen snowballing each other. Meanwhile the Austrians had made their way towards Fredericia. They drove the Danes before them from Gudsö, Taarup, Bredstrap, and other places, all across the isthmus of the peninsula to Fredericia. This fortress was invested, and the towns of Stoutstrup and Erritso occupied by their forces. From these places their artillery commanded the whole sound of the Little Belt, so that all intercourse between Jutland and Alsen had to be carried on by the other side of Fünen. As at Dybböl, no affair of any importance occurred. In one or two skirmishes, however, the Danes lost rather heavily. At Erritso General Wilster, the commander-in-chief at Fredericia, was wounded, and at Gudsö Captain Tane was surprised by a superior force of Austrians, and had to surrender. As soon as Fredericia was invested and its garrison masked, the same inactivity prevailed as at Dybböl. The fires of war blazed out afresh at Dybböl on the 17th of March. The Prussians had not neglected the advantages which the possession of the peninsula of Broagerland gave. They erected batteries all along the cliffs that lined the sound. From these batteries they could throw shot or shell into the town of Sönderborg, and could reach the most distant bastion of the Dybböl forts, while they themselves were entirely out of the range of the Danish guns. Batteries also were built on the heights of Rageböl, a hill to the right of the Danish position. On the morning of the 17th the Prussians opened fire on both town and forts. During the cannonade they advanced with great force against the village of Dybböl and the heights of Arnbjerg. Warned by their previous attack on the 22nd of February, the Danes had done their best to strengthen this position. The churchyard, which had a commanding situation, had been fortified, and here they entrenched themselves. The defence was as obstinate as the attack was violent, and the Danes reconquered lost ground by three successive charges. They had, however, to give way before overwhelming numbers, and as the day closed the Prussians remained masters of the field. The heights of Arnbjerg, as was explained above, closed in the third line of the defensive works of Dybböl. It is on the left of the road, and about the same distance from the Danish bastions as Dybböl. The Danes disputed the possession of this hill with great gallantry. It was taken and retaken, again and again; but the victory in the end remained with the Prussians. With the loss of Arnbjerg the doom of Alsen was sounded, the first knell of which might have been heard when the Prussians were allowed to occupy the Broagerland peninsula. As a strategic position it was of more importance than the possession of the village; for from the top the whole line of forts could be swept by the Prussian fire with ease.

An attempt was made next day by the Danes to recover their lost ground; but the value of their late acquisitions was too well recognized by the Prussians for them to be taken unprepared, and the Danes were repulsed. The Danes made no other attempt to disturb the Prussians in their possessions by assault; but confined themselves to keeping up an incessant firing, to prevent the erection of any batteries. Their guns, however, did not delay their enemies, who proceeded steadily with the work, using field artillery till they mounted their heavy rifled ordnance.

As soon as these guns were placed in position, they began a cannonade which they kept up day after day with great precision and effect.

On the 28th March, under cover of a fire from all their batteries, the Prussians made an assault on the Danish lines. Their chief efforts were directed against the bastions on the extreme left, which they thought had been silenced by the previous day's firing. The Danes had, however, repaired then works, and remounted their guns, which, though smooth bores, were of a very heavy calibre, and made great havoc among the Prussian infantry. An iron-clad of the Danes, the *Rolf-Krake*, steamed into the Vemmingbund Bay, and by keeping under the cliffs of Broagerland succeeded in escaping the guns of the Prussian batteries. When she was in range, she opened a most destructive fire upon the flank of the Prussians, who were then obliged to make a precipitate retreat.

After this repulse the Prussians renewed their former operations, and kept up an incessant storm of shot and shell against the Danish batteries. Bastion after bastion was shattered and the guns dismounted, which the Danes in the lulls of the firing endeavoured, with only partial success, to remount. The Prussians were not merely content with this employment of their guns, but turned them against the town of Sönderborg. This they bombarded till two-thirds were either burnt or levelled to the ground. Nor did the town only suffer, but outlying farmhouses and buildings shared its misfortunes. Nothing was respected that was in the range of the Prussian guns. Besides the destruction of private property, as no notice had been given to the inhabitants to quit the town, a serious loss of life occurred amongst them. It is difficult to discover what object the Prussians had in thus disregarding what has become almost an article of war—the respect due to an unarmed town. Even war has not escaped the influence of civilization, but has grown merciful, in the case of noncombatants and wounded soldiers, to an extent perhaps hardly anticipated in former times. The horrors of war were, however, in 1864, brought bitterly home to the defenceless inhabitants of Sönderborg by the Prussians.

The condition of the Dybböl forts had now got so desperate, that it was not without murmurs that the Danish soldiers marched to their appointed posts. Nor were their complaints without reason. The hopelessness of holding out any longer was seen by every one in Alsen; but orders had come from the government at Copenhagen, that Dybböl was to be held at all costs; and the Danes had no other course open to them than to seek what shelter their fast-falling ramparts gave them from the enemy's shot and shell. They could themselves do no harm to the Prussians, yet even in their batteries their numbers were diminished by a hundred a day.

At length the day came that was to end the sufferings and toil of the besieged and besiegers. On the 18th of April the Prussians swarmed up against Dybböl, accompanied by a furious cannonade from their whole line of batteries, to which the Danes returned what answer their few remaining guns enabled them to make. The ironclad *Rolf-Krake* which had done such service on the occasion of the previous assault of the Prussians, again steamed into the Vemmingbund Bay. But this time the ill-fortune of her owners followed her. As she was passing the Prussian batteries she was struck by two shells. Her deck, which was of one and a half inch plate only, was broken through. Several men were killed, and so much damage done, that she was compelled to return to her anchorage in Hörup Hav.

The Danes made every resistance in their power, but all was useless. They were borne down by the superior numbers of the Prussians from fort to fort; till step by step they were thrust beyond their defences, and over the sound into Alsen. Here they gained a little breathing time by destroying the bridges they had crossed. Their losses in killed and wounded were very serious; and great numbers were left prisoners in the hands of the Prussians. Certainly less than half the army escaped into Alsen. Among the many officers that fell in this engagement was gallant General du Plat. He was at the rear of his retreating columns, encouraging and cheering on his men, when he was struck down by several rifle bullets. The last words he uttered as he fell were: "Hold out, my friends! Hold out for God and Denmark"! The Prussians paid the respect due to his bravery, and sent his body, with those of several other officers, to the Danes for burial. On his head two wreaths of laurel were placed by Prince Frederick Charles and Marshal Wrangel; a token of the high estimation in which they held his heroic resistance. The Prussian loss was comparatively slight.

With the fall of Dybböl the cause of the Danes in Schleswig was lost. The whole province was in the undisturbed possession of the Austro-Prussians; and to fill up the measure of Danish reverses, shortly after the fortress of Fredericia had to be evacuated and abandoned to the Austrians. There was nothing now to prevent the Austrians from overrunning the whole Cimbrian Peninsula from end to end.

To console them in their defeat, the Danes had the consciousness of having done their best to keep what they considered, rightfully or wrongfully, as their lawful possession, and of having succumbed only to superior numbers.

Whatever differences of opinion there may be on the questions involved in the war, no side will hesitate to give the Danes due meed of praise for the manful stand they made in a struggle in which they were over-matched.

Meanwhile it was at length resolved at the conference, that hostilities should be suspended by land and sea from the 12th of May to the 12th of June, Denmark raising her blockades; and at the sitting of the 2nd June this armistice was prolonged, after some difficulty, until the 26th of June. The conference terminated on the 22nd of June, all the belligerents rejecting the mediatory proposals of Great Britain, and at the end of the month hostilities were renewed.

On the 29th the Prussians crossed over to Alsen soon after midnight in considerable force, and landed on the opposite shore without much opposition. The Danish troops in the island soon afterwards came up; but after a sharp engagement they were compelled to retreat with a loss in killed and wounded of between 2500 and 3000 men. The ironclad Danish man-of-war, *Rolf-Krake*, lay in Augustenburg Bay, and attempted to prevent the crossing of the enemy; but she was met by such a concentrated fire from the Prussian batteries, that she was compelled to retire and seek shelter behind an intervening promontory. The Prussians were very proud of their victory, and an official account of the capture of Alsen, which appeared in Berlin, stated that the difficulties of this undertaking were very considerable, and apparent even to an unpractised eye. History contains few examples of the passage of a river in front of the enemy. Here it was requisite to cross an arm of the sea, whose width, depth, and rapid current prevented the erection of a bridge, and whose hostile shore bristled with numerous well-armed batteries and intrenchments. It was necessary to expose the troops to a foreign element in a number of slight boats, not only threatened by wind and weather, but by many hostile war ships commanding the sea, the ironclad vessels in particular capable of inflicting serious losses. Even if the landing of the first battalion succeeded, it was necessary to be prepared for encountering a superior enemy who, long since expecting this attack, would have had time enough, during the suspension of arms, to reorganize his troops and make every preparation for energetically repulsing all attempts to land. When the boats were about 200 yards distant from the hostile shore, the first shots of the enemy's outposts blazed at them through the twilight. The forces in the boats returned the fire, and replied to the first hail of grape from the enemy's batteries with a thundering hurrah. Springing out of the boats, and wading through the shallows, the brave Brandenburgers rapidly gained the opposite bank, stormed the hostile batteries, and drove the enemy back into the Fohlen-koppel wood, notwithstanding his desperate attempts to hold his rifle pits. The capture of Alsen and abandonment of Fredericia decided the issue of the struggle, and Denmark, isolated as she was in the unequal war, found herself compelled to yield and consent to peace.

But her enemies were not at perfect peace among themselves. In the middle of July an ominous quarrel arose at Rendsburg in Schleswig between some Prussian soldiers on the one hand, and some Saxon and Hanoverian soldiers on the other. Much bad feeling had already existed between the Federal and Prussian troops, and the result of the squabble was, that a strong Prussian force was marched into Rendsburg, and Prince Frederick Charles of Prussia, acting upon orders from Berlin, took military possession of the place. General von Hake, who commanded the Saxons, protested against this as an unwarranted act of usurpation, saying that it was impossible for him to consent to the occupation of Rendsburg by Prussian troops, but also clearly out of his power, independent of other important reasons, to think of offering military opposition with a weak garrison of four companies. He declared, therefore, that he should withdraw for the present the Saxon troops from Rendsburg, to avoid a conflict. This affair caused much ill blood against Prussia in Saxony and the minor states of Germany, but in the end good sense prevailed, and possibly a feeling that Prussia was leading them to unity and greatness induced submission to her lead.

Negotiations for peace took place at Vienna between the plenipotentiaries of Austria, Prussia, and Denmark, for the purpose of settling the preliminaries between those powers; and at last, on the 1st of August, they were signed by the respective parties, and were as follows:—1. His Majesty the king of Denmark renounces all his rights to the duchies of Schleswig, Holstein, and Lauenburg, in favour of their Majesties the king of Prussia and the emperor of Austria, engaging to recognize the arrangements their said Majesties shall make in respect of those duchies. 2. The cession of the duchy of Schleswig comprehends all the islands belonging to that duchy, as well as the territory situated upon the mainland. To simplify the boundary question, and put an end to the inconveniences resulting from the portion of Jutland territory situated within Schleswig, his Majesty the king of Denmark cedes to their Majesties the king of Prussia and the emperor of Austria the Jutland possessions situated to the south of the frontier line of the district of Ribe, laid down on the maps. On the other hand, their Majesties the king of Prussia and the emperor of Austria consent that an equivalent portion of Schleswig, comprising, in addition to the island of Arroe, the territories connecting the above-mentioned district of Ribe with the remainder of Jutland, and rectifying the frontier line between Jutland and Schleswig from the side of Cölding, shall be detached from the duchy of Schleswig and incorporated in the kingdom of Denmark. The island of Arroe will not make part of the compensation by reason of its geographical extent. The details of the demarcation of the frontiers shall be settled by the definitive treaty of peace. 3. The debts contracted either by Denmark or any of the duchies, to remain the charge of each country. All war expenses of the allied powers to be paid by the duchies.

A protocol was at the same time signed respecting the terms and duration of the armistice. This provided that there should be a complete suspension of hostilities by land and sea, until the conclusion of the peace. The king of Denmark engaged to raise the blockade of the German ports, and the king of Prussia and the emperor of Austria, while maintaining the occupation of Jutland, under the existing conditions of the *uti-possidetis*, declared themselves ready to keep in that country no larger number of troops than their majesties might judge necessary, according to purely military considerations. A treaty of peace in accordance with the above preliminaries was signed at Vienna on the 1st of October, 1864. The ratification of the treaty was followed by a sharp correspondence between the Prussian minister and the ministers of foreign powers, in which the English minister especially indulged in splenetic observations, which may have been deserved, but were of no use to any person or to any cause. The game to be played out was only begun, and the mighty task which Herr von Bismarck had undertaken was to be accomplished by steps more arduous, if not so unscrupulous, as this conquest of the Elbe duchies.

In a history of the Seven Weeks' War of 1866, it has been observed on this subject, that when, in the first instance, the Germanic Confederation undertook the Danish war, Prussia was not sufficiently confident in her strength to set aside, with her own hand alone, the decrees of the Diet. To have done so would have raised a storm against her, against which she had no reason to suppose that she could successfully bear up. England was excited, and the warlike people of that country eager to rush to arms in the cause of the father of the young princess of Wales. France was discontented with the refusal of the English cabinet to join her proposed congress, but might have accepted a balm for her wounded pride in a free permission to push her frontier up to the Rhine. Austria would have opposed the aggrandizement of Prussia, and all Germany would at that time have supported the great power of the south in the battle for the liberation of Holstein from the supremacy of the Hohenzollerns, as eagerly as from that of the House of Denmark. The efforts made for the independence of Holstein, which could not be opposed by open force, had to be thwarted by stratagem. Prussia sought the alliance of Austria with a proposal that those two great powers should constitute themselves the executors of the Federal decree, in order to put aside the troops of the minor states. Austria agreed, and rues at this hour the signature of that convention. Yet she had much cause of excuse. To allow Prussia to step forward alone as the champion of German national feeling, would have been for Austria to resign for ever into the hands of her rival the supremacy of Germany. Old traditions, chivalrous feeling, and inherited memories caused Austrians to look upon their emperor as the head of Germany, the modern representative of the elected holder of the crown and sceptre of the Holy Roman Empire. Prussia was approaching that supremacy with gigantic strides. Austria was already reduced to the position of being the advocate of German division and of small states, purely because amalgamation and union would have drawn the scattered particles not towards herself, but within the boundaries of her northern neighbour. To permit Prussia to act alone in the matter of the Elbe duchies, would have been to see her surely obtain important territorial aggrandizement, and also to lose the opportunity of creating another independent minor German state, which, if not a source of strength to Austria, might prove an obstacle in the path of Prussia.

The war against Denmark was undertaken. The Danes, terribly inferior in numbers, organization, equipment, armament, and wealth, after a most gallant resistance lost their last strongholds; while the Western powers, which had encouraged the cabinet of Copenhagen in the delusion that other soldiers than Danes would be opposed to the German invaders of Schleswig, calmly looked on. The Danish war terminated in the treaty signed at Vienna in October, 1864; and the duchies of Schleswig, Holstein, and Lauenburg were handed over to the sovereigns of Austria and Prussia. It is noteworthy, says Sir Alexander Malet, that before the invasion of the duchies no precise stipulations had taken place between Austria and Prussia as to the disposal of the conquests which they might safely reckon upon making. This was a grave fault on the part of Austria, and most probably, continues Sir Alexander, a calculated omission on the side of her Prussian ally. Though the condominate rights of the two sovereigns in whose favour the cession of territory was made were equal, the military forces left by each for its occupation differed in strength. Of Prussians there remained eighteen battalions of infantry to five battalions of the Austrians, eighteen squadrons of cavalry to two of theirs, and three batteries of artillery to one of theirs. After the military occupation and a provisional government were settled the popular will was consulted, in a hasty superficial way, as to the future government of the land. At the public meetings held in different parts of Holstein, the generally expressed wish of the population was in favour of a union with the Germanic Confederation, under the sovereignty of the prince of Augustenburg. A small fraction, however, of landed proprietors, led by Baron Scheel Plessen, put forward the wish for annexation to Prussia, which was met by many vehement declarations of a contrary opinion. Against these demonstrations the Prussian government acted in a manner that showed she would not suffer any overt assertion of independence. During a debate on the subject in the Prussian Chamber, Herr von Bismarck said that Kiel, and indeed the entire duchies, were owned by Prussia. True, they were owned in common with the Kaiser; but the share Prussia had in the property would never be abandoned except on condition of Kiel harbour being handed over to her for good. This port was ardently coveted as a nursery for the German navy which would grow out of the Prussian fleet, by developing the maritime resources of the other states of northern Germany. On a similar occasion the minister of state replied in remarkable words to the reproaches of the public press, and of the Chamber of Deputies, who assailed the government for having formed an alliance with Austria. "On this question the future will throw a clearer light. Any other course of policy would have made the late war a war between the Federal Diet and Denmark. The former would have intrusted to us the conduct of the war, but would not have taken into consideration our plans for the organization of the duchies, as does Austria who is friendly to us. . . . I am bound," he said in conclusion, "to limit myself to these statements, on account of the publicity which will be given to my speech." This was spoken in January, 1865, when with all his extreme candour the speaker had things in his mind which Austria, however "friendly to us," would have learned with dismay—things upon which a future of not much more than a year threw a terribly clear light.

A new complexion was ostentatiously given to the co-possession in the month of June, when Herr Wagner, during a discussion in the Chamber at Berlin oh the bill for defraying the expenses of the late war, moved an amendment to the effect, "that the government be requested to endeavour to bring about the annexation of the duchies to Prussia, even by indemnifying, if necessary, any claimant to their possession." The words of the prime minister, in reply, were significant. "The programme for the solution of the question of the duchies," he said, "has been completely carried out, excepting the installation of the prince of Augustenburg as duke of Schleswig-Holstein. This can take place any day upon the prince proving his hereditary right to the duchies, which up to the present time he has failed to do. In a conversation with me last year, his Highness rejected the moderate demands of Prussia, and expressed himself as follows:— 'Why did you come to the duchies? We did not call you. Matters would have been settled without Prussia.' Annexation to Prussia is the best thing for Schleswig-Holstein; but there is no prospect of its accomplishment, on account of the large debts for which it would be necessary for Prussia to render herself liable. After the refusal of our moderate demands by the prince of Augustenburg, we shall be justified in subsequently increasing them." On another occasion the minister declared again and again, that nothing would be abated of the claims which Prussia had on the duchies she had rescued for Germany from Denmark. He professed not to grudge them their duke, nor to trouble himself about any democratic institutions they might be tempted to establish; but it was his duty, he said, to prevent a third Schleswig-Holstein campaign, and to arrange matters in a way which should not expose him to the necessity of taking Dybböl again. As to the concessions made by the duke of Augustenburg, they were dependent on the sanction of the Schleswig-Holstein Estates, even supposing them to be sufficient for Prussian purposes. In reality, no concessions whatever had been made, and nothing remained for Prussia to do but effect an arrangement with the Kaiser on the one hand, and the future duke on the other; if indeed the title of a single person to the whole of the duchies could ever be established. It was growing very clear that neither duke nor Kaiser would stand in the way of Prussian claims while Prussia had the force to prevent it. No votes of the Schleswig-Holstein Estates, no proclamations of the pretenders, would drive Prussia from the duchies. She would stick to her programme, and defend its justice and necessity to her very last man. The people of Prussia and the Chamber at Berlin were no less loath than the minister to give up their hold on the fair prize within their grasp. They too wanted to place Germany in a defensible condition by sea, and to avoid the necessity of another attack upon the Dybböl fortifications. So eager were the Chambers for annexation, that Bismarck endeavoured to wring a money vote from them, by promising that Kiel should become Prussian, adding, "If you doubt our right to it, make a condition with us, and say, "No Kiel, no money." If the pretenders could prove no better title to the dukedom than the right of conquest which Prussia claimed, their pretensions would be disregarded, and no one should contest the right of the sovereigns of Prussia and Austria to make an arrangement between themselves for the disposal of the spoil. Such an arrangement, as will be presently seen, was ere long brought to pass.

Meanwhile co-possession soon disturbed the harmony that seemed to exist between the two great German powers. The double government under an Austrian and Prussian commissioner offered endless opportunities for the old rivalry between the two countries to break out; and the manifest desire of the Prussians to annex the convenient territory served to aggravate the natural jealousy of their ally, who strove to countermine the project by secretly but efficaciously supporting the Augustenburg party. The estrangement between the two powers greatly increased when, on the announcement of the September convention concluded between Italy and France, the Prussian minister refused to acknowledge Austria's claim for assistance founded on promises made during the Danish war. Herr von Bismarck said that their agreement was to assist Austria in case her Italian possessions were attacked in consequence of her share in the Danish war, not otherwise, and that such an engagement could in no way apply to the September convention. The Austrian government felt itself duped, and Count Rechberg, the prime minister, resigned office. The feeling between the two nations increased in soreness, and opportunities were sought for breaking off the now detested alliance. Although several disputes led them to the very verge of a rupture, war was avoided, more especially by Austria, whose finances were so much crippled, and her various subjects so discontented, that she saw how a war at that time would inevitably have led her to bankruptcy and dismemberment. The middle states were willing to help her, but their assistance had very little military or political value, and their opposition to Prussia in the Diet only served to whet the resolution of Herr von Bismarck to accomplish in his own good time a very radical reformation both of the Diet and of the Confederation it proposed to represent.

A commission of crown lawyers was appointed by the two powers to examine into the merits of the claims severally made to sovereign power in the duchies by the king of Denmark, the duke of Augustenburg—the popular candidate, especially in Holstein, who would certainly have been elected duke had the matter been decided by a plebiscitum—and the duke of Oldenburg. Their decision was, that King Christian IX. was by right of succession the undoubted possessor, and that from him the duchies had passed by right of conquest to the victors in the war—the emperor of Austria and the king of Prussia. The three claimants being thus swept out of the way, the scheme of annexation was further developed by a treaty between the conquerors regulating a division of the spoil.

On the 14th of August, 1865, this important convention was signed at Gastein by Herr von Bismarck and Count Blome; and it was afterwards signed at Salzburg by the king of Prussia and the emperor of Austria. The convention began by stating that "their Majesties the king of Prussia and the emperor of Austria, having become convinced that the co-dominion hitherto existing in the countries ceded by Denmark, through the treaty of peace of the 30th of October, 1864, leads to inconveniences which endanger the good understanding between their governments, and also the interests of the duchies; their Majesties have, therefore, come to the determination no longer to exercise in common the rights accruing to them from the third article of the above-mentioned treaty, but to divide geographically the exercise of the same until further agreement."

The following articles were then agreed upon:—

Article I.—The exercise of the rights jointly acquired by the high contracting parties, through the Vienna treaty of peace of the 30th of October, 1864, will, without prejudice to the continuance of these rights of both powers to the whole of both duchies, be transferred as regards the duchy of Schleswig to his Majesty the king of Prussia, and as regards the duchy of Holstein to his Majesty the emperor of Austria.

Article II.—The high contracting powers will propose in the Federal Diet the establishment of a German fleet, and the appointment for that purpose of the harbour of Kiel as a federal harbour. Until the execution of the Diet's resolutions referring thereto, the war-vessels of both powers will use this port, and the command and police of the same will be exercised by Prussia. Prussia is authorized not only to construct the necessary fortifications for the defence of the entrance opposite Friedrichsort, but also to erect marine establishments corresponding with the object of the military port upon the Holstein shore of the bay. These fortifications and establishments are also placed under Prussian command, and the requisite Prussian naval troops and men for their garrison and guard may be quartered in Kiel and the neighbourhood.

Article III.—The high contracting parties will propose at Frankfort to raise Rendsburg into a German federal fortress. Until the settlement by the Diet of the garrison relations of this fortress, its garrison will consist of Prussian and Austrian troops, with the command alternating annually upon the 1st of July.

Article IV.—During the continuance of the division agreed upon by Art. I. of the present convention, the Prussian government will retain two military roads through Holstein; one from Lubeck to Kiel, the other from Hamburg to Rendsburg. The more detailed regulations respecting the halting places for the troops, and also respecting their transport and maintenance, will be settled as early as possible by a special convention. Until this takes place, the existing regulations for Prussian halting places on the roads through Hanover will be in force.

Article V.—The Prussian government retains control over a telegraph line for communication with Kiel and Rendsburg, and the right to send Prussian post vans with Prussian officials over both routes through the duchy of Holstein. Inasmuch as the construction of a railway direct from Lubeck through Kiel to the Schleswig frontier is not yet assured, the concession for that object for the Holstein territory will be given at the request of Prussia upon the usual terms, without Prussia making any claim to rights of sovereignty with respect to the line.

Article VI.—The high contracting parties are both agreed that the duchies shall join the Zollverein. Until this takes place, or until some further understanding, the system hitherto in vogue, and including both duchies, shall remain in force, with equal partition of the revenues. In case it should appear advisable to the Prussian government, pending the duration of the division agreed upon in Art. I. of this present treaty, to open negotiations with respect to the accession of the duchies to the Zollverein, his Majesty the emperor of Austria is ready to empower the representatives of the duchy of Holstein to take part in such negotiations.

Article VII.—Prussia is authorized to carry through Holstein territory the German Ocean and Baltic Canal, to be constructed according to the results of the technical examinations directed by the king's government. So far as this may be the case, Prussia shall have the right of determining the direction and dimensions of the canal; of acquiring the plots of ground requisite for its site, by way of pre-emption in exchange for their value; of directing the construction; of exercising supervision over the canal, and its being kept in repair; and of giving assent to all orders and regulations affecting the same. No other transit dues or tolls upon ships and cargo shall be levied throughout the whole of the canal than the navigation duty, to be imposed by Prussia equally upon the ships of all nations for the use of the passage.

Article VIII.—No alteration is made by this present convention in the arrangements of the Vienna peace treaty of October 30, 1864, with regard to the financial obligations to be undertaken by the duchies, as well towards Denmark as towards Austria and Prussia, save that the duchy of Lauenburg shall be released from all duty of contribution to the expenses of the war. The division of these obligations between the duchies of Holstein and Schleswig shall be based upon a standard of population.

Article IX.—His Majesty the emperor of Austria makes over the rights acquired by the above cited Vienna peace treaty to the duchy of Lauenburg to his Majesty the king of Prussia, in exchange for which the Prussian government binds itself to pay to the Austrian government the sum of 2,500,000 Danish dollars, payable at Berlin in Prussian silver coin, four weeks after the confirmation of this present convention by their Majesties the king of Prussia and the emperor of Austria.

Article X.—The execution of the above agreed division of the co-dominion shall commence as early as possible after the approval of this convention by their Majesties the king of Prussia and the emperor of Austria, and be terminated at latest by the 15th of September. The command-in-chief, hitherto existing in common, shall, after the completed evacuation of Holstein by the

Prussian, and of Schleswig by the Austrian troops, be dissolved, and at latest by the 15th of September.

It will be seen through all the specious wording of the treaty, that Austria had not the best of the bargain, and that Prussia derived immense advantage from her purchase of the imperial rights in Lauenburg for two million and a half dollars in silver, money down. The frugal management of her finances, which kept ready cash in the treasury, for good investments, was never more signally rewarded. The possession of Lauenburg was like the thin end of the wedge, opening the way to further acquisitions of territory. Great was the anger of the other European cabinets when the Gastein convention became known, and another proof was given that all the learned arguing exhibited at the London conference was so much breath thrown away. It is extremely disagreeable to statesmen, as to other men, to have their cherished ideas and traditions summarily and unceremoniously overthrown. Lord Russell wrote to British diplomatic agents abroad a severe letter, in which, among other things, he said, "All rights, old or new, whether based upon a solemn agreement between sovereigns, or on the clear and precise expression of the popular will, have been trodden under foot by the Gastein convention, and the authority of force is the sole power which has been consulted and recognized. Violence and conquest, such are the only bases upon which the dividing powers have established their convention."

M. Drouyn de Lhuys, the French minister for Foreign Affairs, was even more cutting in his tone. "Upon what principle," he asked, "does the Austro-Prussian combination rest? We regret to find no other foundation for it than force, no other justification for it than the reciprocal convenience of the co-partners. This is a mode of dealing to which the Europe of to-day has become unaccustomed, and precedents for it must be sought for in the darkest ages of history. Violence and conquest pervert the notion of right, and the conscience of nations. Substituted for the principles which govern modern society, they are an element of trouble and dissolution, and can only overthrow the past without solidly building up anything new." But though the English fleet was recalled from the Mediterranean, to manoeuvre, by way of menace, with the French fleet at Cherbourg, the great consolidator, Herr von Bismarck, held steadily on his way, and, for all these marks of discontent, firmly resolved to build up something very new and very solid—a united German Fatherland.

The plans of the Prussian premier were ripening; a project he had formed for making an alliance with Italy, at once the oldest and most recent foe of the Kaiser, was becoming feasible. Friendship with the Emperor Napoleon was also being sedulously and successfully cultivated. But above all, the re-organization of the Prussian army, which, since its defects became apparent in 1859, had been proceeding under the able direction of General von Roon, was tolerably complete. This indispensable task had been an arduous one, accomplished in opposition to the repeated decision of the Chamber of Deputies, who on this point were in a state of chronic variance with the king and his minister session after session.

It is not a little remarkable that the popular constitution of the Prussian army, that renders it now so formidable to France, should derive its origin from the arbitrary conditions of peace exacted by the French emperor, Napoleon I., after the battle of Jena. Baron Scharnhorst, says

Alison, contrived to elude the hard conditions imposed on Prussia in the treaty forced upon it by Napoleon in 1806. One condition was to the effect that she must have only 40,000 men under arms, a condition which was kept to the letter, but evaded in the principle by retaining the soldiers only three years with their colours, and training thereby to the use of arms triple the number at any one tune present with the standards. It was this admirable system, gradually adopted in other German state, which was the main cause of the successful resurrection of Prussia in 1813, and the glorious stand she then made on behalf of the liberties of Europe. Everywhere the whole male inhabitants, without distinction of social position, between eighteen and twenty years of age, were liable to serve in the ranks of the regular army, in which they did duty for three years. They then retired into pacific life, to make way for others, who had to go through the same system of military training and discipline, and dismissal. Thus the whole male population was trained to the use of arms, an admirable system for purposes of defence and under a wise and beneficent government, but terrible to bad rulers in times of commotion and revolution. During the convulsions of 1848-49, it was a common saying in Germany that the sovereigns must be overthrown, for their enemies were old soldiers, and their defenders young recruits.

The organization of this army, which will be fully treated of in the second part of this work, underwent considerable changes in 1860 and the following years. These changes made the standing army as large in peace as it would have been before with the addition of the whole first call of landwehr. They were very unpopular changes nevertheless, and for six successive years encountered the firm remonstrance of the Chamber of Deputies, while the Upper House as steadily applauded and supported them. The popular party failed to shake the position which had been taken up by the cabinet, and their efforts had little other effect than to hurry on the foreign policy of the government to the rupture with Austria, for which the transformation of the army had been expressly made.

The Kaiser's vain attempt in 1863 to create a German Parliament, prince-governed and ready to prolong his Imperial Majesty's presidency, taught the bold Prussian minister that the time for action was drawing near, and made him determine to have his instruments of war ready and well in hand. In the Schleswig-Holstein campaign, Prussia, by a bold spring, took the lead in action against Denmark, and placed Austria in the secondary position of a half-willing ally. At the same time the Bund was made to see its own impotence by the joint occupation of the duchies by the two powers, in spite of the decrees of the Diet. Austria was forced from one concession to another, and yet Prussia, while degrading her by policy, feigned just so much unwillingness to quarrel as might avoid giving pretext for foreign interference, or an excuse for the Kaiser to arm.

By the year 1866 the military system of 1859 was fairly complete in all its parts. The active forces were complete in their cadres; the reserve lists full of trained men; and the whole could be made ready for the field at less than a month's notice. The officers were entirely devoted to the crown, and the power of discipline was relied on for carrying the mass as boldly forward through a campaign as though the whole nation had gone to war. The needle gun gave evidence of its enormous power in the Danish war, though its first employment had been against the Baden insurgents in 1849. It was generally thought that its use would tend to so much waste of ammunition as to render it unavailable for general use. By careful instruction, however, and a distribution of small-arm reserves of ammunition, the danger of exhausting the supply before an action is concluded has been avoided, and observers can only wonder at the supineness of other governments and military chiefs who waited to see Prussia gain over Austria the most astounding victories, before they took steps to provide their own soldiers with some weapon as easily managed and as destructive as the breech-loader.

It has just been intimated that the resolution to attempt the forcible expulsion of Austria from the Confederation, took date in Herr von Bismarck's mind from the meeting of the sovereigns in Frankfort, in 1863. Before that, however, in 1862, while exercising for a brief period the functions of Prussian representative in Paris, there is reason to believe that he had found occasion to broach his views on German affairs to the Emperor Napoleon. This at least is the opinion of Sir Alexander Malet, an old diplomatist himself, who was personally acquainted with the Prussian and with many other German ministers at the Frankfort Diet. The same writer goes on to say that Bismarck had taken special care to make Prussian policy agreeable to France, in the matter of the treaty of commerce, so soon as, by taking office at Berlin, the power of influencing his country's counsels fell into his hands. In 1864 a meeting took place between him, then holding office as Prussian premier, and M. Rouher at Carlsbad. Some fraction of the many conversations which are said to have there passed between the two statesmen on European affairs, have taken their place in the domain of public belief, and Herr von Bismarck's habit of speaking his thoughts is so well known, that credence may be given to utterances attributed to him, which from almost any other person living would be counted as extravagances of indiscretion and audacity. Of this nature was the suggestion which he is generally supposed to have thrown out, that France might indemnify herself by taking possession of Belgium, for the contemplated Prussian aggrandizements in Germany and those to be made at the expense of Denmark. Herr von Bismarck's aim was to impress the French minister with the idea, that the advantages he was aiming at for his own country might be compensated to France by equivalent territorial acquisitions. Whether the bait held out was a possible cession of the coal basin of the Saar, of the duchy of Luxemburg, or even the prospect of active assistance in annexing Belgium to France, is immaterial. The general impression sought to be produced, continues Sir Alexander, that Prussia was by no means hostile, that she might indeed be helpful to France, was adroitly produced; and subsequent conversations with the emperor at Biarritz took, there can be little doubt, the same direction, and confirmed the effect. Herr von Bismarck, on his second visit to Biarritz, met indeed with some difficulties. The French circular referring to the treaty of Gastein had been followed by the meeting of the English and French fleets at Cherbourg, apparently as a threat to Prussia, and the king of Prussia raised objections to his minister's taking a journey which, under such circumstances, seemed incompatible with the dignity of Prussia. In this conjuncture, seeing the indispensable need of removing the mistrust of the emperor of the French, Herr von Bismarck contrived to induce the French cabinet to modify the terms of their circular; and the king's consent being thereupon given, he went at once to Paris, and thence continued his journey to Biarritz. His success was complete: how brought about can only be vaguely surmised. One point, however, may be shrewdly guessed at with tolerable certainty, that the alliance of Prussia with Italy, for the purpose of war with Austria, was promised. The emperor did not insist on any positive engagements for contingent advantages to accrue to France. He had not that superb confidence in the ability of Prussia to vanquish Austria, even with Italian aid, indulged in by Bismarck. It is much more likely that he looked forward to the exhaustion of the combatants, when both or either of them might appeal to his not altogether disinterested good offices to appease their strife. The emperor foresaw, however, with tolerable certainty, the probable liberation of Venetia, an object he had greatly at heart; and it is perfectly well known that Herr von Bismarck returned to Berlin with such assurances of sympathy and absolutely benevolent neutrality on the part of France, that he could make his arrangements for employing the Rhenish garrisons, and leaving Saar-Louis, Coblentz, Luxemburg, and Cologne partially stripped of artillery, and with a small force of landwehr for their protection, all which would have been impossible had he been insecure as to the dispositions of France.

These confidences of the veteran British envoy, tinged though they be with a jealous prejudice against the Prussian minister of state, are valuable as evidence of the secret workings of diplomacy in the arrangement of state affairs, and especially in the bringing about of great wars. They recall, too, an expression attributed to the Emperor Napoleon while at Wilhelmshöhe, which merits a permanent record as indicating, by presumption at least, his Majesty's opinion of a formidable antagonist. "The minister of King William," he is reported to have said, "will wind Jules Favre round his finger. I have been quite duped by him—I to whom everybody agrees in attributing penetration and taciturnity. How then will it fare with Monsieur Favre, whose strength lies in fluency of speech? All his words will be turned against him in the form of an agreement with his pacific intentions. Count von Bismarck will throw the responsibility of a refusal on his august Majesty. The talent of this diplomatist consists in his knowing how to throw on others the responsibility of resolutions that have been taken." Surely there is a souvenir here of the interviews at Paris and Biarritz that were so fruitful of consequences. "Count von Bismarck," said the ex-emperor in conclusion, "is an able man, but it is his audacity that makes him so. This is what distinguishes him from Cavour, the greatest politician I have ever met. If Cavour had been the minister of King William, the German empire would have been completed, and that without a shot."

CHAPTER IV.

War between Austria and Prussia—Premonitory Symptoms—Bismarck at Carlsbad in 1865—His conversation with Duc de Gramont—His observations to Herr von der Pfortden—Dalliance with the Central States of Germany—Freiherr von Beust—His desire to reduce Prussia to a level with the minor states—Mental Conflicts of Count von Bismarck—His Impression that he was providentially saved from the Assassin Blind—The Second Chamber at Berlin—Annexation of Lauenberg—The King's reluctance to War with a German State—Gloomy opening of the year 1866—Austrian Liberalism in Holstein antagonistic to Prussian Conservatism—Meeting of Delegates from Schleswig and Holstein Associations countenanced by Austria—Protest of Count von Bismarck and threat of separate policy—Severe decrees of the King of Prussia in Schleswig against supporters of the Prince of Augustenburg—Vienna Government resolve to lay the matter before the Diet—Support of the minor states requested by Austria—Count Karolyi's interview with the Prussian Premier—Alliance between Prussia and Italy—Austria cautiously makes military preparations—The Prussian Minister complains that Austria is arming—Aims a first blow at the Diet, and recounts in a Circular (24th March, 1866) Prussia's grounds of complaint against Austria—Suggests Reformation of the Bund—Austria unwilling to break the Peace—Prussia's readiness for War—Preparations in Italy—Proposal for a common reduction of Armaments—Italy the stumbling-block—Austrian statement of the 26th April—Prussian statement—The negotiations exhausted—Attempt at intervention on the part of other powers—Conference proposed and consented to save by Austria, who objects to the discussion of a cession of territory—Manteuffel marches from Schleswig into Holstein with Prussian troops—Gablenz with the Austrians retires to Altona, crosses the Elbe, and reaches friendly territory—Prussia declares war against Saxony, Hanover, and Hesse—First Prussian army enters Saxony—Overruns Hesse—Proclamation of Prince Frederick Charles—Second army under the Crown Prince—Third army (of the Elbe) under General Herwarth—Movements in Silesia and Bohemia—General Benedek—Crown Prince of Saxony—Clam Gallas—Prussians cross the mountains—Communications kept up by telegraphic wires—Münchengrätz—Turnau—Louwitz—Nachod—Skaliz—Königinhof—Schweinschädel—Capture of Jicin—General order of the Crown Prince of Prussia at Prausnitz—Junction of the Prussian armies—Pursuit of the Austrians to Gitschin—Königgrätz—King of Prussia arrives at Gitschin—His address to the municipal authorities—Great battle—Account of an eye-witness—Village of Chlum—Austrian force and commanders—Artillery contest—Village of Sadowa—Benetak in flames—Attack on Sadowa—Tremendous fire of artillery and needle-guns—Great havoc—Fransky's attack on the wood above Sadowa—3000 Prussians and 90 officers enter the wood, 300 men and 2 officers only leave it—Herewarth's army is engaged with the Saxons at Nechanitz—The first and third Prussian armies brought nearly to a standstill—The moment critical—Village of Chlum on fire—Timely arrival of the Crown Prince of Prussia with the second army on the field of battle—Austrians at a disadvantage—Their obstinate resistance—"All is lost"—Austrian request for an armistice rejected—Forward movement of the Prussians—Remarks on the battle of Königgrätz or Sadowa—The corps of Knobelsdorf and Stabberg in Silesia—

*Generals Goeben and Manteuffel in Hanover—Beyer in Hesse-Cassel—Allies of Austria at
Gottingen, Bamberg, and Frankfort—Prince Charles of Bavaria—General von Falkenstein—
Campaign in Hanover—Armistice—Terms proposed to King George rejected—Battle of
Langensalza on the 27th June—Hanoverians masters of the field—Hemmed in, nevertheless,
by superior numbers, they capitulate to the Prussians, and the king becomes an exile—
Campaign of the Main—Bavarian army—Federal army—Battle of Wiesenthal—Victory of
the Prussians over Bavarians—Battle at Hammelburg on the Saale—Severe engagement at
Kissingen—Actions on the Main between Prussians and the Federal forces under Prince
Alexander of Hesse—Battle of Lanfach—Prussians capture Aschaffenburg—Federals
evacuate Frankfort, which Falkenstein enters at the head of the Prussians—Large sums of
money exacted from the burghers—March from Frankfort southwards—Actions on the
Tauber—Occupation of Franconia by Duke of Mecklenburg-Schwerin—Armistice accorded
at Wurzburg to the Central States—March of Prussians on Brunn, Pressburg, and Vienna—
Preliminaries of Nikolsburg—Peace of Prague—Italian Campaign.*

THE historian Schmidt says that, as early as the month of July, 1865, Count von Bismarck at
Carlsbad had said to the French ambassador at Vienna, the now too famous Duc de Gramont,
that he considered war between Prussia and Austria to have become a necessity. The statement is
disputed, but there is little doubt that the thought was at that time in Bismarck's mind. His
reported conversation, in the same month, with Herr von der Pfordten, the Bavarian prime
minister, is still more remarkable. He said, avers Schmidt, "that war between Austria and Prussia
was very likely, and close at hand. It would be a duel between the two powers only, and the rest
of Germany might stand by as passive spectators. Prussia never contemplated extending her
power beyond the line of the Main. The settlement of the controversy would not take long. One
blow, one pitched battle, and Prussia would be in a position to dictate conditions. The most
urgent need of the central states was to range themselves on the side of Prussia. A localization of
the war in Silesia was determined upon, and was deemed feasible by the best military authorities.
The central states, by proclaiming neutrality, might contribute to this desirable localization, and
Bavaria had only to remember that she was the natural heir to the position of Austria in South
Germany." How deep and far-seeing were these tempting suggestions thrown into the minds of
men who were possible allies or probable foes! The treaty of Gastein, by leaving the central
states in an ambiguous position, had already proved that Austria had not their interests very
deeply at heart.

The leader of what was called the central state policy was Freiherr von Beust, prime minister of
the king of Saxony. His endeavour was to keep alive the old dualism of Austria and Prussia,
conceding nothing to either power, but labouring solely to preserve the independence of the
smaller central states. So long as this policy prevailed, the unification of Germany was
impossible. Had the ideas of the central state party been large and bold, they might have decided
the question of national union, and kept Prussia in a subordinate place, by agreeing with Austria
to form a great state, by means of a solid combination of her German territory and population,
with their own numerous states. But there was no leader among them with power to conceive and

energy to carry out to the end any scheme of this kind, and the genius of the Prussian minister forestalled them. Sacrifices for the sake of unity were demanded of the princes; sacrifices for Germany, not for Prussia, who would have herself to make greater sacrifices than any of them. In the struggles at the Diet, while Austria maintained her ascendancy, great efforts were made to reduce Prussia to an equality with the central states, to their intense gratification. They were ready to make any sacrifice, except independence, if Prussia were subjected to the same; such was their jealousy of Prussian greatness, and their desire to magnify the power of the Federal Diet. For this reason it was that the majority of votes was constantly in support of Austria. They strove to deceive themselves and the world with the notion that Germany and the Federal Diet were identical, and that Prussia was non-German and refractory when she refused to submit to the decrees of Austria and her supporters in the Diet. In combating these principles at Frankfort, Count von Bismarck schooled himself for the greater and more active conflicts that were to follow.

Of extreme interest is the history of the conflicts in the minister's own mind, as the great crisis of his public life approached. The mixture in him of worldly wisdom with unsuspected religious fervour, recalls the history of Oliver Cromwell's great strivings and searchings of heart. The inward strife and agitation which he suffered throughout the spring of 1866 is said actually to have been calmed by the attempt to assassinate him made by the crazy enthusiast, young Blind, on the 7th of May in that year. Bismarck looked upon his escape from death as a sign from heaven, encouraging him to pursue the path on which he had set out. How severe had been the six years' struggle with the second chamber of the Diet on the question of re-organizing the army, can only be known to the participators in that contest. The chamber had both the letter and the spirit of the constitution on its side, and was justified in complaining that the political part of legislation had been brought to a standstill. Important questions of education, trade, and provincial administration, awaiting settlement, were unceremoniously shunted on one side, on account of this unexplained zeal for reforming the army. Bismarck's personal influence could not be exercised over a large assembly, to which it was impossible to reveal a bold and comprehensive plan for revolutionizing Germany without exposing the plan to ruin. The opposition, therefore, in the second chamber was stronger than ever, and early in February manifested itself by voting a resolution to the effect that the annexation of the duchy of Lauenberg to the crown of Prussia should not take place until it had been approved of by both the chambers. Such an interference with the great scheme could not be brooked, and the session was abruptly terminated by the king on the 23rd February. There can be little doubt that the hostile attitude of the faithful commons helped to precipitate the international crisis that was approaching. The minister knew that he was doing right in combating their constitutional views. He alone seems to have had his scheme planned out clearly before him, and when he had successfully defied the Parliament, he had the difficult task of conquering the king. His Majesty's reluctance to go to war with a German state, and with a friendly young monarch like the emperor of Austria, was not easily overcome, but yielded at last to urgent reasons of policy, brought to bear upon his mind with consummate skill and characteristic ardour, by his able minister.

On the opening of the year 1866, symptoms were visible of the dissolution of that hollow friendship between Prussia and Austria, which had been ostensibly cemented at Gastein not many months before. Singularly enough, the first overt ground of offence arose from the liberalism of aristocratic Austria; but it was liberalism in Holstein, where Prussian interests required a strictly conservative and repressive policy. Austria secretly favoured the pretensions of the duke of Augustenburg, which Prussia would not for a moment countenance after the adverse decision of the commission upon the claims to the duchies. The Prussian ministry, moreover, were irritated at perceiving the sympathy expressed by the Austrians for the recalcitrant members of the Berlin parliament, whose opposition to the government seemed a source of weakness in Prussia that was far from disagreeable to the statesmen of Vienna. Thus when the Austrian government was informed of a project for assembling delegates of Holstein and Schleswig associations on January 23, in Altona, it issued a warning against the holding of any such meeting, as calculated to bring new dangers on the country. Upon an assurance, however, being given by the promoters of the meeting, that all agitating questions should be avoided, the Austrian government did not prevent the meeting from taking place. This occurrence drew forth a note from the Berlin cabinet, dated January 26, to their envoy at Vienna, complaining of the conduct of the Holstein government as seriously impairing the relations of the two states. Count von Bismarck appealed to the recollections of the meetings of Gastein and Salzburg, and remarked, that he had allowed himself to hope that at that period Austria was not only convinced of the necessity of combating the revolution, but had agreed as to the mode of combat. The conduct of Austria in the affair of the notes to the Frankfort senate had already somewhat shaken this agreeable persuasion; matters, however, now assumed a far graver aspect. The conduct of the Holstein government could only be designated as aggressive. It ill became the imperial government openly to use against Prussia the same means of agitation against which they fought together at Frankfort. If at Vienna it was thought that they might tranquilly contemplate the revolutionary transformation of the people of Holstein, so distinguished by their conservative spirit, Prussia was resolved not to act in a similar manner. The treaty of Gastein had indeed provisionally divided the administration of the two duchies. But Prussia had the right of claiming that Austria should maintain Holstein in *statu quo*, just as much as Prussia was bound to keep Schleswig in that state. The royal government saw no difficulty in putting an end to the agitation, the scandals, and injuries to the principle of royalty going on in the duchies. The Prussian government entreated the Vienna cabinet to weigh the situation, and to act accordingly. If a negative or evasive reply was given, Prussia would at least be assured that, influenced by her ancient antagonism, Austria could not durably act together with her. This conviction would be a painful one, but Prussia needed to see clearly. Should it be rendered impracticable for her to act with Austria, she would at least gain full freedom for her policy, and might make such use thereof as suited her interests.

This ominous threat of a rupture, which seemed to produce little impression at Vienna, was ere long followed by acts of unmistakable self-assertion in the duchies. Early in March the king of Prussia issued a decree in Schleswig, which declared that any Schleswiger signing an address or delivering a speech in favour of the duke of Augustenburg, would thenceforth be liable to be imprisoned for a period varying from three months to five years; while the actual attempt to abolish the Austro-Prussian sovereignty over the duchies, and hand over the country to any of the rival pretenders, rendered the offender liable to a penalty of from five to ten years' hard labour. This was asserting an authority in matters pertaining to Holstein which Austria could not but resent, as it was tantamount to declaring the treaty of Gastein to be abolished. The government at Vienna, therefore, resolved to bring the matter before the Diet, and let that body decide the question of appropriating the duchies. The minor states were requested to support Austria in the Diet, and to vote for making a summons to Prussia to declare herself; and in case the danger of a rupture of peace became more imminent, they were asked to vote for setting in motion the several army corps, under the command of the Diet, and placing them in communication with the Austrian army. It was in March, according to Sir A. Malet, that Count Karolyi, the Austrian ambassador at Berlin, received orders to ask the Prussian premier if he meant to break the treaty of Gastein. "No!" said his Excellency very decidedly in reply; adding, however, "If I had the intention, do you think I should tell you?" Karolyi hastened to inform his government, which seemed blind to the fact, that he considered war inevitable.

Meanwhile, before the end of March, a secret treaty of alliance was entered into between Prussia and Italy, the terms of which, so far as they were known, show how resolved the two countries were to engage in war with Austria. According to these, Italy engaged to declare war against Austria as soon as Prussia should have either declared war or committed an act of hostility. Prussia engaged to carry on the war until the mainland of Venetia, with the exception of the fortresses and the city of Venice, either was in the hands of the Italians, or until Austria declared herself ready to cede it voluntarily; and King Victor Emmanuel promised not to lay down his arms until the Prussians should be in legal possession of the Elbe duchies.

Austria could not mistake acts of such extraordinary significance as an alliance between Italy and Prussia, although she remained in ignorance of the terms of the treaty. Slowly and hesitatingly she commenced military preparations, which though conducted with great caution, and not calculated to excite serious alarm, were sufficient to furnish Count von Bismarck with grounds of complaint against his Gastein ally, and induce him to make the first openly hostile demonstration.

The Prussian premier struck his first blow at the Diet, and warned the several states of the Confederation, in a circular letter. He complained that Austria had acted in direct opposition to the treaties of Vienna and Gastein, by which the Elbe duchies had been legally transferred to the two powers, and had sought to hand it over to the prince of Augustenburg, "who had no right thereto." The intimate relations of the two powers were endangered by the manifest symptoms of ill-will on the part of the Vienna cabinet. Correspondence had ceased, but no reference to war had been made, nor was war intended. But Austria, while reproaching Prussia with intentions of disturbing the peace, was herself arming and sending from her eastern and southern provinces considerable forces, north and west, towards the Prussian frontier. The gratuitous Prussian supposition that the Kaiser wanted to compel the continuance of the Gastein intimacy, is ludicrously flimsy. Prussia at all events would arm, it being impossible that she could allow Silesia to be beset with troops without making counter preparations of defence. This was not enough; the cabinet at Berlin, having experienced the slight trust to be placed in the Austrian alliance, was bound to look to other quarters for guarantees of safety and peace. National independence was only to be found in the basis of German nationality, and in strengthening the ties which bound the purely German states together. The Bund or Confederation was manifestly insufficient for this purpose, and for the active policy which important crises in Europe might require. Prussia could not rely on the slow-moving Bund for help in the time of need, but must trust to her own good arm and the support of such German states as were friendly to her. The Bund must be reformed, and in a sense that would be for the interest of other German states as much as of Prussia. The interests of the latter state were, by geographical situation, identical with those of Germany, whose fate was involved in Prussia's. If the power of Prussia were broken, Germany would exist on sufferance, and in a great European crisis might undergo the fate of Poland. Strong arguments these to address to a reflective people like the Germans, and they had their effect. In the rupture between the two great powers, the decision of each of the smaller states as to which it would take was of vital importance to itself. Prussia was evidently able and willing to fight, and if she gained the victory it was clear that she meant to have the command of the military force of the proposed new Confederation, at which Count von Bismarck hinted in his circular. Count Karolyi was instructed to answer that circular, by formally assuring the king that the emperor of Austria had not the slightest intention to make a breach of the peace. The reply sent to Vienna was, that nothing could explain away the extensive military preparations made by Austria in the direction of her northern frontier. Owing to the admirably organized military system which they had perfected, the Berlin statesmen were able to make this charge without fear of a retort, for their own army could be mobilized and brought to the field of action in rather less than three weeks' time.

The Prussian force quartered in Silesia at the end of March was about 25,000 men, with eighteen batteries of artillery, while the Austrians had, according to the official Prussian accounts, an army of 80,000 men, with 240 guns in Bohemia, not far from the Silesian frontier. By orders issued between the 28th of March and the 1st of April, Prussia was enabled to put on a war footing considerably larger forces than Austria could possibly oppose to them. On the 25th of March the Italian minister of war gave orders to increase the national force by 100,000 men. Having advanced so far with their preparations, neither party was willing to recede, though King and Kaiser both declared their intention not to commit an act of aggression. Meanwhile, Count von Bismarck created a great ferment throughout Germany by submitting to the Diet at Frankfort his proposition that the Diet should be reformed, and that a national German Assembly should be convoked to consider the means and methods of this said reform. On 18th April the emperor proposed to reduce his armaments if King William would do the same, and the proposal was joyfully accepted by the old king. But other events and other influences were working in a less peaceful direction. Italy was excited in the highest degree at the prospect of another war with Austria, in which the Italians felt presumptuously confident that, with or without the aid of Prussia, they would recover Venetia and the Quadrilateral. Their attitude could not be disregarded by the imperial government, and on the 26th of April a missive from Vienna reached Berlin, which, while expressing the emperor's deep satisfaction at the covenanted disarmament on the Bohemian frontier, informed the royal government that the Austrian army in Italy would have to be put on a war footing, in order to defend the river Po and the sea-coast against the subjects of Victor Emmanuel. The Prussian government expressed grievous disappointment at this announcement, and declined further negotiations unless all the imperial army were reduced to a peace footing. The correspondence rapidly became warm, and Count Karolyi, on the 4th of May, informed the Prussian minister that Austria had now exhausted the negotiation for the simultaneous withdrawal of military preparations on both sides.

The following is the statement made on the 26th of April by the Austrian minister at Berlin:— "The emperor has received with sincere satisfaction the announcement that Prussia has accepted the proposition for a simultaneous disarmament of the two powers. His Majesty had expected nothing less from the conciliatory sentiments of King William. The emperor is now perfectly ready to give orders that the troops which have been directed upon Bohemia for the reinforcements of the garrisons there, shall be withdrawn into the interior of the empire, and thus put an end to any appearance of a concentration of force against Prussia. But we are now in a position which requires us to increase our means of defence in another direction, and we ought to be assured that this circumstance will not prevent the Prussian government from responding to the retirement of our troops from the Bohemian frontier by the reduction of the Prussian corps which have been mobilized. In fact, the latest intelligence from Italy evidently proves that the army of King Victor Emmanuel is preparing for an attack upon Venetia; Austria, therefore, is forced to place its Italian army upon a war footing, by calling in the men on furlough, and by making proper provisions for the defence, not only of its frontier upon the Po, but also of its extended coast line, which cannot be done without the movement of considerable bodies of troops within the interior of the monarchy. We think it necessary to acquaint the cabinet of Berlin with these facts, in order that we may not be exposed to the false interpretations which might be placed upon the circumstance that, while we are withdrawing our troops from Bohemia, we are at the same time making military preparations in another part of the empire.

"I request you, therefore, to explain to the king's government that these preparations are being made solely with a view to the eventuality of a conflict with the Italians, and that we shall begin at once to carry out the proposition of reciprocal disarmament, as soon as we shall be assured that the king's government will not permit the measures which we are compelled to take in our own defence against an attack from the south, to exercise any influence adverse to the re-establishment of the normal state of relations between Austria and Prussia."

Count von Bismarck framed on the 30th of April the following reply to this despatch:—"The Austrian government thus demands that Prussia shall countermand her, in themselves, modest defensive armaments, which have remained unchanged since the 28th of March, while Austria certainly withdraws her reinforcements of garrisons from Bohemia, but extends and hastens her arrangements for the establishment of an army upon a war footing. I cannot conceal from your excellency that, after the exchange of mutual declarations upon the 18th and 21st, hailed by us and by Europe as a guarantee of peace, we were not prepared for this demand. In justification of the altered attitude it takes up in the despatch of the 26th, the imperial government adduces the intelligence it has received from Italy. According to this, the army of King Victor Emmanuel is said to have been placed upon a war footing to proceed to an attack upon Venetia. The information which has reached us direct from Italy, and that we have received through the medium of other courts, coincides in stating that armaments of a threatening character against Austria have not taken place in Italy, and confirm us in the conviction that an unprovoked attack upon the empire is far distant from the intentions of the cabinet of Florence. If, in the meantime and recently, military preparations may have commenced in Italy, these, as well as the measures adopted by us upon the 28th of March, may probably be regarded as the consequence of the armaments begun by Austria. We are persuaded that the Italian armaments would be as readily discontinued as our own, provided the causes through which they have been occasioned ceased.

"In the interest of the preservation of peace, and the cessation of the pressure which at present weighs upon the relations of policies and trade, we therefore again request the imperial government to adhere without wavering to the programme it laid down itself in its despatch of the 18th, and which his Majesty the king accepted without delay, in the most conciliatory sense, and as a mark of his personal confidence in his Majesty the emperor. In execution of the same, we should expect, first, that all the troops sent to Bohemia, Moravia, Cracow, and Austrian Silesia, since the middle of March, should not only return to their former garrisons, but also that all bodies of troops stationed in those provinces should be replaced upon the former peace footing. We await a speedy authentic communication as to the execution of these measures, *i.e.*, of the restoration of the *status quo ante*, as the term of the 25th of April, fixed by the imperial government itself for the return to a peace footing of the troops assembled against our frontiers, has long since expired. We hope that the imperial government will at once, by further inquiry, arrive at the conviction that its intelligence as to the aggressive intentions of Italy was unfounded; that it will then proceed to the effective restoration of a peace footing throughout the imperial army, and thereby enable us to take the same step, to his Majesty's satisfaction."

The manner in which this despatch was received by the cabinet of Vienna, is best explained by the orders issued early in May by the emperor of Austria, authorizing the whole army to be placed on a footing of war, and for directing a part of it to be concentrated upon the frontiers of Bohemia and Silesia; and as early as the 4th of May, Count Mensdorff forwarded an address which he had drawn up, to the Austrian minister at Berlin, which, after referring to the despatch of Count von Bismarck, dated the 30th of April, proceeds, "According to this despatch, the government of his Majesty the king of Prussia thinks there is no reason why Austria should prepare to ward off an attack on her possessions in Italy. It declares that, if Austria should not think fit to place the whole imperial army on a real peace footing, it will not be possible for

Prussia to carry on the important and momentous negotiations with the imperial government in any other way than by maintaining an equilibrium in the warlike preparations of the two powers. Your excellency will understand that we, after this declaration, must consider the negotiations for a simultaneous disarmament on the part of Prussia on the one side, and of Austria on the other, as being at an end. After the solemn assurances given by us in Berlin and in Frankfort, Prussia can have no reason to apprehend aggressive proceedings on our part, and Germany can have no cause to fear that we shall disturb the peace of the German Confederation. Just as little does Austria think of attacking Italy, although on all occasions the forcible detachment of a part of the Austrian territory has been the already pronounced programme of the Florence government. It is our duty to provide for the defence of the monarchy, and if the Prussian government finds in our measures against Italy a motive for upholding her own readiness for war, we can but fulfil that duty—which admits of no foreign control—without entering into any further discussion as to the priority or magnitude of the several military measures. In Berlin it cannot be unknown that we have not only to provide for the integrity of our own empire, but also to protect the territory of the German Bund against an aggressive movement on the part of Italy; and we therefore may, and must, in the interest of Germany, seriously ask of Prussia whether she thinks the demand that the frontiers of Germany shall be left unguarded, compatible with the duties of a German power."

The two opposite influences at work, antagonistic to the welfare of Austria, were shortly to undermine the monarchy, and by their united effect exalt the two countries that exercised them. Italy was to gain a triumphant freedom from Austrian rule, and Prussia an ascendancy long desired, but almost unlooked for. Yet, had the power of Prussia in the north proved as weak as that of her Italian ally in the south, Austria would have had a comparatively easy task, and have gained a double triumph. Austria's mistake was in having almost a needless fear of Italy, mixed with contempt and an affectation of slighting the strength of Prussia.

On another question of moment, that of the Elbe duchies, Austria made a proposal that was excessively disagreeable to Prussia. The proposal was to the effect that the two powers should make a common declaration, that they would cede the rights over the duchies which they had acquired by the treaty of Vienna, to that claimant of the sovereignty whom the Diet should recognize as lawful. Prussia should have the military position of Kiel, Rendsburg, and Sonderburg given to her by the treaty of Gastein; and Kiel should become a federal fort. Austria also would support Prussia's reasonable demands for territory requisite to complete the fortifications of Dybböl and Alsen, and obtain facilities for making the projected ship canal between the Baltic and North seas. Prussia declined to treat with a third party like the Diet on the subject of the duchies, but was willing to make a bargain with Austria if she were disposed to cede her share of the rights accruing by the treaty of Vienna.

Saxony, having made military preparations with a view, as Herr von Beust affirmed, to support her position in the Diet, the Prussian cabinet complained and warned the Saxon government of the consequences. Austria began to arm in earnest. The fortresses of Theresienstadt and

Josephstadt were equipped, Cracow strengthened, Königgrätz made defensible. The regiments in Bohemia, Moravia, and Galicia, were raised to their full war complement.

Early in May a motion was made and carried in the Diet at Frankfort, by the representative of Saxony, to the effect that the Bund should summon Prussia to give a formal declaration that her intentions were of a pacific nature. A week or ten days later there was a conference held at Bamberg, of the middle states, in which the representatives of Bavaria, Würtemburg, Baden, and Grand-ducal Hesse took part with those of the Saxon duchies, Brunswick and Nassau, in formulating the following propositions for the decision of the Diet:—The Diet will request those members of the Confederation which have taken any steps for military preparations beyond their peace establishment, to declare in the next sitting of the Diet, whether, and on what conditions, they will be prepared simultaneously to reduce their armed force to the peace establishment, and on a day to be agreed upon in the Diet's sitting. The vote was to be taken on the 1st June, on which day Baron Kübeck, on the part of Austria, charged Prussia with having made a "lamentable alliance with a foreign opponent of the empire;" adding, that his government, being imperilled on two sides, and uncertain whether the first attack would take place on the south or on the north, must preserve an attitude of defence. Their efforts, he continued, to come to an understanding with Prussia for a settlement on Federal principles of the question of the Elbe duchies, had been frustrated, and they should leave all future decisions with respect to it to the Diet, seeing that all Germany had a common interest in Schleswig and Holstein. This last fling at Prussia's known desire to annex the provinces, struck home, and was followed by orders to General Gablenz, the Austrian governor of Holstein, to convene an assembly of the states for the 11th of June, for the purpose of deciding on their future form of government. By this act, according to Prussian jurists, the treaty of Gastein was abrogated, and the cabinet of Berlin, falling back upon the treaty of Vienna, and the rights of co-possession which it conferred, ordered General Manteuffel to lead a sufficient military force from Schleswig into Holstein. This was done on the 8th and 9th of June, and Gablenz, finding himself outnumbered, and in danger of being caught in a trap the moment war should be declared, wisely withdrew from the duchy to a place of safety. As for the Frankfort Diet, it was informed by Baron Savigny that since they could not restrain Austria and Saxony from threatening Prussia by their formidable armaments, Prussia would protect her own interests without regard to the decisions of the Diet. One more sitting only, of great importance, was the Diet destined to hold. Her decrees were like the fibres of a spider's web, strong enough to hold small flies, but torn to shreds by a bee or a wasp. On the 11th of June, at this memorable meeting, Austria moved that all the Federal contingents saving that of Prussia should be mobilized and placed on their full war establishment, concentrated within fourteen days, and then be ready to take the field within twenty-four hours. This was tantamount to a declaration of war by the whole Confederation against Prussia. Undismayed however, by the formidable aspect of the situation, Prussia replied by the counter proposition of a scheme for reforming the Bund, of which she moved the immediate adoption. This bold scheme consisted of ten articles, the most salient of which were the convocation of a national representative body to be elected by universal suffrage, and to sit periodically, and the exclusion of Austria from the Confederation. The representative of the Kaiser, so long paramount in the Diet as by right prescriptive, must have indeed felt on this occasion that the genius of Count von Bismarck, as Louis Napoleon says, lies in his audacity. The Austrian proposal, however, was carried on a division by nine against six votes. Thereupon Baron Savigny said that his master the king now considered the breach of the Federal compact to be consummated, and his participation in the proceedings of the Diet came to an end. The assembly dispersed on the 14th, never to meet for independent action again, being destroyed, after an existence of fifty years, by the minority of its members. Prussia lost no time in summoning the governments of Saxony, Hanover, and Hesse-Cassel, to declare for or against her, offering to guarantee the sovereign rights of their rulers if they took her side. Saxony refused peremptorily; the other two states delayed their answers; and all three received from Prussia an immediate declaration of war.

One more effort in favour of peace was made by the other great powers, who united in proposing a conference. Prussia, Italy, and the Diet agreed to the proposal, but Austria accepted only on condition that the negotiations should exclude all pretensions on the part of any one of the powers to obtain an aggrandizement of territory. The fulfilment of this condition would have foiled Prussia in her hopes of annexing the Duchies, Italy in her expectation of recovering Venetia, and France in her general views; she being favourable to both of those projects. The idea of a conference was therefore abandoned, and the trumpet sounded for war. "With God, for King and Fatherland," resounded through Berlin and in every town and village of Prussia, while an Austrian archduke, assuming for the first time a national tone, closed an order of the day in Italy with the words, "For God, with Emperor and Fatherland." Bismarck, Moltke, and Roon were now frequently to be seen walking together in the summer evenings under the fine trees of the garden attached to the Ministry of Foreign Affairs at Berlin. There, on the night of Thursday the 14th June, the thought flashed upon Count von Bismarck to set the Prussian army in motion twenty-four hours sooner than was intended. Moltke retired to his cabinet, opened a drawer from which he took out orders that had been carefully prepared, and by means of the telegraph wires delivered those orders to every corner of the kingdom ere the next day had fully dawned. All that thought, knowledge, foresight could do in preparation for a great war, was done by the Prussian government. Austria, on her side, was also full of confidence. She was leader of Germany by prescription, and she certainly did not expect to be overthrown by a power long treated by her as an inferior.

When the prospect of a war, says the "History of the Seven Weeks' War," arose between Austria and Prussia in the spring of 1866, then came Italy's opportunity to complete the work which had been commenced at Magenta, to secure and unite to herself the only province which, still under the rule of the foreigner, prevented her from being free from the Alps to the Adriatic. Italy naturally drew as close to Prussia as she possibly could. Austria requires a long time to mobilize her army, and had begun her preparations for war in the middle of February. Public attention was directed to this fact by a council of war held at Vienna as early as the 10th of March, to which Feldzeugmeister (general of artillery) Benedek was summoned from Verona. At this council the party in favour of war was strongly predominant, and decided that Austria was powerful enough to take the field against Prussia and Italy at the same time, provided that measures were taken to isolate Prussia in Germany, and to draw the states of the Confederation to the Austrian side. The grand error of this council was that too high an estimate was formed of the strength of Austria, and far too low a calculation made of the powers of Prussia; no doubt seems to have been entertained but that Austria would emerge from such a war decidedly the victor. Italy was so detested that every Austrian wished for an Italian war. Prussia, it was thought, weakened by an internal political conflict, could hardly unite her contending parties in a common foreign policy. Nor was a high opinion entertained of her military resources and organization. The professional papers and periodicals of Austria ingeniously demonstrated that Prussia, however hardly pressed, could not place her normal army on a complete war footing, because trained men would be wanting. The writers of these articles calculated that the battalions of infantry could only be brought into the field with a muster-roll of eight hundred men; no consideration was paid to the landwehr; in fact, doubts were in some cases thrown upon the existence of the landwehr soldiers at all, and those who believed in their existence entertained no doubts of their certain disloyalty. It was also calculated that the Prussian army would have to make such strong detachments for the garrisons of fortresses, that a very small force would be left for operations in the field. These false calculations, the first step and perhaps the most certain to the bitter defeat which ensued, were due to defective information. The war office at Vienna was lamentably deficient in those detailed accounts of foreign military statistics, without which any government that undertakes great military operations must necessarily grope in the dark.

Meanwhile the government of Prussia was not idle. By order of the king the entire army was mobilized, five corps d'armée being placed upon a war strength by the 4th of May, while the remaining four corps of the standing army received orders to be augmented and mobilized. The execution of these orders was conducted with such remarkable alacrity and precision as indicated how careful Prussia had been for a considerable period to prepare, in case of the outbreak of war, a force adequate to the severest exigencies of either defence or attack. The equipment of the entire Prussian army was fully effected at the end of a fortnight, when it mustered 490,000 men, unsurpassed in efficiency, and fully provided for a campaign. It was on the 7th of May that the Prussian troops concentrated in Schleswig crossed the frontier, and occupied Holstein; while the Austrians, not having at this point a sufficient body of men to resist their entry, retired to Altona. General Manteuffel, the Prussian governor of Schleswig, then published a proclamation declaring to the inhabitants of Holstein that the provisional government established in 1866 was discarded, and a Prussian president was appointed for the general administration of the affairs of both the duchies of Schleswig and Holstein. The expedition with which Prussia made her preparations appeared a matter of almost as much surprise to themselves as to the Austrians. The army of the latter power, however, although starting with a priority of ten weeks for its formation, was in an incompetent state to open the campaign when the day for action arrived. Had the Prussians then taken advantage of the backward state of their enemy's preparations, the campaign might have been even more marvellously brief and decisive than it was. Why Prussia did not avail herself of the opportunity thus afforded has not been clearly explained. Was

Prussia, it has been asked, really so moderate as her advocates would have the world believe? Was it desire of peace or fear of failure which stayed her hand, and held her marshalled corps on the north of the mountain frontier of Bohemia? It may have been both, but the results of the war show that the latter entered into the calculations of those who planned the Prussian strategy. The army was ready and might have attacked Austria; but it would in its advance have exposed its communications to the assault of the minor states, and until forces were prepared to quell these, the main army could not assume the offensive. This was probably the cause why the troops were not at once concentrated, and pushed immediately into Bohemia. At the very beginning the Prussian army confined itself to taking up defensive positions to cover the provinces most exposed to attack, especially towards Bohemia. The Austrian army of the north had commenced its concentration in Bohemia on the 13th May, and Feldzeugmeister Benedek had there taken over the command-in-chief on the 18th. The first, fifth, and sixth Prussian corps d'armée were posted in Silesia, the second and third corps in Lusatia, and the fourth corps round Erfurt. The guards corps was still left at Berlin, and the seventh and eighth corps were retained in Westphalia and the Rhine provinces, respectively.

Italy had made such progress in her preparations for the coming struggle, that by the end of May her armaments were fully formed. A decree published at Florence having appointed General Garibaldi, the great guerilla chieftain, to the immediate command of twenty volunteer battalions, which were ordered to form under that patriot's standard, the volunteers responded to the call in such numbers that the battalions had to be doubled. Upon this Austria committed towards her Italian dependency one of her last acts of tyranny, by raising a compulsory loan in Venetia of twelve million gulden. This act excited Italian feeling to such a state of desperation, that Victor Emmanuel found the utmost difficulty in restraining his troops from striking the blow for liberty till the proper hour had arrived. Thus Austria was placed between two menacing foes, both acting in concerted measures, yet each relying upon its own strength.

Notwithstanding these active preparations, the actual commencement of hostilites was still averted, and though swords were not imbrued with blood, diplomatic pens, as we have seen, were actively engaged in paper war. Prussia was engaged in putting forward her motion for reform of the Germanic Confederation. The attempt made by the other great powers to bring about a reconciliation between the rival claimants for supremacy in Germany having failed, war became inevitable.

The subjoined chronological table of the principal features of the political prologue is taken from the "History of the Seven Week's War:"—

October 20, 1864.—Treaty of Vienna.

August 14, 1865.—Convention of Gastein.

March 12, 1866.—First preparations of Austria for war in Bohemia and Moravia.

March 30, 1866.—First preparations of Prussia.

April, 1866.—Negotiations concerning those armaments.

April 23, 1866.—Great armament of Austria in Venetia.

April 26, 1866.—Proposal of Austria to submit the question in dispute to the Diet.

May 7, 1866.—Declaration of Prussia of the incompetency of the Diet to decide in international questions, and suggestion of the desirability of the reform of the Confederation.

Until May 28, 1866.—Armaments in all Germany and Italy.

May 28, 1866.—Proposal of a Conference by the three non-Germanic powers.

May 29, 1866.—Prussian acceptance of this proposal.

June 1, 1866.—Submission of the Schleswig-Holstein question to the Diet.

June 5, 1866.—Summons by General Gablenz for assembly of Holstein Estates.

June 10, 1866.—Prussian proposal for the reform of the Federal constitution.

June 11, 1866.—Austrian motion for the decree of Federal execution against Prussia.

June 14, 1866.—Acceptance of the Austrian motion by the Diet.

June 15, 1866.—Declaration of war by Prussia against Hanover, Electoral Hesse, and Saxony.

June 20, 1866.—Declaration of war by Italy against Austria and Bavaria.

It must be remembered that the Westphalian and Rhenish provinces of Prussia were divided from the rest of the kingdom by the interlying territories of Hanover, Hesse-Cassel, and Nassau. Of these powers, all favouring Austria, the first possessed a well-armed, well-trained force of 20,000 men—more than a match, it was thought, for the Prussian landwehr, and fit to be a powerful advanced guard to the forces which Bavaria and her allies upon the Main were about to raise. To meet this danger the Prussian chief ordered half of Vogel's corps to assemble at Minden, where, aided by the southward march of Manteuffel's regiments from Holstein, they were soon in a position to occupy Hanover and overrun Hesse-Cassel. The other half of Vogel's corps was united to Herwarth's, and formed the third or Elbe army, which, after occupying Saxony, became part of the general force employed in the invasion of Bohemia.

The actual commencement of hostilities took place on the 15th June, the day after that on which the Diet had decreed the mobilization of the Federal forces. The Prussians marched into Saxony, and took possession of Leipsic. On committing this bold act of invasion, Prince Frederick Charles, who commanded the Prussians, issued to the inhabitants of Saxony a proclamation, dated Görlitz, June 16, in which he said, "We are not at war with the people and country of Saxony, but only with the government, which by its inveterate hostility has forced us to take up arms." At the same time Hesse-Cassel was also overrun by the Prussians, who met with no impediment. The entire Prussian force was formed into three distinct armies. The first army, under the command of Prince Frederick Charles, was in occupation of Saxony, and threatened the Bohemian frontier. The second army, under the command of the Crown Prince, was in movement in Silesia; and a third army, designated the army of the Elbe, and commanded by General Herwarth, was prepared to march on the right flank of the first army.

The emperor of Austria, on the 17th of June, issued an address "To my Peoples," in which the circumstances which brought about the impending hostilities were reviewed, and reasons given why Austria was under the necessity of entering into the combat. "While engaged in a work of peace," said his Majesty, "which was undertaken for the purpose of laying the foundation for a constitution which should augment the unity and power of the empire, and, at the same time, secure to my several countries and peoples free internal development, my duties as a sovereign have obliged me to place my whole army under arms. On the frontiers of my empire, in the south and in the north, stand the armies of two enemies, who are allied together with the intention of breaking the power of Austria as a great European state. To neither of these enemies have I given cause for war. I call on my Omniscient God to bear witness that I have always considered it my first, my most sacred duty, to do all in my power to secure for my people the blessings of peace."

After alluding to his former alliance with Prussia, and to some minor topics, he says, "The assurances given by my government of my love of peace, and the repeated declarations which were made of my readiness to disarm at the same time with Prussia, were replied to by propositions which could not be accepted without sacrificing the honour and safety of the monarchy. Prussia not only insisted on complete disarmament in the northern provinces of the empire, but also in those parts of it which touch on Italy, where a hostile army was standing, for whose love of peace no guarantee could either be given or offered. The negotiations with Prussia in respect to the Elbe duchies, clearly proved that a settlement of the question in a way compatible with the dignity of Austria, and with the rights and interests of Germany and the duchies, could not be brought about, as Prussia was violently intent on conquest. The negotiations were therefore broken off, the whole affair was referred to the Bund, and at the same time the legal representatives of Holstein were convoked."

The emperor then refers to the intervention of the three powers to avert if possible the outbreak of war, and he attributes the failure of the attempt to the ambitious aims of Prussia. "The recent events clearly prove that Prussia substitutes open violence for right and justice. The rights and the honour of Austria, the rights and the honour of the whole German nation, are no longer a barrier against the inordinate ambition of Prussia. Prussian troops have entered Holstein, the estates convoked by the imperial stadtholder have been violently dissolved. The government of Holstein, which the treaty of Vienna gives to Austria and Prussia in common, has been claimed for Prussia alone; and the Austrian garrison has been obliged to give way to a force ten times as strong as itself. When the German Bund accepted the Austrian proposition to mobilize the Federal troops, Prussia, who prides herself upon being the defender of the interests of Germany, resolved to complete the work she had begun, by violently severing the tie which unites the German races. Suddenly announcing her secession from the Bund, she required from the German government the acceptance of a so-called project of reform, which in reality is a division of Germany, and now she employs military force against those sovereigns who have faithfully discharged their federal duties.

"The most pernicious of wars, a war of Germans against Germans, has become inevitable, and I now summon before the tribunal of history, before the tribunal of an eternal and all-powerful God, those persons who have brought it about, and make them responsible for the misfortunes which may fall on individuals, families, districts, and countries." Turning from this almost pathetic strain, the Kaiser expresses his delight at the patriotic spirit evinced by his people:— "My heart beats high at the sight of my gallant and well-appointed army—the bulwark against which the force of the enemies of Austria will be broken—and of my faithful peoples, who are full of loyal confidence and self-devotion. The pure fire of patriotic enthusiasm burns with equal strength and steadiness in all parts of my vast empire. Joyfully do the furlough men and reserves take their places in the ranks of the army; numerous volunteers present themselves; the whole of the able-bodied population of the countries which are most exposed are preparing to take the field." He also flatters his people with the prospect, that "we shall not be alone in the struggle which is about to take place. The princes and peoples of Germany know that their liberty and independence are menaced by a power, which listens but to the dictates of egotism, and is under the influence of an ungovernable craving after aggrandizement." The emperor ends his lengthy manifesto by testifying his implicit faith in the justness of his cause, and his belief in a consequent success.

On the day of its publication a general order was also issued by Benedek, the commander-in-chief, to the Austrian army of the North, from his head-quarters at Olmütz. In this document the Austrian commander betrays woful ignorance of the quality of the army opposed to him. "Soldiers," he says, "we are on the eve of grave and sanguinary events. I have the full and entire conviction that you are aware of and are worthy of the mission confided to you. Have confidence also in me, and be assured that on my part I will exert my best efforts to bring this campaign to a speedy and glorious termination. We are now faced by inimical forces, composed partly of troops of the line and partly of landwehr. The first comprise young men not accustomed to privations and fatigues, and who have never yet made an important campaign. The latter is composed of doubtful and dissatisfied elements, which rather than fight against us would prefer the downfall of their government. In consequence of a long course of years of peace, the enemy does not possess a single general who has had an opportunity of learning his duties on the field of battle. Veterans of the Mincio and of Palestro, I hope that with tried leaders you will not allow the slightest advantage to such an adversary. On the day of battle the infantry will adopt their lightest campaign accoutrement, and will leave behind their knapsacks and camping material, in order that they may be able to throw themselves with rapidity and promptitude upon the heavily-laden enemy. The officers will discontinue the use of their wide scarves, and all the useless insignia of their ranks, which but renders them too easily distinguishable in action. Every man, without distinction of name or position, shall be promoted whenever he shall distinguish himself on the field of battle. The enemy have for some time vaunted the excellence of their fire-arms; but, soldiers, I do not think that will be of much avail to them. We will give them no time for fire-arms, but attack them with the bayonet and with cross muskets; and when, with God's help, we shall have beaten and compelled them to retreat, we will pursue them without intermission, until you find repose upon the enemy's soil, and those compensations which a glorious and victorious army has a right to demand."

General Benedek distributed his forces along the frontier separating Moravia from Saxony and Silesia; he evidently had no conception of the rapidity of the Prussian movements, but contemplated meeting them at his leisure and cutting them off in detail, while they were traversing the mountain passes that separate the two countries, and entering at various points the Austrian territory.

General von Moltke arranged the plan of the Prussian campaign in Berlin, and to his remarkable foresight and skilful arrangements its crowning success is mainly due. But the shrewd combinations of the able general derived extraordinary strength from the unexpected efficiency of the new weapon that the Prussian government had adopted, the now famous "needle-gun"—a breech-loading arm, which, by the fearful rapidity of its fire, utterly paralyzed the Austrians, and proved to them a terrible engine of destruction. It had been used to some extent in the war against Denmark, but its marked superiority was not made universally manifest till now. The promptness of the Prussians in action was much commented upon at the time. A writer already quoted says, they "were all alert. For some years the king has been fighting his Parliament in order to be in a position to fight Austria and take possession of Germany, and has thus been able to form a regular army. He first used this force to overawe his subjects, and compel them to submit to the new military organization, and then, by calling up the whole adult population of his kingdom, he began the war with an overwhelming force. Austria suddenly found herself overmatched in numbers, while those numbers were trebly multiplied by the superior weapons of the foe. The Prussians came on at a double quick with ambulances, transports, and munitions complete, and even timbers cut to the size of the railway bridges which they expected to find destroyed." Prince Frederick Charles, with the first army, established his headquarters at the village of Hirschfeld, situated on the banks of the Neisse, a short distance east of the frontier town of Zittau, commanding the outlet of the passes stretching from Reichenberg and Friedland, in Bohemia, through the range of mountains into the district in Saxony called Lusatia. It overlooks also the railway lines from Pardubitz to Bautzen.

On the following day the first Prussian army crossed the Bohemian frontier in two columns, one marching by way of Gorlitz, and the other by Zittau; it reached, after a few skirmishes with cavalry, the Bohemian town of Reichenberg. On the 26th of June an artillery engagement took place between an Austrian battery and the Prussian advanced lines, which resulted in the Austrians withdrawing to Münchengrätz. Here, on the 28th, a desperate struggle ensued, and the Austrians, aided by the Saxons, offered a most strenuous resistance; but the Prussians finally drove them back, and pursuing them towards Gitschin, formed in position on the high ground facing that town.

While these engagements were taking place the second Prussian army, commanded by the Crown Prince, had to march into Bohemia from Silesia, through the long and narrow passes of the Sudetian mountains. For the purpose of deceiving the enemy various feigned movements were made on the south-east frontiers of Silesia, the object of the Prussians being to lead the enemy to prepare to meet them crossing into Bohemia from Neisse, through Weidenau. While, however, the Austrians were looking this way for the approach of the invaders, the main body of the second army faced to the right, and appeared, with considerable alacrity on the west at Nachod and Trautenau in Bohemia, having in their march passed the frontier at Reinerz and Landshut without meeting any opposition. The Crown Prince, before traversing the defiles of the mountains separating Silesia from Moravia, on the 20th June, issued from Neisse a general order to his troops, in which he said, "Soldiers of the Second Army—You have heard the words of our king and commander-in-chief. The attempts of his Majesty to preserve peace to our country having proved fruitless, with a heavy heart, but with strong confidence in the spirit and valour of his army, the king has determined to do battle for the honour and independence of Prussia, and for a new organization of Germany on a powerful basis. I, placed by the grace and confidence of my royal father at your head, am proud, as the first servant of our king, to risk with you my blood and property for the most sacred rights of our native country. Soldiers! for the first time for fifty years a worthy foeman is opposed to our army. Confident in your prowess, and in our excellent and approved arms, it behoves us to conquer the same enemy as our greatest king defeated with a small army. And now, forward with the old Prussian battle cry—'With God, for King and Fatherland.' "

The reason why the armies of Prussia debouched into the Austrian territory by different roads, will be understood when it is known that the troops, carriages, &c., of the first army alone, when entering Bohemia, on two lines, covered twelve miles of road; and had the second army and the army of the Elbe marched the same road, any obstructions would have made progress extremely difficult. Nor could the Austrian general hope effectually to repel the invaders by blocking each pass through the mountains, since he would have had to make too many divisions in his forces, and have thus exposed them to the risk of being beaten in detail.

Lieutenant-colonel Cooke, in a sketch of this campaign, says, "The position of the Austrian corps was made known to the Prussians on the 11th June, by means of a little book which had been printed and distributed to the superior officers of the Prussian army. In this small volume the positions of the Austrian corps and their organization were given with great minuteness. Whether the information was obtained by the treachery of some Austrian, or by the exertions of the Prussian Intelligence department, is not known. According to this book, the first corps was at Prague, the second at Hohenmauth and Zwittau, the third at Brünn, the fourth and sixth at Olmütz, the eighth at Auspitz, and the tenth at Brünn. The crown prince of Saxony was to join the first Austrian corps with his army, and take command of both.

On the 22nd the first Prussian army, and the army of the Elbe, prepared to advance. The first army broke up from Görlitz, and moved to the frontier of Bohemia on the Zittau and Friedland roads. The army of the Elbe advanced by the Rumberg road. On the 23rd the "first army entered Bohemia, marching on fine roads towards Reichenberg, and after a halt there made another advance on the 26th, for the purpose of securing the passage of the Iser, over which are bridges at Turnau, Podol, and Münchengrätz. The road from Reichenberg, by which Prince Frederick Charles was advancing, passes through Liebenau, and, when near the Iser, forks to the left to the bridge at Turnau, and to the right to the bridge at Podol, where the road crosses the river, and continues to Münchengrätz. The portion of the Austrian army opposed to the Prussians on this side were behind the Iser, in the neighbourhood of Münchengrätz. They consisted of the first corps, under Clam Gallas, and the Saxons under their crown prince. They held the bridges at Münchengrätz and at Podol, and had an advanced guard consisting of cavalry and artillery at Liebenau, but they seem to have omitted to occupy Turnau in any force. At Liebenau the advanced guard of the Prussian army, consisting of the first division under Horn, met the

Austrian advanced guard, and, after some resistance, drove them back. The latter retreated across the Iser at Turnau, and broke the bridge there; but the Prussians threw a bridge over the river, and occupied the place on the same night with two divisions.

At the same time the Prussians marched on Podol, which they reached at about eight p.m. A severe fight ensued here, which ended in the victory of the Prussians, who drove the Austrians across the Iser, and seized the road and railway bridges. They thus secured the passage of that river, both at Turnau and Podol. Meanwhile the army of the Elbe had continued its advance, and on this day had a successful encounter with the Austrians at Hünerwasser. Prince Frederick Charles determined to endeavour to turn the Austrian right flank by an advance along the Turnau road, while a portion of his army attacked them in front at Podol, and the army of the Elbe assailed them at Münchengrätz. He accordingly advanced on the morning of the 28th with this object; but the Austrians, after a severe fight, in which they lost 2000 men, of whom 1400 were prisoners, abandoned their position in time, and retired towards Jicin.

It is now time to turn to the second army, which entered Bohemia by three different routes; the first corps by the Trautenau road; the guards by Braunau; the fifth corps (followed by the sixth) by Nachod. It had a more difficult task to perform than the first army, as it was nearer the bulk of the Austrian forces. Benedek's headquarters were at Bohmish Trübau on the 25th, and were moved a day or two after to Josephstadt. He appears to have had three corps immediately available, with which to dispute the Crown Prince's advance; the tenth at Trautenau; the sixth at Opoino, to the south of Neustadt; and the eighth in the neighbourhood of Josephstadt.

It is necessary to trace the passage of the left columns of the Prince's army through the mountains, and to show how, on the 30th of June, it was able to effect a junction with the right and central columns on the bank of the Elbe.

On the 27th of June the first corps of the Crown Prince's army, under General von Bonin, seized Trautenau, a town lying on the river Aupa, in a basin surrounded by mountains. A barricade on the bridge having been broken down by the Prussians, the town was entered and a severe street fight ensued, the Austrians being gradually driven back from house to house. After a heavy loss on both sides, the Austrians were thrust out into the open country. There the celebrated Windischgrütz dragoons stood waiting to sweep the Prussians from the ground, as soon as they should emerge from the town. They met their match, however, in the first Prussian dragoon regiment, composed of young Lithuanians, who spend their life on horseback. The two regiments advanced to the encounter without exchanging a shot, and as they closed, both sides raised a cheer, welcoming the hug of battle. For a few minutes the mass of combatants swayed slowly backwards and forwards, and then the Austrians suddenly gave way, scattering in their flight and leaving the Prussians masters of the field. Mondel's Austrian brigade of infantry, posted on the hillside of Capellenberg, were forced to retire by an' attack of Prussian foot. The village of Hohenbrück was occupied by the Prussians, and so confident of victory was Von Bonin, that he declined an offer of assistance made to him by the commander of the Prussian guards, who marching by way of Stcinthal had reached Qualitch, and heard the heavy firing at Trautenau. At three o'clock in the afternoon the action seemed to be over. Half an hour, however, had scarcely elapsed, when the commander of the tenth corps of Austrians, General Gablenz, advanced with his whole force from Pilnikau and attacked the weary Prussians. After an hour's combat he had retaken the village of Hohenbrück, and by five o'clock the Prussians had begun to retreat. This operation was covered by the forty-third Prussian regiment stationed on the hills north of Capellenberg, and supported by the third grenadiers. For some time these regiments, at great loss to themselves, stopped the Austrian pursuit. General von Bonin intended to hold the line of the Aupa on the north of Trautenau, but Gablenz pressed upon him and he was forced to continue his retreat to the position he had occupied on the morning of the 27th. The first Prussian corps lost in this action, in killed and wounded, sixty-three officers and 1214 men, while the Austrian tenth corps, owing to the murderous effect of the Prussian needle-gun, lost 196 officers with 5536 men. The victory of the muzzle-loader was purchased at a cost well nigh as great as that of a defeat. The reverse which the Prussians had sustained under Von Bonin was promptly rectified by the advance of the prince of Würtemberg from Eypel at the head of the first corps of guards early in the morning of the 28th of June. General Gablenz, finding his right flank threatened, had to change his front, a movement which he protected by the heavy fire of sixty-four pieces of artillery that did much damage to the advancing Prussians. The advance of the latter nevertheless was steadily maintained, the Austrians were driven back at Burgersdorf, Alt-Rognitz, towards Koniginhof, and one brigade into Trautenau itself, which the Prussians took by storm, capturing 3000 prisoners and a stand of colours.

To the fifth Prussian corps, which formed the head of the left column of the army of the Crown Prince, was the most difficult task given. Only one narrow road leads from the county of Glatz to Nachod, a road which beyond the Bohemian frontier runs in a winding course near the town of Nachod, through a difficult defile. A corps d'armée, with all its trains and baggage advancing by one road, forms a column of march twenty miles long. If only the combatants themselves and the most necessary train, such as ammunition waggons and field hospitals, form the corps, it still will stretch over ten miles; so that if the head of the column is attacked as it issues from a defile where the troops cannot move off the road, the rearmost battalion will not be able to support the most advanced until four hours have passed.

In order to insure the safe issue from the mountain passes, the advanced guard of the fifth corps, under General von Löwenfeld, was pushed forward as far as Nachod, on the evening of the 26th June. The Austrians held the defile with a very weak force, and did not stand obstinately in the castle of Nachod, so that the Prussian advanced guard occupied that strong post with very slight opposition. General Ramming, who had been posted with the sixth Austrian corps, and a portion of the first division of reserve cavalry at Opoino, about ten miles to the south of Nachod, marched on the 26th towards Skalitz, by order of Feldzeugmeister Benedek. The next day the advanced guard of the Prussian fifth corps brought on the action of Nachod.

On the 27th, the same day that the first corps of the Prussians was defeated at Trautenau, the advanced guard of the fifth Prussian corps d'armée was, about ten o'clock in the morning, moving out of Nachod towards Skalitz, when it was suddenly assailed by a heavy fire from the Austrian artillery, and two Austrian cuirassier regiments drew up across the road to bar the way against the Prussian infantry. These were supported by two infantry brigades, while a third stood in the rear as a reserve. The Prussians were then in a dangerous position, for the road through the defile at Nachod behind them was choked with the carriages of the artillery, and only a few battalions and two squadrons had gained the open ground. General von Löwenfeld, who commanded the advanced guard, threw his infantry into a wood which was beside the road, where, protected by the trees to a certain extent from the shells of the Austrian guns, they maintained their position until their artillery had cleared the defile. At the same time the small body of Prussian cavalry who were with the infantry charged straight down the road against the centre of the line of the cuirassier regiments. The Austrians numbered eight times as many sabres as the Prussians, and their cavalry bore the highest reputation in Europe. All expected to see the Prussians hurled back, broken and destroyed, by their collision with the Austrian line, but the result was far different; the Prussian squadrons thundered down the road, and seemed merely by the speed at which they were galloping to cut clean through the centre of the line of cuirassiers. But though they were thus far successful in their first onslaught, they were quickly assailed in flank and rear by overwhelming numbers, and with difficulty escaped being cut to pieces. Many, however, managed to shake themselves free from the *mêlée*, and, galloping back, rallied under the protection of the fire of their infantry in the wood. The Austrians pressed forward, forcing their foes to retire; and it seemed that the mouth of the defile would be lost, for the Austrian infantry were quickly coming up, and were preparing to attack the wood held by the Prussians. Thus upon Löwenfeld's battalions depended not only the safe passage of the fifth corps through the defile, but also the preservation of the whole of the artillery, for so crowded with carriages was the road that, had the Austrians pressed on, every gun and waggon must have fallen into their hands. But the Prussian infantry proved worthy of the trust placed in them, and nothing availed to dislodge them from the trees, though the shells went whistling in quick succession through the trunks, and the splinters carried away the branches above the heads of the soldiers, and tore up the turf beneath their feet.

The Crown Prince was in Nachod when the firing commenced; he pushed his way with difficulty through the crowded defile, and came to his advanced guard in order to show himself to his soldiers in their time of trial. Behind him followed as quickly as possible the battalions of the main body of the corps, and the guns of the artillery were also pushed forward; but the road was long and crowded, and both regiments and guns made their way with difficulty. In the meantime the Austrians pressed hard upon the little band in the wood, and seemed as though they would pass it by, and close the defile with their columns. But before they could do so the battalions of the main body gained the end of the defile, and the Prussian guns began to come quickly forward; for waggons and all encumbrances had been pushed off the road into the ditches, to facilitate the free passage of the troops going into action. The newly-arrived troops reinforced those in the wood, and the artillery replied to the Austrian batteries; yet at noon the battle was still stationary, the Prussians not having advanced their position since the beginning of the fight, and the Austrian cavalry standing prepared to charge the Prussian infantry if it attempted to move forward on the open ground. The Crown Prince knew that on breaking that cavalry line depended the passage of the fifth corps into Bohemia, and he sent against it the eighth Prussian regiment of dragoons, and the first regiment of Uhlans. It was an exciting moment. The Prussians, nerved by the importance of the issue of their charge, and with the eyes of their infantry upon them, sprang forward readily. The Austrian horsemen, proud of their high renown, and eager to wipe out the memory of the former skirmish, also bounded forward as soon as they saw the Prussians approaching. The two lines met about half way, for one moment formed a tangled struggling crowd, and then the Prussian Uhlans, with their lance points low and heads bent down, were seen pursuing. The most famous cavalry in Europe had been overthrown.

Before and during this charge, both divisions of the fifth Prussian corps had cleared the defile; and scarcely had the effect of the cavalry charge been seen when General Steinmetz, who commanded, determined to assume the offensive. The Prussian infantry and artillery dashed forward after their cavalry. Some of the battalions, turning aside, marched against the village of Wisokow, already in flames from a Prussian shell, with their bayonets at the charge. Among the burning houses the Austrians waited for them; a sharp struggle ensued, but the village was carried, and the Austrians driven out.

In the meantime, the Austrian heavy horsemen had rallied, and again returned to the charge. This time they advanced with skill as well as courage, and bore down upon the flanks of the Uhlans; but their approach was seen, and before they had reached the Prussian line it had quickly changed its front, and met the advancing squadrons face to face. Again the Austrians recoiled, but now without a chance of rallying; they were broken and scattered, and the Uhlans, spreading out in pursuit, went dashing in small knots over the plain after them, and captured two guns from their horse artillery. This cavalry charge decided the fortune of the day, and the Austrians retired, pressed by the Prussian infantry. General Steinmetz, who commanded the fifth corps, which was here engaged, led forward all his troops, having only three battalions of the royal regiment in reserve; and pushed the enemy back. But the most of his men, after a long march and severe action, being too much fatigued to pursue, were halted, and the cavalry, with one or two battalions, alone followed up the pursuit, from which they brought back two thousand prisoners and three guns, besides the two taken by the Uhlans. The Crown Prince thanked General Steinmetz on the field in the name of the king for the victory, and well did the general and his troops merit the compliment, for all the first part of the action was fought with twenty-two battalions against twenty-nine, and with an inferior force of cavalry and artillery.

This victory cost the Prussians a loss of 900 men killed and wounded; among the latter were the two generals, Von Ollech and Von Wuuck. The fifth corps, notwithstanding its march on the 27th over fifteen miles through a narrow defile, and an engagement that lasted eight hours, was still so strong and so confident that General Steinmetz resolved to resume the attack without loss of time.

General Ramming, who had deservedly the reputation of being one of the most able and talented generals of the imperial army, after Having engaged the Prussians at Nachod with his whole force, retreated to Skalitz on the evening of the 27th. On arriving at that place he sent a despatch to the head-quarters of the army, in which he requested that the eighth Austrian corps, which was posted at Josephstadt, might be allowed to assist him with two brigades. Benedek thereupon ordered the eighth corps to advance to Skalitz, and be prepared to engage in the first line, while that of General Ramming should form its reserve. One brigade of the Prussian sixth corps, which was to follow the fifth corps through the defile of Nachod, had reached Nachod on the evening of the 27th, and was ready to advance with General Steinmetz. At the same time the Austrian General Ramming, who had been reinforced by the eighth corps, also advanced from Skalitz in order to drive the Prussians back into the defile of Nachod. Hence arose the action of Skalitz.

The Austrians were soon forced to quit the offensive, and energetically to assume the defensive in front of Skalitz, on the road and railway, which are flanked on the north and south by two woods. The country was entirely unfavourable for the action of cavalry. Either side brought up as much force as possible. The battle swayed hither and thither, but ultimately the superior strength and armament of the Prussian soldier told against his weaker antagonist.

On the north of the railway the thirty-seventh and fifty-eighth Prussian regiments, and the twelfth brigade advanced; while on the south the king's own regiment, though exposed to a terrible fire of artillery, gained the wood on the south of the town, and there succeeded in sustaining the assaults of far superior numbers, until the forty-sixth and fifty-second regiments could come up to its aid, and join in an attack on Skalitz.

The Austrian position was forced, and the Archduke Leopold compelled to fall back to a strong position behind the Aupa, where he intended to hold his ground, supported by his numerous artillery. The position was, however, carried by the Prussians, after hard fighting, and by it they gained the command of the defile of the Aupa. General Steinmetz, by this victory, captured four thousand prisoners, eight guns, and several stands of colours. In the meantime the first Prussian corps had reached Trautenau, and found the Austrian tenth corps posted immediately to the south of the town. They attacked them at once, but were driven back, and not only failed to recover their ground, but were obliged to retire in the night to Liebau. The guards on this day had advanced without opposition to Eypel and Kostelitz. They had offered to come to the assistance of the first corps; but, as the day was then favourable to the Prussians, their offer had been declined. The guards, however, hearing of the check which the first corps had received, advanced at three o'clock in the morning of the 28th to their assistance. They took the Austrians in flank and rear, surprised them, and drove them over the Elbe at Neuschloss, with immense loss. The fifth corps again advanced, and finding the sixth and eighth corps of the enemy drawn up at Skalitz to oppose their progress, they attacked and defeated them. On the actions of the 27th and 28th depended the success of the army of Silesia in effecting its passage over the mountains of Bohemia. The corps of the guards was engaged at Trautenau, the fifth corps at Nachod and Skalitz. The Crown Prince, in person, could not be present at either action. He was obliged to choose a position between the two, whence he could proceed to any point where his presence might be necessary. He accordingly posted himself on a hill near Kosteletz, where the heavy cavalry of the guards took up its position on coming through the hills, and where it was joined at a later period of the day by the reserve artillery of the guards. The time passed heavily on that hill of Kosteletz. The thunder of cannon rose ever louder from Skalitz on the south, and from the direction of Trautenau on the north. With anxious ears the commander-in-chief and his staff listened to the progress of the cannonade, and with eager eyes scanned the positions of the eddying clouds of white smoke which rose from the engaged artillery. It was the instruction of the Crown Prince, if an unfavourable report of the progress of the action on either side was brought to him, to repair to that point, and in person to encourage his pressed troops. But every orderly officer, every aide-decamp, brought the intelligence that the battles in both places were going well for the Prussians.

At last, between three and four o'clock, the commander-in-chief received the positive report from General Steinmetz, that he had stormed Skalitz, and driven back two of the enemy's corps. No longer had the Crown Prince to give a thought to this side. He immediately started for Eypel, in order to be present at the action in which the guards were engaged. At this place the news reached him that the guard had also victoriously achieved its task, and not only had forced the defile from Eypel, but had also opened the pass from Trautenau. Here, then, were the three issues from the mountains, the defiles of Trautenau, Eypel, and Nachod, popularly called the gates of Bohemia, in the secure possession of the second Prussian army, and the junction of the hitherto separated corps almost certain to be effected on the following day. To accomplish the junction of his united army with that of Prince Frederick Charles, the Crown Prince ordered the advance the next morning to be made as far as the Elbe. The Crown Prince had thus successfully brought his whole army across the mountains, and had secured as trophies 9000 prisoners and twenty-four guns.

The Austrians and Saxons, on retreating from Münchengrätz, had taken up an extended position to the north-west of Jicin, between Lochow on the Münchengrätz road, and Diletz on the Turnau road. The crown prince of Saxony is said to have received from Benedek at noon on this day, the 29th, a despatch written on the previous day, to the effect that "the third corps would arrive at Jicin on the 29th, and that four corps of the main army would advance on the 30th against Turnau and Lomnitz." The Crown Prince and Clam Gallas, therefore, prepared to maintain their positions in front of the Jicin. They were attacked in force by the Prussians at about three o'clock. At seven o'clock in the evening a second message was received from Benedek, "to avoid engaging with a superior force, and to effect a junction with the main army, by Höritz and Miletin, and that the four army corps had in the meantime received other instructions." The allied force was, however, already engaged with superior numbers, and only succeeded in effecting a retreat in great disorder, and with the loss of 5000 men, of whom 2000 were prisoners. The Prussians entered Jicin about midnight. On the same day the army of the Elbe made a forward movement towards Jung Bunzlaw, and the advanced guard of the first division of guards drove the Austrians on this day out of Koniginhof, near which place the corps of guards encamped. The first corps advanced to Pilnikau, the fifth corps towards Gradlitz, defeating three brigades of the fourth Austrian corps at Schweinschädel, and forcing them to retreat to Jeromir. On the 30th the first Prussian army was concentrated round Jicin, where it opened communication with the second army, which was between Arnau and Gradlitz, the headquarters of the Crown Prince being at Prausnitz, the sixth corps having already joined the second army from Nachod.

Benedek had taken up his position along the railroad fronting the Elbe, between Koniginhof and Josephstadt; but the capture of Jicin having exposed his left flank, he quitted his position on the morning of the 1st July, and prepared to take up a new one behind the Bistritz.

The strategical operation of concentrating their armies on the other side of the frontier, may now be said to have been successfully accomplished by the Prussians; for although the junction was only actually effected on the field of Königgrätz, yet they were now sufficiently near to afford each other mutual support in case of attack. Before entering upon the description of the battle fought on that field, it will be well to review the operations on both sides which led to it.

The operation which the Prussians undertook was, as before stated, a dangerous one. They entered the mountains at points sixty or seventy miles apart, separated by lofty mountain ranges, and allowing of no lateral communication, and they had to concentrate their armies on some point in the plain which was held by the Austrians.

The control of the operations is generally attributed to General von Moltke. At Berlin the telegraph wires flashed to him from day to day the positions of the armies, and he was able to regulate their movements so that they should advance by proportionate steps. Had one of the armies met with so serious a check as to have compelled it to retreat, he would probably have prevented the others from being compromised by too forward an advance; and the danger of any serious disaster was much diminished by this use of the telegraphic wires. To adopt a homely proverb, he would not let the hand be stretched out farther than the arm could bring it back. But the most important questions in considering the danger and merit of the movements are, how far was the Austrian general prepared to meet them, and what knowledge had the Prussian generals of their enemy's positions? It has been shown that the best situation for the Austrian general would be to have the enemy advancing on him at unequal distances, to keep the one farthest off in check, and to throw himself on the other and crush it before it could receive assistance; and an additional element of success would be, that he should be able to advance on the army nearest him without throwing open his communications to the other.

On July 1 the Crown Prince issued a general order from Prausnitz, in which the brief events of this famous campaign are heralded forth, but without arrogance or vain boasting. "But a few days," he said, "have elapsed since our entering Bohemia, and already brilliant victories have been won, giving us command over the Elbe, and enabling us to effect a junction with the first army. With this our primary task is fulfilled. The brave fifth corps d'armée, under the command of its heroic leader, with distinguished gallantry, on three successive days defeated three different corps of the enemy. The guards gave battle twice, each time discomfiting the enemy with signal triumph. The first corps d'armée, under the most trying circumstances, displayed extraordinary hardihood. Five colours, two standards, twenty guns, and 8000 prisoners, have been captured by us, added to which are many thousand dead and wounded, proving the total loss of the foe to be greater than can now be calculated. We, too, regret the loss of many a brave comrade, removed by death or wounds from our ranks. The consciousness of dying for king and country, and as victors, will have given them comfort in death, and will tend to alleviate the anguish of the sufferers. I pray God to grant future victories to our arms. I thank the generals and officers, as well as soldiers, of the second army, for their gallantry in battle and their steadiness in overcoming the most adverse circumstances, and I am proud to lead such troops."

As before observed, Benedek had taken up his position, on July 1, fronting the Elbe, between Koniginhof and Josephstadt; but Count Clam Gallas having attacked the Prussians contrary to orders, was driven out of his position, pursued by the victorious Prussians through the town of Gitschin, and followed the next day by their cavalry to the river Bistritz. The consequence was that General Benedek's left flank at Dubenec was exposed, and he was compelled to order his army to retire in the direction of Königgrätz. In the words of "a special correspondent," Benedek, who had taken up a strong position, with his centre near Dubenec, his left towards Miletin, and his right covered by the river and by Josephstadt, found himself in the twinkling of an eye placed in a position of the greatest danger; his left was "in the air." The Prussians were not only on his left, but in his rear; and at the same time another great army was marching to effect its junction with them in a direction where he was altogether exposed. He instantly wheeled back his left and centre, and then retiring his right, took up a line at Königgrätz at right angles to the line he had occupied to the west of Josephstadt.

Fully aware of the dangers to which his new position exposed him, Benedek seems to have questioned the *morale* of his troops; for prior to the impending battle he sent a telegram to the emperor at Vienna, bearing the foreboding words, "Sire, you must make peace."

The arrival of the king of Prussia, on the 2nd July, at Gitschin, had a twofold effect, inspiriting his already elated troops, who, flushed with conquest, were prepared to triumph over all impediments. It also had a salutary influence over the tributary states through which his legions had marched. The authorities of Gitschin drew up a petition and laid it before him, when his Majesty thus addressed them:—"I carry on no war against your nation, but only against the armies opposed to me. If, however, the inhabitants will commit acts of hostility against my troops without any cause, I shall be forced to make reprisals. My troops are not savage hordes, and require simply the supplies necessary for subsistence. It must be your care to give them no cause for just complaint. Tell the inhabitants that I have not come to make war upon peaceable citizens, but to defend the honour of Prussia against insult."

On July 2 the disposition of the combined armies of Prussia was as follows:—The first army, commanded by Prince Frederick Charles, formed the centre; the Elbe army, commanded by General Herwarth, the right; and the second army, commanded by the Crown Prince, the left wing. The seventh division marched in front of the first army, through Göritz, Czerkwitz, and Sadowa, to effect a junction with the Crown Prince's right wing. The eighth division marched upon Milowitz, its destination being Königgrätz. The second army was to base its operations upon Donalitz, south of Sadowa. The third army corps formed the centre reserve force. The Elbe army advanced from Smidar towards Nechanitz. The Crown Prince's army was directed from Königinhof, in a direct line, upon Königgrätz.

The Austrian army was extended on a range of small hills between Smiritz and Nechanitz, and ranged over an extent of about nine miles; the position of the centre was on a hill, on which is situate the village of Klum, which formed the key of the manoeuvres; the site was, moreover, distinguished by a group of trees.

The scene of the memorable battle fought here has been well described by one who had the advantage of being an eye-witness of the conflict with the army of Austria, and who obtained a complete prospect of the scene from the top of a tower in the stronghold of Königgrätz.

Lying nearly north of Königgrätz, says this writer, is Josephstadt; but there was nothing going on in that direction at eight o'clock. From the neighbourhood of Josephstadt a continuous line of low undulating hills, with plateau-like tops, or of rolling fields, extends from the right till it slopes away on the left into the meadows watered by the Elbe. Beyond this line, again, and running nearly parallel with the first, about half way where it recedes towards the west and north, is a similar ridge, appearing to be of greater elevation. Further back is still the picturesque broken country, formed by the projecting spurs and lower ranges of the Riesengebirge. This must be taken as a general description of the appearance of the landscape from the spot where I stood. There are many cross valleys permeating both ridges towards the Elbe, and on both there are hills or hillocks, some almost like tumuli, on which villages and their little churches nestle in the woods. In the valley between the first and second ridge runs the Bistritz rivulet, on which Sadowa and Nechanitz are situated. It is traversed nearly at right angles by the main road from Jicin to Königgrätz. In the valley between the first ridge and the rolling ground which lies towards the Elbe runs a road from Smiritz, or Smiric, to Königgrätz, coming out on the Jicin road; and more to the west is another road, branching from the Jicin road, and running by Nechanitz to the main road between Prague and Königgrätz. There are numerous other small roads, connecting the nests of villages which are to be seen in all directions. Immediately below the city of Königgrätz the land is level and marshy; but towards Smiritz, which is nearly halfway to Josephstadt, there is a projecting spur approaching the river, which is one outshoot of the first line of hills, and thence in front of us from left to right a gradual elevation from the river takes place, in a series of irregular terraces. On the top of this first ridge there is the village named Smiritz. This is near the right of the scene of the battle. Then the ridge runs southwestward (to the left) without any more remarkable object on the sky-line than a very large tree, which stands quite alone. There are several villages on the inner side of the slope between Königgrätz and the river. From the big tree the line continues to the left hand till about the centre, where its undulating contour is broken by a wooded knoll or hill, rising rather steeply, on which is placed the church and village of Klum, or Chlum, embowered in thick trees and gardens. Thence to the left the line of the ridges is depressed and carried towards the village of Nechanitz, and gets lost in broken hills, among which are, or rather were, villages unknown to our geographers; now heaps of cinders and ashes, surrounded by dead and dying, for these were the very centres of the tremendous battle. The army with which General Benedek had to defend his position consisted of at least 225,000 men; but a large deduction must be made for the baggage guards, the various escorts, the garrisons of Josephstadt and Königgrätz, the sick and those tired by marching, and the killed, wounded, and prisoners in recent actions; so that probably he had not more than 190,000, or 195,000, actually in hand. The ground he had to cover from right to left was about nine miles in length. On his extreme left in his first line, near the rear of Nechanitz and towards the Prague road, he put the Saxons; the tenth army corps, under Fieldmarshal Lieutenant Gablenz; the third corps d'armée, under Field-marshal Lieutenant Count Thun; the fourth army corps, under Field-marshal Lieutenant Count Festetics (who was wounded early in the day); and the second army corps, under Fieldmarshal Lieutenant Archduke Ernest—were placed from left to right on the slope on the second range or ridge. His second line and his reserves consisted of the eighth corps d'armée, under Fieldmarshal Lieutenant the Archduke Leopold; the first army corps was under Cavalry-general Count Clam Gallas, and the sixth army corps under Field-marshal Lieutenant Ramming. He had at his disposal a grand army of cavalry, composed of the first light cavalry division, under General-major Edelsheim; the second light cavalry division, under Count Taxis; the first heavy cavalry division, under the prince of Holstein; the second heavy cavalry division, under General major Faitseck; and the third heavy cavalry division, under General-major Count Coudenhove. His artillery consisted of about 540 guns.

The Prussian cavalry and horse-artillery were preparing early in the morning of the 3rd of July to commence the attack, and by seven o'clock they commenced their advance down the declivity towards the Bistritz. Here the guns of the Austrians commenced playing upon them, from a battery near the village of Sadowa, at a point where the main road crosses the little river. The seventh division of Prussian artillery bombarded the Austrian right, directing their fire to the village of Benatek, and from the centre of both lines a fearful cannonade was commenced, and equally sustained; neither side appearing to give way. A writer who witnessed the battle from the Prussian side, says:—

While the cannonade had been going on, some of the infantry had been moved down towards the river, where they took shelter from the fire under a convenient undulation of ground. The eighth division came down on the left-hand side of the causeway, and under the cover of the rising ground formed its columns for an attack on the village of Sadowa; while the third and fourth division, on the right-hand side of the road, prepared to storm Dohilnitz and Mokrowens. A short time before their preparations were complete, the village of Benatek, on the Austrian right, caught fire, and the seventh Prussian division made a dash to secure it. The Austrians, however, were not driven out by the flames, and here for the first time in the battle was there hand-to-hand fighting. The twenty-seventh regiment led the attack, and rushed into the orchards of the village, where the burning houses having separated the combatants, they poured volley after volley at each other through the flames, until the Prussians found means to get round the burning houses, and taking the defenders in the reverse, forced them to retire with the loss of many prisoners.

It was ten o'clock when Prince Frederick Charles sent General Stuhnapl to order the attack on Sadowa, Dohilnitz, and Mokrowens. The columns advanced covered by skirmishers, and reached the river bank without much loss; but from thence they had to fight every inch of their way. The Austrian infantry held the bridges and villages in force, and fired fast upon their enemies as they approached. The Prussians could advance but slowly along the narrow ways and against the defences of the houses; and the volleys sweeping through their ranks seemed to mow the soldiers down. The Prussians fired much more quickly than their opponents, but they could not see to take their aim; the houses, trees, and smoke from the Austrian discharges shrouding the villages in obscurity. Sheltered by this, the Austrian jägers fired blindly at the places where they could tell by hearing that the attacking columns were, and the shots told tremendously on the Prussians in their close formation. The latter, however, unproved their positions, although slowly, and by dint of sheer courage and perseverance; for they lost men at every yard of their advance, and in some places almost paved the way with wounded. To help their infantry, the Prussian artillery turned its fire, regardless of the enemy's batteries, on the villages, and made tremendous havoc among the houses. Mokrowens and Dohilnitz both caught fire, and the shells fell quickly and with fearful effect among the defenders of the flaming hamlets. The Austrian guns on their side also played upon the attacking infantry, but at this time these were sheltered from the fire by the intervening houses and trees.

In and around the villages the fighting continued for nearly an hour, until the Austrian infantry, driven out by a rush of the Prussians, retired, but only a short way up the slope into a line with their batteries. One wood above Sadowa was strongly held, and another stood between Sadowa and Benatek, teeming with riflemen, to bar the way of the seventh division. But General Fransky, who commanded this division, was not to be easily stopped. He sent his infantry at the wood, and turned his artillery on the Austrian batteries. The assailants, firing into the trees, found they could not make any impression, for the defenders were concealed, and musketry fire was useless against them. Then Fransky letting them go, they dashed in with the bayonet. The Austrians waited for the onslaught, and in the wood above Benatek was fought out one of the fiercest combats known in that war. The twenty-seventh Prussian regiment went in nearly 3000 strong, with 90 officers, and came out on the further side with only 2 officers and between 300 and 400 men standing; all the rest were killed or wounded. The other regiments of the division also suffered much, though not in the same proportion; but the wood was carried. The Austrian line being now driven in on both flanks, its commander formed a new line of battle a little higher up the hill, round Lipa, still holding the wood which lies above Sadowa.

General Herwarth, the commander of the Prussian army of the Elbe, on the left of the Austrians, was also engaged in an attack on the Saxon troops at the village of Nechanitz, situate on the Bistritz, seven miles from Sadowa. The Saxons fought bravely, but were at length driven back slowly and with great difficulty towards Lipa, contesting every inch of the ground with great tenacity. The Austrians had placed artillery in a wood above the villages of Sadowa and Dohilnitz, which being fired through the trees occasioned considerable losses in the ranks of the Prussian infantry, now making a rapid advance to carry the wood. After a vigorous attack the Austrians were driven back; but at once forming their batteries beyond the trees, their fire told terribly on the Prussians, who were advancing in the wood.

The whole battle line of the Prussians was unable to gain more ground, being obliged to fight hard to retain the position it had won. At one time it seemed as if they would lose that. Some of their guns had been dismounted by the Austrian fire; in the wooded ground the needle gun had not a good field for the display of its superiority, and the infantry fighting was very equal.

Herwarth, too, seemed checked upon the right; the smoke of his musketry and artillery, which had hitherto been pushing forward steadily, stood still for a time. Fransky's men, cut to pieces, could not be sent forward to attack the Sadowa wood, for they would have exposed themselves to be attacked in the rear by the artillery on the right of the Austrian line formed in front of Lipa. All the artillery was engaged except eight batteries, and these had to be retained in case of a reverse; for at one time the firing in the Sadowa wood, and of the Prussian artillery on the slope, seemed almost as if drawing back towards Bistritz. The first army was certainly checked in its advance, if not actually being pushed back.

It was an eminently critical moment, and the Prussian generals were waiting in trepidation for tidings of the Crown Prince, who was to attack the Austrians on the right. This incident recalls that of Napoleon on the field of Waterloo, anxiously awaiting the approach of Grouchy, but with better results for the Prussians than for the French. The Austrian centre was retained by the third and fourth corps in front of Klum and Lipa, constrained to make a backward movement with the first corps in reserve, as was also the sixth corps, on the right facing Smiralitz. The army of the Crown Prince came up at about half past one o'clock in the afternoon, and attacked the right flank of the Austrians. The village of Klum had caught fire, and the troops of the Prussian centre were making desperate efforts to drive the Austrians out of it, when the latter suddenly found their right exposed to a withering cross fire from the advancing army of the Crown Prince. The Austrian army was now in a critical position. The observer who was watching the action from the top of the tower in Königgrätz says, "Suddenly a sputtering of musketry breaks out of the trees and houses of Klum right down on the Austrian gunners, and on the columns of infantry drawn up on the slopes below. The gunners fall on all sides, their horses are disabled, the firing increases in intensity, the Prussians press on over the plateau. This is an awful catastrophe; two columns of Austrians are led against the village, but they cannot stand the fire, and after three attempts to carry it, retreat, leaving the hillside covered with the fallen. It is a terrible moment. The Prussians see their advantage, and enter at once into the very centre of the position. In vain the Austrian staff officers fly to the reserves, and hasten to call back some of the artillery from the front. The dark blue regiments multiply on all sides, and from their edges roll perpetually sparkling musketry. Their guns hurry up, and from the slope take both the Austrian main body on the extreme right, and the reserves in flank. They spread away to the woods near the Prague road, and fire into the rear of the Austrian gunners. The lines of dark blue which came in sight from the right teemed from the vales below, as if the earth yielded them. They filled the whole background of the awful picture, of which Klum was the centre. They pressed down on the left of the Prague road. In square, in column, deployed, or wheeling hither and thither, everywhere pouring in showers of deadly precision, penetrating the whole line of the Austrians, still they could not force their stubborn enemy to fly. On all sides they met brave but unfortunate men, ready to die if they could do no more. At the side of the Prague road the fight went on with incredible vehemence. The Austrians had still an immense force of artillery, and although its concentrated fire swept the ground before it, its effect was lost in some degree by reason of the rising ground above, and at last by its divergence to so many points, to answer the enemy's cannon. . . Cheste and Visa were now burning, so that from right to left the flames of ten villages and the flashes of guns and musketry contended with the sun that pierced the clouds, for the honour of illuminating the seas of steel, and the fields of carnage. It was three o'clock. The efforts of the Austrians to occupy Klum, and free their centre had failed; their right was driven down in a helpless mass towards Königgrätz, quivering and palpitating, as shot and shell tore through it. *Alles ist verloren!* "All is lost!" Artillery still thundered with a force and violence which might have led a stranger to such scenes to think no enemy could withstand it. The Austrian cavalry, however, hung like white thunder clouds on the flanks, and threatened the front of the Prussians, keeping them in square and solid columns. But already the trains were streaming away from Königgrätz, placing the Elbe and Adler between them and the enemy.

General von Gablenz, a brief while after this terrible defeat, was despatched from the Austrian centre to the Prussian head-quarters, to solicit an armistice; but his proposal was at once rejected, as the entire ranks of Prussia were preparing to advance. Prince Frederick Charles directed his army for the road leading to Brünn, the capital of Moravia, the army of the Crown Prince took the course to Olmütz, and the army of the Elbe, under General Herwarth, proceeded to advance westward toward Iglau.

The extreme importance of this battle, whether viewed in a political or military light, will be more strikingly apparent as time goes on. Variously named Königgrätz and Sadowa, the conflict has been the theme of much military criticism. One anonymous writer says, "The Austrians should have been victors here, if positions could win a battle, for better positions they could hardly have had. Their line extended over nine miles, and was throughout one stretch of high ground; while the Prussians advanced through a country rather unfavourable—through woods and villages that afforded cover here and there. Benedek had offered battle at Debenec, but the Prussians having the option in their hands, declined the conflict. This new position left them no choice, and they boldly accepted the gage, though defeat would have been annihilation. They had taken the measure of the Austrian commander; they knew their own strength, and they made their dispositions with a view to victory, not to provide for a retreat. Their line extended from Jicin to Skalitz, but it was of such length that the two divisions wore practically distinct armies, and for some hours were without communication. The centre of the Austrian line was Klum, the headquarters were at Königgrätz, a city at the junction of the Elbe and Adler, strongly fortified, and surrounded by well-filled moats, while a certain area round was inundated by the river. The Austrian line covered the railway station; and while its left was guarded by the fortress of Josephstadt, Königgrätz protected the right. Their force was about 200,000, and that of the Prussians 260,000, a numerical superiority greatly enhanced by the Prussian arm, the needle gun. The battle commenced about eight in the morning; the Austrians having the advantage till about two o'clock, when a fatal oversight gave the victory to the Prussians. The whole line was engaged by ten o'clock, though the division of the Crown Prince had not come up, as it was to approach the field by a detour, so as to fall on the Austrian line at Lipa. The Prussians attacked with superior numbers, yet the Austrians faced the needle-gun without availing themselves of the cover afforded by their position, and again and again drove the enemy back. In like manner the Austrian artillery did yeoman's service in these onslaughts; but from being too closely packed the eight-pounder field-pieces, which are very effective and very well served, did not produce the impression which they are capable of making. On the other hand, the Prussian needle-gun was very efficient, killing at close quarters, and disabling where it did not kill, though owing to the smallness of the ball the wounds were of a character easily cured. The Austrian column bore steadily down through volleys of shot, and through flaming villages, and everywhere beat back the advancing Prussians, who at eleven o'clock were flung panting on the slopes of the opposite hills.

"The Prussians then called in their reserves, and, urged on by their officers, made a furious rush on the Austrian left and centre, at the same time dashing round the Prague road, with the intention of turning the left. They were met with equal ardour, and a desperate conflict ensued, when the Prussians gave way, and were driven further back than before. There was a momentary pause in the struggle. The smoke gathered thick, and hid the armies from each other; then cleared to show the Prussians again reinforced, and once more in battle array. The next assault shook the wearied Austrians; but they yielded no ground, and after a murderous conflict the Prussians recoiled. Here both sides brought up their artillery, and the smoke again favoured the Prussians, who bore down on the Austrian right with irresistible force. The Austrians, victorious on the left and centre, were pushing their advantage, when the success of the Prussians on their right threatened to sever them from Königgrätz. At this juncture the Prussians were joined by their second army, under the Crown Prince, who advanced on the very point the Austrians had left open. The gap seems to have reminded the Prussian commander of Key's project at Waterloo, where the French general, deluded by the ground, thought the English centre unguarded, and rushed to destruction. Nor was the centre at Sadowa really unwatched. The Austrian commander could have confronted the Prussian battalions with 20,000 of the finest cavalry in Europe, cavalry which had already saved his army, and might now have given it the victory. But this supreme moment found the general at the end of his resources, hesitating and bewildered. With the battle won on the left, and in his own hands on the right, he allowed the enemy to reach his centre—to pierce the heart of his army, and thus lost the day. The Austrians retreated hurriedly, but not in disorder, and the cavalry, which might have secured the victory, kept the victors at a respectful distance. Benedek was still at the head of an army, though he left a third of it on the field, or in the hands of the enemy, and his abandoned guns were enough to equip another army for a campaign."

Captain Webber, R.E., who visited the scene of carnage, says:—"On the tenure of the woods and villages depended the success of the Austrians in the battle on the west front. The former appears to have been retained long after the latter had been evacuated. The villages were not placed in a proper state of defence, the entrances not having been even closed. Abattis were insufficiently used, and the strong stone buildings, which were quite capable of resisting field artillery, not loopholed. As some portion of the Austrian army was at Sadowa two days before the battle this would have been practicable. The defences of Chlum were incomplete, the north and north-west only being touched. The Crown Prince attacked it on the north-east side. Breastworks without abattis may be useful to cover a handful of determined men, but advancing troops will run over them. If possible, the one kind of defence should never be used without the other."

The battle, indeed, was a great victory for the Prussians, though its full advantages were not known by them until the following day. One hundred and seventy-four guns, twenty thousand prisoners, and eleven standards, fell into the hands of the conquerors. The total loss of the Austrian army was nearly 40,000 men, while that of the Prussians was not 10,000. The morale of the Austrian army was destroyed, and their infantry found that in open column they could not stand against the better-armed Prussians. The Austrians had hoped to be able to close with the bayonet, and so neutralize the effects of the needle-gun; but the idea of superiority in the use of the bayonet, in which the Austrian army prided itself, is one of those vanities which are common to every nation; and this was proved, that at close quarters the stronger men of Prussia invariably overcame the lighter and smaller Austrians. The number of cartridges fired by the Prussian army in the battle barely exceeded one per man on the ground. Hardly any soldier fired so many as ninety, and few more than sixty. The average number of rounds fired by the artillery of Prince Frederick Charles' army was forty-two per gun, and no gun of that army fired more than eighty rounds. Excellent as was the Prussian artillery it would not have won the battle without brave men to guide and follow it. The quality of the Prussian troops may be illustrated by one anecdote. On the evening of the battle an officer of the Ziethen hussars, who were forward in the pursuit, rode alone as far as the gates of Königgrätz, and finding there was no sentry outside, rode in. The guard, immediately on seeing him in his Prussian uniform, turned out and seized him, when, with admirable presence of mind, he declared he had come to demand the capitulation of the fortress. He was conducted to the commandant, and made the same demand to him, adding that the town would be bombarded if not surrendered within an hour; the commandant, unconscious that he was not dealing with a legitimate messenger, courteously refused to capitulate; but the hussar was conducted out of the town, passed through the guard at the entrance, and got off safely to his troop. The vigilance of the Austrians was often at fault. From the high bank above Königinhof, a staff-officer, lying hidden in the fir-wood, could almost with the naked eye have counted every Prussian gun, every Prussian soldier that the Crown Prince moved towards Miletin. Yet the arrival of the second Prussian army on the scene of action seems to have been a complete surprise. The eyes of the Austrian army failed on more than one occasion during the campaign. The inferiority of their patrol system to that of the Prussians seems to have been due to the want of military education among the officers to whom patrols were intrusted. In the Prussian army special officers of high intelligence were always chosen to reconnoitre—properly so, for the task is no easy one. An eye unskilled, or a mind untutored, can see little, when a tried observer detects important movements. The Prussian system never failed, never allowed a surprise. The Austrians were repeatedly surprised, and taken unprepared.

The telegram in which Benedek first announced to Vienna the loss of the battle, stated that some of the enemy's troops, under cover of the mist, established themselves on his flank, and so caused the defeat. How the Prussian guards were allowed to get into Chlum appears inexplicable. From the top of Chlum church tower the whole country can be clearly seen as far as the top of the high bank of the Elbe. A staff-officer posted there, even through the mist, which was not so heavy as is generally supposed, could have easily seen any movement of the troops as far as Choteborek. A person near Sadowa could see quite distinctly Herwarth's attack at Hradek, and, except during occasional squalls, there was no limit to the view over the surrounding country except where the configuration of the ground or the heavy smoke overcame the sight. The top of Chlum church spire generally stood out clear over the heavy curtain of hanging smoke which, above the heads of the combatants, fringed the side of the Lipa hill from Benatek to Nechanitz. So little apprehensive, however, was Benedek of an attack on his right, that he stationed no officer in the tower; and himself took up a position above Lipa, where any view towards the north was entirely shut out by the hill and houses of Chlum. No report appears to have reached him of the advance of the guards, yet they were engaged at Horenowes, and passed through Maslowed. From that village, without opposition, they marched along the rear of the Austrian line, apparently unobserved, until they flung themselves into Chlum and Rosberitz. It seems that the fourth corps, to whom the defence of the ground between Maslowed and Nedelitz was intrusted, seeing their comrades heavily engaged with Fran sky in the Maslowed wood, turned to their aid, and pressing forwards towards Benatek, quitted their proper ground. A short time afterwards the second Austrian corps was defeated by the Prussian eleventh division, and retreated towards the bridge at Lochenitz. The advance of the fourth corps, and the retreat of the second, left a clear gap in the Austrian line, through which the Prussian guards marched unmolested, and without a shot seized the key of the position. Once installed they could not be ejected, and the battle was practically lost to the Austrians. The Prussian pursuit was tardy, and not pushed, for the men were fatigued, night was coming on, and the Prussian cavalry of the first army had suffered severely. The Austrian cavalry was moving sullenly towards Pardubitz. The Elbe lay between the retreating Austrians and the victorious Prussians. The victory, although fortuitously decisive, was not improved to such advantage as it ought to have been.

Before proceeding to review the events which in the meantime, were taking place in the western theatre of war, it is requisite to cast a glance upon the operations of the two Prussian corps which had been left to guard the province of Silesia. On the concentration of the Austrian army in Bohemia, a corps of 6000 men, under General Trentinaglia, had been left at Cracow. Two Prussian independent corps had been stationed at Ratibor and Nicolai, to shield south-eastern Silesia against a probable attack from this corps. The former was commanded by General Knobelsdorf, and consisted of the sixty-second regiment of infantry, the second regiment of Uhlans, a few battalions of landwehr, and one battery. The latter, under General Count Stolberg, was formed of landwehr alone, and mustered six battalions, two regiments of cavalry, two companies of jägers, and one battery. The corps of Knobelsdorf was to defend the Moravian frontier, that of Stolberg the Galician; and both, in case of attack by overwhelming numbers, were to fall back under the protection of the fortress of Kosel. On the 21st June, Stolberg's corps obtained its first important although bloodless success. On that day it marched rapidly, many of the men being conveyed in waggons, to Pruchna, blew up the railway viaduct there, and so destroyed the communication between General Trentinaglia and the main Austrian army.

On the 24th and 26th June, as well as on the intermediate days, several parties of Austrians made demonstrations of crossing the frontier near Oswiecin, and large bodies of troops appeared to be in the act of concentration at that place. General Stolberg determined to assure himself of the actual strength of the enemy there, by a reconnaissance in force. To aid this, General Knobelsdorf sent a part of his troops to Myslowitz, to cover the rear of Stolberg's corps, while it marched on Oswiecin.

Stolberg, finding in the latter place a considerable force of the enemy, seized the buildings of the railway station, placed them hastily in a state of defence, and determined by a long halt here to force the Austrians to develop their full force. After he had achieved this object, he retired to his position near Nicolai. The detachment at Myslowitz had, at the same time, to sustain an action there, and fulfilled completely its purpose of holding the enemy back from Oswiecin.

On the 30th June, Stolberg's detachment was so weakened by the withdrawal of his landwehr battalions, which were called up in order to aid in the formation of a fourth battalion to every regiment, that it could no longer hold its own against the superior Austrian force near Myslowitz. It retired accordingly nearer to Ratibor in the direction of Plesz, and from this place undertook, in connection with General Knobelsdorf, expeditions into Moravia against Teschen, Biala, and Skotschau, annoying the Austrians considerably, and making the inhabitants of Moravia regard the war with aversion.

CAMPAIGN IN HANOVER.

We turn now to the operations in the western theatre of the German war. The Prussian troops which had invaded Hanover and Hesse-Cassel occupied on the 19th June the following positions:—The divisions of General Goeben and General Manteuffel were in the town of Hanover, and that of General Beyer in Cassel. Of the allies of Austria the Hanoverian army was at Gottingen, the Bavarian in the neighbourhood of Würzburg and Bamberg; the eighth federal corps in the vicinity of Frankfort. The latter consisted of the troops of Würtemburg, Baden, Hesse Darmstadt, Nassau, and Hesse-Cassel, to which was added an Austrian division. The soldiers of the (Hanoverian) reserve, and those who had been absent on furlough, nobly responded to the call of their king, and made their way through the country, which was in Prussian possession, and sometimes even through the lines of the enemy, to join the ranks at Gottingen. By their firm determination to reach their regiments, they afforded an earnest of the gallantry and courage which they afterwards displayed upon the field of battle. On the arrival of these men the army at Gottingen mustered about 20,000 combatants, with fifty guns.

Southern Germany expected great deeds of the Bavarian army. It might have thrown serious difficulties in the way of the Prussian successes, had not uncertainty and vacillation pervaded all its operations. Prince Charles of Bavaria, the commander-in-chief, under whose orders the eighth federal corps was also afterwards placed, seems to have conducted his campaign without a definite strategical object, and without energy in its prosecution. Against him, in command of the Prussian army of the Maine, was a general gifted with prudence and clear foresight, who pursued his aim with iron rigour. The Bavarian is a smart soldier in time of peace, and conducts himself well in battle; but he is too much dependent upon good diet, the want of which grievously maims his capacity for undergoing the fatigues of war. Nor do the ranks of Bavaria contain such intelligence as do those of Prussia; for men drawn for military service are allowed to provide substitutes, so that only the poorer and less educated classes of society furnish recruits for the army. The troops had no knowledge of the causes for which they were to shed their blood, and in this respect contrasted with the Prussian soldiery, which held that the honour, integrity, even the existence of their Fatherland, was in jeopardy. The reader will remember the anecdote current during the recent Rhine campaign, of the Bavarian soldier, who, addressing the Crown Prince of Prussia after a victory, exclaimed:—"Ah! your royal highness, if you had been our commander in the last war, we should have beaten those pestilent Prussians." The Federal troops did not fail in bravery; but no enthusiasm thrilled through their ranks. Individual bodies were doubtless animated by high courage, and in many cases displayed a heroic devotion to their leaders and their princes. But the mass did not work evenly; a want of harmony existed among its heterogeneous units, which, together with the clouded plans of the federal chiefs, facilitated the task of the Prussian general, Von Falckenstein. There was also dissension in the federal councils. Prince Alexander not only habitually disagreed with his superior, Prince Charles, but was often engaged in petty squabbles with the lieutenants who commanded the different contingents. All these things conduced to the catastrophe of the Hanoverian army, which marched from its capital almost totally unprepared to undertake a campaign. It stood in dire need of several days' rest to allow time for the formation of a transport train, as well as for the clothing and armament of the soldiers of reserve who had been recalled to the ranks, and also for the horsing of part of the artillery. It was forced on this account to halt until the 20th June at Göttingen, and the favourable moment for an unmolested march to unite with the troops of Bavaria was allowed to slip away. The Prussian staff took most prompt measures to cut off the Hanoverian retreat, and to occupy the principal points on their line of march with troops. The duke of Coburg had declared openly and decidedly on the side of Prussia, and his troops were in consequence at the service of the Prussian government. On the 20th June Colonel von Fabeck, the commandant of the Coburg contingent, received a telegraphic order from Berlin, to post himself with his two battalions at Eisenach, where it was expected the Hanoverians would first attempt to break through. Three battalions of landwehr, one squadron of landwehr cavalry, and a battery of four guns, were sent from the garrison to reinforce him. A battalion of the fourth regiment of the Prussian guard, which had reached Leipzig on the 19th, was also despatched to his aid, a detachment of which, on the 20th, rendered the railway tunnel near Eisenach impassable. By these movements the king of Hanover was compelled to give up the idea of uniting with the Bavarians, and instead of marching from Heiligenstadt by Eschewege and Fulda, he, on the 21st, ordered his whole army to move upon Gotha, and crossed the Prussian frontier with his troops. He took leave of his people in a proclamation, in which he mournfully expressed his hope soon to return victorious at the head of his army, to the land which he was then temporarily forced to quit.

The Hanoverian army reached Langensalza on the 24th of June. The force opposed to the Hanoverians consisted only of six weak battalions, two squadrons, and four guns. There can hardly be any question but that, if the king of Hanover had marched rapidly on Gotha that day, Colonel von Fabeck would have been quite unable to hold his position. But the Hanoverian leaders failed to take advantage of this last opportunity. The king rejected a proposal made by Colonel von Fabeck, that his army should capitulate; but he applied to the duke of Coburg, and asked him to act as a mediator with the Prussian government. An armistice was agreed upon, but upon some misunderstanding was quickly violated on the night of the 24th by the Hanoverians, who advanced to the Gotha and Eisenach Railway, and broke up the line near Frötestadt. General von Alvensleben then sent a proposal from Gotha to the king of Hanover, that he should capitulate. To this no answer was returned; but the king expressed a wish that General von Alvensleben should repair to his camp, in order to treat with him. His wish was complied with early on the 25th, when an extension of the armistice was agreed upon, and General von Alvensleben hurried back to Berlin for further instructions. It was not at this time the interest of the Prussians to push matters to extremities. The Hanoverians seem to have been ignorant of how small a body alone barred the way to Bavaria, and to have hoped that time might be afforded for aid to reach them. On the night of the 24th a messenger was sent to the Bavarian head-quarters to report the situation of the Hanoverian army, and to solicit speedy assistance. To this request Prince Charles only replied that an army of 19,000 men ought to be able to cut its way through. In consequence of this opinion only one Bavarian brigade of light cavalry was advanced on the 25th of June to Meiningen, in the valley of the Werra, while a few Bavarian detachments were pushed along the high road as far as Vacha. This procedure of Prince Charles of Bavaria was alone sufficient to condemn him as a general; he held his army inactive, when, by a bold advance, not only could he have insured the safety of the Hanoverians, but could in all probability have captured the whole of the enemy's troops at Gotha. Thus he would have saved 19,000 allies, have captured 6000 of his adversary's men, have turned the scale of war by 25,000 combatants, and have preserved to his own cause a skilled and highly-trained army, proud of its ancient military reputation, and only placed in this most precarious and unfortunate position by the faults of politicians.

On the 25th the Prussians were closing in upon the devoted Hanoverians: but telegraphic orders were forwarded from Berlin to all their commanders, not to engage in hostilities until ten o'clock on the morning of the 26th. Colonel von Döring was despatched to Langensalza by the Prussian government, with full powers to treat with the king of Hanover; he proposed an alliance with Prussia, on the basis of the recognition of the Prussian project for reform of the Germanic Confederation, and of the disbandment by Hanover of its army. To these terms King George would not agree; though deserted by his allies, to them he was still faithful, and still expected that the Bavarians must come to his aid.

By the morning of the 26th 42,000 Prussians were placed on the south, west, and north of this devoted army, within a day's march of its position, and all hopes of escape into Bavaria, or of aid from its southern allies, appeared to be vain. On the 26th the armistice expired at ten o'clock in the morning, but the Prussian commander-in-chief did not immediately commence hostilities. His dispositions were not yet perfected. The Hanoverian army drew more closely together, either with the object of accepting battle, or as some say, with the intention of moving by Tennstadt, and endeavouring to join the Bavarians by a circuitous route. In the evening the Hanoverians took up a position between the villages of Thämsbrück, Merxleben, and the town of Langensalza. None of these places were well suited for defence, and no artificial fortifications were thrown up on the southern side of the position, where General Flies lay. On the northern side a few insignificant earthworks and one battery were erected, to guard the rear and right flank of the army against the Prussian corps under General Manteuffel, which lay in the direction of Mühlhausen. The soldiers were weary with marching and privations, but eager to join battle with the Prussians, who of late years had spoken in a disparaging and patronizing tone of the Hanoverian army. The 27th of June had been appointed by royal command to be observed as a solemn day of fast and humiliation throughout Prussia, and the Hanoverian leaders appear to have imagined that on this account the Prussian generals would not attack. In this they were deceived, for before evening there had been fought the bloody battle of Langensalza.

The position occupied by the Hanoverian army on the morning of the 27th, lay along the sloping side of the line of hills which rises from the left bank of the river Unstrut. The right wing and centre rested on the villages of Thämsbrück and Merxleben, the left wing between the villages of Nägelstadt and Merxleben. The third brigade (Von Bülow) formed the right wing, the fourth brigade (Von Bothmer) the left, while in the centre was posted the first brigade (Von der Knesebeck), which at the beginning of the action was held in rear of the general line. The village of Merxleben, and the ground in front of it, was occupied by the second brigade (De Vaux), which had its outposts pushed as far as Henningsleben, along the road to Warza. The artillery and cavalry of the reserve were posted behind Merxleben, near the road to Lundhausen, where the scanty depôts of ammunition and stores were established. The front of the position was covered by the river, which with its steep banks impeded at first the Prussian attack, but afterwards was an obstacle to the offensive advance and counterattack of the Hanoverians.

At about one o'clock on the morning of the 27th, the two Coburg battalions, which formed the advanced guard of General Flies' column, reached Henningsleben, and attacked the Hanoverian outposts there. These withdrew to Langensalza, occasionally checking their pursuers by the fire of their skirmishers. One Hanoverian battalion remained for a short time in Langensalza; but then the whole Hanoverian troops, which had been pushed along the Gotha road, withdrew across the Unstrut to Merxleben, and the Prussians occupied Langensalza before ten o'clock. General Flies then made his arrangements for an attack on the main Hanoverian position. His artillery was very inferior numerically to that of the enemy, so he relied chiefly on his infantry fire. He sent a small column to make a feint against Thämsbrück, while he advanced two regiments of infantry against Merxleben, and detached a column of landwehr to his right in order to outflank, if possible, and turn the Hanoverian left.

On the Hanoverian side the first gun was fired between ten and eleven, from a battery of rifled six-pounders attached to the second brigade, and posted on the left of Merxleben. The first brigade was immediately pushed forward to the support of the second brigade, and took up its position on the right of that village. By a singular error, the Hanoverians failed to hold a wood and bathing establishment, close to the river, on the right bank opposite Merxleben. Into these the Prussian regiments threw themselves as they advanced against the village, and sheltered by the cover, they opened a biting musketry fire on the Hanoverian gunners and troops near the village. This fire caused great loss to the Hanoverians, and rendered their subsequent passage of the bridge most difficult and dangerous. The Prussian columns on the right, pressing forward against the Hanoverian left, bore on their line of retreat, and threatened their flank. The Hanoverian leader seizing his opportunity, resolved to attack with vigour the wide-spread Prussian line. At mid-day the first brigade in the centre, with the third brigade on the right wing, advanced from Merxleben, while the fourth brigade on the left moved forward at the same time against the Prussian right. Here, however, the sides of the river were steep, and the time occupied in descending and ascending the banks, and wading through the stream, permitted only one battalion of rifles of this brigade to take a share in the onset. The rest of the troops, however, supported by their artillery, pressed steadily forward, and bore down upon the Prussians, who retreated. Many prisoners were taken, but not without severe loss to the assailants, who soon occupied the wood and bathing establishment beside the river.

The Prussians then drew off from every point, and a favourable opportunity occurred for a vigorous pursuit. But the disadvantage of a river in front of a position now became apparent. The cavalry could not ford the stream, nor approach it closely, on account of the boggy nature of its banks, and had to depend upon the bridges at Thämsbrück, Merxleben, and Nägelstadt. The duke of Cambridge's regiment of dragoons issued from the latter village and dashed forward quickly, but unsupported, against the Prussians, taking several prisoners. As soon as the heavy cavalry of the reserve had threaded its way across the bridge of Merxleben, it also rushed upon the retreating Prussians. Two squares broke before the advancing horsemen, and many prisoners were made, while Captain von Einein, with his squadron of cuirassiers, captured a Prussian battery. But the Hanoverians suffered fearfully from the deadly rapidity of the needle-gun, and Von Einein fell amidst the cannon he had captured. About five o'clock the pursuit came to an end, and the Hanoverians, masters of the field of battle, posted their outlying pickets on the south of Langensalza. Their total loss in killed and wounded was 1392. The Prussians lost 912 prisoners, and not much less than their enemies in killed and wounded. It is said that the Hanoverian infantry engaged did not number more than 10,000 men, because the recruits were sent to the rear, and during the day 1000 men were employed in throwing up earthworks. The Hanoverian cavalry consisted of twenty-four squadrons, of which eighteen certainly took part in the pursuit, mustering at least 1900 sabres. The artillery in action on that side consisted of forty-two guns. The Prussian force numbered about 12,000 combatants, with twenty-two guns. It is extremely questionable how far General Flies was justified under these circumstances in precipitating an action. The battle of Langensalza was of little avail to the gallant army which had won it. The Hanoverians were too intricately involved in the meshes of Falckenstein's strategy. This general on the 28th closed in his divisions, and drew them tightly round the beleaguered enemy, who, by the action of Langensalza, had repulsed but not cut through their assailants. The division of General Manteuffel, and the brigade of General Wrangel, were pushed into the Hanoverian rear, and took up positions at Alt-Gottern, Rothen, Helligau, and Bollestedt. The division of General Beyer was advanced from Eisenach to Hayna. General Flies was at Warza, and the brigade of General Kummer at Gotha was held ready to move by railway to Weimar, in order to head King George, in case he should march to the eastward on the left bank of the Unstrut. Forty thousand hostile combatants were knitted round the unfortunate monarch and his starving but devoted troops.

When these positions of the Prussians were reported to the king, he determined to avoid a holocaust of his soldiery. An action could hardly have been successful; it must have been desperate. The terms of capitulation which had been formerly proposed by Prussia were agreed to on the evening of the 29th. Arms, carriages, and military stores were handed over to the Prussians: the Hanoverian soldiers were dismissed to their homes: the officers were allowed to retain their horses and their swords, on condition of not again serving against Prussia during the war. The king himself and the crown prince were allowed to depart whither they pleased beyond the boundaries of Hanover. Political errors, and the supineness of Prince Charles of Bavaria, had thus suddenly made a whole army captive, and blotted out from the roll of independent states one of the most renowned of continental principalities. Hanoverians look with a mournful satisfaction on Langensalza, and British soldiers feel a generous pride in the last campaign of an army which mingled its blood with that of their ancestors on the battle-fields of Spain and Belgium.

CAMPAIGN OF THE MAINE.

Opposed to the Prussian army of the Maine stood, after the capitulation of the Hanoverians, the seventh and eighth corps of the Germanic Confederation. The seventh federal corps consisted of the army of Bavaria, which was under the command of Prince Charles of Bavaria, who was also commander-in-chief of the two corps. The Bavarian army was divided into three divisions, each of which consisted of two brigades. A brigade was formed of two regiments of infantry of the line, each of three battalions; a battalion of light infantry, a regiment of cavalry, and a battery of artillery. There was also a reserve brigade of infantry, which consisted of five line regiments and two battalions of rifles. The reserve cavalry consisted of six regiments, the reserve artillery of two batteries. The first division was under the command of General Stephan, the second under General Feder, and the third under General Zoller. The infantry of the reserve was commanded by General Hartmann, the cavalry by a prince of the house of Thurn and Taxis. The whole army numbered over 50,000 sabres and bayonets, with 136 guns. The chief of the staff of Prince Charles was General von der Tann, who was a tried commander of division, but failed to meet the necessities of a position even more arduous than that of commander-in-chief. The Bavarian army in the middle of June was posted along the northern frontier of its own kingdom, in positions intended to cover that country from an invasion from the north or east. Its head-quarters were at Bamberg, its extreme right wing at Hof, and its extreme left wing near the confluence of the Franconian Saale with the Maine, between Schweinfurt and Gemünden.

The eighth federal corps, under the command of Prince Alexander of Hesse, consisted of the Federal contingents of Würtemburg, Baden, Hesse, and a combined division which included the Austrian auxiliary brigade and the troops of Nassau. The whole corps mustered 49,800 sabres and bayonets, with 134 guns. Prince Alexander assumed the command of this corps on the 18th June, and established his head-quarters at Darmstadt. The elector of Hesse-Cassel had sent his troops to the south as soon as the Prussians invaded his territory. By a decree of the Diet of the 22nd June, they were placed under the orders of the commander of the eighth federal corps. On account of their rapid retreat from Cassel, their preparations for war were incomplete, and little could as yet be expected from them in the open field. The troops of Würtemburg and Baden also still wanted time; those of Baden particularly, for their duchy entered unwillingly into the war against Prussia. Würtemburg had sent an infantry brigade, a regiment of cavalry, and two batteries on the 17th June to Frankfort. These were intended to unite with the troops of Hesse-Darmstadt already assembling there. The next Würtemburg brigade joined the corps only on the 28th June, and the last brigade on the 5th July. The first Baden brigade reached Frankfort on the 25th June, where the Austrian brigade had arrived only a few days before. The rest of the troops and the transport trains did not come in till the 8th July, so that the 9th July must be considered to have been the earliest day on which the eighth federal corps was ready to take the field. While these minor governments were still assembling their small contingents, the troops of Prussia had entered into possession of Saxony and Hesse, had caused the surrender of the Hanoverian army, and inflicted a crushing defeat on the main forces of Austria.

The Bavarian army lay along the Maine, with its first division towards Hof, and its fourth towards Gemünden. The Bavarian government was anxious to make an advance upon Berlin, by way of Hof; but the general strategical movements of all the allies of Austria were, in virtue of a convention concluded between Austria and Bavaria on the 14th June, directed from Vienna. The directing genius decided against any offensive movements in a north-easterly direction, and insisted strongly on a junction of the Bavarian and eighth federal corps between Würzburg and Frankfort, in order to make a move against the Prussian provinces on the north-west. The aim of Austria was to compel Prussia to detach strong bodies from her troops engaged with Benedek, and so to weaken her main army. In his own immediate command Prince Charles showed vacillation and uncertainty. He did not strive with energy to liberate the Hanoverians, and failed to unite them with his own force. Nor, when he found himself too late to achieve this object, did he take rapid measures for a concentration of his forces with the eighth corps. On the contrary, instead of making towards his left, he drew away to his right, apparently with the object of crossing the difficult country of the Thuringian forest, and placing that obstacle between himself and his allies, whilst he left the valley of the Werra open to his antagonist as a groove, down which to drive the wedge that should separate the Bavarians entirely from Prince Alexander. On the 4th July news came to the head-quarters of this prince, to the effect that strong Prussian columns were moving on Fulda from Hünfeld and Gerze, towns which lie between the Werra and the Fulda. An advance of the eighth corps, with all precautions and in preparation for battle, was ordered for the next day. Meanwhile, however, the Prussian and Bavarian troops had come into contact.

General Falckenstein, after the capitulation of the Hanoverians, had on the 1st July concentrated his three divisions at Eisenach. To this united corps was given the name of the Army of the Maine. On the 2nd July he took the road which leads from Eisenach by Fulda, to Frankfort, and reached Marksahl that day. His intention was to press the Bavarians eastward. These occupied a position at that time with their main body near Meiningen, on the west of the Werra. Two divisions were posted on that river near Schmalkalden, to cover the passage of the stream against a Prussian corps which was expected from Erfurt. The cavalry was intended to open communication with the eighth corps in the direction of Fulda. On the night of the 2nd July, the same night that the troops of Prince Frederick Charles in Bohemia were moving towards the field of Königgrätz, a Bavarian reconnoitring party fell in with one of Falckenstein's patrols, and on the following day the Prussian reconnoitring officers brought in reports that the Bavarians were in force round Wiesenthal, on the river Felde. It was clear to Falckenstein that this position was held by the heads of the Bavarian columns, which were moving to unite with the eighth corps. The Prussian general could not afford to let the enemy lie in a position so close and threatening, on the left flank of his advance. He ordered General Goeben to push them back on the following morning by forming to his left, and attacking the villages on the Felde in front, while General Manteuffel's division should move up the stream, and assail them on the right flank. The third division, under General Beyer, was in the meantime to push its march towards Fulda.

On the 3rd, the Bavarian general having been informed of the vicinity of the Prussians, concentrated his army, and in the evening occupied the villages of Wiesenthal, Neidhartshausen, Zella, and Diedorf, in considerable strength. His main body bivouacked round Rossdorf, and in rear of that village. At five o'clock in the morning of the 4th July, General Goeben sent Wrangel's brigade against Wiesenthal, and Kummer's against Neidhartshausen. The latter village, as well as the neighbouring heights, were found strongly occupied by the enemy. They were carried only after a long and hard struggle, the scene of which was marked by the numbers of Prussian killed and wounded. Towards noon the Bavarian detachments which had been driven from Neidhartshausen and Zella received reinforcements. Prince Charles determined to hold Diedorf. He ordered a brigade to advance beyond this village, and take up a position on the hills on the further side. The Prussians opened a heavy fire of artillery and small-arms from Zella upon the advancing Bavarians, who could gain no ground under such a shower of missiles, nor produce any change in the positions of the combatants at this point, until the termination of the action. A severe combat, meanwhile, was being fought at Wiesenthal. When General Kummer left Dermbach, he detached two battalions to his left, with orders to occupy the defile of

Lindenau, while Wrangel's brigade advanced against Wiesenthal. Wrangel's advanced guard consisted of a squadron of cavalry and a battalion of infantry, which moved along the road in column of companies. Hardly had it reached the high ground in front of the village, when it was sharply assailed by a well-directed fire of bullets and round shot. Heavy rain prevented the men from seeing clearly what was in their front, but they pressed on, and the enemy was pushed back into the barricaded villages, and up the hills on its southern side. Before the Prussian advanced guard reached Wiesenthal, the rain cleared up, and the Bavarians could be seen hurrying away from the place, in order to take up a position with four battalions, a battery, and several squadrons at the foot of the Nebelsberg. The Prussian battalion from Lindenau had arrived on the south flank of Wiesenthal; another came up with that of the advanced guard, and the Prussians occupied the village. The Prussian artillery also arrived, and came into action with great effect against a Bavarian battery posted on the south-west of Wiesenthal. At the same time the needle-gun told severely on the Bavarian battalions at the foot of the Nebelsberg. Three of these retired into the woods which cover the summit of that hill, while the fourth took post behind the rising ground. Swarms of Prussian skirmishers swept swiftly across the plain in front, and made themselves masters of the edge of the wood; but the Bavarians held fast to the trees inside, and would not be ousted. Two fresh batteries of Bavarian artillery, and several new battalions, were seen hurrying up from Rossdorf. At this moment it was supposed that Manteuffel's cannonade was heard opening in the direction of Nornshausen. It was in truth but the echo of the engaged artillery; but the Prussian columns, animated by the sound, hurried forward, and dashed with the bayonet against the woodcrested hill. The Bavarians awaited the charge, and their riflemen made a serious impression upon the advancing masses, but the men of Westphalia still rushed on. After a short, sharp struggle, the hill was carried; and the Bavarians fled down the reverse slope, leaving hundreds of corpses, grisly sacrifices to the needle-gun, to mark the line of their flight. General Goeben, having achieved his object, halted his troops and prepared to rejoin Falckenstein. Leaving a rear-guard of one battalion, three squadrons, and a battery to cover his movement, and the removal of the killed and wounded, he withdrew his two brigades to Dermbach. The Bavarian march, undertaken for the purpose of uniting with the eighth corps, had been checked, and Falckenstein had lodged his leading columns securely between the separated portions of his adversary's army. The Bavarians in the night, finding their road barred, retired, to seek a junction with Prince Alexander by some other route. They did not, however, move over the western spurs of the Hohe Rhöne, in the direction of Bruckenau, whence they might have stretched a hand to Prince Alexander, who on the night between the 5th and 6th July was only seven miles from Fulda. They preferred moving by the woods on the eastern side of the mountains towards the Franconian Saale and Kissingen. This movement separated them from their allies, instead of bringing the two corps closer together. Prince Alexander had sent an officer to the Bavarian camp, who was present at the action at Wiesenthal, and returned to his head-quarters with a report of the failure of the Bavarians. On the receipt of this intelligence, Prince Alexander appears to have abandoned all hope of effecting a junction with Prince Charles north of the Maine. He faced about and moved back to Frankfort, a town, which, until its subsequent occupation by the Prussians, appears always to have had a singular attraction for the eighth federal corps.

On the same 4th July that General Goeben pressed the Bavarians back at Wiesenthal, the leading division of Falckenstein's army had a singular skirmish in the direction of Hünfeld. As General Beyer, who commanded the Prussian advanced guard, approached that town, he found two squadrons of Bavarian cavalry in front of him. Two guns accompanying these horsemen opened fire on the Prussians. The weather was wet, and a clammy mist held the smoke of the cannon, so that it hung like a weighty cloud over the mouths of the pieces. A Prussian battery opened in reply. The first shot so surprised the Bavarians, who had not anticipated that there was artillery with the advanced guard, that the cuirassiers turned about and sought safety in a wild flight. They left one of their guns, which in their haste they had not limbered up. Beyer pressed forward, and found Hünfeld evacuated by the enemy. It is said that these cuirassiers, who had been pushed forward by Prince Alexander to open communication with Prince Charles, were so dismayed by one well-aimed cannon shot, that many of them did not draw rein till they reached Würzburg. As Prince Alexander withdrew towards Frankfort, Falckenstein pushed forward. On the 6th he occupied Fulda with Beyer's division, while Goeben and Manteuffel encamped on the north towards Hünfeld, and the object of the Prussian advance was obtained. On the 5th July the Bavarians and the eighth Federal corps were separated from each other by only thirty miles; on the 7th, seventy miles lay between them.

On the 8th General Falckenstein commenced his march from Fulda. He did not turn towards Gelnhausen, as was expected in the Bavarian camp, but moved against the position of Prince Charles, reaching Brückenau on the 9th, when orders were given for a flank march to the left over the Hohe Rhön against the Bavarians on the Saale. Beyer's division moved as the right wing along the road to Hammelburg; Goeben advanced in the centre towards Kissingen; and Manteuffel on the left upon Waldaschach. On the morning of the 10th, at nine o'clock, Beyer's division, which had received very doubtful intelligence of the presence of the Bavarians in Hammelburg, began its march towards that town, and in an hour's time the head of the advanced guard fell in with the first patrols of the enemy's cavalry in front of Unter Erthal, a small village on the road from Brückenau, about two miles south of Hammelburg. The patrols retired on the Prussian advance, but unmasked a rifled battery posted between the houses. A Prussian field battery quickly unlimbered and came into action. Under cover of its fire an infantry regiment made a dash at the bridge by which the road from Brückenau crosses the Thulba stream, which was not seriously defended; and after a short cannonade the Bavarians drew back to Hammelburg. At mid-day three Prussian batteries topped the Hobels Berg, and after a few rounds from them, the infantry rushed down with loud cheers to carry the houses. This was not an easy task, for part of the Bavarian division Zoller, numbering some 3000 men, held the town, and determined to bar the passage of the Saale. The odds, however, were too unequal, for the Prussians numbered about 15,000 men. Yet the Bavarians clung with courage to the houses, and opened a sharp fire of small arms on the assailants. Their artillery, too, well supported the infantry defence. Two Prussian infantry regiments threw out skirmishers, and attempted to put down the fire of the Bavarian riflemen. But these were under cover of the houses, and their artillery from the hill of Saalch splintered its shells among the ranks of the Prussian sharp-shooters. For about an hour the fight was equally sustained; then two more Prussian regiments and two additional batteries came into play. The Prussian pieces threw their heavy metal upon the Bavarian guns at Saalch, until the fire of the latter grew weaker, and was at length silenced by superior weight. Some houses, kindled by the Prussian shells, at the same time caught fire, and the town began to burn fiercely in three places. Still the Bavarians clung to the bridge, and stood their ground, careless equally of the flames and of the heavy cannonade. Beyer sent forth his jägers to storm the place, and the defenders could not endure the assault. The quick bullets of the needle-gun rained in showers among the burning buildings, scattering death among the garrison. The stoutly defended town was abandoned, and the Bavarians, pursued by salvos of artillery, drew off to the south-east, while the Prussians gained the passage of the Saale at Hammelburg.

On the day that General Beyer fought the action of Hammelburg on the right, Falckenstein's central column was heavily engaged with the main body of the Bavarians at the celebrated bathing-place of Kissingen. On the 5th July eighty Bavarian troopers, flying from Hünfeld, passed in hot haste through the town. Visitors and inhabitants were much alarmed; but the burgomaster quieted them by a promise that he would give twenty-four hours warning if the place were in danger of being attacked by the Prussians. This assurance had all the more weight, because even so late as on the 8th July Bavarian staff-officers were sauntering about the Kurgarten as quietly as if in time of the most profound peace. Some of the troops which had been quartered in Kissingen and its neighbourhood were, on the 9th, sent to Hammelburg. All appeared still, yet the inhabitants of the neighbouring villages were flying from their houses to avoid the Prussians. The Bavarian intelligence department does not appear to have been well served. By mid-day on the 9th it was too late for the burgomaster to give his warning, that the Prussians were near. The Bavarians concentrated about 20,000 men, and took up their position. Neither visitors nor inhabitants could now retire, but had to remain involuntary witnesses of a battle. Those who lived in the Hotel Sanner, which, lies on the right bank of the Saale, were allowed to move into the less exposed part of the town. No one was permitted to quit the place, lest he should convey intelligence to the enemy of the dispositions of the Bavarian army. Three of the bridges over the Saale were destroyed; but the supports were left to one made of iron, in front of the Alten Berg. It was by the assistance of these supports that the Prussians gained the first passage of the river; for they knew the localities well, many of their staff-officers having frequented the fashionable watering place. The stone bridge was barricaded as hastily as possible, and its approach protected by two twelve-pounder guns. Five battalions, with twelve guns, held the town itself. The Bavarians, who were commanded by Zoller, general of the division, had chosen a very strong position; they held the houses next to the bridge, as well as the bank of the Saale beyond the bridge. Their artillery was posted on the Stadt Berg, but not on the important Finster Berg. A battery on the latter hill would have prevented the Prussians from gaining the passages of the river from the Alten Berg. Behind the village of Haussen guns were also in position. All the bridges outside of Kissingen were destroyed, and all points favourable for defence occupied by infantry.

On the 10th July, at early morning, Prussian hussars made their appearance, and were followed by columns advancing on the roads towards Klaushof and Garitz, west of Kissingen, while a battery came into position on a hill between Garitz and the river. At half past seven in the morning, the Bavarian guns near Winkels and the two twelve-pounders at the bridge opened on the leading Prussian columns, which consisted of General Kummer's brigade. Kummer's artillery replied, and in a short time the rattle of musketry, mingling with the heavier booming of the guns, told that he was sharply engaged.

The main body of Goeben's division had, in the meantime, reached Schlimhoff. Here it received orders to detach three battalions by Poppenroth and Klaushof, who were to attack Friedrichshall under the command of Colonel Goltza. When General Wrangel's brigade approached Kissingen it received orders to advance on the right wing of Kummer's brigade to seize the Alten Berg, and if possible, extending to its right, to outflank the Bavarian position. The Alten Berg being quickly cleared of Bavarian riflemen by the Prussian jägers, a company under Captain von Busche was sent against the bridge to the south of Kissingen, where, though partially destroyed, the piers had been left standing. Tables, forms, and timber were seized from some neighbouring houses, with which very secretly and rapidly the broken bridge was restored so far that before midday men could cross it in single file. Von Busche led his company over the stream, and into a road on the further side, from the corner of which the enemy's marksmen annoyed his men considerably. This company was followed by a second, and as quickly as possible the whole battalion was thrown across the stream and gained the wood on the south-east of Kissingen, where a column was formed, and under the cover of skirmishers advanced against the town. More men were pushed across the repaired bridge, and ere long two battalions and a half of Prussians were engaged among the houses in a street fight. The remaining portion of Wrangel's brigade was at this time directed in support of Kumnier against the principal bridge. Infantry and artillery fire caused the Prussians severe losses; but they pushed on towards the barricade. Their artillery outnumbered that of the defending force, and protected by it they carried the bridge.

The passage of the stream by the Prussians decided the action. They secured the Finster Berg and the Bodenlaube, with the old castle of that name, and pushed forward with loud cheers into the heart of the town. Here the Bavarian light infantry fought hard, and, suffering heavy sacrifices themselves, inflicted grievous loss upon the Prussians. The Kurgarten, held by 300 riflemen, stormed unsuccessfully three times by Wrangel's men, was carried on the fourth assault. A young lieutenant, who commanded the Bavarians, refusing with the whole of his men to ask quarter, fell in the place they held so well. At a little after three the whole town was in possession of the Prussians.

The Bavarians did not yet renounce the combat. The corps which retreated from Kissingen took up a position on the hill east of the town, and renewed the battle. Wrangel's brigade received orders to clear the hills south of the road which leads to Nullingen. The Bavarians had taken up a position on both sides of the road, and greeted the Prussians with an artillery fire from the Linn Berg. They continued the fight till seven o'clock in the evening, when Wrangel occupied Winkels. The Bavarians were supposed to be retiring, and Wrangel's troops were about to bivouac, when a report came in that the Bavarians were advancing in force. General Wrangel in person went to the outposts, and was receiving the reports from the commanding officer of the nineteenth regiment, when some rifle bullets came from the southern hill into his closed columns. The Bavarians, under Prince Charles himself, had come down with nine fresh battalions of their first division, had seized the hills which lie to the north of the road, and were pressing rapidly forward under cover of their artillery. The Prussians were pushed back, and took up a position on the heights south-east of Winkels, where two batteries came into play. From thence troops were sent by Wrangel into the hills north and south of the road flanking the enemy, and immediately afterwards the whole brigade advanced in double-quick time, with drums beating, to a charge that succeeded, though with loss. The Bavarians were driven back, the Prussians regained their former position, and Prince Charles relinquished his attack.

The Prussian left column, which was formed by Manteuffel's division, on the 10th July secured the passage of the river at Waldaschach about five miles above Kissingen, and at Haussen. At neither place did the Bavarians make any obstinate stand. In these actions on the Saale the Bavarians appear to have been taken by surprise. The Prussian march, previous to the battle of Kissingen, was so rapid that their attack was not expected till the following day. In consequence, the Bavarian force was not concentrated on the river. The troops which held Kissingen and Hammelburg were unsupported, those which should have acted as their reserves being too far distant to be of any service. Not reaching the scene of action till their comrades had been defeated, they, instead of acting as reinforcements, met with a similar fate.

The army of Bavaria boasted to have had at that time 126 cannon. Of these only twelve came into action at Kissingen, five at Hammelburg. The rest were uselessly scattered along the bank of the Saale, between these two places. The staff was unprepared, having no maps of the country, except one which the chief of the staff, General von der Tann, had borrowed from a native of one of the small towns near the field.

When Prince Alexander of Hesse turned to retreat on the 5th July, he might still, by a rapid march along the road which leads from Lauterbach to Brückenau, have made an attempt to unite with the Bavarians before they were attacked at Kissingen by the Prussians. This course he appears, however, to have considered too hazardous, for he retired to Frankfort, and on the 9th July concentrated his troops round that town. Frequent alarms made it evident how little confidence pervaded the federal corps of Prince Alexander. The news of the victory won by the Prussians at Königgrätz was widely circulated through the ranks by the Frankfort journals. Every moment reports were rife that Prussian columns were advancing towards Frankfort from Wetzlar, or Giessen; and on one occasion an officer, by spreading the alarm, caused a whole division to lose their night's rest, and take up a position in order of battle.

No firm union existed between the different divisions of the eighth corps, which had not been concentrated for twenty-four years. The organization, the arms, the uniforms, were all different.

The hussars of Hesse-Cassel, for instance, were dressed and accoutred so similarly to Prussian cavalry, that the Austrians fired upon them at Asschaffenburg.

The day after the victory at Kissingen, General Falckenstein turned his attention against this heterogeneous mass without fear of any assault on his rear by the Bavarians, who after the battle of Kissingen had retired in such haste towards the Maine, that Manteuffel's division, sent in pursuit, could not reach them. On the 11th duly Beyer's division marched by way of Hammelburg and Gelnhausen on Hanau, without falling in with the Würtemburg division which held Gelnhausen. On the 14th the Würtemburgers retired in great haste, without throwing any obstacle in the way of the advancing Prussians, either by breaking the bridges or by any other means. The division of General Goeben was directed, at the same time, through the defile of the Spessart, upon Aschaffenburg, and found the passes unoccupied and unbarricaded. Notwithstanding the presence in the district of large numbers of foresters, no abattis or entanglements were placed across the road. None of the almost unassailable heights were occupied, either to prevent the direct progress of the Prussians, or to threaten their line of march in flank. The railway, which was still serviceable, was not used to convey the small number of riflemen and guns, which at Gemünden, as at many other points, might have thrown some difficulties in Goeben's way. Manteuffel's division followed Goeben's, and scoured the country in the direction of Würzburg. Between Gemünden and Aschaffenburg the river Maine makes a deep bend to the south. Into the bow thus formed, the mountainous region of the Spessart protrudes, through which the road and railway lead directly westward from Gemünden to the latter town. On the 13th July, Wrangel's brigade was approaching Hayn, when a report came in that the enemy's cavalry and infantry were advancing from Laufach. They were troops of Hesse-Darmstadt, and were without difficulty pushed back, while the village of Laufach was taken, and the railway station occupied. The enemy with eight or nine battalions—about 8000 men—and two batteries, resumed the offensive. The Prussians occupied the churchyard and the village of Frohnhöfen, and after a severe contest, in which all Wrangel's available troops were engaged, not only repulsed all the assaults of the Hessians, but made a counter-attack which was attended with complete success. The Hessians drew off from all points towards Aschaffenburg, leaving more than 100 prisoners, with 500 killed and wounded, in the hands of the victors. On the Prussian side the loss was very small, twenty men and one officer.

The advantages of ground, disposition, and leading were all on the side of the Prussians, who gained their success, although very weary from a long march, without any exertions worthy of mention. They had so quickly and skilfully availed themselves of each local advantage, for the defence of their line by infantry and artillery fire, that all the reckless bravery of the Hessians had no other result than to inflict upon themselves very severe losses. After the action of the 13th July, Wrangel's brigade bivouacked at Laufach, with an advanced post of three battalions round Frohnhöfen. On the 14th, at seven in the morning, the further march on Aschaffenburg commenced. On the hill of Weiberhofen, Wrangel's brigade fell in with that of General Kummer, which had moved by a route on the south of the railway. General Goeben then ordered a general advance. He moved Wrangel's brigade along the road, Kummer's on the railway embankment; and with a hussar and cuirassier regiment drawn from the reserve, covered his right flank by moving them through the open fields on the south of the road. Hösbach was found unoccupied by the enemy, as was also Goldbach. On the further side of the latter village the infantry fire opened. The Prussian regiments pushed forward to the wooded bank of the Laufach stream. The Federal corps here consisted of the Austrian division under General Count Neipperg, formed of troops which had originally garrisoned Mainz, Rastadt, and Frankfort. There were also some of the Hesse-Darmstadt troops, whose fire caused the Prussians little loss. An Austrian battery, posted on a hill south of Aschaffenburg and admirably served, greatly annoyed the Prussians, and held them at bay until three of their battalions pushed along the stream nearer to the village of Daurm, and made themselves masters of a hill surrounded by a tower walled in. Protected by this the infantry succeeded in forcing the enemy's artillery to retire, and in checking the advance of some squadrons of Federal cavalry. As soon as the Austrian battery drew back, a general advance was made against Aschaffenburg, which is surrounded by a high wall that offered the Austrians cover, and a convenient opportunity for defence. The Prussian artillery coming into action on the top of a hill, soon showed itself superior to that of the Austrians; and after shelling the environs of the town, and the gardens which lay in front of the walls, the Prussians stormed and gained the walls without much loss. There was a sharp conflict at the railway station, but nowhere else in the town. Aschaffenburg having only two gates, the Austrians in their retreat towards the bridge over the Maine came to a dead lock; 2000 of their number, mostly Italians, were made prisoners. Reconnoitring parties were at once pushed on towards Frankfort, and the reward of victory was reaped in the evacuation of that important town, and of the line of the Maine, by the Federal forces.

Wrangel's brigade was pushed forward by forced marches to Hanau. About five o'clock on the evening of the 16th July, the first Prussians, a regiment of cuirassiers and a regiment of hussars, arrived near Frankfort, brought in a train from Aschaffenburg. They got out of the carriages a short distance from the city gates, and took up a position on the Hanau road. At seven a patrol of the hussars, led by an officer, halted before the city gate, and in another quarter of an hour the head of the vanguard passed in. The populace were for the most part sullenly silent. A few insulting cries to the Prussians were occasionally heard from some of the windows, but the soldiers took no notice of them. Generals Vogel von Falckenstein, Goeben, Wrangel, and Treskow, surrounded by the officers of the staff, rode in at the head of the main body, while the bands of the regiments played Prussian national airs. Before ten o'clock the whole line of march had entered. The telegraph and post-office were occupied. The railway station was garrisoned, and guards established over all the principal buildings. The town of Frankfort was virtually annexed to the Prussian monarchy. Next day the remainder of Falckenstein's force entered the town, and some troops, pushing forward south of the city, captured a Hessian bridge train. The general established his head-quarters in Frankfort, and published a proclamation announcing that he had assumed temporarily the government of the duchy of Nassau, the town and territory of Frankfort, and the portions of Bavaria and Hesse-Darmstadt which his troops had occupied. The civil functionaries of these districts were retained in their posts, but were directed to receive no order except from the Prussian commander-in-chief. Several of the Frankfort papers, which had always been distinguished for strong anti-Prussian feeling, were suppressed. The eleven armed unions (*Vereine*) which had existed in the city were abolished; and the functions of the senate and college of burghers established by a general order. Six millions of gulden (£600,000) were demanded from the town as a war contribution, and after much grumbling paid by the citizens. When afterwards, on the 20th of July, an additional contribution of twenty millions of gulden (£2,000,000 sterling) was demanded, a universal cry of indignation and horror arose. In the meantime, General von Roeder had been appointed governor of the town, and to him the burgomaster represented, on the 23rd of July, that the town had already furnished six millions of gulden, and about two millions of rations, and begged to appeal to the king against the second tax. So much did this misfortune of his city weigh on the burgomaster's mind, that he committed suicide the same night. The town sent a deputation to Berlin, which supported by the foreign press succeeded in averting the second contribution. Frankfort shortly afterwards was united definitively to Prussia, and the first contribution of six millions, though not actually returned to the citizens, was retained by the government to be expended in public works for the benefit of the city.

On the 14th July General Falckenstein issued a general order to his troops, recapitulating their victories and expressing his thanks. The thirteenth division, he said, was "fortunate" in being generally at the head of the corps, and the first to come into collision with the enemy. It showed itself worthy of this honourable post, as did the intelligence and energy of its leader in taking advantage of his opportunities. In less than fourteen days this fortunate general had defeated two armies, each as strong as his own, and in a country by no means advantageous for the offensive, had so manoeuvred as to separate by seventy miles adversaries who at the beginning of the contest were within thirty miles of each other. On the 16th of July he was able to report to the king, that all the German territory north of the Maine was in possession of the Prussians.

CAMPAIGN SOUTH OF THE MAINE.

The day that General Falckenstein published his general order to the troops, the army of the Maine lost its commander. For some as yet unexplained offence to the king or his courtiers the rough old general was recalled, and was offered the appointment of military governor-general of Bohemia, an appointment which he did not accept until solicited by the king to do so. The importance of the communications of the main Prussian armies with the provinces of Saxony and Silesia, which were threatened by the three fortresses of Theresienstadt, Josephstadt, and Königgrätz, led the king of Prussia to appoint General Falckenstein as military governor-general of that province.

General Manteuffel assumed the command of the army of the Maine, and on the 18th July occupied Wiesbaden. On the 20th, Kummer's brigade was pushed southwards as an advanced guard, and entered Darmstadt; but the main body of the army halted at Frankfort until the 21st, for reinforcements. Of the 12,000 auxiliaries which came up from the Hanse towns and other places, 5000 men were left to hold the line of the Maine at Frankfort, Hanau, and Aschaffenburg, and the remainder served to raise the active army to a strength of 60,000 combatants.

A second reserve corps to the number of 23,000 men was formed at the same tune at Leipzig, under the command of the grand-duke of Mecklenburg-Schwerin. It was intended to enter Bavaria by way of Hof, and either to act against the rear of the united Bavarian or federal corps, while engaged with General Manteuffel, or to force the Bavarian army to form front towards the east, and prevent Prince Charles of Bavaria from acting in concert with Prince Alexander against Manteuffel.

By the 21st July the railroad from Frankfort to Cassel had been repaired and was available throughout its whole length, not only for military transport, but also for private traffic. On that day the main body of the army of the Maine quitted Frankfort, and moved towards the south, while Beyer's division advanced from Hanau. The Bavarians had concentrated, and were in position near Würzburg. It appeared probable that part of the eighth federal corps intended to hold the defiles of the Odenwald, and the line of the Neckar, while the remainder joined the Bavarians near the Tauber. To take advantage of two roads, in order to move quickly upon Prince Alexander before he was firmly linked with the Bavarians, and to shield his own right flank against any detachments lurking in the Odenwald, General Manteuffel moved Goeben's division by Darmstadt on Könieg, while Flies and Beyer pushed up the valley of the Maine by Woerth.

On the 23rd the army of the Maine occupied a position near Mottenberg and Amorbach. It was found that the enemy was in force on the Tauber, and that his advanced posts were pushed over the river as far as Hundheim. On the 24th two actions took place on the Tauber, an affluent of the Maine, which falls into the latter stream below Wertheim. General Manteuffel moved against the Tauber in three columns. At Tauberbischofsheim the Würtemburg division, under General Hardegg, was posted, to hold the place itself, and then issue from the valley on the road towards Würzburg, in case of an attack by the Prussians. The artillery fire of the advanced guard brigade of Goeben's division caused great loss among the defenders, and soon forced them to retire from the village. General Hardegg withdrew his troops, but endeavoured to hold the Prussians in the houses, and to prevent the advance of their batteries, by blowing up the bridge over the Tauber; he thus for a time prevented the progress of the Prussian artillery. After a hot combat, which lasted three hours, the Würtemburgers were relieved by the fourth division of the eighth federal corps. The action increased in fury, but ultimately the Prussians gained the passage of the Tauber at Bishopsheim, and pushed their outposts a short distance along the road to Würzburg.

After several other conflicts, in which the Prussians were always victorious, the crowning engagement took place when Kummer pushed his skirmishers close up to Marienberg, and with them forced the enemy to quit some earthworks which they had begun to throw up. The whole artillery of the army of the Maine was then posted on the right and left of the road, and opened a cannonade on the houses, to which the enemy's guns actively replied. The arsenal and the castle of Marienberg were set on flames, after which the batteries ceased firing. The day after that cannonade a flag of truce was sent from the Bavarians to General Manteuffel, who announced that an armistice had been concluded between the king of Prussia and the Bavarian government. The cessation of hostilities rescued the allied army from a very precarious situation in the elbow of the Maine, where it was all but cut off from the territories which it had been intended to defend. In these engagements the strength of the Bavarian and eighth Federal corps, which mustered together at least 100,000 men, was frittered away in isolated conflicts, instead of being concentrated for a great battle. Such conflicts could have had no important result, even if they had been successful.

A word or two remains to be said on the occupation of Franconia by the second reserve corps. On the 18th July the Grand-duke Frederick Franz of Mecklenburg-Schwerin assumed command of the second Prussian reserve corps at Leipzig, and on the same day ordered this corps to move upon Hof, in Bavaria. On the 23rd a battalion of the guard crossed the Bavarian frontier, capturing a detachment of sixty-five Bavarian infantry, and on the day following the grand-duke fixed his head-quarters at Hof. There he published a proclamation to the inhabitants of Upper Franconia, informing them that his invasion of their country was only directed against their government, and that private property and interests would be entirely respected by his troops.

In consequence of this assurance he was able to draw from the inhabitants the means of supplying his men with rations. The fine old city of Nürnberg being declared an open town, was occupied without resistance by the Prussian advance guard, and spared the havoc of a bombardment. The Prussian troops were everywhere victoriously pressing forward, and the disruption of the German Confederation became daily more complete.

On the 1st August General Manteuffel, at Würzburg his head-quarters, concluded an armistice with General von Hardegg, for Würtemburg and with the representatives of Hesse-Darmstadt. On the 3rd a plenipotentiary from Baden came to Würzburg, and obtained terms for the grand-duchy. The relics of the Diet advanced rapidly towards dissolution. On the 28th July the troops of Saxe-Meiningen had already been permitted by the governor of Mainz to leave that fortress, which, in virtue of subsequent treaties, was given over, as was Frankfort, by a decree of the Diet, entirely to Prussia. This decree, dated the 26th of August, 1866, was the last act of the Diet of that Germanic Confederation which had been constructed after the fall of the first French empire. In this self-denying document the Diet practically published its own death-warrant.

MOVEMENTS IN MORAVIA.

To return to the Prussian advance from Königgrätz. After Benedek's disastrous retreat from the field of battle he dispatched the tenth corps, which had suffered most severely, to Vienna by railway, and ordered the remainder of his army to move on the entrenched camp at Olmütz, while he left his light infantry division to watch the road from Pardubitz to Iglam, and his second to delay the enemy, if possible, on the road between Pardubitz and Brünn.

On the 4th July he also sent General Gablenz, one of the most able of the Austrian generals, to the Prussian head-quarters, in order to treat for a suspension of hostilities, as a preliminary to the conclusion of peace. This was a new proof of the desperate condition of the Austrian army. Gablenz reported himself at mid-day on the 4th at the outposts of the Crown Prince's army, and received permission to go to the king's head-quarters. He was conducted blindfold through the army to Höritz, and when he reached that town, found the king absent on a visit to his troops in the field of battle. Being taken on to meet him, the general fell in with his Majesty between Sadowa and Chlum, and was thought to be a wounded Austrian general, fit object of royal condolence. King William, being informed of his visitor's mission, ordered the bandage to be removed from his eyes, and bade the Austrian general return with him to Höritz. Here Gablenz expressed Benedek's desire of an armistice; but no truce could be granted, for Prussia and Italy were mutually bound to consent to no suspension of hostilities without a common agreement. General Gablenz returned unsuccessful to the Austrian head-quarters, and the Prussians commenced their victorious march to Brünn, where they halted on the 13th July; having given proofs of power of endurance which have rarely been equalled in the annals of war. Their marches had not been made by small detachments, or over open ground, but in large masses over deep and heavy roads, encumbered with artillery and crowded with carriages.

While the army halted here, reserve troops were being advanced into Bohemia to secure the communications with Saxony, and to keep order in rear of the armies, where the peasantry, having possessed themselves with weapons from the field of battle, had began to plunder convoys and to attack small escorts or patrols. General Falckenstein, as we have seen, was summoned from the army of the Maine to be the commandant of Bohemia. Still it was thought that these preparations were useless, and that the army would never move south of Brünn. The visit of the French ambassador to this town, quickly reported from billet to billet, fell like a cold chill on the enthusiasm of the troops, who longed to conclude the campaign by an entrance into the Austrian capital. The mediation of the emperor of the French with the Prussian court in favour of peace, they looked upon with aversion, and anticipated with disgust an armistice by the conditions of which the army might be retained at Brünn for a considerable time.

Benedek, as observed, did not offer to rally his army beyond the line of the Elbe, or to fortify any position to retard the advancing Prussians. He despatched the tenth corps, the Saxons, and part of the cavalry, to Vienna, and effected a hasty retreat with the remains of his army to Olmütz, expecting the Prussians would not venture to steal a march upon Vienna, with a fortress and army in their flank. He was, however, greatly deceived; for on the 5th the Prussians had crossed the Elbe at three points, and in three columns were advancing towards Vienna.

Archduke Albert, who had recently won a victory at Custozza, superseded General Benedek, on the 12th July, as commander-in-chief of the army of the north. He at once transmitted orders to Benedek to bring his entire force of five corps to Vienna. But as the railroad and nearest road from his position at Olmütz to Vienna were seized by the Prussians, the unlucky general had to effect a difficult march through mountain roads and passes over the lesser Carpathians. The second and fourth corps commenced marching from Olmütz by Tobitschau on the 14th, and Benedek with the first and eighth corps, and the cavalry division of Taxis, followed on the 15th, whilst the sixth corps was sent by Meiszkirchen.

General Bonin, commander of the first corps of the second Prussian army, who was at Pressnitz, received orders on the 14th to destroy the railway bridge at Brerau, south-east of

Olmütz, and in following out these orders his troops came into collision with the retreating Austrian divisions not far from Tobitschau. An engagement took place, in which the latter were defeated with a loss of 1200 men, including 500 prisoners and eighteen guns.

Benedek quickened his retreat across the little Carpathians to Pressburg, at which place the second corps arrived on the 22nd; but the advanced guard of the ex-commander-in-chief only reached Tirnau on the same day, and Benedek himself, with the first, sixth, and eighth corps, did not arrive at Pressburg till the 26th.

The Prussians learnt by the evening of the 14th that the negotiations for an armistice had failed, upon which Von Moltke retired to his quarters and was closeted with his maps, making new plans for the further progress of the campaign, and for the occupation of Vienna. With such leaders, with a better arm than their enemies, with every mechanical contrivance which modern science could suggest, adapted to aid the operations of the army, it is little wonder that the stout-hearted and long-enduring Prussian soldiers proved victorious on every occasion on which they went into action. The Prussian march to the Danube was resumed on the 19th. The advance had been so rapid, that it was almost impossible to realize that the army was within thirty miles of Vienna. The men of the first army would have been glad of some visible proof assuring them of its proximity; but as yet they could have none. Prince Frederick Charles knew that on the 22nd General Benedek would throw his leading divisions over the Danube at Pressburg. If then he could seize that place, the remainder of the Austrian force would have to make a *detour* by Komorn before arriving at Vienna.

The seventh and eighth divisions advancing on Pressburg, engaged the Austrians at Blumeneau on the 22nd. A brigade having crossed the mountains were occupying a position in the Austrian rear, when orders were received that an armistice had been concluded. But the battle had commenced and the fire could not be checked, till an Austrian officer advanced towards the Prussian lines with a flag of truce; the signal to cease firing was sounded along the Prussian ranks, and the combat was broken off. But for this truce the Prussians would undoubtedly have obtained a victory at Blumeneau which would have jeopardized Benedek's army; for on the day of the conclusion of the truce he was at some distance from Pressburg with two of his corps, and in all probability he would have been compelled to fall back.

A curious scene occurred directly the action was over, that illustrates the artificial nature of warfare produced by state policy, and its freedom from personal animosity. The men of Bose's Prussian brigade, who had been planted across the Pressburg road, and a few hours before had been standing ready, rifle in hand, to fire upon the retreating Austrian battalions, were surrounded by groups of those very Austrian soldiers whom they had been waiting to destroy. The men of the two nations mingled together, exchanged tobacco, drank out of each other's flasks, talked and laughed over the war in groups equally composed of blue and white uniforms, cooked their rations at the same fires, and lay down that night, Austrian and Prussian battalions bivouacked close together, without fear, and in perfect security.

For five days longer the Prussian troops remained in the March Feld. The preliminaries of peace had been agreed upon at Nikolsburg on the evening of the 26th, and the war was certainly at an end, as far as Austria and the North German States were concerned. Late at night on the 26th a courier arrived from the king's headquarters at Nikolsburg, with a letter from General Moltke to Prince Frederick Charles, stating simply and without details that a glorious peace had been arranged. The preliminaries, signed that evening at Nikolsburg between Prussia and Austria, included the following terms:—That Austria should go out of the Germanic Confederation, should pay a contribution towards Prussia's expenses in the late war, and should offer no opposition to the steps which Prussia might take with regard to Northern Germany. These steps were, to annex Hanover, Hesse-Cassel, Nassau, and the portion of Hesse-Darmstadt which lies on the north bank of the Maine; to secure the reversion of Brunswick on the death of the present duke, who has no children; to force Saxony to enter into the new North German Confederation headed by Prussia; and to hold the entire military and diplomatic leadership in that confederation. The war contribution to be paid by Austria was fixed at 40,000,000 thalers, of which 15,000,000 were to be paid up: 15,000,000 were credited to Austria for the Schleswig-Holstein expenses, 5,000,000 for the support of the Prussian armies in Bohemia and Moravia, and 5,000,000 to be paid at a future date to be afterwards settled. The Prussian armies were, on the 2nd of August, to retire to the north of the Thaya, but were to occupy Bohemia and Moravia till the signature of the final treaty of peace, and to hold Austrian Silesia until the war contribution was paid.

It was a strange coincidence, says a recent German writer, that the magnificent castle of Nikolsburg had passed through the female line from the house of Dietrichstein to Count Mensdorff of Lothringian descent, like the Hapsburgs, so that peace was actually negotiated in the country house of the Kaiser's minister for foreign affairs. Other historical recollections belong to the place. Napoleon I. sojourned here after Austerlitz, just as William I. did after Sadowa. Bismarck, on his arrival, gazed at the magnificent pile intently, and remarked, with his grim humour, "My old mansion of Schonhausen is certainly insignificant in comparison with this splendid building, and I am better pleased that we should be here at Count Mensdorffs than that he should now be at my house." After the excitement of the battle of Sadowa, and the exposure in the marching which followed, the minister president was assailed by his old complaint of nervous rheumatism. His difficulties at Nikolsburg were neither few nor small. In a letter he wrote in Bohemia, on the 9th July, occur these words: "If we do not become extravagant in our demands, and do not imagine that we have conquered the world, we shall obtain a peace worth the having. But we are as easily intoxicated as cast down; and I have the unthankful office of pouring water into this foaming wine, and of making it clear that we do not inhabit Europe alone, but with three neighbours." Wise words that bore good fruit in 1866, in a peace glorious for Prussia and beneficial to the rest of Germany.

The definitive treaty of peace between Austria and Prussia was signed at the Blue Star Hotel at Prague, on the 23rd August, and consisted of fourteen articles. The ratifications of this treaty were exchanged on the 29th August, also at Prague. As a consequence of the exchange of the ratifications the Prussian troops began to vacate Austrian territory, and by the 18th of September there was not a spiked helmet or a needle-gun in Bohemia or Moravia. There were great rejoicings in Berlin to celebrate the return of the army, and on the 19th of September a public festival in their honour took place. On the evening of the 21st the king assembled at dinner, in the Schloss, 1200 of the generals and principal officers who had served in the campaign. Directly after dark the whole city was lighted up. Special performances were given in all the theatres in honour of the triumphant termination of the war. Prologues were delivered which detailed the glorious deeds of the army; and the plays which were written for the occasion dwelt upon the actions and personal adventures of the heroes of the campaign, and recalled the memories of the concluding wars of the first French empire.

The Prussian government now concluded the programme of events by the formation of the North German Confederation; measures were at once proceeded with, and practically northern Germany was united into one confederate power, under the sceptre of the house of Hohenzollern, by the end of October, 1866.

The fortune that attended Italy during the war will now be briefly touched upon. Her arms had suffered defeat both by land and sea; yet the glorious victories of her Prussian allies procured her the benefits of the peace.

THE WAR IN ITALY.

When Prussia had declared that she regarded the Austrian proceedings at Frankfort as a declaration of war, King Victor Emmanuel, in consequence of his alliance with the government of Berlin, declared war against Austria; and on the 20th of June General La Marmora, chief of the staff of the Italian army, sent an intimation to the commandant of Mantua that hostilities would commence on the 23rd. The Archduke Albrecht accepted the intimation, and made ready for action.

The theatre of war in which the troops of Italy and the Austrian army of the south were about to engage, has often been the battle-field of Europe. It communicates with Vienna by two lines; by the railway, *viâ* Trieste, through Goerz, Udine, Treviso, and Padua to Verona, connecting the Quadrilateral with the capital; and by a line through Salzburg, Innsbruck, Botzen, and Roveredo, which though not completed between Innsbruck and Botzen, afforded a subsidiary way for the supply of troops camped under the protection of the fortresses. The Quadrilateral itself consisted, as our readers know, of the strongly entrenched camp of Verona on the Adige, the less important fortress of Legnano on the same river, the lately strengthened fortifications of Peschiera at the issue of the Mincio from the Lago di Garcia, and the fortress of Mantua, which lies further down the Mincio, with its citadel and fort St. George on the left bank, and its minor works on the right of the stream. The fortified Borgo Forte supports the line of the Mincio in front of the confluence of that river with the Po; while Venice, with many adjacent forts, protected the rear of the Quadrilateral towards the sea.

The Italians, in acting against the Quadrilateral, might either advance across the Mincio, and rush headlong against its parapets and embrasures, or, by advancing from the Lower Po, push towards Padua, and endeavour to cut the main fine of communication with Vienna. General La Marmora had a very difficult problem to solve, and was not fortunate in the conditions he introduced into its solution. His information as to the Austrian designs was greatly at fault, while that of the Archduke Albrecht was excellent. The Italian general was bound to assume the offensive for political reasons. Neglecting a plan of campaign which had been forwarded from Berlin, he adopted one that had, it is said, been determined upon in 1859 by a mixed council of French and Italian officers. The main attack was to be made against the Mincio and Adige, by the principal army, under the personal command of King Victor Emmanuel. The whole army, including the division of reserve cavalry, mustered about 146,000 men, with 228 guns. The Italian staff, presuming that the Archduke Albrecht would await an attack behind the Adige, determined to cross the Mincio, and occupy within the Quadrilateral the ground not held by the Austrians. After taking up this position, and so separating the fortresses from one another, the main army was to give a hand across the Adige to General Cialdini, who was to lead his corps across the Lower Po, from the direction of Ferrara. General Garibaldi, with his volunteers, was to support the movement on the left by attacks on the passes leading from Northern Lombardy to the Tyrol. The day before the declaration of war, the main body of the king's army was moved towards the Mincio, and on the 22nd June the headquarters of the first corps were at Cavriana, those of the third at Gazzoldo, those of the second at Castelluccio, while the king himself went to Goito.

On the morning of the 23rd Cerale's division crossed the Mincio at Monzambano; Sirtori's, at Borghetto and Valeggio; Brignone's, at Molino di Volta; and the reserve division of cavalry, followed by the four divisions of the third corps, at Goito. The two divisions of Bixio and of Prince Humbert were pushed to Belvedere and Roverbella, while the divisions of Govone and Cugia encamped near Pozzolo and Massinbona.

Confident of his information, General La Marmora on the 24th ordered the advance without any preparation having been made for combat. Scouts even were not sent out to observe the roads from the fortresses, and the soldiers were hungry and weary under the broiling sun of an Italian midsummer. This negligence and temerity met with its just reward. The moment news reached the archduke of the entry of the Prussians into Holstein, he concentrated his troops between Pastrengo and San Bonifacio, so that they could easily be united on either bank of the Adige, in case of need, and mustered, after deductions for necessary detachments, about 60,000 foot, 2500 horse, and 270 guns.

BATTLE OF CUSTOZZA.

In the night between the 23rd and 24th a heavy fall of rain took place, which laid the dust, and made the air cool on the following day.

At three o'clock on midsummer morning the sixth Austrian corps moved on Somma Campagna, the fifth on San Giorgio, and the reserve division on Castelnuovo. The cavalry brigades spread over the plain, on the left of the ninth corps, while the advanced guards pushing forward fell in with those of Victor Emmanuel, which were moving in the opposite direction The Italian divisions were engaged under pressure of superior force, and were compelled to retire to Oliosi, where Cerale made a determined stand. The archduke reinforced his reserved division, and after a hot fight, in which great bravery was displayed on both sides, Oliosi caught fire, and Cerale, who was wounded, was forced to retreat to Monte Vento. Here, though reinforced by Sirtori's division, whose advance from Valeggio to Santa Lucia covered his right wing, he could not withstand the assault of the Austrians, who took Monte Vento by storm, and forced Cerale to retreat on Valeggio.

As soon as the Austrians advanced against Sirtori at Santa Lucia, the Italian general quitted his position, and also retreated to Valeggio. Meanwhile General Hartung, having occupied Berettara and Casa del Sole in force, advanced on Custozza, where he fell in with Cugia's division, supported on the right by that of Prince Humbert. The latter was exposed to frequent attacks of the Austrian cavalry, and was often obliged to throw its battalions into square, in one of which the prince himself found shelter from the enemy's horsemen. On Curia's left Brignone's division was led into action by La Marmora himself against the Austrian brigade of Sardier, supported by two other brigades. Shortly after mid-day, and after two commanders of brigades, Gozzani and Prince Amadeus, had been wounded, Brignone was forced to retreat to Custozza, making room for Govone's division, which soon found itself hard pressed by the Austrian seventh corps. Cerale had been driven from Vento, Sirtori from Santa Lucia; and now Cugia, outflanked on his left, was forced to quit Madonna Delia Croce, so that at five o'clock the retreat of the Italian army was general. But so slowly did the third corps retire from the field of action, that it was not till seven o'clock in the evening that the Austrians occupied the heights of Custozza. Bixio's division and the reserve cavalry covered the retreat across the plain, where some detachments of the second corps also came to blows with the enemy.

The Austrians lost 960 killed, 3690 wounded, and nearly 1000 prisoners, who were for the most part captured by Pianelli. The Italians lost 720 killed, 3112 wounded, and 4315 missing. The Italian army required time to recover from this disaster. On the 30th detachments of the Austrian cavalry crossed the Mincio, and pushed as far as the Chiese; but the Archduke Albrecht had no intention or design of invading Lombardy.

The volunteers under General Garibaldi amounted to about 6000 men, the main body of which was collected by the 20th of June in front of Rocca d'Ans, while a small detachment was placed near Edolo, on the road leading through the pass of the Monte Tonale into the Tyrol, and another detachment near Bormio on the road which leads over the Stelvio. The main body crossing the frontier near Storo, found the population of the Tyrol entirely opposed to them, and staunchly loyal to the house of Hapsburg. On the 25th of June a sharp combat took place at the frontier bridge of Cassarobach, in which the Italians were worsted. They retired towards Bogolino, when they were attacked by an Austrian detachment on the 3rd July, again suffered a reverse, and saw their general wounded.

When, after the battle of Königgrätz, Venetia was offered by the government of Vienna to the emperor of the French, the fifth and ninth Austrian corps were withdrawn from Italy, and forwarded to the Danube, leaving, besides the garrisons of the fortresses, only one Austrian corps in Venetia, and in the Tyrol a weak detachment under General Kuhn.

The Italian army rested for a while after the battle of Custozza; but an advance was rendered necessary by the treaty with Prussia. La Marmora's defeat having deprived him of the confidence both of the country and the army, the command-in-chief was given to General Cialdini, who was ordered to cross the Lower Po, and push troops against the Tyrol and into Eastern Venetia. Accordingly on the evening of the 7th July, leaving a division to watch Borgo Forte, and another near Ferrara, he concentrated seven divisions near Carbonara and Felonica, and threw some detachments of light troops across the Po at Massa. On the night following three bridges of boats were thrown across the stream at Carbanarola, Sermide, and Felonica, and on the 9th the army crossed at three points, covered from any attack by the marshes which here lie between the Po and the Adige. Cialdini then made a flank march to his right, gained the high road which leads from Ferrara by Rovigo to Padua, and opened his communication with Ferrara by military bridges thrown across the river, to replace the road and railway bridges which the Austrians had blown up. On the 10th his head quarters were at Rovigo, and on the 14th, after securing the passage of the Adige at Monselice, his advanced guard occupied Padua. Meanwhile the division which he had left under Nunziante, in front of Borgo Forte, besieged that place, which on the night of the 18th was evacuated by the Austrian garrison, and occupied by the Italians, who captured seventy guns, and magazines of all kinds.

As the progress of events in the north pointed to the conclusion of an armistice, the terms of which would compel, in all probability, the troops on both sides to remain in their actual positions, the Italians determined to gain as much ground as possible before diplomacy might cause their army to halt. Cialdini, on the 19th, had with him about 70,000 men, and an expeditionary army of 70,000 more was being prepared to reinforce him. The Austrian troops in Italy which could take the field mustered little over 30,000 men. The Italian general advanced from Padua to Vicenza, along the left bank of the Brenta to Mestre, so as to cut Venice off on the land side, while the fleet should attack it from the sea. At the same time the Austrian field troops under General Maroicie withdrew from the Quadrilateral, and retired gradually behind the Piave, the Livenza, the Tagliamento, and finally behind the Isonzo. On the 22nd they evacuated Udine, which, two days later, was occupied by the Italians. No resistance was made by the Austrians until the Italian advanced guard passed beyond Palmanoro, when a sharp skirmish took place with the Austrian rear-guard, but it led to no results. In the meantime, Cialdini had pushed detachments by Schio towards Roveredo and by Belluno, as far as Avronzo, on his left, while on his right his troops were close up to Venice and Chioggia. A truce was agreed to on 22nd July, which was extended from week to week, until on the 12th August an armistice was concluded. The line of the Indrio was fixed as the line of demarcation between the troops on either side. The conclusion of the armistice between Prussia and Austria had already liberated the Austrian troops which had been transferred from Venetia to the Danube, and they were immediately sent back to the Isonzo, but were not called upon to act.

In the meantime, operations had been carried on against the Southern Tyrol. On the 22nd July Medici with his main body marched against the Austrian works at Primolano, which were promptly evacuated. Next day he entered Borgo, and on the 24th pushed his advanced guards to

Pergine and Vigolo. General Kuhn being reinforced by 8000 men from Verona, determined to fall upon Medici, and thrust him back. A slight combat took place between some of Kuhn's outposts and the Italian advanced guard near Sorda on the 25th, but news of the armistice prevented further conflict. Garibaldi had made some movements from the west against the Tyrol, but without great success. He had captured the small fort of Ampola, and resisted several attacks made by the Austrians; but, though he attempted to gain as much ground as possible, he occupied at the time of the armistice only the valley of the Chiese for a length of ten miles from the Italian frontier, and the Val di Conzei, two miles north of Riva.

NAVAL OPERATIONS.

Of the Italian fleet great things were expected. The long coast line of Italy, and the mercantile habits of the natives of many of her sea-board towns, had for a long succession of years been calculated to foster seamen, and to lay the foundation for an efficient navy. The result of the war, in its naval operations, caused bitter disappointment to the Italian people.

The Italian fleet was assembled at Tarento in the middle of May, under the command of Admiral Persano, who divided his force into three squadrons. The first, under his own immediate command, consisted of seven iron-clad vessels, and a flotilla of five gun-boats. The second, or auxiliary squadron, was formed of seven unplated frigates, and five corvettes. The third squadron consisted of three battering vessels and two gun-boats, while the transport squadron included fifteen vessels, capable of conveying 20,000 men across the Adriatic.

On the declaration of war, the fleets sailed from Tarento to Ancona, where Persano having heard of the disaster of Custozza, resolved to wait until a new plan of operations had been decided on. On the 29th of June the Austrian fleet, under the command of Admiral Tegethoff, appeared in front of Ancona. Some shots were exchanged between an Italian cruiser and the leading Austrian vessel, but no further engagement took place; for before Persano could weigh anchor the Austrian fleet retired. Persano remained inactive in Ancona until Cialdini advanced into Venetia, when being ordered to act he determined to attack Lissa. The island of Lissa lies in the Adriatic, some thirty miles south of Spalatro. Between it and the mainland lie the islands of Lesina, Brazza, and Solta. Between Lissa and Lesina there is a strait about fifteen miles broad. The two ports of Lissa are San Giorgio and Comisa. On the 16th July Persano left Ancona with a fleet of twenty-eight vessels, of which eleven were iron-plated, four screw frigates, two paddle-wheel corvettes, one a screw corvette, four despatch boats, four gun-boats, one hospital ship, and one store ship. The frigate *Garibaldi* remained at Ancona for repairs. Messages were sent to all vessels at Tarento or Brindisi to sail towards Lissa, the *Affondatore* especially being ordered up.

On the evening of the 17th Persano issued orders that Admiral Vacca, with three iron-clad vessels and a corvette, should bombard Comisa; that the main force, consisting of eight iron-clads, a corvette, and despatch boat, should assail San Giorgio; and that Admiral Albini, with four wooden frigates and a despatch boat, should effect a landing at the port of Manego on the south side of the island, in rear of the works of San Giorgio. Two vessels were to cruise on the north and east of Lissa during these operations, in order to give timely warning of the approach of the Austrian fleet. Vacca finding that his guns could not attain sufficient elevation to do much damage to the works at Comisa, gave up the attack and sailed for Port Manego, where Albini attempted in vain to effect a landing. Persano had begun to bombard San Giorgio at eleven in the morning of the 18th, by three o'clock, when joined by Vacca, he had blown up two magazines, and silenced several Austrian batteries. He could not, however, succeed in sending his ships into the harbour, and the prosecution of the attack was postponed till the next day.

The whole of Persano's fleet was now assembled in front of San Giorgio, strengthened by the ram *Affondatore* and three wooden vessels. That evening the admiral was informed that the Austrian fleet was leaving Fasana to attack him. Calculating that the enemy could not approach Lissa before nightfall on the 19th, Persano determined to make a second attack upon the island. But the attack, though well planned, was postponed from hour to hour, in case Tegethoff might arrive; and when in the afternoon the cruisers signalled that no smoke was to be made out on the horizon, the cannonade began. The floating battery the *Formidabile* entered the harbour, and taking post at the extreme end, 400 yards distant from the Austrian batteries, opened fire. A battery on the northern side told severely upon her, and Persano ordered the *Affondatore* to open upon this battery through the mouth of the harbour. This was done, but without much effect.

Vacca formed his three iron-clads in single line, steamed into the harbour, and opened on the batteries inside; but he could not effectually support the *Formidabile*, both because she herself covered the Austrian batteries, and on account of the difficulty of manoeuvring in the narrow space within the harbour, which is only about 100 fathoms wide. He was soon forced to quit the harbour, and was followed by the *Formidabile*, which had lost sixty men, and suffered so considerably that it was sent the same evening to Ancona for repairs. Equally unsuccessful was the attempt at landing. The wind blew fresh from the south-east, and the boats could with difficulty approach the beach on account of the surf. The next day at daybreak, though the weather was still stormy, Persano again ordered a landing to be made. Two iron-clads bombarded Comisa. Albini and Sandri, with the wooden vessels and gunboats, supported the landing at Port Carobert. But the surf was so high that the landing could not be effected, and it was about to be abandoned when a cruiser bore hastily down through the rainy mist, and signalled that the enemy was approaching from the north. Tegethoff with the Austrian fleet was at hand to relieve the beleaguered island.

BATTLE OF LISSA.

On the 17th July Admiral Tegethoff at Fasana heard, by telegram, of the Italian fleet being near Lissa. He concluded that its appearance there was but a demonstration, to draw him away from the coast of Istria. On the 19th, however, being assured by fresh telegrams that the attack on the island was serious, he determined to proceed thither. His fleet was in three divisions, and consisted of seven ironclads under his own immediate command; seven large wooden vessels led by Commodore Petz; and a third division of seven smaller wooden vessels and four despatch boats—making up the number of twenty-five vessels, mounting about five hundred guns.

The Austrian admiral left the roads of Fasana about mid-day on the 19th of June, and on the morning of the 20th his despatch boats reported a vessel of the enemy in sight. The wind was blowing strong from the north-west. At first Tegethoff steered a course from the north-west to south-east, parallel to the Istrian coast; but off Lirona and Solta he altered his course to one directly from north to south. Persano on hearing of the Austrian approach, ordered his vessels to form in line of battle; and by nine o'clock his ironclads formed in a straight line, while steering almost from west-south-west to east-north-east in three divisions. Persano, at the same time, moved in person from the *Re d'Italia* to the *Affondatore*, which he ordered to take up a position on the flank of the column furthest from the Austrian attack. When Admiral Tegethoff could clearly make out the Italian fleet, it was steering from west to east. He bore down upon it in the following order:—His twenty-one vessels were arranged in three divisions of seven ships each, the first consisting of iron-clads; the two others of wooden vessels. The line of iron-clads led, with the admiral's flag-ship slightly in advance, from which the other vessels, falling a little astern, formed a wedge-like order. The seven heaviest wooden vessels followed the iron-clads, and were themselves followed by the lighter vessels in a similar formation.

Tegethoff bore down upon the gap between Vacca's three vessels and the central Italian group, and drove his own flag-ship, the Ferdinand Max, straight upon the *Re d'Italia*, which he rammed several times and sank. Only a small portion of the crew were saved. The *Palestro* attempted to aid the *Re d'Italia*, but Tegethoff turning upon her, ruined her steering apparatus. At the same time she was attacked by other ironclads, and quickly caught fire. She fell away before the wind, and as the fire could not be got under, she with all her ship's company, save sixteen men, was blown into the air. Thus of the Italian central division two vessels were lost, while the *Affondatore* remained inactive, apart from the battle. The third vessel of this division, attacked by the seven Austrian ironclads, as well as by the three wooden vessels, was severely handled, and forced to retreat.

The Italian division under Vacca had, with a north-easterly course, sailed along the flank of the Austrian iron-clads as they advanced, and exchanged some broadsides with them. When his leading ship, the *Carignano*, was clear of Tegethoff's iron-clads, Vacca ordered a change of direction, and brought his three vessels in line between the second and third Austrian divisions. His fire told severely on both, especially on the Kaiser, the flag-ship of the Austrian second division. The Italian division under Ribbotty, when it saw the central division engaged, altered its own course, and moved against the Austrian wooden ships, which were thus brought between two fires. Ribotty fiercely attacked the *Kaiser*, commanded by Commodore Petz. The latter using his wooden vessel as a ram, ran with full steam against the *Re di Portagallo*, and then lay alongside of her. At the same time he was attacked by the *Maria Pia*, and his vessel suffered severely. Tegethoff, by this time, had disposed of the Italian central division, and he brought his iron-clads back to aid his wooden vessels. Under their protection the Kaiser got away, and was taken to Lissa. After this a closer and fiercer battle was maintained between the whole of the Austrian vessels and the six Italian iron-clads, while the Italian wooden squadron, and the *Affondatore* looked on from the distance. The smoke was so thick that either side could with difficulty tell their own vessels; and Tegethoff, hauling off, signalled to his fleet to form in three columns, with a north-easterly course so that the iron-clads formed the northernmost line, nearest to the Italians. By this manoeuvre the Austrian fleet was brought in front of the strait between Lissa and Lesina. Vacca, under the impression that Persano had gone down in the *Re d'Italia*, ordered the Italian iron-clads to assemble, and with them in a single line steered slowly towards the west, waiting for the Palestro. She soon blew up. It was now about two o'clock, and the action had lasted four hours. At this time Persano joined Vacca's squadron with the *Affondatore*, placed her at the head of the line, and ordered the other vessels to follow her movements. These movements appear to have consisted in no more than a steady pursuit of a westerly course to the harbour of Ancona. By the battle of Lissa the Italians lost two ironclads, the *Re d'Italia* and the *Palestro*. The *Affondatore* sunk at Ancona, after reaching harbour. For three days the Italian people were led to believe that a victory had been won at Lissa. The mortification of the defeat, which then became known, was thereby increased. Persano was summoned before the Senate, and was deprived of all command in the Italian navy. One remark appears patent, even to those who are quite unskilled in naval matters, that in the sea-fight Tegethoff led his fleet, Persano only directed his; another, that the Italian admiral, with superior forces at his command, allowed a section of his own fleet to be attacked and defeated at the decisive moment by a smaller force of his adversary.

On the 21st, the Austrian admiral returned, without a vessel missing, to the roads of Fasana.

PEACE BETWEEN ITALY AND AUSTRIA.

The armistice concluded between Austria and Italy was to last from mid-day on the 13th August to the 9th September.

In the meantime negotiations for peace were opened at Vienna; and on the 3rd October a definitive treaty was signed. By it Austria recognized the kingdom of Italy, and sanctioned the cession of Venetia to that power by the emperor of the French. The ratifications were exchanged as soon as possible. The Austrian commissioner-general Moring formally gave over Venetia to the French commissioner-general Leboeuf, when a plebiscite took place. The annexation to the kingdom of Victor Emmanuel was almost unanimously voted by the people of Venetia, and Italy became one great country, united under the sceptre of the House of Piedmont, and free of any foreign dominion, "from the Alps to the Adriatic."

The Austrian surrender of Venetia to the emperor of the French, and not to the king of Italy, was considered at the time a gratuitous insult to the latter power; but whether it was initiated by Austrian or French politicians has not yet been clearly ascertained. Louis Napoleon had reasons for wishing to play the patron to Italy, and may have thought of reviving his plan of an Italian Confederation, with Venetia as a nucleus. Austria, at least, was compelled to show deference to France in some way, if she would make terms with Prussia short of total ruin; and France accepted the present of Venetia for the sake, it is to be hoped, of the magnanimous pleasure of giving it back to its right owner. How far the emperor yielded to the pressure of united Prussia and Italy it would, perhaps, not be polite to surmise; but that the Kaiser was disappointed with the use made of his gift, and the cheapness with which Italy made its acquisition, was generally believed. Yet there can be no doubt, and the Austrians by this time must be willing to admit the fact, that they are as much stronger, safer, and happier without Venetia, as Italy is stronger, safer, and happier with it. To the one nation it was a fretting incumbrance, always breeding sores in the body politic. To the other it is the completion, on one of its sides, of an organic body that will grow and develop with all the more success that its component parts are fairly welded together. Something, no doubt, was due to the policy which dictated Cialdini's march towards Venice after Austria's cession of the territory to France. Viennese politicians imagined that the Italians would not dare to invade "French territory;" but the army of Victor Emmanuel and its leaders were not so easily frightened, and their constancy was rewarded by the non-intervention of the French. The influence exercised by Louis Napoleon on the settlement of the Austro-Prussian quarrel was not so great as had been expected. He secured a nominal independence for the kingdom of Saxony, and a vague promise that the people of North Schleswig, who for the most part are Danes, should some day or other be allowed to settle their nationality, whether they would be German or Danish, by a popular vote. That day has not arrived yet, after a lapse of four years.

Prussia's gain by the war was enormous. Her rival Austria was absolutely turned out of Germany, almost as completely as she had been turned out of Italy. Saxony was completely subordinate to Prussia. Hanover, Cassel, Darmstadt, and Nassau were bodily annexed to her. With a large compact territory north of the Maine, with some thirty millions of people homogeneous in language, culture, taste, and mainly in religion, trained to arms and inspirited with the remembrance of great successes, she found herself at the doors of the smaller states south of the Maine who were unable to resist her influence or her arms, and felt constrained to agree to the military conventions which, for all purposes of peace and war, made the Germans a mighty irresistible nation. Prussia emerged from the war powerful abroad as well as at home. She could show that, having crushed Austria, she was afraid neither of France or Russia, and those great domineering powers found themselves compelled to respect the new power that had arisen in Europe. Well for France had she seen as clearly as her ruler the power of the neighbour who quickly defied him, and denied him the smallest concession by way of restoring the equilibrium of the great powers of Europe.

Much as Prussia has done by her military power and her excellent organization, English readers will do well to recollect the price that is paid for that state of national drill, which makes the whole population a powerful machine in the hands of a king, his ministers, and generals. We as a people should be very loath to sacrifice our personal freedom and individual independence to the exigencies of a rigorous military system, that with harsh if equal legality takes the squire from the hall, the peasant from the plough, the merchant from his counting house, the clerk from his desk, the artist from his studio, the tradesman from his shop, the artizan and the operative from their bench and from their loom, to serve an apprenticeship to the bloody genius of war. The battle for freedom which England fights most successfully has to be waged in the region of opinion and moral influence; though she is obliged by the practices of her neighbours to maintain a large reserve of physical force, she will by her legislation, her literature, and her commerce, encourage peace among nations and the domestic development of individual prosperity in all parts of the world. The glory of carrying on such a work will be far greater than the barbarous *prestige* conceded to military conquerors—a false glory, which it is fervently to be desired will at no distant date disappear, as the renown of being a successful duellist has already ceased to be an object of honourable ambition in civilized society.

The great power and influence acquired by Prussia in her war with Austria and the overthrow of so many of the princelets of Germany was, men feared, to be used in favour of a feudal reaction, that should once more build up society on the basis of the divine right of kings, the blessedness of privilege, and the virtue of blue blood. But there is too much culture on the one hand, and too thorough a love of liberty on the other, for such a reaction to be possible in a territory inhabited by thirty or forty million people of Teutonic race. Despotism tempered by humanity, knowledge, and wisdom may be submitted to by a nation in times of crisis and transition, but its permanent enthronement will never be endured. Nor is it likely that unbridled democracy will gain possession of united Germany; but a peaceful, orderly, representative government, in which every interest is allowed a voice, and a career is open to all talent, is that which seems destined to bind together for ages those parts of the great German family which have been so long separated by the narrow selfishness of feudal lords and petty princes.

CHAPTER V.

Leading Actors in the great Drama—The King-President of the North German Confederation—His Ancestry and their labours for Prussia—Progressive enlargement of Territory and increase of Population—Conquests of Napoleon I.—Restorations and Additions at the Congress of Vienna—Birth of William—Flight from Berlin with Queen Louise—Maxim of Kant the Philosopher—Death of Louise—William in the War of Liberation—His sister Charlotte married to Nicholas of Russia—Friendship of the Brothers-in-law—Journey to Russia—Bite from a chained mastiff—Amateur actor in "Lalla Rookh"—Journey into Italy—Marriage with Princess Augusta of Saxe Weimar—William becomes Crown Prince and Governor of Pomerania—Opposed to violent Changes of the Constitution—Intercourse with Bunsen—Tour in England and Scotland—Conversation with the Duke of Wellington—Attitude of the Crown Prince in 1848—Sudden visit to England—10th April, 1848, in London—Election to the Constituent Assembly—Command in Baden—Political Re-action—Governor of Westphalia and the Rhinelands—Residence at Coblentz—Illness of his brother the King—William made Regent—His first acquaintance with Bismarck—Accession to the Throne—Appoints Bismarck Prime Minister—In Denmark, 1864—At Gastein—Receives an ovation in Berlin, 29th June, 1866—Goes into Bohemia—Risk of Capture—Anxious suspense at Sadowa—The King under fire—Triumphal Return to Berlin—The King's Brothers, Son, and Nephews—The Crown Prince—His Popularity—Military Talent—Domesticity—Prince Frederick Charles—"Always in the Front"—His Campaigns—Important Remarks on the Reformation of Military Tactics—Grand Duke of Mecklenburg, son of the King's sister—General Baron von Moltke—Sketch of his life—In Denmark, Prussia, Turkey, and Bohemia—His Lesson to a French officer—General von Roon, Minister of War—Vogel von Falckenstein in the War of Liberation—In Denmark—On the Maine—In Silesia—Austrian Notabilities—Archduke Albert—General Benedek—Results of the War to the two Antagonists—Prussia's gain—In Territory incorporated—In Influence over the New Confederation of North Germany—Sketch of the Confederation and its Constitution—Austria's loss—Of Territory in Italy—Of Influence in Germany—Her gain in Union with Hungary—New Constitution of the Double Austro-Hungarian Empire—Provincial Diets—Reichsrath—The Executive—Hungarian Chamber of Magnates and Deputies—County Meetings—Executive—Sketch of Count Beust—Speeches of Beust and of the Emperor—Deak Ferencz—History of his Labours for Hungary—Proceedings in Berlin—King's Speech—Coolness towards France—Address of the Chamber—Speech of Count von Bismarck—Application of the Prussian Constitution to the Incorporated States—Possibility of a renewal of War—The right of Prussia to annex is the right of Germany—Bill of Indemnity passed in favour of the Prussian Government—Reconciliation of the Chambers and the Government—The King's apology for annexing Hanover, &c.—Bismarck on the attitude of France in December, 1866—Prussian Indulgence and Modesty—Austria's severance from the Confederation a positive advantage to France—France a match for the North German Confederation—Difficulty of ceding North Schleswig to the Danes with an Ethnological Frontier—Pressure on the Subject from France at Nikolsburg and Prague—Italy's fidelity to

THE elaborate narration of the events recorded in the last chapter was due not only to their intrinsic importance, but also to their especial bearing upon the history which forms the substance of the present work. The Seven Week's War turned into a channel of practical effort all the streaming patriotism that had agitated the German mind for a century. The changes resulting from the successful conclusion of the war were pregnant with other results very momentous, but not necessarily disastrous to Europe. It is necessary now to give a more personal account of the leading actors in that great drama, since they have all survived to play principal parts in the more tremendous tragedy yet to be described.

To begin with King William, the President of the North German Confederation. The kings of Prussia, says Mr. Martin in his excellent "Statesman's Year Book," trace their origin to Count Thassilo of Zollern, one of the generals of Charlemagne. His successor, Count Frederick I., built the family castle of Hohenzollern, near the Danube, in the year 980. A subsequent Zollern or Hohenzollern, Frederick III., was elevated to the rank of a prince of the Holy Roman Empire in 1273, and received the burgraviate of Nuremberg in fief; and his great grandson Frederick VI., being invested by Kaiser Sigismund, in 1411, with the province of Brandenburg, obtained the rank of elector in 1417. A century after, in 1511, the Teutonic Knights, owners of the large province of Prussia on the Baltic, elected Margrave Albert, a younger son of the family of Hohenzollern, to the post of grandmaster, and he, after a while, declared himself hereditary prince. The early extinction of Albert's fine brought the province of Prussia to the electors of Brandenburg, whose own territories meanwhile had been greatly enlarged by the valour and wisdom of Friedrich Wilhelm, the "Great Elector," under whose fostering care rose the first standing army in central Europe. The great elector, dying in 1688, left a country of one and a half millions, a vast treasure, and 38,000 of well drilled troops to his son Frederick I., who put the kingly crown on his head at Königsberg, on the 18th of January, 1701. The first king of Prussia made few efforts to increase the territory left him by the great elector; but his successor, Frederick William I., acquired a treasure of 9,000,000 of thalers, or nearly a million and a half sterling, bought family domains to the amount of 5,000,000 thalers, and raised the annual income of the country to 6,000,000, three-fourths of which, however, had to be spent on the army. After adding part of Pomerania to the possessions of the house, he left his son and successor Frederick II., called "the Great," a state of 47,770 square miles, with 2,500,000 inhabitants. Frederick II. added Silesia, an area of 14,200 square miles, with 1,250,000 souls. This, and the large territory gained in the first partition of Poland, increased Prussia to 74,340 square miles, with a population of more than 5,500,000. Under the reign of Frederick's successor, Frederick William II., the state was enlarged by the acquisition of the principalities of Anspach and Baireuth, as well as the vast territory acquired in another partition of Poland, which raised its area to the extent of nearly 100,000 square miles, with about 9,000,000 souls. Under Frederick William III., nearly one half of this state and population was taken by Napoleon I. At the Congress of Vienna, however, not only was the loss restored, but much territory was added; to wit, parts of the kingdom of Saxony, the Rhinelands, and Swedish Pomerania, moulding Prussia into two separated districts of a total area of 107,300 square miles.

King William of Prussia, as already stated, is the second son of King Frederick William III., and of the heroic Queen Louise, who sustained the spirits of her husband and her countrymen during the terrible trial they underwent at the hands of Napoleon I. He was born in 1797, nine months before his father's accession to the throne. He is therefore old enough to remember the anguish of his parents and the humiliation of his native land. He was one of the children who fled with the beautiful queen, their mother, after the battle of Jena, from Berlin to Stettin, from Stettin to Königsberg, from Königsberg to Memel. Here the royal family lived in a simplicity that approached penury; the king having coined his plate to assist in the contribution exacted by the French. The queen and her eldest daughter were not above helping in affairs of the house. She looked more charming then, says an eye-witness, seated near a shabby table in a simple room, than at the grandest court festival crowded with golden uniforms and stars.

The tutor of the young folks at this time was a Monsieur Chambeau from the French colony, who accompanied the family in their flight. One maxim of Kant's, the Königsberg philosopher, was thoroughly inculcated into the minds of both the princes and princesses—"What a state loses in outward importance, must be replaced by inward greatness and development." Precious are the uses of adversity! and wisely did Prussia, under the guidance of men like Stein, Gneisenau, Hardenberg, and others, apply to practice the profound maxim of her great thinker. It was at Königsberg, to which the simple court returned from Memel after the treaty of Tilsit, that the queen gathered learned Germans to her evening parties, discussed methods of education, and encouraged outbursts of patriotic song, destined to penetrate and elevate the down-trodden nation. To all this young William was not insensible. Bitter to him and to them all was the premature death of their mother, in 1810, a year after her return to Berlin. The prince was bred to arms, and bore a part in the famous campaigns of 1813 and 1814, in which the power of the Corsican conqueror was broken at Leipzig and other places. The Westphalian kingdom of Jerome Bonaparte was restored with other spoils to the Prussian crown, and the four bronze horses were replaced in their rightful position over the Brandenburg gate at Berlin.

When the Grand-duke Nicholas of Russia sought the hand of the Princess Charlotte of Prussia, she made a confidant of her brother William, who was able to tell the Russian prince that his advances were not disagreeable to the young lady. From that time a fast friendship subsisted between the two princes, who, a year or two afterwards, became brothers-in-law. Their predilection for military occupations knitted their friendship with the bond of a common sympathy, as did their high notions of the royal prerogative and the right divine of kings. When the princess, in 1817, after two years' probation in the mysteries of the Russo-Greek Church, proceeded to Russia to her marriage, her brother William bore her company, and participated in the great bridal festivals that took place in Petersburg and Moscow. On their arrival at the Russian capital, the Emperor Alexander introduced the young prince to the empress-mother, with the words, "Allow me to present to you my new brother;" on which the sorely-tried widow of Paul I. replied, as she embraced him, "And I, too, gain a son." This simple record of an act of courtesy is a slender historical link uniting the invader of France in 1870 with the murdered monarch of Russia, who perished in 1801. The gorgeous splendour of the Russian court offered a strong contrast to that of Berlin; but Prince William's mind was always more set on solid advantage than on showy appearance, and he was little affected by the oriental display of magnificence that he witnessed in the ancient and modern capitals of the Czar. His natural easy bearing in his intercourse with Russian society, his activity in movement and liveliness of spirits, contrasted favourably with the stiff and formal manners of the Russian archdukes, and won him golden opinions. While at his sister's country palace of Pavlosk he was one day bitten by a chained mastiff. As no one could say what the consequences might be, he was cauterized, and bore the operation with a good humour that caused the dowager-empress to exclaim, "No wonder! for he is a Prussian prince."

In his old age the gallant king suffers, in the person of his subjects, from a chained mastiff of a fiercer kind, who has both inflicted and received wounds that nothing but the Lethean influence of time can heal or obliterate. Prince William was again in Petersburg in 1819, and was one of the few recipients of that momentous secret which the Emperor Alexander then first communicated to his second brother, to the effect that he proposed abdicating his throne in favour of Nicholas. Constantine had consented to the arrangement, and the king of Prussia was credited with a similar plan in favour of his eldest son. Neither plan came into operation; but on Alexander's death, six years' later, Nicholas did supersede Constantine, the rightful heir to the throne, and had to suppress a military revolt in consequence. It is difficult to imagine the stern King William of the present playing a part on the mimic stage even fifty years ago; yet such was the case in 1820, when he and his elder brother appeared at a court spectacle in Berlin as sons of Aurungzebe in Moore's "Lalla Rookh." Ernest, duke of Cumberland, played Abdallah in the same representation, little dreaming doubtless that the pleasant young man elbowing him in the crowd would one day oust his son and grandson from the crown and kingdom of Hanover. Not long after this, in 1822, the prince went into Italy with his father and brother At Rome, while the learned Niebuhr conducted the king to all objects of interest in the city, the young prince's guide was the scholarly Bunsen, who found Prince William "a sober and manly" young gentleman. The marriage of the latter, in 1829, to the Princess Augusta of Saxe Weimar, sister to his brother Karl's wife, was the occasion of festivities as brilliant in their way, that is, in the frugal, practical, Prussian way, as had been the wedding ceremonies of his sister the empress of Russia. During the life of his frugal father, the prince seems to have received little or no advancement in the public service. Yet his mind, though given principally to military studies, was not indifferent to the art and literature which flourished with so much lustre at his father's and his brother's court. On a visit to Peterhof in 1847 he is found advising with his brother-in-law, the Czar, upon architectural improvements, and discussing the merits of the public buildings, not of Italy only, but of England, a country not generally credited abroad with fine architecture. By the accession of his brother to the throne in 1840 William became Crown Prince, and was that year made governor of Pomerania.

During the discussions on the new Prussian constitution, which took place in 1844, so decidedly opposed was the Crown Prince to certain liberal proposals which the king seemed inclined to adopt, that he avowed his intention of quitting the country if they were adopted. These proposals, it was said at court, emanated from Bunsen, who had been summoned from the embassy in London, and was daily closeted with the king, a circumstance that disposed the prince to regard the ambassador with an unfriendly eye. The feeling, however, quickly passed away; for in August that year his royal highness paid a visit to Queen Victoria on the birth of her second son, and seized the opportunity of making a rapid tour through England and Scotland, with Bunsen for his guide. The king, who had a great liking for Bunsen and reverenced his character, was anxious that his brother should profit by the intercourse which this English trip afforded him. In a letter to his ambassador he wrote, "Talk over with William all things as much as possible, politics, church matters, the arts, Jerusalem in particular. I have begged him, on his part, to discuss everything unreservedly with you; that will be most useful and very necessary." His present Prussian Majesty does not appear to have been deeply impressed with the "Jerusalem" part of the conversations. He took an affection for England, however, and admired her greatness, which he attributed to her religious and political institutions. He took every opportunity of exchanging ideas with English notabilities, Bunsen acting as interpreter. The duke of Wellington readily replied to questions on military subjects. Only one of his answers unfortunately is recorded, and is a reply to a question about military regulations:—"I know of none more important," he said, "than closely to attend to the comfort of the soldier: let him be well clothed, sheltered, and fed. How should he fight, poor fellow! if, besides risking his life, he has to struggle with unnecessary hardships? Also he must not, if it can be helped, be struck by the balls before he is fairly in action. One ought to look sharp after the young officers, and be very indulgent to the soldiers." These words of the veteran were not forgotten by the prince.

Conservative in politics, his royal highness met the democratic outbreak of 1848 with a very different countenance from that of his brother the king, who had dreams of universal philanthropy. So notoriously unpopular was he with the masses, that on news of the revolution being communicated to the alarmed empress of Russia, she fainted away, after exclaiming, "And my brother William!" He did, in fact, take temporary refuge in England, and was in London on the famous 10th of April, when the Chartists carried their monster petition through the streets, and tumults were anticipated. His royal highness was much struck with the duke of Wellington's reply to Bunsen's inquiry, "Your grace will take us all in charge, and London too, on Monday the 10th?" "Yes," was the answer, "we have taken our measures; but not a soldier nor a piece of artillery shall you see, unless in actual need. Should the force of law—the mounted and unmounted police—be overpowered or in danger, then is their time. But it is not fair, on either side, to call them in to do the work of police; the military must not be confounded with the police, nor merged in the police." The prince had arrived in London unexpectedly on the 27th of March, and after a stay of exactly two months he returned to Berlin, having been elected, in May, member of the Constituent Assembly by the constituency of Wüsitz in Posen, and he took his seat in that assembly on the 8th of June. The main cause of his unpopularity was doubtless due to his fondness for arms and the armed force, and his readiness to make use of them lor the maintenance of order. To him in the main is Prussia indebted for coming out of the crisis of 1848—49 in her ancient form of a kingdom, although it was with modifications. In June, 1849, he was appointed commander-in-chief of the forces sent against the revolutionists of Baden; when with the partial use of the needle-gun he quelled the insurrection, and contributed no little to the return of the tide of re-action throughout Europe. He was soon after appointed military governor of Westphalia and the Rhine provinces, and settled in Coblentz. His regard for Prince Albert and the Queen brought him again to England "straight from Russia," in 1850, in order to be present at the christening of their son, his godchild, Prince Arthur. At the time of the war between Russia and the Western Powers he openly expressed an opinion, that if Prussia had assumed a firm attitude the Czar would not have proceeded with his aggression, and war would have been prevented. In that year, 1854, he was appointed colonel-general of Prussian infantry, and governor of the federal fortress of Mayence. The mental disorder of his brother, the king, had reached a very advanced stage in 1857, and long before the men in office would admit his incapacity. The Crown Prince, however, would not accept the responsibilities of a ruler without the full power of regent, to which office he was at length called in October, 1858.

His first acquaintance with his now celebrated minister dates as far back as 1836, when Bismarck and another law student of equally great stature were introduced to Prince William. "Well!" said the prince, gaily, "Justice seeks her young advocates according to the standard of the guards;" a chance remark that, so far as Bismarck is concerned, has been verified in more senses than one. Yet, in 1851, when the Crown Prince was received at Frankfort by the Diet, he rather disapproved of "that militia lieutenant"—for Bismarck had appeared in uniform—being the representative of Prussia in the Diet of the Confederation. He also thought him too young at the age of thirtysix for so responsible an office. He was not long, however, in discovering the ripeness of the minister's understanding, the vivacity of his ideas, and the strength of his character, which rapidly attracted the prince's good will, and a regard which soon ripened into intimate friendship. King Frederick William IV. died on 2nd January, 1861, and William ascended the throne. He spent part of the summer at Baden-Baden, where Bismarck, on leave from his Petersburg mission, had much conversation with his new majesty. Upon one subject these two were thoroughly agreed, that unless a total re-organization of their army were to take place, Prussia would not attain to a high position in the world. The consequence of this agreement became apparent the following year, when the king, after sending his friend on a brief embassy to Paris, appointed him minister-president. Here was the man to battle with liberalism and parliamentarianism, and to make a good army and a strong government! and the liberal ministry had to make way for him. It is a *coup d'état!* exclaimed the democrats, and fiercely angry was the opposition which the appointment roused. Such strife as ensued in the Chamber of

Deputies for the six years following has no parallel in parliamentary annals; but the courage and constancy of the king and his minister triumphed over the fiery eloquence, and the really popular cause, of the opposition deputies. The king owned on one occasion the extent of his debt to his minister's pluck and perseverance. On being complimented during those troublous days on his own good looks, he pointed to Bismarck, and said, "There's my doctor!" In 1863 his Majesty accepted the invitation of the emperor of Austria to a congress of princes at Gastein, where a reform of the Federation was proposed, under the direction of Austria. To this Prussia would not consent, nor would King William attend the subsequent meeting of German sovereigns at Frankfort, which was thus rendered inoperative. After the storming of Düppel by Prince Frederick Charles in 1864, the king proceeded to the seat of war, in order to congratulate his troops on the field of victory. In the autumn of the following year was concluded with Austria the Convention of Gastein, for reasons that probably were based on the king's personal regard for the emperor rather than from motives of policy, for it was plain that it must from political necessity soon be set at nought. The king's life was not an easy one. Working incessantly with his ministers at negotiation, and at administration, military, financial, and general, he had also frequent occasion to know that his life was in danger at the hands of excited enthusiasts of the liberal and democratic party.

At length, in 1866, came the great event, the war with Austria, the triumph and enlargement of Prussia, which, in the eyes of his subjects, condoned all past errors, and made them proud of their king, his ministers, and his generals. The first news of victory over the Austrians was received in Berlin on the 29th June, while the king and Count von Bismarck were still in Berlin. The excitement among the people was tremendous. They sang Luther's hymn in front of the palace, "A strong tower is our God, a trusty shield and weapon," that hymn which ever since the battle of Leuthen has time after time aroused and sustained the Prussian soldier on the march to battle; and the king spoke to them from his balcony words known to be of thanks and congratulation, but inaudible in the deafening roar of human voices below. The minister-president also received an ovation, and ended his reply with a salute to the king and army. As he spoke, a tremendous peal of thunder reverberated over the city, which was illuminated by the accompanying flash of lightning, and Bismarck's ringing voice was heard shouting above the multitude, "The heavens fire a salute." Next day the king set out for the seat of war, accompanied by his ministers. On the way they were so little guarded, that by the admission of Count von Bismarck himself, the Austrians, "had they sent cavalry from Leitmeritz, might have caught the king and all the rest of us." They met Prince Frederick Charles on the road to Gitchin on the 2nd July, and after a council of war held at midnight, resolved on the momentous battle of Königgrätz, or Sadowa, which began amid fog and rain at eight o'clock in the morning of the 3rd. Till mid-day the battle went on furiously, and the Austrians were certainly not worsted. "Noon arrived, says Hezekiel, in a striking picture of the scene, "but no decisive news from the Crown Prince. Many a brave heart feared at that time for beloved Prussia. Dark were the looks in the neighbourhood of the king; old Roon, and Moltke of the bright face, sat there like two statues of bronze. It was whispered that Prince Frederick Charles would have to let loose against the foe his Brandenburghers—his own beloved third corps, whom he had held in reserve—his stormers of Düppel, which would be setting his hazard on the die in very deed. Suddenly Bismarck lowered the glass through which he had been observing the country along which the Crown Prince was expected to come, and drew the attention of his neighbours to some lines in the far distance. All telescopes were pointed thitherward, but the lines were pronounced to be ploughed fields. There was a deep silence till the minister-president, lowering his glass again, said decidedly, ' They are not plough furrows, the spaces are not equal; they are marching lines!' He had been the first to discover the advance of the second army. In a little while the adjutants with the intelligence flew about in every direction—The Crown Prince and victory are at hand! "The warlike old monarch dashed into the grenade fire of the enemy, on which Bismarck, who kept close to him, begged him to pause. ' As a major,' he said, 'I have no right to counsel your Majesty on the battlefield; but as minister-president, it is my duty to beg your Majesty not to seek evident danger.' 'How can I ride off when my army is under fire?' replied the stout-hearted king." The march on Vienna and the armistice of Nikolsburg soon followed.

On the 20th September the victorious troops made their triumphal entry into Berlin, with the king, the royal princes, the ministers, and principal generals at their head. There rode Bismarck, Roon, and Moltke, Voigts-Rheetz, chief of the staff of the first army, Blumenthal, chief of the staff of the second army, and other personages almost as distinguished. Rejoicings and feastings ensued, and the now popular king anticipated a long and steadfast repose on his laurels.

"We have always," said Count von Bismarck, in a speech delivered to some Holsteiners in December, 1866, some three months after the peace of Prague, "we have always belonged to each other as Germans; we have ever been brothers; but we were unconscious of it. In this country there were different races—Schleswigers, Holsteiners, Lauenburgers; elsewhere too, there are Mecklenburgers, Hanoverians, Lübeckers, and Hamburgers. They are all free to remain what they are, in the knowledge that they are Germans—that they are brothers. To the wisdom and energy of one man we owe it, that at length we are able to recognize, vividly and with joy, our common German descent and solidarity. Him we must thank—our lord and king—with a hearty cheer, lor having rendered this consciousness of our common relationship a truth and a fact. Long live his Majesty, our most gracious king and sovereign, William I.!" This pithy expression of satisfaction at the great work achieved is as honourable to the minister who prompted the task as to the sovereign who responded to the call made on his energies in carrying it out.

Other skilful aid he had besides that of his minister-president. More fortunate than many kings, he found conspicuous valour and ability in members of his own family. To say nothing of his brothers Karl, commander of the Prussian artillery, and Albrecht, general of cavalry, who held high military command with credit, there were his son the Crown Prince, and his two nephews, Prince Friedrich Karl and the Grand-duke of Mecklenburg, who distinguished themselves in the field of battle.

THE CROWN PRINCE.

The Hohenzollerns, says Carlyle in his "History of Frederick the Great," are men who seek no fighting where such can be avoided; but who can, when it is necessary, carry on a brisk and vigorous attack. These words apply not only to the present head of the family, but peculiarly to the person of his son. Prince Friedrich Wilhelm of Prussia was born on the 18th October, 1831, the anniversary of the day on which the great battle of Leipzig was fought, the battle of German deliverance from the Gallic yoke. This anniversary has always been marked by the fires which burn on the German hills, and in the year 1831 these fires proclaimed a happy day. From his mother, Queen Augusta of the royal house of Weimar, the prince inherited the unassuming kindness and true-heartedness of disposition which distinguish him, together with a certain gentleness in judging others, and liberality in political affairs, which have not hitherto characterized members of the family. The prince was educated at the University of Bonn, and after finishing college studies, he began the service of the pike and drum. He married on the 28th January, 1858, Victoria, princess royal of Great Britain and Ireland, who has borne him a numerous offspring. A pleasant and genuinely German family life is that of the prince. Art and science are much encouraged by him. A tall stately man, says one who saw him at Berlin in 1867, with a brave handsome countenance, and looking taller in his light blue dragoon uniform with the yellow collar, which he wears but seldom. When engaged in conversation the serious, almost solemn, look which marks his face in repose, gives way to an expression of pleasant animation.

The inexhaustible humour and good temper with which the prince took part in the winter campaign against Denmark, made him beloved by the soldiers. The year 1866 strengthened the confidence he had already won. On the day of Königgrätz he had the difficult task, described in the previous chapter, of debouching with the second army through narrow dales and vast forests, until towards mid-day he succeeded in surrounding the left wing of the enemy. The movement that he effected despite so many difficulties determined the issue of the battle. The correct eye of the prince, which sees quickly the right thing to be done, his indefatigableness and energy, are the theme of admiration to those who know him. One striking proof of the confidence reposed in him by his father's subjects, is the exclamation not seldom heard uttered by parents of the youths summoned to march under the standard: "It's all right if they join the Crown Prince, they will be in good hands." The emphatic testimony of one of the German historians of the war, who compares the generalship of the Crown Prince with that of his cousin Friedrich, is to the effect that the method of the former in conducting the campaign calls to mind the masterly enterprise of renowned captains. The conflict between the Government and the House of Deputies brought him trouble too. It was to the Crown Prince, whose predilection for free parliamentary government he well knew, that Count von Bismarck on one occasion made the remarkable statement of his devotion to the idea of German unity. "What matter," he said, "if they hang me, provided that the rope by which I am hung, bind this new Germany to your throne." Worthy son of a worthy sire, the prince gives promise that the splendid crown awaiting him, will rest on brows which, however they may ache with toil and care, will never harbour an ignoble thought or unmanly purpose.

PRINCE FREDERICK CHARLES.

"Prince always in the front" (*Prinz allzeit vorauf*), thus the people named the Hohenzollern cavalry general in the year 1866, and even as "*allzeit vorauf*" he has lived in the minds of the people ever since cannon shot for the first time crashed around him at Missunde. The German soldiery have a more affectionate regard for that *sobriquet* than for the newer title given by the people, of "Red Prince." Born in 1828, as the son of Prince Karl, brother of the king, he quickly ascended the step-ladder of military honour. With the Hohenzollerns it is an old piece of family pride to show themselves worthy of such honours by unwearied care and study, and in the service of their house to use it for the best interests of the army. In the year 1864 the prince first had an opportunity of showing the world that Prussian skill and bravery had not degenerated during a long time of peace. In 1866 he led the first army into Bohemia, and won the unreserved confidence of his soldiers and the fame of a bold general. A critic, already quoted, says of this prince's conduct of this campaign, that he pursued his way with extraordinary circumspection, following the tactics of a wary general, anxious for the security of his flanks, driving the enemy quietly before him, but leaving little to chance; doing his work cleanly, but too slowly for the attainment of the combined plans. In his operations, as well as in battle, he was always concentrated, and moved frontwise, whereas the Crown Prince generally took up a broad front, threatening and attacking the enemy in flank, forgetting his own line of retreat, but looking sharply after that of his opponent. Prince Frederick's method is correct according to the systematic teaching of the school of Archduke Charles. His leisure after the Bohemian campaign was employed in preparing a pamphlet about French military science, the delicate thorough observations of which show that his courage was coupled with superior intellectual power. Up to 1859 the Prussian tactics, says Colonel Chesney, remained as they were left after Waterloo, and thought was first bestowed upon them when the French fought and won the battle of Solferino. This battle aroused the deepest anxiety in the minds of the Prussians, and the well-known lecture of Prince Frederick Charles, who put before the Prussians the principles upon which the French had fought and conquered, took a deep hold, not merely because the lecturer was a prince, but because men felt that he dealt with a want of their time. The prince pointed out that the French fought in loose formation, but above all, with a design; and from that time the great subject of study was, "How to beat the French by using their own freedom of movement." The result was that the Prussian system was changed in 1861. The Prussian Tactical Instructions of 1861 laid aside all attempts to teach men by rule—officers were given principles, and left to work out their applications by themselves. The proposals of Prince Frederick Charles led to breaking up battalions, so as to allow of the formation of company columns, gaining thereby elasticity in the movements of infantry. The Austro-Prussian war, which followed soon after, was too short to display fully the effect of the new tactics; but there were two remarkable mistakes and failures, at Langensalza and Trautenau, where the defeat of the Prussians occurred from special causes. It is a remarkable fact in favour of the Prussian system, that the general in command at Trautenau is in high favour at the present time, and the subject of that defeat has been a matter of special study by the Prussians since, showing that they are not ashamed of profiting by their own mistakes. If to know his enemy accurately be a condition of victory, the Prussian commander of the first army in Bohemia was well qualified for his position.

GRAND DUKE OF MECKLENBURG.

Another nephew of the king distinguished as a military commander is Frederick Francis, grand-duke of Mecklenburg-Schwerin, son of the Grand-duke Paul Frederick, and of the Princess Alexandra of Prussia. He was born on the 18th February, 1823, and carried on his studies at the university of Bonn, when the death of his father, on the 7th of March, 1842, left him possessor of the grand-ducal throne. The revolutionary movement of 1848 obliged him to make some liberal modifications of the constitution; but in 1851 the aristocratic party among his subjects managed to get the old state of things re-established. In 1849 the grand-duke married Augusta Mathilda Wilhelmina, daughter of Henry, prince of Reuss-Schleiss. By her he has had several children, the eldest of whom, Francis Paul, was born on the 19th March, 1851. In 1866 he was appointed to the command of the second Prussian reserved corps at Leipzig, and on the 18th of July was charged with the duty of occupying Franconia, a task he accomplished with as much promptitude and skill as humanity and kind feeling towards the inhabitants of the invaded territory. He was on his way to unite his forces with those of General Manteuffel, when news of the armistice put a stop to further operations. . The king of Prussia on this occasion sent the "order of merit" to the grand-duke with an autograph letter.

GENERAL BARON VON MOLTKE.

The first rank after the royal commanders of the Prussian forces is unquestionably due to General von Moltke. So unobtrusive has been the life of this eminent man and so opposed to display is his character, that materials for his biography are extremely scanty. "And that is really Von Moltke!" said one who saw the great strategist for the first time; "that tall thin man without any moustache or whiskers, his hands behind his back—the officer with very short greyish hair, and a face cut with many fine lines, his head slightly stooped, his eyebrows pronounced, and the eyes deep set." Yes, there is the man whom the Junkers of Berlin called "the old schoolmaster." "What a lesson he has taught the enemies of his country!" He is the man who caught Benedek in a vice at Königgrätz, and prepared for greater things to come. "He always looks very grave." He is pre-eminently a nineteenth century man, having been born in the year 1800, and a self-made man, having been a soldier since his twentieth year, owing his advancement to his own efforts. "I like self-made men," once remarked Count von Bismarck, "it is the best sort of manufacture in our race." The birthplace of Moltke is Gnewitz in Mecklenburg, the Slavonic name of which signifies "anger." The Christian names of the baron are Helmuth Charles Bernard, the first of which being purely German may be interpreted by the word "heroism." If the general's history should pass, in a remote future, into the mythic stage, here are two points that will be valued by the epic poet who may treat the subject.

On completing his college career young Moltke entered the military service of the king of Denmark, but in 1822 passed over to that of Prussia. By a process of self-teaching he acquired a remarkable knowledge of modern languages, an accomplishment which gave rise to the familiar saying that he was "silent in seven tongues." When he had been ten years in the Prussian service his talents and large information procured him an appointment on the staff. In 1835 he travelled in the East and was presented to Sultan Mahmoud. That sovereign, full of schemes of military reform in his empire, requested the German officer to enter his service; and failing in that request persuaded him to obtain a long furlough for service of a limited period, that he might initiate the Father of the faithful in new theories of strategy, and direct the military reforms his Majesty had so much at heart. The earnest and fruitful study he made of the military art at this time may be seen in his excellent "History of the Russo-Turkish Campaign, 1828—29," which is full of shrewd observation and practical instruction. This work was published in 1845, after his return to Berlin, and was translated into English at the commencement of the Crimean war in 1854; the translator, who is anonymous, makes a statement in his preface that proves how thoroughly Moltke kept out of the sight of the world. "Baron von Moltke, who is now dead, was despatched to the Turkish army by order of his own sovereign, at the express request of Sultan Mahmoud, and served with it through the campaigns here described." The campaign he did serve in was that of Syria, which took place in 1839. He published another work in 1841 concerning Turkey, entitled "Letters on the Occurrences in Turkey from 1835 to 1839." Two earlier literary productions attributed to him may be mentioned here, namely, an historical view of Belgium and Holland, published in 1831; and the year following a paper upon Poland. Soon after his return from Turkey to Prussia he was appointed in 1846 aide-de-camp to Prince Henry, who lived in retirement at Rome, and died there the ensuing year. After executing missions intrusted to him in his capacity of an officer on the staff, Moltke in 1856 became aide-de-camp to Prince Friedrich Wilhelm, the present Crown Prince, who doubtless owes to him much of that military knowledge and skill of which he has proved himself master. Three years later Moltke was made chief of the staff of the army, and his first important task was to draw up a plan of operations with a view to intervention in the Franco-Austrian war in Italy of 1859. The peace of Villafranca obviated the necessity of any military movements at that time; but the effort to be in readiness had revealed to the practised eye of the chief of the staff defects that needed absolute cure ere the Prussian army could become an instrument of any considerable weight in Europe. The maxim of the great Königsberger already quoted fermented in a powerful mind, and "the loss that the Prussian state had sustained in outward importance was now to be rapidly replaced by inward greatness and development in a military sense." The first successful operations of the re-organized army in the Danish campaign of 1864 were conducted on a plan advised by Baron von Moltke, who accompanied Prince Friedrich Karl, the commander-in-chief, throughout the expedition.

The very next year he was actively engaged in preparing a plan of campaign in anticipation of war with Austria, and when war was declared somewhat later, in 1866, his plan was faithfully carried out. Accompanying the king into Bohemia, he directed the march on Vienna which had such a stimulating effect on the Austrian authorities, and induced the acceptance of the preliminaries of Nikolsburg. It was Moltke who on the 22nd June granted the truce of five days, that led to the armistice. The entire confidence of the king in his able lieutenant was pleasantly illustrated by his Majesty's reply to some general who wanted troops detached for his reinforcement, "Ask him there!" pointing to Moltke, with a smile, "he wants them all; I dont know if he will let me have my body guard for long." It was on the occasion of the armistice of Nikolsburg that the king decorated Baron von Moltke with the distinguished order of the Black Eagle. That short and sharp campaign did indeed render fully manifest the remarkable powers of the general, and enforced the claims made for him by his admirers to be the greatest strategist of the age. War has been to him a purely scientific study, wholly devoid of passion, of political or personal feeling. He has acquired his knowledge as a skilful chemist comes to know chemistry— by study, by experiment, and by combination. All possible aids that he can discover or think of are brought in as auxiliaries to victory. The remarkable use made of the telegraph wires in the Bohemian campaign is an instance of this. The carriages conveying the telegraphic instruments formed a nearer adjunct of the staff at head-quarters than the ammunition or provision waggons.

The following interesting glimpse of the general as a teacher is from the pen of a recent French writer:—"MacMahon is supposed to have adopted tactics which are not new; namely, to act above all with his artillery, said to be formidable, and to spare his men as much as possible. Napoleon I., of whom General de Moltke is only the pupil, never proceeded otherwise. He it was who first imagined the great concentration of troops by rapid marches. M. de Moltke, his fervent admirer, has always manifested the greatest contempt for our strategy. I remember having heard quoted some of his very words addressed to a French officer on a mission to Berlin—'Do not talk to me of your military education in Africa. If you have never been there, so much the better; when you become general you will be glad of it. The war you have been carrying on for forty years against the Arabs is a guerillerie of an inferior order. Never any skilful marches, no feints, no countermarches, rarely any surprises. With that school you will do nothing more than form other schools like it. The first great war will demonstrate your inefficiency; and were I not in presence of a man of your merit, sir, I should not hesitate to laugh at your ignorance of the trade to which you devote yourselves. Amongst you—do not deny it—a pioneer is almost a ridiculous person, and in general the working man is one of mean intelligence. Here, on the contrary, the most conscientious studies are in the order of the day, and the lowest captain knows as much as your staff-officers who are so brilliant in the ball-room. Have you even a superficial smattering of the elements of the military art on leaving your special schools? I am tempted to doubt it. Come now,' continued General de Moltke, taking the other by the hand, 'I wager that you do not know what is the most valuable piece of furniture for the chamber of an officer in garrison. Come with me.' So saying, the old Prussian led his interlocutor into a small bed-chamber suited to a sub-lieutenant; a small bed without curtains, three straw chairs, shelves of books from the floor to the roof, and in the middle of the room a black wooden board on an easel, the ground strewed with morsels of chalk. 'It is with this that we beat our adversaries every morning,' murmured the old tactician. 'And for drawing, here is all we want,' and M. de Moltke exhibited some geographical maps."

GENERAL VON ROON.

Albert Theodore Emile von Roon is a general, a statesman, and a man of letters. He was born on the 30th of April, 1803, and after an education at the cadet school, entered the army as an officer in 1821. From 1824 to 1827 he followed the higher course of the general military school, and became instructor in the cadet school at Berlin. He soon acquired the reputation of a master in geography and military science. Some of his works published at this time obtained a large circulation, notably, "Principles of Ethnographical and Political Geography," published in 1832, of which an elementary abridgment appeared two years afterwards. He also published, in 1837, "Military Geography of Europe;" and in 1839, "The Iberian Peninsula in its Military Aspect." This last work refers more especially to the civil wars of Spain. Notwithstanding his literary labours, Herr von Roon pursued his professional career with the utmost regularity. Having made in 1832 a campaign of observation in Belgium at the time of the siege of Antwerp, he was attached first to the topographical department, then to the general staff, and in 1836 became captain. His succeeding grades came at intervals of a few years; major in 1842, chief of the staff in 1848, lieutenant-colonel the year following, major-general in 1856, and lieutenant-general in 1859. From the year 1848 he held various commands, and fulfilled several important missions. On two occasions he was charged with the duty of mobilizing the army, particularly in 1859, when the French emperor's precipitate peace with the Kaiser obviated the necessity of assembling the Prussian army. To Roon was confided the education of Prince Frederick Charles, whom he accompanied to the university of Bonn, and in divers voyages about Europe. On the 16th April, 1861, he was called to preside over the ministry of marine, to which a few months later was added the more responsible function of minister of war, which he has retained ever since. At the head of these united services he displayed much energy and perseverance during the ensuing troublous years of parliamentary warfare, heartily seconding the king's projects for military re-organization. These, as we have seen, he realized, spite of the adverse majority in the Chamber. He had much to do in preparing for the Bohemian and other campaigns of 1866, accompanied the king with other ministers to Sadowa, and contributed no small share to the greatness which his country achieved in that eventful year. Well did the king say of him and his distinguished colleague, "Von Roon has sharpened our sword, Von Moltke has guided it."

EDWARD VOGEL VON FALCKENSTEIN

is one of the most popular men in Germany. He is admired as the veteran soldier of the war of liberation, and for the inexhaustible vigour of youth which leads him at a great age from fight to fight, and from victory to victory. The general was born on the 5th January, 1797, the same year with the king, and at sixteen years of age entered the West Prussian grenadier regiment as volunteer jäger, only to be promoted to lieutenant, after he had fought in the battles of Gross-Görschen, Bautzen, and Hatzbach. The campaign of 1814, in which he fought at Montmirail,

Château-Thierry, Thionville, Mercy, and Laon, brought him the iron cross. In the year 1815 he was on duty in front of Paris. He was in Schleswig for the first time in 1848, and again in 1864. He was appointed in 1866 to be commander general of the army of the Maine, end after a display of consummate generalship entered Frankfort, as we have shown, at the head of the cuirassiers, with his trumpeters pealing out the Prussian national song. A bitter hour was it for the general when he was called away from the command of the army of the Maine, in consequence of events not yet fully explained. He was appointed military governor of Bohemia, which appointment he declined, until reconciled by the kind advances of King William at Nikolsburg. In the autumn of 1866 he received the command of the first army corps, from which the king called him to the shores of the Baltic.

Many other eminent leaders were there in the Prussian army—Manteuffel, Steinmetz, Göben, Voigts Rhetz, and others whose names are emblazoned on the roll of military renown. Of the great mover of this momentous war, the schemer of the mighty changes which have followed it, Count von Bismarck, a detailed biographical sketch is given at the end of Chapter III., in the second portion of this work. To turn to the Austrian side, there were three commanders of their army more distinguished than the rest, though but one of them enjoyed the glory of a victory. They are the Archduke Albert, who was victorious at Custozza, the Crown Prince of Saxony, and General Benedek. Of the Emperor Francis Joseph himself a sufficient account has already been given in the course of this historical introduction.

ARCHDUKE ALBERT.

The archduke was the inheritor of military fame if not of ability, being the son of that Archduke Charles who was the most successful antagonist of Napoleon I. in the early part of the conqueror's career. Albert was born in 1817, and educated for the army, in which he obtained early command, not only as a privilege of his rank, but in deference to his knowledge and merit. He first distinguished himself as a general of cavalry. In the troublous days of 1849 he served under the veteran Radetzky, and bore an important part in the battle of Novara, so fatal to the Piedmontese. At the end of the Italian campaign he was appointed to the command of the third Austrian army corps. On the reduction of Hungary to submission he was appointed governor general of that kingdom, an office which he retained until 1860. The previous year he had been sent on a mission to Prussia, which proved fruitless, and in the Franco-Austrian war he commanded a force that was not called into action. For a short time he took the place of Count Grüner at the head of the war office. In 1861 he replaced Benedek, during a temporary absence, in the command of the Austrian forces in the Lombardo-Venetian kingdom. In the war of 1866 he held the supreme command of the imperial Austrian army of the South, and, as already described, inflicted upon the Italians a severe blow in the battle of Custozza. After the defeat of Sadowa he superseded Benedek as commander-in-chief of the imperial forces.

THE CROWN PRINCE OF SAXONY.

This prince was possessed of excellent military qualities, and would probably have been more fortunate in the war of Bohemia had he not been fighting, in the opinion of many of his father's subjects and soldiers, against the German cause. Descended from one of the oldest reigning houses in Europe, which gave an emperor to Germany in the tenth century, the prince, whose name is Frederick Augustus Albert, was born in 1828. Though his father is known as the German translator of Dante, and his uncle the late king was celebrated as a botanist, the present crown prince was trained to the profession of arms, and as lieutenant-general was made commander of the infantry force of Saxony. Commander of the Saxon army in 1866, he found himself obliged to retire from his own country before the superior force of Prince Frederick Charles of Prussia, and he joined the Austrian army in Bohemia with a force of 25,000 combatants and sixty guns. He was hotly engaged in the battle of Gitschin, and obstinately defended the village of Diletz, but his gallant troops fell in heaps before the murderous needle-gun, and he, his father, and country had to submit to the will of the conqueror, whose terms, though hard enough, would have been still more humiliating to Saxony but for the intervention of the French emperor.

FELDZEUGMEISTER LOUIS VON BENEDEK.

This general was born in 180-1 at Œdenbourg in Hungary, the son of a doctor. He studied military science in the academy at Neustadt, entered the Austrian army in 1822 as cornet, and rose rapidly to the rank of colonel, which he attained in 1843. Two years later, at the time of the insurrection in Galicia, having distinguished himself by his courage and military talents, he was commissioned by the Archduke Ferdinand d'Este to make peace with the western part of the province. His skilful movements there enabled General Collin to march forward and take Podgorze by storm. On this occasion Benedek obtained the insignia of the Order of Leopold. In 1847 he was at the head of the Comte de Giulai's regiment of infantry, when he received orders to rejoin the army of Italy. During the campaign of 1848 he showed much presence of mind in the retreat from Milan, at Osone, and especially at the battle of Curtatone, where he was the last to withstand the enemy's attacks. Lauded for distinguished service in the order of the day by Marshal Eadetzki, he was presented with the Order of Maria Theresa.

On the renewal of hostilities in 1849 he was present at the surrender of Mortara, and fought at the head of his regiment at Novara. On the 3rd April, 1849, Benedek was appointed major-general and brigadier of the first reserve corps of the army of the Danube, and took an active part in the military affairs of Hungary. At Kaab and at Oszöny he commanded the vanguard, and was slightly wounded at Uj-Szegedin. At the battle of Szörnyeozs-Ivány he was hurt by the explosion of a shell. At the end of this war he went into the second corps of the army in Italy, in the capacity of chief of the staff.

During the war of 1859 against Piedmont and France he covered the Austrian retreat from Milan to the Mincio, and at the battle of Solferino he commanded the right Austrian wing, which at one instant had the advantage over the left wing of the allies. He afterwards supplied the place of Marshal Hess in the chief command of the army. After the peace of Villafranca the feldzeugmeister remained in Venetia at the head of the Austrian troops, and the proclamations which he made to his soldiers attracted much notice, as eloquent appeals, calculated to keep them faithful to their allegiance, despite the variety of nationalities and the differences of their political opinions. In 1866, after much caballing and opposition on the part of the aristocratic party at the court of Vienna, which would confer high rank and supreme power on nobody less than an archduke, he was raised to the command of the army, which consisted of 250,000 men, and had a fine artillery of 600 guns. That he was beaten so disastrously by the Prussians was due perhaps as much to the defective organization of the force he commanded, and, as is said, to the reluctant obedience of some of his high-titled subordinates, as to the superior strategy of the Prussian generals.

RESULTS OF THE WAR TO THE TWO COMBATANTS.

The results of the contest carried on by these men and their followers was to Prussia, first of all, a gain of territory to the following extent. To the nine provinces of which the kingdom previously consisted were added by incorporation, Hanover, Hesse Cassel, Nassau, Hesse-Homburg, Schleswig-Holstein, and Lauenburg; that part of Hesse-Darmstadt that lies to the north of the Maine, and the little principality of Hohenzollern—the cradle of the Prussian royal house, situated on the borders of Lake Constance, between Würtemburg and Switzerland. Prussia was thus formed into a compact state of 137,066 square miles, with a population of 22,769,436 souls. Added to this was her leadership of the new Confederation into which Saxony and other minor powers were compelled to fall after the victory of Sadowa. The basis of a new German empire was firmly laid by Prussian genius and valour; and to Prussia rightly belonged the headship which it is fervently to be hoped she will not abuse.

The ancient Germanic empire was dissolved in 1806 by the Conqueror Napoleon I., reconstituted as a confederacy of thirty-nine states by the peacemakers of Vienna in 1815, again dissolved in 1866, and partially restored, without Austria, after the treaty of Prague, as the North German Confederation. Pending their final union under one government, presciently wrote Mr. Martin in his Year-book of 1869—pending that union which every patriotic German felt to be certain of speedy accomplishment—the old states of the Confederation were ranged provisionally in two groups, North Germany and South Germany. The former, including twenty-one states, was placed under the absolute undivided leadership of Prussia; while South Germany, numbering five states, formed an unconnected cluster of semi-independent sovereignties. The two divisions were to some extent bound together by treaties of peace and alliance between Prussia and the three principal states of the south, Bavaria, Würtemburg, and Baden. By the treaty between Prussia and Bavaria, dated August 22, 1866, the two contracting powers mutually guaranteed the integrity of their respective territories, with all the military forces at their disposal; it being further stipulated that, in case of war, the king of Prussia should have the supreme command of the Bavarian army. The treaties between Prussia and Würtemburg, and Prussia and Baden, dated 26th August and 18th August, 1866, were precisely of the same tenour, both providing a strict military alliance and union of armies in time of war. These diplomatic achievements, which in the autumn of 1866 crowned the victorious war, were followed in the spring of 1867 by legislative acts of no less importance. A representative assembly elected by universal suffrage, at the rate of one member for 100,000 souls, met at Berlin on the 24th of February, and by the 16th of April had discussed and adopted a constitutional charter, by which the whole of the states of North Germany were united into a federative empire. The charter entitled "the constitution of the North German Confederation," consists of fifteen chapters, comprising seventy-nine articles, with a preamble declaring that the governments of the states enumerated form themselves into a perpetual confederation or union for the protection of the territory and institutions of the union, and for the care of the German people's welfare. The twenty-one states enumerated in the charter are, Prussia, Saxony, Mecklenburg-Schwerin, Oldenburg, Brunswick, Saxe-Weimar, Mecklenburg-Strelitz, Saxe-Meiningen, Anhalt, Saxe-Coburg-Gotha, Saxe-Altenburg, Waldeck, Lippe-Detmold, Schwarzburg-Sondershausen, Schwarzburg-Rudolstadt, Reuss-Schleiz, Reuss-Greiz, Schaumburg-Lippe, Hamburg, Lubeck, and Bremen. When it is recollected that Henry, the twenty-second Prince of Reuss-Greiz, reigned over a population of about 40,000 souls, and that the public income of his realm was less than £30,000, and that six or seven of his co-princelets were in no better condition, the reader will doubtless sympathize with the strong German feeling that desired to see these frittered atoms of power welded together in one mighty sceptre. The executive power of the confederation was vested in the Prussian crown. The king of Prussia, under the title of Lord President, had to act on behalf of the Confederation in its intercourse with foreign states. To him was given the right of appointing ambassadors, of declaring war, or of concluding peace. He also had to appoint a chancellor of the Confederation, who should preside over the Federal council, and his first and inevitable choice was Count von Bismarck. The lord president enforces the observance of federal laws, and has the right to compel disobedient or negligent members to fulfil their federal duties. He has also the unrestricted command of the army and navy of the federation, the organization of the naval service, and the appointment of all officers and civil functionaries. The contributions of the several states in the Confederation to the cost of the general administration, is regulated by the rate of population.

By the terms of the charter the legislative power of the Confederation was vested in two representative bodies; the first delegated by the various governments, called the Federal Council, or Bundesrath, and the second elected by the population, and styled the Diet of the realm, or "Reichstag." To the council each of the twenty-one governments of the Confederation sends a deputy, who has one vote with the following exceptions:—The deputies from Brunswick and Mecklenburg-Schwerin have two votes each, the delegate of Saxony has four votes, and the representative of Prussia seventeen; making a total of forty-two votes, and giving the Prussian government a preponderance that may easily be turned into an absolute majority, by the subservience of one or two neighbouring states. The Diet is elected by universal suffrage for the term of three years, and meets in annual session. It is independent of the council, but the members of that body have the right to be present at the sittings, in order to make known the views of their respective governments. The initiative of legislative acts belongs to the Diet.

Austria, the other antagonist in the war of 1866, though suffering deeply in every point that was dear to her ancient traditionary policy, was yet not irreparably injured. Indeed, in many respects, she will no doubt discover in the course of time that her disasters of that year were pregnant with future national benefits. She lost Venetia, and with it happily the Lombardo-Venetian debt, which was transferred to Italy by the terms of the treaty of Prague; but her own debt was augmented by the addition of three hundred million florins (£30,000,000), by reason of the war. Her military and financial position was severely shaken, and for a time there was danger of internal disruption, owing to the universal dissatisfaction of the people of Hungary. She was thrust out, too, of the German Confederation, a circumstance far from agreeable to her 8,000,000 German subjects. Grown wiser at last, and profiting by the hard lessons they had received, the emperor and his ministers set sincerely to work at reforming the evils complained of by the several nationalities of the empire. To the Germans were granted free speech, free press, free education, and a popular Parliament. The pope and his cardinals were told that perfect toleration in matteis of religion would henceforth be observed throughout the empire, and that the stringent provisions of the last concordat would cease to operate. To Hungary was restored her national constitution, which is of very ancient date, and is based mainly upon unwritten laws that have acquired authority in the course of centuries. Austria, in fact, became a bipartite state, consisting of a German monarchy headed by the emperor, and a Magyar kingdom, with the self-same chieftain bearing the ancient title of king.

The constitution granted in 1849, after the great revolutionary outbreak, had been repealed by an imperial decree of the 31st of December,1851, which substituted a more absolute form of government. New edicts in the ensuing years altered the national charter, until by a patent of February 26, 1861, the constitution was established which, though suspended in the years 1865 and 1866, has been since 1867 the form of government prevailing in the empire. Very significantly the path of political reform in Austria, and of reconciliation with Hungary, was entered upon by a ministry led by Baron von Beust, an ancient rival of Count von Bismarck in the old Diet, and for some time the prime minister of the king of Saxony. The main features of the new constitution are a double legislature, connected together under one sovereign, the hereditary emperor-king, by a common army and navy and by a governing body known as the Delegations. The Delegations form a Parliament of 120 members, of whom one half are chosen by the legislature of German or Cisleithan Austria, and the other half represent Hungary, the Transleithan kingdom. The Upper House of each kingdom returns twenty deputies, the Lower House forty. In all matters affecting the affairs of the whole empire, the Delegations have a decisive vote, which requires neither the confirmation nor approbation of the assemblies from which they spring Austrians and Hungarians sit generally in separate chambers; but when disagreements arise, the two bodies of delegates meet together, and without further debate give a final vote, which is binding for the whole empire. Specially within the jurisdiction of the Delegations are all matters affecting foreign affairs, war, and finance, involving an executive of three ministers representing those three departments, who are severally and solely responsible to the Delegations.

The separate constitution of German Austria, or Cisleithania, consists, first, of the Provincial Diets, representing the various states of the monarchy; and secondly', a Central Diet, called the Reichsrath, or Council of the Empire. There are fourteen Provincial Diets, namely, for Bohemia, Dalmatia, Galicia, Higher Austria, Lower Austria, Salzburg, Styria, Carinthia, Carniola, Bukowina, Moravia, Silesia, Tyrol and Vorarlberg, Istria and Trieste; all which are formed in nearly the same manner, differing only in the number of deputies. Each consists of one assembly only, composed, first, of the archbishop and bishops of the Roman Catholic and Oriental Greek churches, and the chancellors of universities; secondly, of the representatives of great estates, elected by all landowners paying not less than 100 florins, or £10, taxes; thirdly, of the representatives of towns, elected by those citizens who possess municipal rights; fourthly, of the representatives of boards of commerce and trade unions, chosen by the respective members; and fifthly, of the representatives of rural communes, elected by such inhabitants as pay a small amount of direct taxation. The Provincial Diets are competent to make laws concerning local administration, particularly those affecting county taxation, the cultivation of the soil, educational, church, and charitable institutions, and public works executed at the public expense.

The Reichsrath, or Parliament of the western part of the empire, consists of an Upper and a Lower House. The Upper House is formed—1st, of the princes of the imperial family who are of age; 2nd, of a number of nobles—sixty-two in the present Reichsrath—possessing large landed property, on whom the emperor may confer the dignity of state councillors; 3rd, of the archbishops and bishops who are of princely rank; and 4th, of any other life-members, nominated by the emperor on account of being distinguished in art or science, or who have rendered signal services to church or state, of whom there are forty-seven in the present Reichsrath. The Lower House is composed of 203 members, elected by the fourteen Provincial Diets of the empire, in the following proportions:—Bohemia, 54; Dalmatia, 5; Galicia, 38; Higher Austria, 10; Lower Austria, 18; Salzburg, 3; Styria, 13; Carinthia, 5; Carniola, 6; Bukowina, 5; Moravia, 22; Silesia, 6; Tyrol and Vorarlberg, 12; Istria and Trieste, 6. The election for the Lower House of the Reichsrath is made in the assembled Provincial Diets, the elected deputies to be members of such Diets. The emperor has the right, however, to order the elections to take place directly by the various constituencies of the provincial representatives, should the Diets refuse or neglect to send members to the Reichsrath. The emperor nominates the presidents and vice-presidents of both chambers of the Reichsrath, the remaining functionaries being chosen by the members of the two Houses. It is incumbent upon the head of the state to assemble the Reichsrath annually. The rights which, in consequence of the diploma of October 20, 1860, and the patent of February 26, 1861, are conferred upon the Reichsrath, are as follows:—1st, Consentient authority with respect to all laws relating to military duty; 2nd, Co-operation in the legislature on trade and commerce, customs, banking, posting, telegraph, and railway matters; 3rd, Examination of the estimates of the income and expenditure of the state; of the bills on taxation, public loans, and conversion of the funds; and general control of the public debt. To give validity to bills passed by the Reichsrath, the consent of both chambers is required, as well as the sanction of the head of the state. The members of both the Upper and the Lower House have the right to propose new laws on subjects within the competence of the Reichsrath, but in all other matters the initiative belongs solely to the government.

The executive of Austria Proper consists, under the emperor, of the following branches of administration:—1st, the president of the council; 2nd, the ministry of finance; 3rd, the ministry of the interior and national defence; 4th, the ministry of public education and ecclesiastical affairs; 5th, the ministry of commerce and agriculture; 6th, the ministry of justice. The responsibility of ministers for acts committed in the discharge of their official functions was established, for the first time, by a bill which passed the Reichsrath in July, 1867, and received the sanction of the emperor.

The constitution of the eastern part of the empire, or the kingdom of Hungary, including Hungary Proper, Croatia, Slavonia, and Transylvania, is of very ancient date, and based mainly upon unwritten laws that grew up in the course of centuries. There exists no charter, or constitutional code, but in place of it are fundamental statutes, published at long intervals of time. The principal of them, the "Aurea Bulla" of King Andrew II., was granted in 1222, and changed the form of government, which had until then been completely autocratic, into an aristocratic monarchy. Almost all subsequent rulers endeavoured, though with little or no success, to extend the royal prerogatives, the struggle lasting, with more or less interruption, till the year 1867, when the present king, having failed in his attempt to weld Hungary to his imperial dominions, acknowledged and took oath upon the ancient constitution. The form of government established by it is oligarchical in essence, leaving the whole legislation and internal administration of the country in the hands of the native nobility, comprising above half a million individuals, and giving to the king little more than the chief command of the army, and the right and duty to protect the realm against foreign enemies. The power of legislation and of taxation is vested in two great representative bodies; the first the Diet, or Parliament, and the second the County Meetings. Since 1562 the Diet consists of an upper and lower house, the first known as the Chamber of Magnates, and the second as the Chamber of Deputies. The Chamber of Magnates is composed, first, of the prelates, comprising thirty-five Roman Catholic and twelve Greek archbishops and bishops, headed by the primate, the archbishop of Gran; secondly, of the "barones et comites regni" or peers of the realm, in two classes; thirdly, of the great officers of the crown, with the lords-lieutenant of the fifty-two counties; and fourthly, the barons summoned by royal letters, including every prime count and baron of twenty-five years of age. Magnates who are absent depute representatives, as do also the widows of magnates; but these deputies sit in the second Chamber, where they can speak, but have no vote. The Lower Chamber is made up of representatives of the towns and rural districts of the kingdom, the latter elected at the County Meetings. Much of the business of the Lower Chamber is previously discussed in a committee of the whole house, called a "circular session," in which strict forms are not observed, and each member speaks as often as he can get a hearing. The speeches in both chambers are usually made in Hungarian. Among the magnates some few speak Latin; but this language has almost entirely fallen into disuse. The "personal" or president of the Lower Chamber, who is also chief judge of the "royal table," is appointed by the crown. When the Diet assembles the "propositions" of the crown are first presented to it for consideration, and these form the great business of each session; but proposals also originate in the Lower Chamber, which, when agreed to by the Magnates, are sent to the king, who communicates his assent by a royal "resolution." Many propositions rejected by the crown are voted anew in every Diet, under the title of "Gravamina." Scarcely inferior in political importance to the Diet are the County Meetings. They are of two kinds, called respectively "Restorations "and "Congregations." In the former the parliamentary deputies, as well as all county officers, are chosen, while the latter are occupied with local legislation and taxation, and the general business of the district. A large amount of this business consists in iraming instructions for the representatives at the Diet, who are considered mere delegates, bound to adhere to the will of their constituents, to whom they apply for directions in all difficult or doubtful questions. The County Meeting may even recall a refractory member, and send another in his place, thus assuming direct control over the Diet. The executive is exercised, in the name of the king, by a responsible ministry, consisting of eight departments, namely:—1st, the presidency of the council; 2nd, the ministry of national defence; 3rd, the ministry of finance; 4th, the ministry of the interior; 5th, the ministry of education and of public worship; 6th, the ministry of justice; 7th, the ministry of public works; 8th, the ministry of agriculture, industry, and commerce; 9th, the ministry for Croatia and Slavonia.

The sovereign of Hungary, though emperor of Austria, is styled "king" in all public acts, and the regalia of the crown are guarded by a special corps of halberdiers in the palace at Buda, whence they are only removed for the sovereign's use on state occasions. The grand officers of the court and household are numerous, and are termed "aulae ministeriales." These are the grand justiciary, or "index curiae;" the ban of Croatia; the arch-treasurer, or "tavernicorum regalium magister;" the great cup-bearer, or "pincernarum reg. mag;" the grand carver, or "dapiferorum reg. mag.;" the master of the household, or "agazonum reg. mag.;" the grand porter, or "janitorum reg. mag.;" the master of the ceremonies, or "curiae reg. mag.;" and the captain of the body guard, or "capitaneus nobilis turmae praetorianae." The exchequer is managed by the "Hofkammer," which has its seat at Buda, and under which are the collectors of taxes, the mining boards, and the directors of the crown domains.

Modern history, says a recent writer, exhibits no such example of the hopeless confusion and seemingly inevitable dissolution of a great historical power, as Austria afforded after the defeat of Sadowa. At the close of 1866 men thought that the empire was falling asunder, and that nowhere among its fifteen nationalities, all strangers to each other in language and race, was there any conscious principle of Austrian unity and independence. At least, no such idea showed anywhere signs of life. Many able politicians considered that the disappearance of Austria from the map was only a question of time; and prudent statesmen thought it necessary to make this eventuality a factor in their calculations of the future. Neither Prussia after Jena, nor the French empire after Moscow, Leipzig, and Waterloo, nor Austria herself during the Revolution of 1848, can be compared with Austria after the peace of Prague. Conquered and prostrate, owing her nominal existence to the selfish intercession of doubtful friends, shut out from Germany, despaired of but hardly regretted by her peoples, with her forces demoralized and dissolved in spite of their victories in Italy and on the Adriatic, and on the brink of national bankruptcy, Austria saw her rival and conqueror rise in a few weeks from a dubious rank to be supreme over Germany, and the dictator of Central Europe, whose commands no one of the great powers ventured to gainsay, and whose apparent tendencies to national unity found a ready echo either in the hopes and admiration, or in the fears and hallucinations, of the German populations and their princes.

COUNT VON BEUST.

Three years passed, and the relative position of the two German powers was greatly modified by the revival of Austria and the reform of her institutions. The principal author of these reforms was Count von Beust, whose name will henceforth be inseparably connected with this remarkable epoch in Austrian history. At the beginning of the war of 1866 he accompanied his then master, the king of Saxony, into Austria to oppose the Prussian invasion. There was an ancient antagonism, dating from long past discussions in the Frankfort Diet, between Beust and Bismarck; and when peace was made between Saxony and Prussia after Sadowa, the latter insisted upon the dismissal of the former from the council of the Saxon king. Though the minister of a small state, he had frequently been concerned in questions of European importance. By a curious coincidence, he had taken a peculiar part in the Prussian crisis which ended in the elevation of Count von Bismarck to the premiership, and the count's hostility was not diminished by these little known circumstances.

Frederick Ferdinand, Baron von Beust, was born at Dresden on the 13th January, 1809. Brother to the eminent Saxon geologist, Frederick Constantine Beust, he studied with him at Gottingen, where he acquired a taste for politics and diplomacy, under the teaching of Sartorius, Heeren, Eichorn, and men of like calibre. He underwent his examinations and took his degrees at Leipzig, and on his return to Dresden, in 1831, he entered the foreign office of the Saxon government. After holding the post of assessor of land-survey in 1832, he spent between two and three years in visiting Switzerland, France, and England. He became secretary of the Saxon legation at Berlin in 1836, occupied the same post at Paris in 1838, was chargé d'affaires at Munich in 1841, resident minister in London in 1846, and ambassador to the court of Berlin in 1848. In February, 1849, he was appointed minister for Foreign Affairs for Saxony in the so-called Held cabinet, and received the portfolio for Agriculture in the following May. He took a prominent part in the discussions preceding the treaty of 1852, and in 1853 became minister of the Interior, when he resigned his post as minister of Agriculture. At the time of the crisis brought on by the question of constitutional organization, he declared himself opposed to the constitution, claimed the support of Prussia, and became a member of the Zchinsky cabinet as minister for Foreign Affairs, and of Public Worship also. In this latter capacity he introduced several improvements into the administration of ecclesiastical affairs. On the breaking out of the Danish war in 1863, Baron von Beust distinguished himself by his fidelity to Federal interests, and by a rebuke he administered to Lord Russell in answer to a despatch from the latter. He represented the Germanic Diet at the London Conference of 1864, during the continuance of which he twice visited Paris to confer with the Emperor Napoleon, whose guest he was afterwards at Fontainebleau.

A short time after the peace of Prague, it was proposed to make him foreign minister at Vienna. He had had ample means of studying the affairs of Austria, and had also become acquainted with her populations. But his position only gave him a single voice in the council of ministers, and that not a decisive one in home affairs. There were many people who, at his accession to office, thought it safe to predict for him a speedy fall, as soon as he proved an obstacle to Belcredi and Esterhazy. The public at large received him with little confidence, and with small expectation of his liberal principles being carried out. For they did not reflect on the peculiar conditions which affected the system he had administered amongst the middle states. Napoleon III. showed that he understood him better, when he said to him, "Saxony is too small for you." His first act as minister was to issue the pacific circular of the 2nd November, in which he defined his position. In this circular he protested that he came to his post perfectly free from all resentment and all predilection, and that the imperial government, whose urgent duty it was to efface the traces of a disastrous war, would remain faithful to its policy of peace and conciliation. On the emperor's return to Vienna, Baron von Beust received the further appointment of minister of the household.

To the new minister a hearty reconciliation with Hungary was a matter of primary importance. Renewed negotiations were opened at Vienna with the deputation from Pesth, to which place Baron von Beust went on the 21st December with the Hungarian chancellor. It appeared certain that this business had been taken out of the irresolute hands of Belcredi and the reactionists, and the lock in the cabinet was at an end. Still Beust's original and comprehensive ideas had by no means prevailed. Many such brave beginnings had within the last twenty years withered beneath the powerful court influence of the Austrian nobility and clergy. It was not likely that a foreigner, a Protestant, a "small baron," should succeed in breaking down the bulwark of tenacious traditions, exclusive interests, and inveterate prejudices. Or if he gained a momentary success, there were still intriguers and flatterers to catch him in their more deceitful toils. Again, there was no demonstration that he was master of any extraordinary ideas, bold schemes, or daring resolutions, or that he had the energy and prudence to carry them out. In his new career he had not yet succeeded: in his old one he had been baffled. Thus the year 1866 was drawing to a close, amidst the intense expectation of the patriots, when suddenly, just at its end, on the 28th December, a purely absolutist decree ordered the immediate completion of the army, and a new regulation of public defence for the whole empire, except the Military Frontier. This blunder of his rivals, and similar unconstitutional propositions, brought on a crisis in the cabinet, and Baron von Beust threatened to resign. He gained his point. A complete rupture was made with the system hitherto prevailing; and an imperial decree of the 4th of February restored the operation of the constitution so far as it did not affect the compromise with Hungary. Three days afterwards Belcredi and Esterhazy were dismissed; and Beust then became president of the council, minister for Foreign Affairs, and chancellor of the empire. Deak was called to Vienna, and had an interview of special importance with the emperor. The principles of the revived constitution were clearly defined; and the question now was, whether the practice would answer to the theory. It was a time of deliberate and decisive measures, and complete reconciliation with Hungary was resolved on.

The Reichsrath was not assembled before the 20th of May, nor the convoking patent issued before the 26th of April, because it was necessary that the Hungarian Parliament should have previously accepted a compromise compatible with imperial government. Here also there were difficulties; the democratic party in the Hungarian Parliament maintained an obstinate fight for ten days in favour of the merely personal union; and the victory, at one time considered doubtful, was only obtained by a brilliant speech from Deak, which was followed by a division of 257 against 117 on the 30th of March, 1867.

In the Upper House the compromise was unanimously accepted, after an insignificant opposition, on the 3rd of April. And now the regeneration of the eastern part of the monarchy seemed to be accomplished; and Baron von Beust was entitled to regard with complacency the results of his system and of his efforts. But he could not forget that as yet he had only half finished his task of reconstruction; for he had to persuade the Reichsrath to accept, *après coup*, a compromise on which it had not been consulted, and he had to establish the constitutional institutions of the western portion of the empire on another basis of compromise altogether foreign to Hungarian wants and tendencies.

The chancellor's popularity was rapidly increasing, but he could not easily make a strong ministerial party in the Austrian Chambers. Hungarian jealousy being allayed, however, the questions connected with the army, finance, and foreign affairs were settled in the Reichsrath without much opposition. A very important novelty was introduced at the same time into the administration by the baron, in the form of the Red Book—the first of a series of publications of diplomatic papers and parliamentary debates, on the affairs of the whole Austro-Hungarian monarchy. The documents gave evidence of a clear, consequent, and uniform policy, that inspired confidence both by its directness and its freedom. The Prussian press attacked the Red Book, and suggested to the Hungarians that it was a covert for imperial intrigues; but their inuendoes did no harm to Austria. The Reichsrath, under the guidance of the chancellor, did noble work in the session of 1868; confirmed the compromise with Hungary, reviewed the concordat with Rome, and in fine, rebuilt the constitution of the Austrian empire. The following extracts from speeches of the chancellor and of the emperor will show how minister and master agreed in their views, and what great things they were enabled thus to work out for their country.

At the end of October, Baron von Beust having in his speech on the army budget represented the political situation of Europe as rather critical, was reminded that Lord Stanley, the English foreign minister, had a short time before spoken of it in more favourable terms; upon which he said, "My position differs materially from that of the English secretary of State. Lord Stanley is the minister of a country surrounded and protected by the sea: I have the honour of directing the affairs of a state which has every reason to beware of its neighbours. We should, of course, be glad to be on friendly terms with Prussia, and are even endeavouring to improve our relations with the St. Petersburg cabinet; but, as I said, we must be on our guard, though there is nothing to excite our immediate fears."

There was, however, little confidence at Vienna in either Prussia or Russia. "That Austria's military preparations are merely defensive, remarked the semi-official journal, must be plain to any one that is not wilfully blind. To assume the contrary is simply to offend against common sense, or to enact over again the old story of the lamb and the wolf. But, of course, we owe it to our own interests not to allow ourselves to be netted and bagged. Our rival is showing an unmistakable intention of reviving the Oriental question, to enable him to cross the Maine. It is this policy which encourages Russia to assume a haughty and menacing attitude towards Western Europe, and which is evidently intent on encompassing Austria with flames of revolutionary fire, from the Red Tower Pass to the Alps, from the River Save to the Boeca di Cattaro." In October, Baron von Beust made a speech, justifyingthe necessity of keeping the Austrian army on the war footing of 800,000 men. "Austria," he said, "maintains the best relations with France and England, and is also upon the most friendly footing with Italy. The latter power, however, has not always complete freedom of action. Austria remains unchanged in her resolve to abandon all policy of revenge against Prussia, while with Russia she seeks to maintain friendly relations. In view, however, of the possibility of a conflict between France and Prussia, Austria is obliged to remain armed, as much to cause her own neutrality to be respected, as to keep back other powers who might be inclined to attack."

To the same effect was the emperor's address to the army on the 8th December:—"The monarchy wants peace; we must know how to maintain it. For this purpose I have had presented to both legislatures a bill by which, in case of necessity, the whole population may rise in arms to defend the dearest interests of the country. Both legislatures have passed it, and I have sanctioned it. The re-organization of the empire has been effected on those historical bases on which it reposed in the times when it fought out the most difficult wars successfully. Both sides of my empire will have henceforth the same interests in defending its security and power. My army thereby gains an auxiliary which will support it in good and ill fortune. My people, without distinction of class, will now, according to the law, rank under my colours proudly. Let the army be the school of that courage without which empires cannot maintain themselves. My army has gone through hard trials, but its courage is not broken, and my faith in it is not shaken. The path of honour and loyalty, on which the brave sons of my empire have followed hitherto, may be their path henceforth too. Let them be faithful to their past, and bring with them the glorious traditions of former times. Progressing in science, and in the spirit of the times strengthened by new elements, it will inspire respect to the enemy, and be a stronghold of throne and empire."

In his speech on closing the Diet, as king of Hungary, he said, "We called you together three years ago, under difficult and anxious circumstances, to accomplish a great task. Our common aim and endeavour has been to solve all those questions which, not only in these last times, but for centuries, have been the sources of distrust and of collisions. I having been crowned with the crown of St. Stephen, inherited from my ancestors, the Hungarian constitution has become a full reality. The union of Hungary and Transylvania, of Croatia and Sclavonia, has become an accomplished fact, and the integrity of the empire of St. Stephen has been restored in a way in which it has not existed for the last three hundred years. You have recognized the necessity of a common army; you have inaugurated a system of education which will serve as a support to material and intellectual progress. You have extended the civil and political rights which the citizens belonging to the different races had already enjoyed, to the use of their language likewise, granting all those wishes which are not in opposition to the law and good government. You have extended political rights to the Israelites, who, until now, knew only the charges, and not the advantages, of the constitution. You have regulated the relations of the different confessions on the basis of civil and religious equality. By the new regulation of judicial procedure you have facilitated the prompt administration of justice and the consolidation of private credit. The symptoms of material and moral improvement which are apparent everywhere may fill your hearts with joy, and if once the success follows with which Providence rewards perseverance and energy, posterity will gratefully remember those who have been the instruments of the welfare of the country. May the Almighty make this loyal understanding lasting—this understanding which has not only produced great political results, but which has linked together sovereign and people in the bonds of mutual confidence and love, and which has made us feel that only a happy nation can have a happy sovereign." Noble words spoken with royal frankness and sincerity, and exhibiting a picture of national revival in the space of three years, hardly to be paralleled in the history of nations.

DEAK FERENCZ.

The peaceful restoration of Austria to the rank of a great power could hardly have been brought about in so brief a space of time, spite of the able efforts of Count von Beust, had it not been for the extraordinary influence and wise moderation of one man, Deak the Hungarian patriot. In him, says M. de Laveleye, we see a simple lawyer, unknown to Europe, borne to the head of an heroic nation by dint of his public virtue alone, dictate the conditions of the reconstitution of the Austrian empire, confirm to the descendant of so many emperors the crown of St. Stephen, and by wielding the confidence of his fellow citizens, determine the fate of that powerful state at a time of momentous crisis. A sketch of his life and opinions cannot but be instructive and interesting. Francis Deak, or Deak Ferencz (for in Hungary the practice is to place the baptismal name after that of the family), was born on the 13th of October, 1803, at Sojtor in the county of Zala, the son of a country gentleman, who farmed his own land. He was educated at Kaab, where also he entered the profession of law, and followed at the same time with eagerness the politics of the day. The resistance of the Magyars to the encroachments of the court at Vienna had been suspended during the Napoleonic wars, but broke out with fresh vigour about the time when the young advocate attained his majority. When after long delay the Diet was assembled at Presburg in 1825, a spirit of independence was manifested that thoroughly alarmed the imperial government. That was the "revival Diet." Deak engaged heart and soul in the contest. Entitled to take part in county meetings by his rank of gentleman (of whom there were 600,000 in the kingdom, for the most part poor as Job), and also by his position as member of a liberal profession, he soon distinguished himself as an orator at those quarterly assemblies. The appointment to local offices in Hungary is made almost always by popular election, and gives frequent occasion to animated debates. A strong supporter of modern ideas on the subject of personal freedom and equal justice for all, he was at the same time a staunch maintainer of the ancient privileges of his country, her language, her institutions, her nationality. He soon became the leader of his party in the county, and a fit and proper person to represent it in the National Assembly. He was elected, at the age of twenty-two, to succeed his brother as member for their native county in the Diet of 1825. He was well received by the opposition party, the party of progress, to which he belonged, at the head of which was the celebrated Count Széchenyi, and he was complimented by his first opponent in debate, Pazmandy. It was, however, in the Diet which sat from 1832 to 1836 that he came to the front rank. His speeches were lucid and convincing rather than brilliant, replete with knowledge and sound logic without much ornament. With these he came by degrees to master a most excitable assembly, which he patiently educated up to his own point of view. At the close of that Diet a word from Deak would command a majority. The government at Vienna obstinately opposed all the demands of the Magyars, and the Diet of 1839 came together full of anger. Deak, at the head of the opposition, forced an" amnesty from the government for the politicians of his party who had been imprisoned; and the ministry found it prudent to concert measures with him in order to secure the tranquillity of the country. This eminent position he had attained at the age of thirty-six. A robust broad-shouldered man, with short neck and round head, full of humour and geniality, thick eyebrows shading his shrewd yet kindly eyes. Like his celebrated English contemporary, Mr. Bright, there was no indication in his external appearance of the masterly intellect that controls popular assemblies, and wields them at pleasure by the power of oratory. Dressed in black, with an ivory-headed cane in his hand like a good Presburg burgher, he would meet the members of his party on the eve of a great debate in a club smoking room. After hearing all they had to say, he would give his opinion in a conversational tone, show the points on which all were agreed, and how the end was to be attained; indicate with precision the way to success, the weak point of the other side, what concessions could be made, and those points on which his friends must stand firm. He enlivened this common-sense exposition of the matter in hand with jocular comparisons and anecdotes, and ruled his fellow men with a sceptre of which the weight was not perceptible.

At the election of 1843 Deak had the courage to give his supporters a lesson which they would not soon forget. He had been thrown out at one election, by means of the unscrupulous employment of corruption and intimidation on the part of his adversaries. He was put up again, and his friends resolved to employ similar means to secure his return. Deak protested against this course, and vowed that he would not sit if returned, but they refused to believe him. He kept his word nevertheless, was elected and declined the seat, to the bitter chagrin of men who had spent themselves in conquering success for him, and who could see nothing but overstrained and inflated virtue in this desertion of his party. Deak's absence from the Chamber was deeply felt, and generally bewailed. In 1846 he was obliged to travel for the benefit of his health, and the years that immediately followed were occupied with the sad events of the revolutionary outbreak, and its suppression. He could not agree with the advanced opinions of Kossuth. "I am a reformer," he said, "not a revolutionist." Yet he would not oppose altogether the national party, though he was a firm supporter of union with Austria. The overthrow of 1848 and 1849 filled him with sadness, and drew from him the frequent exclamation, "It is the beginning of the end!" He formed part, however, as minister of Justice, of the ministry of Count Louis Batthyani, and found the labours of office at that period of change in legislation very great indeed. He worked at the emancipation of the peasantry, the amelioration of the criminal law, and the adoption of trial by jury. His desire to accomplish reconciliation and union with Austria by legal means, exposed him in those days of revolution to the charge of treachery, hurled against him by the democrats. He quitted the ministry in October, 1848, but not the Chamber. On the 31st December he was appointed, by a vote of both houses, one of the deputation that attempted to open a negotiation with Windischgrätz in his camp. When that misguided general refused to see the delegates, on the plea that he could not treat with rebels, the dogs of war were let loose, and Deak, who had not wished the revolution, but, on the contrary, had done his best to prevent it, withdrew from public life. He remained in retirement full ten years, living chiefly at Pesth, studying the progress of events around, distributing a share of his modest income in alms, and enjoying the society of his friends. In December, 1860, after the Austrian constitution had been decreed, Deak and his friend Eotvos had a long private conference with the emperor at Vienna, which seems to have given him hope that the breach between his country and the imperial government would soon be closed. On reaching home he at once re-entered public life with his old vigour. He was elected member for Pesth in the Diet of 1861, and had to exert all his talent and influence to induce the extreme radical party to follow moderate counsels. He achieved a great parliamentary triumph on the 13th May of that year, carrying his address to the emperor in the face of an adverse majority. This address was laid, as was well said at the time, on the threshold which divides Hungary from Austria, to be taken up by every emperor who goes to the "hill of coronation" to be crowned king of Hungary. The address was ill-received at Vienna, and met by an imperial rescript that irritated the Chamber at Pesth. The main point of difference was on the subject of representation— whether the Hungarians would, or would not, send their representatives to the German Reichsrath, and abandon their own ancient Diet; a decided negative was skilfully and respectfully drawn up by Deak. The Diet was dissolved on the 21st August, but Deak felt sure of victory sooner or later, and went to play his favourite game of quilles, or skittles, much to the disgust of his more excitable friends. Things went on thus, Deak keeping his people from insurrection, until 1865, when the emperor, aware that danger was thickening around him, made overtures to Deak, and paid a visit to Buda, where he was heartily received. A few months afterwards his Majesty in person opened the Diet in Pesth. Still the separate Hungarian ministry was not accorded, and the war of 1866 had to be borne with Hungary in a bad humour. After the peace of Prague, and the subsequent accession of Baron von Beust to the head of the ministry of Vienna, Deak's programme was accepted without discussion, and the dual form of government for the empire was established, practically leading to what, according to the Hungarians, was the only bond between the two countries of old, a personal union embodied in the sovereign. The Austrian chancellor and the Pesth deputy settled the matter between them. Imperfections in the scheme of dual government there were, which Deak felt equally with other men; but the agreement arrived at by him and Baron von Beust, in all probability, saved Austria from dissolution and Hungary from a dangerous decline. The sage of Hungary, as he was called, would receive no other reward for his services than the satisfaction of having rendered them. The emperor, the Diet, the ministry, pressed upon him various offers, but he declined them all. At the coronation of the king of Hungary, it is an ancient custom for the Count Palatine to ask the assembly present if they accept the sovereign elect, and then to place the crown upon the king's head. In 1867 there was no Count Palatine, the office being about to be abolished. A question arose as to who should have the honour of performing the ancient ceremonial. Every voice pronounced in favour of Deak, the creator of the new state of things, and the Diet by a unanimous vote appointed him to the honour. The patriot declined, gently at first, but when insistance was made, furiously; declaring that he would rather resign his seat in the House than consent to take so prominent and ostentatious a position. Though holding no office, Deak dictates the policy of the Hungarian government, whose supporters are known by the name of the "Deak party." His high position in the opinion of his countrymen does honour to the Hungarians, for he has neither the eloquence of Kossuth nor the brilliancy of Szèchenyi; but he appeals to the reason with all the force of sound logic, and persuades by force of common sense. He offers a striking contrast to the generality of his countrymen, fiery and romantic as they are; but it is by simplicity and purity of life, by earnestness of purpose and thorough disinterestedness, that he has so completely conquered their esteem and respect.

PRUSSIA AFTER THE PEACE OF PRAGUE.

The seal and sanction of public opinion in Germany was given to the great changes wrought by Prussia, by the Chambers which met in new session at Berlin on the 5th of August, 1866. The treaty of peace had not yet been ratified, and some of the speeches delivered in the Chambers exhibited a certain distrust of Austria and other powers. But the king and his ministers were forgiven their unparliamentary offences of preceding years; and the annexation of territory, as well as the subjection of minor states to absolute dependence on Prussia, by the formation of the new League or Confederation of North Germany, was cordially, if not unanimously approved. In the king's speech at the opening of the Chambers, not a word was said about France and the important part taken by the French emperor in bringing the war to a close by his mediation. Nor was Italy even mentioned. All that the king said was, that his army was supported "by few but faithful allies." These omissions naturally gave great offence both to Italy and France; and in France especially much irritation was felt in consequence.

The address of the Upper House sought to remedy the omission, and expressed its recognition of the disinterested mediation of a foreign power in the peace preliminaries. It declared the hopes of the Upper House that the separated portions of the monarchy would be united, and that the future frontier line of Prussia would form a guarantee for her security and her position as a great power. The noble "Herren," or Lords, were further of opinion, that after the withdrawal of Austria from the Germanic Confederation friendly relations would subsist between her and Prussia. The new organization of Germany would be the means of preventing any future bloodshed in conflicts between German states. The reform of the military organization, too, had been put to the test, and had been completely justified by the brilliant results obtained.

In bringing forward a bill for the incorporation of Hanover, Electoral Hesse, Nassau, and Frankfort, with the Prussian dominions, Count von Bismarck said that he hoped the Chambers would leave the details in the hands of the king, who would act with the necessary consideration. The preamble of the bill stated, that "Prussia did not embark in the war with the intention of acquiring territory. The hostile attitude of the above-named states required that their independence should cease. It was to be hoped that, in course of time, the populations of the annexed countries would be thoroughly satisfied with the incorporation." But a strong feeling was manifested by the Chamber that the Prussian constitutional charter should be introduced into the new provinces before the expiration of a year, instead of being postponed indefinitely, as the bill proposed. Count von Bismarck at once assented to this view, and said that, without consulting his colleagues, he would take it upon himself, in the name of the government, to approve of it. A few days afterwards (August 28) he accepted an amendment, which provided that the Prussian constitution should become law in Hanover, Nassau, Hesse-Cassel, and Frankfort, on the 1st October, 1867; and in the course of his speech he made some remarks that have a certain historical value.

"It was just possible," he said, "that Prussia would be called upon to vindicate the possession of what she had acquired. The first Silesian war produced a second and a third, and there was no telling whether they might not have to go through a similar succession of campaigns in the present instance. He therefore wished to have the matter promptly settled, so as to give foreign powers no further opportunity for interference. To do a necessary thing at once was to gain a double advantage from it. The cabinet had difficulties to contend with in various quarters, and might well expect the House to second its action, considering what the circumstances of the times were. The right of Prussia to annex the states mentioned was a more sacred right than that of conquest. It was from the right of Germany to live, breathe, and exist, that Prussia derived her commission to incorporate with her own body politic such *disjecta membra* of the nation as had been won in honest warfare. The interval between now and the extension of the Prussian constitution to the new provinces he would employ to proclaim the laws of military service in them, and establish the right of all subjects of the crown to reside and carry on trade in any part of the united kingdom. He had no doubt that, before loner, all classes in the states annexed would unite in acknowledging the wisdom of this proceeding. This was a transition period; but its attendant difficulties could be easily overcome by the adoption of the proper means. He was not surprised to find that, when people in the minor states had so long enjoyed an existence undisturbed by great political cares, there should be some among them averse to the duties of a more responsible position. But the great majority took a more extended view even now, and the rest would come round soon enough. In point of fact, the only choice they had was to become the citizens of a great German state, or to be at the mercy of foreign powers."

At a later period, a bill of indemnity to save the government from the consequences of having acted in violation of the law in preceding years, by collecting taxes which had not been voted by the Chambers, was passed by a large majority. The minister of the Interior stated, that by the adoption of the bill the government would be morally compelled to act in a friendly spirit towards the House. The indemnity was not an armistice with the government; its adoption would be the preliminaries of a real and lasting peace. This anxious desire on the part of a so-called despotic king and minister, for the sanction of their high-handed dealings by a law to be voted by Parliament, is very significant of the force of public opinion in Germany, and contains excellent promise for the future development of well-ordered freedom in that newly united country.

The king's reply to the address of the Lower House contained a sort of apology for the annexation of neighbouring territories:—"I thank you, gentlemen," he said, "for communicating to me the feelings of your illustrious body. To God alone be all honour. On setting out for the seat of war, I certainly hoped that we should be able to hold our own, as we always have. But I did not expect the rapid victories we achieved, and am doubly grateful to my gallant army for accomplishing them. Since the war I have been obliged to dispossess certain sovereigns, and annex their territories. I was born the son of a king, and taught to respect hereditary rights. If, in the present instance, I have nevertheless profited by the fortune of war to extend my territory at the cost of other sovereigns, you will appreciate the imperative necessity of the step. We cannot permit hostile armies to be raised in our rear, or in localities intervening between our provinces. To preclude the recurrence of such an event was a duty imposed upon me by the law of self-preservation. I have acted for the good of the country, and I beg you to convey my sentiments to the House."

To a deprecatory address from a Hanoverian deputation his Majesty used similar language, to the effect that annexation had become a duty on account of geographical position, and that the rapid victories which led to it were a visible interposition of Providence. Indeed, the national appetite for conquest was clearly not yet satisfied. In the debate on the bill for determining the mode of election to the new German Parliament (September 12), Count von Bismarck had to defend the government against a charge of not having profited sufficiently by the late victories. Again, in December he made a long and instructive speech in the Lower House on the question of the union of the duchies of Schleswig and Holstein with Prussia. It will be remembered that French influence was exerted to secure the cession of the northern part of Schleswig to Denmark, if, on an appeal to the inhabitants, they determined by a plebiscite in favour of such a re-annexation. The passages of the president's speech which relate to the attitude of France, and seem to excuse the deference shown to her in the negotiations at Prague, have no unimportant bearing on the present history. "Foreign nations," said the minister, "were accustomed to look upon us as abandoned to the tender mercies of France, and to make the permanent necessity of help, under which they fancied we were, their reason for speculating upon our indulgence and modesty. By Austria and a portion of our German allies, this speculation had been carried very far during the last ten years. But were they at all right in their fancies? War with France is not in the interests of this country. We have little to gain even by beating her. The Emperor Napoleon himself, differing in this from the accepted politics of other French dynasties, wisely recognized the fact that peace and mutual confidence should prevail between the two neighbouring nations.

But to maintain such relations with France, a strong and independent Prussia is alone competent. If this truth is not admitted by all subjects of Napoleon III., it is a consolation to know that his cabinet, at least, thinks differently, and that we officially, at any rate, have to deal with his cabinet only. Looking upon this vast country of Germany from the French point of view, his cabinet cannot but tell themselves that, to combine it again with Austria into one political whole, and make it a realm of 75,000,000 inhabitants, would be contrary to the French interests. Even if France could make the Rhine her boundary, she would be no match for so formidable a power, were it ever established beside her. To France it is an advantage that Austria does not participate any longer in our common Germanic institutions, and that a state whose interests conflict with her own in Italy and in the East, cannot henceforth constitutionally rely upon our armed assistance in war. It is natural for France to prefer a neighbour of less overwhelming might—a neighbour, in fact, whom 35,000,000 or 38,000,000 of French are quite strong enough to ward off from their boundary line in defensive war. If France justly appreciates her interests, she will as little allow the power of Prussia as that of Austria to be swept away. The present dynasty of France having identified itself with the principle of nationality, always looked upon the question of the duchies in a temperate way, and from the very outset was less adverse to our claims than any of the other powers.

"You are aware that to carry that principle through on the Dano-German frontier is simply impossible. Germans and Danes so intermingle there, that no line of demarcation can be drawn which will separate all members of the one race from those of the other. Yet France, wishing to see her adopted principle acknowledged in this particular instance, as in so many preceding ones, mooted the question, repeatedly bringing on a discussion between us, Denmark, and other powers. In all our communications with the powers, we never concealed it from them, that we would not allow our line of defence to be impaired by any territorial re-arrangement of the kind; but we also intimated that, under certain circumstances, we might be inclined to pay some regard to wishes assiduously uttered by the population, and undoubtedly ascertained by us. Thus the matter stood when, in July last, France was enabled, by the general situation of Europe, to urge her views more forcibly than before. I need not depict the situation of this country at the time I am speaking of. You all know what I mean. Nobody could expect us to carry on two wars at the same time. Peace with Austria had not yet been concluded; were, we to imperil the fruits of our glorious campaign by plunging headlong into hostilities with a new, a second enemy? France, then, being called on by Austria to mediate between the contending parties, as a matter of course did not omit to urge some wishes of her own upon us. We had to determine, not whether we thought the terms offered compatible with the expressed desires of the Schleswig-Holsteiners, but whether we were to accept or to reject in a body the overtures of Austria, as imparted through France. Long negotiations were impracticable under the circumstances. Our communications were interrupted, telegrams requiring three, or even six days to travel from our headquarters to Berlin. In this condition his Majesty determined to adopt the programme submitted to his decision. It is true we were strongly backed by Italy remaining true to her engagements, and standing by us with a fidelity which I cannot too highly appreciate and extol. The Italian government resisted the temptation thrown in its way by a present from Austria, of renouncing its alliance with us, and suspending military operations against the common enemy. This is a fact which I hope guarantees the continuance of friendly relations between Italy and Germany. But, notwithstanding the valuable aid rendered us by our Italian allies, both on the battlefield and in our diplomatic negotiations with friend and foe, we did not think ourselves justified in proceeding to extremities, and involving all Europe in war, merely because a single item of the terms proffered was unpalatable. Had we insisted upon having every thing our own way, the most serious complications might have arisen. I thought it my duty to advise his Majesty to sanction the terms submitted as they stood, rather than jeopardize our previous success and gamble for more."

In the result, the House resolved to postpone the question of the cession of Northern Schleswig to a later period. It has been stated quite recently by an Austrian in authority, that the Vienna cabinet committed an error in accepting French mediation so hastily. The Prussian minister had made proposals for a direct negotiation, in which no mention of any indemnity was made; and Austria would have been spared a fine of thirty million florins if she had only declined to avail herself of the assistance of France.

The failure to carry out the stipulations of the treaty of Prague relating to North Schleswig, has no doubt drawn much obloquy upon the government of King William. Germans in high station have openly disapproved, and some publicists have placed it side by side with the French occupation of Rome as an act politically immoral. The continued occupation, says one writer, of North Schleswig, which is Danish, by Prussia, not as resulting from a compliance with, but in defiance of, the provisions of the fifth article of the treaty of Prague in 1866, is not only a wrong done to Denmark, but it does violence to that European public opinion which Prussia, like France, is so anxious to conciliate. And not merely is this continued occupation a wrong, but it is a wrong of which the treatment and persecution of the Danish inhabitants by Prussia has largely increased the magnitude and intensity. Persecutions are spoken of, and the expulsion of clergymen and others, either actual or virtual, as the result of arbitrary and oppressive measures, in the teeth of the provisions of most solemn treaties. It is to be hoped that the conclusion of war will witness the payment by Count von Bismarck of a debt of strict though tardy justice to Denmark, at the instance of Germans themselves, who are not found wanting as individuals in a sense of justice or in genuine kindness both of heart and sentiment. There can be no reason why the relations between Prussia and Denmark should not be friendly for the future. If, as matter of fact, Germans have, by peaceful emigration, superseded in certain parts of Schleswig the earlier Danish population; and Germany, having taken possession of those parts by conquest, is now desirous of retaining them—that surely is no reason why, in defiance of recent treaty obligations, those parts of Schleswig in which the Danish element is all but unmixed, or at all events, very largely preponderant, should be incorporated with Germany, although the inhabitants most earnestly desire, and have a treaty right, to return to their old allegiance.

That appetite for annexation, which has hitherto distinguished Prussia, will not, it may be well hoped, characterize the policy of a strong united Germany. Germany has won success enough in the field, not merely to immortalize the prowess of her sons and Von Moltke's matchless organizing skill and strategy, but to protect her from all risk through future aggression. It is contrary to her interest to inspire in other nations, by territorial cupidity in Denmark or elsewhere, distrust and suspicion which might lead to a European coalition against her. The prospect for Europe would then be a dark one. To protect the independent and unmutilated existence of a certain number of small states, and to prevent their absorption in the military monarchies, is to maintain the best of guarantees for peace and liberty in Europe. It is this consideration which would seem to have actuated England and the English government in their efforts to maintain inviolate the neutrality and independence of Belgium. Prussia is strong enough to be just in the case of North Schleswig, without fear of consequences. She is victorious, and she is rich enough to be generous. She might now find in North Schleswig and Germany— perhaps may find elsewhere—a fit opportunity for giving to the world an example of those qualities of moderation and magnanimity which form the brightest jewels in the victor's crown. The heart which great successes leave untouched is cold indeed. But such is not the heart of Germany.

The really difficult part of the question so warmly argued is, doubtless, as it was in the case of Hanover, a geographical one. It must be well nigh impossible to draw a distinct line of demarcation between two races that intermingle, and having drawn it, to preserve it. The suspicion that Germany, under the guidance of Prussia, may become an aggressive military nation has almost no foundation. Her power rests upon a military system so onerous to a studious and a commercial people, that it cannot be imposed upon millions of men like the. Germans, save for the most sacred of causes—the spirit-stirring cause of their native country in danger. The vast Teutonic population of Central Europe has been possessed with a dominant idea of unity, that has rapidly increased in intensity in recent years. Germany, one and indivisible, homogeneous, united in policy and in principle, is the thought which inspires the bosom of every ardent German patriot. The realization of this thought involves sacrifice on the part of princes and people. The victory of an idea means the extinction of existing rights. All claims and appeals are silenced before it. The old order perishes to give place to the new. The unity of Germany is inevitable, even though France, the only possible opponent of the unification, should declare herself hostile to it. If France declare war against Germany, wrote a French writer in 1869, she will act for the advantage of militarism and Prussia; if she prove friendly to German unity, she will act for the advantage of European freedom.

DEVELOPMENT OF THE GERMAN FEELING FOR UNITY.

The origin of the enthusiasm that possesses the German race for the unity of their Fatherland, must be sought in past history. The people of Germany have had to undergo a harsh training in the school of adversity, before the need and advantage of having but one common interest have been fully realised. The teachings of this school were, unhappily for Germany, barren of results for nearly four hundred years. From the time of Kaiser Maximilian, the "white king," through the reigns of Charles V. and of the later emperors and empresses antagonists of Louis XIV., XV., and of Frederick, called the Great, down to the era of the French Revolution and the conquests of Napoleon I., Germany was, politically speaking, a sea of trouble, chiefly for want of political cohesion. Not till the beginning of the present century, when, perhaps, the cruelest lesson was given to the Germans, did they begin taking the precepts of calamity to heart, and endeavour to find some good in evil. The sad condition to which their country had been brought by disunion, at length startled them from their apathy. Then was born that passionate patriotism, of which the embers now burn with a brightness and steadfastness unequalled in any other nation.

The utter subjection to which Germany had been brought while the first Napoleon's star was at its zenith, was the immediate cause that kindled this glowing virtue. Nothing less than a national enthusiasm had the power to join discordant elements, and inspire men with that singleness of purpose necessary to break the chains that fettered a great people. The patriot Arndt thus described the manner in which he was affected by the sad consequences of disunion, "When after vain struggles Austria and Prussia both were fallen; then first my soul began to love them and Germany with real love, and to hate the French with a true and righteous rage. Just when Germany had perished by its disunion, my heart embraced the full notion of its oneness and its unity." This was spoken immediately after the heavy blows inflicted on his country by the battles of Austerlitz and Jena; when similar thoughts and feelings began to agitate the hearts of the whole German-speaking folk. Compelled at last by the disastrous plight in which their country lay, to sink their political differences and act in unison, the Germans succeeded in removing the ban of servitude under which they had so severely suffered. Thinking men, too, looked beyond the simple rescue of their land from the tyranny of a foreign yoke in 1813. They looked into the future, and saw Germany occupying the place among the powers of Europe she was entitled to, secured by her strength and concord against interruption from other nations in working out internal reform.

Voices were not wanting to express in ever living words the feelings that then swayed the German race. Nor were the writers of that period singers and preachers only. They were the great movers in the regeneration of Germany; by books and deeds they aroused and fanned the patriotic spirit of their countrymen to enthusiasm. Where statesmen had failed, poets met with success, and created a monument of their labours in the literature of patriotism—the most precious record of that time of Germany's struggle for freedom. Here may be read how the longing ol Germans for unity was engraven in their hearts, and acquired the sanctity of a religion. That, in spite of all opposition made by the jealousy of statecraft, in spite of the long frustration of their hopes, this desire is still so active, may be easily understood, when the influence of popular poetry is understood. "Give me the making of a nation's ballads, and I care not who makes its laws," said Fletcher of Saltoun, whom this sentence has perhaps made more memorable than any other act or speech of his. The history of the patriotic feeling that has pervaded Germany during the last fifty years, is an argument for the justice of the aphorism.

The literature of Germany is peculiarly rich in its store of patriotic songs, forming a reflex of events that have happened from the earliest times. So early as the first century, the Roman historian Tacitus considered the war songs of the Germans worthy of mention, from the influence they exercised on their spirits in battle. There are very few salient features in German history which will not be found registered in popular ballads. Whenever the people have been strongly moved by disaster or triumph, their feelings have sought expression in this shape. During the War of Independence in 1813 this was particularly the case, and from that period till the present day numerous song-writers have appeared, whose productions have acquired a popularity that has been owing as much to the fact of their having given a channel for the thoughts of the Germans, as to the intrinsic merit of the songs themselves.

Among the most distinguished of modern patriotic writers of Germany who stirred their countrymen from base submission, and moved them to throw off the yoke of the stranger, was Karl Theodor Koerner. Although the youngest of the band, his influence was not the least. Perhaps his years and standing lent power to the effect of his poetical talents. He shines out as the representative youth of the time of the war of liberation, and especially of the student class, which has always formed an important element in German society. The manner in which death took him, as he was fighting his country's foes, gave additional lustre to his writings. He had lived but twenty-two years, when Germany put forth her greatest efforts, and, in that short life he had experience enough of the miseries entailed on her by the mischievous policy of the ruling states. What impression these lamentable circumstances made on him, and what influence they had on his genius, can be read in his works. In 1813 he joined the Prussian army as a volunteer.

The regiment in which Koerner enrolled himself began the campaign with a kind of consecration service, when a hymn of his composition was sung. It was while he was performing soldier's duty, at the watch fire, on the march, in the battle even, that most of his battle songs were written, and they were repeated by thousands and tens of thousands as they joyously marched to the places of rendezvous. In the very heart of conflict he bursts out with the following prayer:—

> "Father, on Thee I call!
> Heavy around me the cannon smoke lies;
> Like spray is the flash of the guns in my eyes.
> Ruler of battles, I call on Thee!
> Father, oh lead me!
> Father, oh lead Thou me!
> Lead me as victor, by death when I'm riven.
> Lord, I acknowledge the law Thou hast given,
> E'en as thou wilt, Lord, so lead Thou me!
> God, I acknowledge Thee.
> God, I acknowledge Thee!
> So when the autumn leaves rustle around me,
> So when the thunders of battle surround me,
> Fountain of grace, I acknowledge Thee!
> Father, oh bless Thou me!
> Father, oh bless Thou me!

Into Thy care I commend my spirit;
Thou canst reclaim what from Thee I inherit,
Living or dying, still bless Thou me!
Father, I worship Thee!
Father, I worship Thee!
Not for earth's riches Thy servants are fighting,
Holiest cause with our swords we are righting;
Conq'ring or falling, I worship Thee.
God, I submit to Thee.
God, I submit to Thee!
When all the terrors of death are assailing,
When in the veins e'en the life-blood is failing.
Lord, unto Thee will I bow the knee.
Father, I cry to Thee!"

The same spirit of religious fervour breathes in all his songs. With Koerner it was no war of kings to which he had devoted himself—

"It is no war of which but kings are 'ware—
'Tis a crusade, a people's holy war."

He calls to his companions, you are "fighting for your sanctuary." That old world virtue of patriotism cannot be said to be lost to us of this later time; nor while Koerner's words live in his countrymen's hearts will it ever die.

"One lasting German virtue have we still,
That breaks all fetters with its mighty will.
Let Hell belch out its threats, its power
Reaches not hitherto. It no star can lower
From Heav'n, where our star is steadfast set;
And tho' the night o'ershadow for an hour
Our virtue's joyance, yet our will lives yet!"

So inspired, the German soldier could meet death joyfully, with "Vaterland "upon his lips.

There were other and older men to fan the flame of patriotism, and to prevent disaster and defeat quenching its brightness; who, if more moderate than young poetical students like Koerner, were yet better able to guide this ardour into some practical path. Professors not only shared and fostered, but also directed, their pupils' zeal. In the history of this outburst of enthusiasm the name of Jahn, to which Germany delighted to add the epithet "father," must not be passed over in silence. Though not with songs, he gave much help to the great cause. From his professor's chair he taught that great love of all that was German, which is yet extant in a later generation. That he might give greater force to his teachings, and show by his example that words were worthless if unaccompanied by actions, he served his country as a soldier, nor did he lay down his arms till its foes were conquered. Such was the character of the leading spirits of

Germany in the movement that brought about the decisive battle of Leipzig. Others, too, there were, whose names have become a household possession in Germany, as Arndt and Uhland, who set to music the aspirations of their countryman. The time, as Koerner said, demanded great hearts; and hearts were there to answer.

Arndt was one of the first to perceive the significance of the events of his time, and to recognize the forces that under skilful leadership would bring the German people into a haven of safety. With this conviction, he put out all his energies to procure for his fatherland more than present salvation; and resolutely taking his stand, worked for the present, while he looked to the consequences of his labours in the future. To him belongs the honour of the authorship of that most famous song, "What is the German Fatherland?" a composition which alone would have made his name memorable, from the great part it played in the German War of Independence. This song has become the national anthem of Germany, the textbook of patriotism and of the aspirations of the German race for unity. For the impression it made and the popularity it acquired at the time of its production, it can only be compared to the "Marseillaise," or that old ballad of "Lillibullero," which, its author boasted, had sung king James II. out of three kingdoms; but it has surpassed every other national song, by the hold it has ever since retained on the minds of the Germans. This inspiration of Arndt's, which deserves to be as well known as that of Rouget de Lisle, is quoted as a fact in the history of his country, as worthy to be noticed as any broken treaty or ponderous protocol.

"What is the German Fatherland?
Is't Prussian land or Snabian land?
Where grapes grow thick on Rhine's rich trees?
Where sea-mews skim the Baltic seas?
Oh! no! for thee
The Fatherland must greater be.
What is the German Fatherland?
Bavarian or Styrian land?
Where kine on Holstein's marshes graze?
Where toiling miners iron raise?
Oh! no! for thee
The Fatherland must greater be.
What is the German Fatherland?
Westphalian, Pomeranian land?
Where sand from northern headland blows?
Where Danube's mighty water flows?
Oh! no! for thee
The Fatherland must greater be.
What is the German Fatherland?
Oh! name to me that glorious land!
Can Austria, proud, the title claim,

So rich in victory and in fame?
Oh! no! for thee
The Fatherland must greater be.
What is the German Fatherland?
Tell me, at last, that mighty land!
Wide as is heard the German tongue,
And songs to God in heaven are sung—
That shall it be;
That, valiant German, shall it be.
That is the German Fatherland,
Where close will be the clasp of hand,
Where truth will from the bright eyes start,
And love live warm within the heart.
That shall it be;
That, valiant German, shall it be.
One whole great nation shall it be.
God in heaven, we look to Thee;
Give us the courage, strength, and will,
To keep it safe from woe and ilk
That shall it be;
One whole great nation shall it be."

In 1813, the year of Germany's deliverance from Napoleon, the subject of the most popular song was the Rhine, which has always been associated with the German's patriotic utterances. When, in driving Napoleon back into France, the German soldiers saw the Rhine for the first time, they are said to have broken out into uncontrollable joy. Tears trickled down many cheeks, and the enthusiasm passing from rank to rank, soon a hundred thousand voices joined in one "hurrah!" At this time the Germans began to cast their eyes on the country that lay beyond the Rhine, as the following lines added to the song above referred to will show:—

"The Rhine shall no longer he our boundary;
It is the great artery of the state,
And it shall flow through the heart of our empire."

On this favourite subject the song of Niklas Becker,

"O no! they ne'er shall have it,
The free and German Rhine,"

long possessed the greatest popularity. It is said to have been set to music by no less than seventy different composers, and owed its inspiration to the preparations and menaces of Thiers in 1840. Arndt sent Becker a congratulation on his successful composition:—

"At once, from north to south,

Its echo clear and strong,
Became in every German's mouth
The nation's charter song."

Becker's song subsequently yielded in popularity to one by a man but little known, named Max Schneckinger. This is the famous "Rhine Watch," which has become the lyrical watch-word of the Germans in the present war. The musical setting of the "Rhine Watch" is far superior to any of the seventy to which Becker's song is sung, and is one of the causes of the great hold it has on the Germans. The words of the song, as far as is possible in another tongue, shall speak for themselves.

WHO'LL GUARD THE RHINE?

A cry ascends die thunder crash,
Like ocean's roar, like sabre clash:
"Who'll guard the Rhine, the German Rhine,
To whom shall we the task assign?"
Dear Fatherland, no fear be thine,
Firm stand thy sons to guard the Rhine.
From mouth to mouth the word goes round,
With gleaming eyes we greet the sound;
And old and young we join the hand
That flies to guard the sacred strand.
Dear Fatherland, &c.
And tho' grim death should lay me low,
No prey wouldst thou be to the foe;
For rich, as thy resistless flood,
Is Germany in heroes' blood.
Dear Fatherland, &c.
To Heav'n we solemnly appeal,
And swear—inflamed by warlike zeal:
"Thou Rhine, for all their flippant jests,
Shalt still be German, as our breasts,
Dear Fatherland, &c.
"While there's a drop of blood to run,
While there's an arm to bear a gun,
While there's a hand to wield a sword.
No foe shall dare thy stream to ford."
Dear Fatherland, &c.
The oath is sworn—the masses surge,
The flags wave proudly—on we urge;
And all with heart and soul combine

To guard the Rhine, our German Rhine.
Dear Fatherland, &c.

A song by Ruckert, published in 1865, the year before the battle of Sadowa, will show what development the love of Fatherland reached, in the shape of the idea of unity. The events that happened in the year following its appearance were, however, a practical contradiction to the spirit of Ruckert's composition, which seems to assign to Austria the leading position in the approaching effort to attain national unification:—

> "Against the foe went marching
> Three comrades staunch and good,
> Who side by side together
> In many a fight had stood.
> The first a sturdy Austrian,
> The next a Prussian brave,
> And each one praised his country
> As the best a man could have.
> And where was born the other?
> No Austrian was he,
> Nor yet of Prussian rearing,
> But a son of Germany."

Then as the three were fighting together they were all struck down by the enemy's bullets. The first, in falling, raises a cheer for Austria.

> " 'Hurrah! for Prussia,' cried the next,
> His lifeblood ebbing fast;
> Undaunted by his mortal wound.
> What cry escaped the last?
> He cried 'Hurrah for Germany!'
> His comrades heard the sound
> As right and left beside him
> They sank upon the ground.
> And as they sank, they nearer came
> And close together pressed,
> At right of him and left of him,
> As brothers, breast to breast
> And once more cried the centre one
> 'Hurrah for Germany!'
> The others echoed back the cry,
> And louder still than he."

The love of their land and of freedom, which their poets have raised to the height of a passion, has begotten the all-pervading longing for unity that now possesses the Germans. The disunion, that had rendered humiliation so easy, and that no enemy hitherto had entirely effaced, was a giant which taxed all the strength that enthusiasm gave. Difficulty after difficulty had to be encountered and conquered; now by the slow and doubtful ways of policy, now even by bloodshed of kindred peoples. Those who first worked for this object died without seeing the accomplishment of their desires, and almost despairing of the possibility of an undivided empire. Now perhaps the end is not far off, and the shores of the promised land can be descried without straining of eyes. Aspirations of patriots were despised and looked on with suspicion, if no worse befell. Statesman could understand or recognize no form of thought, that did not emanate from themselves. Arndt, who for his services had in 1818 been appointed professor of history at Bonn, fell under the displeasure of the Prussian government, because he continued to display the same zeal for Germany's welfare, in peaceful times, as that which had effected so much towards her deliverance from the yoke of Napoleon. He had not filled his professor's chair for more than two years, when he was suspected of harbouring designs and thoughts that savoured of republicanism. His papers were seized, and charges brought against him of favouring the formation of secret societies and associations; of misleading the youth, over whom his influence was so great; of dreaming of a rebuilding of the state on republican plans, and reforming the Fatherland. The right and justice of a trial were not accorded to him; he was removed from his post, and lay under the ban of accusation for more than two and twenty years, when, to the unbounded joy of Germany, he was reinstated by the late king of Prussia. In his "Recollections," which he wrote when he was past seventy years of age, he discusses, at length, the offences of which he was accused. "I have, indeed," says he, "preached a dangerous unity of the German people. I am, however, but a miserable late growth, a poor after-preacher, when I recall the many renowned preachers that have spoken before me from quite other hearts and minds. I mean, this sermon is as old as the history of our people." He almost thinks it necessary to write his apology for the vehemence with which he had pursued his idea of an united Germany; and he reiterates in detail the position of his country in Europe, and her many assailable points, for which there was no other defence or protection than the concerted action that a perfect union alone made possible. To his patriarchal years, however, was granted, at last, a glimpse of the goal for which he had so long and so hopelessly yearned and striven.

The conservative spirit of the policy of the ruling states of Germany has always been a great impediment in the way of plans prompted by the popular enthusiasm. In vain might a patriot like Uhland raise his voice in the cause of liberty. He was met everywhere by an overwhelming opposition, against which public opinion was powerless. Whether he combated laws to restrain the freedom of the press, or laws against "public associations," which had been referred to the Diet, the antagonism of the leaders of Germany bore down the weight of his objections. On every possible occasion patriotism met with rebuffs, since it had gravitated to the liberal section in politics, of which it seemed at last to become almost the peculiar possession. Uhland, in a speech made at the Diet in October, 1848, laid bare the stumbling-block that obstructed the agreement of the German people and their rulers. The subject of the debate was the proposition to exclude Austria, the favourite candidate for the imperial sceptre, from the Germanic Confederation; and to make the leadership hereditary with Prussia. Uhland took the popular side, and declared himself in favour of a periodical election of the empire's chief, by a national assembly of the German people. "No head," said he, "can give light to Germany, that is not anointed with a full drop of democratic oil." It was this drop of democratic oil in which the great difficulty lay. All the plans made for Germany's regeneration, that had the sympathy of liberal opinion, were discouraged and frustrated by Prussia and other states. Unity, in the eyes of the men who held the helm of government, appeared to be shorn of its advantages, if it could not be compassed without the alloy of democracy and the admission of the element of personal freedom. While popular enthusiasm contented itself with singing national and patriotic airs, it was borne with; or if it moved men to subscribe towards the purchase of ships to protect the commerce of the Fatherland, under the fostering care of Prussia, the vessels were bought, and the charge accepted.

However wise or unwise the method of the German governments has been, it has certainly made the idea of the unity of the German race a tangible fact to the present generation, which owes no small share of gratitude and praise to those men who were the first to conceive the idea in all its force, and who in fighting against foreign oppression were conscious of the great interests at stake, beyond their own present deliverance. In the words of a biographer of the poet Koerner, they could see that "the further fruit of the struggle would ripen, gradually only, yet surely, in everdeveloping freedom; and that no power on earth would be able to hinder or limit its grand consummation."

CHAPTER VI.

Effect of the Prussian triumphs on the rest of Europe—Proposed division of Germany into a Northern and a Southern Confederation forced upon Prussia by France—Failure of the Plan owing to the Mutual Jealousies of the Southern States and the separate Treaties of each with Prussia—Danger to the Southern States from the Demands of France—Saving Clause in the Treaty on "National Ties"—Parties in Germany that looked to France—Saxony profited by French Interference, and paid a smaller Fine than other States—Meeting of Southern Powers at Nordlingen, in 1868—Dispute over the Federal Fortresses—Rejection of Bavaria's claim to precedence—Project of a Southern Confederation abortive—Austria's patient determination not to re-open the quarrel—The local limitation of Modern Wars due to Commerce, Education, and Public Opinion—Peculiar Situation of the Great Powers affecting International Policy—Warlike Attitude of France alone—Her Demands for a Rectification of Frontier in Compensation for the Aggrandizement of Germany—Incapacity of the French Emperor to resist the Spirit of Nationality—Bearing of the Changes in Germany on the smaller Neutral States—Switzerland a Conservative Republic—A Refuge and a School for the Democrats of Europe—Its Neutrality to be observed strictly by neighbouring Nations— Luxemburg gives rise to a Controversy that threatens War—Anecdote of Count von Bismarck—History of the "Luxemburg Question"—Transfer of the Duchy to Belgium— Eastern portion restored to Germany and the House of Orange—Fortress occupied by a Federal Garrison of Prussians—Neutrality in 1866—Proposal of the King of Holland, Duke of Luxemburg, to sell the Duchy to the Emperor Napoleon—The Proposal entertained, but the Consent of Prussia withheld—War between France and Prussia imminent—Conference proposed by King of Holland—Assembled in London—Guarantee by the Powers of the Neutrality of the Duchy—Fortifications demolished—Roumania—Election of Charles of Hohenzollern Sigmaringen to be Reigning Prince—Attitude of Russia and Turkey—Internal State of Russia after Emancipation of the Serfs—Attempt on the Czar's Life—Reorganization of the Russian Army—Explosive Bullet Treaty signed at St. Petersburg—Erroneous Policy of Russia towards her German Subjects—In England Domestic Affairs divert Attention from Germany—Reform Bill—Change of Ministry—Another Reform Bill—Commercial Panic— Fenians—Foreign Policy of Great Britain—Alabama Claims—Abyssinian War—King Theodore—General Napier—The Nations of Latin Race in Europe and their Attitude to Germany—Italy—Spain—Unpopularity of Queen Isabella—Successive Ministries—Death of Narvaez—Appointment of Bravo—His Arbitrary Conduct—Banishment of the Generals and the Duke and Duchess Montpensier—Insurrection—Admiral Topete and the Fleet—Marshal Serrano—General Prim—Flight of Queen Isabella into France—Provisional Government— The Principle of Monarchy adopted—No Monarch to be obtained—Serrano made Regent— Prim, Prime Minister—Duke of Genoa invited to be King; declines—Prince Leopold of Hohenzollern accepts the offer—To avert a War he afterwards withdraws—Prince Amadens, Second Son of Victor Emmanuel, proclaimed King of Spain—Marshal Prim assassinated on the day before the new King's Landing—Sketch of Prim's Career—The thread of French History resumed with the year 1860—Expedition to China—Syria—Mexico—Withdrawal from the latter of the English and Spanish Contingents—Arrival of General Forey—Capture of Puebla and Mexico—Offer of the Crown to Archduke Maximilian—His Acceptance on Promise of French Support—Unpopularity of the Expedition in France—Menacing Attitude of the United States' Government—Withdrawal of French Troops—Desperate Situation of Maximilian—Journey of Empress Charlotte to Europe—Failure of her Mission—Capture of Maximilian by the Juarists—His Sentence and Execution—Outcry against Napoleon III.— French Policy in Italy—Insurrection in Poland—Probability of French Intervention on behalf of the Poles—Nothing done—Prestige of the Empire rapidly declining—Efforts made by the Emperor to restore Prestige and establish his Dynasty—Concession of Parliamentary Government and Responsibility of Ministers—Appointment of M. Ollivier—General Jubilation checked by the Emperor's recourse to the Plebiscitum—Servility of the Ministry— M. Thiers' Expression of the National Jealousy of Germany—Secret Manufacture of the New Weapon, the Mitrailleuse—Confidence of the Emperor in its Formidable Powers, and in his Complete Readiness for War—Germany, the only possible Antagonist, apparently unprepared and engaged in the Pursuits of Learning or the Peaceful Avocations of Commerce and Agriculture.

IT is necessary now to show the effects produced by the Prussian triumphs of 1866 upon other countries of Europe. It has been stated that Austria, when expelled from Germany by the treaty of Prague, stipulated that the country should be divided into two confederacies, a northern and a southern. It was, in fact, France that made this stipulation, Austria being then too thoroughly humbled to prescribe terms, or do more than appeal for help to France, who gave the solicited aid. Prussia, not wishing to provoke a second war before the first was at an end, accepted the conditions forced upon her; and bisection instead of unity seemed to await Germany, not withstanding the brilliant victories achieved by the Prussians. The Northern Confederacy, as we have seen, was forthwith organized under Prussian auspices, and speedily gained strength and solidity. Not so the Southern. Being too much alike in power and size, none of the southern states were prepared to invest one of their number with the superior dignity and influence of carrying on their common affairs. Meanwhile, Count von Bismarck had boldly and skilfully neutralized the impending danger of a new dualism in Germany, by secretly contracting offensive and defensive alliances individually with each state south of the Maine. They thus enjoyed the protection of the Northern Confederacy, in exchange for the chief command of their armies in time of war, conceded to the king of Prussia. Under these circumstances they had nothing to gain by the additional formation of a southern bund.

The arguments used by Prussian diplomatists to persuade Bavaria, Würtemburg, and Baden to sign the treaties just mentioned, brought forcibly into relief the danger to which they were exposed from the probable demands of France for compensation and rectification of the frontier on the Rhine, in consequence of the unification and aggrandisement of North Germany. France, tormented by envy at the steady growth of German power, might any day fall upon Germany in the midst of peace on the flimsiest pretext. In such case, it was but too evident that Prussia would rather let her neighbours be sacrificed than pay the required compensation with her own territory.

Looking forward, however, with some confidence to the result of a struggle if it should come, the Prussian minister had secured a reservation in the objectionable clause of the treaty of Prague, which he hoped would one day subserve the great interests of German unity. Though north and south were only to be at liberty each to form a separate union, they were at the same time allowed the benefit of "national ties" to bind them together. This is one of those convenient phrases in a treaty, which are found to yield the interpretation most agreeable to the strongest party in any controversy about it. Yet the relations between the North German Confederation and Austria and the South Germans were not very satisfactory during the three years that followed the treaty of Prague. There was a strong party in the minor states that dreaded absorption by Prussia, and looked to France for succour. Saxony had profited considerably by French interference, retaining her king and court and the management of her domestic affairs. Her contribution to Prussia for the expenses of the war was but 10,000,000 thalers (£1,500,000), while that of Bavaria was 30,000,000 florins (£3,000,000). Würtemburg had to pay 8,000,000 florins; Baden, 6,000,000; and Hesse, 3,000,000. Bavaria had also to cede territory—two districts near Orb and Karlsdorf, containing 34,000 souls. Hesse-Darmstadt gave up the landgraviate of Hesse-Homburg, with some other fragments of territory, and as far as concerned her possessions north of the Maine, she entered into the confederation of North Germany. True, she acquired in return some portions of Upper Hesse.

One feeble attempt at united action was made by the southern states in 1868, at the meeting at Nordlingen, and it ended in a lamentable failure. The question was how the old Federal fortresses situated in Southern Germany were to be managed in future. There was Ingolstadt in Bavaria, Ulm in Würtemburg, Rastadt in Baden, and in part Mayence, where Electoral Hesse was obliged to furnish a part of the garrison. Both Ulm and Rastadt are more expensive than Ingolstadt; the tendency, therefore, of both Baden and Würtemburg was to keep the right of garrisoning these fortresses within their territory, and get Bavaria, which is the largest, to pay a part of the expense of keeping them up. Bavaria objected to this unless it was allowed a corresponding influence in the management of these fortresses, to which the others objected. A most original expedient, which well characterizes the whole spirit of this conference, was proposed; namely, to call on Prussia, who contributed most to the garrison of Mayence, to take a share in the expense of maintaining the other fortresses likewise, but without having any voice in the management of the fortresses themselves. All the fortresses in Germany were thus to have been kept up by common expense, to which naturally the North would have contributed most; but all the southern fortresses were to have remained in the hands of the sovereign in whose territory they were situated. This liberal offer was gratefully declined by Prussia; and the only result of the conference of Nordlingen was to prove that it was a hopeless task to try and bring about an understanding between the southern states of Germany on any point whatever.

It was the old story of family feuds and family jealousies, which are invariably more bitter than those with strangers. Bavaria, which is larger in territory and population than all the other three taken together, claimed naturally more or less the position which Prussia held in North Germany, and the others, if they could not maintain their entire independence, would rather make an arrangement with the Northern Confederation than allow Bavaria the precedence. Thus, the project for a Southern Confederation suggested by the fourth article of the treaty of Prague proved still-born; for Hesse could not bring it into being, Baden would not, and Würtemburg and Bavaria would never agree. The idea of such a confederation was nothing more than a sort of political plaster to soothe the wounds of Austria and of the southern states.

While Prussia brooded over the new state of things resulting from her successful war, uncertain whether she should absorb the neighbouring states into her own system, or herself sink into the vast hegemony of a new German empire, Austria patiently and prudently observed a pacific, if not a friendly, line of conduct towards her recent and powerful antagonist. The revelation of the secret military treaties between Prussia and the southern states did not rouse her. Prussia's disregard of the treaty of Prague relating to North Schleswig did not provoke her. In the Luxemburg difficulty she sided neither with France nor Prussia. She made friendly advances to the king and government of Italy, and while anxious for the inviolability of Rome and the pope, would do nothing for his holiness in the way of armed intervention. Indeed, the new laws passed by the legislature at Vienna, on marriage and on education, withdrawing them both from ecclesiastical jurisdiction, did virtually abolish the concordat, and establish religious freedom in Austria. That the Prussian victories should result in substantial benefit to Austria is a fact that, whether foreseen or not by the cabinet of Berlin, is an additional justification of the policy by which they revolutionized Germany.

The great changes that ensued could not but excite fears and apprehensions in other neighbouring states of smaller dimensions. Upon former occasions, the slightest concussion of arms on the Danube or the Rhine was the signal for a general appeal to the sword throughout Europe. No sooner did warriors of Saxony measure swords with Tilly and Wallenstein, than France, Sweden, Spain, and Savoy rushed to the encounter, thinking to make some profit out of the transaction. It was the same when Daun and the great Frederick were pitted against each other; the Czar and Louis XIV. took part, and ultimately changed sides, in the quarrel. In fact, when a musket was fired on the Rhine, the quarrel went on multiplying itself, until the whole world was involved in it. Happily for the rest of Europe, the general conflagration which one spark of war could formerly excite, was not brought on by the very fiery brand of the Bohemian war. Governments had other occupations besides intrigue and war; commerce opened a new sphere for their energies, which were greatly influenced also by the advanced education of the people, and the public opinion that makes itself felt through the press, as well as through representative institutions. Both rulers and the ruled have come to consider it the wisest policy to leave foreign nations to settle their own disputes among themselves, and to adopt whatever institutions are congenial to their tastes, provided these do not become an offence to their neighbours. The peculiar situation of the great powers favoured these views. Spain weakened; Britain pacific; Russia too glad to have a strong barrier against France, in Prussia, and a weak barrier, in Austria, against her own aggressions in the East; Italy only interfering in the dispute to secure Venice as a copestone to the edifice of her own country—all these things gave uncontrolled action to the principles of international policy.

France alone, at the threshold of the dispute, with her hand on the sword, spoke about the necessity of a rectification of frontiers in the event of an aggrandized Prussia. But the French emperor, isolated, felt too weak to struggle alone with the law of inevitable necessity. Outwitted by Cavour in Italy, and foiled by Bismarck in Germany, he was, by the moral forces which those ministers arrayed against him, incapacitated from preventing the universal rally round a national banner of either Germans or Italians. The spirit of nationality, which he was the first to raise effectually, became too mighty for his exorcism when he sought to allay it. For a time, indeed, it was feared that the changes in the political relation and geographical boundaries of the chief continental powers would bear injuriously on the smaller neutral powers, one of which, Switzerland, lies in the midst of three great continental nations, and has a share in the speech and nationality of all three. Germany and Italy might think of claiming the annexation of the German and Italian cantons, while France, it was thought, would hardly be prevented from making attempts on Switzerland or Belgium. But Germany and Italy better understood the teaching of past history, of international law, and of national interest in the higher and wider sense. No design against Switzerland seems to have been entertained by either of these governments. On the ground of nationality France could not claim a single Swiss canton. The small, ancient, conservative republic, in no way threatened the neighbouring monarchies, the republican propaganda forming no part of its policy. For centuries it had ceased to be proselytizing or conquering, and aimed only at preserving its own boundaries and its own liberties. Experience shows that Switzerland can, as a republic, live on the best terms with the neighbouring monarchies. Princes who rooted up commonwealths everywhere else, have shown Switzerland special favour. The elder Bonaparte, who overthrew republics of every variety, from France to Kagusa, showed a real regard for Switzerland, gave her a constitution which was at least an improvement on the previously existing state of things, and inflicted less damage on her than on any other of his dependencies. So, the allied princes who overthrew him showed no jealousy of the republican state, but enlarged its borders and guaranteed its independence and neutrality. Should monarchical Prussia feel jealous of the little state, let her call to mind that the republican spirit which exists in Germany alongside of the monarchic spirit, and which in times past produced German commonweaths and leagues, needs an expression somewhere, and that expression is now found in the Swiss republic. Switzerland has often proved, not only a safe refuge, but a useful school for German democrats. Those who had been dreaming extravagant republican dreams, have gone back to their own country a great deal wiser for their experience of an established and rational republican government, following not the dictates of theory, but those of common sense. It is well for many reasons that Switzerland should remain a neutral ground for all nations, and to this end she must carefully guard the neutrality which she has guarded so long, and which, among other advantages, saved her from the horrors of the Thirty Years' War. "She must stand," says the writer from whom we have quoted, "ready to repel, whether by arms or by diplomacy, any encroachment on her own rights; she must not, whether by arms or by diplomacy, meddle in any way in any possible quarrels of her mightier neighbours."

The fate of another small state locked in between two of the great powers became, in 1867, the cause of great commotion in the cabinets of Europe, and excited very general apprehensions of war between Prussia and France. To Count von Bismarck's firmness and moderation at that time, is probably due the maintenance of peace for three years more. At his dinner-table, a short time after Luxemburg had been declared neutral, a learned man gave an opinion, that Prussia ought to have made the question a *casus belli* with France. Bismarck answered very seriously:—"My dear professor, such a war would have cost us at least 30,000 brave soldiers, and in the best event would have brought us no gain. Whoever has once looked into the breaking eye of a dying warrior on the battle-field, will pause ere he begins a war." And, after dinner, when he was walking in the garden with some guests, he stopped on a lawn, and related how he had paced to and fro upon this place in disquiet and deep emotion, in those momentous days of June, 1867, when he awaited the royal decision in an anguish of fear. When he came indoors again, his wife asked what had happened that he looked so overcome. "I am excited," he replied, "for the very reason that nothing has happened."

The history of the Luxemburg question was briefly as follows:—By the treaties of 1815 the whole of Luxemburg was assigned to the king of the Netherlands, while at the same time the grand duchy was included in the German Confederation. After the secession of Belgium from the Netherlands, it was provided by the treaty of London in 1831, that the western portion of Luxemburg should be assigned to the king of the Belgians in full sovereignty, the federal relations of that part of the duchy being transferred to Limburg, which, together with Eastern Luxemburg, was secured to the king of the Netherlands. The refusal of Holland to accede to the treaty caused the French siege of Antwerp, and the blockade of the Scheldt: and after the termination of hostilities, the whole of Luxemburg remained provisionally in possession of Belgium. In 1839 negotiations for a definite peace were renewed, and Austria and Prussia, on behalf of the confederation, required Belgium to comply with the stipulations of 1831. The western part of Luxemburg was accordingly detached from the confederation, while the remaining portion continued to form a German state under the sovereignty of the house of Orange. The town of Luxemburg, from 1815 to 1866, was a Federal fortress occupied by a Prussian garrison. The plenipotentiary of the grand-duke voted for the motion which provoked from Prussia, in 1866, the declaration that the Bund was dissolved, but no hostile measures were taken on either side; and at the close of the war the Prussian government abstained from including the grand-duchy in the Northern Confederation. The garrison still occupied the fortress, and the king of Holland seemed to take possession of the vacant sovereignty as of a derelict without a claimant. After assuming the right of succession to this member of the defunct confederacy, the king seemed to infer that he had a selling as well as a holding title; and through the medium, it is said, of a lady residing at Paris, he proposed to transfer Luxemburg to the Emperor Napoleon, who was willing, if not anxious, to make the bargain. But the defence of the fortress of Luxemburg had for half a century been intrusted to Prussia, who could scarcely abandon the place in deference to the demand of France.

The Emperor Napoleon committed an error in demanding a concession which could not be granted by Prussia, except at the cost of wounding the national feeling of Germany; while Count von Bismarck, on his side, had been guilty of an oversight in allowing Dutch Luxemburg to remain, even for a time, outside the confederacy. War seemed imminent, for the French emperor having once stated his willingness to bargain for the duchy could not recede without seeming to fear Prussia, and grievously wounding the sensitiveness of the French nation. In order, however, to give him the means of drawing back without discredit, a conference, proposed by the king of the Netherlands, was sanctioned by the neutral powers, and assembled in London, under the presidency of Lord Stanley, the minister for Foreign Affairs. The conference ended in a compromise, in which Prussia conceded something. The duchy was declared neutral, with the guarantee of all the powers represented at the conference. Prussia withdrew her troops from the fortress, and the fortifications were demolished. Thus the crisis was tided over, and hopes began to be once more entertained that Europe was entering upon a long term of peace.

Meanwhile, by a curious coincidence, a prince of a junior branch of the house of Hohenzollern had been raised from comparative obscurity to sovereign power, in the early part of that year which had proved so eventful to the royal family of Prussia. Prince Charles of Hohenzollern Sigmaringen was elected reigning Prince of Roumania in March, 1866, in the twenty-seventh year of his age. He was installed in May, and recognized by the Turkish government in July. Roumania is the name that was given to the two principalities of Wallachia and Moldavia when they were united by a firman of the Sultan, in December, 1861, under Colonel Couza, who had been hospodar of both principalities and assumed the style and title of Prince Alexander John I. With a constitutional form of government, an annual revenue of nearly £3,000,000, a population of about 4,000,000 spread over an area of 45,000 English square miles, Roumania contains the elements of prosperity which wise government may develop and confirm. The reign of Prince Alexander, however, was not a happy one. His government and the popular assembly fell into a state of chronic antagonism on the subject of finance, parliamentary representation, and legislation in general. In May, 1864, the prince issued a decree, proclaiming a new electoral law and certain changes in the constitutional charter. His conduct was approved by a *plebiscitum*, or vote of the people, and the prince began to rule as a dictator, to the depletion of the treasury and the misery of his subjects. In the month of February, 1866, a general insurrection broke out, and the prince, abandoned by the army, was compelled to abdicate and surrender himself a prisoner. After a brief detention, he was allowed to leave the country. The Chambers then proclaimed the Count of Flanders, brother of the king of the Belgians, as prince of Roumania; but the count declined the uneasy throne. The lot then fell upon Prince Charles, whose brother, Prince Leopold, was destined to make so great a commotion in Europe four years later, by his acceptance of the offer of the crown of Spain.

It did not at the time appear that the susceptibilities of either the Russian or the Turkish governments were excited by the apparent extension of Prussian influence to the region where the "Eastern Question" might become the object of renewed complications. Russia, indeed, had her own cares in rebuilding the fabric of her society, which had been seriously dislocated by the humane, but somewhat hasty, scheme of emancipating the serfs. The reckless and profuse members of the upper classes suddenly found themselves brought to the verge of pauperism, their vast estates deprived of labourers, their serfs converted into small landowners, with no capitalists at hand to undertake the farming of the masters' land. The peasantry, however, with few exceptions, used their newly-acquired freedom wisely and moderately. In the communal assemblies they quietly voted for the abolition of all class privileges that pressed unequally on local taxation, and they were generally victorious. By degrees the landholders grew reconciled to the new state of things, finding that with good management their position was materially as well as morally improved by the independence of their peasantry. For awhile the career of reform which the czar had pursued since his accession to the throne was threatened with interruption in 1866, when his majesty's life was attempted by a wild fanatic imbued with the notions of a party styled "the Nihilists," a party that aimed at destroying all existing social differences and distinctions, church and state together, by physical force. The emperor dismissed his reforming ministers, and called conservatives and reactionists to his council. A curb was put on the public press, and governors with repressive tendencies were appointed to all the northern and western provinces, save Poland, which was indulged with a liberal secretary of state. Public opinion, however, reasserted itself ere long, and a vigorous effort was made to reform the military administration and reorganize the army. The old lengthened service of twenty-five years, by which a soldier, before the emancipation, had been able to earn freedom for himself and his posterity, was abolished, and a short term adopted. Corporal punishment was abandoned; new arms of precision were introduced, and improved artillery adopted; the militia was reconstituted on a more popular basis; the cadet schools were reformed, and a more scientific training afforded to the youths destined to become officers. Nor were the Cossacks overlooked; but certain ameliorations in discipline, and improvement in supplies at the military colonies, served to reconcile them to the hardships of their service.

A signal mark of the high position as humanitarians of the leading men in Russia, is to be found in the fact that the "Explosive Bullet Treaty" was signed at St. Petersburg in November by the representatives of Bavaria, Belgium, Denmark, England, France, Greece, Holland, Italy, Persia, Portugal, Austria, Prussia, Russia, Sweden, Switzerland, Turkey, and Würtemburg. The document thus drawn up with a view to mitigate the horrors of war, marks an epoch in civilization and merits record. It is to the following effect:—

"Considering that the progress of civilization ought to result in diminishing as much as possible the sufferings inseparable from war; that the only legitimate object pursued in war is to weaken the force of the enemy; that to attain this it suffices to place as many men as possible 'hors de combat;' that to make use of expedients which will unnecessarily enlarge the wounds of the men placed hors de combat, or entail inevitable death, is incompatible with the before-mentioned object; that to make use of such expedients would, moreover, be contrary to the teachings of humanity; the undersigned, in virtue of the instructions given them by their governments, are authorized to declare as follows:—

"1st. The contracting parties engage, in the event of war between any of them, to abstain from the use of missiles of any description possessing explosive power, or filled with explosive or inflammable material, weighing less than 400 grammes. This restriction to apply to the army and navy alike.

"2nd. They likewise invite all those states not represented at the deliberations of the military commission assembled at St. Petersburg, to subscribe to this mutual engagement.

"3rd. In the event of war this engagement is to be observed only towards the contracting parties, and those that may subsequently subscribe to it. It need not be observed towards any who have not signified their assent to the above stipulations.

"4th. The above engagement likewise ceases to be valid if a state that has not signed it takes part in a war between parties that have signed it.

"5th. Whenever the progress of science results in any new definite proposals being made for improving the equipment of the troops, the contracting parties, as well as those who have subsequently joined this engagement, will assemble to maintain the principles laid down to reconcile the acquirements of war with the demands of humanity."

Turkey, who had not been unprosperous since the Crimean war, not only held Egypt well in check, but showed signs of weariness of her protectors, the western powers. The peace of Paris, in 1856, in laying heavy conditions on Russia with regard to the Black Sea, imposed disabilities on Turkey also. The Sublime Porte did not like its men-of-war to be kept out of the Euxine, nor that the mouths of the Danube and the navigation of that river should be under the control of a European commission. Bather let us have the old state of things back again, muttered the Divan, we have a good army and a good fleet, and Russia will not be in a hurry to quarrel with us. As the government of the czar feels the resentment of that treaty even still more keenly, it is not impossible that the long pending Eastern Question may find a peaceful solution. The war of 1866, though in strengthening Prussia it crippled Austria on the west, yet left the latter power strong on the east, and with a fresh stimulus for extending its influence in that direction, to the detriment of Russian influence in the same quarter. Forces round the Euxine being thus rendered more equal, the temptation to any one of the powers to make a war of conquest is proportionately diminished.

One most unfortunate popular error has been dangerously encouraged by politicians in Russia, who have more zeal for their "nationality "than discretion. It is the prejudice of race against the Germans. The exclusion of Germans from offices of trust has become a popular cry, the fulfilment of which would give a most injurious, if not a fatal check, to the progress of culture and civilization in Russia. How much the development of Russia's power and enlightenment is due to foreigners, and especially to Germans, every student of her history must know. The attempt to develop a Slavonic culture, unsustained by the vigorous qualities of German thought and learning, cannot but end in ridiculous or disastrous failure. In this respect the brotherhood of nations will assert itself; and the Russian, who by nature is volatile and superficial, has more need than other Europeans of the compensating ballast which the deep, meditative character of the German alone can give.

To turn our view homewards, the German war of 1866, fortunately, did not in any way involve the British government in its toils. Occupied by a lively discussion on the domestic question of parliamentary reform, the country paid little more attention to the politics of Germany than that of spectators of the war. Mr. Gladstone, leader of the House of Commons in the ministry of Earl Russell, introduced on the 12th of March a reform bill, which was vigorously opposed, not only by the Conservatives, but by the more timid Whigs, as represented by Mr. Horsman, Mr. Lowe, and Earl Grosvenor. Ministers being defeated on a division by 315 votes against 304, resigned on the 26th of June, not without an effort on the part of the queen to retain them. The earl of Derby became prime minister, with Mr. Disraeli for chancellor of the Exchequer and leader of the House of Commons, the cabinet being completed a few days after the battle of Sadowa. The defeat of the reform bill produced some excitement among the working classes, who felt that they were unjustly deprived of the right of voting for members of Parliament. By way of demonstrating the popular feeling, the Reform League organized a long procession of trades' unions and other societies of working men, to march into Hyde Park. Some foolish writers in the newspapers raised a cry against this meeting, as an improper interference with the comfort of pleasure-seekers in the park. The government ordered the park gates to be shut, and sent a posse of policemen to protect them. The crowd waited patiently outside, until, finding the exclusion continued, they pressed against the feebly rooted iron railings and swayed them from their fastenings. Entrance thus obtained on one side of the park, the railings were uprooted in other quarters, and with little resistance from the police the whole crowd entered the park and held their meeting. Every advantage was sought to be taken by the reactionary press of this scene of violence, such as it was; the Reform League, Mr. Bright, and the Russell ministry incurred much obloquy. Meanwhile the Fenians began to break the peace in Ireland, and a bill was passed for the suspension of the Habeas Corpus Act. A tremendous commercial crisis, too, commenced with the failure, on the 10th of May, 1867, of the celebrated discounting firm, Overend, Gurney, and Co. The widespread ruin that followed penetrated, with various degrees of intensity, to nearly every family in the British islands. Early in the parliamentary session of 1867 Mr. Disraeli introduced a reform bill so very liberal in its principles that three of his most conservative colleagues resigned office. The rest of his party he had "educated," as he said, up to a point that lowered the suffrage to a degree far beyond anything attempted by the Liberals in the previous session. Of this the Liberals could not complain, and they helped the Conservative ministry to pass a measure that practically led to household and lodger suffrage. The result was seen after the dissolution of Parliament, in the return to the House of Commons of a large majority of Liberals, which in the session of 1868 displaced Mr. Disraeli and his friends, and restored to power the liberal leaders.

The reform agitation, the commercial panic, and the Fenian insurrection, diverted the attention which might possibly have otherwise been given to German affairs. Neither the traditional friendship with Austria, nor the dynastic connection with Hanover, served to rouse England from the policy of non-intervention that she had learnt from Mr. Cobden; Whig and Tory, Liberal and Conservative, when in office, alike observed this attitude of abstention. The English government, indeed, offered its services to the belligerents in the interests of peace, and supported France both in the proposal of a conference before the war, and in suggesting an armistice soon after the battle of Sadowa. In the Luxemburg question, which seemed likely to lead to a war between Prussia and France, the British cabinet intervened with effect. The conference proposed by the king of Holland was, as before stated, held in London, and by the treaty then and there signed England, in common with the other powers represented, engaged to guarantee the neutrality of Luxemburg. Favouring the change that had taken place in the Roumanian provinces, yet not encouraging the revolt of the Cretans, England pursued with regard to the Ottoman empire her traditional policy of upholding the strength of Turkey while promoting the improvement of her administration. Crete was not to be made independent, while Moldavia and Wallachia were placed on a vantage ground by the government of Prince Charles, under the nominal suzerainty of the sultan. The relations between Great Britain and France continued very friendly, as did those we had with all the European powers; but there was a coolness in the official intercourse of the United States with the British government, on account of what are called the "Alabama claims." These claims arose out of the depredations committed during the American civil war by the Confederate cruiser, the *Alabama*, which having been built in England, had sailed away before the government in London knew for certain her character and destination. She was far away from England when she received a warlike armament and crew, and commenced a cruise that was fatal to many merchantmen belonging to the Northerners of America. The owners of the merchantmen demanded compensation from the British government, on the ground that it was their duty to prevent the *Alabama* from quitting the English shores. In consequence of this soreness of the Americans, the insurrection of the Fenians was not heartily discouraged in the United States. Raids into Canada were winked at, and the annexation of that colony became a subject of public talk. The subsequent welding together of all the British provinces of North America into one dominion, did much to avert a danger that might have become threatening.

In one memorable instance, England broke through her resolution to maintain peace, and showed to the world how well she could conduct an arduous expedition, when the safety and freedom of her citizens were at stake. The Abyssinian expedition, from its inception to its successful conclusion, is a signal proof that the much decried military administration of Great Britain is quite capable of planning with skill, and executing with vigorous courage, great and warlike enterprises. For four years Theodore, king or negus of Abyssinia, had held in captivity certain British subjects, including an envoy from the queen. Every means of reconciliation were tried with him in vain, and that respect paid to Englishmen in various parts of the world, which is the security for her commercial transactions, was in danger of being forfeited in the East. In the summer, therefore, of 1867, it was resolved that an expedition should be sent from India into Abyssinia, under the able guidance of Sir Robert Napier; and a special session of Parliament was held in November, to vote the sums necessary for the conduct of the war. An additional penny in the pound incometax was agreed to, which produced £1,500,000. There was also a surplus in the treasury, and the Indian government had to pay a large part of the cost. The estimate that £3,500,000 would suffice proved delusive.

The merit of the expedition lay in the completeness of its organization, not in any brilliancy of action. A force of some twelve thousand men, infantry, cavalry, and artillery, with followers at least equally numerous in the transport, commissariat, and kindred services, were conveyed by ships from Bombay to Annesley Bay, and thence marched across the rugged highlands of Abyssinia to Magdala, the mountain fortress of King Theodore, which was stormed and taken without the loss of a man, and with only thirty wounded. Theodore having shot himself rather than be taken prisoner, General Napier returned to the sea-coast with the rescued British subjects, after burning down Magdala and its fortifications, lest it should become a nest of tyranny in the hands of some chieftain of the neighbouring tribes. So well satisfied was England with the completeness of the achievement, and with the respect it procured her among foreign powers, that there was much less murmuring than might have been expected at the undue measure in which the cost of the expedition exceeded the estimate. The total amount of outlay was fully three times as much as the three millions first voted by Parliament. The pasha of Egypt was perhaps not sorry to see this formidable expedition leave the African shore. His relations with the sultan his suzerain were not very cordial, and an old ally of the Ottoman Porte might mean mischief to the commander of the Red Sea. Nothing happened, however, to justify these suspicions.

If the effect produced by the Prussian triumphs was not very distinctly marked in Great Britain, Russia, or Turkey, the Latin race inhabiting Europe was strangely influenced by this new development of Teutonic power. Italy, as we have seen, was a gainer by the defeat of Austria; France, as we shall see, was strangely moved by the same series of events; and Spain, dissevered as she seemed from German interests, became in a singular manner entangled in the mesh of intrigues which rival politicians were weaving. The kingdom of Spain has during these latter years undergone many trials, much suffering, and one great and wholesome change wrought, not by the hands of a foreign enemy or interfering neighbour, but by her native population. The people, spontaneously breaking through the bonds and fetters that held them, hurled the last of the Bourbons from a throne which she had in every sense disgraced. The ague of revolt had afflicted this magnificent country at pretty regular intervals for many years with no positive results, until in April, 1868, an insurrection broke out in Catalonia, and that province was placed in a state of siege. On the 23rd of the month Marshal Narvaez, the prime minister of Queen Isabella Maria, died. In consequence of this event, the ministry resigned and were replaced by a new cabinet under Gonzalez Bravo, whose first important act was to banish the chiefs of the army, and to send them, without trial or notice of any kind, across the sea to the Canary Islands. At the same time her most Catholic Majesty's sister, with her husband the Duc de Montpensier, were ordered to leave Spain. On their refusal to comply with the ministerial order, on the ground that an Infanta of Spain could receive orders only from the sovereign, the queen signed a decree exiling the royal pair, who were conveyed in a Spanish man-of-war, the *Ville de Madrid*, to Lisbon. Some idea of the feeling existing in the navy, and indeed through the entire country, in consequence of the arbitrary proceedings of the new ministry, may be formed from what occurred on board the *Ville de Madrid*. The captain-general of Andalusia was ordered to accompany the royal exiles to the ship, the commander of which, on receiving them, whispered to the duke, "Say but one word, and the captain-general shall remain a prisoner on board, while we sail to the Canaries and bring back the banished generals." The duke declined to utter this word, and lost the crown of Spain, as his father by a similar tenderness of conscience had lost the crown of France. Not long after the perpetration of this arbitrary act, in the month of September, a revolution broke out. The exiled generals were summoned home from the Canaries by the revolutionary leaders, and General Prim, who had escaped to England, returned to his native country. When the latter reached Cadiz the Spanish fleet lying in that port, under the command of Admiral Topete, and the troops of the garrison, declared for the revolution. A proclamation was issued by General Prim in which he said, "Yesterday you were groaning under the yoke of a despotic government; to-day the flag of liberty waves over your walls. Until the moment arrives when Spain, freely convoked, shall decide upon her destinies, it is incumbent upon us to organize ourselves to carry on the struggle, and to save the people from being bereft of all law and authority." A prominent leader of the revolutionary movement was Marshal Serrano, duke de la Torre.

When the province of Andalusia pronounced against the government, the ministry under Gonzalez resigned, and General Concha was appointed by the queen to the presidency of the council. The royal army under the command of the marquis de Novaliches marched upon Cordova, where the insurgents were in force. Upon the issue of this movement depended the future of Spain, and the most strenuous exertions were made by both parties in preparing for action. A severe skirmish occurred at Burgos, at the close of which the royal troops fraternized with the people, a circumstance by no means inspiriting to the gallant and loyal marquis in command, whose fate was worthy of a better cause. Before the end of the month he had reached the river Guadalquiver, and found the insurgents posted at the bridge of Alcolea, about fifteen miles from Cordova, under the command of General Serrano. In the action which ensued the royalist troops were defeated, and their gallant commander fell mortally wounded. The army of the queen broke up and dispersed, while its royal mistress fled from Spain across the Pyrenees into France, reaching Biarritz on the 30th of September. Here she met the Emperor Napoleon, and after a short interview with him proceeded on her journey to Bayonne. On the 20th October a manifesto was issued by the Provisional Government established on the departure of the queen, explaining to the people the necessity which had forced them to rise and expel the Bourbon dynasty. "The people," it said, "must now regain the time which it has lost; the principle of popular sovereignty which is now naturalized in Spain is the principle of national life, and the ideal type of the nation's operations." The document also expressed the desire of the government to keep on good terms with foreign powers, "but if even the example of America in recognizing the revolution were not followed, Spanish independence was not threatened, and there was no foreign intervention to fear."

In another manifesto the government said they should quietly proceed to choose a form of government, without pretending to prejudice such serious questions; though they noticed as very significant the silence maintained by the Juntas respecting monarchical institutions: "if the popular decision should be against a monarchy, the provisional government will respect the will of the national sovereignty." On the 3rd October, Marshal Serrano entered Madrid at the head of the revolutionary army, and was received with enthusiasm by the people, to whom he announced, that after communications with General Espartero, he had been authorized to exercise supreme power and to appoint a ministry provisionally until a constituent assembly should meet. "Let tranquillity," he said, "continue to prevail, and do not allow your confidence in the issue of our efforts to diminish; the unity and discipline of the army, its fraternization with the people, and the patriotism of all, will accomplish the work of the revolution, avoiding equally the impulse of reaction and the discredit of disorder." The affairs of the country were now carried on by a provisional government, a government, as its name implies, existing from hand to mouth, ruling much by circulars and manifestoes. In one of these it was said, "The government has taken in hand the reins of the state, in order to lead the nation to liberty, and not allow it to perish in anarchy." A protest issued by the queen from her asylum in France, met with the following comment:—"Queen Isabella has addressed a manifesto to the Spaniards. The Junta refrains from making any criticism on it. The people have passed their judgment on the acts of the queen, and can now pass their verdict on her words." Meanwhile the Society of Jesuits was suppressed throughout the kingdom and colonies; their colleges and institutions were ordered to be closed within three days, and their property sequestrated to the state. The censorship on literary publications was also suppressed, and the absolute liberty of the press proclaimed.

The ministers of France, Prussia, Portugal, and Great Britain, forwarded despatches recognizing the provisional government. Prim, the guiding spirit of the revolution, was appointed commander-in-chief of the army, and immediately issued an order, forbidding soldiers to interfere in politics, or to attend meetings connected with political objects. A reform bill, or electoral law, was passed by the government, entitling every citizen of twenty-five years to vote at municipal elections, and at elections for the Cortes. An electoral committee, formed to carry out the provisions of the bill, pointed out in a manifesto the form and shape of the future government. "The monarchical form," it said, "is imposed upon us by the exigencies of the revolution, and the necessity of consolidating the liberties we have acquired. Monarchy, by divine right, is for ever dead. Our future monarchy, in deriving its origin from popular rights, will be a consecration of universal suffrage. It will symbolize the national sovereignty and consolidate public liberty, the right of the people being superior to all institutions and powers. This monarchy, surrounded by democratic institutions, cannot fail to be popular." When the provisional government had, as they believed, finally decided on the permanent form of government under which Spain could flourish, the difficulty was to find a man of noble blood, possessing the qualities necessary for a ruler of Spaniards—one who would be acceptable to the Spanish nation, and who would be acceptable also to the various governments of the Old and New World; one who could steer himself and the country through the crooked intrigues and diplomacies continually in action at the European courts, and who could strengthen and consolidate the power of Spain before the eyes of Europe.

At the general election in January, 1869, the monarchical party obtained a large majority of votes in the Cortes, a majority, however, which was divided into two parties—the Unionists, quondam followers of O'Donnell, and the Progressistas, who were attached to Espartero. At the end of this month the governor of Burgos was murdered in the cathedral by some priests, to the great scandal of the church; the pope's nuncio narrowly escaped death by the mob in consequence, and great excitement prevailed. The occasion was not lost by the liberal party, some of whom stimulated the passions of the people against the clergy. Order was at length restored by the trial of the assassins by court-martial, and by the execution of one who was found guilty. On opening the Cortes on the 11th February, Marshal Serrano, the president, invited the representatives of the nation, now that the obstacles to progress were removed, to construct a new edifice, of which the provisional government had prepared the foundations and designed the plan. It proclaimed with enthusiasm the essential principles of the most radical liberalism, namely, liberty of worship, of the press, of public education, of public meeting and association. On the 25th February the marshal announced his assumption of the executive power, simply from patriotic motives and utterly without selfishness; it was impossible, he said, for him to abuse his power, as neither the right of veto or the power of making peace or war had been given to him, so that he had very little power to abuse had he wished to do so. The government, it was said, would endeavour to disarm the republican party by a most liberal policy; yet Senor Castelar's proposal for an amnesty for political offences was opposed by the government and lost by a large majority.

Questions arose from the republican ranks as to the right of the Duc de Montpensier to hold the position of captain-general of Spain, he being brother-in-law of the late queen and son of Louis Philippe, a Bourbon by birth. Prim answered that the appointment was made by the late dynasty, and that the provisional government had no right to interfere. Admiral Topete declared that he would rather have Montpensier as king than a republic. Subsequently when the articles of the new constitution were carried, the minister for the colonies declared that the authors of the revolution would never have undertaken the task, had they suspected that the result would have been the establishment of a republic. In reply to Senor Castelar, Admiral Topete, minister of marine, declared the Duc de Montpensier to be the most eligible candidate for the throne; a monarchy, a regency, or a republic, he said, seemed equally impossible. "Beware," said he, "lest if you make every solution impossible, some insolent daring man undertake to cut the knot you are unable to solve. You will not applaud me now, but you will understand me." This remarkably strong hint had an effect, and on the 6th June Marshal Serrano was elected by a large majority regent of the kingdom. The Cortes with much noise and ceremony sware to support him, and Prim his prime minister. This state of things did not last long; the old difficulty as to who should be king continually cropped up until, on the 28th September, it was resolved to propose the young duke of Genoa as a candidate for the vacant throne. The young gentleman was at this time a student at Harrow school, in Middlesex. His father, the brother of King Victor Emmanuel, died in 1855. His mother was a daughter of John, king of Saxony, and his sister was wife to the heir apparent of the Italian crown. Neither the prince, however, or his relatives would have anything to do at this time with the Spanish crown. His refusal of the proffered dignity occasioned a split in the ministry of General Prim, and the republicans throughout the country, taking advantage of the unsettled state of things, broke out into open insurrection. The regular troops marched against the disaffected, who being once more overthrown, all moderate men became convinced of the necessity of a governing head, capable of wielding supreme power. Prim advised delay, but professed himself a monarchist; "such I was, such I am, and such I will continue to be. The country requires a dynasty." Senor Castelar, professor of history, and leader of the republican party, made a powerful speech, historically memorable, showing that the soil of Spain had never been favourable to dynasties, and that the ancient system of monarchies having died out, nothing was left by which men could enjoy their right of freedom but a republic. In consequence of these cabals and discussions, the year 1869 passed away without giving Spain a king. Matters were, however, rapidly approaching a crisis.

In July, 1870, a deputation was sent from the Spanish Cortes through the prime minister, General Prim, offering the crown to Prince Leopold Hohenzollern Sigmaringen, a very distant relative of the king of Prussia, with, as Prim had every reason to believe, the concurrence of the emperor of the French; this belief is supported by the statement that the prince had offered to communicate his nomination to the court of the Tuileries in person. There had been satisfactory communications with the Spanish minister on the subject, but it has been whispered that, at the last moment, the Empress Eugenie determined to support the pretensions of the ex-Queen Isabella, and of her son. The deplorable result of this most unfortunate determination is before us. M. Benedetti, the French ambassador at Berlin, informed the king of Prussia that his master, Louis Napoleon, would not permit the candidature of Prince Leopold Hohenzollern Sigmaringen to the crown of Spain, and would hold the Prussian government responsible for the consequences if it was persisted in. Prince Leopold, through his father, withdrew as a candidate for the crown of Spain, to the annoyance of the monarchical party in Madrid and the surprise of Europe; but so determined was the Napoleon party in the French government to pick a quarrel, that King William of Prussia had to give a rebuff to the French ambassador in the public gardens of Ems. The ambassadors returned to their respective courts, and in a few days it was known throughout Europe that France had declared war upon Prussia. The powers of Europe stood aloof, as it were, until the fierce onset of the belligerents had shown by its result how greatly the prowess of France had been over-estimated, and the Spanish government being freed from any further dictation from Louis Napoleon, brought their own affairs to a crisis by electing Prince Amadeus of Savoy, duke of Aosta, and younger son of Victor Emanuel, king of Italy, to the crown of Spain. He had been proposed by General Prim in 1868; the offer was then declined by the Italian government in consequence, partly, of the disordered state of Spain at that time, and partly by his position as heir presumptive to the crown of Italy. These difficulties no longer exist. Spain is reduced into order by the energy and patience of General Prim's government, and the crown of Italy is provided for by the birth of a son and heir to the prince's elder brother. We may therefore look forward with hope to an era of increasing power and prosperity to Spain, under the guidance of a prince of the house of Savoy.

General Prim has unfortunately fallen a victim to his fidelity to the cause of monarchy, having been assassinated by political enemies in Madrid, on the very day before the landing of King Amadeus at Carthagena. He was a man holding one of the most exceptional positions known to the students of modern history—that of ruler during an interregnum; a king who was not a king, and never meant to be a king. He ruled a great country with success for two years, yet never looked upon himself as a possible candidate for the permanent sovereignty. He was born in December, 1814, at Reuss in Catalonia, not far from Tarragona, the son of a colonel who had grown old in the Spanish service. With a strong inclination for a soldier's career, Prim at an early period enlisted in the Spanish service as a cadet. Scarcely had he entered the service when the war of the Spanish succession broke out, which lasted from the death of King Ferdinand, in 1833, down to the peace of Bergara, in 1839. In this struggle Prim ranged himself under the constitutional standard, against Don Carlos. He first distinguished himself, not in the regular army, but in one of the free corps. He came to Madrid at the head of one of those wild and lawless bands, the "Marseillais of Spain," which astonished the more sober Castilians by their fierceness of look and bearing, no less than by the strangeness of their attire. Before his twenty-second year he gained his promotion to the rank of captain, and three years later that of colonel, with other military distinctions.

At the end of the civil war, Prim began to devote himself to politics, and was elected a deputy in several successive parliaments. In this capacity he was busy, active, and intelligent, and took a very prominent part in the organization and management of political clubs. He gained rapid promotion, both professional and political, being advanced to the rank of brigadier-general and to the dignity of Comte de Reuss. The year 1844 found him implicated in a conspiracy against Narvaez, then at the head of the Spanish government, who escaped assassination at the cost of his aide-de-camp Rasetti's life. Prim was convicted of participation in the murder, but his sentence was revoked by the queen, and he was afterwards appointed captain-general and governor of Porto Rico. On the breaking out of a negro insurrection at Santa Cruz, he went at once to the rescue of the Danes, and was mainly instrumental in the subjugation of the rebels. His conduct, however, was not satisfactory to the colonial minister at home, who recalled him because he had removed the garrison, and exposed Porto Rico to the attacks of the negroes there, who were as ready for a revolt as their brethren in the Danish colony. Prim's next step was to become involved in a conspiracy against Bravo Murillo, by whom he was banished. However, after a short absence he returned, and in 1854 was sent as Spanish military commissioner to the camp of the allies during the Crimean war. On his return from the East he passed through Paris, where, in 1856, he married a Mexican lady, Senora Echevarria; the marriage was solemnized under the auspices and in the presence of Queen Christina.

On the 31st of January of that year Prim was promoted to the rank of lieutenant-general, and in 1858 he was raised to the senate, where he soon distinguished himself by a very remarkable speech on the Mexican question. The war of Morocco broke out soon afterwards, and Prim, who commanded, attained a high reputation by a variety of exploits, which were crowned by the battle of Castillejos, near Melilla, where, seeing the regiment of Cordova broken and turned to flight, he threw himself on the path of the fugitives, rallied them, and, with their colours in his hand, led them with such impetuosity against the enemy that he secured the victory for the Spanish arms. This heroic deed was rewarded with the title of marquis de los Castillejos, and the rank of grandee of Spain of the first class. In 1861 the joint expedition to Mexico of England, France, and Spain was projected, and Prim was sent out in command of the Spanish contingent, being charged at the same time with the duties of a minister plenipotentiary. How Prim proceeded to Mexico with the French and English contingents, and came back with the latter, leaving to the former alone the task of a complete subjugation of Mexico, and the instalment of an Austrian dynasty there, is related elsewhere. Prim's conduct at this juncture, however severely censured by some of his countrymen, received the fullest sanction of the Cortes. We have not space to follow the career of Prim under the ministry of Senor Mon, or under the Narvaez and O'Donnell administrations. Soon after O'Donnell's accession to power, Prim seemed to recall to memory his former political predilections. He leagued himself with Espartero, and threw himself with all his influence into the interests of the Progressistas. In January, 1866, several regiments in various parts of Spain made demonstrations against the government. Placing himself at the head of the revolted regiments, Prim succeeded in reaching the mountains of Toledo. The royal power, however, was at that time too strong to be overcome. The people failed to respond to the movement; and finding himself unable to cope with the forces brought against him, the leader of the insurrection retreated into Portugal with the bulk of his followers. Prim afterwards repaired to London, where he remained in seclusion until the organization of a counter-movement afforded him the opportunity of re-entering Spain.

After the insurrection which drove Queen Isabella from the Spanish throne, Prim had the singular honour of offering the Spanish crown to some half dozen "eligible candidates," and the mortification of meeting with refusals from all, except Prince Leopold of Hohenzollern (who withdrew his acceptance almost as soon as he had notified it), and Prince Amadeus, the present king of Spain. During these twenty-seven months of difficulty and danger, when a sound head and nerve were required, Marshal Prim was not found wanting in tact and administrative talent. Indeed, it may be safely said that to his firm hand, in a very great measure, Spain owed such tranquillity, as, in spite of at least one insurrection, fell to her lot during the long abeyance of regal authority. In Spain it is as indispensable for every political party to have a military champion, as for a troop of bullfighters to have its own matador. Espartero once held that place among the old Progressistas, Narvaez among the Moderados, and O'Donnell among those who would call themselves Liberal Conservatives, or moderate Liberals. The more advanced Liberals always claimed Prim as their typical hero, and such in reality he was, though some men accused him of inconsistency for accepting the title of Count, while he professed ultra-democratic opinions. The marshal was very strongly addicted to the pleasures of the chase, for the gratification of which taste he kept up a magnificent house and establishment.

In person he was considerably below the middle size, with a small and slender, but wiry and active frame, a lively intelligent countenance, with a very bad complexion. His eyes were large and expressive, his features tolerably regular, with no other marked peculiarity than the high cheekbones. His manners were courteous and winning; his speech fluent, forcible, and not inelegant, both in his native language and in French. He was not a great genius, yet occupied a position very remarkable for a man of ordinary capacity. He was a good officer, possessing that valuable quality of bravery that increases as danger grows more imminent. His idea of government was to maintain military order, and to leave the rest to his colleagues. The wants and grievances of Spain seemed to trouble him but little. He knew the limit of his own powers, and his ambition led him to make a king rather than be a king. His assassination was due, perhaps, as much to the popular hatred of a foreign monarch as to republican hatred of royalty. Anyhow it was a dastardly deed, disgraceful to the party by whom it was instigated or permitted. Meanwhile France, the greatest power among the Latin races, was successfully developing her material prosperity, if not her political institutions, under the rule of Napoleon III. We resume the thread of her history where we left it in Chapter III., namely, in the year 1860. The alliance of France and England continued to grow more close and friendly. The treaty of commerce successfully negotiated by Mr. Cobden gave the two nations a community of interests, and the feeling of amity was strengthened by certain joint expeditions of a warlike nature. In 1880 public attention in France was, for a time, diverted from the Italian question to events in the remote East. Notwithstanding the great distance of China from the West, that country has long enjoyed the advantages, or disadvantages, of foreign intervention. Unlike Mexico, it has no powerful and civilized neighbour jealous of European interference. Both China and Japan are in an unfortunate position in this respect. Possessing no effective means of resistance against the improved appliances of war and the training of the West, they have been unable to withstand the imposition of treaties of trade, and have been compelled, in spite of themselves, to abandon their seclusion and open their ports to foreign commerce. Whatever good may eventually accrue by the opening of the country to Europeans, it is surely the right of the Chinese government to determine whether or not it is for the advantage of their country to open their doors to other nations. Before commercial interests, however, many scruples have to give way. The conduct of Europeans in China, and not least that of the English, cannot be regarded as free from violence and wrong.

When a ratification of the treaty of Tientsin was refused, and the Chinese treacherously opened fire upon the English forces in time of peace, war was again declared by England and France against the government at Pekin. Two separate expeditions were organized without delay, General Montauban, afterwards created Comte de Palikao, commanding the French, and General Sir Hope Grant the English contingent. Baron Gros and Lord Elgin, the English and French ambassadors, suffered shipwreck on their voyage to China, and narrowly escaped with their lives. The allied forces opened the campaign with an attack on a fort at Tangku, which, after an assault, was entered by both armies at the same time. The Taku forts gallantly withstood an assault made by the French, and only yielded to a combined attack of both French and English, leaving the whole of their war material in the hands of the allies. The Chinese government then, as a pretext for delay, entered into negotiations for peace, but faithlessly seized the English commissioners, together with some other gentlemen, and subjected them to many indignities and cruelties. All negotiations were at once broken off, and the allied forces advanced into the country, overcoming all opposition, until they reached the neighbourhood of Pekin, which Lord Elgin threatened to storm unless his terms were acceded to. The Chinese evaded these demands, and the armies advanced, the French making their entry into the emperor's summer palace. The conquerors did not show the virtues of their superior civilization in the face of a semi-barbarous enemy. The acts of the French troops recall the depredations of the early English navigators on the Spanish coast of America. The pillage was wholesale, the destruction most wanton. The public reception hall, the state and private bedrooms, ante-rooms, boudoirs, and every other apartment, were ransacked; articles of virtu, of native and foreign workmanship, taken or broken, if too large to be carried away; ornamental lattice-work, screens, jade-stone ornaments, jars, clocks, watches, and other pieces of mechanism, curtains and furniture—none escaped destruction. There were extensive wardrobes of every article of dress; coats richly embroidered in silk and gold thread, in the imperial dragon pattern, boots, head-dresses, fans, &c., in fact, rooms all but filled with them, storerooms of manufactured silk in rolls, all destroyed.

The English followed the French, and in order to intimidate the Chinese, and to make it plain to them that their semi-barbarism gave them no advantage in the face of Western civilization, burnt the palace to the ground. The Chinese government, now convinced, against their will, of the uselessness of further resistance, accepted the conditions offered by the allies.

It deserves notice that the Emperor Napoleon, in his speech on the opening of the French Chambers in March, 1860, vindicated himself against the charge of meanness in exacting Nice and Savoy as the price of his aid to Italy. "Looking at the transformation of North Italy, which gives to a powerful state all the passes of the Alps, it was my duty, for the security of our frontiers, to claim the French slopes of the mountains. The re-assertion of a claim to a territory of small extent has nothing in it to alarm Europe, and give a denial to the policy of disinterestedness which I have proclaimed more than once; for France does not wish to proceed to this aggrandizement, however small it may be, either by military occupation, or by provoking insurrections, or by under-hand manoeuvres, but by frankly explaining the question to the great powers. They will doubtless understand in their equity, as France would certainly understand it for each of them under similar circumstances, that the important territorial re-arrangement which is about to take place, gives us a right to a guarantee indicated by nature herself."

Neighbouring nations did not take the view of the annexation which the emperor would have had them take. But what could they say when an appeal to universal suffrage among the natives confirmed the annexation?

Switzerland raised a feeble protest against the absorption of these provinces into the empire of France; but she met with a response due to her weakness. About this time the massacre of Christians in Syria by the Mohammedans called the attention of the Western powers to that part of the world. Armed intervention was acknowledged to be the only effective means to quell the disturbances; and a convention was signed by England and France, in virtue of which France, with the consent of Turkey, sent a brigade, under the command of General de Beaufort d'Hautpool, to the scene of disorder, in August, 1860. The appearance of the French flag speedily put an end to the evils under which the Cliristians were suffering. By the terms of the convention the time of the French occupation had been fixed for six months. During this time it had been arranged, that a commission made up of representatives of France and England was to meet at Beyrout, and to concert measures for the maintenance of order, and the safety of the Christian inhabitants of Lebanon. The six months expired on the 3rd March, 1861, and in February the commissioners had not completed their labours. The English government was little disposed to favour an extension of the stay of the French brigade, but consented to a limited delay of four months. On the 5th July the French troops evacuated Syria. A good deal of ill-feeling was excited in France by the conduct of England in this matter. The French could not understand the jealousy with which their sole interference in the affairs of the East was regarded by English politicians.

The French troops had hardly returned from Syria, when fresh employment was found for them in the Western hemisphere. For some years the internal affairs in Mexico had presented nothing but a scene of confusion. Eevolution succeeded revolution. Anarchy alone seemed to possess any stability. This state of things finally called for the intervention of those governments whose subjects had been the chief victims of the exactions of the various Mexican rulers. On the 10th November, 1861, a convention was signed by France, Spain, and England, by which these powers agreed to demand by force of arms redress for their injured countrymen. This undertaking by no means met with universal approval in France. The French people had grown tired of distant campaigns, and showed small desire to have in America a pendant to the wars in Asia. The successes of the French army in Cochin China, where some few thousand men strove bravely against superior numbers and the dangers of the climate, for the sake of establishing a French colony, had not been received with general approbation. It was felt that the losses and the expenses of the expedition would far exceed any substantial gain, and the imperial government was accused of being swayed too easily by the national taste for military affairs. It was thought, moreover, unwise to create complications in America, when so many beset the very borders of France.

At the time the allied expedition set out, Juarez, the chief of the liberal party, held the reins of power. The intentions of the European governments, as officially declared, were "to compel Mexico to fulfil the obligations already solemnly contracted, and to give a guarantee of a more efficient protection for the persons and property of their respective countrymen;" but the allied powers declined any intervention in the domestic affairs of the country, and especially any exercise of pressure on the will of the population with regard to their choice of a government. The first act of the allies was to sign a convention with Juarez at La Soledad, confirming the president's authority. The allied forces were allowed, during the progress of negotiations, to occupy the towns of Cordova, Orizaba, and Tehuacan, places favourable to the health of the soldiers, while the Mexican flag, which had been lowered at the approach of the allies, was allowed to float over Vera Cruz. England, abandoning all intention of advancing into the country, ratified the signature of its plenipotentiary. Spain, though not giving up the enterprise so readily, did not disavow the signature of General Prim. France, however, declared boldly that she could not accept the convention of La Soledad, which was "counter to the national dignity."

This step of the French government at once roused the suspicion that its interference in Mexican affairs was prompted by other considerations than the simple interests of Frenchmen residing in Mexico. As soon as the Spanish and English realized the awkwardness of their position, their only anxiety was not to let slip any opportunity of breaking with their ally. A pretext soon came. Among the French staff had come a Mexican exile, by name Almonte, who was an object of suspicion to Juarez on account of his monarchical opinions. Juarez demanded his surrender as a traitor, and was supported in his demands by England. The French could not in honour, even if they had been willing, listen to a demand of this kind. The result of this difference was that the French, about 5000 in number, were left alone, while the English and Spaniards returned to Europe together. Hostilities soon broke out, and an attempt made by the French to take Puebla signally failed. In the winter of 1862, however, General Forey arrived with 30,000 men, captured that city, and then marched to Mexico, where he met with no opposition. The programme of French policy was now fully declared, and the Archduke Maximilian of Austria was announced as a candidate for the throne of Mexico at the instigation of the church or reactionist party, whose motto, "God and order," was opposed to that of the liberals or Juarists, "Liberty and independence."

Maximilian, on receiving the offer of the sceptre of Mexico, hesitated long ere he yielded to the persuasions of the Mexican commissioners, backed by the French cabinet. His acceptance of the throne took place on April 10, 1864, and was followed by the treaty of Miramar, concluded between him and France, which bound the latter power to maintain a military force in Mexico on certain settled conditions. By the beginning of the year 1865, thanks to General Bazaine's zeal and activity, Mexico, for the first time since its independence, was almost at peace. A national army had been organized; important towns had been put into a state of defence, so far as earthworks and guns availed for that end, and the various government factories of arms had been re-organized and refurnished. Could Maximilian have insured the continued presence of a European force, his plans might have been carried out to a successful issue, and order established in Mexico on a firm basis; but, unfortunately, he soon discovered the futility of single attempts to ameliorate the condition of a degenerate people. Wherever the French troops put down opposition, and confided their conquests to Mexican troops, liberals would immediately reappear in arms and retake their old positions. Not till the end of 1865 was Juarez, who still styled himself the president of the republic, at length subdued. He was driven from Chihuahua, the last stronghold of the liberal cause, into the territory of the United States. The spring of 1866, however, opened unhappily on the new empire. Its resources were not equal to the strain of constant warfare, and the troops, not receiving their pay, resumed their more natural character of marauders. The imperial finances fell into such a critical position, that Bazaine took upon himself to advance Maximilian money, to the no small displeasure of the cabinet of the Tuileries. In fact, the government and people of France were beginning to regret their share in the founding of the new Mexican empire. The French people, who had been induced by the statements of the ministers to take up two Mexican loans, had gradually been enlightened as to the real state of matters, both military and political, in Mexico. Other causes influenced the French government. On the one hand, events happened in Germany in 1866 that made France anxious to have all her available strength within reach; and, on the other, the United States' government had informed the French cabinet, even in 1864, that the unanimous feeling of the American people was opposed to the recognition of a monarchy in Mexico. As time wore on, and the Washington government had more leisure for external affairs, they expressed themselves in more decided terms. To a note addressed to the Tuileries in December, 1865, the French government was constrained to answer that it was disposed to hasten as much as possible the recall of its troops from Mexico. Emboldened his success, Mr. Seward, the American minister, on the 12th February, 1866, worded a still more pressing message, the rudeness of which was very galling to French dignity. Mr. Seward, however, gained the day, and the emperor agreed to make arrangements for the withdrawal of the French troops from Mexico, a step that would leave Maximilian to his own resources, by the autumn of 1867.

Bazaine had the unpleasant task of communicating his orders to Maximilian. The return of Almonte, whom the emperor had sent to Napoleon to endeavour to procure fairer terms, and on whose embassy both he and the empress had built great hopes, in nowise changed the aspect of affairs. The imperial family naturally complained of the breach of faith on the part of France. Maximilian asserted that he had been tricked; that a formal convention had been entered into between the Emperor Napoleon and himself, which guaranteed the assistance of the French troops till the end of the year 1868. He felt that but one course was left for him. On July 7 he took pen in hand to sign his abdication. The empress, however, prevailed on him to delay this step till she had tried in her own person to gain a favourable hearing from the ruler of the destinies of France. With this design the Empress Charlotte landed in France on the 18th August, 1866, and hastened to Paris, where her success was as small as might have been expected. Napoleon tried to evade giving her an audience; but her entreaties were so passionate that he was compelled at last to give way. The answer she received crushed all her hopes, and completely unhinged the poor lady's mind. In the meantime the dissolution of the Mexican empire went on. Maximilian perhaps hastened its pace, by leaving the party which had supported him, because it was the French party, and by selecting his cabinet from the extreme clerical party. The effect was to immediately increase the growing disaffection. On December 1, 1866, Maximilian further crippled himself by signing a convention extorted by France, by which half the proceeds of the customhouses of Vera Cruz and Tampico were assigned to France in payment of her debt. The evacuation of Mexico by the French troops was the signal for risings and desertions. To the trouble of his empire was added the anguish caused by the intelligence of his wife's illness. He then recurred to his former purpose, and prepared to leave for Europe; but the members of the extreme clerical party prevailed on him, by offers of active support in money and men, to change his intention and return to Mexico. The clerical party kept their promises; but their measures excited the opposition of almost every class in the country but the priests. The French withdrew from Mexico even before the time announced to the United States as the term of the French occupation, exacting from their unfortunate protégé heavy pecuniary claims ere they left him. Bereft of every aid save that of native Mexicans, Maximilian's empire quickly fell. His troops, which the presence of French soldiers had not been sufficient to keep in thorough subordination, yielded everywhere to the successful liberals. Town after town fell into the hands of Juarez or of his generals. On the 19th June, 1867, the final act of the tragedy was played, Maximilian, who had foolishly left Mexico for Queretaro, an unfortified town, fell into the hands of Juarez, was tried by court martial, and by the president's orders condemned to be shot. This heinous crime was not without excuse. The refusal of the imperialists in Mexico to look upon Juarez in any other light than as a guerilla chief in rebellion, naturally exasperated the feelings of the liberals, who, as events showed, possessed the sympathies of the majority of the Mexican nation. Juarez was, as he persisted in proclaiming himself, president of the Republic. A decree of Maximilian's issued in October, 1865, had excited feelings of revenge, for it declared that execution awaited every man taken in arms against the emperor, and by virtue of it Generals Arteaga and Salazzar were executed. A few days after Maximilian's death Mexico capitulated; and on the 27th June Vera Cruz was occupied, as the last of the foreign troops were embarking. Thus the attempt to establish monarchical government in Mexico ended in a failure, of which one of the terrible consequences was the cruel death of a distinguished representative of one of the noblest families in Europe. His tragical end, and the scarcely less mournful fate of his brave and amiable consort, must ever remain a dark stain on the history of the second French empire.

Both the military and the political prestige of Napoleon III. were dimmed by the melancholy issue of the Mexican expedition. Complications, too, in other quarters troubled him. His relations with Italy were not the least embarrassing. Committed to the support of the political unity of Italy, he was yet fully aware that the critical position of the pope, in regard to his temporal power, exasperated the Catholic feeling in France. The clergy gave the signal of opposition, and seized every opportunity to hamper the imperial government. In fact, the policy of the French cabinet, like most temporizing measures, was pleasing to hardly any party, either in France or Italy. The friends of Italy in France demanded the recall of the French troops from Rome, while the opposite party still more vehemently urged an energetic intervention in favour of the pope and the dispossessed Italian sovereigns. The emperor had no easy task in mediating between these two extremes. It was not without hesitation and delay that the emperor had recognized Victor Emanuel as king of Italy. In notifying this determination to the cabinet at Turin, the imperial government declared that it declined beforehand every responsibility in enterprises likely to disturb the peace of Europe; and that the French troops would continue the occupation of Rome until the interests which had brought them there were covered by sufficient guarantees. The recognition of the kingdom of Italy put an end to many doubts and uncertainties. Diplomatic relations were renewed with Turin, where M. Benedetti was accredited in quality of minister plenipotentiary. The principal difficulty was, however, with Rome. On the 28th May, the ambassadors of Spain and Austria had addressed joint despatches to offer the aid of their governments, should France think the opportunity a fit one, to unite the efforts of the Catholic powers in securing the pope's temporal power. This proposition rested on the assumption that

Rome was the property of Catholicism, and that its sovereignty could not be placed under the protection of any but the spiritual head of the Catholic church. The French minister of foreign affairs evaded the difficulties raised by this step of Spain and Austria, by declaring that the French government, in its general policy towards Italy, would not join any combination that would be incompatible with its respect for the dignity and independence of the papacy. For that answer the Italians expressed themselves grateful, and the Catholic party could offer no further opposition to French policy.

Napoleon addressed excellent advice to the pope; but his holiness was not of a character amenable to any advice that clashed with his cherished opinions. "The Holy Father," he said, "cannot consent to anything which, either directly or indirectly, ratifies in any manner the spoliation of which he has been the victim." The Gordian knot which diplomatists were endeavouring slowly to untie, Garibaldi resolved to cut with the sword, by the expedition already described, that terminated so unfortunately for him at Aspromonte. It was on the 15th September, 1864, that Napoleon signed, with the Italian government, the treaty which is known as the September Convention, the articles of which were as follows:—1st, Italy engaged not to attack the papal dominions, and to prevent even, by force, every attack upon the said territory coming from without. 2nd, France agreed gradually to withdraw her army from the pontifical states in proportion as the pope's army should be organized. The evacuation, nevertheless, was to be accomplished within the space of two years. 3rd, The Italian government undertook to raise no protest against the organization of a papal army, even if composed of foreign Catholic volunteers, sufficing to maintain the integrity of the frontier of the papal states, provided that the force should not degenerate into a means of attack against the Italian government. 4th, Italy declared herself ready to enter into an arrangement to take the burden of a proportionate part of the debt of the former states of the church.

In accordance with the terms of this convention, on the 11th December, 1866, the French troops left Rome for Civita Vecchia, and embarked for France. The Italians soon began to exhibit signs of impatience at the restraint diplomacy had put on their movements. Insurrectionary committees were formed throughout Italy, with no attempt at repression on the part of the government. Men were openly enlisted by them. Eatazzi, the Italian minister, at length bestirred himself to check any measures the Italian nation might take without the sanction of the government. Garibaldi was arrested on his way to the papal frontier. Everywhere, however, and from all classes, Garibaldi received an ovation, while Eatazzi met with proportionate disfavour. Bowing to this expression of the popular will, he allowed Garibaldi to return to Caprera. He endeavoured to palliate his conduct to the French ambassador by intimating to him that Garibaldi had given it to be understood that he would not leave his island again without the permission of the Italian government—a statement that was denied by Garibaldi as soon as it reached his ears. At the request of Victor Emanuel, Napoleon, who had ordered the French fleet to return to Italy, rescinded his order. Garibaldi, meantime, contrived in a small boat to pass the ships set to watch Caprera, and getting on board an American vessel, landed on the continent. He made no secret of his design, but publicly harangued the populace at Florence. Rejecting the advice offered him by

General Cialdini, he set out in a special train for the frontier. His presence soon united the scattered elements of disaffection; and entering the papal dominions, on the 25th October he gave battle to 3000 pontifical troops, whom he defeated, at Monte Eotondo. His aim was to push on to Rome without delay, and get possession of the city by a *coup de main*, before the arrival of the French troops. His plan was frustrated, however, by the resistance he met with from the pope's forces. The French army, which on the receipt of the intelligence of Garibaldi's escape from Caprera had at once embarked for Italy, landed at Civita Vecchia on the 29th October, and hastened to the scene of action. This second occupation of Rome by foreigners sorely wounded Italian pride; and Menabrea, the general of the regular Italian army, was ordered to enter the pontifical states. Commands were issued to Garibaldi, at the same time, to fall behind the royal lines. In carrying out this order, Garibaldi, with 5000 men, was attacked on the 3rd November at Mentana, by 3000 of the papal soldiers, and 2000 French, under the command of Generals Kanzler and Polhes. The fight lasted four hours. At night, so little was known for certain of the issue of the engagement, that fresh troops were sent from Rome. A little later, however, Mentana capitulated, and Garibaldi, leaving 500 dead on the field and 1600 prisoners in the hands of his opponents, effected his retreat into Italian territory, and surrendered with his followers to General Eicotti, by whom he was sent to Fort Varignano, near Spezzia. He was soon after allowed to return once more to Caprera. The victory of Mentana was in a great measure due to the fact that the French contingent was armed with Chassepot rifles. The advantage the possession of this weapon gave may be estimated by the fact that the Garibaldians left 600 dead and 200 wounded behind them, while the French losses amounted to only two men killed and thirty-six wounded. The pope's soldiers lost twenty men killed and had 123 wounded. After the episode of Mentana the Italians made no further attempt forcibly to dispossess the pope of his temporal power, but resigned themselves to the tedious ways of diplomacy. The only consequence of Garibaldi's efforts in 1867 was that the French tricolor again waved over Italian soil.

In the rest of Europe France had not played the high-handed part she did in Italy. The year 1863 witnessed an act of Napoleon which deserves mention, notwithstanding its failure, as giving signs of a wiser policy than had hitherto prevailed in European councils. The emperor issued to the various sovereigns of Europe letters of invitation to a congress, at which all the questions that were filling the minds of politicians with anxiety were to be settled, and tottering peace established on a surer basis. While the embers of war were smouldering, and before they had kindled into a blaze, Napoleon hoped by an appeal of this nature to stay a conflagration of which he could see the disastrous effects. It seemed, too, reasonable to expect that the patching up of continually widening rents in the old treaties, or their recasting, which would have to follow a war, could be done better and with a greater hope of durability than if the work were left till conflict had exasperated the tempers of nations. To the surprise of France the first refusal, not too courteously expressed, of the emperor's proposal came from England, and produced a soreness in the relations between the two countries. The example of England was soon followed, on various pretexts, by the other great powers. The good intentions of the French emperor were not questioned by any, as every minister in his reply took pains to assure him, but doubts were freely expressed as to any substantial results of the congress. Moreover, Napoleon was informed that no state could allow a representative to take part in any proceedings without a previous knowledge of the questions to be discussed, and their proposed settlements.

The idea of French intervention in Poland had been found impracticable. The insurrection which broke out in that country in 1863 was suppressed by the Russian government with great harshness. Sympathy for the cause of the Poles was pretty general, but in France great indignation was expressed at the treatment they were receiving at the hands of their conquerors. The French government was ready to go to war for Poland, if they could have secured the co-operation of England and Austria. A proposal was, in fact, made to these countries to form an alliance with France, for the purpose of obtaining in concert from Russia some guarantees for the better regulation of Polish affairs. The diplomatic methods were first to be followed, and if these did not succeed other means were to be resorted to. No country except France, however, was prepared to go this length, and the emperor's proposal was declined, though each of the three powers made separate representations to Russia, couched in similar terms. They severally asked Russia to agree to an armistice, that negotiations might be entered into with a view of restoring order in the insurgent provinces, and thus great bloodshed be stayed. Russia replied with an absolute refusal. She would not recognize the right of any other nation to offer advice, or interfere in any manner with her internal policy, and pursued the strong measures which had called forth their remonstrances, with no less harshness than before.

The year 1866 was an eventful year, and full of serious import for all countries in Europe; but nowhere did the circumstances that took place in Germany attract more attention than they did in France. The settlement of the question of the duchies of the Elbe, about which Austria and Prussia had fought side by side two years before, attracted the attention of France in the beginning of 1866 to Germany. The conduct of Prussia in this affair, and the consequences to the peace of Europe that many foreboded from it, added to ignorance of the policy likely to be pursued by the government in the expected crisis, created great uneasiness amongst all classes in France. The mercantile world suffered a panic from this general feeling of insecurity. The funds and personal securities were affected to as great an extent as if France herself had been at war. When, later in the year, the worst anticipations were realized, and the six weeks' war between the leading powers of Germany was waged, the feeling of anxiety and alarm was not lessened by the success of Prussia. With the exception of the actors in this event, no country felt the effects of the victory of Prussia so much as France. For when the North German Confederation became nominally a league of independent states, but really an empire of which Prussia held the entire control, the position of ascendancy in Europe that France had so long occupied was shaken. In face of the new power, which had shown itself possessed of such capital military organization, and had evinced such ability in conducting the operations of war, the French people began to feel distrust in the capacity of the imperial government to vindicate the interests of their country. Suspicions, indeed, floated about, that the neutrality of France in the struggle between Austria and Prussia had been bought with a promise that was not to be fulfilled. The price was even hinted at. There was to be, so went the rumours, a rectification of the frontier at the expense of either Germany or Belgium. The emperor was believed to have been overreached, and to have been unable to get the compensation, whatever it was, which Prussia had engaged to give. Thiers did not hesitate to upbraid the government for its tolerance of Prussia's acts. This statesman's patriotism, which objected to the unity of Italy, would have had France oppose by force the amalgamation into one nation of the separate and independent states beyond the Rhine. Now that Germany had achieved her unity, with the co-operation of the emperor, as he said, Thiers pressed upon the government the adoption of a firm policy, supported by a vigorous organization of the military forces of France. It was in vain that the emperor by his despatches tried to reassure the people of the unaltered position of their country. Popular opinion was on the side of Thiers. With the intent to inspire the people with greater confidence, a new map of Europe was published in 1868, under the auspices of the government. In this map was shown how France in resources and population still surpassed Germany, after all the changes that had taken place in that country. Had only these resources been handled with ability and honesty, France would, indeed, have had no just cause for fear.

The ill-gotten power which Napoleon had wielded for eighteen years in France and Europe was evidently on the wane, and he cast about anxiously for an opportunity of re-establishing his authority, if he could not recover his fame for successful cleverness. Germany, the object of such burning jealousy ever since Sadowa, offered itself as a field for some striking warlike achievement. France has been an evil neighbour to Germany for nearly 400 years, says an eminent writer. All readers of history know what a persistent spirit of universal aggression and dictation set in with the ministry of Richelieu and the reign of Louis XIV. Both the Napoleons upheld France's right to give law to Europe. Details of the negotiations between England and France in 1831 and in 1840, prove that under the Orleanists and the peace-loving monarch, Louis Philippe, the encroaching and dictatorial spirit of the nation was as rampant and ingrained as ever. The whole life of M. Thiers, an eminently representative man, a typical Frenchmen; all his writings, all his speeches, every action of his ministerial career, have been inspired by this spirit, and have breathed the pretension, that France's voice ought to be, and must be made, paramount in determining all political and international arrangements, and that no other nation must be suffered to grow strong lest France should grow relatively weak.

The unfortunate Prevost Paradol, also a leading spirit among the better class of Frenchmen, in the last melancholy chapter of his "France Nouvelle,' warned his countrymen in the most solemn manner, that the unity of Germany, if once accomplished, would be the fall and humiliation of France; that talent, literature, the graces and the pleasures of existence, might still remain to her, but that life, power, splendour, and glory would be gone. At the unification of Germany France would disappear from the political scene.

The Great Frederick of Prussia, wrote one of the most moderate of French organs of public opinion after Sadowa, perfectly comprehended that the expansive force of France was turned to the side of Germany. "France," said he, "is bounded on the west by the Pyrenees, which separate it from Spain, and form a barrier which nature herself has placed there. The ocean serves as a boundary on the north of France, the Mediterranean and the Alps on the south. But on the east France has no other limits than those of its own moderation and justice. Alsace and Lorraine, dismembered from the empire, have carried to the Rhine the frontier line of the domination of France." That this, continues the French writer, the only side on which, according to Frederick, we are not suffocated by the obstacle of a natural barrier, should be closed upon us by the mass of an enormous state, is a fact so contrary to all our national existence, and to the natural constitution of France, that it is impossible that French bosoms should not be oppressed by it. The idea of suffocation is very characteristic of the excitable French mind. England has to endure being suffocated by ocean all round her, and content herself with expansion in colonies and dependencies. Italy is equally shut in by the Alps; Spain by the Pyrenees. But France, like a steam-boiler, must have an open valve—must have the means of expansion; and the spirit of colonisation is not in her people.

The emperor had carefully watched the development in the national mind of that alarmed jealousy of French ascendancy which had been at work ever since 1866. The completeness and unexpectedness of the Prussian victories in the war waged by King William with the rest of Germany, had been fondly attributed to the destructive power of the needle-gun. The emperor, therefore, not only gave the French army a more deadly weapon in the Chassepot rifle, the arm that was used with such fatal effect at Mentana, but applied his own special knowledge of artillery to the invention of a still more formidable engine of destruction, since known to the world as the mitrailleuse. Armed with this new man-slayer he might, he thought, defy the German, and he waited for a convenient moment to throw down the gauntlet and fight for ascendancy in Europe. Meanwhile, to pacify men's minds at home, and perhaps to conceal the real tendency of his foreign policy, he suddenly in December, 1869, announced his intention of abandoning the personal government which he had maintained so long, in exchange for a Parliamentary system that would make the ministers of the crown responsible for their measures to the Chambers, and not to the emperor personally. More than once before had Napoleon shown a desire to relax the restrictions of various kinds with which his reign had been inaugurated, but his hand had always been held back by those partisans who had risen to power with him, who feared to loose their hold from the necks of the people, who were more Bonapartist than the Bonapartes, more imbued with Cæsarism than Cæsar himself. Let every reader remember, as he reads the following pages, that Napoleon III. was no longer an exile, seeing public affairs with disabused eyes; but a man whose high station and considerable power tempted the designing to keep him, for their own selfish interests, in ignorance of much that was going on around him. The more blind they could keep him, the easier for them was it to work out their own ends. His bad health and undecided will favoured then: narrow unpatriotic conduct. Even when he conceived a project evidently safe and calculated to prove beneficial to the country, his ministers, the instruments of his will, as they were supposed to be, took care to pare down every concession to the tone of their own minds, and to the level of their own interests. Such is the inevitable result of personal government.

Whether this truth had impressed itself on the emperor's mind, or no, is not in evidence. Certain it is, however, that two days after the Christmasday of 1869, the imperial cabinet was dissolved, and a letter from the emperor was published, inviting M. Emile Ollivier, an eloquent liberal and opposition member of the Chamber, to aid in the task his Majesty had undertaken, to bring into regular working a constitutional system. There were not unnatural suspicions in the public mind, that the emperor by this step meant rather to give the semblance than the substance of liberty to his subjects; that though he might govern under changed forms, he would govern all the same. Had he been sincerely converted to the theory of constitutional government, it was thought the direction of the new ministry would have been confided to the one man in the Assembly who had more talent, political knowledge, and parliamentary experience than any of his colleagues—M. Thiers. This veteran statesman had for six years occupied a seat in the Legislative Assembly of the second empire, where, by dint of skilful debating and attractive oratory, he had succeeded in forming an opposition to the imperial cabinet which, if not very formidable, was far from despicable. Its influence in the country was undoubtedly greater than its influence in the Chamber, where a majority of imperial nominees did all that could be done to stifle discussion.

In M. Emile Ollivier, a man of unquestioned ability, the emperor expected doubtless to find a more pliable and manageable minister than he would have had in the ex-premier of Louis Philippe, and his Majesty was not disappointed. One great blot of the old system was the injurious pressure by prefects and other officials at the election of deputies, in favour of government candidates. The liberal party in the Chamber disputed the validity of these elections, and attempted to exclude the deputies so returned from the Assembly. M. Ollivier, after his appointment to office, forgetful of his liberal creed, instead of supporting his old friends in carrying out this purification of the Chamber, voted with the government majority that confirmed the election of all the official candidates, with the solitary exception of one, thus rendering the verification of returns as mere a form as it had been in the worst days of personal government. Conduct like this alienated many supporters from the new minister, and excited general suspicion. He found a difficulty in forming a respectable cabinet, and was, it has been conjectured, compelled to promise specific measures of reform, electoral and other, in order to induce men like Count Daru and M. Buffet to accept portfolios. The experiment of a constitutional empire, a compromise between personal government and a republic, was not without its perils. The emperor, though disposed to give it a fair trial, had himself no faith in the system, and unless his ministers could show that they were backed by the majority of the people of France, he would in all likelihood resume the power of which he had lately, by his own free will, relieved himself.

The position of the new ministry was beset by an unexpected difficulty, in an incident that reflected much discredit on the Bonaparte family, and rendered it the object of intense hatred among the extreme republicans. Two or three journalists, including M. Victor Noir, belonging to that party, feeling offended by a letter that Prince Pierre Bonaparte had written, called at that gentleman's house for the purpose of obtaining an explanation. In the interview and altercation which ensued M. Victor Noir was shot dead by the prince, and the other journalists fled from the room. That a savage act of this kind should be committed by a relation of the emperor's, however distant, was enough to serve the purpose of agitators who were greedy for opportunities of attacking the empire. M. Ollivier, as minister of justice, at once announced that a high court of justice would be assembled at Tours to try the Prince Pierre for the crime with which he was charged. There was no truckling to the emperor in that matter. On the other hand, the law had to vindicate itself against the violent and unconstitutional language of the extreme republicans. M. Rochefort, a friend and fellow-journalist of Victor Noir's, and a member of the Chamber, was tried for libel. If the ministers acted without fear of the emperor, they also acted without fear of the mob. These were symptoms of success in the constitutional experiment. The firm attitude of the government overawed the would-be rioters who followed Victor Noir's remains to the grave, and the demonstration which was planned lor the day of the funeral ended in the bloodless discomfiture of Rochefort and his red republicans. The preservation of order, the repression of violent revolution, was, indeed, the only thing now that inspired devotion to Bonapartism. The glory of the first empire, and of its warlike founder, had at length lost its glamour, and well would it have been for France if Napoleon III. had thoroughly understood this fact.

Early in February there was a foolish outbreak of democrats, headed by Gustave Flourens, which aimed at the release of M. Rochefort from prison. It had the effect of keeping Paris uneasy for three days, but in all other respects was harmless; for although six hundred persons were arrested, the greater number of them were speedily released.

As the year advanced it seemed to grow more evident, from speeches of Count Daru and M. Ollivier, that the emperor had adopted the constitutional system in all sincerity. The time had at last arrived, as people thought, for the long promised "crowning of the edifice" of government with liberty. But the emperor found it easier to humble himself before the force of circumstances than to humble some of his servants, and had no small difficulty in inducing the Senate to adopt with him "all the reforms demanded by the constitutional government of the empire." It is possible that his faith in parliamentary rule was no stronger than of yore, and that he had determined to give it a trial under a conviction that it would fail, and personal government again become necessary. Anyhow, a suspicion of this kind was engendered in the minds of some leading politicians on the pubcation of the senatus consultum at the end of March. In this document the imperial government declared that "the constitution cannot be modified except by the people on the proposition of the emperor." The emperor was evidently determined to maintain and extend that untrustworthy political instrument, the plebiscitum. The senatus consultum further limited the succession to the throne, and provided for an election by the people in case of failure of heirs. It vested the government of the country in the emperor, his ministers, the Council of State, the Senate, and the Corps Législatif—the last two assemblies sharing with the emperor the power of legislation. The emperor was made responsible before the French people, to whom he had the right to appeal, his prerogatives being those of chief of the state. His ministers were held responsible to the Chambers, of which they were members *ex officio*. The character of the Senate was considerably changed, and the power given to it in 1852 nearly all transferred to the lower house, the Legislative Assembly. To the surprise of every one who believed in the good faith with which these advances to constitutional freedom had been made, a week had barely elapsed from the publication of the senatus consultum, when the emperor revealed his determination at once to put in practice the principle he had promulgated of his right to appeal to the people. Representative government was at once discredited. Responsible ministers were treated as puppets, and their legislative labours as toys to be cast to the variable winds of a popular vote. The emperor apparently had resolved to show the Chambers that there was a power superior to them in the country, which he could use whenever he chose. What use in legislating for reform, or anything else, if laws, when passed by the Assembly and the Senate, could be reversed by a plebiscitum; for the minister of the Interior, with the army of prefects and local officials at his command, could always insure that the vote should be agreeable to the emperor. How the consent of any of the ministers to this self-stultifying resolution was obtained can only be conjectured. Certain it is that two of the most eminent amongst them, the minister for Foreign Affairs, Count Daru, and M. Buffet, the minister of Public Instruction, resigned office. The Chamber seemed to accept the slight it had received with perfect humility, and an entire sense of its own insignificance; for on a hint from M. Ollivier that it might be in the way during the plebiscitary period, it adjourned, abnegating its functions at the most critical moment of a parliamentary crisis. Personal government was, in fact, restored under the vain show of parliamentary forms.

On the 23rd of April a decree, written, it is said, by the emperor's own hand, was issued, convoking the French nation for the 8th of May in their comitia, to accept or reject the following plebiscitum:—"The people approve the liberal reforms effected in the constitution since 1860 by the emperor, with the co-operation of the great bodies of the state, and ratifies the senatus consultum of the 20th of April, 1870." The votes were to be simply "Aye "or "No," and the manifesto was to be sent to every voter, who would learn, probably for the first time—such was the political ignorance of the majority of the population—that the constitution had undergone a change, and that Napoleon was the author of what was good in that change. Thus the usage of parliamentary government, that the sovereign should not speak in his own name of political matters, but by the mouth of a responsible minister, was unceremoniously ignored. The voters would be led to the polling booths like flocks of sheep, to vote as they were told, and practically to restore their "saviour of society" to undisputed autocratic power.

This series of contradictory transactions, so perplexing to ordinary observers, was very characteristic of Napoleon III., who was always feeling his way and making tentative experiments. The truth seems to be that the emperor and the imperialists had been considerably alarmed at the success of the liberals at the elections in the autumn of 1869, and had made these proposals for a representative government under the influence of fear; but as soon as they discovered that the liberals, after all, formed only a minority that might safely be disregarded, they took measures to retrace their steps, and applied the plebiscitum as a test of their strength. The emperor, in a proclamation, clearly refused to recognize the acts of the Assembly as the acts of the people. "I believe," he said, "that everything done without you is illegitimate."

Representation, delegation of power, was not, in his opinion, good for the people, who, to the number of eight millions, were called upon to give a direct vote; a vote, too, that should show by a large majority how strong the government was in the popular esteem. Virtually the vote to be taken was for the emperor and personal government, against the liberals and parliamentary government. In point of numbers there was no doubt on which side the majority would be, but the minority would include nearly all the intelligence and political honesty of the country. M. Ollivier, whom Guizot styled "a practical Lamartine," cruelly betrayed the cause of liberalism when he consented to remain in office and promulgate the plebiscitum. Had he joined Count Daru and M. Buffet, the whole cabinet would have resigned, and the emperor would have given way rather than face such a crisis. On the 29th of April the French police discovered, or professed to have discovered, a plot against the life of the emperor. Many people were sceptical as to the genuineness of this conspiracy, believing it to be a theatrical invention to prepare the popular mind for the plebiscitum of the 8th of May, by exciting horror of the bloodthirsty projects of the revolutionists, and sympathy for the person of the emperor. The result of the voting on that day was 7,138,367 Ayes, against 1,518,385 Noes. In the towns the majority was generally against the emperor, and a still more ominous preponderance of Noes came from some of the garrisons. To a man in the position of the emperor, dependent as he was upon the army, this partial defection of the troops was food for very serious reflection. These men had not of late been coaxed and petted, and their humour had been soured by the addition to their numbers of men from discontented districts. They had no military employment, but spent an idle, dissatisfying, inglorious barrack life. The emperor showed how sensitive he was on the subject of the army, by writing a public letter to Marshal Canrobert to thank the troops for their admirable behaviour in suppressing some popular riots that took place in Paris the day after the plebiscitum. "He assured them that his confidence in them had never been shaken." No one had said it had; but the military vote of the 8th of May might justify a want of confidence, which his Majesty loudly professed he did not feel. Three important results flowed from the plebiscitum—the liberal party with their parliamentary constitution were overthrown, and their nominal leader, M. Ollivier, politically demoralized, was converted into an obsequious tool of the emperor's will; the emperor was restored to a blind confidence in his power and in the imperial destiny of his son; while at the same time he made the discovery, which ought to have been a warning, that there was no enthusiasm in the army either for him or for his dynasty.

Quem Deus vult perdere dementat is a maxim that many events of history have verified, but of no historical personage can it be said with more truth than of Napoleon III. in the eighteenth year of his reign. With the immense resources that he commanded, the countless channels of information he controlled, he was enveloped in a cloud of ignorance and falsehood both as to his real power and means, and as to his position relatively to his neighbours, that none but an autocrat could have endured. Self-deception bore no small part in the creation of the fool's paradise in which he lived and dreamed. His knowledge of artillery, his success in two wars, the deference paid him by foreign potentates, the number and costliness of his army, the vote of his seven million subjects, the defeat of his political opponents at home, the divisions, as he believed, of his enemies abroad, and the self-seeking flattery of his courtiers and ministers, all combined to make Louis Napoleon resolve on striking a final and victorious blow for the dynasty of the Bonapartes. An ingenious writer has endeavoured to draw a parallel between the Bonapartes in 1869-70 and the Bourbons in 1789-90. At both periods France was engaged in the same kind of task—trying to make a constitution and avoid a revolution. The reigning monarch in each case attempted, with apparently honest intentions, to convert an absolute into a representative government. The elections to the Legislative Assembly in 1869 pointed to a new era, as clearly as did the elections to the Tiers Etat in 1789. The differences in the personages are as striking as the resemblance of the circumstances. Louis Napoleon was neither so dull nor so innocent as Louis Capet, the sixteenth of his name. The Empress Eugenie could hardly be compared with the daughter of Maria Theresa, Marie Antoinette, nor Prince Napoleon Jerome with Orleans Egalité, while Rochefort fell considerably short of Robespierre, and Ollivier missed being a Necker. France, too, in 1870 had no such work before her as that which the first revolution threw upon her hands. The privileges of the church and aristocracy then destroyed had not been restored. Social equality was established, and a career opened every where to talent. Sansculottism, in Mr. Carlyle's words, had got itself breeched, and the mass of the people, knowing the value of property, however small, had come to fear and hate violent revolutions. But as the national rapture and exultation which marked the first revolution was followed by the awful miseries of the Reign of Terror, so, alas! was the corresponding jubilation thoughout France that welcomed the concessions of the emperor at the commencement of 1870, destined to terminate in disaster and mourning and woe. Upon whom was the onslaught of France to be made? the calculated attack that had so long occupied the meditations of Napoleon III? Upon a nation to all appearance lapped in dreams of peace; a people absorbed in the peaceful occupations of art, learning, commerce, and agriculture; the artists of Munich and Dresden; the professors and students of Heidelberg, Göttingen, Leipzig, and Berlin; the merchants of Hamburg, Bremen, and Dantzig; the ploughmen of Bavaria, the fishermen of Pomerania, and the sturdy peasantry of Schleswig and Holstein, quite newly re-united to the Fatherland. All these would have to be summoned to the war, and thousands of them to die; their homesteads left to women and children, their fields standing untilled, their country houses and warehouses closed, and their ships locked in port or captured by hostile men of war. Fearful is the responsibility of those who engage in war, great should be the provocation that can justify it, for awful are the consequences of the first step that sets in motion that bitterest scourge of the human race.

PART II.

CHAPTER I.

THE events narrated in the previous pages have shown that in consequence of the marked success of Prussia in the war between her and Austria in 1866, and the subsequent formation of the North German Confederation, with Prussia at its head, France considered herself menaced by a too powerful neighbour; and it became evident that a struggle between them, for the purpose of deciding their military supremacy and future position in Europe, was only a question of time and opportunity. The circumstance which was at last made the pretext for a declaration of war, was, however, in itself apparently the most unlikely to have led to such a result, and affords one of the most striking historical illustrations of the ancient adage:—

"What mighty ills from trivial causes spring."

The throne of Spain had remained vacant from the flight of Queen Isabella, in 1868, notwithstanding that the Cortes had, by a large majority, decided in favour of continuing the monarchical form of government. Several candidates had been proposed, but all had been deemed more or less unsuitable, until in June, 1870, General Prim, with the full approval of the ministry, offered it to Prince Leopold of Hohenzollern-Sigmaringen, the eldest son of the reigning prince of Hohenzollern, who had, in 1849, surrendered his sovereign rights to Prussia. The prince, who had been married to the sister of the king of Portugal in 1861, was thirty-five years of age, and a Roman Catholic in religion; and the offer was accepted by him subject to the approval of the Cortes, which it was believed was certain to be obtained. No sooner, however, was the news of the event officially made known in Paris, on Tuesday, July 5, than the greatest excitement was caused; the selection of him being regarded there as the work of the Prussian Count von Bismarck, with the view of either causing a rupture with France, or of making Spain little better than a dependency of Prussia. In the Legislative Assembly on the following day, the Duc de Gramont, the foreign minister, in reply to a question on the subject, said that the negotiations which had led to the prince accepting the offer of the crown had been kept a secret from the French government. They had not transgressed the limits of strict neutrality in reference to the pretenders to the Spanish throne, and they should persist in that line of conduct; but, the duke added, amid the cheers of the deputies, "We do not believe that respect for the rights of a neighbouring people obliges us to suffer a foreign power, by placing a prince upon the throne of Charles V., to disturb the European equilibrium to our disadvantage, and tints to imperil the interests and the honour of France. We entertain a firm hope that this will not happen; to prevent it we count upon the wisdom of the German nation, and the friendship of the people of Spain; but in the contrary event, with your support and the support of the nation, we shall know how to do our duty without hesitation or weakness."

This important statement was read, not spoken, thus showing that it had been carefully considered; in fact, the terms of it were settled at a council held at St. Cloud in the morning, at which the emperor presided. The assertion that the candidature of the prince had been kept secret from the French government, and had consequently taken them by surprise, was only true in a technical sense; for it was afterwards proved that the French ambassador at Madrid had known of it as being probable for several months. The matter had also been discussed in the German, and even alluded to in the French press, and on the prorogation of the Spanish Cortes on June 11—three weeks before the excitement in Paris—General Prim made a series of explanations as to the non-success which had attended his endeavours to procure a suitable candidate for the throne; and after alluding to the ex-king of Portugal, the duke of Aosta, and the duke of Genoa, he mentioned a fourth candidate, of whom he said he had great hopes, but who, after going so far as to send two emissaries to Spain, had refused, owing to their report of the divisions in the Cortes, and an insurrection in Catalonia which took place during their stay. He asked to be permitted not to name this candidate—his object being to prevent the raising up of any obstacle to his renewal of negotiations. It was at once concluded, however, that he could be no other than Prince Leopold of Hohenzollern. Baron Mercier, the French ambassador, who was present when the explanation was made, quite agreed in this, and was by no means backward in stating so to his friends in the diplomatic gallery; and it is unreasonable to suppose that, even if he had not done so before, he did not state the fact in his communication to the French government on the following day. The name of the prince was also mentioned in the Madrid papers the same evening, and it would, therefore, certainly appear that the "surprise" of the French government, as expressed by the Duc de Gramont, was feigned; and that whatever other reason may have induced the emperor to delay objecting to the candidature of the prince, it could not have been because he was not aware of its being in contemplation.

At the same sitting of the Corps Législatif, M. Ollivier, the prime minister, declined to accede to a request for the production of documents on the subject. He said that the declaration made by the Duc de Gramont betrayed no uncertainty as to the question whether the government desired peace or war. The government passionately wished for peace, but with honour. The ministry was convinced that the Duc de Gramont's statement would bring about a peaceful solution; for whenever Europe was persuaded that France was firm in her legitimate duty, it did not resist her desire. There was no question here of a hidden object, and if a war was necessary, the government would not enter upon it without the assent of the Legislative Body. Great excitement prevailed in the Chamber during the delivery of both speeches. On the following day M. Picard asked the government to communicate to the House copies of the despatches exchanged since the previous day between the courts of Paris and Berlin. M. Segris, in the absence of the minister for foreign affairs, replied that the government would, when expedient, communicate everything which did not compromise the peaceful settlement it was endeavouring to bring about. M. Jules Favre supported M. Picard's request, and upon M. Ollivier moving the adjournment of the debate, exclaimed, "Then it is a ministry of stock-exchange jobbers." At this there was great uproar, and the speaker was called to order. M. Ollivier afterwards declared that when the government deemed the time opportune, it would lay before the House all the information received at the foreign office. Meantime the country might rest assured of its firmly maintaining its dignity. Orders were immediately issued to the military authorities throughout the empire not to grant any further leave of absence; officers were ordered to return at once to their regiments, and the frontier fortresses were thoroughly inspected.

The French press, with only two or three exceptions, at once assumed a very menacing and hostile tone, and undoubtedly did much to enkindle that bitter feeling against Prussia which it was afterwards impossible to quell, even had such a thing been desired. One important journal declared that if France had once more submitted to be insulted and outwitted by Bismarck, "no woman of character would have consented to be seen on a Frenchman's arm;" another compared Prussia to an eagle, which, drunk with repeated successes, had rashly pounced upon a lamb, not knowing that the shepherd's rifle was ready for her; and, as if determined to do all in its power to provoke a quarrel, it asked if the shepherd was not to fire merely because the eagle might be scared into dropping her prey, although sure some day to return, and then perhaps seize, not lamb, but mutton? "Sooner or later," it said, "France and Prussia must fight, and it is best to get it over at once." Nearly all the papers re-opened the old sore of the rectification of the Rhine frontier—an admirable method of playing into their enemy's hands, by making the quarrel German instead of Prussian; but they were too excited and angry to be diplomatic. One journal had the candour to say plainly that, the instant war was proclaimed, all talk of the Hohenzollern question ought to be at an end: to fight about whether a German prince should or should not sit on the Spanish throne, would, it said, be simply a "*guerre impie*," an iniquitous war.

This warlike tone of the French press, and the uncertainty which consequently prevailed as to the continuance of peace, naturally caused a great convulsion in all the European exchanges, but especially on the Paris Bourse and the London Stock Exchange. The panic in London on Monday, July 11, was more severe than any which had been witnessed there for the previous sixteen years. All kinds of stocks and shares, many totally unconnected with European complications, and some even which would be likely to be benefited by war, were all heavily borne down, and in some instances were almost unsaleable. Consols fell to $91\frac{3}{8}$; a price about 2 per cent, below the average point at which they were maintained during the two years of the Indian mutiny, and exactly the same as during the four equally anxious years of the American struggle. Foreign stocks could scarcely be disposed of at all during the height of the panic. Some of them fell 7 or 8 per cent., and taking them at their money value, Spanish had at one time fallen 25 per cent. The total depreciation during the week, reckoning all classes of securities common to the Paris and London exchanges, could not have represented a sum of less than from £60,000,000 to £100,000,000. Among a few persons at Paris, enjoying early information, great gains were made; but the amount of general distress occasioned was unusually severe, owing to the fact, that for the previous six months operations for a rise had been extensive and continuous in all markets.

In the meantime Baron Werther, the Prussian ambassador at Paris, proceeded to Ems to consult with the king, and received from him an assurance that he had had nothing to do with the selection of the prince of Hohenzollern. The official North *German Gazette*, published at Berlin, also stated that the declaration of the Duc de Gramont, in the French Chamber, that the prince had accepted the offer of the crown of Spain, was the first definitive announcement to that effect received there. The French government, however, responded that it could not accept the answer of the king, and that either he must forbid the prince's persistence in his candidature, or war must ensue. An ultimatum to this effect was presented to the king by M. Benedetti, the French ambassador at Berlin, and in the meantime military preparations were actively pushed on. On Tuesday, July 12, the Spanish ambassador in Paris received a despatch from the father of Prince Leopold, stating that, in consequence of the opposition his son's candidature appeared to have met with, he had withdrawn it in the name of the prince. On the following day the communication was read aloud in the "Salle des Conférences" adjoining the Chamber of the Legislative Body, and M. Ollivier, being eagerly questioned as to what it portended, said, France had never asked for more than the withdrawal of the prince's claims, had said nothing about the treaty of Prague, and the whole affair was therefore now at an end. Shortly afterwards the Duc de Gramont made the announcement officially to the Legislative Body, but added the significant words:—"The negotiations which we are carrying on with Prussia, and which never had any other object in view than the above-mentioned solution, are not as yet terminated; it is therefore impossible for the government to speak on the subject, or to submit to-day to the Chamber and to the country a general statement of this affair." On being pressed, he declined to add anything to his statement, and said he had nothing to do with rumours circulating in the lobbies of the Chamber; evidently referring to the announcement just before made by M. Ollivier, and from which it would appear, either that there had not been complete harmony in the cabinet, or that the Duc de Gramont had been made the special medium of the emperor's wishes. After some discussion it was decided that the question should be debated on the following Friday. Much dissatisfaction and surprise prevailed in Paris at the vague and incomplete character of the duke's statement; but the general opinion was that war had been averted, at least for a time. The *Constitutionnel*, one of the oldest and most respectable journals, said the prince would not reign in Spain, and France asked for nothing further. All her just demands had been satisfied: "We receive with pride this pacific solution, and this great victory which has been obtained without one drop of blood having been shed."

Up to this point the Prussian government and press had preserved great calmness throughout the whole proceedings. The semi-official *North German Correspondent* said, that Prussia had hitherto avoided all interference in the question of the Spanish succession, and was resolved to adhere to the same policy in the future. The Spaniards themselves ought to be the best judges of what was fitting for their country; whether a republic or a monarchy, this prince or that, a Spaniard or a foreigner. The Prussian government, whilst it respected the independence of Spain, was not conscious of having received any special mission to solve the complicated constitutional question on which the attention of Europe was fixed, but believed it would be most safe and politic to leave this problem in the hands of the Spanish people, and their accredited representatives. Similar views were expressed in a communication sent from the foreign office at Berlin to the representatives of the North German Confederation; and it was added that those views were already known to the French government, but explanatory and confidential utterances had been prevented by the tone which the French minister had assumed from the beginning.

On the following day (Wednesday, July 13), everything was changed, and the question again assumed a phase of exceeding gravity. The king of Prussia, unattended by a minister, was at Ems for the benefit of the waters; and as he was walking in the public garden he met M. Benedetti, the French ambassador, and told him he had a newspaper in his hand which showed that the prince had withdrawn his candidature. To his surprise the ambassador then made the further demand of a pledge, that he would never, under any circumstances, approve or give his consent to the candidature of the prince. The king replied that this was a step he could not take, as he must reserve to himself the right of action in future circumstances as they arose. Soon afterwards he found that the ambassador had asked for a fresh audience, and he sent an aide-de-camp to tell him that the prince's candidature had been withdrawn, and that in the same way and to the same extent as he had approved of it, he approved of its withdrawal, and he hoped, therefore, that all difficulty on that point was at an end. On subsequently meeting the ambassador, the king wished to know if he had anything to say to him other than the proposition he had already made, and which he had declined. M. Benedetti replied that he had no fresh proposition, but had certain arguments to adduce in support of the former one, which he had not been able to urge. His Majesty said that with regard to himself he had already given his decision; but that if there were a political question to be discussed, he had better go to Count von Bismarck, and discuss with him the arguments which were to be adduced. M. Benedetti asked if the count was expected the next day, and when told he was not, he said he would be content with the king's answer. Unfortunately the fact of the king's refusing to renew the discussion was telegraphed to Paris without the addition of the reference to Count von Bismarck, and the pressure put upon the king by M. Benedetti was published in Germany without the explanation that it was by way of sequel to a conversation the king had himself initiated. Neither the king nor M. Benedetti realized the offence that had been given and received, till Paris and Berlin informed them that each had been insulted.

It afterwards transpired, from the despatches presented to the North German Parliament, that in addition to this demand on the king of Prussia at Ems. on July 13, in a conversation on the previous day M. Ollivier and the Duc de Gramont requested Baron Werther to communicate to Count von Bismarck their demand that the king should write a letter of apology to the emperor, and that no allusion must be made in it to the fact of the Catholic Hohenzollerns being near relatives of the Bonapartes. In his reply to Baron Werther, Count von Bismarck said he had no doubt misconceived the meaning of the French ministers, and that he had, at all events, better desire them to put their demand down in writing, and have it communicated to the Prussian government in the usual way through their ambassador at Berlin.

The king caused the circumstances connected with the fresh demands made on him by Count Benedetti at Ems, and of his having refused to accede to them, to be immediately telegraphed to Count von Bismarck at Berlin, who lost no time in publishing it; at nine o'clock the same evening boys in great numbers, in all the principal thoroughfares, distributed gratis a special supplement to the official *North German Gazette* relating what had occurred. The effect this bit of printed paper had upon the city was tremendous. It was hailed by old and young. It was welcomed by fathers of families and boys in their teens. It was read and re-read by ladies and young girls, and in patriotic glow finally handed over to the servants, who fondly hoped their sweethearts would soon be on the march. As though a stain had been wiped out from the national escutcheon, as though a burden too heavy to be borne for a long time past had been cast off at last, people were thanking God that their honour had been ultimately vindicated against intolerable assumption. There was but one opinion as to the conduct of the king; there was but one determination to follow his example. By ten o'clock the square in front of the royal palace was crowded with an excited multitude. Hurrahs for the king and cries "To the Rhine!" were heard on all sides. Similar demonstrations were made in other quarters of the town. It was the explosion of a long pent up anger against the French attempts to interfere with the domestic concerns of Germany since 1866, and in the first flush of excitement people absolutely felt relieved at the prospect of circumstances permitting them to fight it out. Thank God! They now could hope to unsheath the sword in a rightful quarrel. Their love of peace, till the day before faithfully preserved even under the trying events of the previous week, had been mistaken for fear by a nation of an entirely different intellectual type. Their king had been affronted beyond endurance, and had given the only possible reply. The crisis had arrived. They yearned to prove the present error of the French in estimating their national character, to avenge past injuries and obviate their recurrence, and so provide against the constant imperilling of peace, industry, and civilization for the future. Everywhere the same sentiments were uttered, the same resolves announced. In all the clubs and taverns, in many a private house, people remained together nearly the whole night, and only at break of day the streets assumed their usual aspect.

The most intense excitement also prevailed in Paris during the night, and on every one's lips was that word of evil omen, "*la guerre.*" Bodies of men paraded the principal streets up to a late hour, mixing up in a very odd fashion the cries of "A Berlin!" "A bas la Prusse!" "Vive l'empereur!" and the singing of the revolutionary war song, the "Marseillaise." It was a somewhat significant fact, that though this public singing of the "Marseillaise" was illegal, and was before occasionally put down with great energy by the gendarmes, even though it was only indulged in by a few revellers returning late from a supper party, and not sufficiently numerous to be very formidable to the safety of the state, it was now allowed to pass without notice; and hence the general impression was that the government were not sorry to give the patriotic anti-Prussian sentiment full play, partly to see what it was worth, and partly to make war popular.

On the morning of Thursday, July 14, the Emperor Napoleon went from St. Cloud to Paris, and presided at a cabinet council, which sat for several hours. The two Chambers expected a communication from the government, but none was made. On the following day, July 15—a day which must now be ever memorable in the history of Europe—a communication drawn up at the council of ministers on the previous day was simultaneously made by the government to the Senate and Corps Législatif, explaining the situation of affairs, and terminating in a declaration of war. The communication was as follows:—

"Gentlemen—The manner in which you received the declaration of the 6th inst., afforded us the certainty that you approved our policy, and that we could count upon your support. We commenced then negotiations with the foreign powers, to invoke their good offices with Prussia, in order that the legitimacy of our grievances might be recognized. We asked nothing of Spain, whose susceptibilities we did not wish to wound. We took no steps with the prince of Hohenzollern, considering him shielded by the king of Prussia, and we refused to mix up in the affair any recrimination upon other subjects. The majority of the powers admitted, with more or less warmth, the justice of our demands. The Prussian minister of foreign affairs refused to accede to our demands, pretending that he knew nothing of the affair, and that the cabinet of Berlin remained completely a stranger to it. We then addressed ourselves to the king himself, and the king, while avowing that he had authorized the prince of Hohenzollern to accept the nomination of the Spanish crown, maintained that he had also been a stranger to the negotiation, and that he had intervened between the prince of Hohenzollern and Spain as head of the family, and not as sovereign. He acknowledged, however, that he had communicated the affair to Count von Bismarck. We could not admit this subtle distinction between the chief of the family and the sovereign. In the meanwhile we received an intimation from the Spanish ambassador, that the prince of Hohenzollern had renounced the crown. We asked the king to associate himself with this renunciation, and we asked him to engage, that should the crown be again offered to the prince of Hohenzollern, he would refuse his authorization. Our moderate demands, couched in equally moderate language, written to M. Benedetti, made it clear that we had no *arriere pensee*, and that we were not seeking a pretext in the Hohenzollern affair. The engagement demanded the king refused to give, and terminated the conversation with M. Benedetti, by saying that he would in this, as in all other things, reserve to himself the right of considering the circumstances. Notwithstanding this, in consequence of our desire for peace, we did not break off the negotiations. Our surprise was great when we learned that the king hail refused to receive M. Benedetti, and had communicated the fact officially to the cabinet. We learned that Baron Werther had received orders to take his leave, and that Prussia was arming. Under these circumstances we should have forgotten our dignity, and also our prudence, had we not made preparations. We have prepared to maintain the war which is offered to us, leaving to each that portion of the responsibility which devolves upon him. Since yesterday we have called out the reserve, and we shall take the necessary measures to guard the interest, and the security, and the honour of France."

In both Houses the ministerial declaration was received with great applause. In the Corps Législatif, however, a considerable minority were indisposed to approve the policy of the government—at least, without fuller information. M. Jules Favre called upon the ministers to communicate the documents which had passed during the negotiations, and especially the Prussian despatch addressed to foreign governments admitting the refusal of the king of Prussia to receive M. Benedetti. M. Buffet opposed the demand for papers, and M. Jules Favre's motion was rejected by 164 votes against 83. An important speech was also made against the proceeding of the government by the veteran statesman, M. Thiers, who eloquently denounced the imprudence and impolicy of the war. He had been as deeply vexed as any one by the events of 1866, and earnestly desired reparation, but he considered the present occasion ill chosen: "for," added he, "when the satisfaction we had a right to demand had been granted; when Prussia had expiated by her withdrawal the grave fault she had committed in stepping beyond the limits of Germany, where lies her strength, and raising hostile pretensions suddenly in our rear; when Europe with honourable readiness declared that we were in the right—then for the government to have listened to susceptibilities upon questions of form might one day cause them regret." The opposition speakers could not, however, get a fair hearing, no tolerance being shown for those who differed from the majority. "I am about to quit the tribune," said M. Thiers, "borne down by the fatigue of speaking to people who will not hear me. I shall nevertheless have demonstrated that the interests of France were safe, and that you aroused the susceptibilities from which war has issued. That is your fault."

In the evening sitting of the Legislative Body, after a noisy debate, a credit of 50,000,000 francs was voted by 246 votes against 10; a credit of 16,000.000 francs for naval purposes was also voted by 248 votes against 1. A motion to call out the Guard Mobile to active service was adopted by 243 votes against 1. Another motion, authorizing the enlistment of volunteers for the duration of the war, was adopted by 244 votes against 1.

During the night, extraordinary animation prevailed throughout Paris. Numerous crowds, each numbering several thousands, came forth from the suburbs and traversed the Boulevards, singing the "Marseillaise" and the "Chant du Depart," and shouting "Vive la guerre! A has la Prusse! Vive l'Empereur! A Berlin!" It has been suggested that these patriotic displays were organized by the police. The soldier, however, became the hero of the hour, and could hardly show himself in the streets without being surrounded and applauded. In fact, the people became intoxicated by martial enthusiasm, and so blinded by jealous passion, that they were really not open to argument as to the right and wrong of the quarrel, and it became far less a question of a Hohenzollern pretension and a Benedetti rebuff, than one of seeing which was the stronger nation. Animosity against Prussia had vented itself so long in words, and it had become such a constant habit with many Frenchmen to speak of some future day of reckoning with their upstart rival as a matter of necessity, that the actual declaration of war seemed to afford relief to a very strong national feeling, and little else was thought of at first. Most Frenchmen had been fighting Prussia in imagination for the previous four years, and giving her the lesson her presumption deserved; the imagination and the longing had been so strong, and the reality for some days so tangible, that the transition from the one to the other was scarcely felt. It is true that the Republican journals, representing the opinions of the mass of the artizans, were from the first against war, nor was it at all popular with the peasantry, to whom it meant only a wider conscription and increased taxation; but in the heat of the excitement all prudential considerations were forgotten, and the voices and opinions of those who deplored the result to which matters had been brought had no influence with those who had the power and were determined to use it. Some attempts made by artizans and others in Paris, on the evening war was declared and on the following day, to get up counter-demonstrations in favour of peace, were immediately put down by the police.

The news of war having actually been declared reached England immediately, and when Parliament met the same afternoon, Mr. Disraeli, the leader of the Opposition, asked the prime minister, Mr. Gladstone, if he could inform the House of the real cause of the rupture, as he could not bring himself to believe that in the nineteenth century, with its extended sympathies and its elevated tendencies, anything so degrading as a war of succession could take place; and he reminded the House that only about two years before, in the matter of Luxemburg, both France and Prussia had invited the good offices of England, and they were successful in removing difficulties which then threatened a rupture. France and Prussia had thus, in his opinion, no moral right to go to war without consulting England, and he wished to know whether the government had taken any steps to impress this upon them. With great solemnity of manner he concluded, "I will only venture to express my individual opinion, that the ruler of any country who at this time disturbs the peace of Europe, incurs the gravest political and moral responsibility which it has ever fallen to the lot of man to incur. I hear, Sir, superficial remarks made about military surprises, the capture of capitals, and the brilliancy and celerity with which results which are not expected or contemplated may be brought about at this moment. Sir, these are events of a bygone age. In the last century such melodramatic catastrophes were frequent and effective; we live in an age animated by a very different spirit; I think a great country like France, and a great country like Prussia, cannot be ultimately affected by such results; and the sovereign who trusts to them will find at the moment of action that he has to encounter, wherever he may be placed, a greater and more powerful force than any military array, and that is the outraged opinion of an enlightened world." Mr. Gladstone, excusing himself from the same freedom of remark in which the leader of the Opposition had indulged, justified the right of England to intervene in the cause of peace, not only on moral grounds, but on the strength of the protocol of Paris in 1856, which set forth the duties of all of the powers there represented to submit to friendly adjudication any causes of difference, before resorting to the last extremity. Neither France nor Prussia had, however, shown any indisposition to listen to her Majesty's government on this occasion, and the foreign secretary had therefore not deemed it necessary to make an express representation, in the sense suggested by Mr. Disraeli.

At a reception of the members of the Senate by the emperor at St. Cloud, on the following day (Saturday, 16th July), M. Rouher, addressing his majesty, said—"The guarantees demanded from Prussia have been refused, and the dignity of France has been disregarded. Your majesty draws the sword, and the country is with you trembling with indignation at the excesses that an ambition over-excited by one day's good fortune was sure, sooner or later, to produce. Your majesty was able to wait, but has occupied the last four years in perfecting the armament and the organization of the army." M. Rouher added his hope that the empress would again act as regent, and that the emperor would take the command of the army. The emperor replied—"Messieurs les Senateurs, I was gratified to learn with what great enthusiasm the Senate received the declaration which the minister of foreign affairs has been instructed to make. Whenever great interests and the honour of France are at stake, I am sure to receive energetic support from the Senate. We are beginning a serious struggle, and France needs the co-operation of all her children. I am very glad that the first patriotic utterance has come from the Senate. It will be loudly re-echoed throughout the country."

In Prussia the news that France had determined upon war was received with enthusiasm. King William arrived at his palace in Berlin on Thursday night, July 14, and was received with the greatest possible loyalty and warmth. Upwards of 100,000 persons were assembled, from the Brandenburg Gate to the palace, cheering loudly and singing the national anthem. The Unter den Linden was illuminated, and decorated with the North German and Prussian flags. King William came forward repeatedly to the windows of the palace, saluting and thanking the crowd.

The following "Proclamation to our Countrymen" by the National Liberal party——the most numerous both in Parliament and among the people—is a fair specimen of the numerous addresses which were at once issued by both public and private societies:—

"War has become inevitable From the plough, the workshop, the office, and the study, our brothers congregate to ward off an enemy that menaces the highest treasures of the nation. The army whose onslaught they are going to encounter is differently composed from our own. It consists of mercenaries and conscripts, without any educated and well-to-do people among them, and for this very reason is liable to be made a tool of by an unjust and frivolous cabinet. Since the Corsican's nephew, by conspiracy, perjury, and every description of crime, surreptitiously obtained the throne of France, his only means of concealing domestic decline was to engage in foreign adventure. The French nation, humiliated at home, was to be reconciled to its fate by martial triumphs, flattering to its national vanity. Through cunning and force France was to be raised to an artificial supremacy over the rest of the world. To disturb the peace of Europe has ever been the only policy of Bonapartism, the vital condition of its existence. Since Louis Napoleon ascended the throne, all his hypocritical assurances of pacific sentiments have never sufficed to give any one a firm confidence in the continuation of peace; since he has been reckoned among sovereigns war has always been considered a mere question of time, and the utmost exertion of the industrious classes has been barely sufficient to cover the military expenditure of the various states. There is no country in Europe with which he has not meddled. He has quarreled with all, menaced all. Even if a state allied itself to him it was not safe from his treachery, as Italy experienced to her cost. The Poles were encouraged by him to rebel, only to be left to their terrible fate when it no longer suited him to play their patron. Neutral Belgium, German Luxemburg, and even some cantons of Switzerland, that tower of peace erected between contending nations, have at various times been the objects of his cupidity, and were only saved by the vigilance of the other powers, and their instinctive opposition to the immorality and mendacity of the Napoleonic polities. As long ago as the Crimean war Napoleon endeavoured to find a pretext for occupying the Rhine province. While we were fighting Austria he again had his eye upon the Rhine, and if we had not so quickly conquered, would have pounced upon us and have kindled universal war. Is it necessary to enumerate other instances of his disgraceful interference? Italy had to pay with two of her provinces for the French alliance, and at his hands, besides suffering many other indignities, was destined to provide the human bodies which first attested the efficiency of the 'miraculous' Chassepot. In Spain French influence has long been the strongest impediment in the way of progress, and although the independence of nations has ever been pompously paraded by him, Napoleon assisted the slave breeders in America, invaded Mexico, and in Germany calculated upon Austria being victorious. That he was mistaken in this latter calculation, and that the German people have at last found, and are steadily marching on, their way towards unity, makes him perfectly restless. It was certainly no very becoming act on the part of French diplomacy, when we had defeated Austria, to come to us begging for a small douceur in the shape of a province or two to reward them for their evil-disposed neutrality; nor was it very honest on the part of the same worthies to attempt to deprive us of our Italian ally by bribery and deceit. Again, it was France, who, by her perfidious intermeddling, prevented us from imposing such conditions of peace upon Austria as would have extended the ties of national unity to the southern states. In thus keeping them out from the Confederacy, Napoleon hoped to make the southern sovereigns tools in his hands and traitors to the Fatherland. We submitted to his arrogance on all these occasions, as also when the Luxemburg affair was brought upon the carpet, because we hoped to be able to avoid war. But his latest demands, and the manner in which they have been preferred, exceed everything that has gone before. To mask his domestic embarrassments, to save his throne, which would otherwise succumb to the hatred and contempt of his own subjects, the sanguinary adventurer has embarked in his last military job. In taking up the gauntlet thrown down to us, we are actuated by a sense of honour, and also by a desire at last to free ourselves from the dangers and solicitudes of the fictitious peace we have endured so long. More injurious than open war, the armed peace to which we have submitted has exhausted our resources, undermined our industry, stopped the advance of our culture, and, worst of all, kept us in constant dread of the sword suspended over us by a hair. In contending against the execrable system of Bonapartism, we shall be fighting, not only for our independence, but for the peace and culture of Europe. Unknown to the Germans is the lust of conquest; all they require is to be permitted to be their own masters. While protecting our own soil, language, and nationality, we are willing to concede corresponding rights to all other nations. We do not hate the French, but the government and the system which dishonour, enslave, and humiliate them. The French have been inveigled into war by their government misrepresenting and calumniating us; but our victory will be also their emancipation. We are firmly convinced that this will be the last great war the German nation is destined to undergo, and that the unity of our race will be the result of it. The God of Justice is with us. The insolent provocation of the French despot has done away with our internal divisions. The Main even now is bridged over. Party divisions are extinct, and will remain so as long as our united strength is required to overthrow the common enemy, who is equally the enemy of Germany and humanity. Inspired by the magnitude of the task before us, we are all united, a people of brethren, who will neither tarry nor rest until the great object has been accomplished."

Not a few passages in the above document would make the reader imagine it proceeded from a radical source. But its authors, the National Liberals, are the most temperate section of the liberals in Germany, and for the most part include the wealth and rank of the nation. If a class of politicians, whose sobriety and, in many instances, tameness had become proverbial, was moved to employ such language as the above, the feeling and expressions of the less moderate can be easily imagined.

The mobilization of the whole of the North German army was ordered on 16th July, and on the following Monday the king received an address from the Berlin town council, thanking his majesty for having repelled the unheard-of attempt made upon the dignity and independence of the nation, and asserting that France having declared war against Prussia, every man would do his duty. The king, in reply, expressed his gratitude for the sentiments contained in the address, and said:—

"God knows I am not answerable for this war. The demand sent me I could not do otherwise than reject. My reply gained the approval of all the towns and provinces, the expression of which I have received from all parts of Germany, and even from Germans residing beyond the seas. The greeting which was given me here on Thursday night last animated me with pride and confidence. Heavy sacrifices will be demanded of my people. We have been rendered unaccustomed to them by the quickly gained victories which we achieved in the last two wars. We shall not get off so cheaply this time; but I know what I may expect from my army, and from those now hastening to join the ranks. The instrument is sharp and cutting. The result is in the hands of God. I know also what I may expect from those who are called upon to alleviate the wounds—the pains and sufferings—which war entails. In conclusion, I beg you to express my sincere thanks to the citizens for the reception they have given me." At the termination of the royal address, which was delivered with much earnestness and gravity, the assembly, in a transport of enthusiasm, shouted unanimously, "Long live the king!"

The North German Parliament was opened on the next day (Tuesday, July 19), with a speech from the throne delivered by King William in person. In the course of it he said:—

"The candidature of a German prince for the Spanish throne—both in the bringing forward and withdrawal of which the Confederate governments were equally unconcerned, and which only interested the North German Confederation in so far as the government of a friendly country appeared to base upon its success the hopes of acquiring for a sorely-tried people a pledge for regular and peaceful government—afforded the emperor of the French a pretext for a *casus belli*, put forward in a manner long since unknown in the annals of diplomatic intercourse, and adhered to after the removal of the very pretext itself, with that disregard of the people's right to the blessings of peace of which the history of a former ruler of France affords so many analogous examples. If Germany in former centuries bore in silence such violation of her rights and of her honour, it was only because, in her then divided state, she knew not her own strength. To-day, when the links of intellectual and rightful community which began to be knit together at the time of the wars of liberation join—the more slowly the more surely—the different German races; to-day that Germany's armament leaves no longer an opening to the enemy, the German nation contains within itself the wish and the power to repel the renewed aggression of France. It is not arrogance that puts these words into my mouth. The Confederate governments, and I myself, are acting in the full consciousness that victory and defeat are in the hands of Him who decides the fate of battles. With a clear gaze we have measured the responsibility which, before the judgment seat of God and of mankind, must fall upon him who drags two great and peace-loving peoples in the heart of Europe into a devastating war.

"The German and French peoples, both equally enjoying and desiring the blessings of a Christian civilization and of an increasing prosperity, are called to a more wholesome rivalry than the sanguinary conflict of arms. Yet those who hold power in France have, by preconcerted misguidance, found means to work upon the legitimate but excitable national sentiment of our great neighbouring people, for the furtherance of personal interests and the gratification of selfish passions.

"The more the Confederate governments are conscious of having done all their honour and dignity permitted to preserve to Europe the blessings of peace, and the more indubitable it shall appear to all minds that the sword has been thrust into our hands, so much the more confidently shall we rely upon the united will of the German governments, both of the north and south, and upon your love of country, and so much the more confidently we shall fight for our right against the violence of foreign invaders. Inasmuch as we pursue no other object than the durable establishment of peace in Europe, God will be with us, as He was with our forefathers."

When the House met in the afternoon for the despatch of business, Count von Bismarck informed the members that the French charge d'affaires had delivered a declaration of war against Prussia. Hereupon all present arose, and greeted the announcement with loud cheering; the persons in the gallery shouting "Hurrah!"

On the following day the Parliament, in reply to his speech, presented the king with an address, in which they said:—

"One thought, one resolve, pervades all Germany at this grave juncture.

"With proud satisfaction has the nation witnessed your Majesty's dignified attitude in rejecting a demand of unprecedented arrogance put forward by the enemy. Disappointed in his hope of humiliating us, the enemy has now invented a sorry and transparent pretext for levying war.

"The German nation has no more ardent wish than to live in peace and amity with all nations that respect its honour and independence.

"As in 1813, in those glorious days when we freed the country from foreign aggression, we are now forced again to take up arms to vindicate our rights and liberties against a Napoleon.

"As in those well-remembered days, all calculations based upon human frailty and faithlessness will be destroyed by the moral energy and resolute will of the German nation.

"That portion of the French people which by envy and selfish ambition has been seduced into hostility against us, will, too late, perceive the crop of evil sure to grow out of sanguinary battlefields. We regret that the more equitably inclined in France have failed to prevent a crime aimed no less at the prosperity of their own country than the maintenance of amicable international relations in this part of the world.

"The German people are aware that they have a severe and portentous struggle before them.

"We confide in the gallantry and patriotism of our brethren in arms, in the indomitable resolve of an united people to sacrifice life and treasure rather than suffer a foreign conqueror to set his foot on German necks.

"We confide in the guidance of our aged and heroic king, who when a young man, more than half a century ago, warred against the French, and who, in the evening of fife, is destined by Providence decisively to terminate a struggle he then began.

"We confide in the Almighty, whose judgment will punish the bloody crime perpetrated against us.

"From the shores of the German Ocean to the foot of the Alps the nation has risen as a single man at the call of its allied princes. No sacrifice will be too heavy for it to make.

"Throughout the civilized world public opinion recognizes the justice of our cause. Friendly nations are looking forward to our victory, which is to free some from the ambitious tyranny of a Bonaparte, and to avenge the injury he has inflicted upon so many others.

"The victory gained, the German nation will at last achieve its unity, and on the battle-field, held by force of arms, with the common consent of its various tribes, erect a free commonwealth, which shall be respected by all peoples.

"Your Majesty and the allied German governments see us and our brethren in the South ready to co-operate for the attainment of this object. The prize of the war is the protection of our honour and liberty, the re-establishment of peace in Europe, and the promotion of the prosperity of nations.

"With profound respect and in loyal obedience,
    "THE PARLIAMENT OF THE NORTH GERMAN CONFEDERACY."

Immediately after the passing of this address, and as an incontrovertible proof that it meant something more than words, a loan of 120,000,000 thalers (£18,000,000) was voted by acclamation. In neither case was there a discussion. As the sum granted was equal to a fourth of the whole Prussian debt, there was a significant eloquence in the figures which ought not to be overlooked by the contemporary historian. Smaller grants, but which in the aggregate reached nearly a third of the Federal loan, were in the next two days likewise devoted to military purposes by the various state parliaments and governments of Northern and Southern Germany.

On Thursday the Parliament was prorogued. Count von Bismarck read a message from the President of the Confederation, and concluded as follows:—"After the words that the king has twice addressed to the Parliament, I should have nothing to add, were it not that his Majesty has commanded me to express his warmest thanks to the Parliament for the rapidity and unanimity with which it has provided for the requirements of the nation. In thus fulfilling the king's order, I declare Parliament closed." Dr. Simson next addressed a few words to the House, and said:— "The labours of the representatives of the people are for the present at an end, and the work of arms will now take its course. May the blessing of the Almighty descend upon our people in this holy war! Long live King William, commander-in-chief of the German army! "The session terminated amid loud and prolonged cheering.

The same day the king issued the following proclamation to his subjects:—

"I am compelled to draw the sword to ward off a wanton attack, with all the forces at Germany's disposal. It is a great consolation to me, before God and man, that I have in no way given a pretext for it. My conscience acquits me of having provoked this war, and I am certain of the righteousness of our cause in the sight of God. The struggle before us is serious, and it will demand heavy sacrifices from my people and from all Germany. But I go forth to it looking to the omniscient God and imploring His almighty support. I have already cause to thank God that, on the first news of the war, one only feeling animated ah German hearts and proclaimed aloud the indignation felt at the attack, and the joyful confidence that Heaven will bestow victory on the righteous cause. My people will also stand by me in this struggle as they stood by my father, who now rests with God. They will, with me, make all sacrifices to conquer peace again for the nations. From my youth upwards I have learnt to believe, that all depends upon the help of a gracious God. In Him is my trust, and I beg my people to rest in the same assurance. I bow myself before Him in acknowledgment of His mercy, and I am sure that my subjects and fellow-countrymen do so with me. Therefore I decree that Wednesday, the 27th of July, shall be set apart for an extraordinary solemn day of prayer and divine service in all our churches, with abstention from all public occupations and labour, so far as may comport with the pressing necessities of the time. I also decree that while the war lasts prayers shall be offered in all divine services, that in this struggle God may lead us to victory, that He may give us grace to bear ourselves as Christian men even unto our enemies, and that it may please Him to allow us to obtain a lasting peace, founded on the honour and independence of Germany.

(Signed)	"WILLIAM.
(Counter Signed)	"VON MÜHLER.

"Berlin, July 21."

On July 21 the Duc de Gramont addressed a circular to the French representatives abroad, with the object of proving that the nomination of Prince Leopold of Hohenzollern for the Spanish throne had been mysteriously promoted by Prussia, in the hope that France would be obliged to accept it as an accomplished fact. The circular stated:—"Either the cabinet of Berlin considered war necessary for the accomplishment of the designs it had long since been meditating against the autonomy of the German states, or not satisfied with having established in the centre of Europe a military power redoubtable to its neighbours, it desired to take advantage of the strength it had acquired to displace definitely, for its own benefit, the international equilibrium. The premeditated intention of refusing us the guarantees most indispensable to our security as well as our honour, is plainly exhibited in all its conduct.

"France has taken up the cause of equilibrium, that is to say, the interest of all the populations menaced like herself by the disproportionate aggrandizement of a royal house. In so doing does she place herself, as has been asserted, in contradiction to her own maxims? Assuredly not. Every nation, we are foremost to proclaim, has a right to govern its own destinies. That principle, openly affirmed by France, has become one of the fundamental laws of modern politics. But the right of each people, as of each individual, is limited by that of others, and any nation is forbidden, under the pretext of exercising its own sovereignty, to menace the existence or security of a neighbouring nation. In that sense it was that M. de Lamartine, one of our great orators, said, in 1847, that in the choice of a sovereign a government has never the right to pretend, and has always the right to exclude. That doctrine has been admitted on several occasions, and Prussia, whom we did not fail to remind of those precedents, appeared for a moment to give way to our just demands. Prince Leopold withdrew his candidateship; there was room to hope that the peace would not be broken. But that expectation soon gave place to fresh apprehensions, and then to the certainty that Prussia, without seriously abandoning any of her pretensions, was only seeking to gain time. The language, at first undecided, and then firm and haughty, of the chief of the house of Hohenzollern, his refusal to engage to maintain on the morrow the renunciation of yesterday, the treatment inflicted on our ambassador, who was forbidden by a verbal message from any fresh communication for the object of his mission of conciliation, and, lastly, the publicity given to that unparalleled proceeding by the Prussian journals, and by the notification of it made to the cabinets—all those successive symptoms of aggressive intentions removed every doubt in the most prejudiced minds. Can there be any illusion when a sovereign who commands a million of soldiers declares, with his hand on the hilt of his sword, that he reserves the right of taking counsel of himself alone, and from circumstances? We were led to that extreme limit at which a nation who feels what is due to itself cannot further compromise with the requirements of its honour. If the closing incidents of this painful discussion did not throw a somewhat vivid light on the schemes nourished by the Berlin cabinet, there is one circumstance not so well known at present, which would put a decisive interpretation on its conduct. The idea of raising a Hohenzollern prince to the Spanish throne was not a new one. So early as March, 1869, it had been mentioned by our ambassador at

Berlin, who was at once requested to inform Count von Bismarck what view the emperor's government would take of such an eventuality. Count Benedetti, in several interviews which he had on this topic with the chancellor of the North German Confederation and the under secretary of state intrusted with the management of foreign affairs, did not leave them in ignorance that we could never admit that a Prussian prince should reign beyond the Pyrenees. Count von Bismarck, for his part, declared that we need be under no anxiety concerning a combination which he himself judged to be incapable of realization, and during the absence of the Federal chancellor, at a moment when M. Benedetti considered it his duty to be incredulous and pressing, Herr von Theile gave his word of honour that the prince of Hohenzollern was not and could not seriously become a candidate for the Spanish crown. If one were to suspect official assurances so positive as this, diplomatic communications would cease to be a guarantee for the peace of Europe; they would be but a snare and a source of peril. Thus, although our ambassador transmitted these statements under all reserve, the Imperial government deemed fit to receive them favourably. It refused to call their good faith into question until the combination which was their glaring negation suddenly revealed itself. In unexpectedly breaking the promise which she had given us, without even attempting to take any steps to free herself towards us, Prussia offered us a veritable defiance. Enlightened at once as to the value to be attached to the most formal protests of Prussian statesmen, we were imperiously obliged to preserve our loyalty from fresh mistakes in the future by an explicit guarantee. We therefore felt it our duty to insist, as we have done, on obtaining the certitude that a withdrawal, which was hedged round with the most subtle distinctions, was this time definite and serious. It is just that the court of Berlin should bear, before history, the responsibility of this war, which it had the means of avoiding and which it has wished for. And under what circumstances has it sought out the struggle? It is when for the last four years France, displaying continual moderation towards it, has abstained, with a scrupulousness perhaps exaggerated, from calling up against it the treaties concluded under the mediation of the emperor himself, but the voluntary neglect of which is seen in all the acts of a government which was already thinking of getting rid of them at the moment of signature.

Europe has been witness of our conduct, and she has had the opportunity of comparing it with that of Prussia during this period. Let her pronounce now upon the justice of our cause. Whatever be the issue of our combats we await without disquietude the judgment of our contemporaries as that of posterity."

Immediately this circular reached Berlin both Count von Bismarck and Herr von Theile issued one, denying most positively that any such pledge was ever given, and in no ambiguous phrase affirming that M. Benedetti had made a statement quite unfounded in fact. On search at the French Foreign Office, however, a despatch narrating the circumstance was found, but as previously stated by the Duc de Gramont, it was marked "under all reserves," a sterotyped phrase of diplomatic phraseology of a rather elastic nature.

On July 22 the emperor received the members of the Legislative Body, and the president, M. Schneider, addressed him as follows:—

"Sire,—The Legislative Body has terminated its labours, after voting all the subsidies and laws necessary for the defence of the country. Thus the Chamber has joined in an effective proof of patriotism. The real author of the war is not he by whom it was declared, but he who rendered it necessary. There will be but one voice among the people of both hemispheres, throwing, namely, the responsibility of the war upon Prussia, which, intoxicated by unexpected success and encouraged by our patience and our desire to preserve to Europe the blessings of peace, has imagined that she could conspire against our security, and wound with impunity our honour. Under these circumstances France will know how to do her duty. The most ardent wishes will follow you to the army, the command of which you assume, accompanied by your son, who, anticipating the duties of maturer age, will learn by your side how to serve his country. Behind you, behind our army, accustomed to carry the noble flag of France, stand the whole nation ready to recruit it. Leave the regency without anxiety in the hands of our august sovereign the empress. To the authority commanded by her great qualities, of which ample evidence has already been given, her Majesty will add the strength now afforded by the liberal institutions so gloriously inaugurated by your Majesty. Sire, the heart of the nation is with you, and with your valiant army."

The emperor replied:—

"I experience the most lively satisfaction, on the eve of my departure for the army, at being able to thank you for the patriotic support which you have afforded my government. A war is right when it is waged with the assent of the country and the approval of the country's representatives. You are right to remember the words of Montesquieu, that 'the real author of war is not he by whom it is declared, but he who renders it necessary.' We have done all in our power to avert the war, and I may say that it is the whole nation which has, by its irresistible impulse, dictated our decisions. I confide to you the empress, who will call you around her if circumstances should require it. She will know how to fulfil courageously the duty which her position imposes upon her. I take my son with me; in the midst of the army he will learn to serve his country. Resolved energetically to pursue the great mission which has been intrusted to me, I have faith in the success of our arms; for I know that behind me France has risen to her feet, and that God protects her."

On the following day, July 23, the emperor addressed the following proclamation to the French nation:—

"Frenchmen,—There are solemn moments in the life of peoples, when the national sense of honour, violently excited, imposes itself with irresistible force, dominates all interests, and alone takes in hand the direction of the destinies of the country. One of those decisive hours has sounded for France. Prussia, towards whom both during and since the war of 1866 we have shown the most conciliatory disposition, has taken no account of our good wishes and our enduring forbearance. Launched on the path of invasion, she has provoked mistrust everywhere, necessitated exaggerated armaments, and has turned Europe into a camp, where reigns nothing but uncertainty and fear of the morrow. A last incident has come to show the instability of international relations, and to prove the gravity of the situation. In presence of the new pretensions of Prussia, we made known our protests. They were evaded, and were followed on the part of Prussia by contemptuous acts. Our country resented this treatment with profound irritation, and immediately a cry for war resounded from one end of France to the other. It only remains to us to leave our destinies to the decision of arms.

"We do not make war on Germany, whose independence we respect. We wish that the people who compose the great German nationality may freely dispose of their destinies. For ourselves, we demand the establishment of a state of affairs which shall guarantee our security and assure our future. We wish to conquer a lasting peace, based on the true interests of peoples, and to put an end to that precarious state in which all nations employ their resources to arm themselves one against the other. The glorious flag which we once more unfurl before those who have provoked us, is the same which bore throughout Europe the civilizing ideas of our great revolution. It represents the same principles and will inspire the same devotion.

"Frenchmen! I am about to place myself at the head of that valiant army which is animated by love of duty and of country. It knows its own worth, since it has seen how victory has accompanied its march in the four quarters of the world. I take with me my son, despite his youth. He knows what are the duties which his name imposes upon him, and he is proud to bear his share in the dangers of those who fight for their country. May God bless our efforts! A great people which defends a just cause is invincible.

"NAPOLEON."

CHAPTER II.

HAVING thus brought the course of events to the declaration of war, it will be better to retrace our steps a little, for the purpose of showing the earnest efforts made by the British government to avert so great a calamity. When, in consequence of the death of Lord Clarendon, Lord Granville became secretary of state for Foreign Affairs in July, 1870, so little was any fear entertained in England of a premature disturbance of the peace of Europe, that Mr. Hammond, the able and experienced permanent secretary at the Foreign Office, told his lordship he had never before known such a lull in foreign politics.

The first intimation of the candidature of Prince Leopold was received officially in England on Tuesday evening, 5th July, in a telegram from Mr. Layard, the British ambassador at Madrid, stating the fact, and that it was expected he would be accepted by the requisite majority. A letter was received the next morning from Lord Lyons, the British ambassador at Paris, stating that the Duc de Gramont had just informed him that France would not permit the selection to be carried into effect: she "would use her whole strength to prevent it." Nothing, the duke added, could be further from the wishes of the French government than to interfere in the internal affairs of Spain; but the interest and dignity of France alike forbade them to permit the establishment of a Prussian dynasty in the Peninsula. They could not consent to a state of things which would oblige them, in case of war with Prussia, to keep a watch upon Spain which would paralyze a division of their army. The proposal to set the crown of Spain upon a Prussian head was nothing less than an insult to France, and with a full consideration of all that such a declaration implied, he said the government of the emperor would not endure it.

It will thus be seen that, from the first day on which the matter was officially made known, the British government were informed that unless the project were relinquished war would certainly ensue. Nothing more would have been necessary to have called forth the immediate intervention of England, but in addition to this, the Duc de Gramont concluded the conversation to which we have referred by expressing to Lord Lyons his earnest hope that the British government would co-operate with that of France in endeavouring to ward off an event which, he said, would be fraught with danger to the peace of Europe.

As will be shown in the following narrative of events, the principle acted upon by the British government throughout, and which secured for it the approval, not only of persons of all parties in England, but the thanks of both France and Prussia, was, that though it could not recognize the election of Prince Leopold as being a danger to France, or that France would be entitled to put it forward as a cause of war either against Prussia or Spain, yet considering the fact that France was violently excited on the subject, and that the imperial government was fully committed to resist the election by force, it was a public duty to obtain the abandonment of the project. In the words of Lord Granville, who so ably conducted the negotiations throughout, its course was to urge the French government to avoid precipitation, and, without dictation, to impress on Prussia and Spain the gravity of the situation. "I felt that our position was very much that of trying to prevent a fire with inflammable materials all around, and with matches all ready to ignite; that it was not the moment to go into any elaborate inquiries as to who had brought the materials, or the rights and wrongs of the case, but that we should endeavour as soon as possible to remove those materials and to prevent one of the greatest calamities which could happen to the world." To this practical end the efforts of the English government were, therefore, directed, and with complete success so far as France had asked for its co-operation—the withdrawal of the prince's candidature.

After writing his letter of the 5th of July, Lord Lyons attended a reception at M. Ollivier's, the head of the French government. The latter took him on one side, and spoke at some length and with considerable emphasis, respecting the news just received. His language was in substance the same as that held by the Duc de Gramont in the afternoon, but he entered rather more into detail, and spoke with still more precision of the impossibility of allowing the prince to become king of Spain. Public opinion in France, he said, would never tolerate it, and any government which acquiesced in it would be at once overthrown. For his own part, he said, it was well known he had never been an enemy to Germany; but with all his good will towards the Germans, he must confess that he felt this proceeding to be an insult, and fully shared the indignation of the public. Lord Lyons urged that the official declaration to be made on the subject in the Chamber on the following day should be moderate, and M. Ollivier assured him that it should be as mild as was compatible with the necessity of satisfying public opinion in France; but in fact, he said, our language is this, "We are not uneasy, because we have a firm hope that the thing will not be done; but if it were to be done, we would not tolerate it." After this conversation, Lord Lyons said, in a despatch written on July 7, that he hardly expected the declaration (which is given in the previous chapter) would have been so strongly worded as it proved to be. He admitted, however, that, forcible as it was, it did not go at all beyond the feeling of the country, and it was only too plain that, without considering how far the real interests of France might be in question, the nation had taken the proposal to place the prince of Hohenzollern on the throne of Spain to be an insult and a challenge from Prussia. The wound inflicted by Sadowa on French pride had never been completely healed, but time was producing its reconciling effects in many minds when this matter had revived all the old animosity: both the government and the people had alike made it a point of honour to prevent the accession of the prince, and had gone too far to recede. Lord Lyons added, however, he did not believe that either the emperor or his ministers wished for war or even expected it: on the contrary, he thought they confidently hoped they should succeed by pacific means in preventing the prince from wearing the crown of Spain, and conceived if that should be so, they should gain popularity at home by giving effect energetically to the feeling of the nation; and that they should raise their credit abroad by a diplomatic success. They were, moreover, not sorry to have an opportunity of testing the public feeling with regard to Prussia, and they were convinced that it would have been impossible, with safety, to allow what, rightly or wrongly, the nation would regard as a fresh triumph of Prussia over France. In the afternoon of the same day (July 7) Lord Lyons had an interview with the Duc de Gramont, and told him he could not but feel uneasy respecting the declaration which he had made the day before in the Corps Législatif, and thought that milder language would have rendered it more easy to treat both with Prussia and Spain for the withdrawal of the pretensions of Prince Leopold. The duke said he was glad Lord Lyons had mentioned this, as he wished to have an opportunity of conveying to the British government an explanation of his reasons for making a public declaration in terms so positive. As minister in a constitutional country, he was sure Lord

Granville would perfectly understand the impossibility of contending with public opinion, and on this point the French nation was so strongly roused, that its will could not be resisted or trifled with, and nothing less than what he had said would have satisfied the public. His speech was in fact, as regarded the internal peace of France, absolutely necessary; and diplomatic considerations must yield to public safety at home. Nor could he admit that it was simply the pride of France which was in question. Her military power was at stake, for, as king of Spain, Prince Leopold could make himself a military sovereign, and secure the means of paralyzing 200,000 French troops, if France should be engaged in a European war. It would be madness to wait until this was accomplished; if there was to be war it had better come at once; but he still trusted much to the aid of the British government, and by exercising their influence at Berlin and Madrid they would manifest their friendship for France, and preserve the peace of Europe. As regarded Prussia, the essential thing was to make her understand that France could not be put off with an evasive answer; it was not to be credited that the king of Prussia had not the power to forbid a prince of his family and an officer of his army from accepting a foreign throne. It was, however, in Spain that the assistance of the British government could be most effectually given to France. The regent might surely be convinced that it was his duty to separate himself from a policy which would plunge Spain into civil war, and cause hostilities in Europe. The same day (July 7) Lord Lyons reported to Earl Granville a conversation he had just had with the Prussian chargé d'affaires at Paris, who considered the Duc de Gramont's declaration to have been too hastily made, and expressed his belief that neither the king nor Count von Bismarck was aware of the offer of the crown to Prince Leopold; but that he hardly knew what power the king of Prussia might possess of enforcing a renunciation, but certainly, being in the army, he could not leave it without the king's permission. Lord Lyons observed that much as they might deplore it, they could not shut their eyes to the fact that the feelings of the French nation would now render it impossible for the government, even if they wished, to acquiesce in the elevation of the prince to the throne. Neither Prussia, nor any other nation that he knew of, had any real interest in making the prince king of Spain; but all nations were deeply interested in preventing war, and that nation would most deserve the gratitude of Europe which should put an end to this cause of disquiet and danger. It seemed to him, therefore, that the king of Prussia, more than any other sovereign, possessed the means of putting a stop to the whole imbroglio in a dignified and honourable manner.

On the previous day, 6th July, M. de Lavalette, the French ambassador in London, had called on Lord Granville, and urged on him the importance of endeavouring to induce the obnoxious candidate to retire; and in compliance with this request, the latter promised to write at once to Lord Augustus Loftus, the English minister at Berlin; but at the same time he expressed his regret at the strong language reported to have been used to the Prussian representative in Paris, and guarded himself against admitting that France was justified in her complaints. In his letter to Lord Augustus Loftus he said, both Mr. Gladstone and he himself were taken very much by surprise by the news received the previous evening; and although the British government had no wish to interfere in Spain or to dictate to Germany, they certainly hoped, and could not but believe, that this project of which they had hitherto been ignorant had not received any sanction from the king. Some of the greatest calamities in the world had been produced by small causes, and by mistakes trivial in their origin, and in the then state of opinion in France, the possession of the crown of Spain by a Prussian prince would be sure to lead to great and dangerous irritation. Of this, indeed, there was conclusive evidence in the statements made by the minister to the French chamber. In Prussia it could be an object of no importance that a member of the house of Hohenzollern should occupy the throne of the most Catholic country in Europe. It was in the interest of civilization, and of European peace and order, that Spain should consolidate her institutions; and it was almost impossible that this should be accomplished if a new monarchy were inaugurated, which was certain to excite jealousy and unfriendly feelings, if not hostile acts, on the part of her immediate and powerful neighbour. He therefore hoped that the king and his advisers would find it consistent with their views of what was advantageous for Spain, effectually to discourage a project fraught with risk to the best interests of that country. Lord Augustus Loftus, however, was cautioned to say nothing which could give ground for the supposition that the English government controverted, or even discussed, the abstract right of Spain to the choice of her own sovereign; and for his own information it was added, that they had not in any measure admitted that the assumption of the Spanish throne by Prince Leopold would justify the immediate resort to arms threatened by France. On that topic, however, he was not then to enter into communication with the Prussian government. The groundwork of the representations which he was instructed to make was prudential. To considerations, however, of that class, Earl Granville said he could not but add the reflection, that the secrecy with which the proceedings had been conducted as between the Spanish ministry and the prince who had been the object of their choice, seemed inconsistent with the spirit of friendship or the rules of comity between nations, and had given, what the government could not but admit to be, so far as it went, just cause of offence.

The following day (July 7) Lord Granville wrote to Mr. Layard at Madrid, calling his attention to the great disfavour with which the candidature of the prince had been received in France, and said that although her Majesty's government had no desire to recommend any particular person whatever to Spain as her future sovereign, or to interfere in any way with the choice of the Spanish nation; still, entertaining as they did the strongest wish for the well-being of Spain, it was impossible that they should not feel anxious as to the consequences of the step thus taken by the provisional government, and they therefore wished him, whilst carefully abstaining from employing any language calculated to offend them, to use every pressure upon them which in his judgment might contribute to induce them to abandon the project.

Similar views were urgently impressed on the Spanish minister in London, who called on Lord Granville the same day; and it was forcibly represented to him that the step, if persevered in, might, on the one hand, induce great European calamities, and on the other, was almost certain to render the relations of Spain with a power which was her immediate neighbour, of a painful, if not a hostile character. A monarchy inaugurated under such auspices would not consolidate the new institutions of the country, and difficulties abroad would certainly find an echo in Spain itself. Senor Rances, the Spanish minister, explained that the project had not been intended as hostile to France; that it was the natural result of other combinations which had failed; and that it was to meet the ardent wish of the liberal party for the election of a king, in order to consolidate their institutions. He promised, however, to represent to his government, in as strong terms as were consistent with the respect due to them, the earnest wish of her Majesty's government, that they would act in the matter with a view to the maintenance of peace in Europe, and the future welfare of Spain.

On July 8 Count Bernstorff, the ambassador of the North German Confederation at London, called on Lord Granville, and informed him that he had received letters from the king of Prussia, and also from Berlin and Count von Bismarck, from the general tenor of which it appeared that the reply of the North German government to the request first made to them by France, for explanation respecting the offer of the crown to Prince Leopold, was to the effect that it was not an affair which concerned the Prussian court. They did not pretend to interfere with the independence of the Spanish nation, but left it to the Spaniards to settle their own affairs; and they were unable to give any information as to the negotiations which had passed between the provisional government of Madrid and the prince of Hohenzollern. He added, that the North German government did not wish to interfere with the matter, but left it to the French to adopt what course they pleased; and the Prussian representative at Paris had been directed to abstain from taking any part in it. The North German government had no desire for a war of succession, but if France chose to commence hostilities against them on account of the choice of a king made by Spain, such a proceeding on her part would be an evidence of a disposition to quarrel without any lawful cause. It was premature, however, to discuss the question as long as the Cortes had not decided on accepting Prince Leopold as king of Spain; still, if France chose to attack North Germany, that country would defend itself. Count Bernstorff went on to say that these views were held by the North German government, and also by the king of Prussia. His Majesty, he added, was a stranger to the negotiations with Prince Leopold, but he would not forbid the prince to accept the crown of Spain. The count dwelt much on the violent language of France. Lord Granville repeated to him the principal arguments of the despatch to Lord Loftus given above, and added that the position of North Germany was such that, while it need not yield to menace, it ought not to be swayed in another direction by hasty words uttered in a moment of great excitement.

The same day (July 8) Lord Granville sent Mr. Layard copies of the despatches just received from Lord Lyons, showing in what a very serious light the matter was received by the French government, and how imminent was the risk of great calamities, if means could not be devised for averting them. The provisional government of Spain would not, he was sure, wish to do anything which would be unnecessarily offensive to France, from whom they had received much consideration in the crisis through which their country was passing. In turning their thoughts to the prince of Hohenzollern they probably looked at the matter in an exclusively Spanish, and not in a European point of view; and being convinced of the necessity of the speedy re-establishment of a monarchy, and disheartened by the successive obstacles which they had encountered in attempting to bring it about, they turned their attention to a prince who might be ready to accept the crown, and who, in other respects, might be acceptable to the Spanish people. Her Majesty's government could quite understand that the excitement which their choice, looked at from a European point of view, had called forth, was unexpected by the provisional government, whose wish, they felt sure, could never be to connect the restoration of the monarchy in their country with a general disturbance of the peace of Europe, and which could not fail to be fraught with danger to Spain itself. The English government had no wish to press their own ideas upon the government of Spain; but they believed it would have been unfriendly to have abstained from thus laying before them some of the prudential reasons which seemed to them of vital importance to the best interests of their country. They hoped that their doing so would be accepted as the best evidence of their anxiety for the greatness and prosperity of Spain, and of their admiration of the wise course of improvement which had been inaugurated under the provisional government; and they trusted that this frank communication might induce the Spanish government to avoid all precipitation, and devise some means, consistent with their dignity and honour, to put an end to the cause of dissension.

On the same day (July 8) Lord Lyons had an interview with the Duc de Gramont in Paris, when the latter expressed great satisfaction with a report he had received from M. de Lavalette, of the conversation between him and Lord Granville on the 6th, and desired that his best thanks should be conveyed to him for the friendly feeling he had manifested towards France. He then went on to say he was still without any answer from Prussia, and that this silence rendered it impossible for the French government to abstain any longer from making military preparations. Some steps in this direction had been already taken, and the next day the military authorities would begin in earnest. The movements of troops would be settled at the council to be held at St. Cloud in the morning. On Lord Lyons manifesting some surprise and regret at the rapid pace at which the French government seemed to be proceeding, M. de Gramont insisted that it was impossible for them to delay any longer. They had reason to know—indeed, he said, the Spanish ministers did not deny it—that the king of Prussia had been cognizant of the negotiation between Marshal Prim and the prince of Hohenzollern from the first. It was therefore incumbent upon his Majesty, if he desired to show friendship towards France, to prohibit formally the acceptance of the crown by a prince of his house. Silence or an evasive answer would be equivalent to a refusal. It could not be said that the quarrel was of France's On the contrary, from the battle of Iowa up to this incident, France had shown a patience, a moderation, and a conciliatory spirit which had, in the opinion of a vast number of Frenchmen, been carried much too far. Now, when all was tranquil, and the irritation caused by the aggrandizement of Prussia was gradually subsiding, the Prussians, in defiance of the feelings and of the interest of France, endeavoured to establish one of their princes beyond the Pyrenees. This aggression it was impossible for France to put up with. It was earnestly to be hoped that the king would efface the impression it had made, by openly forbidding the prince to go to Spain.

There was another solution of the question to which the Duc de Gramont begged Lord Lyons to call the particular attention of the English government. The prince of Hohenzollern might of his own accord abandon his pretensions to the Spanish crown. He must surely have accepted the offer of it in the hope of doing good to his adopted country. When he saw that his accession would bring domestic and foreign war upon his new country, while it would plunge the country of his birth, and indeed all Europe, into hostilities, he would certainly hesitate to make himself responsible for such calamities. If this view of the subject were pressed upon him, he could not but feel that honour and duty required him to sacrifice the idle ambition of ascending a throne on which it was plain he could never be secure.

A voluntary renunciation on the part of the prince would, M. de Gramont thought, be a most fortunate solution of difficult and intricate questions; and he hoped the English government would use all their influence to secure it.

These views were at once communicated to Lord Granville, and hopes were entertained that an amicable arrangement of the difficulty might soon be found. On the next day Lord Granville wrote to Lord Lyons directing him to urge forbearance, and in another despatch, written on the same day, he said her Majesty's government regretted the tenor of the observations successively made in the French Chambers and in the French press, which tended to excite rather than allay the angry feelings which had been aroused in France, and might probably call forth similar feelings in Germany and Spain; and their regret had been increased by the intimation now given by the Duc de Gramont that military preparations would forthwith be made. Such a course, they feared, was calculated to render abortive the attempts which the English government were making to bring about an amicable settlement, and was calculated to raise the serious question as to the expediency of making any further efforts at that time for the purpose, which such precipitate action on the part of France could hardly fail to render nugatory, and of rather reserving such efforts for a future tune, when the parties most directly interested might be willing to second them by moderation and forbearance in the support of their respective views. When these opinions were represented to the Duc de Gramont on the following day, he told Lord Lyons that in this matter the French ministers were following, not leading, the nation. Public opinion would not admit of their doing less than they had done. As regarded military preparations, common prudence required that they should not be behindhand. In the midst of a profound calm, when the French cabinet and Chamber were employed in reducing their military budget, Prussia exploded upon them this mine which she had prepared in secret. It was necessary that France should be at least as forward as Prussia in military preparations.

He said the question now stood exactly thus:—The king of Prussia had told M. Benedetti on the previous evening that he had in fact consented to the prince of Hohenzollern's accepting the crown of Spain; and that, having given his consent, it would be difficult for him now to withdraw it. His Majesty had added, however, that he would confer with the prince, and would give a definitive answer to France when he had done so.

Thus, M. de Gramont observed, two things were clear: first, that the king of Prussia was a consenting party to the acceptance of the crown by the prince; and, secondly, that the prince's decision to persist in his acceptance, or to retire, would be made in concert with his Majesty, so that the affair was, beyond all controversy, one between France and the Prussian sovereign.

The French government would, M. de Gramont added, defer for a short time longer (for twenty-four hours, for instance) those great ostensible preparations for war, such as calling out the reserves, which would inflame public feeling in France. All essential preparations must, however, be carried on unremittingly. The French ministers would be unwise if they ran any risk of allowing Prussia to gain time by dilatory pretexts.

Finally, he told Lord Lyons that he might report to Lord Granville that if the prince of Hohenzollern should, on the advice of the king of Prussia, withdraw his acceptance of the crown, the whole affair would be at an end. He did not, however, conceal that if, on the other hand, the prince, after his conference with the king, persisted in coming forward as a candidate for the throne of Spain, France would forthwith declare war against Prussia.

The next day (July 11) Lord Lyons had another interview with the Duc de Gramont, and stated that the information which had been received from Spain and other quarters, gave good reason to hope that peaceful means would be found for putting an end, once for all, to the candidature of the prince; and he urged that, this being the case, it would be lamentable that France should rush into a war, the cause for which might be removed by a little patience. M. de Gramont replied that the French ministers were already violently reproached, by the deputies and the public, with tardiness and want of spirit. Any further delay would seriously damage their position; and there were military considerations much more important, which counselled immediate action. The government had, however, determined to make another sacrifice to the cause of peace. No answer had yet reached them from the king of Prussia. They would, nevertheless, wait another day, although by so doing they would render themselves one of the most unpopular governments which had ever been seen in France. Lord Lyons replied that the unpopularity would be of very short duration, and that the best title which the ministry could have to public esteem, would be to obtain a settlement of the question, to the honour and advantage of France, without bloodshed. In reporting this conversation to Lord Granville, Lord Lyons stated it was quite true that the war party had become more exacting. It had, in fact, already raised a cry that the settlement of the Hohenzollern question would not be sufficient, and that France must demand satisfaction on the subject of the treaty of Prague.

In a despatch from Madrid, written on July 12, Mr. Layard said the Spanish government fully appreciated the consideration and friendly feeling of that of England, and the equitable and impartial tone of their despatches. They maintained, however, that they had become involved in the difficulty most unwittingly; that they never entertained the remotest thought of entering into a Prussian alliance, or into any combination hostile or unfriendly to France; and they were most desirous of withdrawing from the position in which they had unfortunately placed themselves, if they could do so consistently with the honour and dignity of the country. At Mr. Layard's request they promised to make a communication to this effect to the European powers, as they were desirous to come to any arrangement which might save Europe from the calamities of a war. In an interview, General Prim the same day personally desired Mr. Layard to thank the English government for its good offices, and disclaimed in the most energetic way any intention to take a step hostile to France. He said that he himself was intimately connected with France and

Frenchmen; he had experienced great kindness from the emperor; had married and had many relations in that country; and was consequently the last man to wish to menace or offend France or her ruler. He also desired Mr. Layard to remind the English government of the great difficulties of his position; that when, after the revolution, Spain was without a king, and he was going from door to door in search of one, no European government gave him any help, and that he was everywhere repulsed. But when the Cortes and the country had insisted upon having a king, and when, after having been accused of wishing to maintain the interregnum for personal objects, he had at last succeeded in finding the only eligible candidate, he was immediately accused of having laid a deep plot against France, and of having sought to violate the international law of Europe. He repudiated in the strongest terms any desire of secrecy in order to deceive France or any other power: the reserve which had been maintained during the negotiations was absolutely necessary to save the country from the humiliation of making overtures to a fresh candidate, which might be again refused.

It was on this day (July 12) that the candidature of Prince Leopold was withdrawn, and Lord Lyons then had another interview with the Duc de Gramont on the subject. The latter said the king of Prussia was neither courteous nor satisfactory. His Majesty disclaimed all connection with the offer of the crown of Spain to the Prince Leopold of Hohenzollern, and declined to advise the prince to withdraw his acceptance. On the other hand, Prince Leopold's father had formally announced in the name of his son that the acceptance was withdrawn. In fact, the prince had sent a copy of a telegram which he had despatched to Marshal Prim, declaring that his son's candidature was at an end.

The duke said that this state of things was very embarrassing to the French government. On the one hand, public opinion was so much excited in France that it was doubtful whether the ministry would not be overthrown if it went down to the Chamber the next day, and announced that it regarded the affair as finished, without having obtained some more complete satisfaction from Prussia. On the other hand, the renunciation of the crown by Prince Leopold put an end to the original cause of the dispute. The most satisfactory part of the affair was, he said, that Spain was, at all events, now quite clear of the transaction. The quarrel, if any quarrel existed, was confined to France and Prussia.

Lord Lyons did not conceal from the Duc de Gramont his surprise and regret that the French government should hesitate for a moment to accept the renunciation of the prince as a settlement of the difficulty. He reminded him pointedly of the assurance which he had formerly authorized him to give to the English government, that if the prince withdrew his candidature the affair would be terminated; and he also urged as strongly as he could all the reasons which would render a withdrawal on his part from this assurance painful and disquieting to that government. Moreover, too, he pointed out that the renunciation wholly changed the position of France. If war occurred, all Europe would say that it was the fault of France; that France rushed into it without any substantial cause—merely from pride and resentment. One of the advantages of the former position of France was, that the quarrel rested on a cause in which the feelings of Germany were very little concerned, and German interests not at all. Now Prussia might well expect to rally all

Germany to resist an attack which could be attributed to no other motives than ill-will and jealousy on the part of France, and a passionate desire to humiliate her neighbour. In fact, Lord Lyons said, France would have public opinion throughout the world against her, and her antagonist would have all the advantage of being manifestly forced into the war in self-defence to repel an attack. If there should at the first moment be some disappointment felt in France, in the Chamber, and in the country, he could not but think that the ministry would in a very short time stand better with both if it contented itself with the diplomatic triumph it had achieved, and abstained from plunging the nation into a war for which there was certainly no avowable motive.

After much discussion, the Duc de Gramont said a final resolution must be come to at a council which would be held in presence of the emperor the next day, and the result would be announced to the Chamber immediately afterwards. He should not, he said, be able to see him (Lord Lyons) between the council and his appearance in the Chamber, but he assured him that due weight should be given to the opinion he had offered on behalf of the English government.

The result of this interview was made known at once to the English cabinet, and Lord Granville immediately wrote regretting that the renunciation had not been accepted as a settlement of the question, and said he felt bound to impress upon the French government the immense responsibility which would rest on France if she should seek to enlarge the grounds of quarrel, by declining to accept the withdrawal of Prince Leopold as a satisfactory solution of the question. With regard to the statement made by the Duc de Gramont in the Corps Législatif, that all the cabinets to which the French government had referred the subject appeared to admit that the grievances complained of by France were legitimate, he said such a statement was not applicable to her Majesty's government. He had expressed regret at an occurrence which had, at all events, given rise to great excitement in the imperial government and French nation; but he had carefully abstained from admitting that the cause was sufficient to warrant the intentions which had been announced, while, at the same time, he had deprecated precipitate action, and recommended that no means should be left untried by which any interruption of the general peace could be averted.

In an interview with the French ambassador the same day (July 13), Lord Granville earnestly entreated him to represent to his government that her Majesty's government thought, after their exertions at the request of France, they had a right to urge on the imperial government not to take the great responsibility of quarrelling about forms, when they had obtained the full substance of what they desired, and which M. de Gramont had told Lord Lyons, if obtained, would put an end to everything. All the nations of Europe had now declared their ardent wish that peace should be maintained between Prussia and France, and her Majesty's government believed that the imperial government would not give the slightest pretence to those who might endeavour to show that France was desirous of going to war without an absolute necessity.

The same day Lord Lyons, in a letter which was sent specially to St. Cloud, and delivered at the table at which the ministers were still sitting in council, in the presence of the emperor, again urged upon the Duc de Gramont in the most friendly, but at the same time most pressing, manner, to accept the renunciation of the prince as a satisfactory settlement; and in a personal interview with him in the afternoon—just after his statement in the Corps Législatif, that although the candidature of the prince was withdrawn, the negotiations with Prussia were not concluded—he expressed his surprise and regret that his declaration to the Chamber had not consisted of a simple announcement that the whole question with Prussia, as well as with Spain, was peaceably settled. The duke said he would explain in a few words the position taken up by the government of the emperor. The Spanish ambassador had formally announced to him that the candidature of Prince Leopold had been withdrawn. This put an end to all question with Spain. Spain was no longer a party concerned. But from Prussia France had obtained nothing, literally nothing. He then read to Lord Lyons a telegram, stating that the emperor of Russia had written to the king of Prussia soliciting him to order the prince of Hohenzollern to withdraw his acceptance of the crown, and had, moreover, expressed himself in most friendly terms to France, and manifested a most earnest desire to avert a war. The king of Prussia, M. de Gramont went on to say, had refused to comply with this request from his imperial nephew, and had not given a word of explanation to France. His Majesty had, he repeated, done nothing, absolutely nothing. France would not take offence at this. She would not call upon his Majesty to make her any amends. The king had authorized the prince of Hohenzollern to accept the crown of Spain; all that France now asked was, that his Majesty would forbid the prince to alter at any future time his decision. Surely it was but reasonable that France should take some precautions against a repetition of what had occurred when Prince Leopold's brother repaired to Bucharest. It was not to be supposed that France would run the risk of Prince Leopold suddenly presenting himself in Spain, and appealing to the chivalry of the Spanish people. Still France did not call upon Prussia to prevent the prince from going to Spain; all she desired was that the king should forbid him to change his present resolution to withdraw his candidature. If his Majesty would do this, the whole affair would be absolutely and entirely at an end.

Lord Lyons asked him whether he authorized him categorically to state to his government, in the name of the government of the emperor, that in this case the whole difficulty would be completely disposed of. He said, "Undoubtedly;" and on a sheet of paper wrote the following memorandum, which he placed in the hand of the English ambassador:—

"Nous demandons au roi de Prusse de défendre au prince de Hohenzollern de revenir sur sa résolution. S'il le fait, tout l'incident est terminé." ("We ask the king of Prussia to forbid the prince of Hohenzollern to alter his resolution. If he does so, the whole matter is settled.")

Lord Lyons observed to the duke that he could hardly conceive the French government really apprehended that, after all that had occurred, Prince Leopold would again offer himself as a candidate, or be accepted by the Spanish government if he did; to which the duke replied that he was bound to take precautions against such an occurrence, and that if the king refused to issue the simple prohibition which was demanded, France could only suppose that designs hostile to her were entertained, and must take her measures accordingly. Finally, he asked whether France could count upon the good offices of England to help her in obtaining from the king this prohibition; to which Lord Lyons said that nothing could exceed the desire of her Majesty's government to effect a reconciliation between France and Prussia, but that, of course, he could not take upon himself to answer offhand, without reference to the government, a specific question of that kind.

The substance of this was at once telegraphed to Lord Granville, and the following day Lord Lyons was informed that, in the opinion of the English government, a demand on Prussia for an engagement covering the future could not be justly made by France. Nevertheless, and although they considered that France, having obtained the substance of what she required, ought not in any case to insist to extremities upon the form in which it was obtained, they had at once and urgently recommended to the king of Prussia, that if the French demand was waived, he should communicate to France his consent to the renunciation of Prince Leopold. This renunciation had been placed before the king on behalf of the English government, in the following terms; namely, that as his Majesty had consented to the acceptance by Prince Leopold of the Spanish crown, and had thereby, in a certain sense, become a party to the arrangement, so he might with perfect dignity communicate to the French government his consent to the withdrawal of the acceptance, if France should waive her demand for an engagement covering the future. Such a communication, made at the suggestion of a friendly power, would be a further and the strongest proof of the king's desire for the maintenance of the peace of Europe.

On July 13 Lord Augustus Loftus had an interview with Count von Bismarck, and congratulated him on the apparent solution of the crisis by the spontaneous renunciation of the prince of Hohenzollern. The count, however, appeared somewhat doubtful as to whether this solution would prove a settlement of the difference with France. He told Lord Augustus Loftus that the extreme moderation evinced by the king of Prussia under the menacing tone of the French government, and the courteous reception by his Majesty of Count Benedetti at Ems, after the severe language held to Prussia both officially and in the French press, was producing throughout Prussia general indignation. He had that morning, he said, received telegrams from Bremen, Königsberg, and other places, expressing strong disapprobation of the conciliatory course pursued by the king of Prussia at Ems, and requiring that the honour of the country should not be sacrificed.

The count then expressed a wish that the English government should take some opportunity, possibly by a declaration in Parliament, of expressing their satisfaction at the solution of the Spanish difficulty by the spontaneous act of Prince Leopold, and of bearing public testimony to the calm and wise moderation of the king of Prussia, his government, and of the public press. He adverted to the declaration made by the Duc de Grammont to the Corps Législatif, "that the powers of Europe had recognized the just grounds of France in the demand addressed to the Prussian government; "and he was, therefore, anxious that some public testimony should be given that the powers who had used their "bons offices" to urge on the Prussian government a renunciation by Prince Leopold, should likewise express their appreciation of the peaceful and conciliatory disposition manifested by the king of Prussia. He added that intelligence had been received from Paris (though not officially from Baron Werther), to the effect that the solution of the Spanish difficulty would not suffice to content the French government, and that other claims would be advanced. If such were the case, he said, it was evident that the question of the succession to the Spanish throne was but a mere pretext, and that the real object of France was to seek a revenge for Königgrätz.

The feeling of the German nation, said Count von Bismarck, was that they were fully equal to cope with France, and they were as confident as the French might be of military success. The conviction, therefore, in Prussia and in Germany was, that they should accept no humiliation or insult from France, and that, if unjustly provoked, they should accept the combat. But, said he, we do not wish for war, and we have proved, and shall continue to prove, our peaceful disposition; at the same time we cannot allow the French to have the start of us as regards armaments. He had, said he, positive information that military preparations had been made, and were making, in France for war. Large stores of munition were being concentrated, large purchases of hay and other materials necessary for a campaign being made, and horses rapidly collected. If these continued, they should be obliged to ask the French government for explanations as to their object and meaning. After what had occurred they would be compelled to require some assurance, some guarantee, that they would not be subjected to a sudden attack; and must know that this Spanish difficulty once removed, there were no other lurking designs which might burst upon them like a thunderstorm.

The count further stated that unless some such assurance were given by France to the European powers, or in an official form, that the present solution of the Spanish question was a final and satisfactory settlement of the French demands, and that no further claims would be raised; and if, further, a withdrawal or a satisfactory explanation of the menacing language held by the Duc de Gramont were not made, the Prussian government would be obliged to seek explanations from France. It was impossible, he said, that Prussia could rest, tamely and quietly, under the affront offered to the king and to the nation by the insulting language of the French government. He could not, he said, hold communication with the French ambassador after the menaces addressed to Prussia by the French minister for Foreign Affairs in the face of Europe. In communicating these views to Lord Granville, Lord Augustus Loftus said he would perceive that unless some timely counsel, or friendly hand, could intervene to appease the irritation between the two governments, the breach, in lieu of being closed by the solution of the Spanish difficulty, was likely to become wider. It was evident to him, he said, that Count von Bismarck and the Prussian ministry regretted the courteous attitude and moderation shown by the king towards Count Benedetti, thinking that after the menacing language used in France with regard to Prussia he ought not to have received him at all; and in view of the public opinion of Germany, they felt the necessity of taking some decided measures for the safeguard and honour of the nation. The only means, he thought, which could pacify the wounded pride of the German nation, and restore confidence in the maintenance of peace, would be a declaration of the French government that the incident of the Spanish difficulty had been satisfactorily adjusted; and in rendering justice to the moderate and peaceful disposition of the king of Prussia and his government, a formal statement that the good relations existing between the two states were not likely to be again exposed to any disturbance. He greatly feared that if no mediating influences could be successfully brought to bear on the French government to appease the irritation against Prussia, and to counsel moderation, war would be inevitable.

These views from Prussia were communicated to the English Foreign Office on 13th July, but did not reach there until the 15th. As previously stated, on the previous day, 14th July, Lord Granville had telegraphed to Berlin, and recommended the king of Prussia to communicate to France his consent to Prince Leopold's renunciation, if, on her part, France would withdraw her demand of a guarantee for the future. The suggestion was declined; and Count von Bismarck expressed his regret that her Majesty's government should have made a proposal which it would be impossible for him to recommend to the king for his acceptance. In justification of the reasonableness of the plan suggested by the English government it should, however, be stated, that when the facts became rightly known it transpired that, in his communication with M. Benedetti at Ems on the previous day, as described in the preceding chapter, the king had himself voluntarily taken the identical course they recommended. When declining the suggestion, Count von Bismarck told Lord Augustus Loftus that Prussia had shown, under a public menace from France, a calmness and moderation which would render further concession on her part equivalent to a submission to the arbitrary will of her rival, and would be viewed as a humiliation which the national feeling throughout Germany would certainly repudiate. Under the irritation caused by the menaces of France, the whole of Germany had arrived at the conclusion that war, even under the most difficult circumstances, would be preferable to the submission of their king to any further demands. The Prussian government, as such, had nothing to do with the acceptance of the candidature of Prince Leopold of Hohenzollern, and had not even been cognizant of it. They could not, therefore, balance their assent to such acceptance by their assent to its withdrawal. A demand for interference on the part of a sovereign in a matter of purely private character could not, they considered, be made the subject of public communication between governments; and as the original pretext for such a demand was to be found in the candidature itself, it could no longer be necessary now that the candidature had been renounced.

The fatal telegram, detailing the supposed insult to the French ambassador at Ems, arrived in Paris on July 13, and in a despatch sent on the following day Lord Lyons thus reported the change which immediately occurred in public feeling:—

"PARIS, *July* 14, 1870.

"My Lord,—In my despatch of yesterday I communicated to your lordship the account given to me by the Duc de Gramont of the state of the question regarding the acceptance of the crown of Spain by Prince Leopold of Hohenzollern, and the recent withdrawal of that acceptance.

"My despatch was sent off at the usual hour, 7 o'clock in the evening. During the early part of the night which followed, the hope that it might yet be possible to preserve peace gained some strength. It was understood that the renunciation of his pretensions by Prince Leopold himself had come to confirm that made on his behalf by his father, and that the Spanish government had formally declared to the government of France that the candidature of the prince was at an end. The language of influential members of the cabinet was more pacific, and it was thought possible that some conciliatory intelligence might arrive from Prussia, and enable the government to pronounce the whole question to be at an end.

"But in the morning all was changed. A telegram was received from the French charge d'affaires at Berlin, stating that an article had appeared in the Prussian ministerial organ, the *North German Gazette*, to the effect that the French ambassador had requested the king to promise never to allow a Hohenzollern to be a candidate for the throne of Spain, and that his Majesty had thereupon refused to receive the ambassador, and sent him word by an aide-de-camp that he had nothing more to say to him.

"The intelligence of the publication of this article completely changed the view taken by the French government of the state of the question. The emperor came into Paris from St. Cloud, and held a council at the Tuileries; and it was considered certain that a declaration hostile to Prussia would be addressed at once by the government to the Chambers.

"I made every possible endeavour to see the Duc de Gramont, but was unable to do so. I sent him, however, a most pressing message by the chief of his cabinet, begging him, in the name of her Majesty's government, not to rush precipitately into extreme measures, and, at all events, not to commit the government by a premature declaration to the Chambers. It would, I represented, be more prudent, and at the same time more dignified, to postpone addressing the Chambers at least until the time originally fixed—that is to say, until to-morrow.

"In the meantime, although the news of the appearance of the article in the *North German Gazette* had not become generally known, the public excitement was so great, and so much irritation existed in the army, that it became doubtful whether the government could withstand the cry for war, even if it were able to announce a decided diplomatic success. It was felt that when the Prussian article appeared in the Paris evening papers it would be very difficult to restrain the anger of the people, and it was generally thought that the government would feel bound to appease the public impatience by formally declaring its intention to resent the conduct of Prussia.

"The sittings of the Legislative Body and the Senate have, however, passed over without any communication being made on the subject, and thus no irretrievable step has yet been taken by the government.

"I cannot, however, venture to give your lordship any hope that war will now be avoided. I shall continue to do all that is possible, in the name of her Majesty's government, to avert this great calamity; but I am bound to say that there is the most serious reason to apprehend that an announcement nearly equivalent to a declaration of war will be made in the Chambers to-morrow.

I have, &c.,

"LYONS."

The next day M. Ollivier made, in the Corps Législatif, a statement equivalent to a declaration of war; and shortly afterwards Lord Lyons had another interview with the Duc de Gramont, when the latter desired him to express to the British government the thanks of the government of the emperor for the friendly endeavours which they had made to effect a satisfactory solution of the question with Prussia. The good offices of her Majesty's ministers had, however, he said, been made of no effect by the last acts of the Prussian government, who had deliberately insulted France by declaring to the public that the king had affronted the French ambassador. It was evidently the intention of the government of Prussia to take credit with the people of Germany for having acted with haughtiness and discourtesy, to humiliate France. Not only had the statement so offensive to France been published by the government in its accredited newspaper, but it had been communicated officially by telegraph to the Prussian agents throughout Europe. Until this had been done, the duke said, the negotiation had been particularly private. It had, from the peculiar circumstances of the case, been carried on directly with the king of Prussia. The Prussian minister for foreign affairs, Count von Bismarck, had been in the country, and it had been impossible to approach him. The acting minister, Herr von Thiele, professed to know nothing of the subject, and to consider it as a matter concerning, not the Prussian government, but the king personally. Although the distinction was not in principle admissible, still it obliged France to treat with the king directly, and the French ambassador had been sent to wait upon his Majesty at Ems. The negotiation had not proceeded satisfactorily, but so long as it remained private there were hopes of bringing it to a satisfactory conclusion. Nor, indeed, had the king really treated M. Benedetti with the rough discourtesy which had been boasted of by the Prussian government. But that government had now chosen to declare to Germany and to Europe, that France had been affronted in the person of her ambassador. It was this boast which was the gravamen of the offence. It constituted an insult which no nation of any spirit could brook, and rendered it, much to the regret of the French government, impossible to take into consideration the mode of settling the original matter in dispute which was recommended by the English cabinet.

Lord Lyons having, at Lord Granville's request, called the attention of the duke to the statement made by him in the Chamber, that all the cabinets to whom he had applied had appeared to admit that the complaints of France were legitimate; the duke affirmed that he certainly intended to include the government of Great Britain in the statement, and that he must confess he still thought that he was perfectly justified in doing so. In fact, he said, the friendly efforts made, under Lord Granville's instructions, by her Majesty's minister at Madrid to get the candidature of Prince Leopold set aside, and the representations made for the same purpose by her Majesty's government in other countries, surely indicated that they considered that France had reason to complain of the selection of this prince, and the circumstances which had attended it.

Lord Lyons reminded the duke that the English government had throughout carefully abstained from admitting that this matter was sufficient to warrant a resort to extreme measures: to which he replied, that neither did his statement in the Chamber imply that the governments to which he alluded had made any such admission. The statement had been made at a comparatively early stage of the negotiation, and before the insult which had rendered extreme measures necessary. Finally, he said, he knew the English way of proceeding, and was aware that the English detested war, and therefore were not disposed to look favourably upon those who were the first to commence hostilities. Still, he trusted that France would not lose the sympathy of England. Lord Lyons said that if her Majesty's government had not been able to take exactly the same view of this unhappy dispute as the government of the emperor, he thought that they had, nevertheless, given most substantial proofs of friendship in the earnest endeavours they had made to obtain satisfaction for France. He could not deny that her Majesty's government had reason to feel disappointed, not to say hurt. They had been led to believe that the withdrawal of the prince of Hohenzollern from all pretensions to the crown of Spain was all that France desired. They had exerted themselves to the utmost to obtain this, and were then told that France required more. However this might be, there was, he said in conclusion, most certainly no diminution of the friendly feeling which had now for so many years existed between the two governments and the two nations.

As a last resource, on 15th July Lord Granville wrote simultaneously to the English ambassadors at Paris and Berlin, expressing his deep regret that the breaking out of war between the two countries seemed imminent. But being anxious not to neglect the slightest chance of averting it, the English government appealed to the twenty-third protocol of the conferences held at Paris in the year 1856, in which "Les plénipotentiaires n'hésitent pas à exprimer, au nom de leurs gouvernements, le voeu que les etats entre lesquels s'éleverait un dissentiment sérieux, avant d'en appeler aux armes, eussent recours, en tant que les circonstances admettraient, aux bons offices d'une puissance amie." ["The plenipotentiaries do not hesitate to express, in the name of their governments, their strong desire that states between which any serious difference may arise, before appealing to arms, should have recourse, so far as circumstances will admit, to the good offices of a friendly power."] And they felt themselves the more warranted in doing so, inasmuch as the question in regard to which the two powers were at issue had been brought within narrow limits.

Her Majesty's government, therefore, suggested to France and to Prussia, in identical terms, that before proceeding to extremities they should have recourse to the good offices of some friendly power or powers acceptable to both; the English government being ready to take any part which might be desired in the matter.

This well-intentioned effort on the part of England was decisively but courteously rejected by both countries. M. de Gramont thanked the English government for the sentiment which had prompted the step, but said he must recall to their mind that in recording their wish in the protocols, the Congress of Paris did not profess to impose it in an imperative manner on the powers, which alone remained the judges of the requirements of their honour and their interests. This was expressly laid down by Lord Clarendon, after the observations offered by the Austrian plenipotentiary. However disposed they might be to accept the good offices of a friendly power, and especially England, France could not now accede to the offer of the cabinet of London. In face of the refusal of the king of Prussia to give the French government the guarantees which his policy had forced them to demand, in order to prevent the recurrence of dynastic aims dangerous to their security, and of the offence which the cabinet of Berlin had added to this refusal, the care of the dignity of France allowed no other course. At the eve of a rupture which the kind efforts of friendly powers had been unable to avert, public opinion in England would, he believed, recognize that under the circumstances the emperor's government had no longer a choice in its decisions. On the other hand, Count Bismarck said, the king of Prussia's sincere love of peace, which no one had had a better opportunity of knowing than the English government, rendered him at all times disposed to accept any negotiation which had for its object to secure peace on a basis acceptable to the honour and national convictions of Germany; but the possibility of entering into a negotiation of this nature could only be acquired by a previous assurance of the willingness of France to enter into it also. France took the initiative in the direction of war, and adhered to it after the first complication had, in the opinion even of England, been settled by the removal of its cause. If Prussia were now to take the initiative in negotiating, it would be misunderstood by the national feelings of Germany, excited as they had been by the menaces of France.

In addition to the unceasing efforts of England for the preservation of peace, endeavours in the same direction were made by Russia, Austria, and Italy. Count Beust, the Austrian minister, also told Lord Bloomfield, our ambassador at Vienna, that perhaps no one was better able to judge of the state of feeling in the South German states than himself; and he was convinced that if France counted on the sympathies of those states, she would make a great mistake. With a view, therefore, to discourage her from looking to anything like support from that quarter, he had thought it well, in the interests of peace, to bring this conviction to her knowledge.

War having thus been actually brought about, notwithstanding all they had done to avert it, the English government turned their attention to securing the rights of neutrals. Renewed assurances that the neutrality of Belgium, Holland, and Switzerland would be respected were given by both France and Prussia. Time was also requested for neutral vessels, and protection for neutral property; and both powers at once conceded everything on those points that could, with good grace, be asked. French vessels which were in German ports at the beginning of the war, or which entered such ports subsequently, before being informed of the outbreak, were allowed to remain six weeks, reckoned from the outbreak of the war, and to take in their cargoes, or to unload them. In France the period allowed was thirty days. They were provided with safe-conducts to enable them to return freely to their ports, or to proceed direct to their destination. Vessels which had shipped cargoes for France, and on account of French subjects, in enemy's or neutral ports previously to the declaration of war, were declared to be not liable to capture, but were allowed to land freely their cargoes in ports of the empire, and to receive safe-conducts to return to the ports to which they belonged. The French government, however, declined to extend to the enemy's vessels, with neutral cargoes, the same privileges granted to them with French cargoes. It was also agreed that the following stipulations, agreed to at the treaty of Paris in 1856, should be recognized by both countries during the war:—

1. Privateering is, and remains, abolished.

2. The neutral flag covers enemy's goods, with the exception of contraband of war.

3. Neutral goods, with the exception of contraband of war, are not liable to capture under enemy's flag.

4. Blockades, in order to be binding, must be effective, that is to say, maintained by a force sufficient really to prevent access to the coast of the enemy.

On 19th July a proclamation of strict neutrality was issued by the English government, in which the queen's subjects were expressly forbidden to equip or arm any vessel for the use of either belligerent, and warning all who should attempt to break any blockade lawfully established that they would rightfully be liable to hostile capture, and the penalties awarded by the law of nations in that respect, and would obtain no protection whatever from the government.

A notification was also issued from the Foreign Office, stating that no ship of war, of either belligerent, would be permitted to take in any supplies at any port in the United Kingdom or her colonies, except provisions and such other things as might be requisite for the subsistence of her crew, and only sufficient coal to carry such vessel to the nearest port of her own country, or to some nearer destination. All ships of war were prohibited from making use of any port or roadstead in the United Kingdom, or her colonial possessions, as a station or resort for any warlike purpose; and no vessel of war was to be permitted to leave any port she might have entered for necessary supplies, from which any vessel of the other belligerent (whether the same were a ship of war or a merchant ship) should have left at least twenty-four hours.

As an additional proof of the sincerity of their desire to remain thoroughly neutral during the struggle, and to prevent the possibility of any justifiable complaint from either belligerent, the government introduced and carried a new Foreign Enlistment Act, which went far beyond any law ever before passed in any country for the purpose of enforcing neutrality, and involved a total revolution in the ideas of English statesmen with regard to the duties of neutrals. The chief provisions of the Act are, that a penalty of fine and imprisonment, or both, at the discretion of the court, may be imposed for enlistment in the military or naval service of any foreign state at war with any state at peace with her Majesty, or inducing any other person to accept such service. Similar penalties are imposed for leaving her Majesty's dominions with intent to serve a foreign state, or for embarking persons under false representations as to service. Any master or owner of a ship who knowingly receives on board his ship, within her Majesty's dominions, any person illegally enlisted under any of the circumstances above described, is made liable to fine and imprisonment; his ship may be detained till all the penalties have been paid, or security given for them; and the illegally enlisted persons are to be taken on shore, and not allowed to return to the ship. The object of these latter clauses is, of course, to strike at the former practice of hiring men for an ostensibly peaceful and legal service, and afterwards, with or without their connivance, employing them in a military or naval expedition.

But the most interesting and important division of the Act is that which relates to illegal shipbuilding and illegal expeditions. As in the previous Act, it is declared to be an offence to commission, equip, or despatch any ship with intent or knowledge, or having reasonable cause to believe, that the same will be employed in the military or naval service of any foreign state at war with any friendly state. The offender is punishable by fine and imprisonment; and the ship, in respect of which any such offence is committed, with the equipment, is to be held forfeited to her Majesty. But over and above this the new Act embodies a provision, making the building of a vessel under such circumstances an offence in itself; and what is more, the onus of disproof lies with the builder:—"Where any ship is built by order of or on behalf of any foreign state at war with a friendly state, or is delivered to or to the order of such foreign state, or any agent of such state, or is paid for by such foreign state or their agent, and is employed in the military or naval service of such state, such ship shall, until the contrary is proved, be deemed to have been built with a view to being so employed, and the burden shall lie on the builder of such ship of proving that he did not know that the ship was intended to be so employed in the military or naval service of such foreign state." Further, it is declared an offence to augment the warlike force of any ship for the use of a belligerent. These clauses are intended to check the practice adopted during the American war of building or fitting out a vessel in this country and then sending her either out to sea, or to some other neutral port, to take on board an armament sent to meet her in some other ship. No distinction of this kind as to time or place will, under the new Act, suffice to elude the law. The mere building of a ship with the intent or knowledge that it is afterwards to be equipped and used for purposes of war against a state with whom we are at peace, is ranked as an offence, quite apart from the actual equipment and despatch of the ship for this purpose. The defects of the law were strikingly illustrated by the two cases of the Alabama and the rams. While the former escaped, because the authorities had not authority to seize her, even though her intended use and destination were perfectly notorious, in the other instance the government took the law into their own hands, and arbitrarily seized the rams on their own responsibility. The law is now sufficient to meet all cases of this description, and to spare the authorities any necessity of straining it, in order to discharge the obligations of a neutral. This branch of the measure is completed by two other clauses, enacting that illegal ships shall not be received in British ports, and making it an offence, punishable with fine and imprisonment, to prepare or fit out, or in any way assist in preparing, any naval or military expedition to proceed against the dominions of a friendly state; all ships forming part of such an expedition being forfeited to the crown.

The remaining clauses of the Act relate to the legal procedure in regard to the offences described, the courts which are to try cases, the officers authorized to seize offending ships, &c. A special power is given to the secretary of state, or chief executive authority, to issue a warrant to detain a ship, if "satisfied that there is a reasonable and probable cause for believing "that it is being built, equipped, or despatched for an illegal purpose. The owner of a ship so detained may apply to the Court of Admiralty for its release, and if he can show that the ship was not intended for the use suspected it will be restored to him. If he fails in this proof the secretary of state will be at liberty to detain the vessel as long as he pleases; the court having, however, a discretionary power to release the vessel on the owner giving security that it shall not be employed contrary to the Act. If there has been no reasonable cause for detention, the owner will be entitled to an indemnity to be assessed by the court. The "local authority" may also detain a suspected ship until reference can be made to the secretary of state or chief executive authority. The secretary of state may issue a search warrant in any dockyard in the queen's dominions, and he is to be held free from legal proceedings in connection with any warrant he may issue, and is not bound to give evidence as a witness except with his own consent. The decision of the important question whether a ship is or is not rightly suspected, is withdrawn from the cognizance of a jury and submitted to the consideration of a judge, so that there can be none of those failures of justice which formerly took place in consequence of the misdirected patriotism of juries.

CHAPTER III.

Important Statement of the French Emperor—He declares that he neither expected nor was prepared for War, but that France had slipped out of his hands—A thoroughly National War—His Version of a very important conversation with Count von Bismarck—Publication of a Proposed Secret Treaty between France and Prussia, by which France was to acquire Luxemburg by purchase and conquer Belgium with the Assistance of Prussia, on Condition of not interfering with the Plans of Prussia in Germany—Great Excitement on the Subject in England and Belgium—Statements of the English Government in both Houses of Parliament—Manly Speech of Mr. Disraeli—Letter from M. Ollivier, the Head of the French Government, repudiating the Treaty—General State of Feeling on the Question in France— Explanation of the Journal Officiel—*The Prussian Version of the Transaction—Other Propositions of a Similar Nature made by France to Prussia divulged, including an offer of 300,000 men to assist in a War against Austria, in return for the Rhenish Provinces— Continued Efforts of France to "lead Prussia into Temptation"—Count von Bismarck's Reasons for not divulging the Proposals at the time they were made—Explanation of M. Benedetti, the Proposer of the Secret Treaty—He states that it was well known that Prussia offered to assist France in acquiring Belgium in return for her own Aggrandisement—Such Overtures persistently declined by the French Government—The Secret Treaty written at the Dictation of Count von Bismarck—The Proposals rejected by the French Emperor as soon as they came to his Knowledge—Count von Bismarck's only Reason for publishing them must have been to mislead Public Opinion—French Official Explanation on the same Subject from the Duc de Gramont—The idea of France appropriating Belgium a purely Prussian one, to avert Attention from the Rhine Provinces—Offer of Prussian Assistance to accomplish it— The Emperor steadily refused to entertain the Idea—Emphatic Denial that France intended to offer to conclude Peace on the Basis of the Secret Treaty if it had not been published— Proposals made by France to Prussia through Lord Clarendon to reduce their Armaments— The Proposition rejected by the King of Prussia—Further Proofs adduced by Prussia against France—Anxiety in England—Action taken by the Government—£2,000,000 and 20,000 men enthusiastically voted by the House of Commons—Great Debate on the whole Matter—Mr. Disraeli stigmatises the Pretext for War as "Disgraceful," and Proposes an Alliance with Russia—Guarded Statement of Mr. Gladstone—Dissatisfaction at it in the House—Spirited Speech of Lord Russell in the House of Lords in Favour of supporting Belgium at all Cost— Reassuring reply of Lord Granville—Important Statements in both Houses of Parliament by the Government as to the Course they had adopted, and Comments thereon—The Complete Text of New Treaty agreed on to preserve the Neutrality of Belgium—Feeling of Reassurance in England—Altered State of Feeling in Austria towards France—Biographical Notices of Count vou Bismarck and M. Benedetti.*

In the two preceding chapters the circumstances connected with the war have been consecutively described from the 5th July, when the first official announcement of Prince Leopold's candidature reached England and France, to the 23rd July—a week subsequent to the actual declaration of war by France. Immediately this event took place, both countries commenced massing troops on their respective frontiers, and were so engaged for the next fortnight. Only a few slight skirmishes, however, took place between the reconnoitring parties of the two armies; and before proceeding to describe the more stirring events of the contest, we must, in order to continue the narrative of events consecutively, devote a chapter to the now celebrated "Secret Treaty"—a document which for a time excited even more interest in England than the war itself, and which led to some important steps being adopted by the British Parliament.

Simultaneously with the publication of the Treaty (Monday, 25th July) another communication was published, which would doubtless have created much more attention than it did had it not been that everything else was, for a time, to a great extent overlooked. We, however, reproduce it here, before describing the treaty, and shall then have no further cause to refer to it. It was an account of an interview with the Emperor Napoleon, in the previous week, and was inserted in the *Daily Telegraph* newspaper under the signature of "An Englishman," who said he had his Majesty's free consent to its publication. It stated that the emperor, after speaking upon some private matters, turned suddenly to the political situation of France and of Europe. He said: "One fortnight before the utterance of the Duc de Gramont in the Corps Législatif—which utterance has, as it seems to me, been so unjustly reflected upon by the English press—I had no notion that war was at hand, nor am I, even at this moment, by any means prepared for it. I trusted that, when the Duc de Gramont had set me straight with France by speaking manfully in public as to the Hohenzollern candidature, I should be able so to manipulate and handle the controversy as to make peace certain. But France has slipped out of my hand. I cannot rule unless I lead. This is the most national war that in my time France has undertaken, and I have no choice but to advance at the head of a public opinion which I can neither stem nor check. In addition, Count von Bismarck, although a very clever man, wants too much, and wants it too quick. After the victory of Prussia in 1866, I reminded him that but for the friendly and self-denying neutrality of France he could never have achieved such marvels. I pointed out to him that I had never moved a French soldier near to the Rhine frontier during the continuance of the German war. I quoted to him from his own letter in which he thanked me for my abstinence, and said that he had left neither a Prussian gun nor a Prussian soldier upon the Rhine, but had thrown Prussia's whole and undivided strength against Austria and her allies. I told him that, as some slight return for my friendly inactivity, I thought that he might surrender Luxemburg, and one or two other little towns which gravely menace our frontier, to France. I added that in this way he would, by a trifling sacrifice, easily forgotten by Prussia in view of her enormous successes and acquisitions, pacify the French nation, whose jealousies it was so easy to arouse, so difficult to disarm.

"Count von Bismarck replied to me, after some delay, 'Not one foot of territory, whether Prussian or neutral, can I resign. But, perhaps, if I were to make further acquisitions, I could make some concessions. How, for instance, if I were to take Holland? What would France want as a sop for Holland?'

" ' I replied,' said the emperor, ' that if he attempted to take Holland, it meant war with France; and there the conversation, in which Count von Bismarck and M. de Benedetti were the interlocutors, came to an end.'"

The only notice of importance which was taken of this document was in a debate in the House of Lords, in which Lord Malmsbury said he knew the writer (Honourable F. Lawley) was worthy of all credence, and in the official *North German Gazette*, which admitted the truth of the description of the conversation between Count von Bismarck and the emperor down to the word "resign," but said the remainder of the statement (that concerning Holland) was altogether fictitious.

On the same day (25th July) as this document appeared in the *Daily Telegraph*, the Times startled the world by publishing the "Draft of a Secret Project of Alliance, Offensive and Defensive, between France and Prussia," which, on account of its importance, and the results to which it led, we give both in the original French, and also in an English version. The only variations from the text of the actual proposed treaty, and the copy of it published in the Times, are indicated by italics and brackets.

PROPOSED TREATY BETWEEN FRANCE AND PRUSSIA.

Sa Majesté le roi de Prusse et sa Majesté l'empereur des Français jugeant utile de resserrer les liens d'amitié qui les unissent et de consolider les rapports de bon voisinage heureusement existant entre les deux pays, convaincus d'autre part que pour atteindre ce résultat, propre d'ailleurs à assurer le maintien de la paix générale, il leur importe de s'entendre sur des questions qui intéressent leurs relations futures, ont résolu de conclure un traité à cet effet, et nommé en consequence pour leurs plénipotentiaires, &c., savoir:

Sa Majesté, &c.;

Sa Majesté, &c;

Lesquels, apres avoir échangé leurs plcinspouvoirs, trouvés en bonne et due forme, sont convenus des articles suivants:—

Article I.—Sa Majesté l'empereur des Français admet et reconnait les acquisitions que la Prusse a faites à la suite de la dernière guerre qu'elle a soutenue contre l'Autriche et contre ses alliés [*ainsi que les arrangements pris ou à prendre pour la constitution dune Confédération dans l'Allemagne du Nord, s'engageant en même temps à preter son appui à la conservation de cette oeuvre*],

Article II.—Sa Majesté le roi de Prusse promet de faciliter à la France l'acquisition du Luxembourg; à cet effet la dite Majesté entrera en négociations avec sa Majesté le roi des Pays-Bas pour le déterminer à faire, à l'empereur des Français, la cession de ses droits souverains sur ce duché, moyennant telle compensation qui sera jugée suffisante ou autrement. De son côté l'empereur des Français s'engage à assumer les charges pécuniaires que cette transaction peut comporter. [*Pour faciliter cette transaction, l'empereur des Français, de son côté, s'engage à assumer accessoirement les charges pécuniaires qu'elle pourrait comporter.*]

Article III.—Sa Majesté l'empereur des Français ne s'opposera pas à une union fédérale de la Confédération du Nord avec les etats du midi de l'Allemagne, à l'exception de l'Autriche, laquelle union pourra être basée sur un Parlement commun, tout en respectant, dans une juste mesure, la souveraineté des dits etats.

Article IV.—De son côté, sa Majesté le roi de Prusse, au cas où sa Majesté l'empereur des Français serait amené par les circonstances à, faire entrer ses troupes en Belgique ou à la conquérir, accordera le secours [*concours*] de ses armes à la France, et il la soutiendra avec toutes ses forces de terre et de mer, envers et contre toute puissance qui, dans cette éventualité, lui déclarerait la guerre.

Article V.—Pour assurer l'entière exécution des dispositions qui précèdent, sa Majest'e le roi de Prusse et sa Majesté l'empereur des Français contractent, par le présent traité, une alliance offensive et défensive qu'ils s'engagent solennellement à maintenir. Leurs Majestés s'obligent, en outre et notamment, à l'observer dans tous les cas où leurs etats respectifs, dont elles se garantissent mutuellement l'intégrité, seraient menacés d'une aggression, se tenant pour liées, en pareille conjoncture, de prendre sans retard, et de ne décliner sous aucun prétexte, les arrangements militaires qui seraient commandés par leur intérêt commun conformément aux clauses et prévisions ci-dessus énoncées.

TRANSLATION.

His Majesty the king of Prussia and his Majesty the emperor of the French, deeming it useful to draw closer the bonds of friendship which unite them, and to consolidate the relations of good neighbourhood happily existing between the two countries, and being convinced, on the other hand, that to attain this result, which is calculated besides to assure the maintenance of the general peace, it behoves them to come to an understanding on questions which concern their future relations, have resolved to conclude a treaty to this effect, and named in consequence as their plenipotentiaries, that is to say,

His Majesty, &c;

His Majesty, &c.;

Who, having exchanged their full powers, found to be in good and proper form, have agreed upon the following articles:—

Article I.—His Majesty the emperor of the French admits and recognizes the acquisitions which Prussia has made as the result of the last war which she sustained against Austria and her allies [*as also the arrangements adopted or to be adopted for constituting a Confederation in North Germany, engaging, at the same time, to render his support for the maintenance of that work*].

Article II.—His Majesty the king of Prussia promises to facilitate the acquisition of Luxemburg by France: to that effect his aforesaid Majesty will enter into negotiations with his Majesty the king of the Netherlands, to induce him to cede to the emperor of the French his sovereign rights over that duchy, in return for such compensation as shall be deemed sufficient or otherwise. On his part, the emperor of the French engages to bear the pecuniary charges which this arrangement may involve. [*In order to facilitate this arrangement, the emperor of the French engages, on his part, to bear accessorily the pecuniary charges which it may involve.*]

Article III.—His Majesty the emperor of the French will not oppose a federal union of the Confederation of the North with the southern states of Germany, with the exception of Austria, which union may be based on a common Parliament, the sovereignty of the said states being duly respected.

Article IV.—On his part his Majesty the king of Prussia, in case his Majesty the emperor of the French should be obliged by circumstances to cause his troops to enter Belgium, or to conquer it, will grant the succour [*co-operation*] of his arms to France, and will sustain her with all his forces of land and sea against every power which, in that eventuality, should declare war upon her.

Article V.—To insure the complete execution of the above arrangements, his Majesty the king of Prussia and his Majesty the emperor of the French contract, by the present treaty, an alliance offensive and defensive, which they solemnly engage to maintain. Their Majesties engage moreover, and specifically, to observe it in every case in which their respective states, of which they mutually guarantee the integrity, should be menaced by aggression, holding themselves bound in such a conjuncture to make without delay, and not to decline on any pretext, the military arrangements which may be demanded by their common interest, conformably to the clauses and provisions above set forth.

This treaty had, of course, been supplied to the *Times* by the Prussian government; and in its comments on the matter in a leading article—evidently written under inspiration—the great English journal stated that it was rejected at the time it was tendered, but that it had recently again been offered as a condition of peace. At all events, means had been taken to let it be understood that the old project was open, and that a ready acceptance of it would save Prussia from attack. The suggestion had not, however, been favourably received; on the contrary, matters had, as was well known, been so far advanced that it was impossible to arrest the progress of the war by a *coup de théâtre*.

As will be readily understood, the publication of this document caused the greatest sensation, not only in England, but on the Continent, and especially in Belgium. England was, of course, most deeply interested, because by the treaty of 1839 she, in common with France, Prussia, and other great powers, had guaranteed the independence of the Belgian kingdom. The subject formed the sole topic of conversation in the city during the day, and had a considerable effect on the stock markets, producing a fall both in consols and foreign securities. The excitement at the meeting of the House of Commons in the afternoon was so great, that an octogenarian member said he remembered no more stirring spectacle since 1815. Questions were addressed to the government in both Houses, but they replied that they could give no information as to the source from which the *Times* had obtained the document. They were, however, convinced that, after the announcement of the existence of such a draft treaty, both the governments of France and Prussia would immediately and spontaneously give an explanation to Europe of the matter. In prefacing his question in the House of Commons, Mr. Disraeli, the leader of the opposition, said, amidst loud and general cheering, that the policy indicated in the treaty was one which England had never approved, and never could approve. He should look upon the extinction of Belgium as a calamity to Europe and an injury to England, and therefore he trusted such an attempt would not be made; but if it were, the engagements into which England had entered with respect to that kingdom would demand the gravest consideration. An increase of distrust was observable in all the markets in the city on the following day, the observations in both Houses of Parliament having coincided with the feeling previously entertained as to the gravity of the disclosure regarding the treaty. At the same time, however, there was an augmented sense among all the mercantile classes of the importance of maintaining a strict neutrality.

The same day M. Emile Ollivier, the head of the French government, sent the following letter to a friend in England, evidently with a view to publication:—

"PARIS, *July* 26, 1870.

"My dear Friend,—How could you believe there was any truth in the treaty the *Times* has published? I assure you that the cabinet of the 2nd of January never negotiated or concluded anything of the kind with Prussia.

"I will even tell you that it has negotiated nothing at all with her. The only negotiations that have existed between us have been indirect, confidential, and had Lord Clarendon for their intermediary. Since Mr. Gladstone slightly raised the veil in one of his speeches, we may allow ourselves to say that the object of those negotiations, so honourable to Lord Clarendon, was to assure the peace of Europe by a reciprocal disarmament. You will admit that this does not much resemble the conduct of ministers who seek a pretext for war.

"You know the value I set upon the confidence and friendship of the great English nation. The union of the two countries has always seemed to me the most essential condition of the world's progress. And for that reason I earnestly beg you to contradict all those false reports spread by persons who have an interest in dividing us.

"We have no secret policy hidden behind our avowed policy. Our policy is single, public, loyal, without after thoughts (*arrieres pensées*); we do not belong to the school of those who think force is superior to right; we believe, on the contrary, that good right will always prevail in the end; and it is because the right is on our side in the war now beginning, that with the help of God we reckon upon victory.

"Affectionate salutations from your servant,

(Signed)   "EMILE OLLIVIER."

The excitement created in France was, however, by no means so great as in England. At first the authenticity of the document was boldly denied, but when this was no longer possible, people said, "Well, if it be true, where is the harm of it?" for the idea of annexing Belgium had more than once been broached in the numerous pamphlets which had been published from time to time, advocating a rectification of the French frontiers; and it was! not seriously believed by scarcely one Frenchman in a hundred that England would go to war to prevent it. The first formal notice taken of the matter was on Wednesday, July 27, when the *Journal Officiel* said, "After the treaty of Prague several negotiations passed at Berlin between Count von Bismarck and the

French embassy on the subject of a scheme of alliance. Some of the ideas contained in the document inserted by the Times were raised, but the French government never had cognizance of a written project; and as to the proposals that may have been spoken of in these conversations, the Emperor Napoleon rejected them. No one will fail to see in whose interest, and with what object, it is now sought to mislead the public opinion of England."

The treaty was published in the Berlin journals the same day (July 27), accompanied with the statement that it had been submitted to Count von Bismarck by M. Benedetti, the French ambassador, and that the original, in his handwriting, was in the Berlin archives.

On the following day a long telegraphic despatch was forwarded to the Prussian ambassador in London, to be at once communicated to the English government, with a notification that a fuller account of the whole transaction in writing would be despatched forthwith. This latter document was received a few days after, in the shape of a circular to the North German representatives at the courts of neutral states; and as it contains the complete version of the Prussian side of the question, and is of great historical importance, we give it in full.

"BERLIN, *July* 29, 1870.

"The expectation expressed by Lord Granville and Mr. Gladstone in the British Parliament, that more exact information in reference to the draught treaty of M. Benedetti, would be furnished by the two powers concerned, was in a preliminary manner fulfilled on our side by the telegram which I addressed to Count Bernstorff on the 27th inst. The telegraphic form only enabled me to make a short statement, which I now complete in writing.

"The document published by the Times contains by no means the only proposition of a similar nature which has been made to us on the part of the French. Even before the Danish war, attempts, addressed to me, were made both by official and unofficial French agents to effect an alliance between France and Prussia, with the object of mutual aggrandizement. It is scarcely necessary for me to point out the impossibility of such a transaction for a German minister, whose position is dependent on his being in accord with the national feeling; its explanation is to be found in the want of acquaintance of French statesmen with the fundamental conditions of existence among other nations. Had the agents of the Paris cabinet been competent to observe the state of German affairs, such an illusion would never have been entertained in Paris as that Prussia could permit herself to accept the aid of France in regulating German affairs.

"Your excellency is, of course, as well acquainted as I am myself with the ignorance of the French as regards Germany.

"The endeavours of the French government to carry out, with the assistance of Prussia, its covetous views with reference to Belgium and the Rhine frontier were brought to my notice even before 1862—therefore before my accession to the ministry of Foreign Affairs. I cannot regard it as my task to transfer such communications, which were purely of a personal nature, to the sphere of international negotiations; and I believe it will be best to withhold the most interesting contribution which I could make towards the elucidation of the matter from private letters and conversations.

"The above-mentioned tendencies of the French government were first recognizable by the external influence on European politics and the attitude favourable to us which France assumed in the Germano-Danish conflict. The subsequent bad feeling which France displayed towards us in reference to the Treaty of Gastein, was attributable to the apprehension lest a durable strengthening of the Prusso-Austrian alliance should deprive the Paris cabinet of the fruits of this its attitude. France before 1865 reckoned upon the outbreak of war between us and Austria, and again willingly made approaches to us as soon as our relations with Vienna began to be unfriendly. Before the outbreak of the Austrian war proposals were made to me, partly through relatives of his Majesty the emperor of the French, and partly by confidential agents, which each time had for their object smaller or larger transactions for the purpose of effecting mutual aggrandizement.

"At one time the negotiations were about Luxemburg, or about the frontier of 1814, with Landau and Saarlouis; at another, about larger objects, from which the French Swiss cantons and the question where the linguistic boundaries in Piedmont were to be drawn were not excluded.

"In May, 1866, these pretensions took the form of a proposition for an offensive and defensive alliance, and the following extract of its chief features is in my possession:—

" ' 1. En cas de Congres, poursuivre d'accord la cession de la Vénétie à l'Italie et l'annexion des Duchés a la Prusse. 2. Si le Congrès n'aboutit pas, alliance offensive et defensive. 3. Le roi de Prusse commencera les hostilites dans les 10 jours, la separation du Congrès. 4. Si le Congrès ne se réunit pas, la Prusse attaquera dans 30 jours après la signature du présent traité. 5. L'empereur des Français déclarera la guerre à l'Autriche, dès que les hostilités seront commencées entre l'Autriche et la Prusse en 30 jours, 300,000. 6. On ne fera pas de paix séparée avec l'Autriche. 7. La paix se fera sous les conditions suivantes—La Vénétie à l'Italie, à la Prusse les territoires Allemands cidessous, 7 à 8 millions d'après au choix, plus la réforme fédérale dans le sens Prussien; pour la France, le territoire entre Moselle et Rhin, sans Coblence et Mayence, comprenant 500,000 âmes de Prusse, la Bavière, rive gauche du Rhin, Birkenfeld, Homburg, Darmstadt, 213,000 âmes. 8. Convention militaire et maritime entre la France et la Prusse dès la signature. 9. (Adhésion du roi d'Italie.)'

1. In the event of a Congress, to agree upon the cession of Venetia to Italy, and annexation of the duchies to Prussia. 2. If the Congress come to nothing, an alliance offensive and defensive to be concluded. 3. The king of Prussia to commence hostilities within ten days of the breaking up of the Congress. 4. Should the Congress not reassemble, Prussia to attack in thirty days after the signature to the present treaty. 5. The emperor of the French to declare war against Austria as soon as hostilities shall be commenced between Austria and Prussia, and in thirty days to have 300,000 men in the field. 6. No separate peace to be concluded with Austria. 7. Peace to be made under the following conditions—Venetia to be given to Italy, the German territories, with about seven or eight millions of inhabitants according to their choice, to go to Prussia, besides the prosecution of the Federal reform in the Prussian sense; for France the territory between the Moselle and Rhine, excepting Coblentz and Mainz, comprising 500,000 Prussians, Bavaria, left bank of the Rhine, Birkenfeld, Homburg, Darmstadt, with 213,000 inhabitants. 8. A military and

maritime convention between France and Prussia, dating from the signature. 9. The king of Italy's adhesion to be obtained.]

"The strength of the army with which the emperor, in accordance with Article 5, would assist us was in written explanations placed at 300,000 men; the number of souls comprised in the aggrandizements which France sought for was 1,800,000 souls, according to calculations which, however, did not agree with the actual statistics.

"Every one who is familiar with the secret diplomatic and military history of the year 1866 will see, glimmering through these clauses, the policy which France pursued simultaneously towards Italy (with whom she at the same time secretly negotiated), and subsequently towards Prussia and Italy.

"In June, 1866, after we had rejected the above scheme of alliance, notwithstanding several almost threatening warnings to accept it, the French government began to calculate on the Austrians being victorious over us, and upon our making a bid for French assistance after the eventuality of our defeat, to pave the way for which diplomatically French diplomacy was occupied to the uttermost. That the congress anticipated in the foregoing draught of alliance, and again proposed later, would have had the effect of causing our three months' alliance with Italy to expire without our having profited by it is well known to your excellency, as is also the fact that France, in the further agreements relative to Custozza, was busied in prejudicing our situation, and if possible bringing about our defeat. The patriotic affliction of the minister Rouher furnishes a comment upon the further course of events. Since that time France has not ceased leading us into temptation by offers at the cost of Germany and Belgium. I had never any doubt as to the impossibility of acceding to any such offers; but I considered it useful in the interests of peace to permit the French statesmen to hold these illusions peculiar to them, so long as it should be possible so to do without giving even a verbal assent to their propositions. I imagined that the annihilation of the French hopes would endanger the preservation of peace, the maintenance of which was in the interest both of Germany and Europe. I was not of the opinion of those politicians who considered it unadvisable to shun by all the means in one's power a war with France, on the ground that such a war was in any case unavoidable. No one can so surely foresee the designs of Divine Providence; and I look upon even a victorious war as an evil in itself, which the statesmanship of a country must strive to spare its people.

"I could not in my calculations leave out the possibility that, in the constitution and policy of France changes might arise which would relieve the two great neighbouring peoples from the necessity of war—a hope which was favoured by each postponement of the rupture. For these reasons I was silent about the propositions made, and delayed the negotiations about them, without ever on my side giving a promise. After the negotiations with his Majesty the king of the Netherlands fell, as is well known, to the ground, extended proposals were again addressed to me by France, including in their purport Belgium and South Germany. At this conjuncture comes the communication of the Benedetti manuscript. That the French ambassador, without the consent of his sovereign, and on his own responsibility, drew up these propositions, handed them to me, and negotiated them, modifying them in certain places as I advised, is as unlikely as was the statement on another occasion that the Emperor Napoleon had not agreed to the demand for our surrendering Mayence, which was officially made to me in August, 1866, by the French ambassador, under threat of war in case of our refusal. The different phases of French bad feeling and lust for war which we have gone through from 1866 to 1869, coincided with tolerable exactness with the willingness or unwillingness for negotiations which the French agents believed they met with in me. In 1866, at the time when the Belgian Railway affair was being prepared, it was intimated to me by a high personage, who was not a stranger to the former negotiation, that in case of a French occupation of Belgium, 'nous trouverions notre Belgique ailleurs.' Similarly, on another occasion, I had been given to understand that in a solution of the Eastern question France would seek its share, not in far-off places, but close upon its boundaries. I am under the impression that it was only the definite conviction that no enlargement of the frontiers was to be achieved with us, that has led the emperor to the determination to strive to obtain it against us. I have besides reason to believe that, had the publication in question not been made, so soon as our and the French preparations for war were complete, propositions would have been made to us by France jointly, and at the head of a million armed men, to carry out against unarmed Europe the proposals formerly made to us, and either before or after the first battle to conclude peace on the basis of the Benedetti proposals, and at the expense of Belgium.

"Concerning the text of these proposals, I remark that the draught in our possession is from beginning to end from the hand of M. Benedetti, and written on the paper of the Imperial French Embassy; and that the ambassadors here, including the representatives of Austria, Great Britain, Russia, Baden, Bavaria, Belgium, Hesse, Italy, Saxony, Turkey, and Würtemburg, who have seen the original, have recognized the handwriting. In Article I. M. Benedetti, at the very first reading, withdrew the closing passage, placing it in brackets, after I had remarked that it presupposed the interference of France in the internal affairs of Germany, which I, even in private documents, could not allow. Of his own accord he made an unimportant marginal correction in Article II. in my presence. On the 24th inst. I informed Lord A. Loftus verbally of the existence of the document in question, and on his expressing doubts invited him to a personal inspection of the same. On the 27th of this month he took note of it, and convinced himself that it was in the handwriting of his former French colleague. If the imperial cabinet now repudiates attempts for which it has sought since 1864, both by promises and threats, to obtain our co-operation, this is easily to be explained in presence of the political situation.

"Your excellency will please read this despatch to M. , and hand him a copy.

"VON BISMARCK."

The French side of the question is given in the following explanatory letter of M. Benedetti to the Duc de Gramont, and the latter 's reply to the circular of Count Bismarck:—

"PARIS, *July* 29, 1870.

"M. le Duc,—Unjust as they were, I did not think it proper to notice the observations which were made upon me personally, when it was known in France that the prince of Hohenzollern had accepted the crown of Spain. As in duty bound, I left to the government of the emperor the task of setting them right. I could not keep the same silence in face of the use which Count von Bismarck has made of a document to which he seeks to give a value which it never possessed, and I request your excellency's leave to re-establish the facts exactly as they occurred.

"It is a matter of public notoriety that Count von Bismarck offered us, before and during the last war, to assist in uniting Belgium to France, as a compensation for the aggrandizements of which he was ambitious, and which he obtained for Prussia. I might, on this point, appeal to the testimony of the entire diplomacy of Europe, to whom the whole affair was known.

"The government of the emperor constantly declined these overtures, and one of your predecessors, M. Drouyn de Lhuys, is in a position to give, on this subject, explanations which must remove every doubt. At the moment of the conclusion of the Peace of Prague, and in face of the emotion which was excited in France by the annexation to Prussia of Hanover, of Electoral Hesse, and of the town of Frankfort, Count von Bismarck again showed the strongest desire to re-establish the balance of power, which had been disturbed by these acquisitions. Various combinations having reference to the integrity of the states neighbours of France and Germany were put forward; they became the subject of several conversations, during which Count von Bismarck was always disposed to make his personal ideas prevail.

"In one of these conversations, and in order to give myself an exact idea of his combinations, I consented to transcribe them in a manner ("en quelque sorte") at his dictation. The form, no less than the substance, shows clearly that I confined myself to reproducing a project conceived and developed by him. Count von Bismarck kept this document, wishing to submit it to the king. On my side, I reported in substance to the imperial government the communications which had been made to me. The emperor rejected them as soon as they came to his knowledge. I am bound to say that the king of Prussia himself did not seem to wish to accept the basis of them; and since that time, that is to say, during the last four years, I have never again entered upon any new exchange of ideas on the subject with Count von Bismarck.

"If the initiative of such a treaty had been taken by the government of the emperor, the project would have been drafted by the Foreign Office, and I should not have had to produce a copy of it in my own handwriting; it would besides have been drawn up differently, and it would have led to negotiations which would have been simultaneously carried on at Paris and Berlin. In that case Count von Bismarck would not have been satisfied with indirectly publishing the text, particularly at a time when your excellency was correcting, in despatches which were inserted in the *Journal Officiel*, other errors which attempts were also being made to propagate. But in order to attain the end which he had in view—that of misleading public opinion, and anticipating the revelations which we ourselves might have made—he employed this expedient, which relieved him from the necessity of defining at what time, under what circumstances, and in what manner this document had been written. He evidently flattered himself that, thanks to these omissions, he should suggest conjectures which, whilst freeing his personal responsibility, would compromise that of the emperor's government. Such proceedings need no comment; it is enough to point them out, by submitting them to the appreciation of the public opinion of Europe.

"Receive, etc.,

The following was the French reply to Count von Bismarck, and which was addressed as a circular to the diplomatic agents of France at foreign courts:—

"PARIS, *August* 3.

"Sir,—"We now know the full meaning of the telegram addressed by Count von Bismarck to the Prussian ambassador in London to announce to England the pretended secrets of which the Federal chancellor alleged that he was the depositary. His despatch adds no material fact to those which he has already put forth. We only find in it a few more improbabilities. We shall not attempt to point them out. Public opinion has already done justice to affirmations which derive no authority from the audacity with which they are repeated, and we regard it as completely established, notwithstanding all denials, that never has the Emperor Napoleon proposed to Prussia a treaty for taking possession of Belgium. That idea is the property of Count von Bismarck. It is one of the expedients of that unscrupulous policy which we trust is now approaching its end. I should, therefore, have abstained from reverting to assertions which have been proved to be false if the author of the Prussian despatch, with a want of tact which I noticed in so marked a degree for the first time in a diplomatic document, had not mentioned relatives of the emperor as having been bearers of compromising messages and confidences. Whatever repugnance I may feel at being compelled to follow the Prussian chancellor, and to engage myself in a manner so contrary to my habits, I overcome that feeling, because it is my duty to repudiate perfidious insinuations which, directed against members of the imperial family, are evidently intended to apply to the emperor himself. It was at Berlin that Count von Bismarck, originating ideas the first conception of which he now seeks to impute to us, solicited in these terms the French prince whom, in defiance of all customary rules, he now seeks to draw into the controversy. 'You desire,' said he, ' an impossible thing. You wish to take the Rhenish Provinces, which are German. Why do you not annex Belgium, where the people have the same origin, the same religion, and the same language as yourselves? I have already caused that to be mentioned to the emperor; if he entered into my views, we would assist him to take Belgium. As for myself, if I were the master and I were not hampered by the obstinacy of the king, it would be already done.' These words of the Prussian chancellor have been, so to speak, literally repeated to the court of France by the Count von Goltz. That ambassador was so little reticent upon the subject, that there are many witnesses who have heard him thus express himself. I will add that at the period of the Universal Exhibition the overtures of Prussia were known to more than one high personage, who took note of them and still remembered them. Moreover, it was not a mere passing notion with Count von Bismarck, but truly a concerted plan with which his ambitious schemes were connected; and he pursued his attempts to carry them out with a perseverance which is amply attested by his repeated excursions to France, to Biarritz, and elsewhere. He failed before the immovable will of the emperor, who always refused to connect himself with a policy that was unworthy of his loyalty. I now quit the subject, which I have touched upon for the last time, with a firm intention of never again recurring to it, and I come to the really new point in Count von Bismarck's despatch. 'I have reason to believe,' he says, 'that if the publication of the projected treaty had not occurred, France would have made us an offer—after our mutual armaments had been completed—to carry out the proposition which she had previously made to us, as soon as we found ourselves at the head of a million of well-armed soldiers in the face of unarmed Europe; that is to say, to make peace before or after the first battle upon the basis of M. Benedetti's propositions at the expense of Belgium.' The emperor's government cannot allow such an assertion to pass without notice. In the face of all Europe, his Majesty's ministers defy Count von Bismarck to adduce any fact whatever to justify a belief that they have ever manifested, directly or indirectly, officially or by secret agency, an intention of uniting with Prussia to accomplish together in respect of Belgium the deed she has consummated in respect to Hanover. We have opened no negotiation with Count von Bismarck, either concerning Belgium or any other subject. Far from seeking war, as we have been accused of doing, we besought Lord Clarendon to interpose with the Prussian cabinet, with a view to a mutual disarmament, an important mission which Lord Clarendon, through friendship towards France and devotion to the cause of peace, consented confidentially to undertake. It was on these terms that Comte Daru, in a letter of the 1st of February, explained to the Marquis de Lavalette, our ambasador in London, the intentions of the government:—

" ' It is certain that I should not mix myself up with this affair, nor should I ask England to interfere in it if the question was one simply of an ordinary and purely formal nature, intended only to afford Count von Bismarck an opportunity to repeat once again his refusal. It is a real, serious, positive proposition, which it is sought to act upon. The principal secretary of state appears to anticipate that Count von Bismarck will at first manifest dissatisfaction and displeasure. That is possible, but not certain. With that possibility in view, it will be well to prepare the ground in such a manner as to avoid at the outset a negative reply. I am convinced that time and reflection will induce the chancellor to take into his serious consideration the proposition of England. If at first he does not reject all overtures, then the interests of Prussia and of all Germany will speedily speak out sufficiently to lead him to modify his opposition. He would not be willing to raise against himself the opinion of his entire country. What, indeed, would be his position if we took away the sole pretext upon which he relies, that is, the armament of France?'

"Count von Bismarck at first replied that he could not take upon himself to submit the suggestions of the British government to the king, and that he was sufficiently acquainted with the views of his sovereign to foretell his decision. King William, he said, would certainly see in the proposition of the cabinet of London a change in the disposition of England towards Prussia. In short, the Prussian chancellor declared ' that it was impossible for Prussia to modify a military system which was so closely connected with the traditions of the country, which formed one of the bases of its constitution, and which was in no way abnormal.' Comte Dam was not checked by this first reply. On the 13th of February he wrote to M. de Lavalette:—

" ' I hope that Lord Clarendon will not consider himself beaten nor be discouraged. We will shortly give him an opportunity of returning to the charge, if it should be agreeable to him, and to resume the interrupted communication with the Federal chancellor. Our intention is, in fact, to diminish our contingent. We should largely have reduced it if we had received a favourable reply from the Federal chancellor. We shall make a smaller reduction, as the reply is in the negative; but we shall reduce. The reduction will, I hope, be 10,000 men. That is the number I should propose. We shall affirm by acts, which are of more value than words, our intentions—our policy. Nine contingents, each reduced by 10,000 men, make a total reduction of 90,000 men. That is already something; it is a tenth part of the existing army. The law upon the contingent will be proposed shortly. Lord Clarendon will then judge whether it will be proper to represent to Count von Bismarck that Prussia alone in Europe makes no concession to the spirit of peace, and that he thus places her in a serious position amid other European societies, because he furnishes arms against her to all the world, including the populations which are crushed beneath the weight of military charges which he imposes upon them.'

"Count von Bismarck, closely pressed, felt it to be necessary to enter into some further explanations with Lord Clarendon. These explanations, as far as we are acquainted with them, from a letter from M. de Lavalette dated the 23rd of February, were full of reticence. The chancellor of the Prussian Confederation, departing from his first resolution, had informed King William of the proposition recommended by England, but his Majesty had declined it. In vindication of the refusal, the chancellor pleaded the fear of a possible alliance between Austria and the states of the south, and the ambitious designs that might be entertained by France. But in the foreground he especially placed the anxieties with which the policy of Russia inspired him, and upon that point indulged in particular remarks respecting the court of St. Petersburg which I prefer to pass by in silence, not desiring to reproduce injurious insinuations. Such were the pleas of non-acceptance which Count von Bismarck opposed to the loyal and conscientious entreaties several times renewed by Lord Clarendon at the request of the emperor's government. If, then, Europe has remained in arms; if a million of men are about to be hurled against each other upon the battle-field, it cannot be contested that the responsibility for such a state of things attaches to Prussia: for it is she who has repudiated all idea of disarmament, while we not only forwarded the proposition to her, but also began by setting an example. Is not this conduct explained by the fact that, at the very time when confiding France was reducing her contingent, the cabinet of Berlin was arranging in the dark for the provocative nomination of a Prussian prince? Whatever may be the calumnies invented by the Federal chancellor, we have no fear; he has forfeited the right of being believed. The conscience of history and of Europe will say that Prussia has sought the present war by inflicting upon France, while she was engaged in the development of her political institutions, an outrage which no high-spirited and courageous nation could have accepted without meriting the contempt of nations.

    "Agreez, &c.,   "GRAMONT."

The Prussian reply to this circular was issued a week afterwards, not, it was stated, with the view of taking advantage of the abundant matter it contained for criticism, but of supplying a fresh piece of evidence, and requesting the Prussian representatives at foreign courts to bring it under the notice of the respective governments to which they were accredited. Count von Bismarck said:—"If I have not made use of this evidence before, it was owing to my reluctance, even in a state of war, to drag the person of a monarch into the discussion of the acts of his ministers and representatives; and also because, considering the form of government which avowedly existed in France up to the 2nd of January last, I was not prepared to hear that the draught treaty and the other proposals and arrogant demands alluded to in my despatch of the 29th should have been submitted to me without the knowledge of the Emperor Napoleon. But certain statements which appear in the latest French utterances necessitate my having recourse to a different line of conduct. On the one hand, the French minister of Foreign Affairs assures us that the Emperor Napoleon has never proposed to Prussia a treaty having the acquisition of Belgium for its object (*que jamais l'Empereur Napoleon n'a proposé à la Prusse un traité pour prendre possession de la Belgique*); on the other, M. Benedetti gives out that the draught treaty in question emanates from me; that all he had to do with it was to put it on paper—writing, so to say, from my dictation (*en quelque sorte sous ma dictée*), which he only did the better to apprehend my views; and that the Emperor Napoleon was made cognizant of the draught only after its completion at Berlin. Statements such as these render it indispensable for me to make use of a means at my disposal calculated to support my account of French politics, and to strengthen the supposition I have previously expressed respecting the nature of the connection between the emperor and his ministers, envoys, and agents. In the archives of the Foreign Office at Berlin is preserved a letter from M. Benedetti to me, dated 5th August, 1866, and a draught treaty inclosed in that letter. The originals, in M. Benedetti's handwriting, I shall submit to the inspection of the representatives of the neutral powers, and I will also send you a photographic fac-simile of the same. I beg to observe that, according to the *Moniteur*, the Emperor Napoleon did pass the time from the 28th of July to the 7th of August, 1866, at Vichy. In the official interview which I had with M. Benedetti in consequence of this letter, he supported his demands by threatening war in case of refusal. When I declined, nevertheless, the Luxemburg affair was brought upon the carpet; and after the failure of this little business came the more comprehensive proposal relative to Belgium embodied in M. Benedetti's draught treaty published in the *Times*."

The profound impression created in England by the publication of the treaty increased and deepened with the charges and counter-charges made by and against the respective governments, and the confidence before reposed in the friendship of both countries was put to a severe test. Questions were repeatedly asked of the government in both Houses of Parliament, but without eliciting any further facts than those already given; and the nation became thoroughly in earnest on the subject of its naval and military strength, and the number of breech-loaders already served out and in store.

On Monday, August 2, Mr. Cardwell, the War Minister, laid on the table of the House of Commons a supplementary estimate of £2,000,000 "for strengthening the naval and military forces of the kingdom, including an addition to the army of 20,000 men of all ranks during the European war." There was much cheering on both sides of the House when the estimate was read; and in reply to questions addressed to him immediately afterwards, Mr. Cardwell stated that the whole force of the army was only about 2000 below the establishment; that the militia regiments, with a few exceptions, were recruited up to their full strength; and that the Supply Department was in a position to meet any emergencies.

The same evening Mr. Disraeli, leader of the Opposition, called the attention of the House, according to previous notice, to the position of the country with reference to the war. By way of justification for his interposition, he said that, having witnessed the outbreak of several great wars during his parliamentary career, he had noticed that much injury had been done by the reserve and silence observed by the House of Commons on such occasions, which, instead of assisting and strengthening the hands of the government, had embarrassed it. He spoke contemptuously of the ephemeral and evanescent pretexts for the present war. Whether there was a pretender to the Spanish throne, or whether there was a breach of etiquette at a watering place, or whether Europe was to be devastated on account of the publication of an anonymous paragraph in a newspaper—were pretexts which would have been disgraceful in the eighteenth century, and could not now seriously influence the conduct of any body of men; he pointed out that its real causes were to be gathered from the public declarations of the leading statesmen on both sides, such as M. Rouher and Count von Bismarck; and the recent revelations showed that vast ambitions were stirring in Europe, and subtle schemes were being devised, which had brought about this war, and might produce other events of the utmost importance. After some remarks on the treaties guaranteeing Belgium and Luxemburg—of the former of which he said that it had been negotiated by distinguished Liberal statesmen, and was in accordance with the traditional policy of England—Mr. Disraeli reminded the House that at the Treaty of Vienna England had guaranteed to Prussia her Saxon provinces. That engagement, he contended, ought to have given her an overpowering influence with Prussia; but Russia had undertaken a similar guarantee, and Russia, too, was as anxious to be neutral as England, and in this coincidence he discerned a means by which, from the joint action of these two powers, peace might be restored. The policy of England should be an armed neutrality, and at the proper time she might step in, and in conjunction with Russia, exercise the most considerable effect on the course of public affairs. This led him to consider whether the armaments of the country were in such a position as to enable her to take that line, and to require from the government more complete information as to the strength of the fleet and the army, the condition of stores, and the progress made in the fortifications; insisting that at a crisis like the present no effort should be spared to put the country in a position of complete security. He earnestly urged the House to profit by the lessons of the Crimean war, which might have been prevented had England spoken out at the right moment. She had then as strong a government as at present; but the House of Commons maintained a reserve, and there followed discordant councils, infirmity of action, and, finally, war. If the government spoke to foreign powers with that firmness which could only arise from a due appreciation of their duty, and a determination to perform it, Mr Disraeli predicted that England would not be involved in the war, and her influence, combined with that of Russia, might lead to the speedy restoration of peace. But, above all, England ought to declare in a manner not to be mistaken that she would maintain her treaty engagements, and thereby secure the rights of independent nations.

Mr. Gladstone, the prime minister, confessed that the particular incident out of which the war had arisen had taken him by surprise, though, of course, he was perfectly aware of the state of feeling of which that incident was a symptom. He next sketched the steps taken by the government to preserve peace, which have been fully detailed in Chapter II. During the negotiations, the position of England had been that of a mediator, and her attitude now was one of neutrality; but not an "armed neutrality"—a phrase which he strongly deprecated as having an historical significance totally opposed to the friendly disposition which ought to be preserved towards both belligerents. But he agreed that England's neutrality ought to be accompanied with adequate measures of defence; that it ought to be what he called a "secured neutrality." As to the suggestion of joint action with Russia, he merely said that he saw no objection to coalescing not only with one, but all the neutral powers, for the restoration of peace; but he differed entirely from Mr. Disraeli's idea of the claim which the Saxon guarantee gave England. The dissolution of the German Confederation and the recent aggrandizement of Prussia had destroyed its binding force, and England could not have advanced it without involving herself in the responsibilities of war. Describing next the attitude of the government with regard to the future, he said that the "projected treaty" was considered by the government to be a most important document, giving a serious shock to public confidence, and the country ought to feel indebted to those who had brought it to light. The government had taken the whole circumstances attending it into their consideration, and the propositions they meant to make to the House in their opinion met the necessity of the case, and were calculated to establish perfect confidence and security. Having explained the various steps the government had taken to maintain neutrality, he warmly defended it against Mr. Disraeli's charge of undue reduction of the services in the early part of the year. In every reduction they had made real strength had been arrived at, and efficiency had been increased. The country had 89,000 soldiers at home, there was a considerable Channel fleet afloat, the armament for the forts was ready, the supply of arms of precision was adequate, and stores were in excellent order. The House, to some extent, must rely on the responsibility of the government; but he assured it that they were deeply sensible of the discredit of weakening the power of this country, and that, having made the most careful inquiries, they would take up and maintain that dignified position which would enable England at the proper time to interfere for the restoration of peace.

The studious reserve maintained by Mr. Gladstone throughout his speech upon the obligations of Great Britain under the treaties guaranteeing the neutrality of Belgium and Luxemburg, caused great dissatisfaction, and from the tone of every speech subsequently made, it was evident that the feeling of the House was unmistakable in its recognition of England's duties to the fullest extent. Subsequent events proved that in its negotiations with both France and Prussia the government had been by no means so reticent, and had given them clearly to understand that England felt herself fully bound by the treaty of 1839, and that in case of any violation of the neutrality or independence of Belgium she would at once interfere on her behalf.

On the following evening Lord Russell, in an energetic speech in the House of Lords, which stirred even the well-bred repose of his aristocratic audience, and drew hearty cheers from both sides of the House, asserted the duty of England to defend Belgium to the uttermost. After reviewing the treaty obligations of Great Britain, and referring to the secret treaty, and the explanations to which it had given rise between France and Prussia, he said it would be impossible to feel in future perfect confidence in either of the parties, and unwise to ignore the danger that the treaties in regard to Belgium might be violated. "For my part," he said, "I confess I feel somewhat as if a detective officer had come and told me he had heard a conversation with respect to a friend of mine whom I had promised to guard as much as was in my power against any act of burglary or housebreaking, and that two other persons, who were also friends of mine, had been considering how they might enter his house and deprive him of all the property he possessed. I should reply, under such circumstances, that I was very much astonished to hear it, and that I could not, in the future, feel perfect confidence in either of the parties to that conversation." As to the beginning of the war, it might be a question whether as regards France the charioteer had not himself lashed the horses which he found himself afterwards unable to guide; but, putting aside that point, England's duty was clear. "It is not a question of three courses. There is but one course and one path—namely, the course of honour and the path of honour—that we ought to pursue. We are bound to defend Belgium. I am told that that may lead us into danger. Now, in the first place, I deny that any great danger would exist if this country manfully declared her intention to perform all her engagements, and not to shrink from their performance. I am persuaded that neither France nor Prussia would ever attempt to violate the independence of Belgium. It is only the doubt, the hesitation, that has too long prevailed as to the course which England would take which has encouraged and fostered all these conversations and projects of treaties, all these combinations and intrigues. I am persuaded that if it is once manfully declared that England means to stand by her treaties, to perform her engagements, that her honour and her interest would allow nothing else, such a declaration would check the greater part of these intrigues, and that neither France nor Prussia would wish to add a second enemy to the formidable foe which each has to meet. I am persuaded that both would conform to the faith of treaties, and would not infringe on the territory of Belgium, but till the end of the war remain in the fulfilment of their obligations. When the choice is between honour and infamy, I cannot doubt that her Majesty's government will pursue the course of honour, the only one worthy of the British people. The British people have a very strong sense of honour, and of what is due to this glorious nation. I feel sure, therefore, that the government, in making that intention clear to all the world, would have the entire support of the great majority of this nation. I need hardly speak of other considerations which are of great weight. I consider that if England shrunk from the performance of her engagements, if she acted in a faithless manner with respect to this matter, her extinction as a great power must very soon follow. The main duty of the hour therefore is, how we can best assure Belgium, assure Europe, and assure the world that we mean to be true and faithful, that the great name which we have acquired in the world by the constant observance of truth and justice, and by fidelity to our engagements, will not be departed from, and that we shall be in the future what we have been in the past."

Lord Granville replied briefly, declining to enter upon a general discussion, and justifying the reserve of the government. He gave a positive assurance that the government were aware of the duty this country owed to Belgium, and declared his perfect confidence that if they followed judiciously and actively the course which the honour, the interests, and the obligations of the country dictated, they would receive the full support of Parliament and the nation. He added, that the ministry had taken steps in the previous week to convey to other powers in the clearest manner, though without adopting an offensive or menacing tone, what England believed to be right.

The speech of Lord Granville was received with cheers that testified to a feeling of relief, and when he had concluded, the unfavourable impression which had been produced by Mr. Gladstone's caution on the previous evening was removed. The country now felt it had reason to be satisfied, and waited patiently for the additional communications on the subject which were promised to Parliament as soon as diplomatic considerations would permit. This promise was redeemed on the following Monday (August 8), when statements were made by the ministerial leaders in both Houses. Earl Granville, in the Lords, said that from the first the government were determined to deal in no vague threats or indefinite menaces. At the Cabinet Council of July 30 he was authorized to write to the courts of France and Prussia in the same terms, *mutatis mutandis*, renewing the expressions of the satisfaction of the British government at the assurances given by the emperor and the king respectively, that they intended to respect the neutrality of Belgium. There could be no doubt, he said, as to the duty of both countries to maintain the obligations of the treaty into which they had thus entered with Great Britain and the other signataries; but he pointed out that the assurance was not complete, because each power made a reservation in case the neutrality of Belgium was violated by the other. In the event of a violation of the neutrality by Prussia, France was to be released from her obligation, and in the case of a similar event on the part of France, Prussia was to be released from hers. Her Majesty's government therefore proposed, either by treaty or otherwise, to place on solemn record the common determination of the great powers who were signataries to the treaty of 1839 to maintain the independence of Belgium, and satisfactory replies had been received from Austria and Russia. France also accepted the principle of the new treaty, and as regarded Prussia, Count von Bismarck was ready to concur in any measure for strengthening the neutrality of Belgium, and the king, as soon as he saw the draught treaty, authorized Count Bernstorff, the Prussian ambassador in London, to sign it. Lord Granville next described the treaty, which is given on, and which, as will be seen, renewed all the obligations of the treaty of 1839. It provided that, if the armies of either belligerent violated the neutrality of Belgium, Great Britain should co-operate with the other in its defence, but without engaging to take part in the general operations of the war. The other powers would pledge themselves to a corresponding co-operation, and the treaty was to hold good for twelve months after the war. The government had thus endeavoured clearly to announce their own determination in this matter without menace or offence to the two belligerents, with whom they were still in friendly alliance Expressing a hope that this treaty would remove the alarm which had been felt, while it would in no degree weaken the force or impair the obligations of the treaty of 1839, he said he trusted it would be seen that her Majesty's ministers had not been unmindful of their responsibilities with regard to this great and important question.

The duke of Richmond, the leader of the opposition, expressed a general approval of the attitude of the government, and a fervent hope that Great Britain might preserve her neutrality, and at the same time her honour inviolate during the war.

In the Commons a statement similar to that of Lord Granville was made by the Premier, and Mr. Disraeli, while guarding himself against giving any decided opinion on details so suddenly communicated to the House, expressed his belief that the determination at which he assumed the government to have arrived—to defend the neutrality and independence of Belgium—would give general satisfaction to the country. At the same time he doubted as a general principle the wisdom of founding any other engagements on the existing treaty of guarantee. Neither could he understand how, if England joined with one of the belligerents, her interference was to be limited to the defence of the Belgian frontier, nor how she was to avoid being involved in the general fortunes of the war. Mr. Disraeli concluded by repeating his gratification at finding that the government had pursued a wise and spirited policy, and not the less wise because spirited; and to lay down as a general principle of statesmanship that England, though not merely an European but an Asiatic and Oceanic power, could not absolve herself of all interest in the peace and prosperity of the European states. The coast from Ostend to the North Sea, he held, should be in the possession of powers from whose ambition England and Europe had nothing to fear.

Parliament was prorogued on the following Wednesday (10th August), and in consequence of Lord Cairns' desire to express his opinion on the treaty, and to obtain a fuller and more detailed statement with respect to it, the House of Lords met at the unusual hour of twelve o'clock in the morning. Whilst expressing cordial approval of the object in view—the preservation of the neutrality of Belgium—Lord Cairns objected to the new engagement into which England had entered, as containing the seeds of considerable embarrassment and possible complication. The natural course would have been to announce to the two belligerents, but not by way of menace, that England was prepared to maintain the treaty of 1839, and to oppose any attempt by either or both to violate it. Russia and Austria ought to have been informed of these communications, in order that arrangements might be made for a united course of action in any contingency which might arise. Pointing out certain elements of danger in the treaty, he examined in turn the consequences of its violation by France or Prussia. It would be impossible to agree as to the particular operations which might justly be required of us, while if England joined any of the belligerents the other would necessarily declare war against her, and carry it on wherever she could be struck at and injured. It was the object of each belligerent to obtain the alliance and co-operation of England, and a skilful strategist might so arrange matters as to compel the other belligerent to violate the territory of Belgium. The engagement would be useless if both the belligerents violated the neutrality of Belgium, because there could then be no co-operation with England on the part of either. He also feared that the treaty might involve England in difficulties with Austria and Russia.

Lord Granville denied that the course taken by the government was either menacing or offensive, and argued that the plan proposed by Lord Cairns would not have been successful. The government had received from Austria the assurance of her readiness to adhere to their proposal, assuming that France and Prussia did not object to sign it. Russia sent her most friendly assurances, but declined to join the signataries, because she considered herself as already bound by the original treaty. She also desired an understanding of a much wider description, the effect of which would have been to bring England under obligations by which she was not at present bound. England having now entered upon the treaty was limited to its obligations. He did not believe the contingency contemplated would arise, but if it did England would be obliged to act upon it. It would, however, be an enormous advantage to have a power numbering its soldiers by hundreds of thousands co-operating with the British army and fleet. He repudiated as gratuitous the suspicion that such a piece of strategy as that suggested by Lord Cairns would be attempted, or that after the solemn renewal of this treaty obligation, binding on the personal honour of the emperor of the French and the king of Prussia, they would either of them, within a very few months and in the face of the world, violate such an engagement. While the treaty would, he believed, prevent a particular event which would be most disagreeable and entangling to Great Britain, he strongly denied that it would weaken the obligations of the treaty of 1839. Replying to the objection that the action of her Majesty's government had been disrespectful to Belgium, he stated that she had not been at first consulted in the matter because it was hot desired to compromise her with either belligerent; but he officially informed the Belgian government of the negotiations when they had reached a certain point, assuring them that he wished to act in harmony with Belgium, and that England's sole object was the independence and neutrality of that country. These assurances were entirely satisfactory to the Belgian king and Chambers. So far as the treaty had gone, there was reason to believe that it would be the best means of preventing a great difficulty which had excited much alarm and anxiety both at home and abroad.

In reply to a question of Lord Cairns, as to what progress had been made with the treaty, and whether he could give the text, Lord Granville said the treaty with Prussia was signed by Count Bernstorff and himself on the previous day. The French ambassador had authority to sign as soon as his full powers arrived. He then read the following draught of the treaty between England and Prussia, explaining that the treaty with France was, *mutatis mutandis*, identical with it:—

"DRAUGHT OF TREATY BETWEEN ENGLAND AND PRUSSIA RESPECTING BELGIUM.

"Her Majesty the queen of the United Kingdom of Great Britain and Ireland, and his Majesty the king of Prussia, being desirous at the present time of recording in a solemn act their fixed determination to maintain the independence and neutrality of Belgium, as provided in the seventh article of the treaty signed at London on the 19th of April, 1839, between Belgium and the Netherlands, which article was declared by the Quintuple Treaty of 1839 to be considered as having the same force and value as if textually inserted in the said Quintuple Treaty, their said Majesties have determined to conclude between themselves a separate treaty, which, without impairing or invalidating the conditions of the said Quintuple Treaty, shall be subsidiary and accessory to it; and they have accordingly named as their plenipotentiaries for that purpose, that is to say:—

"Her Majesty the Queen of the United Kingdom of Great Britain and Ireland, &c.

"And his Majesty the king of Prussia, &c.

"Who, after having communicated to each other their respective full powers, found in good and due form, have agreed upon and concluded the following articles:—

"Art. I. His Majesty the king of Prussia having declared that, notwithstanding the hostilities in which the North German Confederation is engaged with France, it is his fixed determination to respect the neutrality of Belgium so long as the same shall be respected by France, her Majesty the queen of the United Kingdom of Great Britain and Ireland on her part declares that, if during the said hostilities the armies of France should violate that neutrality, she will be prepared to co-operate with his Prussian Majesty for the defence of the same in such manner as may be mutually agreed upon, employing for that purpose her naval and military forces to insure its observance, and to maintain, in conjunction with his Prussian Majesty, then and thereafter, the independence and neutrality of Belgium.

"It is clearly understood that her Majesty the queen of the United Kingdom of Great Britain and Ireland does not engage herself by this treaty to take part in any of the general operations of the war now carried on between the North German Confederation and France, beyond the limits of Belgium as defined in the treaty between Belgium and the Netherlands of April 19, 1839.

"Art. II. His Majesty the king of Prussia agrees on his part, in the event provided for in the foregoing article, to co-operate with her Majesty the queen of the United Kingdom of Great Britain and Ireland, employing his naval and military forces for the purpose aforesaid; and the case arising, to concert with her Majesty the measures which shall be taken, separately or in common, to secure the neutrality and independence of Belgium.

"Art. III. This treaty shall be binding on the high contracting parties during the continuance of the present war between the North German Confederation and France, and for twelve months after the ratification of any treaty of peace concluded between those parties; and on the expiration of that time the independence and neutrality of Belgium will, so far as the high contracting parties are respectively concerned, continue to rest as heretofore on the 1st article of the Quintuple Treaty on the 19th of April, 1839.

"Art. IV. The present treaty shall be ratified, &c."

In the House of Commons, on the same day, the treaty was vigorously attacked by Mr. Bernal Osborne, who said he would prefer to have no treaty rather than the extraordinary document which had been laid on the table in so extraordinary a manner, and which he characterized as "a childish perpetration of diplomatic folly." It was not only superfluous, but it superseded the previous treaties; and if it had been submitted to the House he was confident it would have been unanimously rejected. He maintained, too, that England was bound to stand by Belgium, not only in honour but by interest, for her liberties and independence would not be safe for twenty-four hours if Belgium were in the hands of a hostile power.

Mr. Gladstone protested with all the emphasis at his command against Mr. Osborne's extravagant and exaggerated statement that, the liberties of England would be gone if Belgium were in the possession of a hostile power, and maintained that England's concern in the preservation of Belgian independence was substantially no greater than that of the other powers. The government had not been moved by any such selfish spirit, nor had they based their action solely on the guarantees to which an impracticably rigid significance had been attached, against which he felt himself bound to protest. Far wider and stronger than interest or guarantees was the consideration whether England could warrantably stand by and see a crime perpetrated by the absorption of Belgium, which would have been the knell of public right and public law in Europe. He dwelt, too, on the claims Belgium had on their friendship as a model for orderly government, combined with perfectly free institutions; and answering Mr. Osborne's criticisms, he maintained that the treaty of 1839 was not weakened nor superseded by this addition, and that the peculiar circumstances of the case justified this departure from general rules.

It will be seen from the events just narrated, that the uneasiness and excitement which had so universally prevailed on the first publication of the secret project, and the subsequent revelations made in connection with it, were finally allayed; and that the demand of the country that the defence of Belgium against foreign aggression should be again put forward as a cardinal principle of English policy, was complied with by the government in the manner they deemed best calculated to secure, the end in view—although on that point much difference of opinion prevailed. The end, however, having been attained, people cared little about the particular means which had been employed to attain it; and when Parliament broke up the feeling of security which had been somewhat interrupted in the country had quite returned.

The publication of the statement of Count von Bismarck, that before the war of 1866 France had offered her alliance to Prussia, with a promise to declare war against Austria and to attack her with 300,000 men, provided that Prussia would consent to make certain territorial concessions to France on the left bank of the Rhine, had an immense influence in Austria, and put an end to all thought of a French alliance, which up to that time had been considered probable. As a suitable conclusion to this chapter, in which their names have figured so largely, we annex biographical notices of Count von Bismarck and M. Benedetti.

KARL OTTO, COUNT VON BISMARCK, whose name will always be identified with the great work of the unification of Germany, was born at Brandenburg, in 1813, or as some accounts affirm, on the 1st April, 1814. Although the period is comparatively short since his name has become generally familiar in England, he has shared about equally with Napoleon III., for several years, most of the attention bestowed by the readers of English newspapers on continental affairs. His earlier reputation as a Prussian politician is now lost in his renown as one of the greatest statesmen of Germany, and this which is his good fortune now will no doubt be his glory in after ages. His career divides itself naturally into two parts, answering to these two characters: what we may call a Prussian part, in which he figures principally as the most strenuous upholder of divine right in the Prussian monarchy: and a German part, in which his principal *role* is that of the great presiding genius of German unification. Descended from a noble and very ancient family, he was educated at the universities of Göttingen, Greifswalde, and Berlin, and apparently at first was destined for a military career, which he commenced in an infantry regiment as a volunteer, after which he attained the rank of a lieutenant in the landwehr. He became a member of the Diet of the province of Saxony in 1846; and the year following was elected a member of the German Diet, where his character and abilities soon attracted attention, and the reputation which he bore for some years afterwards was fixed by some of those paradoxical utterances in which his toryism and his wit found vent together, such as his reported saying that he wished that "all the large manufacturing and commercial towns, those centres of democracy and constitutionalism, could be abolished from the surface of the earth," so that a purely rural population might submissively obey the king's decrees. One of the earliest notices of his public life which have fallen under our notice, one written shortly after his first appearance in the Diet, speaks of him as, if not a deep political thinker, at any rate an expert debater, whose wit and irony were often displayed with trenchant effect. It would now have to be allowed, perhaps, that the irony and the wit of which he is master, have been often since used to further the plans of a deep enough thinker. In the revolutionary year, 1848, Bismarck was of course one of the most unpopular men in Germany; he was excluded from the National Assembly of that year, but next year he took his seat in the Second Chamber, where he resumed his post of uncompromising opposition to the movements of the liberal party in Parliament. This, if it increased his unpopularity, also marked him out for royal favour. In 1851 he entered the diplomatic service as first secretary of legation to the Prussian embassy at Frankfort, a post which he exchanged after a few months for that of ambassador at the sittings of the Federal Bund. Bismarck's nomination to it was a decisive proof that he was already regarded by the king as his most able as well as most zealous servant. He showed himself worthy of this proof of confidence in his ability and his intentions. Count Rechberg was the representative of Austria at the Diet, and presided at its meetings. Austria, in Bismarck's opinion, was the power that Prussia had to withstand and outwit. Rechberg and Bismarck therefore had frequent encounters, in which the dignity of the one, it is said, suffered terribly from the witty sallies of the other. Till 1858 Bismarck was principally occupied in various places, and on various grounds, in this struggle with the representative of the Austrian empire. It is said that a pamphlet on "Prussia and the Italian question," which appeared in 1858, and which, referring to the ancient enmity between Austria and Prussia, recommended an alliance between France, Prussia, and Russia, was indited or inspired by him. Be this as it may, in the following year he went to St. Petersburg as ambassador, and there gained the friendship and confidence of Gortschakoff, and of his master the Czar, who conferred on him one of his orders of nobility. In the month of May of the same year he was transferred to the capital of France, to the court of the sovereign with whose history his own was afterwards to be mixed up in some of the most remarkable events of this century. He remained in Paris over two years; but in September, 1862, returned to Berlin to undertake the task of forming a new ministry, the previous cabinet having succumbed to adverse votes respecting their war budget. In the ministry which was thus formed by him he retained the portfolio of foreign affairs. The difficulties which in this position he had to face were not those of his own department. They were not of relations to foreign powers, but chiefly of the relations of the government to the representatives of the people. The policy of the administration, which was declared to be violently reactionary in all its tendencies, was especially obnoxious in respect to military re-organization. The Prussian Parliament then became for a period a scene of perpetual struggle of the fiercest description, in which, by large majorities, the deputies opposed the government at every important step. It is curious now, after the wars which Prussia has waged with Denmark, Austria, and France, and waged with such astonishing success, to remark that these fierce struggles were fiercest as to the army budget and military reforms; the administration contending for the extension of the period of compulsory service in the army, and the Chamber bitterly resisting that proposal. Bismarck, who has never been afraid of strong measures when they were required, finding the majorities in the Chamber thus unmanageable, closed the session. His administration, however, continued to be signalized by the same parliamentary scenes which marked its commencement. His policy in respect to Poland was severely blamed; by a majority of 246 to 46 votes he was severely censured for entering into a secret treaty with Russia, having reference to Polish affairs. In 1865—66 the relations of the administration to the Chamber were at the worst. Unable to govern Parliament, the executive governed without Parliament altogether. Stormy debates constantly occurred; there were memorable oratorical encounters between Bismarck and Virschow, but the result, practically, was that military organization, the premier's great project, was proceeded with according to his wish; and several sessions of Parliament were closed or dissolved like that of 1862, by royal decree, and without the sanction of the Chamber. During this period restrictions were laid upon the press, and in several instances opposition journals were subjected to penalties. What the result of all this might have been, had there been nothing to distract attention from home affairs, it would be difficult to say; but the death of the king of Denmark having re-opened the Schleswig-Holstein question, an opportunity was afforded to the administration of exhibiting in actual war the soundness of their policy of military re-organization; and though this did not avail to reconcile to them, the majority of the Chamber, or put a stop to parliamentary recriminations, it materially helped to avert a serious crisis in the relations between the two parties, until a much larger question than that of the duchies began to occupy public attention, and to divert it from home to foreign affairs. This larger question was that of war with Prussia's great rival in the struggle for the leadership of the German empire. The history of this question has been already related in the first part of this work, and need not here be recapitulated, especially as almost every one is familiar with the leading incidents of the period which intervened between the disputes of Austria and Prussia touching the duchies of the Elbe at the beginning of 1866, and the third day of July in that year, memorable in the history of Germany as the day of the battle of Königgrätz, and that which finally determined not so much the ascendancy of one German power over the rest, as the union of all in one great empire. Just before the declaration of war against Austria an attempt was made upon the life of Bismarck. An assassin named Blind fired four times from a pistol at the minister, who however, was only slightly wounded. Bismarck, whose courage and coolness have been tested in various ways, and have seldom failed, himself arrested the criminal. In the year following the conclusion of the war with Austria he had advanced his great project another stage. The North German Confederation was formed—by far the most important political work of this century, yet far more than otherwise the work of one single man. The first chancellor of the Confederation could be no other than Count von Bismarck, who was appointed to that office at the first meeting of the Federal Council. At this point the character of Prussian politician, which he has maintained hitherto, merges in that of the greatest of the living statesmen of Germany. The popularity which in the one character he has despised, now of course pursues him in the other. In the dispute with France respecting the Luxemburg frontier, which followed the Austrian campaign, and which threatened to embroil Europe in war, Bismarck of course played an important part. At the beginning of 1868 he was obliged, on account of his health, which was very seriously impaired, to retire temporarily from public life. His retirement, it was expected, would be lengthy, but it proved to be short. In October he was again at his post in Berlin, and occupying himself as energetically and as ably as ever, in pushing forward the confederation of the various states of the empire. His difficulties in this work were destined to be largely removed by an event, the end of which and the consequences of which it is difficult to foresee. What was needed to do in a day in respect to that work which it would still have taken years to accomplish, was a declaration of war against Prussia, the head of the German Confederation, by some rival power. That declaration of war was made by France in the month of July; and since then Bismarck, whose life has alternated between the camp and the court, has followed the fortunes of the German army in its campaign on the soil of France.

In 1865 Bismarck was promoted to the rank of count. After Königgrätz he was gazetted a general. His great distinction is that, beginning public life as a Prussian, he has made himself at length the representative of Germany. His personal character and manners are well defined and well known. His imperious earnestness and vehemence in public life contrast wonderfully, and yet agree, with his genial humour and merry wit and perfect unaffectedness in private. Not only the stories which are constantly told of him, but letters which he has allowed to be published, exhibit the great statesman of Germany as, in private fife, a brilliant ornament of society.

M. Vincent Benedetti is of Italian extraction, and was born in Corsica about 1815. He was educated for the consular and diplomatic service, and began his career in 1848 as consul at Palermo. From this post he was subsequently advanced to that of first secretary of the embassy at Constantinople. In May, 1859, he was offered, in succession to M. Bourse, the post of envoy extraordinary at Teheran, but he declined to accept that mission, and was shortly afterwards nominated director of political affairs to the foreign minister, and it was in this capacity that he acted as editor of the protocols in the Congress of Paris in 1856, and as secretary to those ministers who drew them up. In 1861, when the French emperor recognized the newly-established kingdom of Italy, M. Benedetti was appointed minister plenipotentiary from his country at Turin, but resigned that post in the autumn of 1864, upon the retirement of M. Thouvenel from the ministry of Foreign Affairs. On November 27 of that year he was appointed to the post of French ambassador at Berlin, a position in which he remained until the outbreak of the war. He was made a chevalier of the legion of honour as far back as June, 1845, and after passing through the intermediate stages of promotion, he was nominated a grand officer in June, 1860.

CHAPTER IV.

Necessity of understanding the Military Organization and Strength of each Combatant—Foundation of Prussia by the "Great Elector"—Its rapid extension—Frederick William I.'s singular passion for Tall Soldiers—His able Military Administration—First Successes of his son, Frederick the Great—The perfection to which he brought his Army—The Seven Years' War against the united forces of Russia, Saxony, Sweden, France, Austria, and the small German States—Its varying results and the state of Prussia at its close—She is admitted as the Rival of Austria for the leadership of Germany—Frederick's Bloodless Campaign, known as the "Potato War"—Policy of his nephew, Frederick William II.—Prussia's share in the spoliation of Poland—The French Revolution opposed by Prussia—Alliance with Austria—War declared against France—Complete failure of the Expedition, and the French frontier advanced to the Rhine—Humiliated and demoralized position of the Prussian Army—Popular fury against Napoleon for forcing a passage through their country, in spite of its neutrality—The King appeased with the bribe of Hanover—Battle of Austerlitz and humiliation of Austria—Insults offered to Prussia by Napoleon—Determination of the people to endure it no longer without a struggle—Battle of Jena and complete defeat of Prussia—The country overrun by French troops, and the King made little better than a vassal of France—Appearance of the great statesmen Stein and Scharnhorst on the scene—Foundation of the present Military System of Prussia with the approval of the whole Nation—Its fundamental principles, and the composition and numbers of the Army and Reserves under it—The Landwehr called out in 1830—The military spirit of the people found to have considerably evaporated—Further defects of the System discovered in 1848, 1850, 1854, and 1859—Material alterations and increase in the numbers of the Army made in 1860—Remonstrances on the part of the House of Deputies useless—Reasons for the alterations and additions—Extension of the term of service—Increased security conferred on the rest of the population—The great advantages of the New System shown in the War of 1866—Extension of the Prussian system to the whole of the North German Confederation in 1867—Present number of the Armies of the Confederation, and of the South German States—Divisions of the Armies in time of War, and their composition—Difference in the numbers of the Armies on paper and those actually engaged on the Field of Battle explained—The requirements of an Army on a Campaign—Extraordinary elasticity of the system proved in 1866 and 1870—The details of it easy enough to be universally understood—Steps taken when the Army is Mobilized, and the rapidity with which they can be executed—The equipment of the different arms of the service after Mobilization—Detailed description of the Prussian organization for insuring regular Supplies to the Army, attending to the Diseased and Wounded, and maintaining the number of Combatants at their full strength during the progress of hostilities—A defect in the Prussian system in the formation of garrison troops—The difficulty of insuring proper Supplies for an Army—Admirable provisions of the Prussian system in this respect, and its great success in the War—The Prussian hospital trains—The employment of Spies—Reconnoitring Parties—Field Signals and Telegraphs—Great ability of the Prussian officers—Peculiarities of the system for obtaining them—Necessity of a previous training in the ranks—Severity of their examinations—The **esprit de corps** *which pervades the whole body, but strong development of class spirit—Special examination for the Artillery and Engineer officers—Admirable system of officering the Landwehr—Re-enlistment of men not much encouraged in the Prussian Army—All ordinary Government Appointments reserved for Non-commissioned Officers after they have served twelve years—Frequent alterations in Prussian tactics—The plan adopted by them at present—Salutary effects of the Military Training on the Prussian population— Economy of the Prussian system—The strain on the Resources of the Country if the Campaign is prolonged—Certainty of any War undertaken by Prussia being a national one— The Prussian Artillery—Description of Krupp's Monster Gun—Description of the Needle- gun—The Prussian Navy.*

IN order to estimate correctly the position and resources of both Prussia and France, it is necessary, before entering upon the detailed record of the deadly struggle in which they engaged, that we should put before the reader a statement of their military growth, their most recently invented weapons, the constitution and strength of their respective armies, and the methods adopted in each country to recruit them.

The "Great Elector," Frederick William, may be regarded as the founder of the present grandeur of the Prussian throne. Under his able rule, from 1640 to 1688, the whole strength of Brandenburg and Prussia was directed to securing the acknowledgment of the independence of the latter dukedom, originally held separately as a fief from Poland. His success in this enterprise was soon followed by claims on Juliers, Cleves, and Berg, skilfully urged by the pen, and boldly supported by the sword; and the limits of the dominions handed to his son were thus extended from the Oder to the Rhine. Lower Pomerania had been among the additions gained by the treaty of Westphalia, and Frederick William used the opening it afforded to the Baltic, to lay the foundation of the navy, which Prussia's statesmen even thus early regarded as essential to support her claim to a distinguished place among the great European powers. The same policy, rather than any love for Austria or hatred of the Turk, led to the despatch of a contingent to the relief of Vienna, when threatened by the Sultan in 1683.

Under his successor, grandfather of the Great Frederick, and first king, the Prussian troops were in constant service as allies of Austria in her Turkish and French wars; and various small principalities, obtained as reward or purchased, swelled his now extensive though scattered dominions. He was succeeded in 1713 by his son, Frederick William I., whose habits were entirely military, and whose constant care was to establish the strictest discipline among his troops. He had such a ridiculous fondness for tall soldiers, that in order to fill the ranks of his favourite regiment, he would use force or fraud, if money would not effect his object, in order to obtain the tallest men in Europe. Indulging freely this singular passion, the father of Frederick the Great was in all else economical to parsimony; and without straining the resources of his five millions of subjects, he left his son an abundant treasury, and the most efficient army in Europe, to be at once the temptation and the instrument for continuing the family policy. The most important measure which Frederick William I. adopted in the military organization of Prussia, was one in which we may clearly trace the origin of her present formidable system of recruiting.

In 1733, seven years before his death, the whole of his territories were parcelled out by decree into cantons, to each of which was allotted a regiment, whose effective strength was to be maintained from within its limits; and all subjects, beneath the rank of noble, were held bound to serve if required. With this ready instrument for supplying the losses of a war, and with an army of 66,000 men, more splendidly equipped and trained than any other of the time, his son, then known as Frederick II., stepped into the field of European politics.

Surpassing his predecessors no less in the scope of his policy than in ability for carrying it out, the new sovereign's ambition was favoured by the stormy times in which he came to the throne. His first success in the seizure of Silesia only fanned his aspirations for further conquest, and he strove next to extend Prussian rule beyond the newly-gained mountain frontier into the northern districts of Bohemia, where his successor's arms in 1866 afterwards met with such signal fortune. On this occasion, however, his strength proved unequal to the new task of spoliation. The king was fairly worsted, and forced out of Bohemia by Daun and Prince Charles of Lorraine; and although the ready tactics of Hohenfriedberg and Sohr proved his increasing dexterity in handling the machine-like army he had trained, he was soon glad to come to terms, and to resign his audacious attempt to aggrandize Prussia upon condition that she retained her late acquisitions.

During the ten years of comparative tranquillity that followed, Frederick employed himself in bringing his troops into a state of discipline never before equalled in any age or country, with the view of concentrating his whole resources on the deadly struggle, not far distant, whose issue, as he foresaw, would be all-important to his dynasty.

Secret information of an alliance between Austria, Russia, and Saxony, gave Frederick reason to fear an attack, which he hastened to anticipate by the invasion of Saxony in 1756. This commenced the Seven Years' War, in which he contended, almost single-handed, against the united forces of Russia, Saxony, Sweden, France, Austria, and the great majority of the other German states. Various were the changes of fortune that befel him during the next six years, success alternating from one side to the other. The glories of Rosbach, Prague, and Leuthen were overshadowed by the disasters of Kollin, Hochkirch, and Kunersdorf. Frederick himself at times seemed to despair of any issue but death for himself and dissolution for his realm. Yet his boldness as a general and readiness as a tactician remained undiminished by defeat, failure, or depression. These qualities, with the excellent training of his troops, his good fortune in possessing the two finest cavalry officers a single army has ever known, and the moral and material support consistently given by England, sufficed to save the struggling kingdom from the ruin that so often, during this tremendous struggle, seemed inevitable. What Prussia suffered whilst it lasted may be conjectured from a few words occurring in the king's own correspondence. On this subject he, of all men, would be little likely to exaggerate. He says, "The peace awakens universal joy. For my own part, being but a poor old man, I return to a city where I now know nothing but the walls; where I cannot find again the friends I once had; where unmeasured toils await me; and where I must soon lay me down to rest in that place in which there is no more unquiet, nor war, nor misery, nor man's deceit." After all his many vicissitudes of fortune, however, the king was left in 1763 in the peaceful possession of his paternal and acquired dominions; the position of his country was assured, and the policy steadily pursued for three successive generations had attained its first great aim. The principality, raised out of obscurity by the Great Elector, and made a kingdom by his son, was henceforth to hold a solid position as one of the first powers of Europe, and the admitted rival of Austria for the leadership of Germany. Her land had indeed a long rest after the great strife for existence; but Frederick, whilst watching diligently over its internal improvement, took care to insure its independent position by refilling as soon as possible the gaps in his army. The standing forces which he maintained and handed over to his successor were scarcely inferior in strength to those which Prussia, with more than three times his resources, kept in pay before the war of 1866; and the greatness of the burden thus imposed is better understood when it is known that the three per cent, of the population which, under Frederick, were actively kept in arms, supply under the present system the whole peace army, the landwehr of the first call, and most of those of the second.

The only other military enterprise of any pretensions undertaken by Frederick was a campaign against Austria, distinguished by its marked difference of character from the somewhat reckless strategy for which he had been famed, and the striking parallel which its opening afforded to that of the great war of 1866; for its scene lay on the very ground where Benedek was afterwards called to oppose another Prussian invasion of Bohemia. The great general's conduct, however, was here in truth very different from that of the Frederick of twenty years before, and we can only account for it by admitting either that his intellect and daring were dulled by coming infirmity, or by supposing that he believed the objects of the campaign could be fully attained without the risk and bloodshed of a great battle. Certain it is, that in this the closing military adventure of his life, he appeared as though utterly foiled by the adversaries he had so often in earlier days worsted in fair field. Frederick, however, if losing some of his military prestige in the bloodless campaign (known familiarly as the "Potato War") of his old age, found sufficient consolation in its political results, and the admission practically made by Austria that her imperial position had sunk to the mere presidency of a confederation. Henceforth, there was recognized in Prussia a power whose consent was a first condition for any action of Austria within the Germanic empire; a power to whom every element hostile to the Kaiser would rally, should the constant rivalry for the control of Germany break out into open hostility.

The military force so ably used by Frederick in enlarging the influence of Prussia at the expense of Austria, was for some years employed with scarcely inferior success in other quarters by his nephew and successor, Frederick William II. Interfering in the civil war in Holland (1787), the well-drilled Prussian battalions without difficulty put down the popular party, and restored the Stadtholder to his shaken seat; and the king had the double satisfaction of increasing the moral weight of his influence in Europe, and of asserting that principle of divine right, to him no less dear than to the first monarch of the line, or to their present representative. A more material gain was that achieved under the guidance of his unscrupulous minister, Herzberg, at the second partition of Poland, when Dantzic and Thorn, districts long coveted as including the mouths of the Vistula, were obtained as the price of Prussia's complicity in a spoliation carried out with an amount of diplomatic fraud even greater than that in which Frederick had shared.

The intervention of Prussia in the affairs of Holland had not long ceased to excite attention, and the final partition of Poland was still unaccomplished, when that mighty storm arose in the west which was destined for a time to extinguish the rivalries and animosities of German powers in their general humiliation, and to school them by common sufferings, by common hatred and fear of a foreign foe, into the union which was only dissolved by the outbreak of 1866. Austria was to be laid prostrate by republican armies, Prussia to be humbled in the dust, and for years to bear the chain of the victor. A new general was to eclipse the achievements of Frederick, and a bolder and more unscrupulous diplomacy than the Great Elector's was to change the whole map of Europe, and remove her most ancient landmarks. The French Revolution and Napoleon came; and the march of Prussian progress was arrested until the overthrow of the latter at Waterloo.

Prussia hesitated considerably before showing any practical opposition to the proceedings of the Republic, and not until the sacred rights of kings were attacked in the person of Louis XVI., after his flight to Varennes, did Frederick William move to the rescue. By the treaty of Pillnitz (August, 1791) he then entered into an alliance with Austria for an armed intervention on behalf of the French sovereign, and with a force mainly composed of Prussian battalions, under the duke of Brunswick, entered Champagne in 1792, having first issued a boastful proclamation against the Revolution and its abettors. Relying too much on the promised support with which they nowhere met, the Prussian staff threw aside the prudent, but cumbrous, arrangements of magazines by which Frederick had always prepared for his offensive movements; and their troops, plunging into an inhospitable district in unusually bad weather, perished by the thousand for lack of supplies. The sickness that ensued, and the unexplained vacillation of the king or of the duke of Brunswick at Valmy, proved the ruin of the expedition, and the turning point of the revolutionary war. Thenceforth the republican armies grew in *morale* as rapidly as in numbers, and a system of tactics destined to replace that which Frederick had bequeathed to Europe, was initiated by the revolutionary generals, and brought to its perfection under Napoleon's master hand, to overthrow the troops of each great power in turn. The failure of the Prussians in their campaign was as great a surprise to Europe in 1792, as the sudden collapse of the Austrian army in 1866, or that of France in 1870. The disasters proved a powerful motive for Frederick William's withdrawal from a struggle in which there was nothing for Prussia to gain, but which had brought a victorious enemy to the borders of her own western provinces. The treaty of Basle soon followed, and Europe saw with dismay the great German power, whose arms, forty years before, had defied France, though leagued with half the Continent, admitting the claim of the aggressive Republic to advance her frontier to the Rhine.

The conduct of the war that Prussia thus relinquished had dimmed her former fame no less than the peace that closed it; yet no administrator rose at this time competent to point out the causes of the ill success which, save in the desultory but brilliant skirmishes conducted by Colonel Blucher and his cavalry, had invariably attended her arms. The activity of this daring trooper was, however, exceptional, and the chief commanders illustrated every degree of military imbecility, while their troops retained only the drill of the battalions of Frederick, and exhibited nothing of their heroic spirit. In spite of the severe system of conscription by districts, enforced by every penalty which the law could employ, a trade in permits for absence had long been established as a perquisite of the captains. Those who could pay well for the exemption were thus allowed to escape the allotted service, the bribes received being partly put in the pockets of the recipients and partly used to attract an inferior class of recruits to the ranks of an army which an iron discipline, maintained in every detail, made thoroughly distasteful in time of peace. Composed thus of indifferent material, brought together by a system of corruption, the companies were as ill-led as they were badly composed, and the army which had once been acknowledged the first in Europe, was now inferior to others in fitness for the field. It was specially ill-suited to meet the growing enthusiasm of the French soldiery, whose ardour, springing from political fanaticism, was sustained through the sternest trials by the hope of professional advancement.

Frederick William III., who succeeded in 1797 to the throne, continued for nearly ten years the neutral policy inaugurated by his father. The indignity, however, which Napoleon inflicted upon Prussia by forcing a passage through the country on his way to Ulm and Austerlitz, excited such a fever of popular fury through the kingdom as shook the royal power, and showed alike the antipathy of the whole German race to the progress of French influence within the empire, and the necessity which thenceforth lay upon the king to adopt a policy more conformable to the wishes of his subjects. To incur the active hostility of Prussia, besides that of Russia and Austria, was what Napoleon was just now anxious to avoid, and he watched with some uneasiness the feeling gathering against him. The entreaties of queen, ministers, and people, had well-nigh swept away the vacillation of the king, and war was to be declared by Prussia on December 15 against the French emperor. At this crisis Napoleon, feigning reconciliation and friendship, adroitly offered a bribe, the temptation of which proved irresistible; and on the very day on which war was to have been declared, Frederick William accepted at the hand of the crafty emperor the coveted gift of Hanover, which now, more honestly won, extends the limits of the once petty margraviate from Russia to the German Ocean.

Austria, meantime, unaided by Prussia, had encountered Napoleon at Austerlitz, and was now writhing under the humiliation of a crushing defeat. The degrading acquisition of territory which Prussia had made was not long destined, however, to reward its public treachery. The bribes of Napoleon Frederick William found to be no free gifts. Bavaria was enlarged at the expense of his kingdom. Cleves and Berg were surrendered to provide the despot's brother-in-law with a new duchy, and fresh insults followed with contemptuous rapidity. From the rank of a great power Prussia found herself suddenly fallen to the condition of a French dependency, and her monarch treated as the French emperor's vassal. Yet she had attempted no struggle and suffered no defeat; had looked on unscathed whilst her neighbours bled; and now, waiting for their loss to make her gain, found herself isolated, exposed, and humbled without pity—a warning for all time to statesmen who make a traffic of neutrality. If the court could endure this, the people could not. Alike the noble, the burgher, and the peasant felt a warlike fever fire their veins, and that tempest of passion swept over the nation, which is to individual fury as the trampling of a multitude to the footfall of a man. Without counting the cost or measuring the odds—without waiting for the aid of Russia, still hostile to France—Frederick William was forced into the struggle he dreaded, and Prussia, single-handed, faced Napoleon and his vassals. Planted already by Bavarian permission within easy distance of the chief strategic points; armed with the might of superior numbers, long training, and accumulated victory; led by a chief whose bold strategy had not yet degenerated into limitless waste of men's lives; the French poured up on the flank exposed by the rash and ill-considered advance of their enemy. Jena was fought and won by the French almost within sight of the little hill of Rosbach, which had given name to their defeat half a century before, and that signal victory was avenged tenfold by the battle which laid Prussia prostrate at the conqueror's feet.

With a rapidity of which even Napoleon's troops were scarcely thought capable, the kingdom was overrun, the remains of its army annihilated, and its cities occupied. The hollowness of its military condition was manifested alike by the evil condition of its fortresses and the overthrow of its columns. Blucher, indeed, fought fiercely to the last; but with this, and two other less noted exceptions to the shameful imbecility of the commanders, generals and governors seemed to vie with each other in surrendering their posts with the least effort at resistance. Reduced, however, as Frederick William was, to a single city and a few square miles of territory, he refused to submit to the harsh terms required of him, until the disaster of Friedland, and the subsequent retreat of the allies, compelled that abandonment of his unhappy kingdom which was one of the conditions imposed by the conqueror when he met Alexander at Tilsit.

No need is there for us to repeat the fatal story of Jena and of Friedland. The bitter lesson taught the nation then has stamped itself ever since upon the national armament, and Prussian administrators strive now as earnestly to be in advance of all Europe in warlike knowledge, as they then clung warmly to the traditions of obsolete tactics which all Europe but themselves had abandoned. But the penalty of truckling policy and pedantic manoeuvring was undergone; and for the next six years the kingdom suffered such humiliation as no other civilized country in modern years has endured. French soldiers swaggered on the pavements of the garrisons. French officers forbade the concert-room its national airs. French generals lived at free quarters in the pleasant squires' houses, which even the all-pervading rapacity of Tilly's and Wallenstein's hordes had not always reached. French battalions lay scattered in the secluded villages, and roused a jealous demon in the dullest Hans whose sweetheart was exposed to the audacious attentions of wandering chasseurs. French *douaniers* checked and controlled and took bribes for the little trade which the long maritime war had spared. And all these intruders were to be maintained at the expense of the quiet orderly land of which they seemed to have taken permanent possession. The Prussian army seemed to have disappeared, so diminished were its numbers. The enslaved monarchy was guarded by the ablest and most feared of the rough soldiers, whom the long course of French victories had brought to eminence; and Davoust headed a garrison so large and highly organized, that even warm patriots shrank from a hopeless contest with its strength. The history of that sad time, with all the irritating details of the French occupation, is written in the municipal records of every Prussian town, in village legend, in popular romance. The burden is always the same: French insults endured in the hope of revenge to come; ardent longing for the day of freedom; tears for the fate of brave Major Schill, warrior of the true heroic type, who, unable to bear longer his country's shame, rode forth one morning at the head of such of his men as would follow him, to declare war single-handed with oppression, and give his life freely in a conflict without hope. Multiply the story of one village by a thousand, the indignation of one citizen by millions, and it will be seen that each day of the French occupation served to give strength and depth to the growing hatred which henceforth must burn in every Prussian breast, and in due time burst forth in furious action.

No doubt the confidence which Bohemian victories gave the nation in its arms has much to do with the readiness for a struggle on the Rhine which Prussia has since displayed. No doubt the vague desire for German unity has been strengthened into passionate longing since Austria has ceased to bar the way. But the ancient loathing of French rule, the ancient detestation of French interference, the deep memory of the time when a Napoleon was indeed "the Scourge of the Fatherland," was all that was needed to touch the heart of the nation with that fire which we have watched this summer so fiercely blaze forth into action.

Stripped of half her territory, the rest a mere field for French tax-gatherers, or exercise-ground for French troops, the policy of Prussia for the six years succeeding Jena seemed to consist but in different degrees of servility to the master whose chains she had no power to shake off. Her revenues were swallowed up by foreign exactions, her army reduced to a mere corps by the decree of Napoleon, and her means of rising against the oppressor seemed hopelessly gone. But whilst despised by both foe and ally, Prussia had yet within her the elements of self-purification. The hard school of humiliation did not break her spirit, nor turn her statesmen aside from the deliberate endeavour to retrieve the past. Frederick William was happy in his counsellors, for there were those among them who never lost sight of the past greatness of their country, and in her hours of deepest darkness strove to fit her for a better destiny than that of a vassal province. Stein, her great minister, laboured indefatigably to prepare her recovery, by raising the legal condition of her peasantry, and breathing into them the spirit of patriotism through measures of domestic reform. Scharnhorst gave no less efficient aid by devising that system of short service in the regular army, on which the existing organization rests. By Napoleon's decree the standing army was not to exceed 40,000 men; but no restriction was named as to the tune the men should serve. By Scharnhorst's plan the actual time of service was limited to six months, with frequent calls of recruits succeeding each other in the ranks, and thence returning home to be embodied in the militia, so as to spread through the suffering nation a general knowledge of arms against the day of need. The laws of promotion were modified, and many of the exemptions from military service abolished; to each company was allotted twice the necessary number of officers; and the disbanded men assembled from time to time in their cantons, and were provided with arms, stores, and clothing from the depôts disseminated over the country.

The immediate result of Stein's reforms was a vast increase of national spirit and strength. The military service of the country was accepted by all without reluctance, in tacit preparation for the day of reckoning with France; and the struggle of 1814 once over, the minister was encouraged by every class to elaborate a complete project for the perpetuation of the system which had restored glory and freedom to Prussia. The foundation of the permanent constitution of the national force was laid by the remarkable law of September 3, 1814—which for more than forty years was the charter adhered to by government and people as binding on both sides, and which in its introduction is declared to be the issue of the wishes of the whole nation—and in the landwehr ordinance of 21st November, 1815.

"In a lawfully administered armament of the country lies the best security of lasting peace." Such is the principle proclaimed as its groundwork, together with the more immediate necessity of maintaining intact by the general exertions the freedom and honourable condition which Prussia had just won. All former exemptions from service in favour of the noblesse were from this time abrogated. Every native of the state, on completing his twentieth year, was to be held as bound to form part of her defensive power; but, with a view to the avoiding inconvenient pressure on the professional and industrial population, the armed force was to be composed of sections whose service should lessen in severity as their years advanced. The whole system comprised, 1st, a standing army, the annual contingent of recruits to which was laid down at 40,000 men, who were to form the nucleus of the regular army of 140,000; 2nd, a landwehr of the first call; 3rd, a landwehr of the second call; and 4th, the landsturm.

The standing army was to be composed of volunteers willing to undergo the necessary examinations for promotion, with a view to the adoption of a regular military career; of men voluntarily enlisting without being prepared for such examination; and of a sufficient number of the youth of the nation called out from their twentieth to their twenty-fifth year—the first three years to be spent by these latter actually with the colours; the other two as "reserved" recruits, remaining at home, but ready to join the ranks at the first sound of war.

The landwehr of the first call, composed of men from twenty-five to thirty-two who had passed through the regular army and reserve, was designed for the support of the standing army in case of war, and was liable to serve at home or abroad, though in peace only to be called out for such exercise as is necessary for training and practice.

The landwehr of the second call was intended in case of war for garrison duty, or in special need, to be used in its entirety either for corps of occupation or reinforcements to the army. It consisted of all who had left the army and the first call. The drill of the second call was in time of peace only for single days, and in their own neighbourhood.

The landsturm was to be called out only in provinces of the kingdom actually invaded, and then must be summoned by a special royal decree. It included all the men up to the fiftieth year who were not regularly allotted to the army or landwehr; of all who had completed their landwehr service; and of all the youth able to carry arms who had attained their seventeenth year. It consisted of civic and local companies in the towns, villages, and open country, according to the divisions of the districts for other governmental purposes. No provision, however, was made for the exercise of these companies, which have, in fact, existed only on paper.

From what we have just said it will be seen that by the law of 1814 every Prussian subject capable of carrying arms was called upon to serve from the age of twenty to twenty-three in the active army; from twenty-three to twenty-five in the reserve; from twenty-five to thirty-two in the first call of the landwehr; and from thirty-two to thirty-nine in the second—the landsturm comprehending all citizens from the age of seventeen to forty-nine who were not incorporated in the army or landwehr. The Prussian forces were therefore composed in the following manner:— 1st. The standing army in time of peace, 140,000; and by the embodiment of the reserve on a war footing, of 220,000. 2nd. The first call of the landwehr, infantry and cavalry, numbering in time of war 150,000. 3rd. The second call of the landwehr, numbering 110,000. If we add to these figures the 50,000 men capable of being recruited by the anticipation of their time of service, we attain a total of 530,000, of which 340,000 composed the armies in the field, and the rest the depôts and garrisons. Only a quarter of these forces were maintained by the state in time of peace.

Such was the achievement of Scharnhorst, and of those patriots whom yet Prussia remembers with gratitude. The organization subsisted, almost without modification, during the two reigns of Frederick William III. and of his son, Frederick William IV., brother of the reigning king. During many years no occasion arose to consecrate on the field the system initiated in 1813. While Prussia seemed for ever condemned to inaction, Russia was skirmishing in the Caucasus, Austria was kept in arms by her Italian difficulties, and France had ever in Algeria a school of war in which to form her officers and prove her troops. It was feared that time had in a great measure deadened the spirit of 1813, and that the enforced military service had become odious to the people. In 1830, under the influence of a strong popular emotion, the Prussian government called out a part of the landwehr, and the result undeniably showed that the enthusiasm kindled by the War of Independence had considerably evaporated. Nevertheless, it was judged dangerous to modify the existing system, since it contained the essential germ of an ideal army: obligatory service. In 1848, in 1850, in 1854, and in 1859, the landwehr was again embodied; and though no hostilities followed to test the system by the stern proofs of war, the government found it unready for action, and ill suited to the needs of a bold policy. On each occasion it was observed that the tactical combination of elements so differently constituted worked badly in practice. The landwehr officers showed a keen jealousy of the assumed superiority, both of their comrades of the line and of the staff, who controlled the whole. Educated in a thoroughly military course: possessed generally of more means than the regulars; and commanding soldiers as good, at the least, as the recruits under the latter; endowed, moreover, constitutionally, with a sort of military equality, they manifested an unmistakable impatience in appearing in the field to support a policy which, in two instances at least, was not heartily favoured by the sympathies of the nation.

The royal government saw clearly enough that an army thus composed could not be relied upon for accomplishing the vast scheme of German supremacy, bequeathed by the Great Elector as his hereditary legacy to the Hohenzollerns. The decrees of November, 1850, and of April, 1852, aimed at remedying these evils. The formation of the army was materially altered. Infantry brigades were thenceforward to be composed of two regiments of the line and one corresponding body of landwehr. In March, 1853, a ministerial order completed this amelioration, and the arrangement was highly effective in amalgamating the two elements which composed the national forces. These alterations, however, were trifling compared to the measures of 1860, in which year the national forces underwent, at the mere will of the executive, a change, in regard to numbers, as great as any ever wrought by republican vote or imperial decree; and notwithstanding six years of firm remonstrance on the part of the House of Deputies, the new system was maintained in every detail until the long-prepared-for war came to justify its authors in the eyes of the nation. At one stroke the annual supply of recruits actually drafted into the line was raised from 40,000 to 63,000. The standing army was augmented by 117 infantry battalions, 10 regiments of cavalry, 31 companies of artillery, 18 of engineers, and 9 battalions of train for the hitherto insufficient transport departments.

The authors of the re-organization took for the starting-point of their calculations the fact that the resources of the country in point of population and revenue had so increased since 1815 that the army was no longer in proportion with them. When the fundamental law of 1814 first took effect, a call to arms was made of $1\frac{1}{4}$ per cent, of the population; and though the standing army was now augmented from 140,000 to 217,000, the proportion still remained below $1\frac{1}{4}$ per cent., so rapid had been the increase of population. The pecuniary sacrifices were also relatively much inferior to those accepted without a murmur in 1814. At that epoch, in spite of the impoverished condition of the nation, the army of 140,000 cost 35 per cent, of the state receipts. On the eve of the Austrian war, the army of 217,000 then absorbed but 29 per cent, of the budget of receipts. It will be thus seen that the augmentation of the active army in 1860 was consistent with the spirit and letter of the law of September, 1814. But the king's object was not only to multiply the numerical force of the army in proportion to the growth of population, but to give that army a permanent consistency that should abrogate the necessity of drawing able-bodied men from "the people under arms," and thus relieve the country from the indisputable evils attendant upon the landwehr system pure and simple.

The most serious innovation of 1860 remains to be noticed. It will be remembered that, under the law of 1814, the recruit owed the state three years of active and continual service, and two years of service in the reserve. The re-organization decree of 1860 prolonged the service in the reserve to four years. The increase of taxation thus caused, and the prolongation of military service, were amply compensated, however, by the security conferred upon the rest of the population. Under the old system the army could only be placed on a war footing by drafting into it large bodies of the landwehr. It is easy to understand the constant perturbation and anxiety the possibility of such an event created among the people. The line of policy that led Prussia into the war of 1866 might not have possessed the suffrage and consent of the whole nation; but the discontent would have been immeasurably more open and serious had the 610,000 men that expressed the strength of the Prussian army in July, 1866, been obtained principally by means of the landwehr. The actual means employed were found to be less costly than the former system. Even a partial mobilization entailed enormous expense, each commune having to be indemnified for its relief of the families left destitute by the departure of the male members. Statistics prove that the cost of each soldier was considerably lessened by the re-organization. In 1820 a soldier cost annually 211 thalers; in 1830 the expense had fallen to 177 thalers; during the mobilization that took place in 1859, the cost reached 214 thalers. After the re-organization it was rated at 196 thalers. Though the Schleswig campaign was undertaken in the winter of 1864, it was not found needful to call upon any part of the landwehr, or indeed to mobilize all the standing army corps. In 1866, however, under the pressure of a heavier strain, Prussia was obliged to have recourse to the landwehr, and the great advantages of the system were then fully demonstrated. The number of men from the landwehr incorporated in the army of 610,000, at the disposition of the Prussian government in 1866, was estimated at 191,500; but of the 261,000 combatants who took part in the battles of Turnau, Münchengrätz, Trautenau, Skaliz, Nachod, Gitchin, and Sadowa, only 27,000 had been summoned from it. How completely the victories of that year swept away all opposition to the Bismarck regime and the royal military system; how the current of democracy, long dashing vainly against the power of the monarchy, turned aside to flow in the tempting channel of national aggrandisement; how German patriots came to look upon their great standing army as no useless attribute of absolutism, but the mighty instrument of completing the once ideal Fatherland, and framing, for the vision of past days, a solid existence: these are now matters of familiar history.

The campaign of 1866 added four millions of the most warlike races of Germany to the Prussian dominions; and to the whole of these the obligation to serve in the army was extended. The eight corps of the old Prussian army were raised to twelve and a half by the formation of one in Schleswig-Holstein, another in conquered Hanover, a third in Cassel and Frankfort, a fourth created out of the fine Saxon army, and a division raised in the northern half of Hesse-Darmstadt. The Prussian system was also introduced into the independent North German States, and every North German is, therefore, now liable to service, and no substitution is allowed. The Federal troops take the oath of fealty to the Federal generalissimo, and all form one army under one command.

Within less than a year of the victory of Sadowa, when the South Germans still sorely felt their defeat, and murmured at their coming Prussianization, and when the new army of the Northern Confederation existed only on paper, Prussia had to face the prospect of a war with France on the Luxemburg question with the lesser resources that had proved so sufficient, and had served her so well, against Austria. But France was then supplied with inferior weapons. Her troops would have had to face the breech-loader at the same risk as those of Benedek; and though the danger of collision passed away for a season, it was certainly not from any fear on the side of the military guides of Prussia, who afterwards avowed that their sole strategy would have been to have massed the armies lately victorious in Bohemia in two great columns on the Rhine, and march straight for Paris, trusting to the needle-gun. The Luxemburg question, however, was solved at the instance of Europe, and by the special interposition of England, and the mortal struggle of the two countries was postponed for three years; and how were these three years spent by the Germans? The field army was vastly increased, as were also the reserves, by the application of the Prussian system to the new Confederation and its allies. These additions were the natural result of annexation and alliance, and concerned the infantry chiefly; but most important changes and additions were also made in the artillery and cavalry departments, which will be alluded to further on in our description of those branches of the service.

In a case where the whole male population may be said to be trained for arms, it is, of course, not an easy matter to arrive at the exact total of men capable of being brought into the field. According to official returns, however, which recent experience has shown to be below rather than above the numbers, the total strength of the army of the North German Confederation amounts to 316,224 men on the peace footing, and to 952,294 men on the war footing. This war establishment comprises:—Field troops, privates and non-commissioned officers, 553,189; depôts, ditto, 185,623; garrison troops, ditto, 208,517; staff, 4965. These are the armies of Prussia, or rather the one army of the North German Confederation. But as the non-confederate states of the South have made common cause in defence of the Fatherland, in the war of which this work treats, we must add their forces to the total. The Bavarian army numbers 73,419 men, or, by calling in the reserves, 96,804. Würtemberg can furnish in war time 29,392 men, and Baden 24,386.

It must not be supposed that the Prussian system involves the training for arms and personal service in the ranks of the *entire* male population. The peculiarity of the system is more in the universal *liability* to service, without any option of substitution. The number of young men who every year arrive at the age of twenty is, however, much larger than the annual contingent to be drafted into the army. Those who are not required for the annual contingent are placed in the second Ersatz reserve. They are liable to be called on in case of war; but as the landwehr have to go first, the chance of their ever being so is exceedingly remote. A very large number of able-bodied men in Germany are never enrolled. It is true that the landsturm includes all men between seventeen and fifty not forming part of the army or landwehr; but this force is only liable to be called out in case of actual invasion.

The Prussian army which takes the field in time of war consists of twelve corps d'armée of troops of the line, and of the corps d'armée of the guard. Each corps d'armée is organized with the intention of being a perfectly complete little army of itself, so that without inconvenience it can be detached from the main army at any time. Each corps d'armée of the line in time of war consists of two divisions of infantry, one division of cavalry, sixteen batteries of artillery, and a military train. Each division of infantry is composed of two brigades, each of which has two regiments, and as each regiment contains three battalions, in a division of infantry there are twelve battalions; to every infantry division is also attached one regiment of cavalry of four squadrons, and one division of artillery of four batteries, making the total strength of the force under the command of every infantry divisional general twelve battalions, four squadrons, and four batteries.

A cavalry division consists of two brigades, each containing two regiments, and as every regiment has in the field four squadrons, the division contains sixteen squadrons; it has also two batteries of horse artillery attached to it. The Prussian cavalry bore itself gallantly in action in the war of 1866, and proved of abundant service in outpost work in Bohemia; but difficulties were experienced from the admixture of half-broken horses and unpractised riders. These evils it was judged necessary to avoid in future, by raising very considerably the peace effective of the cavalry by adding a fifth squadron to each regiment, and increasing the number of regiments—a change which made the Prussians in the war of 1870 show a more marked superiority in that arm over the enemy, than Europe had witnessed since the Archduke Charles outmanoeuvred Moreau and Jourdan on the Danube by the dexterous use of his horse.

The reserve of artillery consists of one division of field artillery, which forms four batteries, and of two batteries of horse artillery, besides an artillery train for the supply of ammunition.

This gives the strength of a corps d'armée as twenty-four battalions of infantry, twenty-four squadrons of cavalry, and sixteen batteries of artillery. Besides this, however, each corps has one distinct "Jaegerbataillon" (battalion of sharpshooters), the men of which are all "picked." The sons of "Waldhüter," "Förster," "herrhosaftliche Jaeger," all from their childhood familiar with the handling of a rifle, are chosen for this service. Their uniform is dark green instead of dark blue. The corps has also one battalion of engineers, besides an engineer train for the transport of materials for making bridges, and a large military train which carries food, hospitals, medicines, fuel for cooking, bakeries, and all the other necessaries not only of life, but of the life of an army, the members of which require not only the same feeding, clothing, and warming as other members of the human race, but also bullets, powder, shot and shells, saddlery for their horses, and who from the nature of their life are more liable to require medicines, bandages, splints, and all hospital accessories than other men.

If we do not consider the train when we are calculating the number of combatants who actually fall in, in the line of battle, every battalion may be considered to consist of 1002 men. Thus the force of infantry and engineers in a corps d'armée numbers over 26,000, and on account of men absent through sickness may in round numbers be calculated at this figure. Each squadron of cavalry may be calculated at 150 mounted men, which makes the whole cavalry force about 3000 men. Each division of four batteries of horse artillery brings into the field 590 actual combatants, and each of field artillery the same, so that the whole artillery force of a corps d'armée is about 2350 men. The actual number of combatants with a corps d'armée is in this way seen to be 31,350 men, which may be stated in round numbers at 31,000. The guard corps d'armée differs chiefly from the Hue corps in having one additional rifle battalion, one additional fusilier regiment, and two additional cavalry regiments, which increase its strength by about 5150 actual combatants; the total number of combatants in this corps may be safely assumed as 36,000 men, in round numbers.

If we turn, however, to the list furnished by the military authorities, we find that the army is said to consist of 553,189 men, with 165,591 horses, of which only about 102,000 belong to the cavalry and artillery, and that it is accompanied by a waggon train of 17,743 carriages, of which only 5000 belonging to the artillery perform any service on the field of battle.

What has then become of these 90,000 men, 60,000 horses, and 11,000 carriages which form the difference between the returns we find of an army on paper and the actual number of men engaged on the field of battle? This difference represents the moving power of the combatant branches; it is this difference that feeds the warriors when they are well, that tends them when wounded, and nurses them when struck down with disease. Nor are these the only duties of the non-combatant branches. An army on a campaign is a little world of itself, and has all the requirements of ordinary men moving about the world, besides having an enemy in its neighbourhood, who attempts to oppose its progress in every way possible. When the line of march leads to a river, over which there is either no bridge or where the bridge has been destroyed, a bridge must be immediately laid down, and, accordingly, a bridge train is necessarily always present with the army. When a camp is pitched, field bakeries have to be immediately established to feed the troops; field telegraphs and field post-offices must be established for the rapid transmission of intelligence. A large staff must be provided for, which is the mainspring which sets all the works going. And these are only ordinary wants, such as any large picnic party on the same scale would require. When we consider that 200 rounds of ammunition can easily be fired away by each gun in a general action, that every infantry soldier can on the same occasion dispose of 120 rounds of ball cartridge, and that this must be all replaced immediately; that all this requires an enormous number of carriages, with horses and drivers; that outside of the line of battle there must be medical men, their assistants, and nurses; that within it and under fire there must be ambulance waggons, and men with stretchers to bear the wounded to them; and that 40 per cent. of the infantry alone in every year's campaign are carried to the rear, we may understand how the large difference between the number of actual fighting men and of men borne upon paper is accounted for.

Each corps d'armée of the line in time of peace is quartered in one of the several provinces of the kingdom; its recruits are obtained from that province, and its landwehr are the men in the province who have served seven years and who have been dismissed from actual service, but are subjected to an annual course of training. The provinces to which the different corps d'armée belong are:—1, Prussia Proper; 2, Pomerania; 3, Brandenburg; 4, Prussian Saxony; 5, Posen; 6, Silesia; 7, Westphalia; 8, Rhine Provinces; 9, Schleswig-Holstein; 10, Hanover; 11, Cassel, &c.; 12, Saxony. The guards are men chosen from the strongest of the military recruits throughout all the provinces of the kingdom. They are from five feet nine inches to six feet one inch in height, and from twelve stones to thirteen and a half stones in weight. The landwehr of the guard consists of the men who have formerly served in it.

The extraordinary elasticity of this organization was first manifested during the campaign of 1866. In a wonderfully short time the large armies which fought at Königgrätz were placed on a war footing, and brought about 260,000 combatants into the very field of battle, besides the necessary detachments which must be made by a large army to cover communications, mask fortresses, and so on; but the detachments made from the Prussian army were very small compared to those which would have had to be separated from an army organized on a different system; for as the field army advanced the depôt troops moved up in rear, and formed both depôts and reserves for the first line, while some of the garrison troops of landwehr came up from Prussia, and formed the garrisons of Saxony, Prague, Pardubitz, and all the other points on the lines of communication. At the same time General Mülbe's corps, formed for the most part of reserve and depôt soldiers, pushed up to Brünn, and was hastening to take its place in the first line, when its march was stopped by the conclusion of the long armistice. In the present war the system was shown to even greater perfection than in 1866; for not only were all gaps in the ranks speedily filled, but the Germans were able to leave 290,000 fighting men for the sieges of Strasbourg and Toul and the investment of Metz, and yet have over 270,000 at the battle of Sedan, and 50,000 men in the line of communication.

Though the part of the Prussian organization which refers to the recruiting of the army and to the filling up of the ranks in case of war had a great deal to do with the success of the campaigns in 1866 and 1870, on account of the facility and rapidity with which by its means the army could be mobilized and brought upon a war footing, the portion of the Prussian organization which relates to the combination of the recruits so obtained in pliable bodies, which can be easily handled, easily moved, yet formed in such due proportions of the different arms as to be capable of independent action, did not fail to be appreciated most fully by those who, with its assistance, gained such tremendous results. This portion of the military organization of the Prussian army is so simple that almost every man in the ranks can understand it. Jealous of expense in time of peace, it allows for a wide expansion, without hurry and without confusion, on the outbreak of war. It provides at the same time for the broadest questions and the most minute details, and is so clearly laid down and so precisely defined, yet at the same time admits of so much elasticity, that the Prussian officers can find no words strong enough to express their praise of it.

As has been previously stated, the Prussian system is a strictly localized one. Every district has its line and landwehr regiment. Adjoining districts are combined in the same military division, and adjoining divisions are united in the same corps d'armée. Each regiment, division, and corps d'armée has thus its local head-quarters, so that the regimental rendezvous is within easy reach, of the soldiers' homes, and the combination of the several regiments into their divisions, and of the divisions into then corps, can be easily effected. The military and civil staff remain at the respective head-quarters, and once a year, after the harvest has been got in, the entire machine is put together, its readiness for service tested, and any defects supplied by calling out the active army for a series of military manoeuvres by which the officers of all ranks, as well as the men, are exercised and instructed.

In peace everything is always kept ready for the mobilization of the army, every officer and every official knows during peace what will be his post and what will be his duty the moment the decree for the mobilization is issued, and the moment that decree is flashed by telegraph to the most distant stations every one sets about his necessary duty without requiring any further orders or any explanations.

When a war is imminent the government decrees the mobilization of the whole army, or of such a portion as may be deemed necessary. Every commanding general mobilizes his own corps d'armée; the "Intendantur" the whole of the branches of the administrative services; the commandants of those fortresses which are ordered to be placed in a state of defence take their own measures for strengthening the fortifications and for obtaining from the artillery depôts the guns necessary for the armament of their parapets. A telegraphic signal from head-quarters puts the whole machinery in operation at once. In the landwehr offices of every village the summonses for assembly lie constantly ready, and have only to be distributed. The mobilization of the whole army is soon complete in every branch. In the present campaign, within four days of the order for mobilizing, military trains began to run at the rate of forty a day towards the Rhine frontier, and in about a fortnight every arm of the service was deposited in their selected places, completely equipped for the field, even to the removers and helpers of the wounded.

The process of the mobilization may be classed under the following five heads:—1, The filling in of the field troops to their war strength; 2, the formation of depôt troops; 3, the formation of garrison troops and the arming of the fortresses; 4, the mobilization of the field administration; 5, the formation of the head-quarter staffs, &c., who are to remain in the different districts to supply the places of those who march to the seat of war.

The completion of the rank and file of the field troops to war strength is effected by drawing in some of the reserve soldiers, who supply half the total war strength of the infantry, one-third of that of the artillery, and one-twenty-fifth of that of the cavalry. The cavalry has, of course, on account of being maintained in such force during peace, a superabundance of reserve soldiers available on a mobilization; these, after the men required for the cavalry itself have been drawn from them, are handed over to the artillery and military train, so that these services thus obtain many valuable soldiers, well accustomed to mounted duties. The reserve soldiers who are to be enrolled have orders sent to them through the commanding officer of the landwehr of the district in which they live, who can avail himself of the services of the provincial and parochial civil authorities to facilitate the delivery of these orders. The men are, immediately on the receipt of their orders, required to proceed to the head-quarters of the landwehr of the district, where they are received, medically inspected, and forwarded to their regiment, by an officer and some non-commissioned officers of the regiment which draws its recruits from the district. Officers who are required to fill up vacancies in the regular army on a mobilization are obtained by promoting some of the senior non-commissioned officers and calling in reserve officers.

A great advantage accrues to the Prussian army from the fact, that the country supplies horses in sufficiency for every branch of the service. Of these, as of the men, the local authorities in every hamlet keep a register, and the requisite number is called for as the demand arises. On a mobilization, the whole army requires about 100,000 horses more than it has in time of peace; in order to obtain these quickly the government has the power, if it cannot buy them readily from regular dealers, to take a certain number from every district, paying for them a price which is fixed by a mixed commission of military officers and of persons appointed by the civil authorities of the district.

Each regiment of field artillery forms nine ammunition columns, in each of which are waggons to carry reserve ammunition for infantry, cavalry, and artillery, in the proportions in which experience has shown that ammunition is usually required. In the field these ammunition waggons follow directly in rear of the field army, but are kept entirely separate from the field batteries, the officers of which are justly supposed to have enough to do in action in superintending their own guns, without being hampered with the supply of cartridges to the cavalry and infantry.

Every battalion of engineers forms a column of waggons which carries tools for intrenching purposes, and also a heavy pontoon train and a light field bridge train for which all is kept ready during peace. If a portion of the army is mobilized merely for practice, or goes into camp for great manoeuvres, as is done nearly every summer during peace, one, or perhaps two or three, engineer battalions make their trains mobile, in order to practice the men and to accustom them to the use of the matériel. Arms and ammunition which are required to complete the war strength of regiments are supplied from the artillery depôts. Officers are allowed soldier servants on a more liberal scale than in the English army, but no officers' servants are mustered in the company; they form, with all the non-combatant men of each battalion of infantry, the train which is attached to every battalion: this consists of the officers' servants and the drivers of the regimental waggons; every one else borne on the muster-roll draws a trigger in action, so that the muster-rolls actually show the number of rank and file who are present, and do not include any of the followers, who often never come up into the line of battle at all. On service the captain of every company is mounted, and is required to have two horses, to aid in the purchase of which he is allowed a certain sum of money by the state.

The strength of an ordinary battalion on active service is one field-officer, four captains, four first lieutenants, nine second lieutenants, one surgeon, one assistant-surgeon, one paymaster, one quartermaster, 1002 non-commissioned officers and privates. The train attached to this battalion is, besides officers' servants, the drivers of the ammunition waggon, which has six horses; of the *Montirung Wagon*, which carries the paymasters' books, money chest, and a certain amount of material for the repair of arms and clothing, and is drawn by four horses; a hospital cart with two horses, an officers' baggage waggon with four horses, and men to lead four packhorses, each of which carries on a pack-saddle the books of one company.

The baggage of a cavalry regiment on service consists of one medicine cart with two horses, one field forge with two horses, four squadron waggons, each with two horses, one officers' baggage waggon, with four horses; the total strength of a cavalry regiment in the field being 23 officers, 659 men, of whom 600 fall in in the ranks, 713 horses, and seven carriages.

The nine ammunition columns which are formed by each artillery regiment for the supply of ammunition to the artillery and infantry of the corps d'armée to which the regiment belongs are divided into two divisions, one of which consists of five columns, and has a strength of two officers, 175 men, 174 horses, and 25 waggons; the second, consisting of four columns, has two officers, 173 men, 170 horses, and 24 waggons. This division is made to facilitate the dispatch of the two divisions separately to the ammunition depôt to have the waggons refilled after then first supply of cartridges has been exhausted, or to allow one division to be detached with each infantry division, in case of the corps d'armée being divided, in which case four columns can conveniently be attached to each infantry division, and one column to the cavalry division of the corps.

The reserve ammunition park from which these ammunition columns are replenished, is also divided into two divisions, each of which has a strength of nine officers, 195 men, 264 carriages, and is further subdivided into eight columns of thirty-three waggons each. It is brought into the theatre of war either by railway or water carriages, or by means of horses hired in the country where the war is being conducted. Generally it is one or two days' march in rear of the army.

A siege train for attacking fortresses is not generally organized at the beginning of a war, unless the general plan of the campaign should be likely to lead the army into a country where fortresses exist, which could not be either neglected or masked, and which must be reduced. If a siege train is organized, it is formed with especial reference to the fortresses against which it is to act, and follows the army in the same manner as the reserve ammunition park.

It is thus that the Prussian army is formed in peace, that its field forces can be made ready to march in a few days in case of war, and that the troops in the field are supplied with the powder and shot which give them the means of fighting. But *l'art de vaincre est perdu sans l'art de subsister* (the art of conquering is as nothing without the art of maintaining the conquering army). An organization of even more importance lies still behind—the organization of the means of supplying the warriors with food when in health, with medicine and hospitals when diseased or wounded, and for filling up the gaps which are opened in the ranks by battle or pestilence; an organization which has always been found to be more difficult and to require more delicate handling than even strategical combinations, or the arraying of troops for battle.

The Prussian army can enter the field with 760,000 men in its ranks; but, as is well known, no army, nor any collection of men, can maintain its normal strength for a single day; in such a host, even of young healthy men, ordinary illness would immediately cause a few absentees from duty, much more so do the marches, the hardships, and the fatigues to which a soldier is exposed on active service before the first shot is fired. Then as soon as an action takes place, a single day adds a long list to the hospital roll, and the evening sees in the ranks many gaps which in the morning were filled by strong soldiers, who are now lying torn and mangled or dead on the field of battle. The dead are gone for ever; they are so much power lost out of the hand of the general; nor can an army wait till the wounded are cured and are again able to draw a trigger or to wield a sabre. Means must be taken to supply the deficiencies as quickly as possible, and to restore to the commander of the army the missing force which has been expended in moving his own army through the first steps of the campaign, or in resisting the motion of his adversary. What is the amount of such deficiencies may be estimated from Prussian statistics, which have been compiled with great care, and from the experience of many campaigns; these state officially that at the end of a year's war 40 per cent, of the infantry of the field army, 20 per cent, of the cavalry, artillery, and engineers, and 12 per cent, of the military train would have been lost to the service, and have had to be supplied anew.

It is for the formation of these supplies of men, and for forwarding them to the active army, that depôts are intended. The depôts of the Prussian army are formed as soon as the mobilization takes place, and it is ordered that one half of the men of each depôt should be soldiers of the reserve, who, already acquainted with their drill, can be sent up to the front on the first call; the other half of each depôt consists of recruits who are raised in the ordinary way, and of all the men of the regiments belonging to the field army which have not been perfectly drilled by the time their regiment marches to the seat of war. The officers of the depôts are either officers who are detached from the regular army for this duty, or are officers who have been previously wounded, and who cannot bear active service, but can perform the easier duties of the depôt, besides young officers, who are being trained to their duty before joining their regiments.

Since the re-organization of 1859, the number of depôt troops kept up during a war has been quite doubled; formerly every two infantry regiments had one depôt battalion, and every two cavalry regiments one depôt squadron. When the army was re-organized, it was foreseen that this amount of depôt troops would never be sufficient in case of a war of any duration or severity, so by the new regulations each infantry regiment has one depôt battalion of 18 officers and 1002 men; each rifle battalion, a depôt company of 4 officers and 201 men; each cavalry regiment, a depôt squadron of 5 officers, 200 men, and 212 horses; each field artillery regiment (96 guns), a depôt division of one horse artillery battery, and three field batteries, each of four guns, with 14 officers, 556 men, and 189 horses; every engineer battalion, one depôt company of 4 officers and 202 men; every train battalion, a depôt division of two companies, which muster together 12 officers, 502 men, and 213 horses. All this is required to feed the army in the field with supplies of men to take the places of those who pass from the regimental muster roll into the lists of killed, died in hospital, or disabled; for those who are only slightly wounded return to their duty either in the depôt or at once to their battalions, as is most convenient from the situation of the hospital in which they have been.

As a rule, four weeks after the field army has marched, the first supply of men is forwarded from the depôts to the battalions in the field. This first supply consists of one-eighth of the calculated yearly loss which has been given above. On the first day of every succeeding month a fresh supply is forwarded. Each of these later supplies is one-twelfth of the total calculated yearly loss. If a very bloody battle is fought, special supplies are sent at once to make up the losses of the troops that have been engaged.

The troops in depôt are provided with all articles of equipment with which they should take the field. When a detachment is to be sent to the front, all who belong to one corps d'armée are assembled together; the infantry soldiers are formed into companies of 200 men each for the march, the cavalry into squadrons of about 100 horsemen, and are taken under the charge of officers to the field army, thus bringing to the front with them the necessary reserves of horses. The places in the depôts of those who have marched away are filled up by recruiting.

An army, though of great strength and well provided with supplies of men, cannot always be sure of taking the initiative, and by an offensive campaign driving the war into an enemy's country. Judging from the experience of both the Prusso-Austrian and Franco-Prussian wars, there seems no doubt that an offensive campaign is much better for a country and much more likely to achieve success than a defensive one. But political reasons or want of preparation often force an army to be unable to assume the offensive, and with the loss of the initiative make a present to the enemy of the first great advantage in the war. In this case the theatre of war is carried into its own territory, when an army requires fortresses to protect its arsenals, dockyards, and its capital, to cover important strategical points, or to afford a place where, in case of defeat or disaster, it may be re-organized under the shelter of fortifications and heavy artillery. It has been seen in this war that small fortresses do not, as a rule, delay the progress in the field of a large invading army, which can afford to spare detachments to prevent their garrisons from making sallies. Bitsche, Phalsburg, and Thionville did not delay the German armies for a day, though they are each strong places; but they were masked by detachments, the loss of which from the fine of battle was hardly felt by the main body, and the great lines of the German armies passed in safety within a few miles of their paralyzed garrisons.

Under certain circumstances, however, it was found that small fortresses may prove a very serious inconvenience to an invader, who generally counts upon using the main roads and lines of railway of the country through which he passes. In the case of Toul, during the late war, a third-rate fortress, with a garrison ridiculously small compared with the overwhelming number of besiegers, prevented the Germans for full six weeks from using the main railway to Paris; thus obliging them to make a wide detour over a toilsome road, with all their heavy guns and provisions. It was a double inconvenience, inasmuch as the very essential Prussian field telegraph could not be attached to and used with the ordinary lines, but was obliged to be laid across the open country, where, notwithstanding the innumerable patrols, it was being constantly cut by the French peasants.

As long as fortresses exist they require garrisons, but the troops which are formed in Prussia on the breaking out of a war are not intended, in case of an offensive campaign, only to hang listlessly over the parapets of fortified places. When an army pushes forward into a foreign country, it leaves behind it long lines of road or railway over which pass the supplies of food, clothing, medicines, and stores, which are vitally important to the existence of an army. With an unfriendly population, and the enemy's cavalry ready always to seize an opportunity of breaking in upon these lines of communication, of charging down upon convoys, and destroying or burning their contents, and of thus deranging seriously what might be called the household economy of the army, it is necessary, especially on lines of railway, that strong garrisons should be maintained at particular points, and that patrols should be furnished for nearly the whole line. Towns have to be occupied in rear of the front line, depôts of stores have to be guarded and protected, convoys have to be escorted, telegraph lines watched, the fortifications which may fall garrisoned. To detach troops for the performance of all these duties dribbles away the strength of an army. To provide for these duties, and to allow the main armies to push forward in almost unimpaired strength, Prussia forms on the mobilization of the field army her so-called garrison troops.

For the formation of garrison troops the Prussian government makes use of the landwehr men, or men who have passed through the army and reserve, and are between twenty-seven and thirty-two years of age. The landwehr battalions can be called out either of a strength of 402 men each, by calling in the younger men of the landwehr, or as it is technically called, the first augmentation of the landwehr. By calling in the older men in the second augmentation each battalion is raised to a strength of 802 men. These battalions can be placed in the field formed into divisions of the same number of battalions as the divisions of the regular army. In the campaign of 1870 five such landwehr divisions were actively employed in France.

In some respects, which are easily seen, the Prussian landwehr resembles the British militia, but there are two vital differences between our organization and that of Prussia. The first is, that in England when a militia regiment is formed it is made up of men who are not old soldiers, and consequently, if the regiment is for some years disembodied, all its late recruits know nothing of their work except what they can pick up in the short period of annual training; so that in course of time, if a regiment remains for many years without being embodied, the mass of the ranks contain men who from want of training are not qualified to step at the outbreak of war into the line of battle. In the second place, the landwehr is as much an attendant and concomitant of an army in the field as the park of reserve artillery; and it is this which makes the landwehr so valuable, because it thus takes up the duties which otherwise would have to be performed by detachments from the active army. If the Prussian armies in 1866 had been obliged to leave detachments in Leipsic, Dresden, Prague, Pardubitz, and along the railway from Gorlitz to Brünn, besides troops in Hanover, Hesse, and on the lines of communications of the armies which were fighting against the Bavarians, how many troops would have formed the first lines of battle either on the Danube or in the theatre of war near the Main? The armies which were collecting, together 225,000 regular troops, for the attack upon Vienna, would, unless they had had these landwehr behind them, have been reduced to under 125,000 men. In fact, an English army under the same circumstances would have been shorn of almost half its strength.

When a Prussian army with its unimpaired strength is preparing to fight a battle in an enemy's country, when supplies of men are already coming up in anticipation of the losses which the action will cause, and when its lines of communication are guarded and secured by the garrison troops in its rear, it musters an enormous number of soldiers, who must every day be provided with food, without which a man can neither fight, march, nor live; and not only must it provide for itself alone, but also for the prisoners of the enemy who may fall into its hands—not only food, but hospitals, medicines, and attendants for the sick, surgeries, assistants, and appliances for the wounded, and the means of conveying both sick and wounded from the places where they fall helpless to convenient spots where they may be tended and healed at a safe distance from the danger of battle, or of being taken in case of a sudden advance of the enemy. It is extremely difficult from mere figures to realize what a gigantic undertaking it has been to supply even food alone to the armies which have fought in the late campaign. The difficulties of such a task may be conceived if we remember that the front line of the Prussian armies invading France, while Metz, Strasburg, and Toul were still unsubdued, mustered twelve times the number of British troops with which Lord Raglan invaded the Crimea; that close behind this line lay a second large army, and that this army and the army which was besieging Strasburg were alone stronger by 200,000 men than all the British, German, and Spanish troops that fought at Talavera; that behind them again was a large mass of landwehr; that during the siege of Sebastopol the British army was stationary, and had the great advantage of sea transport to within a few miles of its camps, while in the late campaign the Prussian army moved forward at an enormously rapid rate; and that the men to be fed in the front line alone numbered about 270,000—a population larger than that of the twelfth part of London. He would be a bold man who would undertake to supply the twelfth part of the whole population of the metropolis with one day's food; a bolder still who would undertake the task if this portion of the population were about to move bodily on that morning down to Richmond, and would require to have the meat for their dinner delivered to them the moment they arrived there, and who, without railway transport, agreed to keep the same crowd daily provided with food until moving at the same rate they arrived at Plymouth; and yet a general has to do much more than this in giving food to his men—he has, besides the ordinary difficulties of such a task, to calculate upon bad roads, weary horses, breaking waggons, the attacks of an enemy's cavalry; he has not only to get the food to the troops, but in many cases he has to provide it in the first place; he has to keep his magazines constantly stocked, to increase the amount of transport in exact proportion as his troops advance; to feed not only the fighting men, but all the men who are employed in carrying provisions to the combatants, to find hay and corn for all the horses of the cavalry and for the horses of the transport waggons, and to arrange beforehand so that every man and horse shall halt for the night in close proximity to a large supply of good water. This is not the lightest nor the least of a general's duties. It was the proud boast of England's great soldier that "many could lead troops; he could feed them." When the enemy is in front, and any moment may bring on an action, a general has little time to turn his mind to the organization of a system of supply. Then he must sift intelligence, weigh information, divine his adversary's intentions almost before they are formed, prepare a parry for every blow, and speed a thrust into any opening joint of his antagonist's harness. The means of supplying troops ought to be given ready into the hands of a general; they should be all arranged and organized beforehand, so that he has but to see that they are properly administered and made use of.

The transport which follows a Prussian army in the field, exclusive of the waggons of each battalion, the artillery, engineer, and ammunition trains, and the field telegraph divisions, is divided under two heads. The first and larger portion is under the direction of the Intendantur department, and is maintained solely for the supply of food, forage, money, and extra clothing to men and horses. The second portion is also under the Intendantur, but is placed at the disposal of the medical department, and carries the medicines and hospital necessaries for the sick and wounded, together with the means of carrying disabled men.

The first portion in charge of the Intendantur department consists, in the first place, of a certain amount of waggons, which are in time of peace always kept ready in case of war, and immediately on the mobilization of the army are provided with horses and drivers from the military train, who are entirely under the control of the principal officer of the Intendantur. Each army has a principal Intendantur officer; each corps has with its headquarters an Intendantur officer of high rank, and one of the next inferior grade is attached to each division. These officers, with their subalterns and assistants, form the first links of the chain by which a general draws food to his troops. The Commissariat columns of each corps d'armée, which are always retained in peace ready to be mobilized, consists of five provision columns, each of which has 2 officers, 101 men, 165 horses, and 32 waggons. If the corps d'armée is broken up into divisions, a certain portion of these columns accompanies each infantry division, the cavalry division, and the reserve artillery, and to each of these divisions an officer of Intendantur is attached. The Prussian plan of thus giving each column a "Proviant Meister," with waggons, &c., under his command, and making him responsible, has been proved beyond all doubt to be the best in practical working—far superior indeed to the French *Intendance*, to the utter failure and breakdown of which their earliest disasters are believed to have been due. Under the Prussian system of dividing the responsibility into sections, not only is everything more manageable and simple, but the blame can be laid on the right shoulders when anything goes wrong; whereas in a great cumbrous central organization like that of the French it is difficult to make any single individual responsible. In the present war the Prussians, at a distance from their own supplies, and consequently compelled to maintain a long line of communication through an enemy's country, were actually better furnished with material and food than the French. They succeeded in moving their wounded more rapidly from the field of battle; and their operations were never once impeded by a want of transport. The French system is described in the next chapter, and it will be seen that it is essentially one of centralization, whereas that of Prussia is exactly the reverse; and instead of providing one *Intendance* of the whole army, it makes each corps d'armée complete in itself.

The Prussians carry no tents, and sleep with nothing but their cloaks between them and the ground. They, however, secure a slight protection from the weather when convenient and necessary by constructing *tentes d'abri* with the boughs of trees. When the men arrive at the end of their day's march, they select the driest and most convenient place of ground they can find, and set to work at once to bivouac. Having halted, the arms are piled, the battalions being drawn up in line of contiguous columns at quarter distance; the men then take off their helmets, and each man places his helmet on his rifle, which acts as an effectual protection from any wet getting down the barrel; the companies then break off by subdivisions to the right and left of their arms, the knapsacks are placed in a row, the camp kettles taken off, and the fatigue squad falls out from each company to draw water. Meantime the remainder dig small, oblong holes in the ground for their fires; a couple of sticks at each end, and another resting across, completes the simple but practical arrangement. On this stick hangs the camp kettles, generally speaking by twos—one for the potatoes, and the other for the soup and meat. This soup is the mainstay of the German as well as of the French, and indeed of most continental armies. It is very simply made. Into the camp kettle is put very much whatever comes to hand, and a savoury mess, at least for hungry men, is soon made. At night big fires are got to burn, cloaks are then spread upon the ground, and in ten minutes the bivouac is complete. The officers are exactly on the same footing as the men, and quite as much exposed. Upon coming to the ground where it is intended to halt for the night, the officers commanding battalions tell off an officer and twelve men to bring up provisions for the troops. There is no pillaging of the villages permitted; the strictest orders protect the inhabitants everywhere, although it is difficult to prevent the cavalry from making free quarters of every village they come to, inasmuch as they are in the advance of every column of troops. The men sometimes think it hard that in a conquered country they are not allowed to dig the potatoes; but the general's order is strict, and a speedy punishment awaits the offender.

The 160 waggons which form the Commissariat columns carry three days' provisions for every man in the corps d'armée; as soon as the waggons which carry the first day's supply are emptied, they are sent off to the magazines in rear, replenished, and must be up again with the troops to supply the fourth day's food, for in the two days" interval the other waggons will have been emptied. As it is easier to carry flour than bread in these waggons, each corps d'armée is accompanied by a field bakery, which consists of 1 officer and 118 men, 27 horses, and 5 waggons, which are distributed among the troops as may be most convenient; and as the horses of both the provision columns and field bakeries have very hard work, a depôt of 86 horses, with 48 spare drivers, accompanies each corps d'armée. These provision columns thus carry three days' provisions, but in a country where supplies are not very abundant they can do nothing in the way of collecting food; their duty is simply to bring provisions from the magazines where they are gathered together, and to carry them to the troops. It is evident, therefore, that as the army advances these magazines must advance also, and that means must be provided for keeping the magazines fall. The collection of food in such magazines entails an enormous amount of transport; this transport is obtained by hiring waggons and carts in the country where the war is being carried on, or in the countries near it. Waggons hired in the country are also used for carrying forage for the horses of the cavalry and artillery from the magazines to the front, for the provision columns only carry food for the men.

When it was found that the country was not laid waste, the provision waggons in some cases were filled in the neighbourhood of the troops by requisitions; but this was found not to be so good a plan as to send them back to the magazines where the provisions were collected ready for them, because the time taken up in gathering together driblets of food and forage from each village, and the great distances over which waggons had to move, imposed an enormous amount of work on both the men and horses. Although the requisition system was very useful, it was only regarded as an auxiliary means of supply, for the armies moved prepared every day to find that the country in front of them might be devastated, and Germany was always looked upon as the real source of supplies; and this was absolutely necessary, because it would have been impossible to feed such a large force as the Prussian armies presented by requisitions alone: for requisitions cannot conveniently be made at great distances from the direct line of communications, and in a very short time the quarter of a million of men who were in the front line alone would have eaten up everything in the country around them if they had been dependent on that tract of country only for supplies. Then, even if the troops could have got food from more distant places, the villagers and country people would have starved; and it is the interest of a general to make his requisitions so that they do not drive the inhabitants to destitution, for terrible sickness always follows in the train of want, and if pestilence breaks out among the people of the country, it is certain immediately to appear in the ranks of the invading army. A Prussian regiment of infantry (3006 men, with 69 officers) has a medical staff of six surgeons attached to it. All these belong to the highest class of the profession, and have passed their degrees as physicians. Each cavalry regiment (602 men, with 26 officers) has three surgeons, and each detachment of artillery (540 men, and 18 officers), likewise three surgeons in its train. Accordingly, there is more than one surgeon to every 500 combatants, apparently an ample provision when it is considered that the ordinary proportion in Prussian society is one to 2000. In addition to the medical there is a special *Krankenträger* or sick-bearer service. This is divided into detachments, three detachments belonging to each corps d'armée. Each detachment comprises 150 bearers, eight nurses, eight lazarethe assistants (a lower order of the craft), one apothecary, seven doctors, and three military officers. Six carriages for the transport of the wounded, and four carriages with bandages, lint, medicine, &c., are allotted to a detachment. To assist the *Krankenträger* in their work, four men in every company of infantry (250 men) have been instructed in the best way of lifting and carrying the wounded from the field. When fighting occurs, one half the doctors attached to each regiment accompanies the combatants into action; the other half, at a short distance in the rear, dressing the wounds of those whose cases were not attended to on the battle-field itself.

Each soldier carries in his breast some lint and a bandage, so that when he falls the surgeon can instantly run up, open his coat, and apply a bandage. A certain number of tourniquets are also carried by the non-commissioned officers of each regiment; and, although in the heat of a pitched battle the non-commissioned officers could not stop to apply tourniquets to the wounded, yet, as a proportion of these also fall, the instruments are always at hand for the surgeons, and in the skirmishes, or in regiments not exposed to the full brunt of a conflict, there will yet be a certain number of wounded, many of whose lives, which would otherwise be lost, may be saved by the prompt application of a tourniquet or bandages. Round each man's neck as he goes into action, also, is a card upon which is his name. As he falls the surgeon who examines and binds up his wounds sees at once whether it is of a nature which will permit of the patient being moved to a distance or not. According to its severity, then, he writes on the card whether the man is to be taken to the field hospital close at hand, or to the hospitals further in the rear. Accordingly, when the ambulance arrives, it is seen at once where the wounded man is to be conveyed.

A field lazarethe is provided with everything necessary for 200 sick and wounded. Five doctors, a number of inferior assistants, and from three to four carriages, form its staff, which in case of need is augmented by *Krankenträger* or common soldiers. Each army corps has twelve field lazarethes, or, to give it in figures, there is provision made for the perfect and scientific treatment of 2400 out of every 30,000 men. If sufficient formerly, this was found inadequate in this first breech-loading campaign, when it has occurred that every third man in a regiment has been disabled. The field lazarethe moves with the troops. Modern warfare involving many battles in a short space, it would be impossible to detain the staff of the field lazarethes long in one locality. Accordingly, all the slightly wounded, as soon as they can be transported, are sent off to the war hospitals in Germany—institutions both public and private, the extent of which may be gathered from the fact that they contain a total of 65,000 beds. The number of the reserve doctors, which has always been found too small, in this sanguinary war has proved so utterly insufficient as to cause the appointment of 200 extra surgeons to be employed wherever most required. The action of the medical service on the battle-field is directed by division doctors. The next above them in rank are the *General Aertze*, or physicians-general, one to each corps d'armée, who receive their instructions from the *General Stabs Arzt*, or chief of the medical staff. To give the soldiers the benefit of the best help, all the most eminent surgeons of the country were besides requested to repair to the front, and accept high military grades, created for them on purpose, and held only during the war.

To convey the wounded from France into the home hospitals, thirty physicians and some hundred lazarethe assistants and nurses were engaged by the government. Each transport of a hundred wounded had an escort of one or two doctors, two lazarethe assistants, and thirteen nurses. The thirty physicians set apart for this duty saw their melancholy convoy only as far as one of the three *Haupt Etappen* or principal stations on the frontier, by which the army communicates with home. Thence to the hospitals the journey was made under the direction of one of another body of thirty physicians distributed over the *Etappen*. The sum total of the doctors employed in the army at the time of the battle of Sedan exceeded 2700.

To facilitate the treatment by successive doctors, the one who sees the patient first writes his diagnosis on a card, which is fastened round the sufferer's neck. This useful bit of pasteboard is, of course, attached only when a man falls ill; but another is fastened to his arm the very day he leaves his garrison for the field. Containing the number of his regiment and his number in the regiment, it serves for identification in case of death. The men are perfectly aware of the reasonableness of this novel arrangement, and regard it as a proof of the anxious solicitude borne them by the government; yet they have an instinctive dislike to the fatal badge, and, in grim allusion to its purpose, dubbed it their "tombstone" (*grabstein*).

Special arrangements are made for the conveyance of the wounded by rail. The fourth-class carriages of German lines are entered by doors at each end, and thus a considerable space can be obtained when the seats are removed. The space is made available by screwing into the opposite sides of the carriages stout hooks, from which the field-stretchers, bearing the wounded, are suspended by elastic rings. There is, therefore, no transfer of the patient from one bed to another, and the motion of the carriage is very little felt, less even than on board ship in a hammock.

When the field army, the depôt and garrison troops, and the provision and medical department trains have been mobilized, the Prussian army is fit to take the field. The necessary commandants and staffs of the districts where the depôt troops are stationed, are composed either of officers detached from the regular army, or of reserve or landwehr officers. When the army takes the field, its movements must be directed not only so as to pursue the original plan of the campaign, but also so as to keep pace with the enemy's combinations, and the movements of its different parts must be guided by orders from the directing general.

The Prussian army has its own arrangements for feeling its way through a hostile country. The commander of the advancing corps selects a clever and determined officer, and in the Prussian army such men are numerous. Some fifteen or twenty picked horsemen are confided to him, and the officer then takes a man previously acquainted with the country to serve as guide. The spot which the party desires to investigate has been explained to him, and pointed out on an excellent map carried by the officer. The place is often twenty or twenty-five miles from the Prussian lines. To the rear of the first horseman, who is ordered to proceed slowly, following byroads and sometimes going across country, at a distance of 200 paces, follow two light troopers. A hundred paces behind them comes the officer, followed at a short distance by eight or ten of his men, charged to protect him if necessary, The rear guard is like the advance guard. If the foremost horseman is surprised he fires off his carbine and the band takes to flight, with the exception of the officer and his escort, who advance to reconnoitre before flying. Even in the case of an ambush, it is almost impossible to prevent two or three of the scouts getting back to camp.

The above is a sketch of the general system on which the Prussian army is normally organized. How such an army is worked in the field, how its resources are made available, and how it achieves the objects for which it has been mobilized, must depend in a great measure upon the skill of the general to whose direction it is intrusted. What an army so organized can effect when its motions are guided by a skilful hand and far seeing intellect like that of Moltke, the rapid victories of the late campaign have shown. When the field army enters on the theatre of war, the organizer and administrator has done with it; his province is then to take care that its recruits are forthcoming and its supplies are ready when required. But when an army is handed over to the general who is to use it, he has a right to expect that when he receives his divisions he shall also receive the means of manoeuvring them; and when he assumes the command of his corps he shall be provided with every appliance which can help him to move them in the combination and unison without which different bodies of troops are not an army, but a series of scattered detachments, which must be easily defeated in detail, or in isolation taken prisoners by an active and energetic enemy. After the plan of a campaign has been once decided upon, the means by which a general moves his troops into positions where they may act most advantageously, and from which they may strike the heavy blows that will gain a speedy and profitable peace—for a peace is the ultimate object of all wars—may be classed under the heads of Information, Intelligence, and the Transmission of Orders. Information of the enemy's preparations, of the number of troops he can put into the field—how those troops will be armed, organized, and administered—should be obtained by the government of the country to which the army belongs, and communicated to the general when he takes the command of the army.

To acquire this information concerning foreign armies during peace every country in Europe devotes a special department of its war office, which is ever busy collecting and compiling statistics of every foreign army, because, however friendly the relations of any two countries may be, it can never be known how long they will remain so. As soon as hostilities are imminent, a war office has little chance of obtaining much information from inside the lines of the probable enemy; then the duty of collecting information devolves upon the general himself, who must, by every means he can avail himself of, discover, as far as possible, every position and intention of his adversary's troops. For this purpose, during war, spies are generally employed. Spies have a dangerous task, and not an honourable one; consequently, except in very rare and extreme cases, officers will not accept the invidious duty, and it is often extremely difficult to find persons who will consent to act as spies sufficiently conversant with military matters to make their information worth having. Money is the great means of obtaining good spies; needy adventurers and unscrupulous men will, if well paid, do the work, and for the sake of a sufficient sum run the risk of the certain death which awaits them if discovered in disguise within the hostile outposts.

The information collected from spies is not, in most cases, completely trustworthy. In the first place, the men who undertake this duty are nearly always mercenary wretches, who will sell friend and foe alike as best suits their own interest; in the second place, spies are seldom sufficiently acquainted with military matters not to exaggerate movements of slight importance and miss observing vital combinations. To test the accuracy of their reports intelligence is collected by means of reconnoitring officers, who, either alone or attended by a few troopers, get as close as they can to the enemy's posts; observe as far as possible, without the use of disguise and in full uniform, the positions of his troops; and when discovered and pursued by his patrols, fight or ride to bring their intelligence safe home to their own outposts. In the Prussian army the Uhlans, or lancers, are often employed in this service, and their great successes in the present campaign proved how admirably they were suited for it. Intelligence is also culled by every vedette and every advanced sentinel, but the reconnoitring officer is the main source. To reconnoitre well requires not only a brave but a very able officer, with a quick eye, a ready memory, and a great knowledge of the indications which tell the presence of hostile troops, and allow an estimate to be formed of the force in which they are. When the reconnoitring officer regains the shelter of his own outposts, he must either personally bring or by some means send his intelligence as quickly as possible to headquarters. The plan usually pursued in European armies has been for the officer himself to ride quickly to his general, and to be the first bearer of his intelligence. This means has, however, been found by experience to be too slow, and the Prussian army in the late campaign was accompanied by a telegraphic corps. By means of this corps signals were flashed from post to post, and the intelligence collected by the reconnoitring officer sometimes arrived at headquarters within a few minutes after the officer had reached the outposts.

When a general receives intelligence, he has to weigh it, consider it, and often strike the balance between conflicting information. He has then to move his own divisions in accordance with his deductions, and must send word to any co-operating force of what he has heard, and what he is about to do. Undoubtedly, the quickest way for a reconnoitring officer to despatch his reports to his general, and for the general to communicate with his own divisions and with his colleagues, would be by electric telegraph; but it would be almost impossible for a reconnoitring officer always to communicate with head-quarters by electricity. Reconnoitring expeditions are made so suddenly and so uncertainly that, quick as the Prussian field telegraph is laid down, this means of communication is not always available with the outposts. Nor is the electric telegraph easily used to communicate with every division: it might be so used, but its application would require a number of extra waggons to be attached to every division, and would bring a confusing number of lines into the office of the chief of the staff. During the late campaign orders were sent to the divisional commanders by mounted officers, who were attached to head-quarters for this special purpose. Besides these officers a certain number of picked troopers are selected from every cavalry regiment, and formed into a special corps at the beginning of a campaign, and a certain number attached to every general. These troopers form the general's escort, and act as orderlies to carry unimportant messages. When an officer is sent with an important order, one or two of these soldiers are sent with him, in case of his being attacked to act as a defence as far as possible, to yield up a horse to him in case of his own breaking down, or, in case of his being killed, to carry the order themselves to its destination, or, at any rate, to prevent its falling into the hands of the enemy if the officer is wounded and likely to be taken. During the campaign the communications between head-quarters and divisions were usually kept up by means of mounted officers; but communications between the head-quarters of each army and the king were always maintained by means of the field-telegraph.

To understand the Prussian field telegraph system, it should be borne in mind that the army is composed of various corps d'armée, and each corps of two divisions; therefore the telegraph is divided into three sections—1, the station at the commander-in-chief's; 2, the station at each corps; 3, the station at each division. Each station has one inspector and five secretaries or clerks, four carriages, two smaller ones, and six waggons. The first-named contain the cable, the second the apparatus and batteries, and the last-named the posts upon which the wires are fixed. Each carriage contains twenty English miles of cable, and the average time it takes to lay it is three hours to every four miles. The process of laying is naturally the most scientific part of the arrangement, and is conducted in the following manner:—An intelligent officer from the army with some assistant with him, is intrusted with the general supervision of the telegraph of each army, and to him is committed the task of directing where the main line shall run. He rides on ahead of the waggons, which proceed at a footpace, the cable being passed out over a wheel, and indicates to the drivers by means of a piece of paper stuck on a stick or a blazed tree the direction they shall follow. In the meantime, the foot soldiers attached to the telegraph, who are selected from the regiments for superior intelligence, and wear a different uniform, with a large T on the shoulder-strap, are divided into what is called troops, or, in navvy language, "gangs," of three men each. The first take the wire as it is payed out, lay it on the ground, and on it a post for every 100 yards; the second, coming after them, twist the cable round the insulator, which is made of gutta-percha, not glass as with British telegraphs, and erect the posts in the ground. This is a matter of great ease, they being about twelve feet high, and about the thickness of the butt end of a salmon rod, slightly tapering towards the top. The third troop strain the wire, and ascertain that it is clear of all wood, &c., and, in short, "runs clear." Whenever it is possible, the trees are used as telegraph posts, being easily ascended to the requisite height by means of a light ladder. The whole of the cable carried is seldom all required, for the lines of the communications of armies usually run along railways, and as far as possible the permanent wires are repaired by the men of the division, and made use of for the telegraphic communication of the army. The obstinate resistance, however, of several fortified places, Toul especially, prevented the carrying out of this plan for several weeks in the late war. Each division carries with it five miles of insulated wire for the purpose of laying through rivers or lakes, if these should come in the way of the line. The wires are coiled inside each waggon on rollers, from which they can be uncoiled as the waggon moves along, or in bad ground the roller can be transferred to a stretcher, which is carried between two men. The wire is carried about ten feet high, so that where it crosses roads it may pass clear over the heads of mounted men. As it is equally culpable in war to prevent communication by unfair means within the lines of an army, as it is to seek to obtain the same in disguise between the enemy's sentries, any enemy not in uniform, or any one in the enemy's pay who is detected cutting the telegraph wire, is regarded as a spy, and treated accordingly. When on the field of battle, the telegraph is worked by a machine fixed inside one of the carriages, unless a house is obtainable, when a room is instantly turned into an office.

One of the most highly prized services of the army is the Field Post. Each corps d'armée has a head postmaster, under whom are the following staffs:—Six clerks attached to the office of the head-quarters, four at the head-quarters of each division, and three with the reserve of each corps. Besides this he has fourteen letter-sorters and nineteen postillions. The head-quarter's staff post of a corps d'armée has three waggons, one chaise, and one fourgon. The first ply with the letters, the second carries the postmaster and his second when on the march, as well as small parcels; and the third carries the luggage, such as tables, chairs, sorting-boxes, &c., necessary for the despatch of business. Each division of each corps has two waggons. The authorities issue cards to each regiment, on one side of which is printed,

"Feld Post Corremspondenz Karte.

To

Address,"

and on the other side the letter is written in pencil or ink. If in the former, it is rendered perfectly secure against being rubbed out by the application of a wet cloth across it, which, thanks to some preparation on the surface of the card, secures its legibility to the end of its journey. Early each morning the field post rides through the camp or past the ranks of the troops on march, to collect the letters written during the preceding evening. Armed with posthorn and leathern bags, he rides up and down the ranks, receiving right and left, with both hands, the letters the soldiers hold out to him. On some days the task of this galloping letter box is much heavier, owing to most of the troops, in view of an impending battle, of which notice has been issued, having on the evening before written their letters of farewell. The number of letters sent off after a battle also are almost incalculable. In order that every chance of writing should be given, postillions ride over the field with cards and a pencil the day after the battle, and any wounded man who is still there can either write or dictate his message home. Poor fellows thus left have frequently been noticed to hold up their arms to attract the postillion's attention in preference to waving for the ambulance waggon. Remembering that in no country is education so universal as in Prussia, and that from the very composition of the German army no soldiers of any country have so many home connections, it will not be surprising to hear that during the first three months of the war upwards of twelve million letters were transmitted through the Field Post.

Another humane improvement has been introduced to lessen the horrors of war. By order of the postal department letters to soldiers who die in the war will be returned to the writers, not by the ordinary postmen, but by the civil authorities. The latter are charged in each case to prepare the writers for the melancholy intelligence they have to impart.

The pages describing the chief engagements of the war will show how greatly the Prussian army has been changed from the stiff unbending machine which was transmitted by his father to Frederick the Great, and which, in his hands, won the victories of the Seven Years' War. On the conclusion of that war, all Europe hastened to adopt the Prussian model, and England, more than other countries, blindly accepting the outward appearance without the principle, padded, starched, and strangled with stocks her soldiers, under the impression that by obtaining the rigidity, she would also obtain the discipline and vigour of the Potsdam grenadiers. And even now, with but slight alterations, the system of drill and military carriage introduced into Prussia by the greatest sergeant-major that ever lived may be observed by the antiquary on the hills of Aldershot or the parade-ground of St. James'. But in the country where it was produced and perfected, it is a thing of the past. The crowning disaster of Jena proved to Prussia the antiquity and weakness of its military tactics, and convinced her administrators of the necessity of adapting their military tactics to altered times and circumstances. On this principle they have since unswervingly acted, and every decade has seen a steady advance in the tactical organization of the Prussian army. The present system may be briefly described. The front line of battle engaged with the enemy is composed of long lines of skirmishers, supported by small columns, which take up convenient positions wherever they can be sheltered from the enemy's fire by any variations of the ground. In the rear of these supports, reserves are stationed to reinforce the first line, or to repulse an attack made through or over it. These reserves and the first line are supposed, under the guidance of the officers who lead them, to carry out the general object of the commander-in-chief, who himself keeps in hand the chief reserves, to be moved to a flank which may be threatened by the enemy, or to drive home an offensive movement undertaken by the troops in front. The consequence of this precaution is, that a long thin line is spread in front of the hostile position, which is probably outflanked at the very commencement of the action, while behind the skirmishers and their supports, additional forces are held ready to decide victory or avert defeat. This practice, no doubt, is the secret of those sudden flank attacks which have so surprised the French officers in the late war, and caused them such severe losses in prisoners. Its usefulness in resisting the most impetuous onslaughts of the French will be especially seen, as early in the campaign as the battle of Woerth.

Manoeuvring on Prussian field-days is quite a different matter from the displays to which the British soldier is accustomed. At Aldershot marshes are drained, turf walls levelled, all difficulties cleared away, and the men are put through the routine farce of a sham fight, every detail of which is known to them all from the beginning. In Prussia, on the contrary, everything is arranged with a view of inculcating thorough self-reliance, and to drawing out the individual abilities of those in command. The positions chosen for exercising are those with considerable natural obstacles, such as might be met with in actual warfare, and the following sentence occurs in the official instructions:—It will be perceived by those who understand the purport of these exercises, that no movement is dictated, no time fixed; all must be left to the discretion of the commander. Beyond the general idea, he has received no instructions defining the issue of the affair. In fact, the situation at the end of the manoeuvre should be the *bona fide* result of his own dispositions.

During the war of which the present work treats, the excellence and military aptitude of the Prussian officers have been the subjects of frequent comment. All accounts agree in crediting the Prussian officer with a knowledge of his work, and a professional zeal, which have contributed in a very marked degree to the successful issue of the various brilliant operations upon which the army has been engaged. It is therefore worth while to inquire what the system is under which such officers are produced. Its main peculiarity is that in all cases, with one single exception, a certain length of service in the ranks is an indispensable condition of obtaining a commission; and that proof of having received, first, a good general education, and, secondly, a certain amount of professional instruction, is required from every one before appointment to the rank of officer. The one exception to the rule about a preliminary service in the ranks occurs in the case of the young men who, after a course in one of the preparatory cadet schools, obtain admission to the highest class—the Selecta—of that institution. But of these young men there are only fifty annually commissioned; all other officers must go through a certain preliminary training in the ranks. There are two main classes of officers:—1. Those who enter from civil life. 2. Those who enter the army from a cadet school.

The military schools of Prussia are under the general control of an inspector-general of military education, who is assisted by a council called the supreme board of military studies. To this department also belongs the military examination commission. As already stated, the first examination of the aspirant for a commission, the ensign's examination, is in subjects of general knowledge. But the rank of ensign, or *Portépée-fahnrich*, cannot be obtained until after six months' actual service in the ranks. The young Avantageurs on joining their regiments have the rank, and receive the pay and clothing, of private soldiers. The mode of treating them during their service in the ranks depends much upon the commanding officer of the regiment, the regulations in some regiments being much stricter than in others. For a certain time they have to perform the actual duties of private soldiers, to mount guard, and in the cavalry to clean their horses. In some regiments they are even required to live, sleep, and mess with the privates, though the period for which this is exacted seldom exceeds six weeks. In most regiments they are allowed to find their own lodgings, and to mess with the officers, by whom, except when on duty, they are treated almost as equals. The general principle which regulates their treatment is that they should, by actual performance of the various duties, learn the work of privates, corporals, and non-commissioned officers. There are thus two qualifications for the grade of *Portépée-fahnrich,* the test of the examination and the six months' service in the ranks. The examinations are held in Berlin before the supreme military commission. They are held constantly every week for about nine months of the year, each examination occupying a week. There are thus about forty examinations in all during the year, at each of which on an average twenty-five candidates present themselves, making in all about 1000 candidates yearly. The examination, after a nomination is obtained, is partly on paper and partly viva voce. The following subjects are obligatory:—German, Latin, French, mathematics, geography, history, and drawing, including hill sketching. The questions are fewer in number and more comprehensive in character than in the military examinations in England; the answers are expected to approach nearly to the form of short essays. The main object is to find not so much positive knowledge as intellectual capacity to put knowledge to a useful purpose. There is no competition; the candidates are only required to come up to a certain qualifying standard. A candidate failing is allowed a second trial, or even a third frequently; the number of final failures does not exceed 10 per cent.

A certificate of having passed the *abiturient's*, or leaving examination of a gymnasium, or *real-schule*, which qualifies for admission to a university, exempts from this ensign's examination; and young men entering from the Cadet Corps are examined while still at the Senior Cadet House at Berlin. At least 200 *abiturienten* enter the army yearly, and are said to prove a very superior class of officers. The second or officer's examination is in purely professional subjects. Ten months in a war school is the usual preparation; but a small number of cadets, who have obtained admission to the highest class (the *Selecta*) of the Berlin Cadet House, receive their military instruction in this class instead of at a war school, and pass their officer's examination before quitting the Cadet House; and exemption from attendance at the war school is also granted to young men who have studied for at least one year at a university before entering the army, and to landwehr officers who have received permission to be transferred to the active army. About 800 candidates are examined yearly for the rank of officer. The examination is not competitive. The subjects are tactics (including drill), science of arms, fortification, surveying, knowledge of military duty, and military drawing. Those who fail are allowed another trial, after a certain interval; but failures are very rare, and this examination is considered much less severe than that for the grade of ensign. Those who succeed are qualified for commissions as second lieutenants. But they must wait, according to seniority, for vacancies; and on a vacancy the senior ensign's name cannot be submitted to the king for his appointment without a document stating, on the part of the officers of the regiment, that he has the requisite knowledge of the duties of the service, and that they consider him worthy of admission among them. If the majority is opposed to his admission, the name of the next ensign in order of seniority is brought forward. Comparatively few cases of veto occur; it is generally ascertained at a prior stage of a young man's career that he will not be ineligible. Still, the existence of the right of veto exercises an influence on conduct. In the majority of cases the officer's examination is passed between the ages of eighteen and a half and twenty-one.

The Royal Cadet Corps is under the command of a general officer, and is intended as a nursery for officers of the army. It includes pensioners, or paying pupils, and the king's cadets, who are educated at the cost of the state. After receiving a general education in the junior schools the cadets proceed at fifteen or sixteen to the upper school at Berlin, where they pass one year in the *secunda* class and one year in the *prima*. About seventy of the best pupils are retained for a third year to go through a special course of military instruction in the *Ober-prima* and *Selecta* classes. The discipline is strict. The most scrupulous neatness in dress is enforced; and any cadet seen in public, on leave, without his gloves or with his belt improperly put on would be severely "chaffed" by his comrades. The cadets appear upon the whole to work steadily, and few fail to pass the ensign's examination. The universal liability to military service in Prussia supplies a most powerful incentive both to industry and to good conduct. Idleness or bad conduct may entail the forfeiture of all prospect of obtaining a commission, and necessitate the performance of the legal period of service in the ranks. The advantage of passing through the Cadet Corps is that a general education is obtained at a cheap rate, and that a commission can be gained at an earlier age than by entering the army direct from civil life. It cannot be said that cadets as a rule show more professional ability, or rise to greater distinction in the service, than men who have not passed through the Cadet Corps. Equally distinguished officers are to be found in both classes; General Steinmetz and Herwarth von Bittenfeld are old cadets; General von Moltke entered the army from civil life. Among commanding officers of regiments there appears to be generally a feeling unfavourable to the cadets, partly perhaps because every cadet who is appointed to their regiments deprives them of the patronage of a nomination, but mainly because they prefer their young officers to be men who have had the more liberal education afforded by civil schools. It is maintained by many distinguished officers that the exclusively military atmosphere by which cadets are surrounded from so early an age has a narrowing effect upon the mind, and that the almost monastic, system in which they are brought up is fatal to freedom of thought and development of character. Others are of opinion that the admixture of the two classes is of advantage to the service.

The war schools afford to candidates for commissions, after a certain length of service in the ranks, the professional instruction necessary to fit them for the duties of regimental officers. The subjects of instruction are tactics, the science of arms, fortification, drawing and surveying, military regulations, and military correspondence. The system of small classes is adopted, not exceeding thirty in each. Each class attends lectures separately. A certain portion of each lecture is devoted to questioning, and the students are frequently set to write essays and memoirs. Progress is tested by quarterly examinations, both on paper and viva voce; great importance is attached to the latter as a means of cultivating readiness of resource and rapidity of judgment. Practical as well as theoretical instruction is given. The students have fencing and gymnastic lessons every second day, alternately with riding; they have artillery gun drill and aiming drill about once a week, and two hours' practice weekly in the regimental drill of their own arms, in addition to the more general instruction in drill which they receive during the lessons of application in connection with the course of tactics. The ensigns of artillery and engineers have additional instruction in the special duties of their corps. The students are more particularly instructed in the drill of the arms to which they respectively belong, but they also learn the general elements of that of the other services, and both the infantry and cavalry ensigns go through a course of instruction in the service of field guns. Battalion and regimental movements are practised by means of skeleton drill. The chief object kept in view in teaching both drill and gymnastics is that of fitting the young ensigns for the duty of giving instruction in these subjects when they become officers; and for this purpose individuals are constantly called out to put their comrades through field movements. There is a course of swimming for those who are unable to swim. The last portion of the ten months' course is termed more especially the "practical course." Reconnaissances of military positions are then executed and reported, and dispositions for attack and defence have to be described by the students; there is musketry practice, and artillery practice is attended; field works are traced, and operations in sapping, bridging, &c., attended. Schemes are set for putting villages or houses into a state of defence, throwing up hasty intrenchments, and the like. Great importance is attached to rapid sketching without instruments, and to sketching on horseback. Some days are spent at a fortress.

The final examination on which depends an ensign's fitness for the rank of officer is held at the war schools, under the superintendence of the supreme examination commission. The paper work occupies about four days; the viva voce examination then follows. Candidates for the scientific corps, after some months' service with the troops, and passing through the war schools, go through a course of special instruction in the artillery and engineer school, and pass a further examination in their special subjects. They also, for practical instruction, serve with their regiments as supernumerary officers for a time, before receiving their definitive commissions. A thorough acquaintance with practical duty, acquired thus by service, is enforced before their special instruction as officers of the scientific corps commences. This system is considered by Prussian officers superior to that by which, as in England and France, the theoretical instruction is given before any regimental duty is performed. It is maintained that theory can be more easily understood if it is based upon a groundwork of actual experience; and that officers of the age of twenty-three or twenty-four, with a practical knowledge of their duties, derive more advantage from study than young men of seventeen or eighteen who have no practical acquaintance with the subject to which their studies relate.

The French and Prussian systems agree in this, that no attempt is made to give a special military education at an early age; that a general education is made the groundwork of the professional training; and that at least up to the age of seventeen or eighteen the future officer receives the same kind of education as the civilian. But the principle of deferring military education to a comparatively late age is in Prussia carried even to a greater extent than in France, for all professional instruction is postponed until after the service has been entered, and regimental duty been performed for nearly a year. The theory of the profession is not studied until after the practice of it has been learnt. Much of the progress made is ascribed to the unity now given to the whole system of instruction. The general management of military education is vested in a single officer, the inspector-general; but he is assisted by the board of studies and the supreme examination board, and at the same time each of the educational institutions has its own board of studies, on which the civilian professors are represented. In discipline the heads of the various schools are almost entirely supreme. A marked point of contrast between the French and Prussian systems of military education consists in this, that in Prussia the principle of competition is little adopted, and never, perhaps, strictly adhered to. In a country where military service is compulsory, the desire to escape duty as a private soldier is a great inducement to exertion, and the object is to form a general estimate of the abilities, character, and military capacity of each man, rather than a comparison of the attainments of several. A remarkable feature of the system of teaching is the care bestowed upon the higher objects of education, upon forming and disciplining the mind and encouraging habits of reflection. The teachers are instructed to endeavour to develop the faculties, and to cultivate powers of thought and reasoning. The system of small classes enables them to devote attention to each student, and adapt the instruction to varieties of ability. The examination questions are framed with a view to test an intelligent acquaintance with a subject, and the power of turning knowledge to a useful purpose. In the Prussian method of instruction there is almost an entire absence of the minute detail as to numbers, dates, and facts, to which importance is attached in military teaching in England. The students are left to study in private in order to teach them self-reliance and encourage habits of work. The aim throughout is the development of the mind. The cultivation of special talents is ever kept in view at the war schools; the attainment of a high standard in individual subjects is regarded as of much greater importance than average requirements in all.

It follows from the above that those who regard the Prussian system of officering the army as a system of promotion from the ranks, in the ordinary sense of the phrase, are greatly mistaken. Promotion from the ranks is, on the contrary, extremely rare, and the few individuals who obtain commissions in this manner are seldom left with the army, but are pensioned off or provided with civil appointments. The result is that admission to the *offizier corps* of the Prussian army is regarded as conferring distinctive privileges. The strong *esprit de corps* which pervades the whole body of officers undoubtedly creates an extremely high tone and a gentlemanly feeling which resents any conduct that might be considered discreditable to the character of an officer; on the other hand, its tendency is to make the officers of the army somewhat of an exclusive caste. There is probably no service in the world in which class spirit is so strongly developed, or which is so aristocratic in character, as that of Prussia. It is necessary to point this out, because otherwise there might be a tendency to entertain the erroneous idea—an idea which in one form or another is continually cropping up—that the only way to obtain a professional body of officers is by an indiscriminate system of promotion from the ranks. By observing the Prussian system we may see how at once education and professional requirements of an exacting order can be combined with careful selection, a high tone, and much esprit de corps.

Promotion in the Prussian service is by seniority, tempered by selection. If an officer is passed over two or three times, he generally accepts it as a hint to retire. If he does not take the hint, he is gazetted out. There are no examinations for promotion, except in the artillery and engineers. Not the slightest favour seems to have been shown to rank or position, as such, in the appointment of officers at the commencement of the war; but in all cases the men who occupied high command were such as had proved title to it by their experience and proved ability. The government, thinking it better to hurt the feelings of a man than to confide the fate of many thousands to him, if doubting his military talent or health, in several cases promoted juniors over the heads of the highest officers.

The landwehr is officered either by officers of the regular army who have quitted it within the limits of age, which render them liable to serve in the landwehr, or by means of an important provision which allows all young men of the educated classes who can clothe and arm themselves, to take service in the rifle corps and other light infantry; and after completing one year at their own expense to receive furlough to the end of their regular call, upon application. This rule was introduced, no doubt, to save the wealthy and well-born the degradation which, in a country essentially aristocratic, the mixture in a barrack-room with recruits of the lowest classes would necessarily imply; and there has been built upon it, during the last half century, the elaborate system of *Einjahrige*, or one-year volunteers, which has solved at once two difficult problems. The universality of the conscription has been maintained without open opposition from that important middle order, the wealth and influence of which has grown in Prussia as much as in any part of Europe, and which, notwithstanding its claims, is excluded from the higher parts of the army; while a body of efficient officers, trained in all the duties of the line, has been provided for the staff of the landwehr without expense to the state. As a necessary consequence of the growing wealth of the commercial classes, the number of these *Einjahrige* has annually increased; and it has long been a regular part of the education of the son of every manufacturer, proprietor, professional man, and even of every well-to-do shopkeeper, to spend one of the three years between his seventeenth and twentieth birthdays in passing through his volunteer course.

As might be expected where military service is compulsory, there are comparatively few among the privates who make soldiering a profession, and re-enlistments into the ranks of the standing army are not very numerous nor much encouraged. If a man wishes to re-enlist after the completion of his three years' term of service he is allowed to do so, provided the general commanding his brigade approves him; but he only re-enlists for one year, at the end of which either party can break off the engagement: or, if both consent to continue, a reenlistment can be effected for another year, and so on. In time of war the soldier cannot break off his engagement at the end of the year, but must continue to serve till the war is over. At any time he can be discharged for misbehaviour. A man who re-enlists, generally, if well educated, becomes a non-commissioned officer; but neither the pay nor the position of a non-commissioned officer is high enough to induce men to stay long in the army under ordinary circumstances. But a sufficiently powerful inducement is found in the fact that, after a man has served twelve years, during nine of which he has been a non-commissioned officer, he is certain to obtain a good civil appointment; for all vacancies among railway and telegraph officials, government clerks, overseers of the public forests, gendarmes, non-commissioned officers of police, post-office clerks, and gaolers, are filled from the ranks of the non-commissioned officers whose times of service in the army have expired:

As regards dress, the German army exhibits less variety than the soldiers of any other country. The prevailing colour, however, is such as not to unduly expose the men to the observation of an enemy. The uniform of the Prussian guard differs only from that of the line in having white ornaments on the collars: they wear the helmet, dark-blue tunic, white belt, and black trousers with red stripes, similar to that of the British line. Their knapsacks, and those of the whole Prussian army, are of brown, undressed cowhide. The artillery differ from the line soldiers only in wearing black sword-belts instead of white, and in carrying a short rifle with a sword-bayonet, instead of the long rifle and straight bayonet of the line. This general uniformity between infantry and artillery gives a certain monotony to the appearance of large bodies of Prussian troops, as compared with those of other nations. There are exceptions, however. The chasseurs are dressed in dark green, with shakos similar to those of the British infantry, but larger; they carry a short rifle and short bayonet. The artillery carry their blanket, which is green, in a roll over the shoulder. Upon the whole, the only distinguishing mark of the various regiments is the colour of the facings. The Hessian contingents are distinguishable by their light-blue facings. The Bavarian infantry has not adopted the Prussian style of uniform, and retains the national green with red facings. The dragoon regiments are light blue. The hussars are red, black, green, brown, and light and dark blue. They wear shakos of miniver fur, and braided jackets. The Uhlans are principally dark blue, with laneer caps; they are the heaviest cavalry of the Prussian army, with the exception of the ten cuirassier regiments, who wear white uniforms, with steel breast and back plates and helmets, with high buff leather boots and gauntlets.

In the face of the astounding events of the late campaign, the Prussian system needs no one to point out its superiority in the attainment of its one great object—success in war. But nations do not live for war, and people may well ask themselves what sort of effect the organization has on the nation at large apart from its warlike ends?

The serious disadvantages of universal military service are of course obvious to every one. The ordinary German is compelled to serve for three years; for three years, therefore, his regular occupations are interfered with; and though this drawback is to some extent remedied by the one year's service of those who have received a certain amount of education, fixed by government, the interference is, no doubt, very serious. This objection really sums up nearly every disadvantage which has been ascribed to the Prussian military system; and without denying its validity, it may be well to ask what the system has to give in return for so great a sacrifice?

The first point, which may sound very like a paradox, is that the Prussian military organization is essentially anti-warlike; it affords a guarantee against war. Just because every man is a soldier, just because war leaves hardly a home in Germany unscathed, just because every mother and every wife is "feelingly persuaded" what war means, the system tends to discourage war. The army is not composed of a set of professional soldiers to whom war means wealth, honours, and advancement, but of peaceful citizens called from their occupations, from the plough and from the study, from the workshop and the law court, who fight with a savage indignation, which carries all before it, when provoked, but at the same time affords a safe guarantee that war will not be undertaken for purposes of conquest or the establishment of a dynasty. Other advantages of the system are that, in addition to its military character, it is at the same ,time a system of education. Every soldier has had a certain amount of education in his youth; but when he comes to serve his time it often happens that his knowledge is, to say the least, very rusty, and sadly in want of a little brushing up. This the recruit receives with his drill, and what he then learns is not so easily forgotten, owing to his riper age. But the Prussian system does more than merely freshen up the memories of those who come immediately under it. It stimulates education throughout the country by dismissing, after one year's service, those who possess certain attainments fixed by government, and by requiring every officer to pass a special examination.

Almost of equal importance with the mental is the bodily training which every German has to pass through as a soldier. Even in England a little drilling is considered a good thing for young men; at any rate we have our games, our cricket and football, our rackets and fives, to strengthen our muscles and lengthen our wind. The Germans have nothing of the sort. To such a people the value of drilling, and the installation of a little soldierly pride, is hardly to be over-estimated. In his soldier-life the German learns habits of self-control and neatness, and a certain amount of dandyism which to him at least is little more than a wholesome corrective.

In another respect the military system does what in England is one of the most valuable results of her public schools and universities. It brings together on a footing of perfect equality high and low, rich and poor. It is a mill in which men "rub each other's edges down." The aristocrat learns to understand the feelings of the democrat, and the democrat finds that the aristocrat is after all a man very much like himself. Of greater value still is military service to that class rapidly increasing in Germany, which is devoted to the pursuit of money. A young banker's son, who hardly knows what hardship means, suddenly comes to know that other things have a value besides money. He finds no amount of money will save him from exactly the same duties which his groom has to perform, and learns military obedience and devotion.

Among the lower orders, the necessity of military service encourages saving, while it delays marriage till the time of service is past. The German knows that he will have to leave his farm and occupations for a time, and therefore prepares for the time of need. At the same time his absence raises the importance of the women of his family. They must be prepared to undertake the management of his business, and must be acquainted with all its details, so that to a certain extent the position of the women is elevated.

The benefits derived from such a system are thus many and obvious. Its economy is also evident when we reflect that Prussia conducted two European campaigns (1864 and 1866) at about the same expense that England incurred in the expedition to Abyssinia. Although the Prussian is the most perfect of all armies in its equipments, the Prussian soldier is maintained at an average cost of about £29 10s. per head per annum. The French army, which shared with it the economy resulting from compulsory, and therefore underpaid labour, and which could not boast of anything like its efficiency in the noncombatant departments, cost above one-third more, or £41 10s. per head; whilst in England the expense is three times as great, being over £90 a year per man.

Another immense advantage, at least to a nation with a free form of government, is the absolute certainty that no such nation would ever incur the horrors of war except in a truly national cause and as a case of necessity. While hostilities last Prussia and North Germany have only one business in hand—the war. All other labour and industry is in abeyance, and every one out of three in the million of men under arms represents the sustenance of a family, a unit in the aggregate sustenance of the state. What a strain a campaign of twelve months' duration would be upon a community organized on Prussian military principles has not yet been tried; but it is an experiment from which Prussian rulers must at all times shrink. War reduces Germany to a state of suspended animation. Were the ordeal indefinitely prolonged, utter exhaustion must ensue. In England, a man may say, "Well, it will cost me twopence, perhaps fourpence, or even sixpence in the pound additional income tax; but that is the worst that can happen, and if we only win, I can stand that." But the same individual would think, speak, and vote very differently if he knew that he himself would have to shoulder his musket, leave home, friends, and comfort, to brave the perils of the field.

The Prussian system, brought as nearly as can be to perfection, has been seen to work admirably in the last three campaigns in which the nation has been engaged. It has been tried to the uttermost, and unmistakably asserts its superiority over every other. In fact, it is undoubtedly the greatest triumph of perfect organization the world has ever seen. On the 15th of July war against Prussia was declared by France, and no great difficulty was supposed to stand in the way of a rapid dash across the Rhine and a triumphant progress to Berlin. On the 17th of July, however, General von Moltke is reported to have said, "Give me to the 3rd of August, and we are safe." Just three days after the given date, on the 6th of August, the French army was driven back, and the German nation in arms commenced its victorious progress into the very heart of France.

The lessons taught by every campaign of modern times have been carefully studied by Prussia with a view to improvement. While Europe gazed astonished at her successes in 1866, the Prussians themselves, so far from boasting, were not at all satisfied, and set to work immediately to remedy what experience showed to be the weak points of their army; notably in the case of their artillery, to the performances of which much of their success in France was due, and to which the emperor attributed the disasters to his army, resulting in the most memorable capitulation ever recorded in history—that of Sedan.

Part of the Prussian batteries at Sadowa were of the old smooth-bore construction, but of the breech-loading guns many batteries had been carried into the field. In the war of 1870 all confusion and uncertainty had passed away, and the simplest and most efficient breech-loading piece had been adopted throughout. The artillery service and the proportion of horses and drivers maintained in peace had also been brought up to a higher standard; the experience of 1866 having clearly shown that a large infusion of raw elements into the field artillery, to strengthen it suddenly, defeated its object by crippling the efficiency of the batteries. A full comparison between the Prussian and French artillery, and the system generally pursued in each arm by this branch of the service, is given in the next chapter; but as relating exclusively to Prussia, we give here a description of the great Prussian gun, illustrated on Plate 4, which was one of the articles sent by the firm of F. Krupp, of Essen, in Rhenish Prussia, to the Paris exhibition, 1867. At the commencement of the war of 1870 it was placed to defend the naval port of Wilhelmshaven. It is a rifled breech-loader, made entirely of cast steel, and supported on a steel carriage. The central cylindrical tube forming this piece of ordnance is made of a solid forging of steel, and weighs by itself, in its finished state, about twenty tons. The weight of the cast-steel block employed in the manufacture of this tube was forty-eight tons, there being a waste of more than 50 per cent, of the original ingot caused by the operations of forging, turning and boring, and by cutting off the crop ends of the rough block. There are three superposed rings shrunk on to this central tube, the last ring inclosing the breech being forged in one piece with the trunnions, and made without any weld. The rings are of different lengths, as usual with built-up guns; and the whole is diminished in thickness towards the muzzle, only not tapered, but turned in parallel steps of decreasing diameter. The three superposed rings weigh thirty tons in all, and they are produced by a process similar to that followed in the production of weldless steel tyres. All these parts were hammered under the fifty-ton hammer constructed by M. Krupp for his own use. The weight and dimensions of this gun are as follows:—

Total weight, including breech, ...	50 tons.
Weight of breech-piece, ...	15 cwts
Diameter of bore, ...	14 inches (English).
Total length of barrel, ...	210-25 inches.

Rifling.

Number of grooves, ...	40.
Depth of grooves, ...	0-15 inch.
Pitch, ...	980 inches and 1014-4 inches

Projectiles.

Weight of solid steel shot, ...	1212 lbs. (English).
Total weight of steel shell, ...	765 lbs.
Lead coating, ...	200 lbs.
Charge, ...	16 lbs.
	981 lbs. Pruss. or 1080 lbs. Eng.
Weight of powder charge, ...	110 to 130 lbs. (English).

The gun carriage weighs about fifteen tons, and is placed upon a turntable, the total weight of which comes up to twenty-five tons. This also is made wholly of steel. The arrangements for working the gun are such, that it can be managed by two men with sufficient speed and accuracy for all practical requirements.

The manufacture of this piece of ordnance occupied a time exceeding sixteen months, the work being carried on without interruption day and night, including Sundays. There were no railway trucks in existence sufficiently strong to transport this gun, so M. Krupp designed and built a special truck at his own works for that purpose. This truck is made entirely of steel and iron, runs on six pairs of wheels, and weighs, when empty, twenty-three tons. The price of the gun was 105,000 Prussian dollars, without the carriage. The complete piece, with carriage and turntable, cost 145,000 thalers, or £21,750.

It will be a fitting conclusion to our explanation of the Prussian military system, if we give a description of the weapon which Prussia was the foremost nation to adopt, and the remarkable success of which has caused quite a revolution in the manufacture of small-arms. To be loaded at the breech, and to be fired by the penetration of a needle into a detonating cap within the cartridge, are distinct attributes in a weapon. And although the latter system has only been before the public for about thirty years, systems for breech-loading have been tried, accepted, and abandoned without number during the last three centuries. Indeed, a sort of instinct dictates that loading at the breech is the preferable course; and all the earlier muskets were so made, the system being doubtless abandoned from the difficulty of accurately closing the breech, in those days of rough workmanship. The extraordinary efficacy, however, of these combined principles only came into special prominence during the Prussian wars of 1864 and 1866. In the face of such an irresistible argument, every other power hastened to either prepare new arms, or to convert their existing stock into needle-firing breech-loaders of as good a construction as circumstances would permit.

The first patent for the needle-gun was taken out in England, December 13, 1831, by one Abraham Adolph Moser, who pressed his invention upon the British government, but meeting with no encouragement tried his fortune abroad, and at last obtained the patronage of the Prussian war office. Various improvements were suggested by Dreyse, a gunmaker of Sömmerada, and the perfected arm was put into the hands of the Prussian infantry in 1848. Other modifications have since been introduced, so as to render it lighter and more manageable, and considerable improvements were about to be introduced into it just as the present war broke out, and which were in consequence postponed. On Plate 3 two engravings of the weapon are shown, and in its present stage of development it may be described as follows:—

The barrel is closed by a sliding plunger or bolt, which can be pushed forward against the barrel, or withdrawn for the admission of the cartridge. In the former position it is secured by turning it, with the assistance of a small knob or lever, a quarter circle to the right, on the principle of a common door bolt. The plunger is hollow; its front end forming, when the arm is shut, a sort of cap to the back end of the barrel, the two being coned to correspond with each other. The long steel needle, from which the gun derives its name, and by which the explosion of the charge is effected, works in the hollow bolt, being driven forward by means of a spiral spring. The spring and needle are set, and the needle, so to speak, cocked by means of a trigger. The action of the trigger likewise releases the needle, which is shot forward into a patch of detonating composition in the centre of the cartridge.

The ammunition consists of an egg-shaped bullet, whose base is imbedded in a *papier-mâché* sabot. The fulminate is placed in the hinder part of the sabot; and behind this again, in a thin paper case which is choked over the apex of the bullet, is the powder.

The alterations proposed in the needle-gun, but which were deferred by the advent of war, are very slight. The whole change consists in the insertion of a caoutchouc ring, which does not increase the efficiency, but facilitates the handling of the arm, and in a new cartridge with a smaller ball, and a proportionate increase in the thickness of the case. As the barrel remains the same, both the old and new cartridge may be employed indiscriminately, the only difference being that the smaller ball would have a wider range than the larger one. A comparison of the relative merits of the needle-gun and the Chassepot, as also of the artillery of the two countries, is given in the next chapter.

A characteristic of the Germans during the war with France was the deliberation with which the men aimed and fired, though they had in their hands a needle-gun, tempting them to fire eight shots a minute. As long as the Prussians had their old firelocks they stood in three ranks, if standing in line of battle. The two foremost ranks fired only; the men in the third rank had only to charge their guns, and to exchange them for the empty ones of the second rank. Now two ranks only are formed in battle, but the great amount of firing is done by skirmishers kneeling or lying. It is an old experience that the soldiers, if firing quick, very frequently do not take time to bring their guns in the right position, but fire without aiming, and before the barrels of their guns are in a horizontal position. Those that fire in a kneeling position cannot fire high, without doing it purposely.

The formation of the Prussian navy only dates from 1848, and even up to 1864 it was very insignificant. But the result of the Danish war in that year, and the annexations made in 1866, rendered the possession of a powerful navy more than ever necessary to the welfare of Prussia. At the commencement of the present war she had six powerful iron-clads, the largest being the *König Wilhelm*, designed by Mr. E. J. Reed, then chief constructor of the English navy, and originally built for the Turkish government at the Thames Ironworks. The Sultan, however, being unable to pay for her, she was offered at the same price to the Board of Admiralty, who declined to buy her, and Prussia at once came forward and offered £487,500, or £30,000 more. Seeing their mistake, the English Admiralty then tried to outbid, but was too late. The vessel has a speed of fourteen knots, is plated with eight-inch armour, and carries twenty-eight guns, four 300-pounders, and twenty-four rifled 96-pounders made of Krupp's hammered steel, and capable of being fired with seventy-five lbs. charges twice in a minute. Besides this and five other iron-clads, there were nine screw frigates and corvettes, and eighty-six small vessels and sailing ships, carrying in the whole 542 guns, and manned by 5000 men and marines. The sailors and marines are raised by conscription from amongst the seafaring population, which is exempt on this account from service in the army. Great inducements are held out for able seamen to volunteer in the navy, and the number who have done so in recent years has been very large. The total seafaring population of North Germany is estimated at 80,000.

During the last few years Prussia has done her best to strengthen her power in the Baltic and North Seas. On both these seas she has an important and an uninterrupted line of coast, where she has endeavoured to establish ports which might be useful either in time of peace or war. On the Baltic she has three ports: Dantzic, on the extreme east; Stralsund, midway between Memel and Holstein; and Kiel, the most important, which is established in a fine bay in Holstein. Of these three ports Kiel is the strongest and most formidable, and is supposed to be regarded by Russia with some degree of suspicion and alarm. The most superficial glance on the map will show its importance to the Prussians. When complete, it is so well situated, both geographically and locally, as to show that it may easily be made the Cherbourg of the Baltic. It is said that the Baltic will then be merely a Prussian lake, and that Prussia, without any difficulty, will not only be able to close the entrance to foreign fleets, but will possess the most complete power over Copenhagen. Wilhelmshaven, in the bay of Jahde, in the North Sea, one of the most important harbours for the newly-founded German navy, was opened by King William I. in 1869. It forms a vast artificial construction of granite, and comprises five separate harbours, with canals, sluices to regulate the tide, and an array of dry docks for ordinary and ironclad vessels. Its total cost of construction was I £1,500,000.

CHAPTER V.

Sketch of the Organization of the Regular Army in France—State of things prior to the time of Louis XIV., and from that period to the Great Revolution—"Levée en Masse" in 1793— The Genius of Carnot—Wonderful Successes of the French Army in 1794—Introduction of the Law of Conscription—Nothing done by Napoleon to improve the Organic Constitution of the Army—Exhaustion of France after the Battle of Waterloo—Re-establishment of the Army in 1818—The State of the Army under the Second Empire—Alarm at the Success of Prussia at the Battle of Sadowa—Most important alterations made in 1868—The chief provisions of the Army Re-organization Act explained—The system of purchasing Substitutes—Broad Results of the New Act, and the Number and Composition of the Army intended to have been secured by it—Great Power given to the Emperor—Comparison of the French and Prussian Systems—Objections to the former—Serious effect of the Conscription on the Population in France—Failure of the Act of 1868—Reasons of Failure stated—Delusion entertained as to the National Guard—Actual Force in France at the commencement of the War—Weakness of the French Commissariat—The System explained—Contrast with that of Prussia—Rapid Strategy and Mobility of Force essential to Modern Warfare—Favour shown in France to the Corps d'Élite a weakness to the general Army—The Accoutrement of the French Soldier far too heavy—No important alteration made in the System of Tactics in France for nearly eighty years—Prussian Tactics the subject of incessant study and improvement—Enthusiasm of the French Troops of no use against Modern Weapons—Difference of Discipline in the French and Prussian Armies—Want of respect for their Officers amongst the French—Causes of the absence of Discipline on the part of the French traced chiefly to the tone of Society under the Empire—The Conscription now regarded only as a Blood-tax on the Poor for the benefit of the Rich—Evils of the "Exoneration" system—Paper Soldiers—Corruption on the part of the Government—Education and Training of the French Officers not calculated to create habits of command—Too many Court Generals, and incapacity of the État Major—The Destructive and Marauding Habits of the French Troops increased of late years—Rapidity of the decline in the Prestige *of the French Army—Full description of the Chassepot and its Cartridge— Comparison with the Needle-Gun—The Mitrailleuse—Description of the Weapon, and also of the Gatling Gun—Importance of Artillery in War—-Superiority of the Prussian Field Artillery over that of the French—The Guns and Projectiles, and the practice of firing in both Armies explained and contrasted—Breech* versus *Muzzle Loaders—The Strength and Composition of the French Navy.*

THE history of the organization of the regular army of France commences in the middle of the seventeenth century. Prior to the reign of Louis XIV. war was carried on by men-at-arms, troops of horse, and bodies of sharpshooters who bore little relation to a modern army. The soldier was equally brave, and more independent; but the art of acting in great masses, and the discipline by which the individual is entirely merged in the corps to which he belongs, is of comparatively recent date. The formation of regular armies required systematic organization—uniformity of arms and dress, regularity of advancement, stricter conditions of service, graduated pay, and more certain methods of insuring the sustenance of troops.

These are the elements of which Louvois was the first great master, and by his careful application of them he contributed more to the success of the arms of Louis XIV. than Turenne and Luxemburg, who led the French forces to victory in the field. The organization of Louvois lasted, with no material changes, until 1793; it perished in that great convulsion which overthrew the monarchy and the privileged classes, who had played so great a part in it. In the French army, thus constituted during the eighteenth century, most of the peculiarities prevailed which have now disappeared from every European army but that of England. The men were raised by voluntary enlistment. The regiments retained a local name and character from the districts to which they belonged; the brigades of Picardy, Normandy, Champagne, and Auvergne corresponding to the Coldstream Guards, Sutherland or Gordon Highlanders, Connaught Rangers, or Welsh Fusileers in the United Kingdom. The king's household troops were a privileged corps, with this distinction, however, that in the Royal Guards and Musketeers the purchase system never obtained, and that they were open to all ranks of society. In the rest of the army, regiments and companies having been originally raised by private persons for the service of the crown, had become a species of property, like commissions in the British army. The old French army was a highly aristocratic institution; for although the purchase of commissions was tolerated, Louvois had contrived to make the military service rather onerous than profitable, and the consequence was that the rich and the noble alone could hold them. The French nobility served with unflinching courage and enthusiasm; they were as ready to spend their fortunes in the purchase of a step as to spend their blood on the field of battle. Commissions were sometimes vouchsafed by the king to private soldiers of signal valour and merit, but the noblesse d'épée may as a rule be said to have officered the army. The latter was essentially royal and aristocratic when the revolutionary storm of 1789 burst on France, and swept away both the nobility and the throne.

In 1791 the French army consisted of 166 regiments of foot and horse. These troops were well trained, but the corps were numerically weak; and the political agitation of the time had shaken the unity and self-reliance of the army. The consequence was that the outset of the war was disastrous; and the prodigious enthusiasm and energy of the volunteers of 1792 and 1793 alone restored victory to the standards of the Republic. The events of these years proved at once the value and the weakness of a great volunteer movement. The popular movement of 1792 saved France; but in the following year, when it was opposed to the renewed operations of regular troops, the spell was broken, the charm was over. The army of the Rhine was thrown across the Lauter; the army of the north was driven out of Belgium; and it became more than ever difficult to raise men for the necessary service of the country. On the 1st of January, 1793, the eight armies of the French republic had not more than 150,000 men in their ranks. For, as the Duc d'Aumale, in an able work on the military institutions of France, has said:—"It is of the essence of special volunteer corps not to renew their strength, although the mere existence of these corps seriously interferes with and may arrest enlistment for the line." It might be worth while for the leaders of public opinion in England to consider how far this remark applies to our popular volunteer movement, as well as to the great French rising of 1792. The French patriots of 1791 having enlisted for one year, took their discharge when that time had elapsed, and 60,000 of them returned home. The Convention called out 300,000 national guards, but the measure failed for want of authority to raise them. Toulon was taken by the English, Lyons was in insurrection, the eastern departments were invaded, the country was in a supreme hour of danger, when Carnot joined the Committee of Public Safety, and six days afterwards the "*levée en masse*" of the nation was decreed by the Convention. At that moment sprang to life the national army of France. A former law had placed all citizens from the age of eighteen to forty (at one moment even from sixteen to forty-five) under the grasp of arbitrary rule, and subjected them to the caprice of a local authority. The law of the 20th August, 1793, was more harsh in appearance, but less vexatious and oppressive in reality. It abolished the local discretionary power, confined itself to men from eighteen to twenty-five, but within those limits *took them all*. In six months all the pressure of the Reign of Terror had failed to raise 300,000 men under the earlier law. In three months the general levy was effected without serious opposition under the later law, and on the 1st January, 1794, the strength of the army had risen to 770,932.

This vast army was consolidated by the genius of Carnot into one uniform machine. All distinctions of corps, and even the grades of the non-commissioned officers, were abolished. Local appellations of regiments were superseded by numbers, and the uniform of the whole army became identical; the white livery of the Crown being exchanged for the blue tunic of the Republic. Such was the constitution of the immortal armies of the "Sambre et Meuse," and of the "Rhin et Moselle," which saved France on the plains of Fleurus, won twenty-seven victories in a year, captured 3800 guns, and dissolved the European coalition.

The law of conscription was first established in France on the 5th September, 1798, fourteen months before the 18th Brumaire; and the statute which placed the population at the disposal of the state, as each succeeding generation completed its twentieth year, preceded the power which was to make so tremendous a use of it. From that time to the present, the youth of France just entering upon manhood has been cropped by law, like the tracts in a forest set apart for annual felling; and though the amount has varied, the principle of conscription is now deeply rooted in the law and the habits of the nation, although it devours so large a proportion of the adult male population. The first act of the First Consul was to demand, not an instalment of the conscription, but the whole class of the year, amounting to 100,000 men, and to take severe measures against every evasion of the law. These demands and measures increased in intensity throughout his reign. It is remarkable, however, that Napoleon, the greatest master of the art of modern warfare, did nothing to improve the organic constitution of the army. He employed the military resources of the country with consummate ability, and with insatiable rapacity; but he consumed everything that he created. The permanent military strength of France could not keep pace with his extravagant demands upon it; and the termination of the empire was the annihilation of the force by which it had been raised to the highest pinnacle of power and glory.

For three years after the battle of Waterloo France remained without an army, and the allied forces were not all withdrawn from her territory, when Marshal Gouvion Saint-Cyr, minister of war under the Restoration, undertook hi 1818 the difficult task of re-organizing the military institutions of the kingdom. The peace establishment of the army was fixed at 240,000 men, to be raised by an annual conscription of 40,000 men, enlisted for six years. The reserve was to be composed of soldiers belonging to the levies of the preceding ten years, but this part of the scheme failed. No man could be an officer, who had not passed a certain time in the ranks, or gone through one of the military schools. The guard was retained, and consisted of 30,000 men. The annual conscription on the peace establishment was raised successively to 60,000 and 80,000 by the government of Louis Philippe. Under the second empire it became at least 100,000; and during the Crimean and Italian wars 140,000 men was the annual contingent. The efficient strength of the French army in 1867, including the staff, the gendarmerie, and the military train, was 389,604 men; of whom 23,105 were officers, 70,850 non-commissioned officers, 26,374 unclassed companies, musicians, &c., and 229,275 private soldiers. From this number, 80,000 must be deducted for home garrisons, depôts, and the force serving in Africa. A further deduction must be made of at least one-seventh for the raw conscripts of the year, and of another considerable fraction of men entitled to their discharge, as having served their time. By calling in the whole reserve of the contingents, the nominal strength of the army might have been raised to 600,000 men, but the actual strength was very far below that figure. As conscripts were allowed to commute or buy off their actual service by paying a certain sum to the military chest, a further deduction must be made for those who paid their debt of military service in money, and not in person. From 1856 to 1865 the average annual number of these exceeded 20,000 men, or one-fifth of the whole conscription, in years of peace; but in 1859 and 1860, when the army was on a war footing, and the conscription was raised to 140,000, the number of "exonerations" exceeded 44,000, or nearly *one-third of the whole* contingent.

The result is, that in the wars of the Crimea and of Italy, France could only send to the field, and maintain by reinforcements, an army not much exceeding one-fourth of her nominal effective strength; and it is well known that in 1867, when the Luxembourg question was supposed to threaten war, the Emperor Napoleon could not immediately have sent above 150,000 men to the Rhine, and these, in case of a check, could not, under several months, have been supported by a second army. The startling success of the campaign ending with the battle of Sadowa caused a shock of surprise and alarm through France; and in the uneasiness that followed, the highest military authorities of the nation came to the conclusion that they were not in a position to meet on an equal footing the state of things which the system of the Prussian armies and the consolidation of Germany had produced in Europe.

Accordingly, in 1868, most important alterations were introduced by the "Army Re-organization Act." The conscription system was still retained, and the forces of the country classified in three divisions: the Active Army, the Army of Reserve, and the National Guard. The duration of service in the active army was fixed at five years, at the expiration of which time the soldier had to enter the reserve for four years longer. The period of service of the young men who had not been comprised in the active army, was four years in the reserve, and five in the national guard. The young men drawn for the active army were permitted to purchase substitutes from the government, but the privilege was withheld from the men of the reserve. They might, however, interchange with those of the National Guard, or furnish as substitute a man under thirty-two years of age, fulfilling the conditions required for military service, and liberated from all other obligations. Substitutes were formerly procured through private agencies, but an imperial decree in 1855 made the right to furnish them a government monopoly. The price to be paid for substitutes was fixed annually, and varied. In 1868 the minister of war settled it at 2500 francs, or £100. This sum, increased by various other items, was supposed to be thrown into an army fund, out of which the substitutes were paid a certain amount at the time of enlistment, besides receiving an increase of pay at the end of seven years, another increase at the end of fourteen, and a pension of one franc, or tenpence a day, was to be given after a service of forty-five years. Soldiers were allowed to re-enlist as long as they were fit for service, and re-enlistments were greatly encouraged, so as to give the army a standing nucleus of experienced troops, who had made the military service their life-profession.

By the terms of the Act of 1868, the number of men to be drafted every year was fixed at 160,000, but more might be voted. The number to be called out in each department was settled by imperial decree, and the contingent for each canton by the prefect. The broad result of the law was to give the emperor the absolute command, for military purposes, of the entire male population between the ages of twenty and thirty. Every Frenchman, on attaining his twentieth year, was liable to nine years' military service. Previous to 1832, the period of compulsory enlistment was eight years, and from 1832 to 1868 seven years. Under the new system, not only were two years added to the enlistment, but the chances of escaping it were greatly curtailed. It was intended to maintain about 400,000 men in the active army, 430,000 in the reserve, and 408,000 in the national guard. The latter force was destined as an auxiliary to the active army in the defence of the fortresses, coasts, and frontier of the empire, and in the maintenance of order in the interior. The preceding figures give a total of 1,238,000 men, but the emperor could increase the force at pleasure. In any year he could, if he chose, call on the whole "class" of young men twenty years old, supposed to number about 300,000; the reserve could be rendered available for service in the field on the same conditions as the army; and the national guard called out for active duty in the room of the reserve by a special law, or, in the interval of the session, by a decree which was to be presented within twenty-one days to the legislative body. It will be thus seen that from 1868 conscripts were for nine years at the call of the government, their service being divided between the army (five years) and reserve (four years), or between the reserve (four years) and the national guard (five years). The regulation stature was reduced to 5 feet 1¼ inches, a modification favourable to tall men, as the number of conscripts was thus increased, and they had a better chance of not serving in the active army. The reserves could, it is true, be called out by the emperor in time of war, but it was understood that such expeditions as those of Rome, or Mexico, or China, or Syria, did not constitute a time of war, which term, in fact, implied a serious menace of collision with some great Continental power. A French soldier was able to many after having passed one year in the reserve, unless stopped by an imperial decree calling out that force. The married men of the reserve had to perform the same duties as their single comrades. Substitutes were again allowed, and the old offices where a man could step in and purchase another fellow to serve in his stead rose from their ashes. The movable national guard consisted of such Frenchmen as did not belong to the active army or reserve, and had no legal cause of exemption. If a man had a substitute in the active army or reserve, he must, nevertheless, belong to the national guard. These men served for five years, and in this force no substitutes were allowed, as in time of peace the duties would be light, and in time of war every man would be required at his post.

The amended plan was avowedly based on the Prussian system, but with two important differences. The period of service in the active army, which was five years in France, is only three years in Prussia. Again, only half of the French reserve was composed of conscripts who had seen actual service—the other half were of inferior efficiency. In Prussia, on the contrary, the reserve is wholly composed of experienced troops, who have spent three years under colours. In France the conscript was free at the age of twenty-nine, while in Prussia the war office retains its hold over him till he is thirty-two, and, indeed, if the landsturm is taken into account, for a longer period. But in peace a Prussian conscript is after three years practically at liberty to return to civil pursuits, the distribution of the reserve being so arranged that the men composing it can remain in their own town or village among their friends and associates, except during the brief annual exercises. The French conscript, however, was bound for five years in the army; and if the reserve had been made really efficient, the conscripts who there began their military career would have had to devote more time to it than the Prussian reserve men (who have already been trained, and need only a little "setting-up" drill to freshen their recollection), and would have found the requirements of the service injuriously interfere with their ordinary occupations. The French plan, therefore, while more oppressive than the Prussian one, provided a less efficient reserve.

When the proportion between the conscription and the population is considered, a still more serious objection arises to the French system. It is calculated that about 320,000 young men every year reach the age of twenty in France, but of these quite *half* obtain exemption from military service on account of being included in one or other of the following classes:—Those below the standard; those whose infirmities unfit them for soldiering; the eldest of a family of orphans; the only son or eldest son, or, in default of son or stepson, the only or eldest grandson of a widow, or of a blind father, or of a father aged seventy; the eldest of two brothers drawn for service, if the younger is fit to serve; those who have a brother actually serving, not as a substitute; those who have had a brother killed or disabled in the service. Hence there were only some 160,000 men to supply the contingent of the year. Formerly the contingent stood at 100,000 in times of peace, but the Act of 1868 having raised it to 160,000, it will be seen that the conscription every year carried off every young man who was twenty years of age, and fit for service; and no margin was left for the necessities of war. Accordingly, the whole able-bodied male population of France was bound to military service of one kind or another between the ages of twenty and thirty. In Prussia there is some chance of escape from the army, even for those who are not cripples or invalids. The nominal "class "of the year is 170,000; deducting men unfit for arms, there remain some 75,000 to supply the annual contingent of 60,000. In Prussia, a conscript can marry after his three years' service under the colours. In France, six years at least was the period during which marriage was forbidden.

If we consider the French conscription in its effect upon the population, the case assumes a most serious aspect. At least a century of peace was necessary after 1815, to enable the population to recover from the tremendous drain of the wars of the first empire. Statistics prove that the levy of 100,000 men, more or less, under arms, instantly produces a marked effect on the population. When the conscription was 40,000 men the population rapidly increased; with 60,000 the progress was slower; with 80,000, slower still; with 100,000 it was arrested; with 140,000 (in 1854 and 1855) it positively declined. The population of France has for many years increased more slowly than that of any other country, and under the Army Act of 1868 there seemed no prospect before it but rapid decline. No surprise can be felt at such a phenomenon when we remember that 160,000 stout and able-bodied young men were marched off every year to the barracks or the camp; that for at least six years they were unable to contract marriage; and that their more fortunate contemporaries who remained at home, cultivated their fields, married, and reared children, were precisely those who were rejected by the conscription on account of their diminutive size, their feeble constitutions, or other infirmities.

So far as results are concerned the Act of 1868 may really be said to have been a failure. In execution it fell very far short of its express intention, viz., of enabling the emperor to have 800,000 fighting men at his disposal, and of raising the available military strength of the empire to upwards of 1,200,000 men. The reasons of its failure are not hard to find. The imperial government did not possess the unequivocal or undivided confidence of any class of French citizens. The emperor, whose will was the only tangible form of authority, could not boast of high military talents, and had been unfortunate in several of his military experiments. After him there had not been for many years in France any general of such indisputable pre-eminence and authority, that he could at once give the vigour and unity of paramount command to the whole military system. As there did not exist any immediate and stirring motive for such a measure of national armament beyond the successes of a neighbour, the measure did not meet with popular sympathy; and a government whose relations with the people were never the most cordial, hesitated to enforce to the letter an objectionable law. The government even lacked the courage or strength to put into execution some of its mildest and least vexatious provisions, such as the training and arming of the garde mobile. If the policy of Napoleon III., after the passing of the Act of 1868, had not been characterized by such infirmity of purpose and fatal timidity and vacillation, the so-called "Army of the Rhine" of 1870 would not have been so hopelessly overwhelmed, outnumbered, and broken up as it was by the Prussian forces.

The great national guard, of which so much was expected, having been wilfully maintained in a condition which rendered it perfectly worthless in time of war, the notion that France had a great reserve on which to fall back, was found, when too late, to have been a delusion. The regular army were soldiers; but the national guard had neither drill, nor arms, nor officers worthy of the name. The reason of this is manifest enough in the extreme reluctance of the Bonapartist ministry to place arms in the hands of the civil population; and it must be remembered that before the French army had suffered a single reverse, the disaffection of the garde mobile had been so abundantly demonstrated in the camp at Châlons, that it was thought prudent to teach the bulk of the men drill with sticks instead of Chassepots.

At the commencement of the war the regular army of France was 400,000 men, of whom 40,000 were at Cherbourg getting ready for the Baltic, 5000 in Italy, 10,000 in Algeria, 35,000 in Paris and Châlons, 10,000 in Lyons, and at least 30,000 more in Marseilles, Toulon, Bordeaux, Toulouse, L'Orient, Rochefort, and the hospitals, leaving only 270,000 efficients for the front—that is, eight corps d'armée of 30,000 each, and the guard. On this army rushed, by German official accounts, the Crown Prince with 210,000 men, Prince Frederick Charles with 220,000 more, and Steinmetz with 90,000, or 520,000 in all. In addition to these, to reinforce German losses, there was "the second line"—the 200,000 soldiers encamped between the Rhine and the Weser.

An element of very considerable weakness in the French system, was to be found in what is called the administration of the army, better known in England as the commissariat. In time of peace it is difficult to learn the art of supplying an army in the field. In peace the delivery of contracts is perfectly simple, regular, and easy. In war everything—time, place, and demand—is urgent, difficult, and irregular. The only method of dealing with so many unforeseen contingencies is not by military routine, but by a ready and complete knowledge of business. But all the officers of the French commissariat had served for years in the army itself; and the heads of the department, or intendants, were superannuated generals. The consequence was, that these persons knew nothing of the operations of trade, by which alone supply can adjust itself to demand. During the Italian campaign of 1859, the French troops were often without bread, in one of the richest corn-bearing regions of Europe. Biscuit was equally deficient, and an attempt was made to supply the place of these necessaries by polenta, which the men could not eat, because they did not know how to cook it! The commissariat knew nothing about buying and selling food; they could only distribute it.

It will be seen, therefore, that the French were not only outnumbered and out-generalled, but that their organization completely broke down. The Prussians, at a distance from their own supplies, and consequently compelled to maintain a long line of communication through an enemy's country, were better furnished with matériel and food than the French. They succeeded in moving their wounded more rapidly from the field of battle; and their operations were never impeded by a want of transport. It is impossible, on the other hand, to explain some of the delays of the French generals except on the supposition that their transport failed them. Even the great disaster at Sedan might have been averted, or lessened, if MacMahon had been able to move at the rate of twenty miles a day. An admirable organization enabled the Prussians easily to accomplish distances which a want of it made it hopeless for the French to attempt.

On the French system the ministry of war, through a great department—the Intendance—monopolizes the whole business of the army. It musters the troops, checks the pay lists, issues provisions, fuel, forage, and clothing, supervises the hospital service, manages the whole transport of the army, and takes charge of all the matériel of war. The system of the Prussians is the exact reverse. Instead of centralizing, they have decentralized. Instead of providing one intendance for the whole army, they have aimed at making each corps d'armée complete in itself. Each corps has its own stores and its own reserves, and draws its supplies from its depôts without the necessity of reference to a central authority. In France the entire transport is under the control of the Intendance, and the vehicles may be used for any purpose or for any regiment for which they may be temporarily required. In Prussia the duties of the central authority are confined to the simple task of replenishing the depôts from which each corps draws its stores; every corps Intendance has control over its own carriages, which can only be used for the service of the particular corps to which they are attached. Each corps has means at its disposal for the carriage of its reserve ammunition, its hospital service, its stores, and its supplies, and not only is adequate transport provided for each corps, but sufficient vehicles are furnished for each object. The ammunition waggons, the hospital carts, the store train, are all distinct from each other, and under the orders of separate officers, though subject to the commands of the general of the corps. The preference which has been shown by many high authorities for the French plan, is based on the supposition that the requirements of an army are so various and so incapable of being foreseen, that it is wasteful to maintain separate matériel for each regiment. One regiment may be stationed in a barren country, the other in a fertile one. The one may be far from its resources, the other near them. In either case the one would require more elaborate means of transport than the other, and, if each were provided with the same amount, half the horses in the one case would be standing idle, while all the beasts in the other would be worked to death. But this criticism overlooks the fact, that the Prussians knowingly provide a transport which in some cases may prove extravagant, in order that they may be quite sure that in every instance it may be adequate. And thus, at the outbreak of war, each regiment in the Prussian army is ready to move at a moment's notice, while the French cannot move a step till the Intendance has undertaken a preliminary distribution of stores, matériel, and transport. The French, from the nature of their system, were organizing while the Prussians were marching. Their organization may prove admirable, if they can fight at their own time. It must fail before an enemy prepared to assume at the very outbreak of the war an active offensive. In short, it is suited for the dilatory operations of ancient warfare. It is wholly unfitted for the sudden and rapid movements of modern armies.

The same principles of rapid strategy and mobility of force have ever been the keys of victory, whether this rapidity and mobility have been gained by improvement of roads, improvement of organization, adaptations of scientific discoveries, or superiority of armament. The same skilful application of the science of war has turned the scale in every campaign from the days of Alexander to those of Moltke. Every great general who has handed down his name as a mighty master of his art has owed his successes and his reputation to the discovery or appreciation of some new means of rendering his army more easy to move, or more easy to concentrate for decisive action, than that of his opponent. Alexander conquered by means of the discipline and equipment of the troops handed down to him by his father, which enabled them to move more rapidly than the cumbrous forces of his enemies, in exactly the same manner as Frederick the Great triumphed over his enemies by means of the discipline and equipment of the troops handed down to him by his father. Caesar gained victories by the mobility of the legions, exactly in the same manner as Napoleon did by the adoption of the system of divisions and corps d'armée, first advocated by Moreau. Wherever we turn in the history of war, we find the same broad principles the foundation of success. The French gained the great victory of Jena by having adopted a system of manoeuvre which was as superior in mobility to that handed down from the time of Frederick the Great as is the system of the present day, by which the Prussians have turned the tables on the French, to that of the first Napoleon. The art of war, like every other art, is ever progressive, ever advancing. There is no such thing as chivalry in war. A general who gave up an advantageous position nowadays to meet an enemy on equal terms, would be thought as great a madman as a knight would have been considered in the so-called days of chivalry, if he had taken off his armour and fought without protection. War is, always has been, and always must be, the means of doing the maximum of damage to an enemy with the minimum injury to oneself. And the principles of war have remained the same in all ages. They may be summed up briefly as the means of moving most rapidly against your enemy when he is unprepared, and of hitting him hardest when you get near him. Could soldiers fight more bravely than those of the French army did in the war? They showed a courage in the field of battle which allowed them to retire from even an unsuccessful struggle with every honour. Yet of what avail was their gallantry for the defence of the country which they were maintained to defend? Their enemy had mastered the present conditions of the art of war, and all their gallantry and bravery was ineffectual and abortive.

The favour shown by the French military authorities to their *corps d'élite*, has a tendency to drain the line of its best men. By common consent the infantry of an army is its most essential and important element. The foot soldier of the French army, carrying on his back a weight of thirty-five kilogrammes, or seventy-five lbs., which is more than one-third of the regulation burden of a camp mule, has to march, to watch, to work, and to fight, for the support and defence of the whole service. In the Chassepot the voltigeur certainly has a much lighter weapon than the old muzzle-loader, but "the pack" is still greater than any man can be expected to carry on a long march without exhaustion. First, there is the Chassepot, 7½ pounds; next, the sword bayonet and scabbard, 3 pounds; 10 pounds of ammunition, distributed partly in two pouches, and partly in his knapsack; a pair of shoes; a four-pound loaf of bread; a canvas bag slung over the left shoulder, and containing any creature comforts the man may have procured; Over the knapsack—first, a great-coat; secondly, a blanket; thirdly, his share of the canvas for the *tente d'abri*, and sticks for the same; and fourthly, a huge camp kettle. Inside the knapsack he has a second pair of trousers, comb, brushes, needles, thread, buttons, a pair of gloves, a couple of pairs of socks, and three shirts; in addition, a flask capable of containing about a quart of liquid is flung over the right shoulder. A long march with such a weight must incapacitate all but the very strongest men. Yet how is the infantry of the line formed? It is what may fairly be called the *residuum* of the conscription. The artillery and engineers have the first choice, as they must have men of physical strength and superior intelligence. Then the big men are taken for the heavy cavalry regiments. Then the most agile and hardy men are selected for the light infantry corps (*chasseurs à pied*); and when the regiments of the line are formed, the best men are drafted out of them to serve in the imperial guard, or to form the two picked companies of each battalion. What remains after all this selection, is of necessity the dregs of the whole mass. No error can be more fatal than this fostering of picked bodies of troops at the expense of the whole army. The forces are weakened by continually subtracting their strongest ingredients; and the army, as a whole, loses that uniform solidity which is essential to great operations.

When we remember that it was the Emperor Napoleon I. who said that, to preserve the superiority of an army in war, the system of tactics required to be changed every ten years, it seems remarkable that the French military authorities should have been the last in Europe to act upon the principle. Yet such was the case. The exercises and manoeuvres of the French line when the war with Prussia commenced were still almost those of 1791; indeed, they were introduced and copied from the drill of Frederick II., after the battle of Rosbach. In process of time these regulations, revised and amended in a thousand ways, reached an enormous bulk— some 846 articles of evolutions, most of which could not be executed in actual war. They are still essentially the regulations of Potsdam, devised by Leopold Von Dessau, soon after Frederick had adopted the iron ramrod, which was the needle-gun of the last century. The minuteness and complexity of these details exceeds all belief, and the study of them diverts the mind of an officer from the true objects of war. The whole drill should be reduced to a few pages; and now that the inflexible rigidity of the old Prussian line of battle has been superseded by elasticity, mobility, and the relative independence of its components parts, it is evident that simplicity and clearness in theory, and rapidity in execution, have become the absolute law of modern manoeuvres and tactics. While French infantry tactics are thus complicated and old-fashioned, those of the Prussian army were the subject of incessant study and improvement from the battle of Jena, when their old system broke down, to the battle of Sadowa, when their new system culminated in victory. The German armies are now in the highest state of efficiency which can be reached by scientific preparation for war, by concentration, by compact discipline, and by forethought.

The French army has always been remarkable for a degree of enthusiasm in their fighting far beyond that of other nations; and the wars of the present generation show that this peculiarity has not altered. It is due, in the first instance, to the nervous, high-spirited temperament of the men; but it has been increased, rather than counteracted, by the influence of the campaigns in Algeria, the great school of modern French arms. The loose formation and desultory warfare of Africa against the Arab tribes, have given to men and officers a high degree of individual resource and self-reliance, but they have weakened that severe discipline and close connection which is essential to regular movements against an enemy in line of battle. French soldiers take up their ground with extreme promptitude and gallantry: when the fire of the enemy begins to tell upon them they rush forward with irresistible ardour, but with some degree of confusion. In their European campaign of 1859, the French beat the Austrians by furious assaults with the bayonet; but that sort of thing, it was found, would never do with the present range and rapidity of firearms, and a novel system of movements had therefore to be introduced. The Prussians supplied this want, simultaneously with the adoption of the breechloader, and successfully practised their new manoeuvre of fighting in dispersed columns four years ago. The French have yet to adapt themselves to this particular requirement of the age. Their noisy and impetuous movements are ill-timed and inconvenient; and in the event of a check inflicted by an enemy under stricter discipline and control, are followed by the most disastrous consequences.

In most of their campaigns of late years, before the war with Germany, the French troops were opposed to an enemy far inferior to themselves in soldierly qualities. They found that a well-directed attack generally secured them victory, and became, therefore, confirmed in the belief that nothing could withstand their rush. They seem to have forgotten that Germans, the most military of the continental nations, fighting for all they held dear, and imbued with the deepest feelings of nationality, were not men likely to yield without a desperate struggle. They did not recognize that with arms of precision, and especially with breech-loaders, calmness, steadiness, and resolution are more than a counterpoise for dash and enthusiasm. Even French writers noticed that the French conscripts fired wildly, and what does firing wildly with the Chassepot mean? It means a useless expenditure of ammunition from a rapidly loaded rifle, and an utter disregard of the value of accuracy. Possibly breech-loading arms may be better adapted for the slow and steady German than for the eager and impetuous Frenchman. It now requires a great degree of calmness on the part of the soldier, when under a heavy fire, to refrain from expending his ammunition. Courage, apart from excitement, is necessary to enable him to keep cool and to use his arm of precision. Few who have studied the events of the war will be able to avoid the thought that, armed as soldiers now are, steady troops will have the advantage over those who trust to *élan* for their superiority, and seek by enthusiasm to replace the firm persistency which characterizes the northern nations.

It will not be out of place if we indicate here one or two other features of the campaign, which will to a great extent account for the overwhelming reverse of fortune which has overtaken the military power of France. No doubt a very large portion of the Prussian success may be accounted for by the superiority of numbers and the great talents of the strategists and generals who have planned and executed the various movements; but it would show a disregard of the lessons of war if the influence attaching to the composition of their rank and file were overlooked. In the first place, few can fail to be struck with the difference between the discipline of the German and French regiments, not only when defeat had tested to the utmost the quality of the latter, but even before the war had actually commenced, and during the inarch of the troops to the front. There was an earnestness and determination among the German soldiers which contrasted favourably with the excitement and effervescent enthusiasm of the French troops. What can be more marked in their difference than the narratives of the departure of the regiments from Berlin and Paris! In the former city quiet, order, and determination not unmixed with sadness, characterized the march of the men who had left home and family to fight for a cause which they believed to be identical with the existence of Germany as a nation. In Paris, on the contrary, the wild conduct of the Zouaves and Turcos was applauded as the natural outbursts of soldiers who by mere *élan* were to overcome their enemies and override Europe. To hold within bounds of discipline such soldiers requires a strong hand and a firm will. Neither of these seems to have been employed. Unprejudiced spectators have narrated how French regiments behave on the line of march; how the soldiers straggle, fall out, and lag behind; how the officers ride in front, careless of their men, and intent only on securing for themselves good quarters and good food. The necessary results follow. The stragglers, released from the restraints of discipline, plundered and oppressed even their own countrymen, and in some instances, without the excuse of hunger or want, sacked the baggage of the army, which had been left without a sufficient guard. On the other hand, the marching of the Prussian regiments received the well-merited commendation of all who witnessed it, while their conduct in the enemy's country showed how well discipline had been preserved, not only by the power of military rule, but by the influence of men of education and good character on their comrades in the ranks. Neither the officers nor men of the German army shrunk from the hardships of war; all equally experienced them; and the generals, the staff, and the regimental officers, alike shared with their men the bivouac in the open and the inconvenience it entailed. The French officers do not appear to have considered necessary such a similarity of life between themselves and their men. Take the account of the capture of St. Privat by the Prussian guards, on the occasion of the battle of Gravellotte. They advanced across the open, up a steep hill, their generals and mounted officers in front, in face of a most withering fire from an enemy entrenched behind the walls and houses. Their mounted officers were all either dismounted or killed, their ranks were more than decimated; but they pressed on, drove the French from their position, and took their camp. The captured camp afforded unwonted luxuries. These Prussian guardsmen, men of the highest families of Berlin, were amazed at the comforts which abounded in the tents of the French officers. Their own generals and officers of all ranks were accustomed to sleep on the ground; but these gentlemen of France had beds, chairs, carpets, curtains, and looking-glasses, and, as a Prussian staff officer naively remarked, "we then quite understood why the French could not march so rapidly as we do."

The French army did not bear well the strain of disaster. To judge by the narratives of eyewitnesses, the soldiery appear to have broken loose from the bonds of discipline, and the officers to have lost all control over their men. The climax of this absence of discipline and of the good feeling which in a well-regulated army exists between all ranks, was reached in the last hours of the terrible battle of Sedan. In that awful time, when the organization of the best troops would have been subjected to the severest trial, the discipline of the French army completely succumbed. Soldiers fired on their officers, and officers who surrendered themselves as prisoners were not ashamed to curse their men in the presence of their captors. But it may be said these troops by their behaviour on the battlefield wiped out any stain that might attach to their conduct in camp. Doubtless they showed great courage, which was worthily recognized by their enemy, and the whole world beside; but does not the cool determination of the soldiers of Germany appear to be more suitable for the proper use of the weapons of modern war, than the fierce enthusiasm of the French with its accompanying disorganization? The breech-loading rifle requires a steady and a thinking man to appreciate the effects of its power of accurate shooting, and the necessity of carefully husbanding every cartridge. Nor when the time arrived for attack over the open did the German soldiery fail. With a patient endurance and hardy courage contrasting greatly with the favourite French quality, no men, nevertheless, could have faced death more readily than they did when ordered to assault the French in their entrenched positions; while, probably for the first time in war, skirmishers in extended order not only received the charge, but actually advanced to the attack of heavy cavalry.

It is well worth while to ask what cause lay at the bottom of this absence of discipline on the part of the French? were similar faults observed in the great wars of the first empire? and are all armies when tried by defeat equally insensible to the calls of duty? These questions are difficult to answer, because their solution lies in a correct idea of what discipline implies, and on the means by which it can be best secured. An army is only an integral part of a nation, and as such contains within itself the particular virtues and vices of its society. This is especially true of armies raised by conscription, as they necessarily embrace representatives of all classes. Now the tone of society, using the term broadly, of the French nation under the empire was eminently selfish, luxurious, and vicious. Noble aims and worthy ambitions were set aside. Material prosperity alone was extolled. The rich lived for pleasure, and neglected all the duties of their position. The poor, longing for pleasures in which their superiors indulged, and envious of their supposed good fortune, imbibed eagerly the doctrines of Socialism. Amid the many changes of government loyalty became extinct, and even party was regarded solely as a means of enriching self. The army did not escape these influences. The good feeling which in Great Britain unites class with class, and which may be observed in the village equally as in the barrack, did not exist. No common bond of sentiment united officers and men. Each acted for himself. The officers, looking for promotion, attached themselves to the party in power; the soldiers, imbued with Socialistic ideas, regarded their superiors with envy.

Another cause of an evil so novel and so strange, we believe will ultimately be found in the fact that the moral force of the conscription has at last entirely broken down. It is now considered not a blood-tax on France, but a blood-tax on the poor for the benefit of the rich. Owing partly to the spread of habits of comfort, partly to the demands for Algerine service and the frequency of foreign expeditions, but chiefly to the new development of the desire to make money, the reluctance to enter the service has of late years greatly increased; the mothers save more carefully to purchase immunity for their sons, and the whole burden of the war falls upon the poor, who again have been aroused by the liberal press and the artizans in the ranks to a perception that it is so—that equality before the law is a mere phrase. This feeling has sunk deeply into the peasantry, so deeply as to produce a deadly hatred of all who purchase exemption, and a bitter dislike of the service, and distrust of those in it who are above themselves. This feeling, which in Picardy especially has been openly manifested, has been fostered by the workmen ever since the soldiery were employed to put down strikes, and though quiet in ordinary times, breaks out under defeat with terrible violence. Then the conscript remembers that he is serving under compulsion, while the rich are exempt, and while his officer, whose mistake, as his men think, exposes rank and file to slaughter, is serving voluntarily. A spirit first of grudging, then of disaffection, and then of disgust springs up, which any accident, a defeat, a want of food, a harsh commandant, or even a severe order, may exasperate into a fury fatal to discipline and wholly incompatible with success in the field. It must be remembered that the defect of the French character, its special and persistent foible, is envy, and that the love of equality is in all classes, and more especially among the peasantry, a passion which is capable of inciting them to terrible acts, and undoubtedly fosters that spirit of Socialism which the officers complain has crept into the army.

In enumerating the causes of the French misfortunes in the war, too much stress cannot be laid upon the evils of the "exoneration" system. Formerly substitutes were procured through private offices, but as before stated, of late years this business was made a government monopoly; and it became not only the means of infinite corruption, but a source of incalculable evil to the country. In theory France had an immense army; but when actual service was required, the nation, waking from a terrible and fatal delusion, found that its forces were largely composed of mere paper soldiers. If a young man who had drawn an unlucky number did not wish to be a soldier, his parents went to the government office appointed for that purpose, and paid, say, two thousand francs. Their dear lad was exonerated. Now, it was understood that with the two thousand francs a substitute, a *remplaçant*, was bought. This was the bargain between (1) the exonerated youth, (2) the government, and (3) the nation. While the traffic in men was in the hands of private companies the government took care to have their substitutes, since they had no interest in suppressing them. But when they turned dealers themselves, their interest lay at once in a different direction. They took the money from the pockets of families, and put it into their own. The substitute money did not buy a substitute. The effect of this was that the right number of men were put upon paper. To the public, who knew nothing of the dishonest transaction, the companies of French regiments were a hundred strong; and consequently the regiments, it was believed, had each 3000 men under the flag. But, what was the actual truth? That in many instances the actual available men were not more than thirty to the company. Regiments that upon paper were at their full strength would barely muster 1800 fighting men, and some even less than this. This might almost be said to have been the key to the disasters which redden the brow of every Frenchman.

The education of the French officer does not seem calculated to create habits of command. A large number are trained in the great military schools of St. Cyr and Metz, which they enter by competition. They are then kept under the closest surveillance, and are forced to acquire in a short time a great amount of knowledge. No responsibility is allowed them, and until they become officers they are treated in a way which no English schoolboy would endure. They consequently never attain habits of command; and, as the majority do not enter from the higher classes of society, have never, even as boys, received the rudimentary training which teaches how to rule and how to obey. Another portion of the officers (nearly a third) enter from the ranks, and are selected either by favour or merit from the noncommissioned officers. These seldom attain a higher grade than that of captain, and consequently continually see young men who have merely passed through the schools promoted over their heads. Again, the staff form a distinct corps, and are almost entirely separated, even at the commencement of their career, from the regimental service. Consequently they are ignorant of the feelings and prejudices of the soldiery, and have little or no sympathy with them. In times of victory, when success glosses over defects and even crimes, all goes well. The martial spirit of the French troops carries them through difficulties and dangers; while lookers-on are so dazzled by the blaze of glory that they fail to perceive the defects which lie beneath the surface. Ambition has been always held up to French soldiers as the incentive to action. Phrases, such as the soldier carrying in his knapsack the baton of a marshal, have been repeated until it has been forgotten that those who are left behind in the race for glory may possibly feel a keen discontent, unknown to those who have been actuated by the humbler aim of doing their duty and being a credit to their regiment.

A country paying 600 million francs for its army, as France did, should have had the right of expecting itself always prepared for war, but the money was to a great extent thrown away in the pay of the generals and marshals who spent their lives at the court. The Etat Major, a body whose chief duties ought to consist in the study, in time of peace, of strategical positions all over Europe, and of reconnoitring in time of war, were officers who were not apparently up to their work. The Prussians sent usually a couple of dozen of Uhlans, as they call their lancers, using their original Polish name, with three or four officers, and if one of them came back safely with some useful information they were quite satisfied, thinking the purchase worth the expense. Thus they knew everything about the French army, while the French knew nothing about them.

The destructive and marauding habits of the French troops are well known. In the war the French villagers said they were often much worse treated by their own soldiers than by the Prussians. The difference between them and the English in this respect particularly struck General Trochu in the Crimea, and when asked how he would propose to correct this license, so common to French soldiers, he answered, "En les faisant vertueux." He had soon the opportunity of showing how far this assertion was neither paradoxical nor pedantic; for in the Italian war his division combined all the military qualities with a regard for the persons and properties of non-combatants hitherto unexampled. He began by degrading a non-commissioned officer to the ranks for insulting a peasant woman, and through the whole line of march the site of his encampment was always distinguishable by the uninjured dwellings and the mulberry trees still clothed with vines green amid the field of desolation. This power of restraining military disorder was, however, given to very few French commanders in recent years. For a long time two causes operated to the damage of the traditionally amiable and friendly character of the French soldier. The first was the prominent position given to the Zouaves, and the infection of their rowdy and violent spirit. The other, and far more serious, was the recruitment of the old soldiers. These are generally men who have failed to establish themselves in civil life, and who re-enter the army with the worst habits and principles. It may have been the hope of the originators of this system that the veterans who returned to the service would infuse into the younger portion of it certain imperial associations of which it was deficient; but the effect is acknowledged on all hands to have been most detrimental to discipline. Indeed the quiet, gay, gentle, and simple *piou-piou* (infantry soldier) of the French line became the exception rather than the rule.

The decline in the *prestige* of the French army is the more surprising from its extreme rapidity. If we only recur to 1854, we find that France then possessed a great many comparatively young officers, who had served in high positions in Africa at the time when there was still some serious fighting there; and that in the Algerian special corps were troops undoubtedly superior to any other in Europe. The numerous substitutes and re-enlistments (which latter were much encouraged by the emperor), provided a larger number of professional soldiers who had seen service, real veterans, than any other continental power. The one thing necessary was to elevate as much as possible the mass of the troops to the level of the special corps. This was done to a great extent. The *pas gymnastique* (the "double" of the English), hitherto practised by the special corps only, was extended to the whole infantry, and thus a rapidity of manoeuvring was obtained previously unknown to armies. The cavalry was mounted, as far as possible, with better horses; the *matériel* of the whole army was looked to and completed; and, finally, the Crimean war was commenced. The organization of the French army showed to great advantage beside that of the English; the numerical proportions of the allied armies naturally gave the principal part of the glory—whatever there was of it—to the French; the character of the war, circling entirely round one grand siege, brought out to the best advantage the peculiarly mathematical genius of the French as applied by their engineers; and altogether the Crimean war again elevated the French army to the rank of the first in Europe.

Under these circumstances the Italian war was undertaken, resulting in additional "glory" and increased territory to France. If after the Crimean war the French *chasseur à pied* had already become the *beau ideal* of a foot soldier, this admiration was now extended to the whole of the French army. Its institutions were studied; its camp became instructing schools for officers of all nations. The invincibility of the French became almost a European article of faith. In the meantime, France rifled all her old muskets, and armed all her artillery with rifled cannon. But the same campaign which elevated the French army to the first rank in Europe, gave rise to efforts which ended in procuring for it, first a rival, then a conqueror. The year 1870 came, and the French army was no longer that of 1859.

In point of armament, the Prussians forestalled the other armies of Europe in the introduction and use of the breech-loading rifle; but this inequality in their favour disappeared after the introduction of the French Chassepot, a weapon which will be better understood from the accompanying illustrations. Fig. 3, Plate 3, is an elevation of this rifle, the bolt being shown elevated to a vertical position, and the hammer cocked; and fig. 4 is a longitudinal vertical section of the arm, with the hammer in the position it assumes after firing, and the breech closed by the bolt, the handle of which assumes a horizontal position. The breech, *a*, is screwed on to the barrel; it is open on the upper surface, as well as on the right hand side, in order to allow of the working of the bolt, *g*. It is through this lateral opening that the cartridge is introduced. The rear face or end of the barrel serves as a stop to the front, *h*, of the bolt, *g*. The trigger mechanism, for holding the hammer when cocked, consists of two pieces, *c* and *d*, connected by a screw, *e*. The piece, *d*, tends always to project in the interior of the breech by the action of a spring, *b*, which forces upon the trigger the rear end of the piece, *c*, working on a centre at *f*. The pressure exerted upon the trigger is transmitted to the tumbler, *d*, which on being depressed releases the hammer, and allows it to act under the influence of a balance spring, and to strike the priming of the cartridge. The bolt, *g*, serves to open and close the chamber. It carries a piece, *h*, provided with a handle, *i*, for actuating it. Between the end of the bolt, *g*, and a shoulder formed on a movable head, *j*, there is fitted a washer of vulcanized india-rubber, composed of three superposed layers of different degrees of hardness. At the moment of igniting the charge the pressure exerted on the movable head, *j*, of the bolt is transmitted to the washer, which, being thus compressed, forms a perfect packing, and prevents the escape of gas. The portion which terminates the piece, *j*, is intended to form a space behind the cartridge for the expulsion and combustion of the fragments of paper which may remain in the barrel after the charge has been fired. The rear and upper part, as well as the left side of the bolt, *g*, are provided with two longitudinal slots of unequal size; the first acts as a safety notch, and the other forms the working notch. There is between the axle of these two grooves or slots a space of 90° when the breech is open. The cock or hammer is in front of the safety notch, so that if it accidentally becomes released no dangerous result will follow; it only corresponds with the working groove when the bolt closes the breech and is firmly held in its position by the handle, *i*, which will then be in a horizontal position. The bolt is also provided with a groove or notch opposed to the piece, *h*, the object of which is to permit, when charging, of drawing the bolt back without it being stopped by the trigger piece. A second groove formed on the right-hand side serves as a stop for the bolt, and prevents it leaving the breech when the screw, *r*, is in place. The hammer is composed of four parts, connected together with pins; these are, the hammer proper, *k*, the roller, *l*, the tumbler, *m*, and the spring-bearing spindle, *n*. The gun is cocked, not, as formerly, by causing the hammer to describe an arc of a circle, but by pulling it back longitudinally. The front part of this hammer terminates in an extended portion, *p*, which engages in the upper opening of the breech, and to the end of which is fixed the screw, *q*. It is this screw which, on penetrating one or other of the two grooves before referred to, brings the hammer into the safety notch, or permits it to strike the needle. The sliding of the hammer is facilitated by the roller, *r*.

The helical spring on the rod, *n*, is intended to give the impact of the needle on the priming, and has its bearing at *s*. The striking end of the needle is pointed, whilst the opposite end is fixed in a small holder, *t*. The following are the movements in using this arm, it being held in the left hand, with the butt pressed against the right side:—*First movement:*—Place the forefinger against the trigger guard, and draw back the hammer with the thumb. *Second movement:*—To open the arm, turn the lever from left to right, and draw back the bolt. *Third movement:*—To load, seize the cartridge in the right hand, and insert it into the barrel through the opening made in the right side of the breech. *Fourth movement:*—To close the arm, push the bolt forward, and turn the lever from right to left. *Fifth movement:*—To fire, press upon the trigger. In order to place the arm upon the safety notch after the breech has been closed, the handle of the bolt must be elevated so that the smallest notch in the bolt shall be opposite the hammer, which must be followed up till its screw, q, arrives at the bottom of this notch. When it is desired to fire, it is simply necessary to turn the bolt to the side and draw the trigger.

The following is a description of the cartridge intended to be used with the Chassepot arm. Fig. 5 is a longitudinal section of the cartridge. It is composed of six elements, namely, the priming, powder case, powder, cardboard wad, ball case, and ball. The priming consists of a copper cap, w, similar to those used in the army, but rather smaller. It is perforated at the bottom with two holes, diametrically opposite to each other, and which are intended for the free passage of the flame. The fulminating powder, v, is placed at the bottom of the cap; a small wad, x, of cloth or wax covers it in order to preserve it from external shock. The cap thus prepared is fitted with a small washer, y, of thin tin; this washer is connected to a paper disc, intended to form the bottom of the cartridge, when the priming will be complete. The powder case consists of a band of paper, z, rolled on a mandril, and cemented at the edges. The charge of powder introduced therein, equal to five grammes five decigrammes, is slightly rammed to give rigidity to the cartridge. A wad of card, b^1, is placed on the powder, of about two millimètres in thickness, and having a perforation therein of about six millimètres in size, through which the ends of the case, z, are pressed; the excess of paper being removed with a pair of scissors. The ball case consists of a covering of paper, c^1, making two turns round a conical mandril, and cemented at the base only. The ball, the form of which is shown in Fig. 5, weighs 24 grammes 5 decigrammes. After having placed this ball in its case, the cartridge is completed by uniting the ball-case to the powder-case by a ligature in a groove made a short distance in the rear of the cardboard wad. As a final operation, the whole height of the cartridge corresponding to the ball, less the ogive or tapered end of the bullet, is to be greased, when the cartridge will be ready for use. The Chassepot carries a sabre bayonet, and the length of the two is 6 feet 1½ inches.

The Chassepot has a longer range, but less precision, than the Prussian needle-gun. The Chassepot has an incipient velocity of 1328 feet per second, the needle-gun of only 990; but the semi-diameter of the scattering circle at a distance of 300 paces is as much as 13½ inches in the case of the former, and only 7¼ inches in that of the latter. This circumstance, coupled with the fact that the range of the needle-gun is quite as far as the eye can aim with anything like accuracy, considerably reduces its inequality as compared with its rival. Under some circumstances, however, the longer range of the Chassepot gives tremendous advantages to the troops who use it, but the experience of the war shows it to have been a superior weapon badly handled. The Chassepot allows of about ten or eleven, the needle-gun only of seven or eight discharges per minute; but as to fire even seven effective rounds per minute is beyond the capacity of the ordinary soldier, the advantage the Chassepot has in this respect is again imaginary rather than practical. It is, moreover, counterbalanced by a serious drawback; in rapid fire the Chassepot barrel has, after twelve or fourteen rounds, to be cleared of the remnants of cartridges. A really strong point of the Chassepot, the smallness of its calibre, which permits a Frenchman to carry ninety-three cartridges against the seventy-two lodged in the German pouch, has been likewise secured for the needle-gun by the alterations which have been adopted. Besides, the smaller number of cartridges is a disadvantage which tells considerably less against a German soldier than it would against a Frenchman. Far from being taught to blaze away as rapidly as possible, the German soldier is educated not to use his rifle, except when he has a fair aim; and as the instances rarely occur when "quick fire" can be of any good, troops no longer fighting in massed columns, the German soldier, upon the whole, has been found to have enough and to spare in his seventy-two shots. To meet extraordinary exigencies, however, an additional allotment of cartridges is sometimes carried in the knapsacks. The effective range of the Chassepot is 1800 paces, and that of the needle-gun only 600. Such a superiority of range was severely felt on several occasions by the Prussians in charging, when they had to traverse a distance of 1200 paces entirely exposed to a destructive fire to which they were powerless to reply. It is inexplicable, however, why the French did not make use of the boasted long range of their Chassepots to pick off the Prussian gunners on many occasions, especially at the battle of Gravelotte, where the Prussian artillery was extremely destructive.

The campaign of 1870 tried a previously unknown weapon, the mitrailleuse; but the rough verdict of war has been, upon the whole, unfavourable to the novelty. The words mitrailleur and mitrailleuse are indifferently employed to denote a class of arm which has imitated but not surpassed the mitraille or case shot fire of our present field pieces. The new mitraille is hurled by engines which avail themselves of rifling, of breech-loading, and of the skill of the mechanical engineer, and seek to prolong the scathing effects of the old case, which barely reached to 400 yards, to at least 2000; but they are not so useful as ordinary field-guns in practical war.

The principle of the French mitrailleuse will be seen from the accompanying engravings. Fig. 1, Plate 1, represents the weapon in action; fig. 2 is a sectional elevation of the weapon and carriage; fig. 3 is a section of the breech end; fig. 4 is a section of the breech end, with the block or closer drawn down, leaving the barrels free to be loaded; and fig. 5 is a sectional plan, with the cartridges in the barrels and the closer screwed home. This compound gun is composed of a series of barrels, which are fitted between plates, A A, which stretch across from one side to the other so as to firmly unite the two side plates, B B, upon which the trunnions are formed for supporting the mitrailleuse upon a carriage, so that it can be removed from place to place and employed in field operations. The rear ends of the side plates, B B, are of greater thickness than the other portions, and are slotted so that the guide plates of the closer can work therein. These plates are centred upon pins, which are kept in position without working loose by means of tappets acting upon the nuts on their ends. The breech-closer plates, G, extend a distance beyond the rear end of the barrels, and have near their ends long holes, which serve to hold secure a transverse bar, J. The central portion of the transverse bar is of larger diameter, or is thicker than the other parts, so that the threaded rod, L, which passes through it, may be turned so as to bring the breech-closer nearer to or further from the rear of the barrels. The front of the threaded rod, L, is rounded, the rounded portion being fitted between two half plates, q q.

The under side of the closer plate has lugs, v v, for carrying a pin, V, to which the upper end of a link or lever bar, U, is jointed. The lower end of the link is pinned to a lever, Q, so that the closer, when released from the barrels, can be raised and lowered upon their joint pins, H H, which are fitted in the side plates, B B. The under side of the rear of the side plates has projections for the closer to slide upon as it is being moved, and when it has travelled such a distance as to be tilted, it rests upon a plate, h, which forms part of the closer frame, G G. The front of the closer or breech block, O, has a face plate, P, secured thereto. This plate is provided with a series of holes corresponding to the number of barrels fitted in the frames upon the carriage. The holes are threaded for the reception of screw plugs or nipples, through which pins are fitted. The inner ends of these pins rest upon a disc of horn or other yielding material, so that when the explosion takes place the force of the recoil is diminished. The distance the pins may project is regulated by a washer or plug screwed into the back of the plate, P. Under the rear of the breech end of the barrels is attached one end of an elevating screw, by which the depression or elevation of the barrels is governed. The lower end of the screw works in a block or socket on the carriage.

The drawing back of the breech-closer is regulated by the hand lever, Q, and it can be retained at the required point by means of a pawl working in the teeth of a ratchet wheel fitted on the side of the frame. When the barrels are filled or loaded with cartridges, and the breech-closer brought in contact with the rear of the barrels by means of the lever handle, the fire can be communicated by means of a percussion cap or fuse or quickfire at one side of the barrel framing, which fire is instantly forced through a hole, and impinges against the cartridge case with sufficient impulse lo break it and explode the powder therein. The explosion in the barrel causes fire to be driven through another hole, which leads from the first barrel to the second, and this causes the second charge to be fired in the same manner as the first and from the second to the third barrel in succession until the whole of the barrels on that level have been discharged. The fire then passes up to a second series of barrels, placed above the lower series in succession, and in a similar manner to a third series of barrels.

The French were foremost in adopting the new weapon, but various other powers now use machine guns of different constructions, mostly embodying the principle of the mitrailleuse. The United States of America, from which, we believe, the original invention came, have adopted one known as the Gatling gun. Russia has been supplied with the same. As the British government has also favoured the Gatling mitrailleuse, we give an illustration of the gun and of its cartridges. (Plate 2, figs. 1, 2, and 3).

It is said by those who have carefully studied the subject, that when war must be undertaken it is practically less destructive to life to employ the most potent and fatal agent in its prosecution. In this view of the case scarcely any modern implement of war can equal the Gatling battery gun, which, from its wonderful powers of destruction, may be said to take rank as the foremost of philanthropists. To give the reader an idea of the character of this gun, it may be said that it can be fired, when well manned, from 400 to 500 times per minute. Its main features may be briefly summed up as follows:—First, it has as many locks as there are barrels, and all the locks revolve with the barrels. The locks also have, when the gun is in operation, a reciprocating motion. The forward motion of the locks places the cartridges in the rear ends of the barrels, and closes the breech at the time of each discharge, while the return movement extracts the cartridge shells after they have been fired. When the ten-barrel gun is being fired, there are five cartridges at all times in the process of loading and firing; and at the same time, five of the shells, after they have been fired, are in different stages of being extracted. These several operations are continuous when the gun is in operation. In other words, as long as the gun is supplied with cartridges (which is done by means of "feed-cases," in which they are transported), the several operations of loading, firing, and extracting the cartridge shells are carried on automatically, uniformly, and continuously. The locks operate on a line with the axes and barrels, and are not attached to any part of the gun; but as the gun is made to revolve, they play back and forth in the cavities in which they work, like a weaver's shuttle, performing their functions of loading and firing by their impingement on stationary inclined planes or spiral projecting surfaces. Second, it can be loaded or fired only when the barrels are in motion, that is to say, when the barrels, the inner breech, &c., are being revolved. Third, it may justly be termed a compound machine gun; since the ten barrels, each being furnished with its own loading and firing apparatus, form, as it were, ten guns in one. This is a valuable feature, for in the event of one of the locks or barrels becoming impaired, the remaining ones can still be used effectively. The Gatling also has a feeding drum into which 400 cartridges can be poured, materially increasing the rapidity of firing; and an automatic mowing movement, which distributes the fire of the mitrailleuse horizontally, and thus removes the chief fault of the French piece—a too concentrated delivery. The gun bears the same relation to ordinary fire-arms that the printing press does to the pen, or the railway to the stage coach. It may safely be said that no other gun which can be rapidly fired has so great a range and accuracy as the larger-sized Gatling guns, which have an effective range of 2000 to 3000 yards.

The Prussians, a long time previous to the war with France, tried both the Montigny and Gatling mitrailleuses, but rejected them as useless for field purposes, at the same time admitting their utility for fortresses, ditch defence of intrenchments, and defiles. In the early part of the campaign they were supposed to possess a mysterious weapon, called the *kügelspritzen*, but nothing transpired respecting its special performances. The new weapon will never supersede artillery or small arms, and it is doubtful if it will ever hold an important position as a powerful adjunct to them.

All accounts of the battles during the late campaign concur in ascribing much of the success of the Prussians to their superiority in field artillery. The Chassepot is acknowledged to be a quicker shooting and further ranging rifle than the needle-gun, and more accurate, though the excitability of French troops has apparently prevented them from making the most of their weapons. But, on the other hand, the Prussian artillery fire has almost invariably triumphed over the opposition of the enemy; and it is evident from such descriptions of battles as have reached us, that the German infantry could never have stormed the positions taken up by the enemy in every battle, but for the strong protecting fire of the guns.

The first Napoleon, himself an artillery officer, was deeply impressed with the value of field artillery. No one knew better than he how to prepare the way for the advance of his infantry by concentrating a powerful artillery fire on one portion of the enemy's position; and, what is more, his generals learnt from their great chief the art of using field artillery as a separate arm, and not merely as scattered throughout the divisions of an army. At Eylau and Friedland Senarmont handled his artillery admirably. At Friedland it is related by General Marion—

"That thirty-six pieces of artillery did what Ney and Dupont, with more than 20,000 men, had been unable to do, and what the three reserved divisions of Victor would probably not have done; in view of the steady courage with which the Russians, when their retreat had been cut off, resisted the attacks of the triumphant army, it may well be assumed that victory would have been impossible to any other arm than artillery; but Senarmont advanced his guns and obtained the most brilliant success."

It is important to understand that, though in this battle Senarmont concentrated thirty-six guns in a small space, it was only when the nature of the ground obliged him to do so. As long as he could, he carried out the great law of distributing the guns but concentrating their fire.

When rifled small-arms came into use, field artillery fell for a short time into the shade; for it became very dangerous to bring the smoothbore guns into action against infantry at short ranges, and their fire at longer ranges was, comparatively speaking, inefficient. It may almost be said that, if breech-loading rifles had been brought into use before rifled artillery, the employment of field guns would have ceased. But, as the range of the infantry weapon was increased to 600 and 800 yards, the action of the field guns was made available at a distance of 2000 or 3000 yards, while their accuracy was equally improved.

In the campaign of 1859 the French obtained great advantages by the use of their rifled field guns. In 1866 the Austrian rifled field artillery, acting independently, saved the infantry from annihilation after the battle of Königgrätz; and 1870 proved again and again the invaluable services of field artillery, culminating in the grandest achievement of modern times. At Sedan the numerous and gallant army of MacMahon, defended by the ramparts of a fortress, had to lay down its arms, not because of any immediate want of food, not in expectation of the place being stormed, but because the Prussian rifled field guns were disposed upon every hill in the neighbourhood of the fortress, at a distance outside the range of smooth-bore guns, but yet so near that resistance would only have converted the town into a slaughter-house. The battle preceding the capitulation was a great proof of the value of field artillery; for a vital position, rendered almost unassailable by the fire that came from behind its earthworks, was converted from unassailable to indefensible by the enfilade fire of Prussian rifled guns.

Sir Joseph Whitworth sent to the last Paris Exhibition two specimens of his steel field-pieces, the one a ten-pounder, and the other a three-pounder. These guns, having attracted the notice of the emperor, were sent by his desire in the first instance to Versailles, and afterwards to the camp at Châlons, for exhaustive experiment. The result of repeated trials clearly proved the great inferiority of the field guns, made of bronze, with which the French artillery was equipped in the war with Prussia, at least as compared with English steel guns. This evidence is supplied by a series of tables in the official report, in which the performances of these latter guns are compared with those of the *canon de quatre de campagne*, as regards range, lowness of trajectory, retention of velocity at long distances, and accuracy. In all these particulars the French bronze gun was much inferior to both of the steel guns, and in some respects is so inferior as to bear no reasonable comparison with them. Even at five degrees of elevation, the range of the three-pounder exceeded that of the French ten-pounder by 290 mètres, while the English ten-pounder exceeded the other by 440 mètres. But as the range increased, the inferiority of the French became much more marked. Thus, at ten degrees the French gun ranged 2350 mètres, the English three-pounder 3120, and the English ten-pounder 3320. At twenty degrees the ranges were 3480, 5000, and 5490 mètres respectively; and at thirty degrees, while the range of the French gun was but 4100 mètres, the English three-pounder had a range of 6100, and the ten-pounder 6890 mètres. These inferior ranges of the French gun are associated, as they must be, with correspondingly high flights or trajectories, rendering the aim of the artilleryman very uncertain in the field, where distances have to be judged hastily and by the eye alone. In ranging 2000 mètres the French shell rose to a height of eighty-three mètres, while the highest point of the trajectory of the three-pounder was fifty-four mètres, and of the ten-pounder only fifty-one mètres. At 3000 yards' range the *maximum* ordinate of the trajectory of the last-named gun was 136 mètres, that of the three-pounder 137, and that of the French gun 253 mètres! Those who understand the relation between a low trajectory and good aim in the field will discern the immense disadvantage of the French gun in this comparison. Not less remarkable is its want of *conservation de la vitesse*, or the quality of keeping up the power to hit hard throughout its flight; and as the penetrating effect of a shell depends upon its velocity, it is easy to see how inferior the French arm must be in this respect likewise. Its inferior accuracy is also very remarkable, especially at long ranges, but we have not space to record all the figures. Those already given are taken without alteration from the official report. It is only necessary to add that bronze is of less than half the strength of good steel, or of Whitworth metal, and that much of the inferiority of the French gun is attributable to its use; it being quite impossible to fire the full charges of powder and length of projectile from a bronze gun of given bore without speedily destroying it.

The Emperor Napoleon, after his terrible experience of the Prussian artillery at Sedan, is said to have remarked that the German victory was due to the "superiority of their artillery, not in numbers, but in weight, range, and precision." His Majesty was, however, mistaken. The Prussian field-pieces were considerably superior in number, which is almost enough in itself to account for their success, supposing them to be even equal in power and equally well handled. The word "weight" in the emperor's dictum, whether it applies to the guns or the shells, is quite incorrect, unless we suppose that the heavier class of the Prussian guns (six-pounders carrying 15 lb. shells) were opposed to the lighter class of the French guns (four-pounders carrying 9 lb. shells), a most improbable supposition, considering the enormous number of guns engaged on either side.

Superiority in range and precision the Prussian guns undoubtedly had; but it must be remembered those of the French were the first rifled guns made, and that other powers, having had the benefit of previous experience, improved upon the French model in establishing their own patterns. The main cause of this inferiority is to be found in the large bore adopted. The

French four-pounder (9 lb. shell) has a bore of 3-41 inches in diameter, and the area of the cross section opposed to the resistance of the air is, in round numbers, 9 square inches; the bore of the Prussian four-pounder (9 lb. shell) is 3-089 inches, and the area opposed to the air is 7.5 square inches. Again, the French gun, with a larger relative charge of powder of between one-seventh and one-eighth of the weight of the projectile, has an initial velocity of 1066 feet per second; while the Prussian gun, with a relative charge of one-eighth, has a velocity of 1184 feet per second. We thus see that the French shell starts at a slower rate than the Prussian, and as it opposes a larger area to the resistance of the air in the ratio of 1-27 to 1 (the shells being of the same weight), it loses its velocity much more quickly. The trajectory, therefore, is more highly curved.

The Prussian artillery has but one explosive projectile, a common shell burst by a concussion fuse. The French have common shells and shrapnel, some three-fourths of the ammunition being of the former nature, both usually exploded by time fuses. Now, all artillerymen know that common shells are most efficient when burst by concussion fuses, because the pieces of the shell are more likely to hit the object fired at when exploded on flat, hard ground, than when the shell bursts in the air by a time fuse, and because, under the former circumstances, the pointsman at the gun can see better whether his shells are bursting correctly, by observing the relative position of the cloud of smoke of the bursting charge and the front of the enemy, than when the cloud is up in the air. In addition, then, to the Prussian guns having greater range and precision, their shells during the late actions, for the reasons adduced, were more correctly burst by their concussion fuses than the French shells by their time fuses.

Another point of difference is that the Prussians fired slowly and the French quickly. The simple consequence was an immense waste of ammunition. Did not common sense show us, *a priori*, how much more efficient and in every way advisable deliberate fire is than quick fire, the English experiments at Shoeburyness have proved the point to a demonstration. The Prussian books giving instructions in laying a gun and correcting the practice are elaborate, and go to the bottom of the question. What is called "the light of nature" is in no wise depended upon. Every gunner is taught what the difference of range will be by the addition or subtraction of one-sixteenth of an inch to or from the height of his tangent scales. Again, he learns what the mean difference of range at any given distance may be expected to be. If his shell falls at an estimated distance from his enemy within double the mean difference of range, he knows that he will not improve matters by altering his elevation, as his error is within that inherent to the gun. If, after two or three shots, he finds they all err in the same way, all being too short or too long, he then alters his elevation, allowing as many sixteenths on his tangent scales as he knows will give an increase or decrease of range equivalent to the amount of his estimated error. In French drill-books the question of laying a gun is much more generally treated, and no minute instructions for correcting the practice are there to be found.

There is also a great difference in the mobility of the pieces, for the French, like the English, carry the gunners chiefly upon the waggons, and the waggons do not go into action with the guns. The men, therefore, must run on foot if they would keep up with their guns when the latter move with any rapidity. On the other hand, the Prussians have comfortable seats for two gunners above the axle-tree of the gun-carriage. The Austrians and Russians effect the same object by slightly different means. Whatever, therefore, be the speed at which the gun is called upon to move, it always carries with it sufficient men to serve it in action. This is a very considerable advantage. The exigencies of modern warfare require guns to be moved swiftly from one part of the field of battle to another; and of what possible utility are the guns if the men who serve them come up heated, breathless, and well-nigh exhausted with running?

The artillery practice of the war does not seem to have exhibited any very decided advantages to be derived from breech-loading over muzzle-loading guns. Because the Prussians, armed on the breech-loading system, have in two gigantic campaigns beaten their adversaries, armed on the muzzle-loading system, it does not therefore follow that the former system is better than the latter for field-guns. It is easy to see how false such a conclusion is, by applying the argument to the respective merits of the needle-gun and Chassepot. Because the Prussians beat the French, ergo the needle-gun is better than the Chassepot. An artillery officer standing ten yards in rear of a Prussian four-pounder battery in action, describes the loading of the guns as anything but easy, inasmuch as after each discharge the gunner had to tug very hard at the breech-closing apparatus to get it open, and that on one occasion a lever had to be used for that purpose. Proof enough and to spare has been found during English experiments, that muzzle-loading guns properly made shoot as rapidly and accurately as breechloaders; that a stronger powder charge may be used, thereby obtaining higher velocity and lower trajectory; while the simplicity both of gun and projectiles is greatly increased, and everybody is now familiar with the phrase, "What is not simple in war is impossible."

Although they did so very little with it, the French had the advantage of a navy which, for age, tradition, and size, far exceeded that of Prussia. As in the case of the army, the navy is manned by conscription; but the marine conscription is of much older date than that of the land forces, having been introduced as early as the year 1683. On the navy lists are inscribed the names of all individuals of the "maritime population;" that is, men and youths devoted to a seafaring life, from the eighteenth to the fiftieth year of age. The number of men thus inscribed fluctuates from 150,000 to 180,000. Though all are liable, the administration ordinarily dispenses with the services of men over forty and under twenty, as well as of pilots, captains, fathers of large families, and able seamen who have signed for long voyages. The law of maritime conscription was modified by an imperial decree of October 21, 1863. The decree was intended to give greater encouragement to voluntary enlistments, by allowing youths from sixteen to twenty-one to enlist for four years, in order to make themselves sailors, and those of more than sixteen and less than twenty-three to engage for seven years as apprentice seamen. Every one whose name stands on the maritime inscription continued, as before, to be liable to conscription at the age of twenty, unless he can furnish legal claims to exemption. Formerly the custom was to keep sailors on board for an obligatory period, which was generally three years, after which they returned to their homes. Many, however, finding the advantage of immediately fulfilling their full period of six years, re-engaged, in order that at the expiration of their full term they might be no longer liable to be called upon, unless by an extraordinary decree. This plan was continued, but with the modification that during the six years renewable furloughs were given, with or without pay, according to the occupations in which the men might employ themselves during such leave of absence. They were at liberty to enter into any kind of seafaring pursuit; but those who engaged in coasting or home fishery only received a quarter of the pay allowed them when on shore by way of pay, *en disponibilité*.

The ordinary number of sailors in the French navy is about 35,000, which, together with officers, navy surgeons, and other *personnel*, brings the grand total of men engaged in the service of the fleet up to 43,000. On the war footing, the number of men is raised to 66,535. From these figures are excluded the marines and coast-guard.

The progress of the French navy in the course of nearly a century is represented by the following figures:—In 1780 the fleet of war consisted of 60 first-class ships, 24 second-class, and 182 smaller vessels: altogether 266 ships, with 13,000 guns and 78,000 sailors. In 1790 the number had decreased to 246 ships, with 51,000 sailors and less than 10,000 guns; while at the battle of Trafalgar, 1805, in which the greater part of the imperial naval force was engaged, there were only 18 French men-of-war, with 1352 guns. In 1844 the navy had increased to 226 sailing vessels, and 47 steamers, with 8639 guns and 24,513 sailors; and this strength was not increased till the year 1855, when the government ordered the entire re-organization of the navy, including a substitution of iron-clads and steamers for wooden and sailing vessels.

The actual strength of the French navy at the commencement of the war was: 59 iron-clads, including 27 floating batteries, carrying a total of 810 guns; 237 unarmoured vessels, including ships of the line, frigates, corvettes, transports, gunboats, &c., mounting 956 guns; 73 paddle, steamers, with 208 guns; and 111 sailing vessels, carrying 776 guns. Total: 480 ships and 2750 guns.

The most remarkable among the iron-clads are—the *Magenta, Solferino, Couronne, Normandie, Invincible*, and the cupola ship *Taureau*, all heavily plated and armed. The *Taureau* carries a single 20-ton gun, and her deck is covered for its entire length with a cylindrical ball-proof dome, so inclined that it is not practicable to walk on it. Four of the iron-clads are turret ships; another, the *Rochambeau*, formerly the *Donderberg*, was bought from the United States for £480,000. Several are armed with heavy spurs or beaks, and all the first-class vessels can be driven at a high speed.

CHAPTER VI.

French hopes of support from South Germany—Searching Questions of the French Government for obtaining information on this point—Real State of Feeling seriously misrepresented to them—Germany thoroughly united through the action of France—Enthusiastic Meetings on the subject in various parts of Germany—Concurrence of all Parties for the Defence of Fatherland—Ultimatum of the French Government to the South German States—French Official Repudiation of any desire to make War on Germany—Decisive means adopted to prevent the Enlistment of a Foreign German Legion in France—Hopes in France of an Alliance with Denmark—Position taken by Russia and Austria—State of feeling on the War in England and Ireland—Soreness in France at the want of Sympathy for her in England—Complaints from Prussia as to England's one-sided Neutrality—Important Official Circular by Lord Granville, and correspondence between the two Governments on the Subject—Policy of the French Government towards the Press—Correspondents peremptorily forbidden to accompany the French Armies—Different system pursued by Prussia—Wonderful Organization displayed throughout Germany—The temper of the People—Contrast with the feeling manifested before the War with Austria in 1866—Enthusiasm throughout the whole country—Rapid Mobilization of the Army—Sacrifices made by all Parties—More Volunteers for the Army than could be accepted—Closing of the Universities to enable the Students to join their Regiments—The Enthusiasm spread even among Boys—Societies universally established for the Benefit of the Army and the Relief of the Wounded—Refreshment Associations formed in most towns to supply the Soldiers on their way to the Front—Assistance from Germans in Great Britain and America—No fear of ultimate defeat in Germany, but determination to become thoroughly united whatever might be the result of the struggle—Departure of the King from Berlin—Enthusiastic Demonstration—Proclamation to the Prussian people—Resuscitation of the much-valued Order of the Iron Cross—Departure of the Emperor from Paris for Metz—The young Prince Imperial and his Mother—Proclamation to the French Army—Delusions in France as to the state of preparation of the Army and what it would be able to accomplish—Change of feeling after the Emperor's Proclamation—Recapitulation of what had been accomplished in the fortnight from July 15—Composition, Numbers, and Positions of both Armies on the Frontier—The Address of the Crown Prince on taking the command of the South German Forces—Large number of German Princes in the field against the French.

WHEN contemplating the struggle which the Emperor Napoleon foresaw would be certain to take place sooner or later between France and Prussia, one of his great hopes was to obtain the support of the South German states, or at all events, to insure their isolation from the North German Confederation, and also to take advantage of the disaffection which prevailed in some of the northern provinces acquired after the war in 1866. If either the active or passive support of the southern states could have been insured, the French, by a rapid dash across the Rhine, with as large a force as could be collected, somewhere between Germersheim and Mayence (Mainz), and an advance in the direction of Frankfort and Wurzburg, would have found themselves virtually masters of the situation, and would have compelled Prussia to bring down to the Main, as hastily as possible, all available troops, whether ready or not for a campaign. The whole process of mobilization in Prussia would have been disturbed, and all the chances have been in favour of the invaders being able to defeat the Prussians in detail as they arrived from various parts of the country. With the object of ascertaining the state of feeling in South Germany, and the amount of support to be expected there, the following searching questions were confidentially addressed by the French minister of foreign affairs to the imperial envoy at Stuttgard, the capital of Würtemburg, some months before the war took place:—

1. What was the state of parties previous to the war of 1866?

2. What changes in the division of parties have been caused by the war of 1866?

3. What is the relative strength of the democratic party? What of the Catholic party, the conservative party, and the Prussian or unity party?

4. What means are employed by the various parties to promote their objects? What are their journals, their leaders, and their most important members?

5. Which party is the most popular, and has the greatest chance of success?

6. What opinions are entertained by the different classes of society?

7. Is the dynasty popular? Has it a party? Would any particular exertions be made to defend it?

8. Which have been the principal political events in Würtemburg since the war?

9. Which are the principal laws enacted since that period?

10. What has been the relative position of parties since the war in the First Chamber? What in the Second?

11. What impression has been produced in the country by the new laws enacted in consequence of the military and financial connection of Würtemburg with the North German Confederacy— viz., the army bill, the introduction of the impost upon tobacco and salt, and the new government loan?

12. Is the new distribution of the franchise in favour? Is universal suffrage liked?

13. What influence on the future of the country can universal suffrage be expected to exercise?

14. Are people satisfied with the re-organization of the army? And has it been successful?

15. How is Würtemburg situated respecting its commerce and industry?

16. What influence have recent events had upon its commerce and industry?

17. Has prosperity increased since 1866?

18. What is the amount of the Würtemburg imports? What of the exports?

19. Have the events of 1866 had any permanent reaction on the state of the money-market?

20. The creation of the Customs' Parliament, being the most important event in the last few years, what is thought of it? What is anticipated concerning its future?

21. Why have the Prussian party been defeated in the late elections to the Customs' Parliament?

22. What prevented the establishment of a South German Confederacy?

23. What are the reasons of the jealousy which keeps the South German states separate?

24. Are there any pecuniary interests opposed to the formation of a South German Confederacy?

25. Are the interests of the South bound up with those of the North? Would it be possible to separate the two?

26. Are there no ties of common interest binding the southern states to Austria?

27. Would it not be possible to create a flourishing commerce between Southern Germany and the Adriatic, and make it a connecting link between the Levant and Western Europe?

28. What is Prussia's policy towards the southern states?

29. Has Prussia abandoned the thought of German unity?

30. How is it that Austria does not seek to regain her former influence over Southern Germany?

31. What are the present politics of the Würtemburg government? What are its relations to the various political parties in the country. What attitude does it maintain towards Austria and Prussia?

32. Does the Würtemburg government regret the offensive and defensive alliance binding it to Prussia?

33. In the event of war, would the Würtemburg government side with Prussia?

34. In the event of war with Prussia, would France find any allies in Southern Germany?

35. How is the Würtemburg army disposed?

36. Why does the Würtemburg government Prussianize (*prussianiser*) the organization of its army?

37. Does the Würtemburg government intend to join the North German Confederacy?

38. What are the political opinions and tendencies of the leading members of the Würtemburg Cabinet?

39. What influence has Queen Olga on the politics of the kingdom?

40. Does Russia support Würtemburg?

41. Will the present state of things last? And what may one expect in the future?

The replies returned to these questions were generally favourable to France; and the press of the ultra-democratic party in all the southern states tended to foster the delusion by its continual tirades against Prussia. The whole of the extreme Ultramontane party went, of course, in the same direction, and did much to deceive the French government, and involved them in many of their subsequent disasters. In fact, could they have foreseen anything like that which subsequently took place with regard to this particular matter, it is scarcely credible to believe they would have ventured on war at all. It is true that now and then a journal with German affinities, scientific and religious—such as the *Temps*, for example—warned the public not to trust to German quarrels for furnishing French alliances in the hour of need; but the caution thus thrown out was quite powerless to destroy the pleasing delusion that an invading army would be hailed as liberators. In vain it was urged that a few Ultramontanes in South Germany, who hated Prussia, especially as a Protestant power, or a few discontented Hanoverian officers, were all that could be relied upon. France insisted on regarding the South German states as distinct from Prussia, and resolved to declare war against the latter power exclusively.

As soon, however, as matters had begun to assume a really serious aspect—even before the interview between M. Benedetti and the king of Prussia at Ems—Bavaria and Baden tendered an all but unqualified promise to stand by Prussia; and on July 19 the Bavarian Chambers rejected, by a majority of 101 to 47, the proposition for an armed neutrality that had been brought in by some of the Ultramontane members, and at once granted subsidies to the government to carry on the war; Würtemburg almost immediately afterwards gave in her adhesion; and immediately after the declaration of war the Saxon war minister waited upon the king of Prussia, to solicit for the Saxon army the honour of forming the van of the German forces. Only four years before, in the campaign of 1866, the Saxons were the most dangerous of all the enemies of Prussia! A great opportunity for a demonstration of the public feeling was also given at Leipzig by the performance in the new theatre of Schiller's "William Tell." Every line in which an allusion to the then position of the Fatherland could be detected was received with a storm of sympathetic applause. This was especially the case when it came to the Rüttli scene; the words of the sworn liberators:—

> One single people will we be of brothers,
> We will not part in any need or danger,

were drowned in the shouts of appreciative patriots, and the public showed equal excitement when Tell exclaimed—

> The best of men can never live at peace
> If 'tis not pleasing to his wicked neighbour.

In fact, France found to her cost, when too late, that Germany was thoroughly united, and that her action had at once done more to cement that unity firmly, than ordinary causes could have effected in several years. No sooner was war declared than enthusiastic meetings were held in many parts of Germany, with the view of expressing popular opinion on the subject, and it was unanimously resolved to withstand the aggression of France to the utmost. Some of the largest meetings were held in places in which the anti-unity party were supposed to muster in considerable strength. Thus, for instance, amongst the towns were Hanover, where many of the inhabitants cherished a lingering predilection for the old regime; Schleswig, where local interests were ever uppermost in men's mind; and Munich, whose ancient and not unjustifiable pride had revolted at the idea of being absorbed by a larger state, and of thus being reduced to a provincial town. The more notorious these places had been for the strength of the anti-unity party within their walls, the more anxious they were in the present emergency to testify to their love for the common Fatherland. If there was any town in Germany where a hostile feeling to the Prussian government had been kept up it was Frankfort. Yet this city, where the French hoped to find almost partisans enough to enact the old comedy of liberating one part of Germany from the alleged yoke of another, was among the most forward to show her hatred of the invader. On the Senate of the city asking the town council for 100,000 florins to defray certain local expenses incidental to the war, the council voted twice that sum, and offered to bear any other burdens that might be required. All the officers of the late Frankfort troops, who resigned on the annexation of the city in 1866, asked permission to rejoin the service, and in no town in Germany was more enthusiasm observable. In Munich, the old stronghold of the Ultramontanes, fifteen thousand people—nearly a tenth of the inhabitants—went to the palace and congratulated the king for siding with the North; and so many students in that city volunteered, as to obtain the permission of the military authorities to form a battalion of their own. Similar demonstrations took place at Stuttgard; in Hanover the Guelphian party, called together by their leading paper, passed a vote repudiating the assistance of the foreigner for the attainment of their purposes; in Schleswig the particularists, in Brunswick the socialists, and in Stuttgard the republicans, were likewise prompted to declare that, although opposed to the present political arrangements of Germany, they would not be outdone by any other party in defending its independence against all comers.

It was this marvellous concord between the various local and political parties which constituted the strength of Germany; this political unity, so firmly established, even before the first shot had been fired, which so completely frustrated the calculations of France. Never since the days of the Hohenstaufens had the like been witnessed. National feeling may have been strong enough long after that date, and remained a living force until it evaporated in the religious wars of the sixteenth and seventeenth centuries; but apparently there never existed such a willingness to merge local in common interests, and obey the dictates of the leading sovereign, as in the memorable summer of 1870. This intensely unanimous feeling of the people was naturally reflected in the press, and to whatever journal one refers—north or south, democratic or conservative, Prussian or Suabian—the same tone prevails in every article. Intense hatred of the French emperor and his supporters, mingled censure and compassion for the French people, and determination to put an end to a state of things which exposed to the periodical recurrence of massacres a pacific, industrious, and highly cultivated race—such are the contents of the thousands of leading articles that were then composed on the one absorbing topic of the day.

After this outburst of feeling it was of course more as a matter of form than in the hope of its leading to any practical result, that France addressed an ultimatum to the South German states, leaving them the option between neutrality—in which case their territory was not to be touched—or war, when they would be treated with the utmost severity. To the last, however, France maintained that she had not gone to war against Germany, but against Prussia, or rather against Count von Bismarck's policy. This may easily be seen from the following manifesto, published in the *Journal Officiel:*—"It is not with Germany we are at war; it is with Prussia, or, more properly, with the policy of Count von Bismarck. Careful of patriotic sentiments, and respecting the principles of nationality, the emperor and his government have never assumed towards the great German race any but the most friendly attitude. By arresting at Villafranca the victorious march of our troops, his Majesty was influenced by a desire to spare himself the regret of being compelled to fight Germany in order to liberate the peninsula. When in June, 1860, he visited Baden, he there met King William, then prince regent of Prussia, the kings of Bavaria, Würtemburg, Hanover, and Saxony, the grand-dukes of Hesse-Darmstadt, Baden, Saxe-Weimar, and the dukes of Coburg and Nassau, and by tendering them the most cordial assurances he offered loyally to those princes his friendship and that of France. When King William, in 1861, visited Compiegne, he received a cordial and courteous welcome. Previous to Sadowa the emperor wrote to M. Drouyn de Lhuys, at that time his minister for Foreign Affairs, a letter which sketched out the programme most favourable to the prosperity of the Germanic Confederation and most congenial with the aspirations and the rights of the German nation. To yield to Prussia all the satisfactions that were compatible with the liberty, the independence and the equilibrium of Germany, to maintain Austria in her great position among the Germanic populations, to assure to the minor states a closer union, a more powerful organization, and a more important position—such was the plan proposed by his Majesty. The realization of those ideas, so consistent with the desires and the interests of all the German populations, would have been the triumph of right and of justice; it would have spared Germany the misfortunes of despotism and of war. Let us compare the emperor's programme with the theories which Count von Bismarck has succeeded in carrying out in practice. For many years profound peace had existed among all Germans. For that peace the Prussian minister substituted a war which broke up the Germanic Confederation, and created an abyss between Austria and Prussia. By excluding from Germany a monarchy which was one of its principal sources of strength, Count von Bismarck was a traitor to the common country. In order to augment Prussia he sensibly diminished Germany, and the day is not far distant when all true patriots across the Rhine will reproach him bitterly for it. Not content with destroying the bonds which connected Prussia with the Germanic Confederation, he has not shrunk from brutally despoiling princes whose only crime was their fidelity to federal duties. Let the countries which have been annexed to Prussia compare their present lot with their situation before 1866. Tranquil, rich, honoured, lightly taxed, they presented a pattern of moral and material prosperity. Popular dynasties established an intimate relationship between the people and the government. To-day those countries profoundly regret their princes. Crushed under the weight of excessive taxation, ruined in the manufacturing and commercial life, compelled to leave agricultural work to be done by the women, they are now required to lavish their gold and their blood for a policy whose violence is hateful to them. Hanoverians, Hessians, inhabitants of Nassau and Frankfort, it is not enough that you should be the victims of Count von Bismarck's ambition. The Prussian minister desires that you should become his accomplices: you were worthy of a better cause. It is lamentable to behold to what lengths a monarch may be led who, instead of listening to the dictates of his heart and mind, places himself under the control of an unscrupulous minister. How far distant is the time when King William said, upon accepting the regency, 'Prussia should make none but moral conquests in Germany.' If that prince, whose intentions were loyal, and who had a respect for right, had then been told that a day would come when, without cause or pretext, he would violently dispossess the most respectable princes of Germany, or that he would seize not only the crown but the private fortune of a sovereign so irreproachable as the king of Hanover, or that in the ancient free city of Frankfort he would give a slap in the face to the long-established glories of Germany, he would never have credited such a prediction. Will he, then, not distrust a minister who only yesterday dared to reproach him for giving a courteous reception to the representative of France, and who maintained to the English ambassador at Berlin that that conduct had provoked general indignation throughout Prussia? If we have witnessed with sorrow the excesses committed against the princes of North Germany, we have not been less grieved at the treatment to which the princes of Southern Germany have been submitted. Can the peoples of Southern Germany have any ground of resentment towards France? Bavaria, immediately after Sadowa, did she not address herself to us to preserve the integrity of her territory? and did we not hasten to respond to her desire? Who was it that demanded for the states of the South an independent national existence? Who was it that desired that the sovereigns of those countries, instead of being transformed into crowned prefects, should preserve all the prerogatives of a real sovereignty, which would have been the guarantee of the independence and liberty of their states. Full of respect for the qualities of those fine populations, honest and laborious, we knew that, ready as they might be to take part in a truly national war, they would be afflicted by being called upon to join in a purely Prussian war. Our traditional sympathies with the states of the South survive even in the present war, and we hope that the hour will come when the people of those states will perceive that we were their real friends. The emperor has said so in his proclamation. He desires that the countries which compose the great Germanic race should freely dispose of their own destinies. To deliver Germany from Prussian oppression, to reconcile the rights of sovereigns with the legitimate aspirations of the people, to put an end to incessant encroachments which are a perpetual menace to Europe, to preserve the Danish nationality from complete ruin, to conquer an equitable and lasting peace, based upon moderation, justice, and right—such is the general idea which governs the present contest. The war now beginning is not on our part a war of ambition—it is a war of equilibrium. It is the defence of the weak against the strong, the reparation of great iniquities, the chastisement of unjustifiable acts. Far from being influenced by motives of rancour or hatred, we enjoy that calmness which arises from the performance of a duty, and we appeal in full confidence to public opinion, the arbiter of peoples and of kings. We desire that Germany, instead of placing her strength at the disposal of Prussian egotism and ambition, should re-enter the paths of wisdom and of prosperity. The future will prove the elevated views which govern the imperial policy, and the Germans themselves will unite to render justice to the loyalty of France and her sovereign."

This appeal was reprinted in several of the South German journals, and commented on in terms of scorn and derision. The *Darmstadt Gazette*, the official organ of the Hesse government, said that only "a born idiot" (*gimpel*) would trust the emperor. For the authorized organ of a royal government this was certainly strong language, but it only re-echoed public opinion, and was a verdict alike approved by peasant and king.

As soon as war was actually declared, the French ministers to all the minor German courts had their passports delivered to them, and even the French consuls resident in localities where military movements could be advantageously observed were requested to withdraw. At the same time, another more serious measure was taken by the government. Having ascertained that the emperor of the French intended to form a Hanoverian legion, the chancellor of the Confederacy published a decree, commanding all North Germans serving in the French army to return home without delay. Those not obeying the summons, if taken prisoners, were to be shot. The proclamation applied equally to German volunteers in the Algerian force, a class not very numerous, but which had never been entirely wanting since the first landing of the French in Africa. South Germans were also informed that they would experience the like treatment at the hands of their respective sovereigns.

In addition to their hopes of support from South Germany, the French were exceedingly desirous to enter into an alliance with Denmark—chiefly for the purpose of being able to disembark safely and without molestation a force sufficiently large for the invasion of Northern Prussia; and so far as the majority of the people was concerned such an alliance would at one time have been very agreeable, for the Danes have never forgiven the Prussians for the loss of Schleswig-Holstein. But from the first the king and the government determined on the observance of a strict neutrality, foreseeing doubtless that if Germany were victorious their country would be annexed to Prussia, and that even if victory remained with France the lost provinces could never be regained. As the news of the successive French reverses reached them a re-action set in on the part of the people, who then saw reason to be thankful to their government for not having thrown their fortunes and hopes into the same scale with France, and thus have saved them from a complete overthrow in her downfall.

Immediately after the declaration of war Count Beust issued a circular stating that, like England, Austria had not attempted to pass judgment on the question in dispute between France and Prussia, but had confined herself to recommending the withdrawal of the prince of Hohenzollern's candidature. Now that war had been declared, it was her wish to moderate its intensity, and in order to arrive at that result she would maintain a passive and consequently neutral attitude. That attitude did not, however, exclude the duty of the government "to watch over the safety of the monarchy, and protect its interests by placing it in a position to defend it against all possible dangers," and accordingly a loan of 12,000,000 florins was immediately raised to increase the army to the ordinary peace establishment.

These military preparations in Austria drew Russia into the field. For a short time it seemed uncertain whether the Emperor Alexander would be prevailed upon to side with his old ally of Berlin, or whether, in return for French connivance in the East, he would leave Prussia to fight it out single-handed, even against more than one adversary. It soon became evident, however, that if Austria came forward as an ally of France (as was thought highly probable before the publication of the proposals made to Prussia by France with regard to Austria in 1866, Russia would join Prussia and Germany. The official journal of the Russian government said, "The Czar is determined to observe neutrality towards both belligerent powers, as long as the interests of Russia remain unaffected by the eventualities of the war." The meaning of this announcement was plain. As Russia's interests in the war could be touched much more easily by Austria and France, her competitors in the East, than by Prussia, who had always been comparatively indifferent to the affairs of the Levant, it was evident that the victory of the two former powers would have been more prejudicial to her than the triumph of the latter. Such an interpretation of the official language, conclusive enough in itself, was moreover supported by direct intelligence from the Russian metropolis, and was gladdening news indeed to the Prussians, as it freed them from danger in the rear, and left them at full liberty to ward off the attack in front. To prepare for all eventualities Russian troops were concentrated on the southern confines of Poland.

At the commencement of the quarrel nearly the whole of the English press sided with Prussia. One strong reason for this was the general reprobation always felt in England towards the aggressor in a quarrel; towards him who strikes the first blow, especially when he can show no other reason for doing so than is involved in a long argumentative recrimination. It was felt, too, that with France on the Rhine and in Belgium, and with no hope of reversing the issue, England's influence as a European power would be curtailed; while a German coalition dictating terms of peace at Paris could scarcely by possibility have any demands to make incompatible with the honour and advantage of England.

There were, however, many well wishers to France, and many whose reasons for being so, as well as their openness in avowing them, were very honourable. Many, for instance, could not overcome their hostility to Prussia as the originator of the complications which indirectly led to the war of 1870, by her, in their opinion, overbearing injustice to Denmark and her well-timed assault on Austria. Many, too, were influenced by a strong sense of the loyal friendliness of France towards England for many years previously, and on them the memories of the joint contest in the Crimea acted more forcibly than the fears or jealousies of the present. And there were more than might have been at first supposed, belonging at least to the higher, if not the more powerful classes, in whose eyes the quarrel assumed something of a religious complexion. The French Roman Catholic journal, the *Monde*, assured the public the war was to be regarded as a crusade; that it was imperatively necessary, in order to check the progress of German Protestantism and infidelity. Strange as such an appeal to the God of battles in such a cause may have been, it undoubtedly struck an answering chord in many hearts in England. Such sentiments, more or less pronounced, were not confined to Romanists, but were shared by the section of the English upper classes whose feelings lead them into the nearest approximation to Rome, and whose favourite object of aversion is crude Calvinistic Protestantism. In Ireland, also, the feeling was enthusiastically on the side of the French amongst the Catholic portion of the population, but the Protestants were generally in favour of Prussia.

The fact of nearly the whole of the English press siding with Prussia created a feeling of soreness and disappointment in France, where it was said, and doubtless believed, that all the faults were on the side of Prussia; and even if it were admitted that they were equally divided, and that both sides were bent on a fight and took the first opportunity of engaging in it, the French people could not understand why England should not wish them success. They seemed to forget the great efforts she had made to preserve peace, at the request of France, which efforts were rendered of no avail, through what was generally believed in England to have been her too precipitate action, and they also appeared to lose sight of the obligations of a neutral power. The English had, however, so long been on the most friendly terms with France, that the latter could scarcely, perhaps, feel otherwise than pained and aggrieved at not enjoying their full moral support.

On the other hand, notwithstanding this general feeling in favour of Prussia, and of the issue of the proclamation of neutrality and the passing of the Foreign Enlistment Act described in a previous chapter, scarcely had war been declared than the Prussian official newspapers commenced making accusations against the good faith of England and its one-sided neutrality, accusations which soon bore their intended fruit in the shape of a marked soreness on the part of the Prussian people. The chief charges made against England were that she allowed the export of coal, arms, and ammunition to France, and thus benefited her at the expense of Germany. It was afterwards shown from official statistics, that the reports of the exportations had been enormously exaggerated, and that in reality unusually small quantities of the articles named had been sent from this country; and with the view of setting the whole matter right, a diplomatic circular on the subject was written by Lord Granville, stating that the English government had learnt with much regret that an impression existed in Germany that Great Britain was deviating from the attitude of neutrality which she had announced her resolution to observe, by giving France facilities for obtaining certain articles useful to her for war purposes, such as munitions of war, horses, and coal, while such facilities were not accorded in an equal degree to the allied German states. It was not unnatural that, in a moment of excitement like the present, the German people should be more than ordinarily sensitive in watching the attitude of nations which were taking no part in the struggle; and it could not be wondered at that they should for a time accept as facts unfounded rumours, and that they should somewhat hastily condemn as breaches of neutrality proceedings which, at a calmer season, they would not hesitate to pronounce, with that impartiality of judgment for which they were distinguished, to be strictly in accordance with the usages of international law and comity. Her Majesty's government lost no time, after the declarations of war had been exchanged, in announcing the determination of Great Britain to maintain a position of neutrality between the contending parties; and that position had been faithfully observed. It was not true that any facilities had been given, or any restrictions imposed, which were not equally applicable to both belligerents. The steps taken by her Majesty's government had been strictly in accordance with precedent, and with the principles by which neutral nations, including Prussia herself, had been guided in recent wars. But it now appeared to be wished that Great Britain should go further; and that she should not only enjoin upon British subjects the obligations of neutrality, but that she should take it upon herself to enforce those obligations in a manner and to an extent wholly unusual. It was demanded that she should not only forbid, but absolutely prevent, the exportation of articles contraband of war; that is to say, that she should decide herself what articles were to be considered as contraband of war, and that she should keep such a watch upon her ports as to make it impossible for such articles to be exported from them. It required but little consideration to be convinced that this was a task which a neutral power could hardly be called upon to perform. Different nations take different views at different times as to what articles are to be ranked as contraband of war, and no general decision had been come to on the subject. Strong remonstrances, for instance, were made against the export of coal to France; but it had been held by Prussian authors of high reputation that coal was not contraband, and that no one power, either neutral or belligerent, could pronounce it to be so. But even if this point were clearly denned, it was beyond dispute that the contraband character would depend upon the destination; the neutral power could hardly be called upon to prevent the exportation of such cargoes to a neutral port; and if this were the case, how could it be decided, at the time of departure of a vessel, whether the alleged neutral destination were real or colourable? The question of the destination of the cargo must be decided in the prize court of a belligerent, and Prussia could hardly seriously propose to hold the British government responsible whenever a British ship carrying a contraband cargo should be captured while attempting to enter a French port. Her Majesty's government did not doubt that, when the present excitement had subsided, the German nation would give them credit for having honestly acted up to the duties of neutrality to the best of their power; and they were confirmed in that conviction by the recollection that, when Prussia was in the same position as that in which Great Britain now found herself, her line of conduct was similar, and she found herself equally unable to enforce upon her subjects stringent obligations against the exportation even of unquestionable munitions of war. During the Crimean war, arms and munitions were freely exported from Prussia to Russia, and arms of Belgian manufacture found their way to the same quarter through Prussian territory, in spite of a decree issued by the Prussian government prohibiting the transport of arms coming from foreign states. Reflection upon these points would doubtless make the German nation inclined to take a juster view of the position occupied by her Majesty's government.

Some further important correspondence on the subject took place between the two governments; and although it will slightly anticipate its proper position, according to the chronological order of events, which we wish to maintain as far as practicable, we give the substance of it here, so that there may be no necessity to refer to the matter again. On August 30, the North German ambassador at London, in a despatch marked "confidential," reminded Lord Granville that English public opinion, as well as English statesmen, had unanimously pronounced the war on the part of France "a most flagitious breach of the peace." The right of Germany, on the other hand, to enter upon a defensive war was freely admitted. Germany was therefore led to expect, that the neutrality of Great Britain, her former ally against Napoleonic aggression, however strict in form, would at least be benevolent in spirit to Germany, for it was impossible for the human mind not to side with one or the other party in a conflict like the present. But in what way had England shown the practical benevolence Germany had a right to expect? It was best to reverse the question, and to put it in this shape:—If Germany had been the aggressor, and consequently condemned by public opinion, in what way could the government and the people of the United Kingdom have been able to avoid taking an active part in the struggle, and, at the same time, to prove to France their benevolent intentions? Being short of coal, the French would have been allowed to find here all they needed for their naval expeditions. Their preparations for war not being so far advanced, and not so complete as they first thought, the French would have found the manufacturers of arms and ammunition in this country ready to supply them with, and the British government willing not to prevent their obtaining here, all the material they wanted. This, Count Bernstorff thought, would have been the utmost aid which Great Britain could have granted to France, without transgressing the letter of the existing neutrality laws, had the parts of aggressor and attacked, of right and wrong, been the reverse of the present condition. Facts, however, openly boasted of by the French minister of war, and not denied by the British government—the continuous export of arms, ammunition, coal, and other war material to France—proved that the neutrality of Great Britain, far from being impartial towards that party which had been pronounced to be in the right, was, on the contrary, such as it might possibly have been if that party had been wrong in the eyes of the British people and government. Count Bernstorff did not admit that there was any necessity, in order to carry out such a neutrality as he conceived ought to have been maintained, to hamper the trade with neutral countries. Had the government declared such exportation to the belligerents to be illegal, it would have remained an exception, subject to penalty if detected. The *bona fide* trade with neutrals would not in the least have been affected thereby. But the government, far from doing this, refused even to accept such propositions as might have prevented direct or clandestine exportation of contraband of war to France; besides, it could not be admitted that such prohibitive measures could in reality damage the regular and lawful trade of the English people at large. They would merely prevent some rapacious individuals from disregarding the verdict of the nation, and realizing enormous profits, which never would have legitimately been made under ordinary circumstances. The rapid increase of the private fortunes of a few tradesmen by such ventures, could not appreciably add to the national wealth of the country. But, on the other hand, the nation could be held morally responsible for the blood which was being shed through the agency of those individuals. It would be said that the war would have ended sooner, and that fewer German soldiers would have been killed and wounded, had not the people and government of England permitted such abuses. It hardly could be seriously meant to say that the Germans were at liberty to bring each case before their prize courts, for it would be out of place thus to taunt Germany with not being mistress of the seas. . . . The policy of the British government, notwithstanding the verdict of public opinion in this country in favour of the German cause, was, if not intentionally, at least practically, benevolent to France, without there being any real foundation for the excuse that the commercial interests of the country would be seriously affected by a different course. The allusion which had been made in England to Prussian neutrality during the Crimean war was disposed of by Count Bernstorff by the remark, first that the cases were in no way parallel: but even if they were, Great Britain remonstrated at the time against the alleged wrong of Prussia. There was (Count Bernstorff proceeded) but one possible alternative. Either the complaints of the British government were well founded, or they were not. If they really were, how could it be maintained at present that the complaints of Germany were unfounded, should even the great difference of the two cases be entirely disregarded? By declaring the present grievances of Germany devoid of foundation, the British government disavowed implicitly the bitter charges they preferred at the time, and condemned the ill-feeling created by them, and partly entertained ever since in England against Prussia.

Count Bernstorff concluded by remarking, that should the position occupied by the British government in regard to Germany, notwithstanding the admitted justice of her cause, continue to be maintained, it would be difficult even for the stanchest advocate of friendship between England and Germany to persuade the German nation that they had been fairly dealt by.

Earl Granville's reply, which is dated the 15th of September, extended to twice the length of the ambassador's remonstrance. The foreign secretary pointed out that the demand for "benevolent," as distinct from impartial neutrality, was something new, and therefore it was necessary at the outset to consider what it meant and what would be its practical effect. The new principle, if accepted, could only be accepted as a principle of international law, and as such susceptible of general application. Thus applied, then, its effect would be as follows: that on the outbreak of a war between two nations, it would be the duty of each neutral to ascertain which belligerent was favoured by the public opinion of its subjects, and to assume an attitude of neutrality benevolent towards that belligerent. But such neutrality should not, as he gathered from his Excellency's memorandum, be confined to sympathy, but should be exhibited in practice; that is to say, the measures adopted by each neutral should be favourable to one belligerent, and proportionately unfavourable to the other. It seemed hardly possible to push the examination further without being met by insuperable difficulties. Where could the line be drawn between a departure from the usual practice in order to confer material advantages on one belligerent state to the exclusion of the other, and a participation in hostilities? The sympathies of nations, as of individuals, were not invariably influenced by abstract considerations of right or wrong, but swayed by material interests and other causes. Neutrals would probably, therefore, be found ranged on different sides. What would be the material relations of such neutrals? What their relations with the belligerent to whom they were opposed? It seemed hardly to admit of doubt that neutrality, when it once departed from strict impartiality, ran the risk of altering its essence; and that the moment a neutral allowed his proceedings to be biassed by predilection for one of two belligerents, he ceased to be a neutral. The idea therefore of benevolent neutrality could mean little less than the extinction of neutrality.

Earl Granville examined at length Count Bernstorff's two propositions, that the conduct of Prussia during the Crimean war was not applicable in the present argument because the cases were not parallel, and that, whether the cases were parallel or not, England remonstrated with Prussia. The foreign secretary insisted that the' cases were parallel, and then proceeded to deal with the dilemma in which it was sought to place her Majesty's government. "You observe," he says, "that Great Britain remonstrated strongly against the state of things above described, and you add that either those remonstrances were founded, or they were not. If founded, how, you ash, can the present complaints of Germany be held to be unfounded?"

Her Majesty's government do not complain, continued Earl Granville, of the Prussian government making an effort to alter a state of things which they conceive to be at this moment disadvantageous to them; but her Majesty's government are of opinion that the answers which the Prussian government made during the Crimean war more than justify the reply which, to my great regret, I have been obliged on several occasions to make, and now again to repeat, to your

Excellency. The nature of those answers will be seen on referring to the correspondence which passed at the time between the two governments, which shows also the nature of the remonstrances addressed to Prussia by Great Britain. On ascertaining that the Prussian government did not mean to restrict the export of arms or contraband of war of native origin, but intended to prohibit the transit of such articles, her Majesty's government consulted the legal advisers of the Crown as to the extent to which they would be justified in making representations founded on their rights as belligerents. The answer was clear, that her Majesty's government would be entitled to remonstrate only in the event of violation of Prussian law; and it will be found, on reference to the correspondence, that though the large direct exportations from the states of the Zollverein certainly formed occasionally the subject of representations and discussions, the strong remonstrances to which your Excellency alludes were, with few exceptions, made on the subject of the continuous violation of the injunctions of the decrees forbidding the transit of arms, which violation was so systematic that, in only one case, of the stoppage at Aix-la-Chapelle of some revolvers concealed in bales of cotton, were the customs authorities successful in interposing a check on it.

Pointing out that what Prussia seemed to require was alterations of practice and the creation of restrictions on trade in a sense favourable to Prussian interests, Earl Granville went on to dispute the statement that the policy of her Majesty's government had been practically benevolent to France, and that the British nation, which had not prevented the export to France of contraband of war and supplies useful for warlike purposes, would be held morally responsible for the blood which was being shed. Admitting to the fullest extent the difficulty of defining the rights of belligerents and the duties of neutrals, and fully recognizing that the present feeling of the German nation was under the circumstances not unnatural, Earl Granville said both belligerents entered on the war with a full knowledge of the rules of international law, and of what had been the almost uniform practice of neutrals; and each belligerent had consequently a right to expect that the existing rules and former practice would be maintained, and might with reason have complained if any change had been made. It must be remembered that obligations upon neutrals had become more strict with the progress of civilization; but the present question was one which was not raised or discussed at the Congress of Paris in 1856; and the Royal Commission, composed of some of the most eminent jurisconsults in England, who inquired into the neutrality laws in 1867, decided that to prohibit the export of munitions of war was impracticable and impolitic.

Turning next to the German specific demand that the export to France of arms, ammunition, coal, and other contraband of war should be prevented, the foreign secretary said there was no doubt that the executive had, under the Customs Consolidation Act of 1853, the legal power to prohibit the export of contraband of war; but the highest authority could be adduced to show that such exportation was not forbidden by English municipal law, and it had not been the practice to prohibit it except when the interests of Great Britain, as in the case of self-defence, were directly and immediately concerned in the prohibition: and even in some of these cases, such as the Crimean war, considerable doubts arose during its continuance whether the prohibition, when actually attempted to be enforced, was as disadvantageous to the enemy as it was inconvenient to ourselves.

Earl Granville argued that if the export of arms were prohibited a clandestine traffic would be carried on, in order to prevent which the most vexatious interference with neutral vessels would be necessary, and, with regard to coal, observed:—"Your Excellency includes coal among the articles to be prohibited, on the ground that coal is more useful to France than to Germany during the present war. This raises the question of the prohibition of all articles, not contraband of war, which might be of service to a belligerent. But if this principle were admitted, where is it to stop? In the American war no cargoes would have been more useful to the Southern states than cloth, leather, and quinine. It would be difficult for a neutral, and obviously inadmissible for a belligerent, to draw the line. It must be remembered, too, that the features of a war may change. Articles invaluable to a belligerent at one period may be valueless at another, and *vice versâ*. Is the neutral to watch the shifting phases, and vary his restrictions in accordance with them? Again, the XIth Article of the Treaty of Commerce between this country and France expressly provides that the contracting parties shall not prohibit the exportation of coal. Can this solemn treaty stipulation be lightly disregarded, as long as we remain neutral!"

In conclusion, Lord Granville said that her Majesty's government feared that no means could be devised for securing, at that moment, a calm discussion of the subject. "They by no means desire to claim exceptional rights for this country. They would be prepared to enter into consultation with other nations as to the possibility of adopting in common a stricter rule, although their expectations of a practical result in the sense indicated by the North German government are not sanguine. We took the course which appeared to be according to the dictates of practice and precedent, at a time when it was impossible to know how the fortune of war would turn. Since then France, notwithstanding the display of her usual courage and gallantry, has met with nothing but reverses. Germany has, on the other hand, given extraordinary proofs of her military ability and power, accompanied, as it has been, by continuous success. Your Excellency, as the representative of a great and chivalrous nation, must agree with me that it would not be possible that we should now change the policy which we declared to our Parliament to be usual, just, and expedient, because it was stated by the victorious belligerent to be in some degree favourable to the defeated enemy."

In his reply, dated October 8, Count Bernstorff, the North German ambassador, informed Lord Granville that he delayed answering him because he hoped the conclusion of peace might have rendered an answer unnecessary, as he would have much preferred to discontinue the controversy. As, however, that hope had disappeared for the present, he felt bound to reply. The answer which he made divided itself into two parts: a complaint that the attitude of the British government in the dispute had changed, and an endeavour to prove that the new attitude it had taken up was unjustifiable either by English municipal or by international law. What Count Bernstorff said in effect was, that up to the 13th of September Earl Granville had never questioned the German position, that the government ought to prevent the export of articles contraband of war. In answer to numerous complaints the foreign minister had asked for proofs, but none of his replies contained a positive statement to the effect that her Britannic Majesty's government regarded the traffic in contraband of war compatible with their neutrality, and that they could not interfere. On the contrary, said Count Bernstorff, it had been repeatedly left to him to search after particular cases with the means at his disposal, in order to bring them under the notice of her Majesty's government. He proceeded to say:—"After I had succeeded by my notes of the 1st, 2nd, 3rd, 6th, 7th, 8th, and 9th ult., in bringing a series of irrefutable facts before her Britannic Majesty's government, a sudden change took place. In your note of the 13th ult., while acknowledging the correctness of a large number of cases pointed out by me, your Excellency declared that the traffic, which had been quite openly carried on, was legitimate, and that the customs authorities had no power to stop it. Had her Majesty's government from the commencement of the discussion taken this standing point, they would certainly not have induced me to institute the above inquiries; and far less would they have had reason to subject the correctness of my information to a practical test. I therefore consider myself justified in concluding, that her Britannic Majesty's government, since the receipt of my memorandum, has materially changed the position previously occupied in regard to our complaints. It was unavoidable that this change should be reflected in the answer to my memorandum penned under different conditions; for I had started with the supposition that the legal means at the disposal of the executive had hitherto not been applied simply from motives of convenience. I had been under the impression that it would only be necessary to prove the serious extent of the supply of France with arms and ammunition on the part of England, in order to convince the British government that the time had arrived to make use of their powers. I had therefore not entered upon a judicial examination of the question of English neutrality, not because I had reason to shun its discussion, but merely because I had hoped that by abstaining from it I should be bringing about a more rapid practical decision, and therefore considered it sufficient to restrict myself to the practical and political aspect of the question."

In answering Lord Granville's arguments contained in his lordship's despatch of the 15th of September, Count Bernstorff commenced by denying that he ever asked from England "a benevolent neutrality." On the contrary, he said, "I have on the one hand merely given expression to my satisfaction that the public opinion had ranged itself on our side in this war wantonly thrust upon us, and had on the other hand combined with it the reflection, how difficult it is to reconcile the faith in the practical value of public opinion with the neutrality policy actually pursued by her Britannic Majesty's government." He had only wished a return from a lax neutrality, whereby one party was benefited, to a strict and really impartial neutrality. "For I am unable to admit that it is compatible with strict neutrality that French agents should be permitted to buy up in this country, under the eyes and with the cognizance of her Britannic Majesty's government, many thousands of breechloaders, revolvers, and pistols, with the requisite ammunition, in order to arm therewith the French people, and make the formation of fresh army corps possible, after the regular armies of France have been defeated and surrounded."

Before proceeding to his main argument Count Bernstorff drew Earl Granville's attention to the extent to which arms and ammunition were being exported from England to France. According to his information, which could be partly tested upon oath if that should appear desirable, the number of fire-arms shipped from England to France since his memorandum of the 30th September was treble and fourfold the number of 40,000 announced by Count Palikao; and a number of manufactories, especially in Birmingham and London, were working day and night for French agents and their men of straw. He was in possession of authenticated copies of contracts concluded between the French government and English contractors. The events of the war had quite recently delivered into the German hands an official letter of the French minister of War, dated the 18th September, to a French officer at the French embassy in London, and in which the then expected despatch of 25,000 Snider rifles was mentioned, and reference was made for the payment to the funds at the disposal of the French charge d'affaires for the purchase of arms in general. In like manner authentic proofs were before him that the export of fire-arms and ammunition to France has been thoroughly organized in some British ports.

Taking advantage of Lord Granville's own admission, that the executive had the power to prohibit the export of contraband of war, but that the practice was to make use of this right only in the interests of England, as in the case of self-defence, Count Bernstorff quoted a letter of the duke of Wellington to Mr. Canning, dated the 30th of August, 1825, and reprinted in a London newspaper immediately "after the indiscretion of Count Palikao," which, he said, refuted this assumption, proving that England, as a neutral, had repeatedly prohibited the export of arms by an "Order in Council." In one part of the duke's letter the words occur, "I am afraid, then, that the world will not entirely acquit us of at least not doing our utmost to prevent this breach of neutrality of which the Porte will accuse us."

Count Bernstorff quoted the Customs Consolidation Act, 1853, cap. 107, sec. 150, to prove that her Britannic Majesty's government had at their disposal the means to put a stop to the traffic objected to, without the necessity of introducing a new machinery of officials for the purpose. Some other sections of the same Act were referred to, and were held by the ambassador to prove that only the right intention of her Majesty's government was required. That British action in such matters varied from time to time was proved, he thought, by the different language of two instructions issued to the customs authorities of the United Kingdom on the 2nd of June, 1848, and the 8th of September, 1870, respectively. In the first, which originated at the time of the Danish-German complications, Sir Charles Trevelyan, one of the secretaries to the lords commissioners of her Majesty's Treasury, informed the commissioners of customs in a Treasury minute, that if they should be satisfied that any arms or warlike stores were embarked to be sent from the United Kingdom for the purpose of being employed in hostilities against the Danish government, they were to give instructions to prevent the exportation. On the other hand, the instructions dated September 8, 1870, were as follows:—"The board directs you, when it is supposed that arms and ammunition are being exported, to ascertain the fact, and, if so, what is the nature of the arms and ammunitions, and in what quantities, by whom, and to what destination they are to be shipped; but you are not in any case to delay the shipment longer than is sufficient to obtain the above particulars."

After quoting from the French law for the sake of proving that it was not impossible for a government to secure that articles cleared for a neutral port should really be delivered there, Count Bernstorff went on to the behaviour of Prussia in the Crimean war, respecting which he still held that, if the complaints of England against Prussia at the time of the Crimean war were warranted, those of Germany against England at the present time were at least equally well founded.

In the course of his arguments on the international aspects of the question, the North German ambassador said, "The present controversy simply centres in the question whether the refusal of her Majesty's government to prohibit the export of arms is not at variance with the still unaltered general rules of international law regarding the duties of neutrals towards belligerents, and with the laws of this country not yet repealed by the legislature for the better fulfilment of these duties. That such is the case I believe I have proved by the existing facts and the laws themselves."

The ambassador thus concluded, "As for the hope expressed by your Excellency, that the German people will in a cooler moment judge less severely the attitude of the government of Great Britain in this question than now in the heat of action, I regret that, in consequence of your Excellency's note of the 15th ultimo, added to the knowledge that our enemy is being daily equipped with British arms, I cannot share it. Should this state of things continue, I could only look forward to the soothing influence which the numerous and actual proofs of sympathy given by the English people, and the manifold testimonies of public opinion in favour of Germany and its good right, may have upon the feelings of the German nation."

In his reply to this note of Count Bernstorff, dated October 21, Lord Granville expressed a hope, that the calm discussion of the subject would not only remove present misunderstandings, but pave the way for an eventual solution. He denied that there had been since the beginning of the war a change in the policy of the British government, as alleged by the Count. "From the date of the outbreak of the war the cabinet has never hesitated as to the course which should be pursued. The views of the House of Commons were clearly manifested when, on the 4th of August, an amendment, by which it was proposed to insert in the Foreign Enlistment Act, then under discussion, a clause prohibiting the exportation to belligerents of arms or munitions of war, was rejected by a large majority; and the same opinions were shown to be held in the House of Lords in the debate of August 8, on the same bill, in which the lord chancellor, the lord privy seal, and Lord Cairns took part. I myself, in answer to a question addressed to me in the House of Lords by the marquis of Clanricarde on the 22nd of July, went so far as to express some doubts whether a policy of prohibition was advisable even in self-defence; and in the constant conversations on the subject which I have had with your Excellency since the commencement of the war, I have invariably explained to you that the new Foreign Enlistment Act neither diminished nor added to the powers of the government as regarded the exportation of munitions of war, and that it was our intention to adhere, on that point, to the usual practice of this country, which practice we believe to be in conformity with the established principles of public law."

The foreign secretary further pointed out that the mere fact of the English government having instituted inquiries into the truth of certain alleged exportations did not imply an acknowledgment that such exportations, if they had actually taken place, constituted an offence on the part of England. These inquiries were called for by the "wild rumours" which were in circulation, and by the anxiety of the government to make sure that the shipments of arms were not of such a nature as to bring them within the operation of the clauses of the Foreign Enlistment Act, forbidding the despatch of store-ships or the fitting out of military or naval expeditions. Independent information from the customs officials, from the Board of Trade, from the police, and from the small-arms department of the War office, must, of course, be more trustworthy than information from the sources to which the German government had access, and Lord Granville could not, of course, suppose that any importance would be attached by his Excellency to reports given in return for pecuniary rewards.

After reminding the Count that his former "series of irrefutable facts," as he called them, had nearly all been shown to be quite unfounded, Lord Granville proceeded to demolish his fresh accusations. Count Palikao's statement, as reported in the *Journal Officiel*, was merely that arms had been ordered *à l'étranger*, not in England; no trace could be discovered of the order ever having been received in this country, and it was certain that if it was received it was not executed. Again, full returns showed that the supplies of arms drawn by France from the United Kingdom, between the two specified dates, were less than those drawn by her from the United States. This reference to the United States suggested an expression of surprise that a monopoly of the German complaints have been reserved for Great Britain, while the exports from the United States and the positive assertion of the president of the privileges of neutrals had elicited no remark from the North German government. In conclusion, Lord Granville congratulated his Excellency on having withdrawn from the untenable doctrine of "benevolent neutrality," for though "good offices may be benevolent, neutrality, like arbitration, cannot be so;" and, repudiating all jealousy of German unity, repeated his assurance of the friendly and sympathetic feelings of Great Britain towards Germany.

From the first the French government adopted the policy of keeping the public as much in the dark as possible with regard to the progress of events, and an Act was passed inflicting heavy fines and suspension on any newspaper which published war news other than that supplied officially. This measure raised such a protest from the journals of all parties, that the government were obliged to give way to the extent of allowing them to deal with all the past events and accomplished facts of the war, and only to abstain from revelations which might possibly be useful to the enemy. Nothing, in fact, was to be said of "operations and movements in course of execution," but as regarded other matters the papers were free to discuss and publish them. Formal orders were, however, issued by the emperor that no journalist whatever, French or foreign, was to be permitted to accompany the army, and very many who attempted to do so were arrested as spies, and in some cases treated with considerable severity. His Majesty's feeling was that the encounter would be so severe, that he could not afford to give the enemy even the slightest, and, apparently, most superficial advantage; and he believed that assistance furnished to the opposite side by a band of correspondents in the French camp, eagerly reporting whatever news they could pick up, would be by no means slight. However much this might have been the case with some of the less thoughtful of the French writers, the experience obtained in all previous wars in which duly authorized English correspondents had been permitted, might have convinced him that his fears were groundless so far as they were concerned; and it is undeniable that the belligerent from whose camp the most minute and well-written intelligence is forwarded, is sure to obtain the greatest amount of sympathy as regards neutral nations. In the present instance the exclusion of impartial and friendly representatives of the press from the French armies is to be especially regretted, as it prevented that full record of their gallant conduct from being given to the world which would otherwise have been obtained, whilst shortcomings would have been more fairly extenuated, and the blame of disasters would have been more conclusively laid where it was to a great extent due—not on the brave soldier, whose conduct in most of the earlier battles at least was beyond all praise, but on the incapacity of those in supreme command.

Before the actual outbreak of hostilities, the Prussian government felt it necessary to warn the press of their country against publishing matters which would not only be likely to direct the enemy's attention to supposed weak points in their line of defence, but which might show him the ways and means by which he could best profit by this information. They, however, as in the war of 1866, freely permitted duly authorized representatives of the press, both English and German, to accompany the armies, relying on their good judgment for suppressing anything which was likely to prove of service to the enemy; and as a natural consequence, we have such a true and faithful record of the war, as could not possibly have been obtained by any other means.

The wonderful combination of activity and quiet which characterizes Prussian institutions, were peculiarly remarkable during the days occupied in sending the troops to the front; and nothing could possibly have been more admirable than the manner in which the railway transport was worked.

On July 17 orders for the mobilization of the army were issued from Berlin, and within a fortnight there stood massed on the French frontier upwards of half a million of men, with all the supplies and provisions needful for such a host. Incessantly, by day and by night, hourly, and in some instances half-hourly, trains filled with soldiers, horses, and artillery ran on the three main arteries of railway communication that converge on the Rhine district. From every part of Germany the available rolling stock was impressed into the service of transport, and, with a regularity and punctuality which amounted almost to perpetual motion, at identical intervals, long trains laden with men and stores hurried along the lines towards the central stations which constituted the points of disembarkation, in a curve extending from Bingerbrück to Rastadt. But if the celerity and perfect system exhibited by so rapid a concentration were astounding, there was something yet more deserving of admiration, and something yet more significant of the temper in which the struggle was being entered upon, in the frame of mind universally exhibited by the soldiers and the population. What made this especially noteworthy was its contrast with the disposition exhibited in 1866 on the outbreak of the war against Austria. On that occasion demonstrations were made against the war by corporations, by mercantile communities, and, in more than one instance, by the landwehr regiments summoned from their avocations of peaceful industry by a then unpopular minister, to fight for his ambitious aims against an empire of German affinities and German relations. But now from one end of the country to the other the movement was one of spontaneous, heartfelt, undeviating, and unlimited enthusiasm, but an enthusiasm manifested in a calm, collected, and earnest way, which had in it no swagger and no levity. In fact, although the excitement among such usually quiet persons was wonderful, what Macaulay said of the Prussians fighting at Leuthen was equally true now—their excitement was shown after the fashion of a grave and earnest people. The sternness of their military organization, which inflicts death for desertion or disobedience, was not needed, for all were willing; but the sternness made men prompt, and in all parts of the country the same spectacle was presented; the announcement of war arrived at noon, at night came the summons to all enrolled citizens, and the next day all those of the youth who were liable, ready as veterans, and as skilled, were on their way to the headquarters of their divisions. Entering at one gate of the barracks, clothed in every variety of mufti, they emerged in a few moments from the opposite entrance in complete uniform, with their trusty needle-gun in hand, ready, without the least confusion, to take the place in the ranks they had occupied during their period of training. Never, probably, in the history of the world had anything more striking been observed than this great military exodus; for it was literally the exodus of a people going forth to do battle in defence of their own, and in what they believed to be a holy cause. To show, however, how grossly the French people were deceived on this, as on most other points, at this time, it may be as well to quote a despatch sent from Metz to the *Gaulois*, a very widely circulated Paris newspaper, on July 21st:—"Calling out of the landwehr difficult; conscripts weep; great fear of the French, especially of the Turcos; they are carried off by force in waggons."

To those not specially conversant with the social condition of Prussia, it would be difficult to realize the intense personal sacrifices of such a mobilization as that of 1870, which invaded almost every household that comprised male members in the bloom of life, and brought under arms a million subjects of the North German Confederation. It was needful to be on the spot to have brought home to your mind in all its force the full practical working of such a system that so sharply, and without distinction of persons, gathers in all liable to service, whatever might be their social position. Of course such a summoning to arms strikes heavily, not merely individual existences, but also the country, through the disturbance it creates in many industrial establishments. By way of exemplifying the public loss, it is known to every one what an enormous foundry is that of M. Krupp, at Essen, in Rhenish Prussia. Nearly 8000 workmen are employed in it, and of these on the present occasion no fewer than 1500 had to join their colours, to the great loss of the foundry, as they were the skilled and absolutely indispensable artizans. Yet nowhere did the least murmuring arise among the population at the calls imposed on them. Nobles and peasants, men and women, were all equally determined, and ready to make the greatest sacrifices. Those amongst the male population of the proper age, who found themselves forcibly exempted from service for infirmity, frequently had recourse to various devices to obtain admission into the ranks, and those only were disheartened who were doomed to remain in fortresses, without any prospect of facing the enemy.

Volunteers flocked to the army in thousands, but most of them were not accepted, as there was no need for more than those who could be legally called upon. No less than 400 young men, all just below the regulation age, asked permission to volunteer into one regiment at Berlin—the 1st Dragoons. Several of the universities had to close on account of the students leaving to join the army in such large numbers; in fact, the movement which converted incipient scholars into warriors extended even to the first form of the grammar schools. In Glogau alone fifty "Gymnasiasten" left Sophocles for the stern realities of life; at Berlin, Trèves, Cologne, &c., many more flung Cicero into the corner and put on the spiked helmet, in proof that the lessons of civic virtue inculcated into their ripening minds by the classics had not been thrown away upon them. The enthusiasm even caught boys (as in the time of the Crusades), and on one occasion seventy-two of them concealed themselves under the seats of the railway carriages going from Berlin to the PJüne. The boys, from ten to fourteen years of age, wanted to enlist, and cried with vexation when they were discovered and pulled out of their hiding places.

For that part of the population physically incapacitated from taking the field, but financially able to contribute to the expenses, the establishment and support of relieving societies became an earnest and well-observed duty. In every town, and almost in every street, offices were opened for the reception of subscriptions and of the thousand-and-one articles which an army in the field or a soldier in the hospital stand most in need of. Wine, coffee, extract of meat, lint, linen, stockings, and cigars, were the principal commodities brought forward; and to regulate and control the action of the many local societies established for this purpose, some central commits tees, all co-operating with each other, were set afoot in Berlin. To give a tangible reward to courage, at least fifty gentlemen offered prizes to soldiers who might capture French flags and cannon. In most towns refreshment committees and associations were established for the purpose of providing refreshments for the soldiers as they passed through, and it was a very touching sight to see the little maidens, and boys and old men with red and white rosettes and ribands, with their baskets and trays, distributing the supplies.

Congratulatory telegrams and promises of assistance were also received in large numbers from Germans in America; those resident in St. Louis alone telegraphed to the speaker of the Federal Parliament that they would send him a million dollars as their contribution to the expenses of the war. In many parts of the United Kingdom, too, enthusiastic meetings were held and large sums subscribed, and most of those residing in this country who were liable to serve in the army, left to join it of their own accord, and before the notices from their government could possibly have reached them.

Throughout the whole of Germany the idea of defeat—ultimate defeat—seemed out of the question. Whatever happened, people said, they must ultimately be the gainers. Whatever success might attend the French arms, it was utterly impossible that France could retain possession of an inch of German soil. Were the whole country to be overrun and the nation paralyzed for a time, the struggle would be renewed again and again until Germany was free once more. Should, on the other hand, their efforts be crowned with that success which a just cause merited, and which they confidently believed would attend them, then would victory over a common foe be the keystone of German unity, binding all the Fatherland into one whole and undivided nation. But even if the fortune of war were against them, if reverses followed and the blood of thousands of their countrymen were poured out for hearth and home—still would their newborn unity, baptized in that blood, bound and sanctified by the bond of common suffering, rise triumphant at the last, so firm, so fixed, that no petty jealousy, no internal quarrels, could ever again cause dissension among them.

The king of Prussia left Berlin for his headquarters at Mayence on the evening of 31st July, his departure being made the occasion of a most moving popular demonstration. The way to the station was lined with a dense crowd of enthusiastic subjects, who gave vent to their feelings in the most unmistakable manner. His Majesty was accompanied to the station by the queen, who graciously responded to the cheers of the public, but was unable to repress her tears at the thought of the perils her husband was about to encounter. At the terminus, which was decorated with flowers, and occupied by an immense multitude, the king was received by General von Moltke and Count von Bismarck, his military and diplomatic premiers. As on a preceding occasion of a similar nature, the well-matched couple were to be his companions in the coming eventful journey. It was a moving scene when the king embraced his queen, when all voices were hushed while the two were shaking hands for the last time, and when the hurrahs which had momentarily ceased thundered forth again directly his Majesty had taken his seat in the carriage. His Majesty evidently suffered from feelings of deep emotion, which he could with difficulty restrain. For some days previous—in fact, since the declaration of war—it was noticed that he was not in his usual joyous spirits. He spoke with devout confidence, and trusted in the justice of his quarrel, but nevertheless appeared unusually grave. Count von Bismarck and General von Moltke, as well as the king, became the heroes of a perfect ovation before they could enter their carriage.

Before his departure the king issued the following proclamation:—

"To my People!—On my departure to-day for the army, to fight with it for Germany's honour and the preservation of our most precious possessions, I wish to grant an amnesty for all political crimes and offences, in recognition of the unanimous uprising of my people at this crisis.

"I have instructed the minister of state to submit a decree to me to this effect.

"My people know, with me, that the rupture of the peace and the provocation of war did not emanate from our side. But being challenged, we are resolved, like our forefathers, placing full trust in God, to accept the battle for the defence of the Fatherland.

"WILLIAM."

How much in earnest the Prussians were in all military matters was proved by his Majesty on his journey, which occupied thirty-six hours from Berlin to Cologne. The distance in ordinary times occupied only twelve hours; but though the king was the passenger, and was an aged gentleman to boot, who must suffer severely from the fatigue of a long journey, the arrangements for the transport of the troops occasioning the delay were not in the least interfered with. Before military law all Prussians are equal, the king not excepted.

His Majesty arrived at Mayence on August 2, and at once issued the following proclamation to his army:—

"All Germany stands unanimously in arms against a neighbouring state, who has surprised us by declaring a war against us without any motive. The defence of the threatened Fatherland, of our honour and our hearths, is at stake. To-day I undertake the command of the whole army, and I advance cheerfully to a contest which in former times our fathers, similarly situated, fought gloriously. The whole Fatherland, as well as myself, trusts confidently in you. The Lord God will be with our righteous cause."

His Majesty also revived the Order of the Iron Cross, than which, among all the orders and medals of honour known to history, none have ever shown more brightly or decorated its bearers more gloriously. It was first instituted on March 10, 1813, by Frederick William III., and was conferred only for gallantry against the French. Its very simplicity and lack of intrinsic value were intended to bring back to memory the hard iron times by which it was called into existence, the terrible hand-to-hand fight with an over powerful enemy, and the noblest treasures of a nation that were to be regained by the war: freedom and independence of the Fatherland, moral and political honour, security of the fireside, of the family, of law, and of religion. Thousands of these iron crosses were distributed among the patriots who, fired with the love of country, and full of indignation against the foreign usurper, performed deeds of intrepid valour and noble self-sacrifice. The cross insured its wearer a small pension, but especially the grateful esteem and reverence of his countrymen. Fifty-five years, however, had elapsed since the close of the war which called it into existence, and the large number of knights of the iron cross had consequently dwindled down to a small handful, while the comparatively small number of iron crosses transmitted to the present generation were beginning to be looked upon as relics of a great and glorious age, and the time did not seem to be far distant when the only iron cross on exhibition would be that of Blücher, which is preserved in the historical museum in Berlin. The few survivors who were entitled to wear them were, in late years, on all public occasions treated with the honours accorded to the high dignitaries of state.

The only difference between the old and the new cross of iron is in the initials of the king, and the number of the year, 1870, being used instead of 1813—14; in all other respects, and also in the classes of the order, the new order is exactly like the old. The form of the cross is the same as that of the order of the Teutonic knights, the founders of old Prussia. It is made of black cast-iron with silver borders. As when first instituted, the order included two classes, with a grand cross as a third; but the latter could only be conferred on a general in command for gaining a battle, capturing a fortress, or some such decisive exploit. Had anything in the world been possible to have increased the enthusiasm and valour of the Prussian soldiers of all ranks during the forthcoming campaign, it would certainly have been the resuscitation of this much-coveted order of the iron cross.

On Wednesday, July 27, a decree was published appointing the empress regent during the absence of the emperor, and on the following day his majesty left Paris for Metz, for the purpose of assuming the command. Instead of proceeding publicly through the city, as was at one time intended, his departure was conducted as privately as possible, which proceeding had a bad effect on the lower orders, who inferred from it that he did not go willingly, or that his health was bad, and also indulged in some other unfavourable suppositions. He was accompanied by his only child, the Prince Imperial, only fourteen years of age. The latter had previously worn his hair rather long and curling, but just before his departure he had it cut to the French military regulations, which was not quite so becoming, but which his mother thought suited him extremely well. Before leaving he gave a lock of his hair to all the ladies of the palace. The empress superintended the preparation of the young soldier's "kit," and packed his trunk with her own hands. As usual on occasions when firmness and energy were required, she showed to great advantage—bearing the parting with much fortitude, and replying cheerfully to those who condoled with her on the separation. It was right, she said, that the prince should thus early begin his apprenticeship to the noble profession of arms, and prove himself worthy of France, of the name of Napoleon, and of that of the valiant race of Guzman, from which, on her side, he sprang.

The emperor was enthusiastically received on his arrival at Metz, and immediately issued the following proclamation to the army:—

"Soldiers,—I am about to place myself at your head, to defend the honour and the soil of the country. You go to fight against one of the best armies in Europe, but others which were quite as worthy have been unable to resist your bravery. The same thing will occur again at the present time. The war which is now commencing will be a long and severe one, since it will have for the scene of its operations places teeming with fortresses and obstacles; but nothing is too difficult for the soldiers of Africa, the Crimea, China, Italy, and Mexico. You will again prove what the French army, animated by the sentiment of duty, maintained by discipline, and inspired with love of country, can perform. Whatever may be the road we take beyond our own frontiers, we shall everywhere find glorious memorials of our fathers. We will prove ourselves worthy of them. All France follows you with her ardent wishes, and the eyes of the world are upon you. The fate of liberty and civilization depends upon our success.

"Soldiers,—Let each one do his duty, and the God of armies will be with us.

"NAPOLEON.

"THE IMPERIAL HEAD-QUARTERS, METZ, July 28."

This proclamation had an important effect in France. As stated in a previous chapter, when war was first declared, it was openly announced that for four years France had been specially providing for the crisis which had now arrived, and therefore it was presumed that little remained for her to do. General Leboeuf, the responsible minister for war, on being interrogated by his imperial master as to the efficiency of the army, replied with epigrammatic brevity, "Nous n'avons qu'à ouvrir nos armoires." The military wardrobe of France was complete: all that was necessary was to place the army in the field. For this purpose the network of rails which connected the capital with the eastern provinces was more than sufficient. The activity and precision, it was said, which on all former occasions had distinguished the French military system, would suffice to concentrate an army on the frontier which, before the slow and ponderous forces of the North German Confederation could be mobilized, would be prepared to enter at once upon its triumphal progress to Berlin. The *matériel* of the French army was magnificent. The common soldier was armed with the Chassepot, which had worked such marvels on the field of Mentana. The majority of the staff, from the imperial commander downwards, had learnt the art of war at Magenta and Solferino, or beneath the burning sun of Mexico. Many had distinguished themselves at Alma and Inkermann, and had gathered laurels at the glorious storming of the Malakoff. The cavalry of France was the finest in the world. Her artillery had no superior and few equals. The habits of organization so distinctive of the French people, had been exercised to perfection in the civil departments of her forces. The commissariat was more than equal to any strain that could be put upon it. Above all and for the first time, the mysterious and dreaded *mitrailleuse* was to assist the chassepot and the field gun in clearing the way to the capital of Prussia. That the enemy would content itself with harrassing the flanks of the steadily advancing legions was possible; that it would offer compact resistance in the open was an idea too absurd to be entertained for a moment. It was true that the battle of Sadowa was still fresh in the memories of men, where the Prussians beat the Austrians. But then the Austrians were at best, and notwithstanding their magnificent appearance on parade, merely an inferior kind of Prussians. Germans might beat Germans, but nothing could contend against the *élan* of the French soldier in the peculiar tactics of the Zouave and the Turco. (The employment of the latter troops by France in a purely European contest, was considered by many a disgrace to her, and a strange commentary on the emperor's proclamation, describing the war as a "mission of civilization" on the part of France.)

The estimate by which the French soldier was taught to gauge his German antagonist was well illustrated in the pages of *Charivari*, where a Turco, with laboured politeness, thus addressed Count von Bismarck:—"Pardon, m'sieu, peut être vous me croyez un nommé Benedek." In another cartoon a French soldier was represented working a mitrailleuse; in the distance was a field covered with dead Germans, and the soldier was made to exclaim, "Dear me, I have only been working ten minutes, and the battle is over; I suppose I must have turned the handle too fast." With these feelings so general in France, it is perhaps no wonder that M. Ollivier, the head of the government, surveyed General Leboeuf's preparations for a holiday campaign with conscious pride; and that the "lightness of heart "with which that statesman said he entered on the campaign should have found a ready echo in the feelings of his too confident countrymen.

As another specimen of French arrogance at this period, we may quote a few fines from a thoroughly representative and able Frenchman, M. Edmond About, who was sent to the seat of war as correspondent for the *Soir* newspaper, and whose letters to that journal obtained an exceedingly wide circulation. He thus described the passage of the first French soldiers across the Saar:—"Our advanced posts are in Prussia: they mean to pass the night there. Not only have we violated the inviolable soil of Germany, but the French soldier even prepares to sleep quite comfortably upon it. An event so overwhelming does not astonish, or excite, the manly population of this place. No one seems greatly moved at hearing, or even seeing, that our troops have crossed the frontier. If it were our territory, ours, that was invaded, every man would be furious; every pulse would give 120 beats to the minute; that fatal day would engrave itself ineffaceably in the recollection of every spectator. But it seems as if the neighbouring territory were made to be conquered right away, and confiscated in a trice. Tradespeople and the peasantry, like the soldiers, seem to think the thing quite natural. They have made no more ceremony about taking the country of ale than about drinking a glass of its brew. The enemy's bayonets shine by their absence on the horizon. We are free to suppose that the army of King William has chosen another field of battle, and does not mind abandoning the provinces to us."

The importance, and still less the possible duration of the war, was for some time by no means clearly apprehended in France. The popular idea put into popular language, was that France was about to send her army across the frontier to give the Prussians a good lesson, the result of which would be, perhaps, a territorial aggrandizement on the Rhine, and certainly, what was far more important, the recognition of French military supremacy by the rest of Europe. The notion of the war going beyond its professional limits, of war on French soil, of war involving not only the possibility of national gains, but the risk of national losses—of war, in a word, with its horrors and its hazards, entered very few heads. Moreover, as has already been stated, though a fight with Prussia for military supremacy was not only admitted but desired, it is an undeniable fact that war with united Germany, a battle of nations, was never contemplated by the vast majority of Frenchmen. When, therefore, in his "Proclamation to the Army," the emperor spoke of the war being a "long and severe one," it came as a discouragement to the country at large, and as the time to commence drew nearer, the immense difficulties of the enterprise revealed themselves, confidence diminished, and the directors and promoters of the vast operations thought it prudent to be less sanguine in their assurances.

After his arrival at Metz, the empress telegraphed to the emperor, saying she desired to come to see him, to embrace her son, and to show herself to the army and endeavour to increase the enthusiasm for the war, as it was apt to be increased on such occasions by a woman's presence. She had previously gone to Cherbourg, to be present at the departure of the fleet for the Baltic. The emperor replied, thanking her for her wishes and intentions, but requesting her not to carry them out, as he should have left Metz before she could arrive there, and he was unable to tell where she would be able to find him.

We have now traced the events connected with the war to the time at which the armies of France and Germany were brought face to face, in the valley of the Saar, to commence the struggle which was to decide for this century the leadership of Europe; and have described, as impartially as possible, the different feelings by which the inhabitants of the two countries were animated. The emperor of the French had allowed his great adversary, whose fearful strength, as we have already seen, scarcely any one in his empire but himself seemed to have thoroughly comprehended, to secure the fourteen days which was all he needed for preparation. And what had been accomplished in those fourteen days? In a silence like that of the grave, silence absolutely without precedent, and explicable only by a willing submission to an inexorable rule,

Germany, from Memel to the Lake of Constance, rolled itself together in arms to bar the invader's road; the whole country was turned into a camp, her youth, *en masse*, into soldiers, and her cities into fortified positions. More than a million of men, three-fourths of them (on July 14) peaceful citizens, scattered over countries many times the size of England, had flung down their tools, stepped silently into places marked out for them for years, and on railways, turned at an hour's notice into a branch of the transport service of the state, had been carried as fully-equipped and organized soldiers to points selected for their rendezvous by Baron von Moltke years before. Through great provinces, which but a short time before were independent; amidst "tribes" divided or hostile for centuries; using governments whose manifestoes against Prussia were hardly dry as trusted instruments—the splendid Prussian organization had worked as smoothly as some magnificent machine.

Before proceeding to describe the first engagements between the two armies, a short description of the armies themselves, and the positions they occupied, will be useful.

The following was the number and position of the French army about the fourth week in July:—

	Infantry.	Cavalry.	Guns.
IN FIRST LINE.			
Strassburg, 1st Corps, MacMahon,	35,000	3,500	90
Bitsche, 5th Corps, De Failly, . . .	26,250	2,600	72
St. Avold, 2nd Corps, Frossard, . .	26,250	2,600	72
Thionville, 4th Corps, L'Admirault,	26,250	2,600	72
. . . .			
IN SUPPORT OF THIONVILLE AND ST. AVOLD.			
Metz, 3rd Corps, Bazaine, ...	35,000	3,500	90
IN SECOND LINE TO SUPPORT EITHER FLANK: MOVED AFTERWARDS TO METZ.			
Nancy, Imperial Guard, Bourbaki. . .	16,650	3,600	60
Forming a grand total of,.	165,400	18,400	456
IN RESERVE.			
Forming at Châlons—			
6th Corps, Canrobert, ...	35,000	3,500	90
Cavalry Reserve, ...		6,250	36
Forming at Belfort—			
7th Corps, Felix Douay	26,500	2,600	72

Total Reserve, ...	61,500	12,350	198

The above force, numbering altogether 226,150 infantry, 30,750 cavalry, and 654 guns, together with the African army of from forty to fifty thousand men, one division watching the Spanish frontier, and the troops destined for the Baltic expedition, exhausted all the regular troops of France immediately available. Outside these were the fourth battalions, very imperfectly drilled, and the garde mobile, totally untrained, which supplied the only means of increasing the strength of the army in the field.

Looking at the positions of the different corps d'armée on the map, it will be seen that they possessed remarkable facilities for concentration and mutual support by means of frontier railroads; Strassburg, Bitsche, St. Avold, Metz, and Thionville being all situated on the same line of railroad, while a second line in rear of the first placed Strassburg in communication with Nancy and Metz by Saverne, Sarrebourg, and Luneville. Strassburg and Nancy, again, communicated to their rear by two railroads, placing both these towns in connection with Belfort, where Felix Douay's corps was and with Lyons; while Nancy and Thionville respectively communicated with Paris by two railroads, the one passing by Toul, Vitry, Châlons, and Epernay; the other by Montmèdy, Mézières, Rheims, and Soissons.

Thus the French were in possession of railroad communication all along their strategical front, as well as to their rear from the centre and from both flanks; and their general position was strengthened by the strong fortresses of Metz and Strassburg, by the forts of Bitsche, Petite Pierre, and Phalsbourg, blocking passes over the Vosges mountains; and by the fortified places of Thionville and Toul, both on the Moselle river, and both commanding railroads which lead to Paris. Strassburg was the base of supply for MacMahon and De Failly on the right; Metz for the remainder of the army.

The German army consisted of:—

1st or East Prussian Corps,.	General	Manteuffel.
2nd Pomeranian, ...	"	Fransetzky.
3rd Brandenburger, ...	"	Von Alvensleben II.
4th Prussians, Saxons, and Thuringians, . . .	"	Von Alvensleben I.
5th Poseners, ...	"	Von Kirchbach.
6th Silesians, ...	"	Von Tümpling.
7th Westphalians, ...	"	Von Zastrow.
8th Rhineland, ...	"	Von Göben.
9th Schleswig-Holstein, ...	"	Von Manstein.
10th Hanoverians, ...	"	Von Voigts Rhetz.
11th Hesse and Nassau, ...	"	Von Böse.
12th Saxons, ...	"	the Crown Prince of Saxony.

The Guards, under Prince Augustus of Würtemburg, and the armies of South Germany—Bavaria, Würtemburg, Baden, and Hesse Darmstadt.

These forces were divided into three armies as follows:—

First Army.—The army of the Saar, under General von Steinmetz—the 7th and 8th and part of the 10th corps, and the 4th or Brandenburg division of cavalry, with thirty-one batteries of artillery. Total strength, 70,000 men and 186 guns.

Second Army.—The army of the Rhine, under Prince Frederick Charles—the 1st, 2nd, 3rd, 4th, 9th, 10th, and 12th corps, the Hesse Darmstadt division, the garrison of Mainz, and the 1st, 2nd, 4th, 10th, and 12th cavalry divisions, with 110 batteries of artillery. Total, 250,000 men with 660 guns.

Third Army.—The army of the South, under the crown prince of Prussia—the corps of the Guard, the 5th, 6th, and 11th corps, with the 6th cavalry division, the Würtemberg, Baden, and Bavarian contingents, and 110 batteries of artillery. Total, 250,000 men, with 660 guns.

The total strength of the three German armies was therefore 570,000 men, with 1506 pieces of artillery.

In addition to these immense forces there were 200,000 men in the second line, between the Rhine and the Weser; 150,000, under General von Falkenstein, in the coast provinces in the North; and 150,000 in garrison eastward, especially in Posen and Silesia. This gives a total of 1,070,000 troops in actual readiness. The numbers, as numbers of efficients, seem almost incredible, but they correspond almost exactly to the number of efficients which would be produced by a conscription throughout Germany of all men of 21, 22, 23, and 24 years of age. Such a conscription would yield 1,600,000 men, and the Germans, whose surgeons are not to be bribed, do not reject more than one in four.

Up to the 28th July, the first army had alone reached the frontier, where it occupied the line of the Saar; from Saarburg on the right, with advanced posts at that place and at Merzig, Saarlouis, Saarbrück, and Bliescastel, with its main body massed somewhat behind in convenient situations for support at Ottweiler, Neuenkirchen, Homburg, and Landstuhl.

The second army, under Prince Frederick Charles, with the royal headquarters, having crossed the Rhine at Mayence and Mannheim, was pressing on in the rear of Steinmetz, and on the 1st August prolonged the line of that general's outposts towards the left by the occupation of Zweibrücken and Pirmasens; and having the main body echeloned from the left of the first corps at Landstuhl, along the line of railway joining that place with Landau, at Kaiserslautern and Neustadt.

About the 2nd and 3rd August the third army, under the Crown Prince, coming from the east bank of the Rhine by Mannheim and Germersheim, took up the line from the left of the second army, occupying as outposts Bergzabern, on the road leading to Weissenburg and Wenden, the junction of the railroads coming from Carlsruhe in one direction and from Mannheim by Neustadt in the other, and having its main body at Neustadt, Spire, Landau, and Germersheim.

By again referring to the map it will be seen that the Prussians, like the French, obtained great advantages of concentration from their system of railways.

Beginning on the right, Steinmetz communicated with Prince Frederick Charles, and he with the Crown Prince, by the railroad passing from Trèves, through Merzig, Saarlouis, Saarbrück, Ottweiler, Homburg, Landstuhl, Neustadt, and Landau, all occupied by their troops, to Wenden junction, the extreme left outpost of the Crown Prince's army The course of this railroad between Saarbrück and Wenden is in the form of a curve, concave towards the French; that is, having the flanks advanced and the centre retired, and it obviously gave remarkable facilities for massing troops on the flanks, which were the only parts of the German line exposed to attack.

The different armies communicated to their rear as follows:—Steinmetz, by the railroad to Mayence, which passes by Wenden, Sobernheim, and Bingen; Prince Frederick Charles, also with Mayence, by the railroad passing by Neustadt, Mannheim, and Worms; or, if preferable, by Mannheim with Heidelberg; while the Crown Prince had the choice of two lines of retreat equally secure—the one by Mannheim either to Mayence or Heidelberg, the other by railroad from Wenden junction to Carlsruhe.

The strong fortresses of Mayence, Landau, and Germersheim greatly strengthened the Prussian general position, which was far more compact than the strategical position of the French army.

The appointment of the Crown Prince to the head of the army in which the South German forces were to be included, caused great satisfaction in those states, and it was regarded by them as an especial compliment. On assuming the command he issued the following address:—

SOLDIERS OF THE THIRD ARMY.

Appointed by his Majesty the king of Prussia to the command in chief of the Third Army, I send greeting to the troops of Prussia, Bavaria, Würtemburg, and Baden, who from this day are united under my command.

It fills me with pride and joy to march against the enemy at the head of the united sons of every part of the German Fatherland, to fight for the common national cause, for German right, for German honour.

We are entering on a great and severe struggle; but in the consciousness of our good right, and confident in your valour, your perseverance and discipline, I rely on a victorious issue.

Let us then stand together like true brothers in arms, and with God's help let us unfurl our standards to new victories, to the glory and peace of our now united Germany.

FREDERICK WILLIAM,
Crown Prince of Prussia.

Before placing himself at the head of their troops his Royal Highness, in accordance with military etiquette, paid a flying visit to the three southern sovereigns, and was most enthusiastically received at Munich, Stuttgard, and Carlsruhe. The courts and people absolutely vied with each other in showing their regard for the heir to the Prussian throne, and their joy at his having been appointed to take the command of their armies. The Prussian generals, too, who had been appointed to command in the south, met with the cordial sympathy of the people and troops.

It was also a strange commentary upon the value of the information which had been supplied to the French emperor, and the trustworthiness of his envoys, that when the German armies were on the eve of their advance, Bismarck and Von Moltke sat down to dinner on South German territory with men sentenced by Prussia in 1849 to death and imprisonment, and that aristocrats and extreme democrats clinked their glasses in German fashion as they pledged the German arms in the national war.

The Crown Prince had Lieutenant-general von Blumenthal as chief of his staff, as at Königgrätz; Prince Frederick Charles had with him in a like capacity Colonel von Stichle; and General Steinmetz was advised by Major-general von Sperling. Lieutenant-general von Obernitz commanded the Würtemburg division, and General von Beyer the Baden division.

The king was the commander-in-chief of the German armies, but all the strategical operations were directed by General von Moltke. In addition to the king of Prussia, the Crown Prince, and Prince Charles, several other German princes took the field against the French. The king was attended in his headquarters by the grand-duke of Saxe-Weimar, the grand-duke of Mecklenburg-Schwerin, the crown prince of Mecklenburg-Strelitz, Prince Luitpold of Bavaria, and Prince Charles of Prussia. The duke of Saxe-Coburg Gotha accompanied the Crown Prince, and some other illustrious personages were in the camp of Prince Frederick Charles.

CHAPTER VII.

Early Skirmishes in the neighbourhood of the River Saar—Description of the River and surrounding Country—Dash and Enterprise shown by the Germans—Destruction of the Bridge of Kehl by them—The French cross the Frontier and fire at a Military train—Attempt to destroy the German Railway repulsed—Brilliant Exploit of the Prussian Lancers— Skirmish at Niederbronn—Death of the First Officer, an Englishman in the service of the Grand-duke of Baden—Delay of the French after the Emperor's Arrival at Metz on July 28— The Great Opportunity of inflicting Serious Injury on the Germans lost—Contrast of the Strategy on both sides—The Emperor's own Version of his Proceedings up to this point— Alteration of the German Plan of the Campaign in consequence of the French delay— Determination of the French to strike a blow for Political rather than Military Purposes— Description of the town of Saarbrück, the Scene of the First Engagement—The French Attack and "Victory" on August 2—The Prince Imperial's "Baptism of Fire"—Sketch of the Engagement by the Prince—Return of the Emperor to Metz—Enthusiasm and Admiration of the Inhabitants—Intended departure of the Emperor for Strassburg postponed through Illness—Detailed Description of the Position of both Armies on August 3—The French Situation very badly chosen for Defence—Their Inaction and Carelessness a source of great Assistance to the Germans—French Council of War on August 4—A previous German Council of War has unanimously determined to assume the Offensive—Position and description of Wissembourg and surrounding Country—The Battle there on August 4—The German Tactics—Heroism displayed on both sides—The Attack on the Geisberg—Superior weight of the Germans—The Bayonet and the Breech-Loader—Results of the Battle, and Losses on both sides—Position of the Crown Prince during the action—Generous Rivalry caused by placing the Prussian and Bavarian Regiments side by side—Feeling of Satisfaction throughout Germany at the Result of the Engagement—The Moral Effect of it on both Armies.

ALMOST immediately after the declaration of war, the usual skirmishes which always precede more serious engagements, consequent upon the reconnaissances made by two hostile armies in order to obtain information, took place in the neighbourhood of the river Saar, as it is named in German, or Sarre, as it is called in French.

This river rises in the Vosges mountains, in Alsace, and flows northward to Sarreguemines, whence it enters the Prussian territory, bending to the north-west, and passing the towns of Saarbrück, Saarlouis, and Merzig, till its junction with the Moselle, above the city of Trèves (which the Germans name Trier), finally sending its waters into the Rhine at Coblentz. The valley of the Saar, lying deep between wooded hills, crosses a tract of uneven country, some thirty miles wide, inclosed by the Vosges mountains on the south, and the Hochwald, or highlands of the Moselle, on the north. It is not unlike the valley of the Wye, or that of the Lynn in Devonshire.

In most instances the early skirmishes were little more than an interchange of shots between videttes, without leading to any definite result; but in all the Prussians showed a dash and enterprise which might more naturally have been expected from their adversaries.

The first really important act of the war occurred on July 22, when the Prussians blew up the railway bridge between Strassburg and Kehl. This handsome structure, which crossed the Rhine and effected the junction between the French and German railways, was built between 1858 and 1861, at the common expense of both nations, and was so formed that communication could be broken off by either side in a few hours. The bridge was built in three portions; the central one, which consisted of an iron trellis on stone piers of three spans, each about sixty yards long, was fixed, while that at each end was movable, swinging round on a pivot. At the commencement of hostilities the German, and subsequently the French portions, were swung round, thus destroying communication without permanently injuring the bridge. Teutonic prudence, however, did not stop here, and accordingly the German division of the bridge was blown up—an act which called forth from the French the most bitter accusations of Vandalism; but it was in reality an evidence of the stern reality with which the Germans had entered upon the struggle. The explosion was terrible; large masses of stone and iron being projected as far as the French bank.

On July 23 the French, crossing the frontier with a couple of guns, north of Forbach, fired at a military train between Burbach and Linsenthal, two villages on the Saarlouis-Saarbrück line. The soldiers escaped unhurt; but four peasants in an adjoining field were slightly wounded. On the evening of the same day the French, having again crossed the frontier, and penetrated as far as the neighbourhood of Saarlouis, fired at a Prussian patrol and wounded two horses. Early on the morning of the 24th, another reconnaissance led to a more sanguinary result. From Forbach, where a French division had been stationed for the previous few days, a strong detachment marched to endeavour to destroy the Prussian railroad at Volklingen, between Saarlouis and Saarbrück. Soon after establishing themselves on German territory they were met by the Germans and repulsed with the loss of ten men. A rival exploit performed on the same night by the Prussians was much more successful, and was altogether a feat of considerable brilliancy. The railway on which Saarbrück stood, after it crossed French territory, and passed Forbach, threw out a connection at a little place called Hochern. This connection ran eastward, skirting the frontier at a greater or less interval, till it reached Haguenau, where it turned southward to Strassburg. It is easy to see what a valuable line this would have been to the French, as a feeder to their forces on the frontier. By it they could concentrate or disperse, reinforce or withdraw. The task of interrupting the continuity of the line was committed to Lieutenant von Forght and thirty picked men of his regiment, the seventh lancers. They first proceeded to Neuenkirchen, from the ironworks and collieries around which they obtained a supply of artificers conversant with blasting operations. Thence they went to Zweibrucken, and from that base reconnoitred the frontier. They found the French in considerable strength, and after the frustration of two direct attempts, it became evident that a sudden dash from the flank was the only means of reaching the viaduct of the railway, which had been selected as the most eligible point for destruction. It was a work of considerable magnitude, crossing, in arches, a valley a few miles to the west of

Bitsche. Some riding lessons having been given to the civilian engineers, to enable them to sit troop horses at a gallop, the party, on the night of July 24, penetrated the French territory at an unfrequented point on a forest road, galloped forward some seven miles to the viaduct, dropped the engineers, and extended in covering order. In a remarkably short space of time the centre arch of the viaduct went up in the air with a loud explosion, which brought the French outposts inland from the frontier at speed. The Uhlans, as the Prussian lancers are called, kept them off, however, till the engineers had completed the demolition of the viaduct, destroyed a quantity of railway and other matériel, and caused damage which it would have taken some weeks of uninterrupted labour to have repaired. Then the lieutenant, having quietly drawn in his covering parties, remounted his engineers, and cantered off over the frontier, without suffering the slightest casualty in an enterprise which for sagacity, courage, and success, deserved the highest credit.

On July 25 a skirmish took place at Niederbronn, which was chiefly noticeable from the fact that it resulted in the death of the first officer killed in the war—a young Englishman named Winsloe, in the service of the grand-duke of Baden—and in the capture of the first prisoners by the French. The French journals at the time greatly exaggerated the importance of the affair; but the real facts were, that a captain, two lieutenants, and twelve troopers of a regiment of Baden cavalry, were sent to obtain information, and cut the telegraphic wires on the French frontier. They crossed on the Sunday morning near the French town of Lauterburg, were seen by numbers of people, cut the wires at the Huntspach station while the inhabitants were at church, passed the day in riding about the country, and advanced no less than thirty miles into the enemy's territory. Early on the following morning they found themselves on the height of Neiderbronn. Wishing to rest and refresh themselves, they halted at an inn, which was in part also a large barn; and, although they were close to the enemy, they had the imprudence to unsaddle and unbridle their horses. A platoon of French cavalry on the scout discovered them, and took ten of the troopers prisoners without any difficulty. The other two escaped over a wall, but eventually were captured and conveyed to Metz. All this time the officers were breakfasting in the inn, when a sergeant of the French cavalry, impetuously and single-banded, rushed into the room. He was at once shot by the captain of the Baden cavalry, who had the presence of mind to spring into the saddle of a cavalry horse—that belonging to the French sergeant—and so effected his escape. In the firing which took place during the scuffle, the Englishman was mortally wounded, and died the same evening. Count Zepplin, the captain, escaped amidst a shower of rifle balls, and successfully carried off to the Crown Prince the information which the party had come to seek. An English journal stigmatized them as "madmen," but there is no reason to suppose that their madness was without method. At all events, twelve days after the reconnaissance, the headquarters of the victorious German army were established near the very scene of Mr. Winsloe's death.

On 28th July the Emperor Napoleon reached Metz, and on the following morning he assumed the command of the army of the Rhine. According to Napoleonic traditions, that date ought to have marked the beginning of active operations; but day after day passed, and nothing was done. It is now well known that when the Emperor left Paris for Metz, his intention was to advance across the frontier at once; and had he done so he would have been able to have disturbed his enemy's plans very materially. The military force of France was a standing army, and this was so organized that at the beginning of a war it was supposed to be superior in strength to anything that Germany could bring into the field, though in the long run it would be weaker in numbers, because its mode of recruitment was slow, and it was only fully upheld by the national levies which, in imitation of the German system, had been recently arrayed to give it support. But Germany was an armed nation; if at the outset her standing army would be much less numerous than that of France, it would quickly assume immense proportions; and behind it were vast masses of reserves, composed of the martial flower of the race, which experience had shown would flock to the standards of the regular troops with astonishing speed, and which, if once collected, would form an array far exceeding the united musters of France. The great hope of France lay, therefore, in assuming the offensive as rapidly as possible.

On the 29th and 30th of July, the German armies were still far from being concentrated. The south Germans were still converging by rail and road towards the bridges of the Rhine. The Prussian reserve cavalry was passing in endless files through Coblentz and Ehrenbreitstein, marching southwards; and a resolute advance at that time could scarcely have failed to have brought the French up to the outlying forts of Mayence (Mainz), and to have insured them considerable advantages over the retiring columns of the Germans; perhaps it might have enabled them even to have thrown a bridge over the Rhine, and protected it by a bridge-head on the right bank. At all events, the war would have been carried into the enemy's country, and the moral effect upon the French troops must have been excellent.

Who, indeed, can tell what the result would have been, had a general like the first Napoleon at this time commanded the army which, in the pride of its strength, already grasped with its leading divisions the as yet unprotected German frontier? It is by no means improbable, that if he had been in the field in such circumstances, he would have completely changed the character of the campaign. But feebleness and indecision occupied the place of genius and skill in the camp of France, and the occasion was lost on which, perhaps, the destiny of two nations depended. The emperor had delayed at Paris some time longer than he ought to have done; and the long and irresolute pause which he made after actually assuming the command, was of evil omen to his future operations. The excuse put forward by him, as we shall hereafter see, is, that he discovered that his corps was weaker than he had supposed, and that his commissariat was extremely defective (and that such was the fact is certain); but in the actual position of affairs, when a rapid attack was still the true game, considerations of this kind would not have paralyzed a really great commander.

The delay which had allowed Germany to arm and pour into the Rhineland had caused the French army to be outnumbered nearly two to one on the line chosen by its own commanders; and, literally before a blow had been struck, its chances of success had well nigh vanished. A mere calculation of numbers, however, will not convey an adequate notion of the danger in which it was now placed, and of the difference between the energy and skill displayed conspicuously by the German leaders, and the false strategy of the French commanders. A glance at the map will show that the corps which, from Thionville to the north of Strassburg, formed the advanced line of the French army, were not only scattered on a wide front and feebly connected, if at all, but were thrown too far beyond their supports at Metz, and were thus liable to be isolated, and beaten in detail by a daring enemy. This was especially the case with the corps of Frossard, De Failly, and MacMahon, which, separated from each other and from the bodies in the rear, were in a position somewhat similar to that of the French before the first Napoleon succeeded in the operations of Landshut and Ratisbon. On the other hand, the corps of the Germans, collected upon a narrow front from within Saarlouis to Wissembourg, with their supports close at hand from Neuenkirchen to Homburg, Kaiserslautern, Neustadt, and Landau, and holding three railways and numerous roads, were already in a position to throw a preponderating force on the French line at almost any point of attack; and, having driven it in, to roll into France an overwhelming tide of invasion. In fact, as regarded the French front, they were in possession of the chord of the arc, from Thionville to Bitsche and Strassburg, with easier means of concentration; and they had the power of seconding a vigorous advance by an offensive movement of crushing strength. The combinations which produced these results reflected the highest credit on the German commanders, and on the martial arrays they led; they showed skill, forethought, energy, and boldness; and they were conducted with that secrecy and swiftness invaluable in military operations. Already the cloud of war which overhung the Saar threatened the forces of France with serious disaster.

As it is our wish above all things to give a thoroughly impartial account of everything connected with the war, it is only fair, perhaps, after what we have just stated, that we should, in justice to the emperor, give his own account of the proceedings up to this point, and in which it will be seen he endeavours to excuse himself from much of the blame that is generally laid to his charge. In a now celebrated historical pamphlet, published at Brussels under the title of "Campagne de 1870: des Causes qui ont amené la Capitulation de Sedan, par un officier attaché à l'Etat Major-General," and which was dictated by the emperor himself during his retirement at Wilhelmshöhe, it is stated that when war was declared, and the emperor assumed the command-in-chief, he frequently gave expression to the thought, reflected in his initial proclamation, that the campaign about to open would be surrounded by the greatest difficulties. In the midst of the satisfaction occasioned by the enthusiasm which everywhere greeted his footsteps, many observed the look of sadness with which he listened to shouts of "Onward to Berlin!" uttered by the excited multitude—as if the enterprise was destined to be merely a military promenade, and a march forward would suffice to vanquish the European nation most thoroughly exercised in the profession of arms, and best prepared for war.

The emperor knew that Prussia was ready to call out, in a short time, 900,000 men, and, with the aid of the southern states of Germany, could count upon 1,100,000 soldiers. France was only able to muster 600,000; and as the number of fighting men is never more than one-half the actual effective force, Germany was in a position to bring into the field 550,000 men, whilst France had only about 300,000 to confront her. To compensate for this numerical inferiority, it was necessary for the French, by a rapid movement, to cross the Rhine, separate Southern Germany from the North German Confederation, and, by the éclat of a first success, secure the alliance of Austria and Italy. If they were able to prevent the armies of Southern Germany from forming their junction with those of the north, the effective strength of the Prussians would be reduced 200,000 men, and the disproportion between the number of combatants thus much diminished. If Austria and Italy made common cause with France, then the superiority of numbers would be in her favour. The emperor's plan of campaign—which he confided at Paris to Marshals MacMahon and Leboeuf alone—was to mass 150,000 men at Metz, 100,000 at Strassburg, and 50,000 at the camp of Châlons. The concentration of the first two armies, one on the Sarre, and the other on the Rhine, did not reveal his projects; for the enemy was left in uncertainty as to whether the attack would be made against the Rhenish Provinces or upon the duchy of Baden. As soon as the troops should have been concentrated at the points indicated, it was the emperor's purpose to immediately unite the two armies of Metz and Strassburg; and, at the head of 250,000 men, to cross the Rhine at Maxau, leaving at his right the fortress of Rastadt, and at his left that of Germersheim. Reaching the other side of the Rhine, he would have forced the states of the south to observe neutrality, and would then have hurried on to encounter the Prussians. Whilst this movement was in course of execution, the 50,000 men at Châlons, under the command of Marshal Canrobert, were to proceed to Metz, to protect the rear of the army and guard the eastern frontier. At the same time, the French fleet cruising in the Baltic would have held stationary, in the north of Prussia, a part of the enemy's forces, obliged to defend the coasts threatened with invasion. The sole chance of this plan succeeding, was to surpass the enemy in rapidity of movement. To accomplish this it was necessary to muster, in a very few days, at the points decided upon, not only the number of men required, but also the essential accessories of the projected campaign; such as waggon equipages, artillery parks, pontoon trains, gunboats to cover the passage of the Rhine, and, finally, the commissariat necessary to supply a large army on the march.

The emperor flattered himself with the hope of attaining these results, and in this he was deceived; as, in fact, everybody was led astray by the supposition that, by means of the railways, men could be concentrated, and horses and matériel brought forward, with the order and precision indispensable to success, where preparations had not been made long in advance by a vigilant administration. "The delays incurred arose," said the emperor, "in a great measure from the defects of our military organization, as it has existed for the last fifty years, and which revealed themselves from the very beginning." Instead of possessing, as was the case with Prussia, army corps always in an organized state, recruited in the province itself, and possessing on the spot their *matériel* and complete accessories, in France the troops composing an army were dispersed over the whole country, whilst the *matériel* was stored in different cities in crowded magazines.

In case it was decided to form an active division upon any given point of the frontier, the artillery generally came from some distant place, and the train equipage and ambulances from Paris and Verdun. Nearly all the munitions and provisions were brought from the capital; and as for the soldiers of the reserve, they rejoined their regiments from all parts of France. The consequence was, that the railways were insufficient for the transportation of the men, horses, and matériel; confusion took place everywhere; and the railway stations were often encumbered with objects of which the nature and the destination were equally unknown.

In 1860 the emperor had resolved that the recruits of the second portion of the annual contingent should be drilled in the depôts of their respective provinces, thence to be drafted, in time of war, into the regiments destined for the campaign. This plan combined the advantages of the Prussian with those of the French system. The men belonging to the reserve, being simply obliged to go from their place of residence to the principal town of the department, were there assembled, speedily equipped, and divided among the different regiments. Still, although rapidly completed, the regiments were not, as in Prussia, made up from the population of an entire province. Unfortunately, this plan was modified by the war office in 1866, and each soldier, after being mustered into the service, was immediately assigned to a regiment. The result was that, in 1870, when the reserve was called out, the men belonging to it, in order to rejoin their various regiments, were in many instances obliged to follow a long and complicated route. Thus, for example, the men who were at Strassburg, and whose regiments were actually stationed in Alsace, instead of at once joining the ranks at Strassburg, were sent to their respective regimental depôts, which might be in the south of France, or even in Algiers, and were thence obliged to return again to Strassburg for incorporation. It may be easily conceived what delays in the assembling of the troops were caused by so defective an organization. The same fact existed with respect to the camping material, the ambulance waggons, and the officers' transportation. Instead of being distributed among the depôts, in the centre of each department of the empire, they were all stored in a limited number of military warehouses; so that many troops belonging to the reserve were forced to join their corps only imperfectly equipped, destitute of haversacks, *tentes d'abri*, pannikins, saucepans, and camp-kettles—all objects of first necessity.

To these defects must be added the limited power intrusted to the generals in command of the departments, and to the military commissariat. The most trifling thing required a ministerial authorization. It was, for instance, impossible to distribute to officers or men the most indispensable adjuncts, even the necessary arms, without an express order from Paris. This administrative routine deprived the generals of the activity and foresight which may sometimes remedy defective organization.

"We hasten to add, however," continues the pamphlet, "that, to make up an army, less account must be taken of individual intelligence than of substantial organization, moved by simple machinery, and capable of working regularly in time of war, because it has been habituated to working regularly in time of peace. Yet, notwithstanding all the deceptions we encountered, justice must be rendered to the functionaries at the war office, who, at a moment of profound tranquillity, were invested with the task of setting in motion the entire military power of France. Taking into consideration the defective French administration, it was in reality a *tour de force* to bring into line, in so brief a period, armies incompletely formed; no previous measure for the purpose having been carried into effect.

"No doubt the objection will be made that some, at least, of the faults heretofore mentioned ought to have been remedied in advance. But the difficulty of conquering inveterate habits and prejudices must not be forgotten. The Chambers, too, persistently refused the aid necessary to accomplish the most important reforms. Who does not remember the objections and protestations to which the bill providing for a new military organization gave rise? The opposition adhered to their vain theory of levies *en masse*, and the bill was everywhere badly received. On the other hand, the emperor, confident in the armies which had achieved such glorious successes in the Crimea and in Italy, was not indisposed to believe that their irresistible rush (*élan*) would compensate for many deficiencies, and render victory assured. His illusions were not of long duration.

"The army of Metz, instead of 150,000 men, only mustered 100,000; that of Strassburg only 40,000, instead of 100,000; whilst the corps of Marshal Canrobert had still one division at Paris and another at Soissons: his artillery, as well as his cavalry, was not ready. Further, no army corps was even yet completely furnished with the equipments necessary for taking the field.

"The emperor gave precise orders to the effect that the missing regiments should be pushed on with all possible speed; but he was obeyed slowly, excuse being made that it was impossible to leave Algeria, Paris, and Lyons without garrisons.

"Nevertheless, the hope of carrying out the (original) plan of the campaign was not lost. It was thought that the enemy would not be ready before us. His movements were not known, nor in what quarter his forces were being massed; but all uncertainty on this point was soon cleared away by the events in the first week in August."

As might have been expected, the delay on the part of the French produced an evident change in the German plan of operations. Originally believing the French would force the fighting, they had shown no other anxiety than to be prepared to resist their impetuosity. They deemed it inexpedient to await an onset on the Saar, but wished to decoy the French away from their base of operations at Metz, and to await them in their own formidable position near Mayence. The whole district between the Moselle and the Rhine was left almost defenceless. Moltke had resolved on sacrificing no men in detail, and in fact on the spur of the moment he had no men to mass; but with each day of reprieve his forces accumulated in geometrical progression, until at length he could draw a sigh of relief, satisfied that Germany had both the generalship and the soldiers; and as action was felt to be necessary to them, it was resolved, that as the French delayed making the expected advance, they would assume the offensive, so that the parts assigned to the two countries by long-established traditions were reversed. With this object in view, a general advance of the German troops was made from their second line on the Rhine, to their more advanced one between it and the Lauter.

General Steinmetz with the first army came from Cologne across the Eifel mountains, and from Coblentz up the Moselle to Trèves and Saarlouis. The Crown Prince moved onwards from Speyer, across the Rhine to Germersheim and Landau; while Prince Frederick Charles brought forward the centre by Kaiserslautern and Birkenfeld, towards Saarbrück.

Prepared or not, however, political considerations compelled the French emperor to make at least some show of actual hostilities, for the Parisian public were already murmuring loudly at the delay; and it was accordingly decided to strike a blow at one of the least defended and most accessible points on the frontier. The place thus chosen was Saarbrück, a manufacturing town of considerable importance, situated in a rich coal district, and which has, with its suburb of St. Johann, with which it is connected by two bridges, a population of 14,000. The town stands on the south, or French side of the river Saar, and consists of long streets, with a slight ascent, running parallel to the river. A broad hill rises immediately behind the town, from whose summit there is a good view of the broad valley, bounded in front by the heights of Spicheren. These latter hills are called—to commence from the left—the Winterberg, Reppersberg, Frilles, and Galenberg, and the Exerciesplatz. The town is an open one, and being completely commanded by heights, its defence entered so little into the plans of Prussian strategists, that it had at first hardly any garrison at all. In fact, had they cared to have done so, almost as soon as war was declared the French could easily have gained possession of the place without firing a shot, and the major in command had been only left in his exposed position whilst the mobilization was proceeding, at his own urgent request. For several days in the last week of July the French from Forbach and from Sarreguemines, under Generals Frossard and De Failly, had been occupying the surrounding hills, unimpeded by the Prussians, and rearing their batteries, under cover of the woods on the plateau at Spicheren, on the right of the road from Forbach, and advancing with heavy columns upon the village of St. Arnual on the right, and Gersweiler on the left of the central plateau. From this height the range of the French cannon had been tried at 1800 mètres' (about 2100 yards') distance with perfect success. A reconnaissance and attack on the town by the French, which took place on Saturday, July 30, was, however, repulsed; but on the following Tuesday, August 2, the attack was renewed with much greater force, and with ultimate success. The attacking troops consisted of the second division (General Bataille) of the second army corps (General Frossard). The advance was made by the Forbach road, the first object to be attained being the complete occupation of the heights immediately commanding Saarbrück. This was easily accomplished, the Prussian videttes falling back as the enemy advanced. There was indeed but little opposition until the French were fairly posted on this vantage ground, from which their guns commanded the town where the Prussians were posted. The combat then became one of artillery, and, on the part of the French, of mitrailleuses, from which so much was expected. The town was held by three companies of the fortieth regiment, amounting to about 800 men, supported by two light guns (four pounders) and about 250 cavalry. The emperor and prince imperial left Metz by special train about half past eight in the morning, so as to be present at the engagement, which commenced at about eleven, and was continued for nearly three hours. At the end of that time, the position being evidently untenable, was evacuated by the Prussians, who retired by way of Grosswald, and it was during their retreat across the bridge that the mitrailleuses were brought into play upon two detachments of troops. The effect was said by the French to have been marvellous, "the enemy being at once scattered, and leaving half their number dead or wounded;" but the Prussian official statement of their whole loss was only two officers and seventy men, and a trustworthy Englishman, who witnessed the action from the town, said he noticed particularly that nearly all the mitrailleuse bullets fell short. He said the pluck and enthusiasm with which the Prussians contested every inch of ground, in spite of being so much outnumbered, showed of what material they were made; and the steady way in which they brought their needle gun up to their shoulder and deliberately took aim, contrasted favourably with the excited random shots of the French with their Chassepots; the French idea apparently being that it was desirable to consume as much ammunition as possible, regardless of results.

The following was the account of the action supplied to the emperor, by the general commanding the troops engaged on the French side:—

August 2.

Sire,—I have the honour to report to your Majesty the movements effected this day by the second army corps in pursuance of your orders, to take possession of the positions on the left bank of! the Saar, which command the heights of Saarbrück.

General Bataille's division, supported on the right by that of General Laveaucoupet and one of the twelve-pounder batteries of the reserve, and on the left by the first brigade of the division of General Vergé, with a second battery of twelve-pounders, formed the first line. General Bastoul, encamped at Spicheren, and intrusted with the duty of directing the movement on our right, was ordered to send two battalions to occupy the village of St. Arnual and the heights above it; whilst the remainder of his brigade, crossing the ravine in front of Spicheren, was to make a front attack on the positions to the right of the road from Forbach to Saarbrück. The other brigade of the Bataille division was to move on to the position known as the exercising ground. Three squadrons of the fifth mounted chasseurs preceded it to clear the way. Finally, Colonel du Ferron, of the fourth mounted chasseurs, with two battalions of the first brigade of the Vergé division, was to push on a reconnaissance to Guerswiller to connect the movement of the second corps with that of Marshal Bazaine. The troops left their bivouacks between nine and ten o'clock. Lieutenant-colonel Thebeaudin, with two battalions of his regiment (the sixty-seventh), in advancing to the attack of the village of St. Arnual, found it strongly occupied and defended by batteries of position planted on the right bank of the Saar. To demolish this artillery, General Micheler, whose brigade had come forward to support the movement of General Bastoul, ordered into action a battery of the fifteenth regiment, which effectually opened fire on the Prussian guns. Supported by a battalion of the fortieth regiment of the line, and by the company of sappers and miners of the third division, materially assisted by the flank movement of Colonel Mangin, who, with the remainder of the sixty-seventh regiment and the sixty-sixth regiment, descended the heights on the left, Lieutenant-colonel Thebeaudin was able to carry the village of St. Arnual, and occupied it with a battalion of the fortieth regiment and the company of sappers and miners. The battalions of the sixty-seventh, with great 4lan, rushed up the slopes of the hillock of St. Arnual, and established themselves on the crest opposite Saarbrück. The sixty-sixth, with equal resolution, took possession of the heights up to the exercising ground, driving the enemy from all his positions. At the same time, General Bataille rapidly moved his first brigade to the rising ground on the left of the Saarbrück road, connecting his movement with that of his second brigade by advancing a battalion of the thirty-third regiment. Advancing in line, the battalions of the twenty-third and eighth regiments, their front covered by numerous skirmishers, resolutely carried the many ravines which run across the ground, which is very difficult and thickly wooded. One battalion of the eighth regiment, working its way across the woods, followed the railway as far as the village of Frotrany, where it effected its junction with the other battalions of the regiment, and together they attacked the exercising ground of the right. On gaining the heights, General Bataille planted one of his batteries in front of the lines of the sixty-sixth regiment, and another on the exercising ground, to fire on the railway station and silence the enemy's artillery, which had taken up a position on the left of Saarbrück. It was unable to sustain our fire, and had to fall back. The twelve-pounder battery of the reserve was ordered by me to support the fire of the batteries on the exercising ground, and finally a battery of mitrailleuses of the second division threw into utter disorder the enemy's columns of infantry, which were evacuating the town. During this artillery duel the troops were able to acclaim his Majesty the emperor and the prince imperial, on the very ground from which they had just dislodged the enemy. The movements of the infantry were excellently seconded by the fifth regiment of horse chasseurs, under the orders of Colonel de Seréville. The squadrons, supported by infantry in skirmishing order, searched every nook in the ground, and rapidly gained all the crests of the hills whence they could descry the enemy. The twelfth battalion of foot chasseurs, and the company of sappers and miners of the second division, formed the reserve of General Bataille; they joined the troop of the first brigade on the exercising ground. The first brigade of the Vergé division, which formed the second line, constantly kept at 400 or 500 mètres from the first line, and availed themselves of every rise in the ground to cover themselves. The reports I have received up to this time announce the following losses:—The sixty-sixth regiment had one officer killed, M. de Bar, lieutenant of the francs-tireurs; Captain Adjutant Major Privat has a very dangerous gunshot wound; Lieutenant Laramey received a bullet through his shoulder; fifteen or sixteen rank and file were killed or wounded. The sixty-seventh had no casualty among its officers. Rank and file, twenty men killed or wounded. The eighth regiment, two rank and file wounded. The third division reports a sergeant killed and a private wounded. I have not received the report of Colonel du Ferron. I am told that he was engaged, and had about ten men wounded. Neither have I received the report of the commander of the tenth battalion of foot chasseurs, which has pushed forward on the right along the road from Sarreguemines to Saarbrück. The troops are encamped on the ground they have gained. I have had a few entrenchments thrown up in front and flank of their position. Some *epaulements* have also been established to protect our guns and gunners. I was greatly pleased with the dash and resolution of the troops. They showed great energy in marching up steep ground, and also in action. The heads of the several corps congratulate themselves on the steadiness of their men, their intrepidity, and the growing confidence they show in their weapons. I will make known to your Majesty the names of the officers and men of all ranks who specially merit being pointed out. Our losses amount to six killed, and sixty-seven wounded.—Receive, &c.,

The "victory" was of no importance whatever to the French in a military point of view, as no further advance was made, and no advantage taken of the success. In fact, the town, which had some of its houses burned during the fight, was not even occupied, as the Prussian guns completely commanded it from the heights behind. The "victory," however, enabled the emperor to send the empress a telegram which has now become historical, announcing the fact that the young prince imperial had received his "Baptism of Fire." The document ran thus:—"Louis has just received his baptism of fire. He showed admirable coolness, and was not at all affected. A division of General Frossard has captured the heights which overlooked the left bank at Saarbrück. The Prussians made but a short resistance. We were in the front rank, but the bullets and cannon balls fell at our feet. Louis has kept a bullet which fell quite close to him. Some of the soldiers wept at seeing him so calm. We have lost one officer and ten men killed.

"NAPOLEON."

At the same time the emperor's private secretary announced the victory to the minister of the Interior as follows:—

"METZ, *August* 2, 4.30.

"By the emperor's orders, get the following inserted in the *Official Journal*, in the non-official part, and give a copy to all the Paris papers:—This day, August 2, at eleven in the morning, the French troops had a serious engagement with the Prussian troops. Our army assumed the offensive, crossed the frontier, and invaded Prussian territory. In spite of the strong position of the enemy, a few of our battalions succeeded in taking the heights which command Saarbrück, and our artillery very soon drove the enemy out of the town. The engagement began at eleven o'clock, and was over at one. The emperor was present at the operations, and the prince imperial, who accompanied him throughout, received the 'baptism of fire.' His imperial highness's presence of mind and his *sang froid* in danger were worthy of the name he bears. The emperor returned to Metz at four o'clock."

In the evening after the combat the prince, who has a great natural taste for drawing, made a sketch of the engagement, and presented it to M. Tristan Lambert, who was a great friend of his, and who had volunteered as a private in one of the regiments of the guards for the campaign. ' This sketch was very exact and precise, the march of the troops, the encounter, the bridge, the spot where, with the emperor, he stood during the affair, all being clearly indicated. In one corner of the sketch were written these lines:—"A mon ami Tristan Lambert. Le 2 Aout, après avoir vu le feu pour la premiere fois.

"LOUIS NAPOLEON."

On the return of the emperor to Metz in the evening (or, as was officially announced, "in time for dinner"), he sent for the mayor, and after an interview of a few moments' duration the latter stated publicly to his friends and acquaintances on the Place Napoléon that the French troops had taken the town of Saarbrück, that the town was on fire, and the Prussians running away. The inhabitants immediately gave themselves up to the most extravagant expressions of joy. In some parts of the town music, singing, and dancing were kept up all night. Some of the oldest inhabitants reminded the mayor that the custom of Metz was to ring a merry peal from the bells of the cathedral at every victory of France over her enemies, and regretted that he did not order it to be rung immediately. They also suggested that an official notice of the victory might be very conveniently posted up at the Prefecture, and also at the Hotel de Ville. The mayor, upon this, returned to his Majesty to ask permission both to ring the bells, and to post up the bulletin of the entrance of the French army into Saarbrück. But he came back considerably disappointed: the emperor had said, in answer to his loyal application, "Never mind about the bells nor the official notice either." This was considered by the masses as an example of the most admirable modesty and abnegation in which an imperial sovereign could possibly display his *haute sagesse*, and when at last people did betake themselves to bed, they amused themselves by constantly repeating the words *sage, prudent, modeste et grand homme!* During the night and all the following morning, officers who had been in the affair came to Metz, and when the real truth came out it considerably reduced the noisy enthusiasm of the citizens and the soldiery.

Marshal MacMahon went from Strassburg to Metz on Sunday, July 31, and had a long interview with the emperor; and after his departure orders were given to prepare for the emperor's departure for Strassburg on Wednesday morning, August 3, at five o'clock. Every thing was ready accordingly, but when the time came it was found that the emperor's state of health did not permit him to make the journey; the travelling and the excitement of the previous day had exhausted his strength so much that neither physician nor surgeon would consent to his leaving the house.

For the purpose of more clearly understanding subsequent events, it may be well if we here briefly recapitulate the general situation of the two armies at this time (Wednesday, August 3). The emperor kept his corps scattered along the Prussian and Bavarian frontiers, MacMahon covering the right, between Strassburg and the Lauter; L'Admirault on the left at Thionville; Frossard overlooking Saarbrück and at Forbach, on the left centre, supported by Bazaine and the guards in rear; and De Failly about Bitsche, protecting the branch railroad from Sarreguemines to Haguenau. Marshal Canrobert's corps was in second line at Châlons or Nancy, and Douay's to the south-east of the whole at Belfort. Most of these positions had been occupied for many days, and an advance by Forbach and Saarbrück was looked for by the main body as the natural complement of the attack on Saarbrück of the 2nd; for although suited for attack, the whole French position was about the very worst that could have been chosen for defence, the outstretched wings being distributed over a front 100 miles long, and inviting attack at half-a-dozen points from a vigorous enemy.

The position of the four French front corps, though too scattered for defence, might have been turned by the staff to one special end with great advantage. Had each chief exerted himself to the full to gain intelligence of the enemy's proceedings, had they impressed this necessity on their subordinates, their cavalry might in their earlier days of expectation have penetrated every point of the Prussian and Bavarian districts before them, and done such service as at least to have changed the aspect of affairs at the outset. Frossard's advanced troops should have destroyed the junctions of the three railroads which met from Trèves, Bingen, and Mayence, within twenty miles of his front. L'Admirault might have discovered the truth of the reports already rife, of an assembly of Germans behind Saarlouis about Trèves. De Failly's horse should have penetrated into Rhenish Bavaria, at least sufficiently far to discover whether Landau was being garrisoned in force. Without doubt, a little exertion on the part of the two former would have at least discovered the enemy's plan sufficiently to have made known the vital importance to the coming German concentration of the railroad junctions of Saarbrück and Neuenkirchen. Had De Failly been moderately active, he would have infallibly discovered that a third of the German armies were being gathered within a morning's ride of his videttes. As to MacMahon's own share in this strange state of indolence, it is beyond question that he had about Strassburg some means at least of feigning a passage of the Rhine in force, and so drawing his enemy's attention that way. But not one of these things was even attempted.

The following was the Prussian situation at the same time (August 3). On the right, the first army, organized by Herwarth at Coblentz, had General Steinmetz, another veteran of the Waterloo period, assigned to its head in the field. It consisted of the seventh, eighth, and half of the first corps; but in spite of every exertion, only three of the five divisions had reached the district where the Saar flows into the Moselle above Trèves (Trier). The central, or second army, was less advanced. Prince Frederick Charles had only taken up his head-quarters at Mayence (Mainz) on the 1st, and was occupied in pushing his leading corps (the third, under Alvensleben), direct through the Vosges towards the point of junction on the Saar, so long threatened by the French troops of Frossard.

Marching partly, and partly using the Kreutznach-Bingen line of railway, this corps was now more than half over the hundred miles which lie between Mayence and Forbach. How important to Prince Frederick Charles was the inaction of the French we have already alluded to, may best be understood by again observing, that their advance for fifteen miles only beyond Saarbrück would have brought them upon the second junction station before them, that of Neuenkirchen, where the Kreutznach-Bingen line unites with the main railroad from Metz to Mannheim. The French main body, therefore, if they had pushed less than twenty miles from the Saar, would have completely severed the communication of the troops on the Bingen line from those on the Mannheim, and both of course from that to Trèves by Saarbrück, except so far as the Prussians might have used the cross-roads of a difficult country.

"Whilst the right and centre of the Prussians were thus still far from facing the enemy in strength, the case was very different with their left, where General Moltke had directed so large a force to assemble as to give to the Crown Prince and his army (the third) great independence of action. Here were no mountains to be passed, no wide districts to be traversed before the enemy was found. The river Rhine and its petty affluent, the Lauter, had from the first separated the outposts of MacMahon from those of the Badish and Bavarian levies first summoned to cover the frontier. Dashing expeditions of horsemen were made across it, chiefly from the German lines; and whilst these occupied the attention of the French, the third army was being collected undiscovered in their front. The fifth and eleventh Prussian corps, and the first Bavarian, were the earliest to arrive at the designated passages of the Rhine at Germersheim and Mannheim, and for fourteen days consecutively 5000 men a day were passed through the latter city alone, and sent on by rail to Landau, where the Crown Prince had his head-quarters on the 3rd, and where he was joined also by divisions from Baden and Würtemburg, the latter only that evening.

The fortress of Landau is but a short march from the frontier on the Lauter, and as the German side of that stream was wooded, it was not difficult to mass a great part of the allied troops close to it on the 3rd. The line of the stream was observed by the French with a single division of MacMahon's corps, under General Abel Douay, who, though ignorant of the movements on the other side, was so rash as to keep the bulk of his troops almost upon the frontier. It was open to him to have held the fine with pickets of his cavalry, and kept his command so far to the south as to have had ample notice of the advance of the Prussians over the stream.

Trusting, however, to a vague idea that the enemy were on the defensive, he neglected this obvious precaution, although aware that there were other unguarded passages by which he might be attacked, as that of Lauterburg, a small place ten miles to his right, near the Rhine. His position, therefore laid him at the mercy of the superior numbers who were gathering before him unobserved, and as will be immediately described, the Crown Prince promptly used the advantage thus offered by the enemy, whose camp was but a mile beyond the Lauter. The secrecy preserved by the Prussian generals, and in some measure, too, the carelessness of the French authorities, prevented the latter from ascertaining the true strength and position of their adversaries, whilst the Prussians were kept unusually well informed as to the movements and strength of the French, and availed themselves of every opportunity to obtain such information, and without much impediment being placed in their way. It was, for instance, only natural that the Prussians should obtain information from some of the peasants of Alsace and the German part of Lorraine, and the first measure taken by the French should have been to prevent all communication on the frontier. Instead of this, up to the very moment that an attack was made by the Prussians, women and children living in the various villages adjacent to the Palatinate and the Rhenish provinces went daily across the frontier, pursuing their usual trade in rural produce; and a girl thirteen years of age gave, for a thaler, much useful information concerning the division of General Douay. It is thus obvious that the Prussians, exerting all their efforts for getting news, and speaking German with the borderers, who are German all along the frontier, had an enormous advantage over the French in this respect; for they neither took the trouble to send reconnoitring detachments across the frontier, nor could expect Prussian or Bavarian peasants to come over to talk with them. No wonder then they were taken so completely by surprise! The country itself, too, broken by ravines and densely wooded, was admirably adapted to conceal the movements of the German troops.

No important event occurred on Wednesday, August 3; but on the following day a French council of war was held at Metz, at which MacMahon and Bazaine were present; and at which, it is believed, an advance in force was decided upon, involving an independent movement of MacMahon's corps towards the Rhine, while Bazaine was to force back the troops in front, and cut off all communication with Trèves. A German council of war held earlier in the week, at Mayence, immediately after the arrival of the king of Prussia, was unanimously of opinion that the German armies should act on the offensive.

The South German army was already massed between Landau and Bergzabern, before the French could be persuaded that the Crown Prince had emerged from the Black Forest; and while the French council of war was assembling at Metz, on Thursday, August 4, the first great battle of the campaign had already been decided.

On the morning of that day the Prussians and Bavarians crossed the Lauter by various passages near Wissembourg (or Weissenburg, as spelt by the Germans), a frontier town which forms the western apex of a triangle, of which the Rhine forms the base, and the little streams of the Otter and the Lauter the sides. It formed the extreme right of the French position, commanding the railway to Haguenau and Strassburg, as well as the high roads to Niederbronn and Bitsche. The town was formerly a free city of the German empire, and was ceded to France by the Treaty of Ryswick. For six years, 1719 to 1725, it was the residence of the unfortunate Stanislas Leczynski, duke of Lorraine, and elect king of Poland. It has more than once owed its selection for a battleground to the works with which its neighbourhood was furnished by Marshal Villars, in the reign of Louis XIV., after his conquest of Alsace. In 1705 the marshal caused a series of redoubts and intrenchments to be constructed from near the Geisberg, which stands near the town, above the southern bank of the Lauter, to nearly as far as Lauterburg; and these lines have, time after time, been captured and recaptured. They were stormed more than once during the War of the Succession; and on October 13, 1793, they were carried by the Austrians, under Prince Waldeck. It is somewhat remarkable too, that its loss on that occasion by General Beauharnais, the maternal grandfather of Napoleon III., was expiated by that unlucky servant of the Republic on the guillotine. The Germans, however, held them only for a short time, as on Christmas Day of the same year they were retaken by the French; and from that time Wissembourg enjoyed an interval of peaceful existence as the chief place of the department of the Bas-Rhin. It was, until 1867, a fortified town, and although it is now dismantled, is still naturally protected by the hills upon which stood once the redoubts of St. Germain, St. Paul, and St. Remy. The town is distant twenty-seven miles north-east from Strassburg, by the railway which passes through Haguenau, seven miles from Wissembourg, and which there forms a junction with the main railway, the Great Eastern of France, leading to Luneville, Nancy, Châlons, and Paris. The valley of the Lauter at Wissembourg forms a gorge which opens upon the Rhenish plains to the south, and into the Vosges on the west. About two miles and a half to the west, upon the road to Bitsche, is a hill, which rises nearly 2000 feet above the valley of the Lauter. The ground from Wissembourg to this peak, for about half a mile, rises gently; and then suddenly at the bend of the Bitsche road to the right the ascent becomes more steep, and the road climbs up it with many easy gradations. The road to Climbach, shown in our battle-field plan, runs through a woody country, easily defended, traverses the forest of Mundat, and after running rather more than a mile beyond, reaches the little village of Lembach, which lies on high ground.

The road then descends, passes through the forest of Ratzenthal, lying in a small valley, and terminates at Bitsche, a fortress of great natural strength, twenty-five miles distant.

Early, then, on the morning of Thursday, August 4, the Crown Prince emerged from the Bienwald, at Schweighoffen, a Bavarian village just over the frontier, and surprised the town of Wissembourg, in which, as we have stated, MacMahon's second division was posted under the command of General Abel Douay, brother of the commander of the French seventh corps d'armée. The French had made a reconnaissance on the previous day, but had not discovered the neighbourhood of their enemy, although within a short distance of the heights of Schweighoffen, from which the attack was first made, there were drawn up the greater part of the fifth and eleventh Prussian corps and the first Bavarian corps, numbering at least 50,000 men. It is easy, however, to understand how this surprise was effected. The Crown Prince's advanced posts were at Bergzabern (which lies nearly due north of Wissembourg little more than six miles distant by road), and at Wenden Junction, on the north-east of Wissembourg, distant from that place by rail eleven miles, and from Bergzabern also by rail six miles. Troops massed at these places could therefore easily be brought down under cover of the night. Besides, the road from Bergzabern skirts the forest of Mundat, on the lower spurs of the Vosges, which afforded facilities for concealment. The French reconnaissance had been superficial, or had not been pushed far enough. Parties of a few daring troopers radiating from Wissembourg on the 3rd in all directions, would have revealed to Douay that a concentration of hostile forces was taking place dangerously near to his isolated position. The French troops at and near Wissembourg consisted of three regiments of the line, the sixteenth chasseurs, the zouaves and turcos of General Pellè, three batteries of artillery, and one mitrailleuse battery—the total force being about 8000 men. The attacking force of the Germans numbered altogether about 40,000 men, and the Baden division occupied Lauterbach and Hagenbach at the same time.

A Bavarian division commanded by General Bothmer led the assault, which was covered by a powerful cannonade. The French, as we have said, were utterly surprised, not having had the slightest idea that the Crown Prince was so close upon them. In fact, the men of one of the regiments were busy cooking their morning meal when the shells and bullets began to rain into their camp. General Douay was riding away from the town to examine the adjacent country, when he was recalled by the firing. The troops in the town, having been reinforced by some of those who had been stationed on the adjoining ridges, held their own stoutly; and the Bavarian division, consisting of 10,000 infantry and 500 cavalry, made little impression in their attack on the town, till the ninth division of the fifth corps (Von Sandrart) came up and turned it on the south-east by Altenstadt, which was taken at 11-30 a.m. Then, whilst one of its brigades (Voight Rhetz), stormed the position on the Geisberg, part of the other joined the Bavarian attack on Wissembourg. The attack on the Geisberg was further sustained by the forty-first brigade (Schachtmeyer) of the eleventh corps. The French fought desperately—in fact, throughout the day they made almost superhuman efforts to east back the enemy's masses beyond the Lauter; and although so enormously outnumbered, they charged again and again, as if under the idea that mere valour would stop bullets. Whilst the attack on the Geisberg was proceeding, the gates of

Wissembourg had been demolished by artillery fire, and the place stormed; and after attempting a counter attack on the summit of the Geisberg at two o'clock, the French were compelled to retreat on all sides. Before three there was a general advance of the German troops. The French continued fighting along the main road, but gradually quickened their pace as they were pressed; although they made a stand at two of the villages on the way, and were only dislodged with loss. The Germans also behaved remarkably well during the engagement; their advance up the hill of Geisberg being, in the opinion of an English officer (Colonel Walker) who was present, like that of the British troops at the battle of the Alma, to which the position offered some resemblance. "Upon the crest were the French with their Chassepots and mitrailleuses. When the order to storm it was given, the Germans went at it without flinching. A storm of balls rained upon them. Whole ranks were swept away, but the rest rushed on without a pause. No single shot was fired in return. They trusted entirely to the bayonet, and the instant they gained the crest they swept the French before them by sheer weight." The king's grenadiers (7th regiment) of the guard and the fifty-eight regiment of Silesia advanced at a run with shouts of "Up, Prussians! the Bavarians need help!"

The German advantage in weight was very great, as was afterwards found by weighing some prisoners; two Germans on an average weighed nearly as much as three Frenchmen. In a hand-to-hand struggle this difference of weight gave a preponderance to the German which was overwhelming, and as just stated, the French lines were broken instantly by the impetuous onslaught of the Prussian and Bavarian troops. It was certainly very singular, that whereas military men had almost come to the conclusion that the bayonet was a weapon which had ceased to be of any great utility, for that it was next to impossible that cavalry could ever come to close quarters with infantry armed with breech-loaders, or that two infantry regiments could ever come to a hand-to-hand struggle; that upon their first battle between troops alike armed with breech-loaders one party should have charged and defeated the other with the bayonet and clubbed muskets. Theoretically, and upon paper, it would seem impossible for troops to charge up a hill exposed to a fire from breech-loaders and mitrailleuses; and the fact that the feat was here performed, showed that improved arms after all have not modified the system of fighting, as military men had concluded that it must do, and that weight and strength, when accompanied by desperate courage, still count for much.

In their retreat the French lost their baggage, camp equipments, &c., and left about 500 killed and wounded on the field, besides 800 prisoners (including 18 officers) and one six pounder, of which, however, all the horses had been killed, and which had been spiked before it was abandoned.

Most of the prisoners were taken as skirmishers in a cave, which formed their cover, and where they were cut off by the rapid and continuous advance of the Prussians. A few others, who were taken on the field, had expended all their ammunition (as at Saarbrück on the previous Tuesday, the French fired at such a distance as made hitting a mere matter of chance, and also very rapidly, and consequently widely); but they refused to surrender, and kept on fighting at the point of the bayonet. As the Prussians did not wish to kill them, they rushed at last in a body upon them and threw them down wrestling. The Turcos behaved infamously; many of them, after asking for and receiving quarter, stabbed with their sword bayonets the soldiers who had spared them, or snatched up the muskets they had thrown down, and treacherously shot the victors.

General Douay himself was killed by a shell early in the action while rallying his troops, and Brigader Montmarie was wounded. The former was buried in the town the day after the battle, with full military honours; his body was followed to the grave by an entire German regiment of infantry and a battery of artillery, and the last salute was fired by a whole company. On the way to the churchyard the band played the French national hymn, and, returning after the burial, the popular German song, "Die Wacht am Rhein." The French regiments which suffered most in the engagement were the Turcos (of whom 500 were taken prisoners), and one of the regiments of the line. The German loss amounted to 700 men, including 76 officers, which accounted for the telegram from the Crown Prince announcing the victory, and describing it as a "brilliant but bloody" one. General Kirchbach was wounded, and the king's grenadiers and the fifty-eighth regiment suffered very severely. The casualties amongst the inhabitants of the town were three killed and fifteen wounded; amongst the former a young girl, the acknowledged beauty of the town, who was standing at her father's house-door with a younger brother, talking to a neighbour, when a shell burst close to the group. One fragment struck her in the body, and another took off her brother's hand and wrist. She died next day in great agony.

The German front extended altogether over a length of two miles. During the chief part of the engagement the Crown Prince and his staff were on the left of their line, the artillery was in the centre, and the columns of their troops were massed on the right.

The disposal of Prussian and Bavarian regiment side by side evoked a rivalry in daring most honourable to both; and if anything could have enhanced the satisfaction felt at the success throughout Germany, it was the fact that the first action in the war had been gained, to a great extent, through the assistance of the very South Germans from whom the French emperor had hoped so much; and the convincing proof that it afforded, that although divorced from each other for centuries by religious animosity and political differences, the two great sections of Germany had, in an age of mutual tolerance, been reunited at last by patriotism and a sensible appreciation of their common interest.

Throughout the action the Prussian artillery was splendidly served.

Although the fight lasted so long, no supports were sent' to the French general from Marshal MacMahon; but in the midst of the battle a detachment of the line happened to arrive by rail, entirely ignorant of what was going on. The soldiers immediately joined in the engagement, but were of course powerless to avert the disaster. In fact, the engagement was conducted by the Germans with such a superiority of numbers as to make success, sooner or later, almost certain. For the isolation of his division MacMahon must be held in some degree responsible; but Douay had himself chiefly to blame for the temerity which exposed his troops to a surprise by a greatly superior force. There was no military purpose gained by thrusting his camp close to the frontier which would not have been in every sense better answered by keeping it ten miles to the south, and watching the passages of the little stream with detachments of cavalry. Probably the convenience of being near the town, and the fact that there was a good position behind looking towards the Lauter, decided the general's choice. Choosing thus, however, he put himself, as we have seen, completely at the mercy of his enemy, and the Crown Prince, like a judicious commander, took care to insure success, and to make it certain that the first blow he struck—a matter of vital importance in war—should be irresistible and completely decisive.

To prevent their retreat on Bitsche from being intercepted, the French retreated by their left, and by the Col de Pigeonnière, in the direction of that fortress.

The moral effect of the battle on both armies, as the first serious engagement of the war, was of course great, and the result was exceedingly useful to the victors as giving their arms that credit and presumption of success so valuable at the outset of a campaign: Confident though the Germans were that victory would sooner or later crown their cause, they were yet extremely anxious about the issue of the first battle. It was felt by them that the alleged superiority of the Chassepot might prove to be a reality, and that the dash of the French soldiers might be irresistible. With a feeling of relief as much as of satisfaction they learned that the confidence they entertained as to their own strength was not misplaced. On the other hand, at the French head-quarters at Metz the news fell like a thunderbolt, and, of course, the emperor's plans were completely deranged.

CHAPTER VIII.

BATTLE OF WOERTH.

THE Crown Prince established his headquarters at Schweighoffen on the night of August 4, and on the following day pushed boldly into the French territory. He did not turn to his right, and pursue the road along the frontier towards Bitsche, but came down that leading nearly due south to Soultz (Sous Forêts), where it touches the railway from Haguenau to Wissembourg, He had, as we know, suffered a good deal the day before; many stragglers encumbered the march of his columns, and if De Failly, from Bitsche, with the French fifth corps, combining with a French force in front, had vigorously attacked the Germans in flank, as they threw their right wing forward, it is not impossible that a check might have been inflicted on the Prussian commander. Nothing, however, of the kind was attempted; and while De Failly sent one division, which could be of little avail, across the hills, he misinterpreting, it is said, his orders, remained immovable with his main force, while the German army was being concentrated.

The Crown Prince did not descend quite as far as Soultz, but kept a little to the west, near to the slopes of the Hoch Wald; for during the day authentic intelligence was received at the German headquarters that Marshal MacMahon was busily engaged in concentrating his troops on the hills west of Woerth, and that he was being reinforced by constant arrivals by railway. In consequence of these advices the Germans resolved to lose no time in effecting a change of front, which had been determined upon a few days previously, but not yet executed. The second Bavarian and the fifth Prussian corps were to remain in their respective positions at Lembach and Preuschdorf; the eleventh Prussian corps was to wheel to the right and encamp at Hölscbloch, with its van pushed forward towards the river Sauerbach, and the first Bavarian corps was to advance into the neighbourhood of Lobsann and Lampertsloch. The cavalry division remained at Schoenenbourg, fronting the west. Werder's corps (the Würtemburg and Baden divisions) marched to Reunerswiller, with patrols facing the Haguenau forest.

The fifth Prussian corps, on the evening of the 5th, pushed on its van from its bivouac at Preuschdorf to the heights east of Woerth, and on the other side of the Sauerbach numerous camp fires of the French were visible during the night. The village of Woerth is a small place of about 700 inhabitants, lying in a valley between two rows of long low hills, covered with vineyards, corn and potato fields, and woods; and beyond these again are higher ranges of hills, on which the contending armies were posted. Woerth lies on the direct road from Soultz to Niederbronn. Above the village there is a height of considerable extent, on which stand the villages of Froeschwiller and Elsasshausen, the road from Woerth traversing this height through the former village, and thence to Reichskoffen and Niederbronn.

MacMahon had heard of the disaster of his lieutenant at Wissembourg too late to remedy the fault which had exposed a small division to be crushed by an army; and having rallied the troops flying from that town upon his other divisions, he advanced from Haguenau, took up a strong defensive position fifteen miles to the south-west of Wissembourg, on the lower spurs of the Vosges, and drew his forces together with the object of covering the railway from Strassburg to Bitsche, and the chief channels of communication between the eastern and western sides of the Vosges. The position occupied by his troops, according to his own report to the emperor, was as follows:—

The first division was placed with the right in front of Froeschwiller, the left in the direction of Reichshoffen, resting on a mound which covers that village. It detached two companies to Neehwiller, and one to Jaegersthal.

The third division occupied, with its first brigade, the jutting hill which detaches itself from Froeschwiller, and terminates in a point towards Goersdorf. The second brigade rested its left on Froeschwiller, and its right on the village of Elsasshausen.

The fourth division formed a broken line on the right of the third division, its first brigade facing Gunstett, and its second vis-a-vis with the village of Morsbronn, which it was unable to occupy from want of sufficient force. The Dumesnil division of the seventh corps, which joined early on the morning of the 6th, was placed in rear of the fourth division. In reserve was the second division, placed behind the second brigade of the third division and the first brigade of the fourth. Finally, further in the rear was the brigade of cavalry under the orders of General de Bonnemain: the brigade of Michel cavalry, under the orders of General Duchesne, was placed behind the right wing of the fourth division.

It will be thus seen that MacMahon's front, looking generally north-east, was semicircular, the right thrown back so as to be parallel to the great road and railroad from Wissembourg along the Rhine to Strassburg, while his left pointed rather to the west, covering the railroad which turns off from the main line just mentioned, at Haguenau, and traverses the Vosges by the pass of Bitsche. In fact, the position taken up by Marshal MacMahon formed, so to speak, the keystone of the whole French system of communications across the Vosges; that is, between the main army and its right wing, which originally rested on the Rhine, below Strassburg.

The nature of the country was difficult and broken. The crests of the hills in that part of the Vosges are wooded, and the ravines, though not precipitous, are usually deep, with steep descents on either side. The plateaux above are smooth and often open, and the difficulties of the ascent before MacMahon—with the occupation of the villages of Froeschwiller in his centre, Reichshoffen to his left, and Elsasshausen, covering his right, wooded patches lying all about them—formed the strength of his position. It was impossible that an enemy's force could pass by towards Haguenau and Strassburg without danger to its flank, whilst to penetrate into the Vosges the Germans must dislodge him by direct attack. He had also so placed himself that he could draw supports from De Failly, should that general come to his aid, and, unless in the event of an utter rout, he could fairly cover his own line of retreat. In fact, he had done the best that could have been expected from an able commander, and his position was not only strong in itself, but strategically well-chosen, had the opposing forces been anything like fairly matched. As before stated, however, the Crown Prince pushed on steadily from Wissembourg on the 5th, and was close to MacMahon that evening with 130,000 men, while the French had not more than 50,000, even with the reserves which arrived on the morning of the 6th. The French, moreover, had a front to defend exceeding four miles in length; a fact which made the disproportion in number all the more serious, notwithstanding that the Germans would be compelled to cross the valley under the fire of their artillery before they could commence the work of driving them from their fastnesses.

The Crown Prince had been kept admirably informed of the strength and position of MacMahon; but the latter, with utter disregard of the consequences of such a want of foresight, and in spite of the surprise at Wissembourg, although he knew that the prince was marching upon him with an army flushed by victory, had no idea of that army's strength, and was even unaware of its exact whereabouts or proximate approach until within a few minutes of the hour at which he saw its vanguard appearing on the summits of the hills, exactly over against his own ground, and about a mile and a half distant from him. He had no scouts or spies thrown out, no organization of outposts, none of the precautions usually adopted by a leader of armies to warn him of his enemy's vicinity.

The general opinion in the French camp seemed to be that they would have to fight only two Prussian corps, or, altogether, from 60,000 to 65,000 men, and at these odds they felt convinced that their triumph would be complete. In fact, the word "convinced "only half expresses the absolute certainty the French entertained of gaining the battle, and of driving the German force back beyond the frontier.

A military correspondent of the Temps—usually one of the best informed of the French journals—stated, that as soon as the marshal became aware of the superior forces before him, he telegraphed to headquarters stating such was the case. "Attack them," was the reply. He telegraphed again, insisting on the disproportion of strength; but still the wires reiterated "Attack!"

On the afternoon of the 5th three shots were fired by the French into the opposite woods, to which, of course, there was no reply; and during the whole of the day men were hard at work destroying the bridges across the Sauerbach, so as to prevent the passage of the German army. About six o'clock in the evening several German columns were seen from the French camp to be taking up their position at Dieffenbach and Goersdorff. At seven, the mayor of Gunstett and some country people arrived at Woerth, and reported that the Germans were occupying their village, which is about a mile and a half distant.

During the night Woerth was evacuated by the French, and was not occupied by the Germans. The former left it as a trap for the latter, and *vice versâ*. From nine P.M. until after daybreak the rain poured down in torrents, and with the exception of a few random shots, there was no firing until nearly six A.M., when a few companies of Prussians pushed up to the village to feel for the French army, and were met by a patrol of the latter on the same mission. Some shots were exchanged, but nothing more happened till about seven, when the Germans sent a couple of shells into the steeple of the village church. Just before, a battalion of Zouaves had come down the hill to reconnoitre. The men were pitiful to see. They were wet through and through, and had had nothing to eat for twenty-four hours. They were, however, in excellent spirits, and were joking that they would eat the Germans' dinner before night; but of this very regiment there were, four hours later, little more than half left, and most of those were prisoners! Immediately the church was struck, all the French soldiers rushed back to the camp, and the streets cleared as if by enchantment. A few moments of quiet followed this signal of combat. Some German sharpshooters, who had arrived by the road to Soultz, next crossed the only bridge which had not been destroyed. They passed through the village, and went towards the French centre, being followed by other troops, who took possession of the hill of Dieffenbach, and the meadows on the Prussian right. The sharpshooters commenced firing into the vine-clad hills at the foot of Elsasshausen, and the artillery of both armies at once opened fire, the discharges being slower on the German side than on the French; so slow, in fact, that it was evidently rather a reconnaissance in force than an attack.

MacMahon himself did not believe he should be attacked till the 7th, and the Crown Prince would have preferred waiting till that day, for he had made a long march on the 5th, and had left many stragglers on the road; in addition to which some regiments of the fifth corps had suffered severely at Wissembourg, and found their muster rolls already strangely weakened. By waiting till the 7th, too, the cavalry would have arrived, and been able to have rendered him much valuable assistance after the battle; the nature of the ground being such as to prevent their use to any large extent during the fight. The impatience of his outposts, however, as we have seen, brought on heavy firing at Woerth early on the 6th, and almost immediately afterwards, the battle was fairly joined, but in another direction; for the first real attack was opened by the Bavarians, who, holding to their own right along the base of the steeper heights, debouched by Goersdorf, and with great determination endeavoured to turn the French left.

They attacked so vigorously, that MacMahon, to prevent his general position being turned by its left, executed a change of front by wheeling up his left wing on Froeschwiller as a pivot, so that his position now extended nearly in a straight line—as shown in our plan of the battle. At eight o'clock the steady firing in this direction, and the French fire directed against Woerth, caused the Prussians to station the entire artillery of their fifth corps on the heights east of that place, and they thus succeeded in relieving the Bavarians. A little later the fifth corps was ordered to break off the engagement, it being the intention of the German generals to begin the battle against the concentrated forces of the French only when the entire German army was ready to be brought into action. At a quarter to eight o'clock Bothmer's fourth division of the second Bavarian corps (Hartmann's) induced by the heavy fire of the outposts near Woerth, had left their bivouac at Lembach, and, proceeding by Matistall and Langen-Soulzbach, after a sharp engagement penetrated as far as Neehwiller, where they spread, fronting to the south. At half past ten this Bavarian corps, supposing the order to break off the engagement, which had been given to the fifth Prussians, to extend to themselves, withdrew to Langen-Soulzbach. The French, being thus no longer pressed on their left, turned all their strength with the greatest energy against the fifth Prussians at Woerth, and endeavoured to crush this isolated part of their antagonist's forces. Finding them so earnest on this point, and perceiving the eleventh Prussians approaching vigorously in the direction of Gunstett, the fifth Prussians immediately proceeded to the attack, so as to defeat the French if possible, before they had time fully to concentrate. The twentieth Brigade was the first to defile through Woerth, and marched towards Elsasshausen and Froeschwiller. It was promptly followed by the nineteenth Brigade. Eventually, the ninth division being drawn into the fight, the whole fifth corps found itself involved in the sanguinary conflict raging along the heights west of Woerth.

For more than three hours the battle raged here with the greatest fury. Chassepots, needleguns, mitrailleuses, field artillery, and shells, all played their part in the terrible fray. Undismayed by the havoc spread through their ranks, the Germans marched down the eastern slopes, across the valley, and attacked the opposite heights in the face of a tremendous fire.

The most sanguinary part of the strife commenced at the foot of the hills occupied by the French. In the vineyards the Zouaves and Turcos had taken up their position, and they possessed the twofold advantage over the impetuous advance of the Germans, of being under cover, and of being in a position to take good aim at their foes; the Germans at the same time being entirely exposed, and compelled to fire almost at randon. Two, three, and in some places even four times, were the Germans repulsed, but on each occasion they fell back on their reserves, and the reserves again on their supports, in the best order. In fact, nothing could possibly have exceeded their steadiness and coolness under fire. The French, too, fought with the greatest bravery, and twice did they succeed in recapturing Woerth: in fact, at one period they looked upon victory as almost certain, and the state of affairs was decidedly critical for the Germans. As a proof of the determined manner in which the French fought at this time, we may state that, on one of the occasions when the first and second Zouaves were pressing the Prussians back through the streets of the village, they were taken in flank and rear, completely cut off, and, after heroically striving to fight their way through to their supports, were all killed, wounded, or captured. A single incident will suffice to show the terrible nature of the struggle at this point. A captain of the first Zouaves, who was wounded in the village, had been ordered to advance to the support of another company of his regiment engaged in the streets. He had with him sixty-eight men and two subalterns when he entered the place; by the time (about twenty minutes later) his sergeant-major informed him that the rear of his company was threatened, only thirty-six remained; and when he had broken through the first lot of Prussians that attempted to stop his retreat, he found himself at the head of eleven men. Things looked so bad—more Prussians hurrying up and a fire from the houses being sustained—that he stopped, and said to his men, "Eh bien! que dites-vous?" to which all replied, "Nous allons nous defendre." On he went, with his small but heroic following. When he got into the open ground by the river, his eleven men were reduced to three, besides his sergeant-major, who, as well as himself, fell the next moment, the one wounded in the shoulder, the other through the leg.

At last the French, who were threatened with being outflanked, were compelled to fall back inch by inch on their own centre, and it was now the turn of the Germans to again advance.

At half-past one o'clock orders were given to the first Bavarian corps (Von der Tann's) to leave one of its two divisions where it stood, and sending on the other as quickly as possible by Lobsann and Lampertsloch, to seize upon the French front in the gap between the second Bavarian corps at Langen-Soulzbach, and the fifth Prussian corps at Woerth. The eleventh Prussians were ordered to advance to Elsasshausen, skirt the forest of Nieder Wald, and operate against Froeschwiller. The Würtemburg division was to proceed to Gunstett, and follow the eleventh Prussians across the Sauerbach; the Baden division was to remain at Sourbourg.

At two o'clock the combat had extended along the entire line, and the struggle was most severe. The fifth Prussians were fighting at Woerth; the eleventh Prussians near Elsasshausen. At the strong positions of the French on and near the heights of Froeschwiller, they offered the most intense resistance. The first Bavarian corps reached Goersdorf, but could not maintain their ground; the second Bavarian corps had to exchange the exhausted troops of Bothmer's division, who had spent all their ammunition in the fierce fights of the morning, for Walther's division. While Bothmer's troops fell back, Schleich's brigade, belonging to Walther's division, marched upon Langen-Soulzbach, and the Würtemburg division approached Gunstett.

At two o'clock fresh orders were given by the Germans. The Würtemburg division was to turn towards Reichshoffen by way of Ebersbach, to threaten the French line of retreat. The first Bavarian was to attack at once and dislodge them from their position at Froeschwiller and in the neighbouring vineyards, and thus roll up the right of the French lines.

Clouds of German skirmishers crossed the marshy bottom to the east of Woerth, between Elsasshausen and Morsbronn, under the cover of a tremendous artillery fire from sixty guns, posted on the opposite heights of Gunstett; large masses of infantry pressed forward in support, and the Germans made vigorous endeavours to force the French right wing back upon the Haguenau-Bitsche road, so as to compel it to retreat towards Bitsche—a movement that would have been fatal. The conflict raged with tremendous fury; prodigies of valour were displayed by the French, who, anticipating the hostile attack, advanced again and again to the charge, only to recoil before the fresh troops whom the Germans incessantly brought up, "as if," said a captured officer, "they sprang out of the ground."

The village of Froeschwiller, which was burnt during the struggle, was at last carried by a fierce hand to hand encounter; the houses being stormed one by one, the doors burst open by the butt ends of the guns, and many Zouaves and Turcos made prisoners. The assaulting parties of Würtemburg and Prussian troops, fighting their way from opposite sides, met in the centre of the village, at the foot of the church tower.

Between two and three o'clock the French, bringing fresh troops into the field, and advancing with consummate bravery, assumed the offensive against the fifth and eleventh Prussian corps; and about three o'clock it appeared as if MacMahon would so far carry the day, that he would take possession of the only bridge upon the Sauerbach, and break through the German centre. Had he done this, and been able to hold what he was possessed of, he would have captured a vast portion of the German artillery, and have inflicted a fearful punishment upon every battalion of them that had crossed the bridge. But the French had to deal with a much larger force, far more orderly, and better handled, than their own. The Prussians fought like soldiers in the highest state of discipline; the French now seemed to behave more like a gallant mob. There appeared to be no order in their formation after the first ten minutes of their being under fire. Any advantage which they had in the superior range of the Chassepot over the needle-gun they threw away, by advancing—rushing would be the better word—so near their enemy that they were placed upon an equality with him. In numbers, also, they were less than one to two.

A little after three came the turning point of the battle. After some sharp fighting, the Prussian advance against the French left was so far successful that the village of Reichshoffen was carried; but not until the Crown Prince had developed his chief and crowning effort against the French right centre, where the fifth corps, supported by the second Bavarian, advanced in heavy columns, covered by a tremendous cannonade, and carried at a rush the village of Elsasshausen, from which MacMahon's third division had hitherto commanded the wide valley of the Sauerbach, which before divided the opposing armies at this part. From the moment at which this movement commenced, it was evident that the French were outnumbered, outflanked, and beaten; and nothing was left to MacMahon but to throw his right completely back upon the centre—a movement so finely executed in the face of adverse circumstances and a superior force, as to win admiration from his enemy.

The pressure soon became overwhelming, and, assailed fiercely in front and flank, the French right and centre were cut in two, and rolled away in shattered and divided fragments. About the same time the Crown Prince made his last manoeuvre by bringing up some Würtemburg troops not previously engaged, beyond the extreme right flank of the French; and the whole right being thus completely outflanked, was driven in and crushed, and the magnificent and renowned Algerian army, which had crowned the range of Woerth at sunrise, soon became a ruined mass of disheartened fugitives.

A fierce charge of the French cuirassier regiments against the fifth and eleventh Prussian corps, was made at the close of the fight, in the hope of either retrieving the day, or at all events of facilitating the retreat of the rest of the army. Nothing could possibly have been more brilliant than the manner in which they advanced; but it ended, as such charges of heavy cavalry must almost of necessity do in the face of modern artillery and the breech-loader, in the all but annihilation of the daring horsemen. The artillery awaited them in a stationary position, and inflicted on them a very heavy loss. The infantry, too, with their needle-guns, were many of them placed in the protecting orchards, and from behind the trees came another terrible fire through which the men rode to their death. As they came within range they were swept down, and not a single man reached the German line. It was simply destruction; but having received their orders, they charged again and again (according to some accounts not fewer than eleven times), and rode as gallantly to be shot down without a chance of retaliation, as though they were following up a victory. When the battle was ended, the ground over which they had charged was strewn with the steel helmets and cuirasses of the extinct regiments. Some 200 prisoners were taken, and a few stragglers were left to take part in the subsequent flight; but the brave regiments were no more, and when asked, during the retreat, "Where are the cuirassiers?" MacMahon replied that they did not exist. In the destruction of these troops the Coburg Gotha regiment greatly distinguished itself, and Duke Ernest, who rode throughout the day by the side of the Crown Prince, having witnessed their bravery, galloped up to them and expressed his pride and gratitude at their gallant conduct. A little incident in connection with the charge of the cuirassiers is worth mentioning, as showing the bravery of the Germans as well as of the French on the occasion. In a hop plantation lay a company of the ninety-fifth regiment, and some pioneers of the eleventh battalion, the latter armed with the short-barrelled needle-gun. The lieutenant-commander of the latter was a man of dauntless bravery and coolness. To these troops, covered by the hops and tree trunks, presently approached one of the cuirassier regiments. Until within a distance of fifty paces, when the French word of command to push forward was called out, the Germans believed them to be Bavarians. No further doubt was, however, possible, and for the moment the German position seemed a fearful one; it looked like madness for a few infantry to attempt to withstand that mass of cavalry, charging with uplifted sabres, and so the Germans turned to the right-about, to retire as fast as possible. But the lieutenant stood firm and cried out, "Children, are you going to leave me here alone?" His brave fellows instantly stood still, and at a few steps' distance, fired rapid volleys which greatly decimated the horsemen, and those who charged were shot down by other troops. The colonel, the beau ideal of a soldier, a stately, handsome, middle-aged man, had led the charge to the very fine of the needle-guns, and came down, as his horse rolled dead, with a heavy crash in his cuirass. He was afterwards presented to the Crown Prince, and was forwarded to the railway station on foot, his cuirass being taken off, with orders that he should receive every attention.

An unusually horrid circumstance occurred during the third charge of the cuirassiers; for the Germans saw coming towards them at full speed a horse carrying a rider whose head had just been carried off by a cannon ball. This mutilated corpse was that of M. de la Futzun de Lacarre, of the third regiment. The same ball had cut the trumpeter of the regiment in two, and carried off the hand of the captain who was by his side.

About four o'clock the troops of MacMahon, thoroughly broken and exhausted, retired in great confusion towards Reichshoffen and Niederbronn. Here a new engagement took place. Niederbronn is the point at which the roads to Bitsche and Saverne diverge: and the Prussians strove hard to seize that village. The Bavarians pressed forward over the heights by Neehwiller, now abandoned by the French left; and they might have succeeded in occupying the cross-roads, but for the fortunate arrival of a division of the fifth French corps, which had been sent by De Failly by rail from Bitsche, and which had been prevented from coming up in time for the battle in consequence of the mistake of a telegraphic operator. It took up a position covering Niederbronn, and maintained itself there until night had fallen, and some of the remnants of MacMahon's corps had gained the road to Saverne. We say, some of the remnants, because many others escaped by way of Haguenau, towards Strassburg. The retreat of the latter, which had chiefly formed the French right during the engagement, was in reality a panic-stricken rout, although they were not pressed at all after their ground was once yielded. In fact, nothing worse has occurred in modern history, except, perhaps, the flight of the raw fugitives at the battle of Bull's Bun on the opening of the American War. Fleeing madly, though wholly unpursued, crowds of men on foot, or worse, on horses stolen from the guns and trains, rushed pell-mell through Haguenau. The scene was vividly sketched by the correspondent of the Vienna *Wehr Zeitung*, who happened to be a witness of it. "About four o'clock," he said, "a riderless horse galloped into the town, then a second, and a third; but the first intimation of how the day had gone was brought by a cuirassier, who came spurring through without cuirass or arms, his horse covered with foam and blood. Next arrived an artillerist on an unsaddled horse, his face distorted with inexpressible alarm. Some minutes later a mob of some twenty horsemen hurried past, among whom two Zouaves clinging upon one horse were conspicuous; the others were cuirassiers in every stage of fright and terror, some wildly swinging their sabres; others as if out of their wits, flogging their poor exhausted horses, several without saddles, most of them without arms. One cuirassier halted his horse just before me, loosened his cuirass, threw off his helmet, next his heavy sword, lastly his weighty breast-plate, and then, laughing contentedly, rode leisurely on. A pause of some five minutes followed. The townsmen had all fled inside the gates. Presently, up gallops a field gendarme, halts his half-dead horse, and calls out ' Shut the gates instantly, the Prussians are at my heels.' The field-watch turned white. I exclaimed, 'What madness! Haguenau is an open town. There can be no defence, and if the Prussians are really at hand, the best thing for the town is to open the gates as wide as possible.' His face brightened up. The tumult, however, became greater. Among a crowd of cuirassiers some lancers were mixed up; then came hussar uniforms. The road becomes thronged; unmounted horses gallop past as if driven on by panic; on all sides are swarms of artillerymen in shirt-sleeves, many of their horses with the traces cut, ridden by infantry or artillerymen, but having no officers with them.

"While this motley crowd of cavalry was galloping through, a train rushed past laden with infantry. All the waggons were filled—on the roofs, hanging on by the handles, with half their bodies in the air, on the gangway boards, some fully accoutred, some half naked, no wounded. By five o'clock the rush of horsemen began to abate, and then came a stream of conveyances, four or five carriages all completely harnessed, yet without their guns. Then jolted and rattled past a broken ammunition waggon crammed with Turcos; next a peasant's waggon filled with bedding and household gear, but no owner; a Zouave led the horses; two frightfully wounded Turcos lay on the top, a cluster of unarmed soldiers of all arms clung round it. Now followed infantry on foot. It was about half past five; still no officers. In dense swarms come the chancery cars, the carriages of three general brigades, the archives of a division, four or five empty ammunition trucks, every kind of ambulance waggon, all packed with uninjured soldiers. On one car lay three corpses, and a few pitifully draggled Turcos followed in the crowd in dumb resignation. Then came a lot of sutlers and camp-followers. The infantry had all flung away their packs, many their guns, some were in their shirt-sleeves, most of them had loaves stuck on their swords and swung on their shoulders. About half past six an orderly troop of cuirassiers, under the command of a captain and two subalterns, about forty men strong, rode past. They were almost all properly accoutred, and kept step. Between four and seven o'clock a disorderly rabble hurried by absorbed in themselves and in their miserable existence; in the whole body not more than forty in marching order, altogether some 8000 to 10,000 men, very few wounded, some three or four cavalry officers, two artillery, and about eight infantry officers in the entire swarm."

Shameful as the disorder was on this side, the centre and left of MacMahon's forces behaved hardly better in their retreat after leaving Niederbronn, which, in fact, their own misconduct turned into a disastrous rout. Their officers, who had neglected to maintain order in time of peace, found it impossible to rally them under the pressure of panic, and when MacMahon, on the following evening, reached Saverne after a cross march through the hills, but three of his infantry regiments had kept their ranks. The fatal disregard of discipline, the total want of mutual confidence between officers and men, the utter prostration under reverse which constantly characterized the army of the Second Empire during the war, were at once fully manifested in this shameful retreat—the sad presage of greater misfortunes to come.

The official statement of the loss of the Germans in the battle was 8000 men. The regiments which suffered most may be estimated from the number of officers they lost. The fifty-eighth lost thirty-two; the fifty-ninth, twenty-three; the seventh (guards), thirty-five; the forty-seventh, twenty-nine; the forty-sixth, thirty-three; the fifty-seventh, thirty; the sixth, twenty-eight; the thirty-seventh, twenty-five. It is perhaps worthy of notice, that of the troops engaged, nearly all were non-Prussians; that is, the fifth corps, Poseners; eleventh, Nassauers, Hesse Casselers, Saxe Coburgers, &c., and the rest Southern Germans.

The French loss in killed and wounded was almost as great as that of the Prussians, and in addition the Germans captured 6000 prisoners on the field, and about 4000 afterwards. The disastrous rout already described must also have entailed on the French a loss, chiefly in stragglers, of nearly a third of the whole army; for the highest estimate ever given of those rallied afterwards mentioned no more than 18,000 men, including; 3000 who escaped to Strassburg, where they were at once incorporated in the garrison.

The French also lost thirty-six cannon, six mitrailleuses, two eagles, innumerable arms, their entire baggage and treasure, and two railway trains containing provisions. Even MacMahon's personal baggage, his official and private letters, the plan of the French campaign in cipher (which was soon deciphered), &c., fell into the hands of the conquerors. It was characteristic of modern French strategy, that no maps of France, especially of the Vosges, were found in the officers' baggage; while routes to Coburg, Berlin, &c., were discovered, as well as sketches of the country beyond the Rhine. It was also significant of the luxury which was too prevalent in the French army, that among other trophies was a gaudy collection of ladies' dresses and female finery.

At Solferino the French took 6000 prisoners, thirty guns, and two standards. The tactical importance of Woerth was therefore quite equal to that of Solferino; and the moral effect on the German forces of such a signal success over the best general and one of the finest armies France could place in the field was, of course, exceedingly great. The fearful havoc inflicted on MacMahon's troops and the disastrous nature of his rout, not only quite freed South Germany from any fear of invasion, but on the other hand laid open the whole right of the French line of defence, and left Marshal Bazaine with two armies to watch, where he was already overmatched with one.

As early as half past four in the afternoon the Crown Prince had sent home the following despatch announcing the victory:—

"*Battle-field near Woerth, Saturday, August* 6, 4.30 *p.m.*—Victorious battle near Woerth. I have completely defeated Marshal MacMahon, with the greater part of his army. The French were driven back to Bitsche.

"Friedrich Wilhelm, Crown Prince."

A little later the king informed her Majesty, Queen Augusta, of the result as follows:—

"Wonderful fortune! This new great victory won by Fritz. Thank God for his mercy! We have taken thirty cannons, two eagles, six mitrailleuses, 4000 prisoners. MacMahon received reinforcements from the main army."

The scene at the close of the battle was well described in a letter from the duke of Saxe-Coburg, from which we annex an extract:—"We were able to watch the whole battle from the nearest proximity; and where we stood the Crown Prince was in a position to give his command. When the last "hurrah" had rung forth, we chased into the line and up the hostile height, after we had for hours witnessed around us the explosion of shells. But what a sight presented itself close by! It is indescribable. A beautiful calm summer's evening, and straight along burning farms and villages; between, accumulations of the dead and the dying, and the exulting outcry of our victorious troops The banners were displayed, the military bands were playing the national hymn, men embraced and fondled each other in joy, and the hand of many a dying comrade was yet clasped. And I heard no one complain, notwithstanding the horrible devastation. Eight on we went, through thousands of French prisoners, and through the captured fire-arms, around which the serving men lay in heaps of dead and wounded. There was no eye without a tear. It was the grandest and most appalling sight that can be witnessed in life. Slowly night set upon this awful scene, and wiped away the terrible view. How can I find words for my joy and sorrow when I came to our decimated regiment, which had taken a glorious part in the secured laurels?"

The district in which the engagement took place, of course, suffered terribly. Many of the houses in Woerth were destroyed, and at Froeschwiller it was even worse. In this village, too, the church was shelled, and then burnt down after a fearful hand-to-hand combat had taken place within its walls. The orchards in all parts of the battle-field were knocked to pieces: the vines and hops ruthlessly cut down, the potatoes annihilated, and the meadows turned into desolate tracts of rugged soil.

All the German troops which had taken part in the engagement bivouacked on the battle-field that night. On the following morning the cavalry corps began the pursuit of the disorganized French troops; and for some days after they were continually capturing fresh prisoners, and finding the shattered *débris* of MacMahon's army.

After the battle great animosity was displayed by the peasants, and some of them were guilty of the grossest barbarity towards the wounded Germans. At Gunstett alone, twenty-eight peasants, caught red-handed gouging and maiming, were tried and shot; and at one time as many as forty lads, between the ages of twelve and eighteen, were in the hands of the provost marshal, under accusation of having committed similar outrages. In fact, the fanatic hatred of the Alsatian peasants against the German invaders excited much surprise and regret. In no case did the soldiers take the law into their own hands, but brought in the persons whom they found committing the outrages to the proper military authorities.

In consequence of the fearful losses on both sides and the hasty flight of the French, the sufferings endured by the wounded were unusually great; for even twenty-four hours after the engagement hundreds of them still lay untended, and the air was polluted with the stench of unburied corpses blackening in the sun's hot rays.

In calmly reviewing the whole circumstances connected with the battle, it must be admitted that the manner in which it was contested was honourable alike to conquerors and conquered. The Germans certainly were in irresistible force; but this was not felt until after mid-day, and for several hours the French possessed the advantage of a formidable position. When the German attack was fully developed, it proved, as might have been expected, crushing; yet for some time they fought with a superiority of numbers not too great to render the struggle wholly unequal. On the other hand, the French attacked frequently with splendid courage, and resisted with determined resolution; they generally manoeuvred, too, with the ease, the celerity, and the precision of a well-trained army. Yet, as we have seen, they showed signs of panic towards the close of the fight; they broke up rapidly on being outflanked, and fled from the field in wild confusion. The terrible defect of the French troops—their inability to resist the temptation to hasty firing offered by the breechloaders—began to tell as early as two o'clock in the afternoon, for by that time there was a want of ammunition on several parts of the French lines. It would appear, too, that this characteristic of the French was aggravated in some parts of the field by the orders given by MacMahon. His experience had chiefly been in Algeria, where the troops are often ordered to put off their knapsacks, with a view to move more freely, and this was the order he gave his troops at Reichshoffen. The result was, that out of the ninety cartridges which a French soldier is provided with, he had only thirty; the remaining sixty having been left on the battle-field, together with the knapsacks. On the other side, the steadiness, rapidity, and accuracy of the German fire was such, that the French believed they were using mitrailleuses (as will be seen further on, it was so stated in the telegram from the emperor announcing the result of the engagement), and to these they attributed much of the terrible slaughter in their ranks. One chief result of the battle was, in fact, the demonstration of the close connection between the value of arms of precision and the constitutional temperament of those in whose hands they are placed. The best troops of France were mown down because the German soldier kept cool and took good aim, while the effect of the rapid firing of the French was greatly inferior.

The Germans, like generous enemies, frankly admitted the gallantry which could not withstand them; and the soldiers who were present on both occasions said that nothing in the hottest of the fighting at Königgrätz could at all compare with the fighting at Woerth. The German generals, too, admitted that they never witnessed anything more brilliant than the bravery of the French troops, but their own troops were not to be denied. With tenacity as great, and a fierce resolution, they pressed on and on, up heights where the vineyards dripped with blood; and although checked again and again, still persevered with a furious intrepidity which the French could not, at last, withstand. In fact, the Germans showed such an absolute disregard of death, and such a desperate valour, as excited the astonishment and admiration of the French. Their steadiness, in spite of the most frightful carnage, was abundantly proved by the returns of killed and wounded.

Personally, MacMahon acted throughout the fight in the bravest possible manner. Nearly all his staff were killed; and he himself, after having been fifteen hours in the saddle, was found in a ditch, faint with fatigue, and revived by a soldier with a draught of brandy. He remained all night on the heights of Phalsburg, and when in the morning he tried to count his losses, and to rally the remains of his unfortunate divisions, the great heart of the brave marshal failed at the task Overcome by emotion, tears were seen flowing from his eyes, and his head was bowed under the weight of his disasters.

The following was his address to those of his troops who remained with him a day or two after the battle:—

"Soldiers!—On the 6th of August the fortune of war betrayed your courage. You only lost your positions after an heroic resistance which lasted not less than nine hours. You were 35,000 against 140,000, and were overwhelmed by numbers. Under such conditions a defeat is glorious, and history will record that at the battle of Froeschwiller the French displayed the greatest valour. You have experienced heavy loss; but that of the enemy is heavier still. If he did not pursue you, it was because you had hit him so hard. The emperor is satisfied with you, and the whole country thanks you for having so worthily upheld the honour of your flag. We have had a great ordeal to go through. You must forget it. The first corps is about to be re-organized, and, with God's help, we shall soon take a brilliant revenge.

"MACMAHON."

The *Figaro* opened a subscription, which was liberally responded to, for the purpose of presenting a sword of honour to the general, whose defeat it regarded as one of the most brilliant achievements in the history of France!

As regards the tactics displayed by the two commanders, the movements of the Germans at the beginning of the day scarcely seem to have been well timed; their attacks were partial and disunited, and MacMahon had more than one chance, especially against the centre at Woerth, which, had De Failly's corps been added to his own, might have caused the result to have been very different. It is acknowledged, too, by the Germans themselves, that their cavalry ought to have done more. Had that arm been boldly and vigorously employed after the French flanks had been finally turned, MacMahon's army might have been destroyed; it is at least probable that it would have been more cut up than it was, and that it would have lost nearly its whole artillery. The manner, however, in which the Crown Prince disposed his forces for the double attack on both the French flanks was admirable, if not altogether free from danger; and though it may be said that he acted cautiously, with some hesitation, and perhaps without the hope of great success, he nevertheless gave proof of the powers of a real general at the decisive moment. MacMahon's conduct in the first part of the day was worthy of his high reputation. He made the most of his troops and his ground, and handled his army with quickness and skill; but probably he ought to have effected his retreat while as yet an opportunity remained, when the great flanking attacks were being developed.

A slight incident of the battle revealed very strikingly the want of information among the French troops of what was happening, and had happened, in their vicinity. After the Crown Prince had completely beaten MacMahon, and the whole line of communication was in German hands, a train started from Haguenau with 1000 French soldiers, who steamed away quietly and comfortably to find themselves prisoners in the centre of the German army.

As a fitting conclusion to our description of this battle, in which MacMahon played such an important part, and as an accompaniment to the annexed portrait, a few particulars respecting the previous career of the French general will not be out of place. His full baptismal name is Marie Edme Patrick Maurice, and by his surname he recalls one of the noblest families of the old Celtic princes of Ireland, who suffered severely in the wars of Cromwell in that country, and who risked and lost their once proud position in the cause of the last of the Stuart kings. It is said that the sept of MacMahon carried their national traditions, their ancestral pride, and their historic name, to France, where they mingled their blood by intermarriages with the old nobility of their adopted country. The future marshal was born in the year 1808, at the Château de Sully, near Autun. Up to seventeen years old young MacMahon was educated at the quiet seminary of

Autun. He was then, however, transferred to the military school of St. Cyr, which, two years afterwards, he left as *sous-lieutenant éléve*, and as such joined the Staff School of Application.

His first fighting experiences were made in Algeria in 1830, while acting as orderly officer to General Achard. In this capacity he accompanied the first Medéah expedition, and greatly distinguished himself in an engagement on the Mouzaïa by carrying an important despatch through a whole army of Arabs to Blidah, escaping his enemies by leaping down a frightful abyss. Though his horse was killed, the young lieutenant escaped with a severe shaking, and accomplished his mission in safety. For this gallant exploit he received the cross of the Legion of Honour. In 1832, still with General Achard, MacMahon was present at the siege of Antwerp, at the close of which he was created captain. Returning to Algeria in 1836, he was wounded at the second siege of Constantine in the following year, while acting as aide-de-camp to General Damrémont. Recompensed here with the rank of officer of the Legion of Honour, we subsequently find him, in 1840, aide-de-camp to General Changarnier in Algeria, where, shortly after, he obtained the command of a regiment of Chasseurs a pied, a body afterwards greatly relied on by the French, but which were then being organized by the duke of Orleans. With these he gained fresh honours, commanding several expeditions against the Kabyles, and assisting to subdue the renowned Arab chief, Abd-el-Kader.

In August, 1855, he replaced General Canrobert, who was obliged to return invalided, in the command of the 1st Division of the French Crimean Army, and when the chiefs of the allied armies resolved upon the final assault of Sebastopol, they assigned to General MacMahon the post of carrying the works of the Malakoff. The well-known storming of this strong fort rendered his name famous in European, as it already was in African annals. Elevated to the dignity of Senator in 1856, he again returned to Algeria, and took an active part in the campaign of 1857, and in 1858 was named commander-in-chief of the whole Algerian forces. Summoned in the following year with his troops to the Italian war, he gained on two successive days, the 3rd and 4th of June, the celebrated victories of Turbigo and Magenta. This latter success won him his baton and the title of Duke of Magenta, both being granted on the field of battle.

Amongst the romantic and sentimental incidents of the war of Italian liberty, one of the most characteristic was General MacMahon's triumphal entry, at the head of his troops, into the city of Milan; carrying on the pommel of his saddle a little Italian child, whom he had picked up on the road. The enthusiastic Milanese wept for joy. He represented France in 1861, as ambassador extraordinary to Prussia, on the coronation of the king. He was soon afterwards made governor-general of Algeria, in which position he remained until called to the chief command of the first corps d'armée in the campaign against Germany.

BATTLE OF FORBACH.

On the same day as that on which the battle of Woerth was fought (Saturday, August 6), from before noon till after seven in the evening, the Germans and French were engaged in a not less desperate battle near Saarbrück, on the same hill of Spicheren, and near the same village of St.

Arnual, where the emperor and the prince imperial had witnessed a mere rehearsal of a battle on the Tuesday, only four days before.

The news of a sudden advance of a force of unknown strength through Wissembourg, and of the disaster that Douay's division had suffered, reached the French headquarters on the 5th, and spurred the emperor's staff to take steps for that concentration which had hitherto been only generally designed. Though even yet neither L'Admirault nor Bazaine was moved up to support him, orders were given to General Frossard to withdraw the troops left overlooking Saarbrück on the previous Tuesday, consisting of the second corps, numbering about 28,000 men, with 72 guns, lest a similar surprise to that of Douay should be attempted from the woods beyond the German frontier-line. On the morning of the 6th, therefore, the French had evacuated the position gained by them with so much pomp and superfluous energy four days before, and were out of sight of the town. They were encamped chiefly on the heights of Spicheren, which consist of an abrupt hill (or rather a spur of a range of hills), possessing naturally great strength for purposes of defence, and which was reinforced by field works most scientifically thrown up. The distance from Saarbrück is about two and a half miles, and the last cover which the Germans (advancing from that town to attack the heights) could have, before arriving at the base of the hill, is about 1900 paces. They had to advance this distance over a plain with occasional slight undulations, none of which, however, were of sufficient depth to afford them shelter from the fire of the heights. The entire plain is destitute of trees, hedges, bushes, or natural cover of any kind, and had been mostly cultivated for potato crops. Between the town of Saarbrück and this plain lie the range of hills which had been occupied by the French after the affair on the 2nd, and which are inferior in elevation, and nearly parallel to the Spicheren heights. These latter commence by a gentle slope from the plain for about 200 paces; then rise with great abruptness to an elevation of 110 to 130 feet; and are so steep that it is exceedingly difficult to ascend them, even without the encumbrance of rifles and knapsacks. In fact, as an old Crimean officer remarked, the ascent of the Alma was almost child's play compared with climbing them. They form a natural fortress, which needs no addition from art to be all but impregnable. Like so many bastions the hills project into the valley, facing it on all sides, and afford the strongest imaginable position for defence. Some French officers who were taken prisoners confessed to having smiled at the idea of the Germans attacking them in this stronghold, and there was scarcely a man on the French side who was not persuaded, that to attempt to take the Spicheren hills must lead to the utter annihilation of the attacking force. Fortunately for the Germans, the French were left by their generals with a most inadequate supply of artillery—one of those unaccountable mistakes which marked French generalship as a main cause of the disasters to the imperial armies in the campaign.

As we have said, the heights form the spur of a range running in a general direction from east to west, but at this spot taking a southwest turn towards the village of Forbach, where the French left was placed, and distant about three and a half miles as the crow flies. The hills themselves are thickly wooded; but this portion is tolerably bare of trees. Forbach lies in the valley, and on the other side of that village the ground again slopes up to other woods. A country road from

Saarbrück runs across the plain, and winds round the east side of the spur to Spicheren village, rather more than a mile in the rear of the heights which bear its name. Bound the top edge of this spur a parapet was thrown up from the inside, before the engagement, which formed an earthen breastwork extending all across the front and along the western side of the spur for about 180 or 200 yards; the eastern side being almost precipitous. The spur itself on the summit is about 100 yards broad, and 250 or 300 yards long.

On the forenoon of August 6, the seventh German corps of the army of the centre pushed its vanguard to Herchenbach, about five miles north-west of Saarbrück, with outposts stretching as far as the river Saar. They did not intend to commence hostilities that day; but, as before stated, the previous night the French had evacuated their position on the drill ground of Saarbrück, and about noon on the 6th the German cavalry division, under General Rhein Göben, passed through the town. Two squadrons formed the van; and the moment they reached the highest point of the drill ground, and became visible to spectators on the south, they were fired at from the hills near Spicheren.

The French, however, were not anticipating an engagement on that day; in fact, General Frossard was still in the act of further withdrawing a portion of his troops when the Germans arrived, and he mistook their first advance for a reconnaissance in force. Even when a German battery had been brought up and posted on the external slope of the heights abandoned by the French the night before, and had commenced a sharp fire, the arms of the French infantry regiments were still piled, the men were lounging about in easy *déshabillé*, some of them lying in their *tentes d'abris*, some cooking, and some cleaning their accoutrements: the same symptoms were observable among the gunners, and nothing betokened any expectation of trouble or disturbance from the enemy.

Immediately, however, all was hurry and bustle, and orderlies and aides-de-camp began to tear backward and forward along the road to Forbach. A battery of artillery was got into position facing up the valley, the arms of the infantry were unpiled, their tents were struck as quick as lightning, a working party were hard at work throwing up an intrenchment in front of their position, and those troops which had been withdrawn were at once turned round to re-occupy the heights.

Between twelve and one o'clock the fourteenth German division arrived at Saarbrück, and proceeding south, it encountered a strong French force in the valley between Saarbrück and Spicheren, and opened fire forthwith.

The division at first had to deal with far superior numbers; and yet to have limited the attack to the French front would have been useless, as their left could have come down the slope and closed in force upon their enemy. General von Kamecke, therefore, while engaging the front, also attempted to turn the French left flank by Stiring. The troops he could spare for these operations were, however, too weak to make an effectual impression upon the much stronger numbers of the French, and two successive assaults on the steep range of heights in the French centre, and forming the key of their position, were successfully repulsed by General Frossard, the Germans leaving long fines of dead and wounded on the slopes of the hill.

Eventually, however, the roar of the cannon attracted several other German detachments. The division under General von Barnekow was the first to be drawn to the spot. Two of its batteries came dashing up at full speed, to relieve their struggling comrades. They were promptly followed by the fortieth infantry (the regiment which had been engaged at Saarbrück on the 2nd) under Colonel Rex, and three squadrons of the ninth hussars. At this moment the vanguard of the fifth division was espied on the Winterberg hill. General Stülpnagel, whose van had been stationed at Sulzbach the same morning, had been ordered by General von Alvensleben to march his entire division in the direction from which the sound of cannon proceeded, and two batteries advanced in a forced march on the high road. The infantry were partly sent by rail from Neuenkirchen to Saarbrück.

As early as half-past one the woods near Stiring, on the opposite side of the plain to the French left, were filled with German infantry, who were keeping up a murderous fire on the French infantry in the open, and on some artillery which was replying to certain German guns now in position in the plain below, and firing up the valley in the direction of Forbach.

It was here that the heavy losses of the French were sustained. Obviously they fought at a tremendous disadvantage, and the effect produced by the fire of their tirailleurs upon the enemy, who kept themselves carefully concealed, must have been infinitely less than of that which was directed against them from the dense cover of the woods. It would be impossible to over-rate the dash and valour of the French infantry at this point, or to pay too high a tribute to their endurance under such trying circumstances. A hundred times they advanced close up to the wood with a desperate impetuosity; but although they did all that could be expected of brave men, they were time after time obliged to retire, dropping in scores at each successive advance or retreat. This sort of fighting went on steadily for a couple of hours. At one time the Germans were so far successful that they carried the village of Stiring and captured several mitrailleuses, but the repeated attacks of their companions in the front having totally failed, both the village and mitrailleuses were retaken, and for a time the Germans in both places were thrown on the defensive.

At about half-past three o'clock Kamecke's division had been sufficiently reinforced to enable General von Göben, who had arrived in the meantime and assumed the command, to make a more vigorous onslaught on the enemy's front. He therefore ordered the attack to commence, at the same time massing a large body of cavalry, composed of cuirassiers, lancers, hussars, and dragoons, on either flank. Skirmishers were also deployed to harass the French right from the woods of St. Arnual. The chief aim of the attack on the centre was the wooded portion of the declivity of Spicheren. The fortieth infantry, supported on its right by troops of the fourteenth division, and on its left by four battalions of the fifth division, made the assault. A reserve was formed of some battalions of the fifth and sixteenth divisions, as they came up.

About six German batteries opened fire on the French position to cover the advance of the first line, which this time gained the foot of the hill with but little loss. The conflict then became sanguinary, as every inch of ground was most obstinately disputed, and the continual roll of musketry was terrific. Gradually, however, the French retired and the wood was occupied. Still ascending, the Germans at last drove the French to the top of the hill. Here the latter made a stand, and combining the three arms of the service for a united attack, endeavoured to retrieve the day. The loss to the Germans was now fearful, and it is believed that about nine of them fell for every Frenchman. They were only about sixty yards distant, were ill-concealed and had to fire up and climb an exceedingly steep height, whilst the French were naturally protected by the crest of the hill, and had the advantage of firing down on their enemy.

For an hour, the struggle for possession of the crest of the hill was hot and furious. At length the French gave way, and the German infantry steadily advanced. No sooner had the French reached the suburbs of Forbach, than they opened a hot fire of artillery upon the right of the German line, causing the cavalry placed there to change their position to the left flank. Here the whole cavalry division, some 8000 sabres, were massed behind a sheltering hill. It was at this juncture that the artillery of the fifth German division accomplished a rare and most daring feat. Two batteries literally clambered up the hills of Spicheren by a narrow and precipitous mountain path, and contributed materially to the success of the day; for with their help a fresh attack of the French was repulsed. A flank attack, directed against the German left from Alsting and Spicheren, was also warded off in time by battalions of the fifth division stationed in reserve.

About five o'clock the battle languished all along the fine, and, in fact, died out altogether for a little time; but shortly after a tremendous cannonade recommenced, for the French had received reinforcements from General Bazaine from the direction of Sarreguemines, consisting of four or five regiments of chasseurs and dragoons, and several regiments of infantry.

The cavalry pushed rapidly up the inner section of the valley, but were not advanced into the outer plain. The infantry, on the other hand, were thrown at once into the woods on the right, and were advanced to reinforce the French line all along its extent. The battle now recommenced with redoubled vigour; but the efforts of the Germans were apparently directed for the time chiefly against the French right.

They were also at this time strongly reinforced, and an immense column of their infantry descended into the plain from the direction of Saarbrück. Their cannonade then became more and more vigorous, and the whole French line gradually gave way. At this critical juncture a sudden cannonade was opened in a totally new direction, for the Germans had suddenly descended from the heights and shown themselves in force opposite the French left, which their fire, directed across the railway and high road, was threatening to turn and cut off from their communication with Metz. The French reply was as feeble as possible, and already along the road ominous symptoms of retreat began to be visible. The Germans had been strongly reinforced, simultaneously, at either extremity of their line; whereas the French reinforcements had been sent away to their right and right-centre, and there was nothing to meet the Prussian attack when it fell thus unexpectedly on their left.

The German troops which arrived so opportunely at the crisis of the engagement, were part of the corps d'armée of General Zastrow, which in the early part of the day were on the line of railway connecting Saarbrück with Trèves, where they were informed by telegraph of the state of affairs. Beyond Volklingen, at a distance of some eight or nine miles from Saarbrück, the disposable regiments of Zastrow's corps—among them the fifty-second and the seventy-seventh—crossed the Saar, and the lofty range of hills which there surmount its left bank, hurried on at a run for two miles and a half, and, entering the wood which closed in the French position on the left, attacked the French in flank and in rear, inflicting terrible losses upon them and deciding the day. While the battle was raging on Spicheren hill, the thirteenth German division crossed the Saar at Wehrden, and carried the town of Forbach by assault.

Great carnage took place here: out of a whole battalion of chasseurs de Vincennes only three were left alive. The Germans not only succeeded in driving out the French, but seized vast magazines of food and clothing, and forced General Frossard to withdraw to the south-west, leaving free the road to St. Avold and Metz. The town of Forbach had been set on fire during the latter part of the engagement, and the inhabitants were flying in wild terror, not only before the flames, but also before the shower of bullets.

The command of the Germans was taken by General von Steinmetz towards the close of the battle, and shortly afterwards Prince Frederick Charles arrived.

Darkness fast setting in, afforded its valuable aid to the French in effecting their retreat. To cover this backward movement their artillery were stationed on the hills skirting the battle-field on the south, where they kept up a continuous but harmless fire for a considerable time.

The ground was too difficult for the German cavalry to take any part in the action. Nevertheless, the fruits of the victory were very remarkable; the corps under General Frossard being entirely demoralized and dispersed. The road it took in its hasty flight was marked by numerous waggons with provisions and clothing; the woods were filled with hosts of stragglers, wandering about purposeless (altogether 2000 prisoners were taken); and large stores and quantities of goods of every description fell into the hands of the Germans. Among the stores were several railway vans full of confectionery! The losses were exceedingly heavy on both sides; but no official return of either has ever been published. The fifth German division alone had 230 dead, and about 1800 wounded. The twelfth infantry had 32 officers and 800 men dead or wounded, and next to them the fortieth, eighth, forty-eighth, thirty-ninth, and seventy-fourth German regiments suffered most. Some companies left nearly one-half their men on the spot, as for instance the fifth company of the forty-eighth (Rhinelanders), which went with 250 men into the fire and came out with 129, and the first company of the eighth (King's Own—Brandenburgers), which, on the evening of the battle, consigned 107 comrades either to the grave or the hospital. The batteries, too, encountered terrible loss. The success of the fortieth regiment in scaling the height was accomplished at a cost of 600 men and 16 officers. Their advance in face of the fearful fire that was poured upon them was magnificent. They were as steady as if on parade, and although on the first two occasions they were unsuccessful in their endeavour, they retreated in the best order. The thirty-ninth regiment had only forty men left in one company, and no officers; and in one grave were buried the captain, lieutenant, and three ensigns.

The awful slaughter thus caused in particular regiments in this and succeeding battles, showed in one respect, perhaps, a disadvantage in the German system of recruiting. As we have fully explained in Chapter IV., in that country every regiment is recruited on its own ground; first, to intensify its *esprit de corps*, the soldier fighting, as it were, among his kinsmen and neighbours, so that he must stand his ground or be condemned to local infamy as a coward; secondly, to keep up social discipline, the squire commanding the peasants, who think him their natural leader; and thirdly, to make the evasion of a summons more difficult. Under this system, however, heavy slaughter in a corps d'armée may throw a province into mourning, and the loss of a division often decimates a whole district. The majority of the Prussian reserves are married men, and if their regiment or division suffers severely, in the districts to which they belong there is scarcely a family which is not thrown into mourning. The husbands and sons and brothers of a whole neighbourhood are swept away at a single blow, and the distress caused is terrible. By no other method of recruitment could such a calamity as this be possible. In any other army, were three or four brothers forced away to the war, the chances, at least, are that only one of the four regiments to which they would be allotted would suffer greatly. By the Prussian system they would stand shoulder to shoulder, and all might fall together. What heart-rending affliction, for instance, must the official list of killed and wounded in this battle, which was very far from being the bloodiest of the war, have carried into many a quiet hamlet! Half the able-bodied population swept away at once! This is, indeed, to intensify the horrors of war, by making them fall with crushing severity upon localities. By ordinary systems, although a heavy loss may be widely spread, it is at least diminished by the wideness of its dissemination. A village could scarcely lose more than two or three of its able-bodied men. The gap would not be so noticeable; if some loved ones were gone, many would be spared. In Prussia, as we have seen, the whole of the male population in the army from each district are ranged side by side, and their destruction throws those dependent on them upon the country for subsistence.

To show the spirit with which the German soldiers were animated, it may be stated that the matter which chiefly troubled the wounded, both after Woerth and Forbach, was their being prevented from taking their part in the fighting, and in many cases convalescents protested against being sent to distant hospitals, as it would interpose unnecessary delay, they said, in the way of rejoining their regiments.

The French losses at Forbach, as well as the German, were exceedingly severe; the seventy-seventh, seventy-sixth, sixty-sixth, sixty-seventh, third chasseurs a pied, with the twenty-third and thirty-second regiments, one regiment of dragoons, and one of chasseurs a cheval, being almost destroyed.

The way in which the people of Saarbrück behaved to the wounded offered a very pleasing contrast to the feeling manifested by the peasantry at Woerth. The women were absolutely running about on the field of battle giving drink to the wounded, and every house in the town at once turned itself into an hospital. Country carts, with wine and eatables, lined the road to Forbach, and all possible means to alleviate suffering were employed.

As we have already described, at the battles of Wissembourg and Woerth the French were not only out-generalled, but also crushed by superior numbers. The latter, however, was by no means the case at Forbach; where the advantage in this respect was for a long time in their favour. The attack was made by the fourteenth division, supported by the fortieth regiment—in all fifteen battalions. They alone, of infantry, fought for hours against the three divisions, or thirty-nine battalions, which Frossard brought up successively. When they were nearly crushed, but still held their position, the fifth division came up, and took part in the engagement—all in all, twenty-seven battalions of Germans. They drove the French from their position, and it was only after the retreat had commenced that the head of the thirteenth division reached the field of battle, fell upon Forbach, and turned the retreat into a rout by cutting off the direct road to Metz. Thus, if at Wissembourg and Woerth the French were crushed by superior masses, they were beaten by inferior numbers at Forbach. The troops on both sides showed a degree of valour and heroic endurance which it is impossible to overpraise. Telegrams from Wissembourg, announcing the German victory at Woerth on the same day, were communicated to many of the troops before going into action, and naturally incited them to deeds of greater daring.

The movement by which General Göben, finding another corps joining his left, allowed them to occupy the attention of the enemy, whilst he transferred the weight of his attack to his right, and thus, without difficulty, mastered the main road the French should have covered, was as remarkable an instance of tactical readiness as any modern action has displayed.

All through the battle, indeed, the dispositions of the German commanders were very able, even if the advance of their first troops was premature. Their reinforcements were quickly brought into the field; they chose the right points of attack, and with great skill used the cover of the woods to harass and ruin the French. On the other hand, while the French soldiers fought gallantly, they were very badly handled; in fact, the tactics of their commanders could not well have been worse. They were surprised in the morning, while they ought easily to have crushed the first German division, and they attacked in force only when it was altogether too late. They were left with no reserve echeloned in their rear, except at a great distance, and some of the troops sent to help them only came up in time to assist, or rather impede them in their retreat. There is no precedent in war for supposing that French soldiers, properly supported, could have been turned out of such a position as they occupied—which must be seen to be realized in its full strength.

It seems almost incredible, but according to the Comte de la Chapelle, the correspondent of the *Standard* English newspaper, who was present at the engagement, and who not only stated it in his letter from the field, but has since deliberately repeated it in his little work, "The War; Events and Incidents of the Battle Fields,"—while a similar statement has also been made by others— General Frossard, with inconceivable carelessness, left the battle-field after giving a few orders, treating the affair as a mere engagement without importance. He quietly remained several hours in the house of his friend, the mayor of Forbach, enjoying a luxurious lunch, and discussing with that worthy magistrate the magnitude of his arrangements; and in the meantime new German columns had arrived on the battle-field. The French soldiers, headed by the brave General Bataille, had to sustain the tremendous shock of an enemy increasing continually in number. Message on message was sent to the general-in-chief, but to no purpose; and instead of a new combination, or a movement of retreat which might have saved the day, the French divisions were left without new order, and had to succumb by degrees under the tremendous shock of their opponents.

Had the Germans known the full extent of their victory and pursued in earnest, Metz might have been taken and the first campaign ended; for during some hours after the engagement the town was in anarchy. The emperor and his staff were in the railway station ready to start for the battle-field, when the news of the defeat and retreat was brought by a messenger on an engine. This, of course, completely altered his Majesty's plans, and he at once started for the prefecture, consternation being plainly visible on his countenance. The staff, by the testimony of all eye-witnesses, utterly lost its head, did not know where the different sorps were, could give no orders, and expected to see the enemy before the town every moment. The emperor sat writing despondent telegrams. Metz was full of beaten soldiers, and but one perfect corps was within the lines. The Germans, however, did not at first realize the extent of their success; they also wanted ammunition and reinforcements, and contented themselves with throwing forward their immense strength of cavalry.

The two Prussian divisions camped on the roadside and on the heights for the night; next morning they crossed the French frontier and marched on Forbach, which, to their great surprise, they found totally abandoned. The French retreat had been so precipitate, that they did not even destroy the railroad nor blow up a single bridge.

The result of the two actions of August 6 to the French was a loss of between 20,000 and 30,000 men, killed, wounded, missing, and prisoners, and the complete defeat and dispersion of two of their best corps. The engagements also compelled them to assume a purely defensive attitude.

The emperor himself was obliged to admit his defeats, and he did so in the two telegrams annexed:—

"METZ, *Sunday*, 3.30 a.m."

"My communications with MacMahon being interrupted, I had no news from him up to yesterday. It is General L'Aigle who announces to me that MacMahon has lost a battle against considerable forces, and that he has retired in good order. On another side on the Saar an engagement commenced about one o'clock. It did not appear to be very serious, when little by little masses of the enemy considerably increased; without, however, obliging the second corps to retreat. It was only between six and seven o'clock in the evening that the masses of the enemy becoming continually more compact, the second corps and the regiments which supported it retired on the heights. The night has been quiet. I go to place myself at the centre of the position.

"NAPOLEON."

"In yesterday's engagement at Forbach only the second army corps was engaged, supported by two divisions of other corps. The corps of General L'Admirault, that of General Failly, and the imperial guard did not take part in the fight. The engagement commenced at one o'clock, and appeared unimportant, but soon numerous troops concealed in the woods endeavoured to turn the position. At five o'clock the Prussians appeared to be repulsed, and to have abandoned the attack, but a fresh corps arriving from Wehrden on the Saar obliged General Frossard to retreat. To-day the troops, which had found themselves divided, are concentrated on Metz. In the battle which took place near Froeschwiller, Marshal MacMahon had five divisions. The corps of General Failly was unable to join him. Only very vague details have been received. It is said that there were several charges of cavalry, but *the Prussians had mitrailleuses, which caused us much harm.*

"NAPOLEON."

When the defeats of both MacMahon and Frossard became generally known in Metz on Sunday morning, a spirit of despair for a time seemed to have seized both officers and troops. The former considered and acknowledged that all was lost for France; and amongst the latter "Tout est perdu" was the motto which within a few days had replaced the boasting of a military promenade to Berlin.

"The Germanic Empire is made "was the sentence repeated everywhere; and whatever victories the French might win in the future, they would not be able to shake the Prussian influence and prestige. Such was the prevailing opinion.

A panic also seized the civil population; the disposition to exaggerate so inherent in French minds had already created imaginary dangers; and the Germans being momentarily expected, all the carriages and vehicles were chartered to convey the alarmists and their families far from the seat of war; the emperor himself was preparing for departure, and it was asserted that the quartier impérial and the état-major of the armée du Rhin would be immediately transferred to some other city in the interior.

Later in the day the equipages of the emperor and some officers of his staff actually left the town; but at the same time a somewhat reassuring feature was observed in a large assembly of the citizens of Metz, who had congregated in the court of the Hotel de Metz, and swore to put aside all causes of political antagonism, and to join in the defence of their city.

Amongst the lower classes the excitement reached almost to madness; bands of men paraded the streets, clamouring for revenge, and stopping any looker-on who had a foreign appearance. Several English and American correspondents were roughly handled by the mob; and the authorities were compelled to put them under arrest to protect them from the infuriated people, who fancied they saw in them Prussian spies.

An exceedingly painful episode of the battle of Forbach was the flight of the villagers, disturbed in their homes in the valleys between Saarbrück and Forbach. They would not have been ill-treated by the Prussian soldiers had they remained, but hundreds of families, amazed by the French defeat, hurried off in the utmost terror. The correspondent of a daily journal, who was a witness of the scene, thus described their condition:—

"Among this panic-stricken crowd we found ourselves, and we thought it better to continue with them and avail ourselves of their knowledge of roads and byways, whereby to get, at all events, to a more comfortable distance from the Prussians. When we had reached the summit of the heights, and were actually out of immediate danger of the Prussian shot and shell—when, in fact, the poor people could think of something beyond the instant peril of life and limb—they seemed suddenly to realize the entire ruin which had fallen upon them; they also began to think of their families and friends, who were all scattered, flying in desperation through the deep woods, where the darkness was deepening with the falling night. Such scenes of anguish and misery I never saw before, and hope never again to see. Mothers, who had lost their children, seeking for them with frantic cries and gesticulations; old, tottering men and women stumbling feebly along, laden with some of their poor household gods, silent with the silent grief of age; little children only half conscious of what all these things meant, tripping along, often leading some cherished household pet, and seeking for some friendly hand to guide them; husbands supporting their wives, carrying their little ones (sometimes two or three) on their shoulders, and encouraging the little family group with brave and tender words; the woods ringing with shrieks and lamentations—with prayers to the Saviour and the Virgin. It is impossible to describe in language the sadness and the pathos of that most mournful exodus. If all the world could only catch a glimpse of such a scene, I will venture to say that war would become impossible; that fierce national pride and Quixotic notions of honour, and the hot ambitions of kings and emperors and statesmen, would be for ever curbed by the remembrance of all the pity and the desolation of the spectacle."

It is a fact worthy of record, as showing how instantaneously the spark once kindled burst out into the full flame of war, that three weeks before the two battles near Saarbrück we have described in this and the preceding chapters, the Peace Society of Paris sent their deputies to that town, to celebrate an international festival held there by the corresponding society in Prussia. It was held at the station, one of the first places in flames on Tuesday, August 2. The German soldiers rechristened the hill on which the prince imperial stood on that day, and on which part of the deadly contest raged on the 6th, which before was known as the Speikerberg, "Lulu-berg;" Lulu being the sobriquet by which he was known.

In the previous chapter we have alluded to the fatal mistake of the French in allowing their troops to remain scattered over so wide a line (nearly a hundred miles), by which they laid themselves open to defeat in detail at the hands of a vigorous enemy with superior forces. In this we have seen that the attempt of MacMahon to retrieve the disaster of Wissembourg had the effect of separating the right wing still more from the centre, and laying open his line of communication with it. While, too, the right wing was being crushed at Woerth, the centre was severely beaten at Spicheren! The other troops were too far away to come up to their assistance. L'Admirault was still near Bouzonville, the rest of Bazaine's men and the guards were about Boulay, the mass of Canrobert's troops turned up at Nancy, part of De Failly's were lost sight of completely, and Felix Douay, on the 1st of August, was at Altkirch, in the extreme south of Alsace, nearly 120 miles from the battlefield of Woerth, and with but imperfect means of railway conveyance. In fact, the whole of the French arrangements from the commencement indicated nothing but hesitancy and vacillation. Could anything possibly have been worse than allowing three of the eight corps of the army to be defeated in three days, and in each case in detail? and where was the generalship which permitted Frossard to fight at Forbach all day, while to his left, and within about ten miles from the line of the Saar, seven divisions were looking on?

Everywhere along the whole front line of the French army there was the same story. Supreme incapacity presided, and hurled it hopeless on its fate. Not the faintest attempt was made to ascertain the movements of the enemy or to combine the movements of the troops until too late. The French soldiers fought splendidly; but they were sacrificed, and fought and died knowing that they were sacrificed, by the utter imbecility of those at the head of affairs. In fact, the French strategy was only worthy of the Austrians in their most helpless times; and, as will be shown in Chapter X., it enabled the Germans to advance at once into France and do what they liked.

On the German side, from the first, everything had been carried out in the most admirable manner. The concentration of their troops took place rapidly but cautiously, and every available man was brought to the front. The effect of their enormous numerical superiority was yet further increased by superior generalship and splendid strategy; for, as has been seen, they at once altered their whole plan of intended operations, entered upon an offensive instead of a defensive campaign, and carried it out successfully without a single hitch or flaw at any point. In fact, no more perfect or awful implement of destruction than the German army ever did its destined work. It was the physical force of a nation brought together and driven against its enemy after such training and discipline, and with such a ready co-operation of every man in the array, that it acted like a single individual.

CHAPTER IX.

To give a clear and consecutive form to our narrative of the incidents connected with the war, it is necessary to retrace our steps to Paris. As already stated in Chapter VI., the warlike enthusiasm of the capital materially subsided after the departure of the emperor for the scene of operations, and the issue of his proclamation to the army. It had become increasingly evident that a contest with Germany meant a prolonged struggle against a million of armed combatants, determined to defend their own country, and, if possible, to give the French such a lesson that for the future the emperor's peculiar mode of making his reign an era of peace by attacking his neighbours should be rendered impossible. The announcement that the fortifications of Paris were to be placed in a condition of defence, and the emperor's admission that the war would be a long one, greatly damped the ardour of those who imagined that within a fortnight a glorious peace, re-establishing the supremacy of French arms, would be signed in Berlin. The calling out of the garde mobile, too, caused much distress and discontent throughout the country, and a bad spirit prevailed in that force, which the Republican party did its utmost to heighten. The press was requested not to speak of it, but it is a fact, that when the first battalion of the mobiles went off by railway to the camp at Châlons, seditious cries were heard, both from the soldiers and a great crowd which had assembled to see them depart. There were shouts of "Down with Napoleon!" "Vive la République!" "A bas Ollivier!" "Les Ministres à Cayenne!" and the mob sang scurrilous songs, abusive of the government, to the hackneyed revolutionary air of *Les Lampions*. Another matter, also, threatened to disturb the anticipated course of events. An official intimation was given on the Tuesday following the emperor's departure that the spirit of reform was so strong in France, that during the progress of the war his Majesty would no doubt make several visits to Paris, and the Bourse experienced a shock when it became known that the celebrated surgeon Nelaton had left the capital to fulfil a promised visit to the emperor. As yet, however, although no forward movement of consequence had been made by the army, the Parisians awaited the development of the campaign with confidence.

It was on the evening of Tuesday (August 2) that Paris received the news of the "first victory "at Saarbrück. The emperor's despatch was handed to the empress as she was walking in the park at St. Cloud. On perusing it her Majesty burst into tears, walked straight to the guardroom, and read it aloud to the soldiers, by whom it was received with deafening cheers. By the Parisians generally the announcement was also accepted with extravagant delight. Everything thus far had succeeded *à merveille*, and the first step had been taken on the road to the Prussian capital. Both the emperor and the heir to the throne had been present, and the young prince, on whom were fixed the hopes of France, had escaped the bullets which fell around him. The language in which the emperor's telegram was couched, his reports of the "baptism of fire," and the soldiers shedding tears at the sight of the Prince Imperial, excited at the time the liveliest enthusiasm, and called forth apparently sincere expressions of attachment to his dynasty. At a later period, however, it formed the basis of insulting and injurious aspersions on the courage and patriotism of the imperial family.

When hostilities had actually commenced the inner heart of Paris was greatly moved at the dangers of the battle-field. All day long, at the great old-fashioned church of Our Lady of Victories, the open space in front was crowded with carriages, while a continuous stream of anxious people poured into and out of the edifice. In the huge antique interior, hung round with enormous oil-paintings, the altar and all about it was ablaze with votive candles; and there the mothers and sisters of Paris, praying, formed a touching scene. There, too, were Frenchmen and French officers, with sons, perhaps, at the front. The scene was fitted to increase their devotion, as every inch of the walls of the church is incrusted with small marble tablets, literally in thousands, each with an inscription of acknowledgment for some prayer heard or favour received.

The ill effects of the government regulations respecting the supply of news from the seat of war soon became apparent. The dearth of information was a cause of uneasiness, and the position taken by the authorities tended to the worst results. Towards the end of the week it gradually dawned upon the capital that something had happened to Marshal MacMahon, but no one distinctly knew what. On Friday (August 5), it was rumoured from the Bourse that he had captured Landau, taken forty guns, and held the Crown Prince and 20,000 Prussian prisoners. So eagerly was the rumour embraced, that many flags were hoisted, and signs of rejoicing everywhere displayed. The Rentes went up, the people prepared to illuminate, and kissed each other in the streets, amid shouts of victory! Popular singers were compelled to sing the "Marseillaise" in the public thoroughfares, and the judges sitting in the Palais de Justice stayed proceedings to announce the triumph of the imperial arms.

The rumour, however, proved false, and had been got up only to serve the purposes of the Stock Exchange. The real fact was the defeat of Wissembourg, which the ministry concealed for some twelve hours after it was known in England; and then simply published a laconic despatch from the emperor. This appeared just as the London papers arrived with fuller particulars, and the real truth created tremendous excitement. Crowds of people rushed through the streets, many of them armed with cudgels; compelled the flags to be taken down from the houses from which they had been displayed; and subsequently threatened to burn the Bourse. A couple of unfortunate money-changers with German names, though of French and Belgian origin, had their shops attacked and their windows broken; the one for having made some unguarded remark on the success achieved by Prussia, the other because he was believed to be engaged in supplying specie to the enemy. On the shutters of the latter the following notice was posted—"Shut up till Berlin is taken." The inflamed mob also rushed to the Place Vendôme, demanding that the originator of the false reports should be exposed. M. Ollivier appeared on the balcony, announced the arrest of the author, and promised that precautions should be taken to prevent the repetition of so scandalous an act. He further intimated that, confiding in the patriotism and patience of the people, all news should in future be immediately published, whether good or bad. The minister then besought the crowd to separate with the cry of "Vive la Patrie," reminding them that such proceedings as theirs, often repeated, would be a great victory for Prussia. Later in the evening the council of ministers issued an address to the same effect. On that day, also, the first cannon was placed upon the fortifications of the capital.

The Parisians already began to doubt the wisdom that presided over the conduct of the campaign; but their confidence in the army itself was rather raised than weakened by the reports of heroic feats performed by individuals and separate corps, and they firmly believed that Wissembourg would be terribly avenged.

But while Paris felt thus, the emperor, away at Metz, was despatching the dismal news of repeated defeats, which appeared on the following morning, Sunday, August 7, in the annexed telegram:—

"Marshal MacMahon has lost a battle. General Frossard, on the Saar, has been compelled to fall back. The retreat is being effected in good order. All may be regained (*tout peut se rétablir*).

Subsequent despatches acknowledged that MacMahon's communications had been intercepted, that the defeat of Frossard had been a surprise, and that the emperor was going to place himself "in the centre of the position." A message at half-past four conveyed the re-assuring statement that the troops were full of spirit, and the situation was not compromised, although the enemy was on French territory, and could only be repelled by a serious effort. Such was the discouraging intelligence that reached Paris on the day after the disasters of Woerth and Forbach. As early as five o'clock in the morning the empress had hastened from St. Cloud to the Tuileries, summoned MM. Rouher and Schneider, the presidents of the Senate and Corps Législatif, and at once issued the following proclamation:—

"Frenchmen!—The opening of the war has not been in our favour. Our arms have suffered a check. Let us be firm under this reverse, and let us hasten to repair it. Let there be among us but a single party, that of France; but a single flag, the flag of our national honour. I come into your midst. Faithful to my mission and to my duty, you will see me first, where danger threatens, to defend the flag of France. I call upon all good citizens to preserve order; to disturb it would be to conspire with our enemies.

"EUGENIE.

"THE TUILERIES, *August* 7."

The council of ministers remained sitting *en permanence*, and issued an address on the state of affairs which concluded as follows:—"In the face of the grave news which has come to hand, our duty is clear. "We appeal to the patriotism and energy of all. The Chambers are convoked. Let us first place Paris in a state of defence, in order to facilitate the execution of the military preparations. We declare the capital in a state of siege. Let there be no weakness, no divisions. Our resources are immense. Let us fight with vigour, and the country will be saved."

During the day the following report from General Dejean, the ad interim minister of war, was addressed to the empress regent:—

"PARIS, *August* 7, 1870.

"Madame,—Existing circumstances require that measures be taken for the defence of the capital and for the raising of fresh troops, which, combined with those remaining under the orders of the emperor, will be enabled to fight in the open field against an enemy emboldened by his first successes to attempt to march upon Paris. But Paris will not be taken unawares. The external forts have long since had their protective armament. Great efforts have been made to complete it, and the armament of the *enceinte* was commenced at the outbreak of the war. The completion of this state of defence, moreover, is connected with the execution of certain works, the plans of which have been prepared, and which will be begun to-morrow. It will be speedily done. The exterior forts will be put into a condition to sustain a regular siege; and within a few days the *enceinte* will be in the same condition. Neither the labour nor the good-will of the inhabitants of Paris will be wanting for this work. The national guard will defend the ramparts which it has contributed to render impregnable. Forty thousand men taken from their ranks, added to the present garrison, will be more than sufficient to offer a vigorous and efficient defence against an enemy presenting a very extended front. The defence of Paris will therefore be assured. But it is a point of not less essential importance to provide for the voids which have occurred in the ranks of our army. With the aid of the marine troops, of the regiments still available for service in France and in Algeria, of the 4th battalions of our 100 infantry regiments, completed to the strength of 900 men by the incorporation of gardes mobiles, and by the formation from a portion of our gendarmerie of regiments which should be constituted as corps d'élite, a force of 150,000 men can, without difficulty, be placed in the field. Then, again, the calling out of the conscripts of 1869, the young soldiers forming which will join their corps between the 8th and the 12th of August, will give us 60,000 men, who, within a month, will be true soldiers. Thus, without reckoning what could be furnished by the cavalry, artillery, engineers, and others arms, 150,000 men can at once be obtained, and at a later period, another 60,000 to place in front of the enemy. But the garde nationale mobile may take part in the struggle, as also the volunteer companies of francs-tireurs, which are everywhere asking for permission to organize themselves. They would amount to 400,000 men. Finally, we could rely upon the sedentary garde nationale; so that France can call to arms 2,000,000 of defenders. Their muskets are ready, and there will still remain 1,000,000 in reserve.—I am, &c.,

"GENERAL V. DEJEAN."

The report was followed by the annexed decree:

"Napoleon, by the grace of God and the national will, emperor of the French, to all present and to come—Having heard the counsel of our ministers, we have decreed and do decree:—

"Article 1.—All capable citizens between thirty and forty years of age, not already forming part of the sedentary garde nationale, shall be incorporated in it.

"Article 2.—The garde nationale of Paris is intrusted with the defence of the capital, and the placing in a state of defence the fortifications.

"Article 3.—A projét de loi will be prepared providing for the incorporation in the garde nationale mobile of all citizens under thirty-three years of age, who are not at present included in that force.

"Article 4.—Our ministers of the interior and of war are charged with the execution of this decree.

"Done at the Palace of the Tuileries, August 7, 1870. For the emperor, by virtue of the powers he has confided to us,

"EUGENIE."

Later in the day another proclamation, signed by all the ministers, was issued:—

"Frenchmen!—We have told you the whole truth; it is now for you to fulfil your duty. Let one single cry issue from the breast of all—from one end of France to the other. Let the whole people rise, quivering, and sworn to fight the great fight. Some of our regiments have succumbed before overwhelming numbers, but our army has not been vanquished. The same intrepid breath still animates it; let us support it. To a momentarily successful audacity we will oppose a union which conquers destiny. Let us fall back upon ourselves, and our invaders shall hurl themselves against a rampart of human breasts. As in 1792 and at Sebastopol, let our reverses be the school of our victories. It would be a crime to doubt for an instant the safety of our country, and a greater still not to do our part to secure it. Up, then, up! And you, inhabitants of the Centre, the North, and the South, upon whom the burden of the war does not fall, hasten with unanimous enthusiasm to the help of your brethren in the East. Let France, united in success, be still more united under trial, and may God bless our arms!"

These proclamations were read by the disappointed crowds with a deep melancholy, and with conflicting speculations as to the utility of a "state of siege;" which they knew, at all events, would interfere largely with the liberty of the subject. The law giving this power to the ministry was passed in 1849, and provided that the military tribunals could take cognisance of crimes and offences against the security of the state, against the constitution, against order and the public peace, whatever might be the quality of the principal offenders or of their accomplices. It also gave the authorities the right to search by day or night in the houses of citizens; to remove returned convicts, and any individuals not domiciled in the places subject to the state of siege; to order the surrender of arms and munitions, and to take measures for seeking and removing them; to forbid such publications and such meetings as might be held to be of a nature to excite or prolong disorder.

The Parisians, however, were now thoroughly aroused, and in the evening a demonstration was made in the Place Vendome in favour of a general arming. There was also extraordinary excitement on the Boulevards, where vast crowds were carrying flags and singing the "Marseillaise." A fear possessed the people that the events were even worse than reported, and deep were their murmurs when they learnt from the foreign journals how large were the numbers of killed, wounded, and prisoners.

On the morning of Monday, August 8, the feeling of alarm manifested itself in a run upon the Bank of France, and other similar establishments, by persons wishing to change their securities and notes for cash. The ministry showed themselves fully alive to the critical nature of the situation, and to calm the public excitement issued the following proclamation:—

"Parisians! Our army is concentrating itself, and preparing for a new effort. It is full of energy and confidence. To agitate in Paris would be to fight against our army, and at the decisive moment to weaken the moral force necessary to conquer. Our enemies reckon on this. A Prussian spy, brought a prisoner to headquarters, was found with the following paper in his possession:— 'Courage! Paris is in a state of revolt. The French army will be taken between two fires.' We are preparing the armament of the nation and the defence of Paris. To-morrow the Corps Législatif will join its action to ours. Let all good citizens unite to prevent crowds and manifestations. Those who are in a hurry to get arms may have them directly by presenting themselves at the recruiting offices, where they will be at once supplied with a musket to go to the frontier."— (Signed by all the Ministers.)

Such sentiments, however, failed to influence the conduct of the people, and the government summoned General Trochu to Paris, and asked him to take the post of minister of War. The general peremptorily refused, unless the empress should lay down the regency. This drove the ministers to their wits' end, and they convoked the Chambers for the following day (Tuesday). The evening *Official Journal* also published an extraordinary address, not only to the French nation, but to the European courts generally. This remarkable document said:—

"There exists in the life of nations solemn and decisive moments, in which God gives them an opportunity of showing what they are and of what they are capable. That hour has come for France. It has sometimes been asserted that, though intrepid in the dash of success, the great nation supports reverses with difficulty. What is now passing before us gives the lie to this calumny. The attitude of the people is not one of discouragement; it is one of sublime and patriotic rage against the invaders of France, who in France must find a tomb. All Frenchmen will rise like one man; they remember their ancestors and their children. Behind them they see centuries of glory, before them a future that their heroism shall render free and powerful. Never has our country been better prepared for self-devotion and sacrifice, never has "it shown in a more imposing and magnificent manner the vigour and pride of the national character. It shouts with enthusiasm, 'Up; to arms!' To conquer or die is its motto. While our soldiers heroically defend the soil of France, Europe is rightly uneasy at the successes of Prussia. People ask themselves to what lengths the ambition of that insatiable power would carry her if she were intoxicated with a decisive triumph. It is an invariable law of history that any nation which by unbounded covetousness disturbs the general equilibrium challenges a reaction against its victories, and turns all other countries into opponents. This truth cannot fail to be again demonstrated by the results. Who is there interested in the resurrection of the German empire? Who is there that desires the Baltic to become a Prussian lake? Can it be Sweden, Norway, or Denmark—countries that a Prussian triumph would annihilate? Can it be Russia—Russia which is more interested than any power in saving the equilibrium of the North against German covetousness? Can it be England, which, as a great maritime power, and as the protector of Denmark, is opposed to the progress of the Prussian navy? Can it be Holland, which is already so much threatened by the audacious intrigues of Count von Bismarck? With regard to Austria, the restoration of the German empire to the advantage of the House of Hohenzollern would be the most fatal blow, not only to the dynasty of the Hapsburgs, but to the existence of the Austro-Hungarian monarchy. . . . The decisive victory of the Hohenzollerns would not be less fatal to Italy than to Austria, and the regeneration of the former would be compromised. We appeal with confidence to the wisdom of governments and peoples to root Prussian despotism out of Europe, to aid us, either by alliance or sympathy, in saving the European equilibrium."

The address also intimated that England was fully satisfied with the declarations given with regard to Belgium. Sweden, Norway, and Denmark showed an attitude "trembling with patriotism." The emperor of Russia honoured their ambassador with his particular good will. The emperor of Austria and the king of Italy, with their governments, manifested dispositions more and more satisfactory. In conclusion, it was added—"Our diplomacy will not be less active than our army. France is making a supreme effort, and our patriotism rises equal to every danger. The more serious the circumstances, the more will the nation be energetic. All divisions cease, and the French press unanimously express the most practical and most noble ideas. The concurrence of the Senate and Legislative Body is about to lend fresh strength to our troops, and the France of 1870 will show the peoples of Europe that we have not degenerated."

Before the commencement of hostilities the emperor had said France did not seek any allies; but on the first experience of disaster this melancholy wail was immediately issued and telegraphed in full to all the courts of Europe. Even before the assembling of the Chambers, the address had sealed the fate of the ministry, and to none could it have caused more consternation than to the emperor himself. To the losses on the field was now added the incompetence of the government, and thus were intensified those feelings of wounded pride and fierce anger, which were subsequently displayed both inside and outside the Legislative Assemblies.

Tuesday (August 9) was a day of such tumult and excitement as even Paris had seldom seen without bloodshed. No further despatches having arrived from the seat of war, the popular interest was concentrated on the Chambers. Long before noon a dense crowd thronged the quay in front of the palace of the Corps Législatif, the court of which was occupied by large bodies of troops, 10,000 men of the infantry of marine having arrived from Cherbourg and other ports on the previous day. The ministers were received with shouts of "Vive Rochefort!" "Des Armes!" "A bas les Ministres!" M. Jules Favre made an attempt to address the crowd, but failed to secure a hearing. Seizing the hand of a national guard, he gave the mob to understand that that force sympathized with the people, an announcement which called forth applause, the national guards waving their shakos on the ends of their rifles. On the arrival of Marshal Baraguay d'Hilliers, commandant of the army of Paris, he ordered the drums to beat, and summons to be made to the crowd to retire. But though it was repeatedly charged with cavalry, there was happily no bloodshed. The troops were assailed with such cries as "Lâches, fainéants, à la frontière; battez vous avec les Prussiens!" but the majority of the crowd contented themselves with shouting "Vive la Liberté!" "Vive la République!" and, above all, "Des Armes! des Armes!" The readiness with which the crowd took advantage of any bit of scaffolding or broken wall, which the cavalry could not get over, showed their hereditary turn for street fighting, and what mischief they might have done had their appeal for arms been heard. "Once," said an eye-witness, "the pursuers were thus rendered so baffled and helpless that they were glad in their turn to retreat before the merciless volley of abuse heaped upon them, though they got their revenge by running another group into a *cul-de-sac*, and belabouring them with the flat of their drawn swords."

At the meeting of the Senate little business of any interest was transacted. M. de Parieu, president of the council of state, delivered a speech intended to re-assure the members of the body, upon which discussion was not allowed, and the proceedings closed.

The scene inside the Corps Législatif, however, was very exciting. When M. Schneider proceeded to read the decree of the emperor convoking the Chambers, no sooner had he uttered the words, "Napoleon, by the grace of God and the national will emperor of the French," than he was assailed with cries to pass it over. M. Ollivier, while explaining why the Chambers had been convoked, was subjected to continual interruptions. One member, on an allusion having been made to the valour of the troops, chimed in with, "Yes, lions led by asses; as was remarked by

Napoleon I." M. Arago called upon the ministry to "retire, and then the army would conquer." M. Jules Favre said the presence of the ministry in the Chamber was a disgrace. When M. Ollivier remarked that the Chamber would be wanting in its duty if it supported the government, having the smallest want of confidence in it, and said that he was probably addressing them as minister for the last time, the Left shouted out, "We hope so, for the salvation of the country!" The minister of War having introduced a project of law ordaining the embodying of all citizens of thirty years of age in a national garde mobile, M. Jules Favre, amid breathless attention, proposed the immediate arming of all French citizens, and the appointment of a committee of fifteen deputies charged with the defence of France. He also called for the return of the emperor. "The fact is," said M. Favre, "that the fate of the country is compromised, which is the result of the operations of those who have the direction of military affairs, and of the absolute incapacity of the commander-in-chief. It is therefore necessary that all our forces should be placed in the hands of one man, but that man must not be the emperor."

This movement of the leader of the opposition had an indescribable effect on the Chamber; it was like throwing oil on fire. In the tumult which followed it was impossible to hear any of the speakers, who, in spite of the president's efforts to maintain order, indulged in an angry discussion across the Chamber. The proposition of M. Favre, enthusiastically approved by the Left and Left Centre, was most violently protested against by M. Granier de Cassagnac, who increased the turmoil by declaring that, were he the government, he would have the whole Left tried by court-martial, and shot. M. Ollivier for some time vainly tried to obtain a hearing, but at length succeeded in intimating to the House that several of his colleagues had asked him if he meant to have the Left shot. Here M. de Gramont was understood to interrupt his chief (although he afterwards denied it) by exclaiming superciliously, "Seulement!" At this supposed insult M. Estancelin rushed across the Chamber, and shook his fist in the face of the foreign minister; he was followed by M. Jules Ferry, while M. Jules Simon, inaudible from the uproar, beat his breast to signify that he longed for the government bullet. A battle appeared imminent; but the Right intervened, and under its sheltering wing M. de Gramont left the Chamber. The president put on his hat, and the sitting was suspended.

On the resumption of business M. Clément Duvernois, who was in the confidence of the emperor, proposed a resolution to the following effect:—"That the Chamber is determined to support a cabinet which is capable of providing for the defence of the country." This resolution was carried, under the protest of the ministry, with only six dissentients, whereupon M. Ollivier, with his colleagues, retired to the Tuileries. On his return, the prime minister rose and said— "After the vote of the Chamber the ministers have tendered their resignations to the empress regent, who has accepted them, and I am charged by her to declare that with the assent of the emperor she has intrusted Count Palikao with the task of forming a cabinet."

The sitting then closed amidst great excitement, and the result speedily became known throughout Paris. The crowd outside the Palais Bourbon was immense, and the ministers were again received with loud cries of "Vive Rochefort," "A bas les Ministres," "Des Armes!" M. Jules Ferry had a perfect ovation, and M. Jules Simon was carried through the streets in triumph.

The crowd, however, soon dispersed, and Paris had a few hours of quiet after the intense excitement of the previous days.

It is here worthy of remark, that whatever were the failings of M. Ollivier as prime minister of France, he was not responsible for the war, having in the first instance opposed it. But defeat had overtaken the imperial arms; it became necessary that he should be sacrificed in the interests of the dynasty, and hence the resolution moved by a favourite courtier of the emperor, who was more afraid of the republicans than of the Prussians.

The new ministry was formed without a moment's delay. General Cousin Montauban, Comte de Palikao, having received his commission at the hands of the empress, appointed his cabinet as follows:—M. Chevreau, minister of the Interior; M. Magne, minister of Finance; M. Clément Duvernois, minister of Commerce and Agriculture; Admiral Rigault de Genouilly, minister of Marine; Baron Jérôme David, minister of Public Works; Prince de la Tour d'Auvergne, minister of Foreign Affairs; M. Grandperret, minister of Justice; M. Jules Brame, minister of Public Instruction; M. Busson-Billault, president of the Council of State.

General Montauban, the head of the cabinet and minister of War, was a thorough soldier. Born in 1796, he entered the army at an early age, and greatly distinguished himself as a cavalry officer in the Algerian wars. Major in 1836, he was gradually promoted, and became a general of brigade in 1857. His most notable exploits were performed in China, where, appointed French commander-in-chief of the Anglo-French expedition of 1860, he gave proof of great military talent by the way in which, with but a very small army and with literally millions of opponents, he conquered the fort of Takow, gained over the Chinese general, Sang-ko-lin-sin, the celebrated victory of Palikao (whence his title was derived), and triumphantly entered Pekin itself. From that war Montauban came back enriched with plunder. He was rewarded with the grand cross of the legion of honour, the title of count, and the dignity of senator; but the Corps Législatif refused to vote him a pension, and he retired into comparative obscurity as commander of the fourth corps d'armée. In the dilemma of the 9th August he was summoned by the empress and chosen as the safest Napoleonic premier. With regard to the other members of the new cabinet, they were statesmen of but ordinary mark, although of a thoroughly imperialistic and military character.

The Palikao ministry was avowedly constructed as a "Cabinet of Defence," and instead of representing any particular party in the legislature, was pronounced a ministry of "Arcadians." There was abundant reason why the new body should be composed of men of military energy. But the Parisians were mistrustful. Great indignation was displayed at the incapacity of the emperor, who was tabooed even by the Legislative Body, and whose name was carefully omitted in all official documents. The empress, who had never been a favourite with the people, was regarded with suspicion in her conduct of the regency, as it was believed that she had attempted to infuse her influence into public affairs. Added to these considerations, the antecedents of the Comte de Palikao gave rise to fears of overt acts of indiscretion on his part. "Montauban," it was said, "is very firm; but he is not very scrupulous."

On the first appearance of the Palikao cabinet in the Corps Législatif (August 10), great precautions were taken for the protection of the Chamber. In addition to the cavalry and infantry force previously on duty, two batteries of artillery were put in requisition. The proceedings, however, were comparatively quiet. A proposal was adopted to declare urgent a resolution to postpone all payments for one month. M. Forcade de la Roquette read the report of the committee appointed to consider the means of raising new levies, and the House unanimously adopted a proposition to call out the soldiers no longer liable to serve of the classes from 1858 to 1863, by which might be obtained 300,000 men who had seen service; that a levy should be made of all citizens who had been under arms; and that all men between twenty-five and thirty-five who were unmarried, and had no children, should be required to join the army. It was further agreed to raise the grant of 4,000,000 francs for the assistance of the families of the national guard to 20,000,000 francs. M. Forcade de la Eoquette then moved a vote of thanks to the French army, as having deserved well of the country. Enthusiastic cheering, three times renewed, greeted this motion, and the Chamber decided that the president should transmit it to the army. M. Estancelin moved that the Legislative Body should sit *en permanence* until the Prussians evacuated France; but on a vote there were 117 ayes against 117 noes, and the motion was consequently lost. M. Jules Ferry questioned the cabinet as to the use it intended to make of the powers conferred upon it by a state of siege, and criticised the repressive measures resorted to; but no reply was given by the government. M. Lecesne proposed a resolution with a view to establishing the forced currency of bank-notes; but the urgency of such a measure was disputed, and the House quietly separated.

Outside the Chamber, also, peace reigned, the excitement of the previous day having in a great measure subsided. But 40,000 regular troops and marines were retained in the capital to keep down the Republicans, and the old policy of repression was pursued, as if France were in insurrection against the Empire instead of Prussia.

It began to be feared, too, that increased troubles would come from without, and preparations were commenced against the contingency of having the German battalions before the walls of the city. Among the first acts of the Ministry of Defence was the demolition of the little memorial chapel of St. Ferdinando, erected by Marie Amélie to the memory of the duke of Orleans, who was killed on the site in 1848. The emperor had often wished to get rid of that interesting relic of the Orleans family. The district of Belleville (Rochefort's circonscription) also fell in the way of the preparations, and much of it was destroyed, as well as many of the trees in the city, which might hinder defensive operations.

The Germans residing in Paris were reduced to great hardships in consequence of the state of siege. Immediately after the declaration of war, both the Prussian and Saxon ambassadors placed their diplomatic archives under the protection of the American Legation. Mr. Washbourne also applied to the Duc de Gramont to allow German subjects to leave France for the Fatherland; but the request was refused, on the ground that all able-bodied Germans were liable to military duty, and would at once take up arms against France. A change of policy, however, had ensued. As early as the 5th of August the prefect of police had issued an edict, rendered necessary by the "internal manoeuvres of certain foreign residents against the safety of the state;" and the Legislature subsequently decreed that the Germans (to the number of some 40,000) should be expelled the capital—a "humane" precaution, it was said, as Paris was too excited to tolerate foreigners. German residents had been menaced, many "spies" shot, and one poor workman killed with spades. The decree was effectively enforced, and hundreds of German families had to make a hasty flight. On arriving at Berlin, many of these refugees presented a petition to the king, in which they complained that, in the department of the Seine alone, 80,000 persons had been obliged to leave their business, their property, many even their wives and children, and flee like criminals from a country whose prosperity they had for years done much to secure. Three days only had been granted to them—the same time as ordinarily intervened between a sentence of death and its execution—and in a period so brief no effective arrangements could be made. "In the places of business, the workshops, and the dwelling-houses, everything had to be left as it stood; they were locked and left to the care of Providence, and we fled the country where Germans were deprived of their rights, and left without protection to the rage of a fanatical people." The official journals of Germany threatened revenge, though not in the form of expelling Frenchmen from the country. "Frenchmen residing among us," said they, "may tranquillize themselves; they will, like the rest of the world, become convinced that it is Germany that marches at the head of civilization."

The expulsion was entirely without precedent, unless it be in the first Napoleon's detention of the English in Verdun; still it was not contrary to the principles of international law, as every nation maintains an Alien Act, which may be enforced in any special emergency.

At this period, also, it is notable, that all the members of the Orleans family visited Brussels, whence they addressed letters to the French government, offering their services in defence of their country. Prince de Joinville wrote to Admiral Rigault de Genouilly, the French minister of marine:—"In presence of the danger which threatens our country, I ask the emperor to be allowed to serve on the active army in any capacity, and request my old comrade to assist me in obtaining this permission." The Duc d'Aumale, writing to the minister of War, said—"You call out all Frenchmen to fight for the defence of the country. I am a Frenchman, an able-bodied soldier, and have the rank of general of division. I ask to serve in the active army." The Duc de Chartres wrote—"As a Frenchman, and as a former officer in the American and Italian wars, I request to be employed on active service. My most ardent wish is to fight for my country, even if it be only as a volunteer." For obvious reasons these several offers were declined.

It was about this time that the damaging stories in regard to the malversation of stores, the rottenness of the administration, and the incompetence of the emperor to lead armies or to continue the system of personal government, became rife in Paris, and most of them were at once received as foregone conclusions. The cry of treason was raised against the blunderers of the war and the plunderers of the commissariat, in which both Napoleon and his marshal, Leboeuf, came in for their share of the popular indignation. Bitter also was the feeling against the government for placing France in so ignominious a position, and warnings were thrown out of a day of future reckoning. "Give us news of the war," said the Parisians. "Let us be satisfied that Paris is safe, and that the honour of France can be redeemed; we can settle such a minor matter as our next form of government later."

During these events, however, no contrast could have been more complete than that between Paris and the rural districts of France. Having recovered from the panic caused by the affair of Woerth, the capital, moved by alternating hopes and fears, was full of excitement; but in the villages there was generally a blank look of misery and submission to their fate. Soldiers left Paris in uniform for the scene of conflict, gaily singing patriotic songs; but each individual warrior left his hamlet, in his blouse and wooden shoes, with a heavy heart. At almost every provincial railway station groups of sorrowing rustics waited for the train to carry them to the camp. But they left their peaceful avocations behind them, with the feeling that the tillage of the land and the various industries of their districts would suffer ruin. "Why," said the peasantry, "did you not tell us the plebiscite meant war? We would never then have said 'Yes.' "

Even in most of the large towns of France there was comparatively little excitement. The influence of affairs at the front told by far the most heavily upon the capital, giving a colouring to the egotistic boast of the Parisians that "Paris is France."

It is here necessary to turn again to the proceedings in the Legislative Body, where on Thursday, August 11, M. de Keratry caused a mighty uproar, by proposing the appointment of a committee to try Marshal Leboeuf. Not another word of his, however, could be heard for a time; but the senator folded his arms and leant back in an attitude of supercilious endurance, while the members shouted and gesticulated at him and at each other. This scene lasted for some minutes, when "the order of the day, pure and simple," was voted. Nothing daunted by his colleague's failure, another member of the Left, M. Guyot Montpayroux, insisted on being told whether Marshal Leboeuf was still *Major-Général de l'Armée.* The previous uproar was instantly renewed in a longer and far more furious style. The minister of War contrived to say that he considered that *les convenances* precluded a reply, at which M. Montpayroux flung himself in the direction of the minister, literally foaming at the mouth; but not a syllable he shouted was audible. Physical exhaustion compelled him to resume his seat; but at the first lull in the storm he again sprang up, and insisted on an answer, "Yes or no," fiercely challenging every member of the House to rise and express approval of the conduct of Marshal Leboeuf. The Right replied with a shout of defiance and derision; the Left rose as one man, and after gesticulating with such violence that a hand-to-hand fight seemed imminent, prepared to leave the House. At this juncture M. Thiers, whom Right and Left were eager to hear, was observed slowly making his way to the tribune. He began in tones so low that every head was bent forward to catch his words, and the deep stillness, following such a storm, was singularly impressive. He said that the present was not the time for raising such discussions, and appealed to his hearers whether it was right to call to the bar of the House a brave soldier, who was baring his breast to the bullets of the enemy. The speech of M. Thiers, though short, produced the desired effect, and the House, which from all parts loudly applauded him at the close, settled down to business at once in real earnest.

The ministerial programme carried through at this sitting was of a remarkable character. Soon after the war broke out the *Journal Officiel* contradicted a rumour that it was the intention of the bank of France to obtain a forced currency for its paper, and stated that the bank possessed 1,200,000,000 francs in specie to meet 1,400,000,000 francs in notes. Thus there was no reason for establishing a forced currency, nor was any such design entertained. Within a month, however, of the declaration of war, the Palikao ministry proposed this very measure, and the Corps Législatif voted it with only one dissentient. Article 1 declared that from the date of promulgation, the notes of the bank of France should be received as legal tender by the public treasuries and by private persons. Article 2 relieved the bank from the obligation of cashing its notes. Article 3 limited the issues of the bank to 1,800,000,000. Article 4 applied the law to the bank of Algeria; and article 5 permitted the issue of 25-franc notes. These legislative enactments produced a marked effect. The suspension of specie payments by the bank of France, the increase of the war credit from £20,000,000 to £40,000,000, and the granting of a period of grace for the payment of bills and other liabilities, gave rise to much discussion on the London Exchange.

The authorized issue of the bank under the forced currency was limited to £72,000,000, and as the amount of notes in circulation was £63,340,000, the balance available for increasing it amounted to £8,660,000. The bullion during the week, August 6 to 13, experienced a further decrease of £2,730,000, making a total reduction of £11,630,000, and the sum of £41,140,000 remained in hand. The war demand, coupled with that on the part of the people, must in a very short time have caused another heavy diminution, which would probably have swept away the balance. It was therefore thought better that it should remain in the vaults of the bank, to serve as the foundation for a resumption of payment at the proper time. Of course, as a natural result of the measure, gold rose to a premium throughout France, and extra prices had to be paid for all imported necessaries of the people; but in such a crisis a more promising or practicable method could not have been resorted to, and its efficiency in carrying countries through the most severe trials, and enabling them to raise any amount of loans, has been exemplified from the time of the earlier wars of England down to the more recent American struggle.

In the Corps Législatif on Friday, August 12, Count Palikao announced the resignation as major-general of the army of the Rhine of Marshal Leboeuf, who had been universally impeached of presumption, negligence, and ignorance. The minister was loudly cheered while describing some vigorous measures which had been taken for raising troops, and promising that, within two days, two *corps d'armée* of 35,000 men each should be sent to the front. M. Gambetta, on behalf of the Left, expressed strong approval of the ministerial action.

On Saturday, August 13, the Legislative Body unanimously adopted the bill raising the issue of bank notes to 2,400,000,000 francs. A bill, opening a credit of 5,000,000 francs in the budget of Paris for the distressed families of mobile guards who were engaged at the front, was also urgently pressed. In the course of the sitting the minister of war stated that Marshal Bazaine had been appointed sole commander-in-chief of the whole army, and that the defences of Paris would soon be complete. Replying to M. Gambetta, Count Palikao said that the ministers, placing confidence in all parties of the Chamber, and claiming like confidence in return, would accept a discussion on the question of appointing a committee of national defence. The president likewise requested the deputies not to leave Paris, so as to be at hand if required.

Meanwhile the work of completing the defences of the city was rapidly pushed forward, and detachments of naval gunners arrived from Cherbourg to work the cannons at the gates. Although the measures of the government placed at its disposal millions of men, and consequently many more than it could possibly arm, the cry was still for more. The Left demanded that the youths who had taken refuge in the religious colleges should be dragged thence, and take their share in the defence of the country; and a bill was also brought in demanding that all persons born in France should be drafted into the army. The consequence was that crowds of Englishmen, born of British parents and not in the enjoyment of civic rights in France, claimed their passports and prepared for a hegira. Lord Lyons very properly protested against the proposed law in a semi-official manner, and asked that, in the event of its being carried, Englishmen should at least be allowed forty days to reflect whether they would risk life for the French government or return to England.

Both Chambers met on Sunday, August 14, the first meeting that had been held on a Sunday since the establishment of the empire. In the Corps Législatif there was a most animated debate, brought on by M. Gambetta accusing the government of withholding news; the entrance of the Prussian cavalry into Nancy at three on Friday afternoon not being made public in Paris till nine o'clock on Sunday morning. Page and confusion seized the Chamber, and M. Schneider strove in vain to restore order. Many had a suspicion that the emperor interfered with the military operations, and M. Jules Favre presented a petition signed by a large number of Parisians, urging that the emperor should come back to the capital, and that all military men should be sent to the front. The reading of this petition produced a strange sensation, which boded ill for the future of his imperial majesty.

The stormy scenes of the Chamber on this particular Sunday found a reflex on the boulevards and in the city. In the afternoon a disgraceful riot occurred in the north-eastern suburb of La Villette, where a body of about sixty armed men attacked the firemen's barracks, shot down a solitary fireman who was on guard, and mortally wounded the first sergent de ville who arrived on the spot. The mob then plundered the post of a few Chassepots and some ammunition, after which they beat a hasty retreat to the heights of Belleville, shouting "Vive la République! "and firing off their revolvers. Sudden and unexpected as was the dastardly attack, a strong body of police was soon in pursuit, and most of the rioters were captured.

Throughout the entire night of the 14th disturbance and disquiet reigned in Paris. Arrests of spies, real or supposed, were made by the authorities; acts of violence were committed in the streets; and thus the morning of August 15, the day of the "Fête Napoleon," was heralded in by ominous disorder.

That day, so long identified in the minds of sightseers of every nation with brilliant reviews, salvos of cannon, and monster displays of fireworks, found France invaded and the Empire tottering. The previous year had celebrated the centenary of the first Napoleon amidst great splendour, and for nearly twenty years the fete-day had been distinguished by galas and rejoicings, garlands of light and wreaths of flowers. But the imperial festival of 1870 saw no such signs. The times were too mournful for holiday sports; the workshops were shut, but the people were in no mood for pleasure and gaiety. The Corps Législatif, however, did not assemble; business was partially suspended; the, churches were open, their candles ablaze, and their priests in their richest canonicals, while the solemn chant rolled out into the streets; and truly there never was more occasion for singing *Domine, salvum fac Napoleonem.*

It had been confidently expected that this day would bring tidings of a victory from the army of the Rhine; but the official news of a Prussian attack on the banks of the Moselle at Longueville having been repulsed after four hours' fighting, did little to remove the gloom hanging over Paris; nay, it was even felt as a just source of dissatisfaction, that the intelligence was not conveyed by Marshal Bazaine to the minister of War, but sent in a telegram from Napoleon to the empress. The people read the despatch with incredulity, which was turned into wrath by the fact that French territory was the scene of the reported events.

The night closed in on Paris without a solitary token of rejoicing; there were no fireworks and illuminations; the theatres were but scantily filled, and many were entirely closed. In fact, throughout the city the spirit of gloom rested heavily, the counterpart of that which must have pressed on the mind of the emperor away at the front.

The day of the emperor's fete, according to the French idea at the beginning of the war, was to have found the imperial troops in the "Unter den Linden," at Berlin. When the day came, it only served to show in stronger colours the great fall which the empire had sustained. To many of the thoughtful inhabitants of Paris it seemed surprising that the emperor should have hazarded so much on the war. He left with the full knowledge that defeat would imperil his dynasty. The Germans in front were scarcely more formidable than enemies left at home. But justice requires it to be noted, that in the eyes of most of the French his crime was, not the going to war, but commencing it before France was ready; and therefore on his head the results of defeat ought to fall, for to the French mind their troops were invincible. To add to the crushing effect of disaster in the field, not one among his thousand servants showed sign of real devotion to him. The first thing done by his council was to omit his name in ah proclamations; and the first thought of his ministry was to summon the rival power—the Legislative Body. Deserted by his flatterers and enfeebled in bodily health, his fete-day, about which he was always wont to have a superstitious feeling, as if it were a day of destiny, brought ample food for gloomy memories and still gloomier anticipations.

Whilst the remarkable proceedings narrated in the previous pages were occurring in the distracted capital of France, a widely different feeling pervaded Berlin and the entire German nation. France was prepared only for success, failing which anarchy and disorganization threatened the empire; Germany awaited with calmness either victory or defeat, regarding it as quite probable that the emperor's troops would gain a few dashing triumphs at the outset, and even advance a longer or shorter distance beyond their frontier; but the Teutons none the less firmly believed in their power ultimately to hurl back the enemy with disastrous effect. The *élan* of the French was to be met and conquered by German "phlegm." "We shall, perhaps, be beaten at first," said the Crown Prince, as he started for the front; "but do not mind: we are quite sure to win in the end."

Nevertheless, the official announcement of the evacuation of Saarbrück had at first a somewhat depressing effect on the capital. It was not supposed that actual defeat had been sustained, and the accuracy of the bulletin was unquestioned, seeing that during the war with Austria the Prussian government carefully avoided either exaggerating its successes or glossing over its losses. The inhabitants, however, from the queen downwards, were grave and anxious, less from the fact that the opening of the war had witnessed a slight check to their army, than the feeling engendered by the danger of their friends in the ranks, now that hostilities had commenced in earnest.

On the afternoon of Thursday, August 5, imperfect accounts of the affair at Wissembourg were circulated throughout Berlin, and the tidings that the Crown Prince had crossed the Rhine and was fighting on French ground caused great excitement. The ordinary business of the city came to an immediate standstill, and a crowd assembled before the king's palace, in which many of the first bankers and merchants were content to jostle with people of all sorts and conditions. It soon became known that a telegram of vital importance had been received by the queen, who delegated a general officer to report the news from the king of the first Prussian victory, in the following terms:—

"MAINZ, *August* 4.

"To the Queen Augusta.

"Under Fritz's eyes to-day a brilliant but bloody victory has been won by the storming of Weissenburg, and Geisberg behind it. Our fifth and eleventh corps, and the second Bavarian army corps fought. The enemy in flight: 500 unwounded prisoners, one cannon, and the encampment in our hands. General Douay dead. Of us, General von Kirchbach slightly wounded. My regiment and the fiftieth heavy losses. God be praised for the first glorious action! May he help us further!"

This despatch was posted up about the streets, and gladdened the hearts of the entire population. "God be praised." That was the universal feeling; and the terrors of Chassepots and mitrailleuses ceased to disquiet the minds of the people. The news of the victory was announced after nine in the evening, and in less than half an hour all the windows of the principal streets were lit up in token of the general rejoicing. The feeling of jubilation lasted far into the night, and was renewed on the morning of Friday by a message which raised the number of French prisoners from 500 to 800, and stated that batches of them might shortly be expected in Berlin.

The afternoon of Saturday (August 6) brought the tidings that the Crown Prince had beaten MacMahon at Woerth, and driven his army in headlong rout. The inhabitants turned out *en masse* at this news, and the telegram announcing the victory was read by General Hanenfeld from the balcony of the royal palace. It caused a burst of joy through all Berlin. Till midnight the crowd continued crying, "Long live the king!" and "Long live the Crown Prince!" Four tunes the queen came forward, waving her handkerchief, while the people responded in loud hurrahs.

Unter den Linden, Friedrich-strasse, and all the leading thoroughfares, were illuminated, and the signs of rejoicing continued through the night. Early on Sunday morning the bands of the different regiments played in honour of the victory, and the event was celebrated by salvos of artillery.

The news of the successful engagement on the heights of Spicheren, under General Steinmetz, on the 6th, did not arrive till late at night, and only became generally known on Sunday morning. It was reported in the simplest language, and not even called a victory, although quite as important as Woerth.

These successes left in the hands of the Germans some 20,000 wounded and unwounded prisoners, who were distributed in Posen, Passau, Glogau, Spandau, Berlin, &c. On the 6th August, a first batch of 600, part of those taken at Wissembourg, were lodged in the casemates of Graudenz. On their passage through Frankfort, Berlin, and other cities, these prisoners were lionized, and treated with the utmost kindness by the public, which stared at, talked to, and good-naturedly cheered them by thousands. The Berlin police had previously issued a notice that French prisoners were coming through the city, and begged the people to show that they knew how to treat a vanquished enemy with courtesy. This intimation was more than fulfilled. The Frenchmen were regaled with huge piles of butterbrödchen and other delicacies, and with unlimited quantities of sausages, cigars, tobacco, wine, and beer. The ladies who supplied the viands, as well as the officers and many of the privates forming the escort, spoke French fluently, to the great surprise of the prisoners, many of whom seemed to have been persuaded that they were warring with a race of semi-barbarians, ignorant of everything save their own jargon.

It was originally intended that the French prisoners for Spandau, viâ Berlin, should be marched through the capital, and a crowd of 100,000 assembled to witness the spectacle. At the request of the queen the intention was abandoned; the prisoners were conveyed across the city by the connecting line of rails, and forwarded to the Frankfort station.

The Turcos, of whom a large number were captured, excited the greatest curiosity. Ugly, swarthy, slight in physique, they did not improve on acquaintance. Even their fellow-prisoners appeared ashamed of their companionship. It was likewise rumoured that they had been caught mutilating and massacring the wounded on the battle-field, which created in Germany a strong feeling of repulsion against them, and of indignation that the emperor should have employed such savages in European warfare.

More slowly the wounded Prussians, as well as the wounded French who had been captured, were forwarded to Berlin, and many a moving scene took place at the Potsdam railway station on their arrival. It was likewise noticeable, that the spirit in which the Germans received the news of the brilliant victories of their armies, contrasted favourably with that excited by the fictitious tidings of MacMahon's triumph in Paris, already described. From the sovereign who led them to the poorest subject, the one cry which arose was that of Luther's grand old hymn, "Nun dankt alle Gott"—Now let all thank God—mingled with an honest pride in the fearless courage of their civilian army. The first natural impulses of joy were succeeded by thoughtful sympathy and care for the wounded. In every town and village systematic means were taken to lighten the sufferings of the sick and disabled.

The joy of the people was far beyond that caused by the triumphs of Prussia in 1866. After Königgrätz, many of the chief cities of the Fatherland were sorrowful and humiliated. German had shed the blood of German. But in the war of 1870 they had united against a common enemy; while the brilliant exploits of the campaign were fully shared by the southern Teutons, whose apocryphal enfranchisement was one of the pretexts advanced by the French emperor to justify the war. In fact, throughout Germany, at this time the war was felt to be but a means to an end, and that end was not so much the humiliation of France as the construction of Germany. And what could draw the bonds of union tighter than common sufferings and mutual services? A Bavarian corps comes to the rescue of a Prussian one in the hour of need; North German soldiers have every attention lavished on them as they pass South German Mayence; South Germans are cared for tenderly at Prussian Saarbrück and Trèves. The religious barrier also was breached, and Catholic priests and Protestant clergymen were busied in smoothing the same pillow, and Sisters of Charity glided about the beds of the Northern Lutherans and Calvinists. In fact, the Bavarian, the Swabian, and the Prussian, each rejoiced in the prowess of their brothers and sons, and looked forward with fervent hope and prayer for their speedy and safe return to Fatherland.

Meanwhile, still poring over its war maps and tracing out the line of opposed army fronts, Berlin waited in the assurance that genius, courage, and numbers combined to make failure all but impossible. Success also led the Prussians to consider what they should exact from the vanquished, and already it was said that Alsace must once more be German territory.

As the days advanced towards the 15th August, by which time the French had calculated to enter Berlin in triumph, it became increasingly gratifying to all with German sympathies to see how large a tract of French ground was held by King William, who had issued proclamations addressed to the French inhabitants of the provinces held by the Prussian army, intimating that while the Germans were fighting the emperor's troops, they were desirous to live at peace with the French people.

United Germany had formed a determined purpose to make it the last war with France. They were afraid otherwise that their dearly-bought victories would prove fruitless, by having the work to do over again. "Stop short of Paris," they said, "as we stopped short of Vienna! certainly not. *They* were for marching into Berlin. *Their* cry of invasion was 'to the Rhine!' We have beaten them back to the Moselle, and are masters of all the country between. We have nearly regained our old province of Alsace. We shall starve out Strassburg. We shall starve out Metz or take it, and shall keep beating them back and back to Châlons. Paris will be ours; and, come all Europe, we will not be denied our triumph and revenge."

CHAPTER X.

Brief Recapitulation of the Results of the Battles of Woerth and Forbach—The Scene at Saverne on the arrival of the débris of MacMahon's Army—The Troops of the Crown Prince advance to Haguenau—Surrender of the Town—MacMahon's retreat westward—Capture of Lichtenberg and La Petite Pierre—Resistance of Bitsche and Phalsbourg—Description of both Fortresses—The Baden Contingent despatched to besiege Strassburg—Address of the Baden General to the Alsatians—General description of German advance into France— Proclamation of the Crown Prince—Arrival at Nancy—Panic in the Town—It is actually taken by Four German Soldiers—Junction of the Crown Prince with the other German Armies—Position of the Different French Corps after the Battles of Woerth and Forbach— Generous Conduct of Canrobert—Another Fatal Delay on the part of the French—The Advance of the First and Second German Armies—Address of the King to the Soldiers— Gallant Conduct of a Young German Lieutenant in the Capture of Saargemund—The German Tactics as regarded the Advance of their different Armies—Their Commissariat— Novel description of Food introduced—Praiseworthy Conduct of the Troops at St. Avold— Passage of the Moselle at Pont-à-Mousson by the Germans—Proceedings at the French Headquarters—Removal of Marshal Leboeuf—The Emperor resigns the Command-in- Chief—Arrival of General Changarnier at Metz—Appointment of Marshal Bazaine as Commander-in-Chief—Biographical Notice of him—The Evils of a Divided Command— Bazaine Resolves on a Retreat—Departure of the Emperor from Metz—Proclamation to the Inhabitants—Attempt of the Prussians to capture the Emperor—His Flight to Verdun, and Ride to Châlons in a Third-Class Carriage—Comments on the Cruelty of uselessly exposing the Prince Imperial—General Review of the Situation at this time—The Tactics which might have saved France—The Emperor's own Explanations of his Proceedings—Description of the City and Fortress of Metz.

THE first act of the military drama of 1870 may be said to have closed with the battles of the 6th of August, described in Chapter VIII. Their result was the evacuation of Northern Alsace and the retreat of the French army—now thrown entirely on the defensive—beyond the line of the Vosges; the main body falling back upon Metz, the right wing making its way as best it could, in utter disorganization, towards Nancy and Châlons. The following week was employed by the Germans in bringing up their second line, composed almost exclusively of regiments from the old Prussian provinces; while the troops which had been already engaged were pushed forward as fast as supplies could be procured and communications established with the rear, with the double object of preventing the reunion of the two sections of the French army, and either intercepting the main body in its retreat, or forcing it to fall back upon Châlons by a northerly and circuitous route, along which it could be incessantly harassed, or, if necessary, even thrown back upon the Ardennes, where it would be compelled to give battle in a district devoid of supplies, and with a neutral territory in the rear.

But we must not anticipate. As we have already briefly described in Chapter VIII., after the terrible defeat which MacMahon's army had suffered at Woerth, it was dispersed, and a large part of his broken right wing escaped towards Haguenau and Strassburg, while the remains of his other troops were scattered over the roads that ran southwards athwart the Vosges. The marshal made an effort to reach De Failly's corps and Bitsche, in order to rejoin the main army, and attempted a stand at Niederbronn; but his troops gave way at the sight of the Germans, and he fell back hastily upon Saverne.

When they arrived at this town a complete panic seized the inhabitants. According to a correspondent of the *Siècle*, who happened to be present, "all the houses were closed—hotels, cafés, beer-houses. I was scarcely half an hour in my chamber when the landlord entered, and told me to leave as soon as I could, for he was going to conceal himself in the mountains of the Vosges. I was shortly in the street, and beheld hundreds taking the paths which lead to the mountains. The army also thought it wise to retreat, and to fall back on Sarrebourg. Not being able to follow the army, I followed the people on foot, as neither vehicles nor horses were to be had. I left my luggage in the house of a person whom I do not know, and who had the politeness to open the door and pitch it inside, when he locked the door and was off to the hills as fast as his feet and legs could carry him. I do not know exactly where they are going, but I know where the crowd is going, and what a crowd—old men, women with their babes, and little girls of some four years climbing across chamois paths, amid cries, tears, and desolation. They brought with them as much as they could, and more than they could carry. Men bend under the load; even the children have their burdens. All these people speak German. After an hour's march we arrived at the first village, which has already heard the news, and is itself preparing to decamp. Oxen, cows, &c., are driven before us. Beds, linen, &c., are heaped in carts, and at each step the number of the flying is increased. I ask some persons whom I hear speaking French, where we are going, and when will our journey come to an end. I am told we are going to a plateau where we will encamp for the night as best we can after a journey of five or six hours."

M. Edmond About, who also contrived to reach the town on Saturday night, after a very perilous journey, thus described the state of affairs:—

"At the gates of Saverne, the panic-stricken were flying along the railway or hiding in the gardens; but some good regiments of the line were tramping in step through the streets. Their passage, calm and courageous, was not over before eleven o'clock at night. I found the little town a prey to a panic really fabulous. In the twinkling of an eye Saverne saw itself filled with the first corps, which the foe, very luckily, believed to have retired upon Bitsche. They massed themselves together where they could—those most fortunate in the houses of the townsmen; those who had brought away their knapsacks and camp equipage, under their tents; many upon the pavement, in the fields, under heaven's canopy. The night was passed in terror. If the enemy had known how to profit by the opportunity, he might have made 10,000 or 15,000 prisoners at one blow. The population was only half re-assured by the presence of troops broken-down, starved, and discomfited. Some families got off by the mail-train at mid-day, the last that went from Strassburg to Paris. Some others regained confidence in waiting for the officers, who said,

"You have nothing to be afraid of so long as we are here." But on Sunday at six o'clock, upon I know not what false alarm—perhaps only because three or four scouts of the enemy were announced on the side of Steinburg—the Duc de Magenta caused the *générale* to be beaten, and Saverne thought itself lost. Whilst officers and soldiers threw themselves pell-mell upon the Phalsbourg road, three-fourths of the people went off wildly towards the neighbouring forests. The example—a sad example—was set by the gendarmes and the sergents-de-ville. The townsfolk closed the shops, piled up the furniture upon carts; some farmers drove their cattle before them as in the time of Abraham; there were incredible accumulations formed, both of men and animals, in the houses of the foresters and in the ruins of old castles.

"Poor France! She granted all and pardoned all to a man who said to her at first, 'The Empire is peace!' who said to her afterwards, 'The Empire is glory and victory, the revision of shameful treaties, the rectification of frontiers, war for principle, war for interest, war for luck, but war always successful, and the prestige of the French name always more dazzling every day! France believed all she was told; she believed in her master's 'star.' What an awakening! To-day the empire means defeat by the incapacity of its chief, panic of the generals, invasion with all its following of grief and misery, the Prussian soldier tramping triumphantly over three or four departments after a campaign of eight days!"

On Sunday the 7th the troops of the Crown Prince, following the track of the French, proceeded to Haguenau. The capture of 200 French soldiers and an enormous mass of military stores at this town, by about a dozen German dragoons, headed by a couple of young lieutenants—Von Schonau and Von Freydorf—was one of the most brilliant little episodes of the war, and illustrated the utter demoralization of the French troops. About one o'clock p.m. the first and second dragoons took possession of the town, and the two lieutenants just named, followed by a few troopers, rode off to the great barracks, which were still in the hands of some 200 French soldiers. The pair summoned the occupants to surrender, which they at once did, marching out and piling their arms.

MacMahon commenced his retreat from Saverne, westwards, on Sunday afternoon. The same evening the town was occupied by the advance troops of the Crown Prince, who with the bulk of his army afterwards pressed forward in the same direction, taking care, however, to send strong detachments to his right, either to capture or mask the fortresses of the Vosges in their way. The small hill fort of Lichtenberg was taken, after some resistance, on the 9th, and shortly after another post of some importance, commanding a pass to the westward, called La Petite Pierre by the French and Luetzelstein by the Germans, where a stout resistance was expected, was abandoned by the French in such haste that they left large quantities of ammunition and some guns behind them. This fort is situated on the very crest of the Vosges, in a country covered with forest, and looks down from the Altenberg on the little town at its feet. Its advanced works, cut in the rock, are strengthened by thick walls, but it offered in its mass of exposed masonry a huge target to artillery fire. By capturing it the passage of the Vosges may be said to have been accomplished, and the way opened to Sarre Union, Sarre Albe, Sarre Werden, and further, to Fenestrange, Gros Tenquin, and other villages more immediately on the road to Nancy.

The Germans had, however, been compelled to mask the fortresses of Bitsche and Phalsbourg, as both refused to surrender, and in fact withstood longer sieges than any other places during the war. The first-named fort commands a main road, and also the railway from Sarreguemines to Haguenau, with its guns only a few score yards off the line. A proof of the value of even a small fortress in impeding an army, was afforded in the detours the Germans were obliged to make to avoid it. The fortress is situated about thirty miles north of Strassburg, and fifteen from Sarreguemines. The citadel stands in a valley upon a steep rock, 1000 feet above the level of the sea. The town, formerly called Kaltenhausen, nestles at the foot of the threatening cliff, near a large shallow lake, whence the Rome takes its source. The 3000 inhabitants live on the profits of the fine pottery for which they are famous, construct paper snuffboxes, or labour in the great glassworks of Munsthal. The rock, vaulted and casemated, with four bastions and a half-moon battery, mounts eighty pieces of cannon, and has a good supply of water. Though not a Gibraltar, or even an Ehrenbreitstein, Bitsche, as the events of the war proved, is quite inpregnable to ordinary artillery.

In the détenus' time (1803—1814) the garrison consisted of seventeen gendarmes and one hundred veterans. "The place of tears," as the English prisoners during the old Napoleon war used to call it, for it was then the depôt for the lees and dregs of Verdun, is ascended on one side by a zigzag footpath, on the other by a winding carriage road. Both these roads meet at a drawbridge that communicates with an inclined plane raised upon arches, leading to a gate at the entrance to the fort, the approaches to which are swept by the fire of ten heavy guns. The entrance is by a tunnel cut through the rock, 120 feet long, with a massive gate at each end, and one in the centre. The rock is cut through in two places as low as the ditch, one extremity being called the Grosse Tête, and the other the Petite Tête, and both are connected with the body of the fort by drawbridges. On the west side there is a mortar battery. In the centre of the fort stand two large barracks, and at the two ends are storehouses and magazines. The rock is hollowed to contain the garrison and the provisions, and is divided by compartments connected by narrow passages with massive doors. There is also a subterranean passage communicating with the town below. Although the fort is of solid rock, cut down perpendicularly 90 to 150 feet, it is faced nearly all round with masonry. The place cost so much to fortify, that Louis XIV., when asked for more money to complete it, inquired with a smile if they were building it of louis-d'ors.

Phalsbourg, the other fortress which was left in the hands of the French, is on the high road from Strassburg to Paris, overlooking the lull of Saverne, and commanding the mountain defiles of the Upper Barr, the Roche Plate, the Bonne Fontaine, and the Graufthal. Its bastions, demilunes, and advanced outworks, extend in zigzag lines over a rocky platform. From a distance the walls appear so low that one might expect to stride over them; but on approaching nearer, further advance is stopped by the moat, 100 feet wide and 30 feet deep, beyond which are the grim ramparts, cut out of the solid rock. The buildings of the town are concealed behind the glacis, except the churches, the townhall, and the gatehouses, with their fronts shaped like a mitre, erected at the two entrances, named the Porte de France and the Porte d'Allemagne. Such is the little town of Phalsbourg. It is not without a certain grandeur of appearance, and is especially imposing when one first crosses the drawbridge, and enters by the deep and massive gateway, defended by an iron portcullis and chevaux-defrise. The whole place has a military aspect, and is well known to all who have read Erckmann-Chatrian's charming tales of French popular life and soldiership during the wars of Napoleon I. It was here that Joseph Bertha, the conscript of 1813, lived as apprentice to the good watchmaker, M. Goulden; and his sweetheart Catherine lived at the adjoining village of Quatre-Vents. The sufferings of the town in 1814 are vividly pourtrayed in "Le Blocus." The railroad, avoiding the rugged eminence on which the town stands, is carried some distance to the south, beyond the reach of the guns of the fort, and therefore, when the line was completely in the hands of the Germans, and in working order, the place proved much less inconvenient than would have been the case had their troops and supplies required to be taken along the main road, as in former times. The garrison was commanded by General Talhouet, and made a stout resistance on the 14th, when the town was cannonaded by the Germans. Some of the houses were burned by the shells, but the guns were too light to make any breach in the ramparts; and the place was then regularly blockaded.

In addition to capturing or masking these forts in the Vosges, the Crown Prince, on his arrival at Saverne, executed a much more important operation of a similar kind, in detaching lüa Baden contingent, under General Beyer, to lay siege to Strassburg—-an operation which its position on the frontier, and close to the main lines of the German railways, rendered comparatively easy. The commandant, General Uhrich, resolutely rejected the summons of the besiegers, and prepared for a vigorous defence. All the approaches were barricaded, and the obstructions on the glacis cleared away. The details respecting its siege and capture are given in Chapter XVIII. Its investment so very early in the war caused no surprise; for when MacMahon, after his defeat at Woerth, retreated to Saverne, twenty miles northwest of Strassburg, he virtually abandoned that place to its fate; as his position could only secure his own retreat towards Nancy, while it could not prevent an overpowering hostile force from throwing off a comparatively small part of its strength to invest or mask the fortress, and to destroy its communications with the country on every side.

Soon after his appointment, the Badish general issued the following address to the inhabitants of Alsace:—"I have to address to you a serious word. We, your neighbours, used amicably to confer with each other in times of peace. We speak the same language. To you I appeal. Let the language of the heart, let the voice of humanity, reach you. Germany is engaged in war with France—in a war which was not desired by Germany. We were compelled to invade your land. But we regard every human life, and all property that can be spared, as a gain which is blessed by religion and by humane sentiments. We stand in the midst of war. The armed fight with the armed in honest open contest. But we will spare the unarmed civilians, the inhabitant of the towns and the villages. Maintaining severe discipline, we expect—nay, I demand it most rigorously—that the inhabitants of this country shall refrain from overt or secret hostility. To our deep sorrow we have been compelled with severe retribution to visit provocations, cruelties, and savage acts; I therefore expect that the local authorities, the clergy, the schoolmasters, will charge the communes, and the heads of families will charge their relatives and subordinates, that no hostilities be practised upon my soldiers. All misery that can be averted is a benefaction in the sight of Him who watches over mankind. I admonish you, I warn you, be mindful of this!"

The sixth German corps, which had been in the rear on the day of Woerth, was further detained by reports that De Failly, with the fifth French, having got away from Bitsche and Sarreguemines, across their front, was holding the branch railroads to the south of them, with the design of slipping round and raising the siege of Strassburg. When this sixth corps reached the city, they supplied the place of some of the original besiegers, who were moved along the great route which leads westward into the interior.

In their march across the Vosges, most of the infantry of the Crown Prince used every available path and by-road, to leave, as far as possible, all the main routes for artillery, cavalry, and baggage, but still holding them in immense force. The general scene was thus described by an eyewitness:—

"There has been a shifting of quarters from village to village since I last wrote; indeed, the army of the Crown Prince is so active, that this shifting of quarters is an almost daily occurrence. Everything is done in perfect order. The carriages are told off in a slow moving column, with mounted troopers at intervals to regulate the line of march, and when all are placed, there is a halt of a few minutes to allow the prince and his staff to pass. The style in which the troops march is such as to justify all the praise lavished on the Prussian infantry. The usual walking pace of a good horse is considerably faster than that of an ordinary march. The prince's staff scarcely ever check that pace of their horses. Mile after mile the infantry, carrying knapsacks, coats, and cooking-tins, in the very heaviest marching order, go on in front of the horses in a six hours' march, mostly up a series of ascents, and only halt once, except for half an hour in the middle of the day. There is little talking in the ranks as they march, but the men sing, a few beginning, and the rest joining in chorus with very pretty effect. With each advance, the Prussians bring forward their field-post and their military telegraph. A more perfect system of organization it is difficult to imagine. The columns of provisions creep like great serpents over the country. The active detachments of telegraph men push on, with their light poles set up at intervals, and their slowly decreasing coil of wire; and the field post-office brings letters to the different divisions. From side to side for many a mile, the whole country is on the move. Well may the villagers stare at the show, for they are not likely to see again so many fine horses and bright uniforms. Old and young crowd the wayside as his royal highness goes by, and doff their caps respectfully, but without any sign of welcome. It is curious to see these German Frenchmen, or rather these Gallicised Germans, dealing with the invaders. The power of understanding one another makes their intercourse much less disagreeable than might be supposed. Yet, nevertheless, there is a strong sympathy with France among the Alsatian peasants, because they have, thanks to the conscription, such a number of their sons serving in the French army. I notice that the younger folks can all speak a little French, though they answer the question of the soldiers, "Parlez vous Chassepot," with a sententious "nein," which seems to imply utter ignorance of the language referred to. Poor souls! They are very much frightened by this astounding invasion, and make the most of their rough Alsatian dialect, as a means of propitiating the new and dreaded invaders of the empire. I must say, in justice to the German troops, that this dread is founded on a notion of what might be, rather than what really happens. Beyond compulsory service in country waggons to carry wounded men or loads of hay, and compulsory sales of provisions to the military authorities, there is little to complain of. It is as with Wellington's army in Southern France in 1814, rather than as with the Allied armies in that memorable year. No invasion can be pleasant to the conquered people; but this one of 1870 is conducted on the humane principles of modern warfare. The Crown Prince of Prussia has resolved to strike only at the French government, and at the armed forces which oppose him. The consideration and gracious courtesy of his royal highness to all brought in contact with him, are quite beyond acknowledgment when one reflects on the cares which press upon his mind in this tremendous moment; and whatever may be the necessities and severities and horrors of this war, there is not a member of the Peace Society, nor a humanitarian in England, or out of it, who is more profoundly moved by the sufferings inflicted on the people, and so averse from war for its own sake, as the Crown Prince. He possesses the confidence and affection of those serving under him, and never comes in sight without their giving him the hearty cheer which cannot be simulated, and which is the most grateful sound to a leader's ear."

The following proclamation was issued by his royal highness soon after reaching French territory:—"We, general commanding the third German army, seeing the proclamation of his Majesty the king of Prussia, authorizing the generals commanding-in-chief of the several corps of the German army to frame special regulations with relation to the measures to be taken against communes and persons who may be acting in contravention of the usages of war; and with relation to the requisitions which may be judged necessary for the wants of the troops, and to fix the difference in the rate of exchange between German and French moneys—have decreed, and do decree the following regulations, which we make known to the public.

"1. Military jurisdiction is established by this decree. It will be extended to all the territory occupied by German troops, to every action tending to endanger the security of those troops, to causing them injury, or lending assistance to the enemy. Military jurisdiction will be considered as in force, and proclaimed through all the extent of a canton as soon as it is posted in any locality forming part of it.

"2. All persons not forming part of the French army, and not proving their quality as soldiers by outward signs, and who (a) shall serve the enemy as spies; (b) shall mislead the German troops when charged to act for them as guides; (c) shall kill, wound, or rob persons belonging to the German troops, or making part of their suite; (d) shall destroy bridges or canals, damage telegraphic lines or railways, render roads impassable, set fire to munitions and provisions of war, or troops' quarters; (e) shall take up arms against the German troops—will be punished by death. In each case, the officer in command will institute a council of war, with authority to try the matter and pronounce sentence. These councils can only condemn to death. Their sentences will be executed immediately.

"3. The communes to which the culprits belong, as well as those whose territory may have been the scene of the offence, will be condemned in a penalty for each case equalling the annual amount of their taxes.

"4. The inhabitants will have to supply all necessaries for the support of the troops. Each soldier will receive daily 750 grammes of bread, 500 grammes of meat, 250 grammes of lard, 30 grammes of coffee, 60 grammes of tobacco or 5 cigars, ½ litre of wine, or 1 litre of beer, or 1-10th of brandy. The rations to be furnished daily for each horse will be six kilogrammes of oats, two kilogrammes of hay, and one and a half kilogramme of straw. In case of the inhabitants preferring an indemnity in coin to one in kind, it will be fixed at two francs each soldier daily.

"5. All commanders of detached corps will have the right to order a requisition of provisions needful to the support of their troops. The requisition of other articles judged indispensable to the army, can only be ordered by generals and officers acting as such. In all cases, nothing will be demanded of the inhabitants except what is necessary for the support of the troops, and official receipts will be given for everything supplied. We hope, therefore, that the inhabitants will not offer any obstacles to the requisitions which may be deemed necessary.

"6. With regard to individual bargains between the troops and the inhabitants, we fix as an equivalent for 1 franc, 8 silbergros or 28 kreutzers.

"The general commanding-in-chief the third German army,

"FREDERIC WILLIAM,
"Prince Royal of Prussia."

The Germans had succeeded in forcing the beaten French troops so far south, that they could only rejoin the rest of the army by taking a very circuitous route; but they still kept close after them, marching straight on to Luneville and Nancy. Their advanced troops reached the latter city—the old capital of Lorraine and one of the prettiest towns in France—on Friday, August 12, but the prince's headquarters were not established there till five days later. The town is open, and proclamations had been issued by the authorities enjoining the inhabitants to offer no resistance to the troops. There was not, however, much necessity for this, as a day or two before the arrival of the Germans, a few carriages of wounded, brought from MacMahon's corps, threw the whole town into despair; and the men who a fortnight before frantically sang the "Marseillaise" along the pretty street, were now running away and spreading alarm everywhere. Inhabitants of Saverne and similar places, arriving at Nancy on their way from the parts of the country actually occupied, deepened still more the despair and demoralization of the people of the very places which had in former times been distinguished for valour and courage. The readers of Erckmann-Chatrian's romances will remember that the action of the best of them takes place near where Marshal MacMahon lost in two battles more than 10,000 men, and whence the inhabitants now ran away as if none of them had either bone or muscle to defend their native soil. Seeing the long train of chariots loaded with peasant families, about to take their refuge in the forests between Nancy and Commercy, or the noisy groups of the bourgeois with weeping women and children assembled before some crowded hotel, unable to give them anything in the shape of a bed, one could not help thinking that either Erckmann-Chatrian had too much idealized their heroes, or that human nature had greatly changed in that part of France since the beginning of the century.

Nancy, the chief town in the department of the Meurthe, containing 40,000 inhabitants, was actually taken possession of by four German soldiers, who reached it about three o'clock in the afternoon. About half an hour later a detachment of twenty-six Germans marched through the city and took possession of the railway station; the station-master was made prisoner, but left at liberty on parole. The mayor was ordered to wait upon the German commander, encamped on the road between St. Max and Pont d'Essey. Meanwhile an officer of Uhlans followed by two orderlies galloped over the town to reconnoitre. On the mayor's return the municipal council was compelled to vote 50,000 francs to the victorious Germans, together with large rations of oats; and some of the inhabitants were compelled to tear up more than a mile of rails, from Nancy to Maxville, which the Germans flung into the canal. They also cut down the posts for the telegraphic wires.

The French troops—retreating to Châlons—had only abandoned the town at a very early hour the same morning, and much indignation was expressed in Paris at the conduct of the municipal or military authorities in not making an attempt to defend it.

As already stated, the Crown Prince himself did not reach Nancy till August 17, but three days before he had effected a junction with the other German armies at Gros Tenquin, and on the 14th, troops of both the second and the third armies occupied Pont-à-Mousson, a railway station about midway between Metz and Nancy. The third army was, therefore, now so placed as to be ready if necessary to carry out General Moltke's original design, which was to bring it on the southern flank of the French forces defending the Saar or Moselle against the first and second. As it happened, however, the combinations against the French main body had been so hurried forward by the force of events as to leave no room for the action of the Crown Prince; and having thus traced the progress of his army from the battle of Woerth to the occupation of Nancy, in pursuit of MacMahon, with the débris of his corps, to Châlons, we now leave them for awhile, and return to the remaining French corps and the first and second German armies.

After the rout of MacMahon at Woerth, the other French corps, in endeavouring to effect their junction in Lorraine, were swayed to and fro by the pressure of the enemy, and compelled to make more than one false movement in consequence of the distance between their first line on the Saar, and their second at Metz. Of the fifth French corps (De Failly's), which had lain between the armies routed at Woerth and Forbach, we know that a division arrived at Niederbronn on the afternoon of the 6th, just in time to cover the retreat of MacMahon's broken battalions upon Saverne. This division afterwards retreated by Bitsche, and ultimately effected its junction with Bazaine at Metz, but the other two divisions, finding that the defeats on both sides of them had rendered their position untenable, retreated southwards with the greatest precipitation, and was lost to view for ten of the most critical days of the campaign. After having made an immense détour, they only succeeded in joining MacMahon at Châlons on August 20. Frossard, after the rout of Forbach, had fled with the wrecks of his corps towards Metz, abandoning St. Avold and several good positions. L'Admirault, also, though as yet unassailed, but involved in the common disaster, evacuated Thionville with the fourth corps, and was in retreat towards Metz along the Moselle. Bazaine, meanwhile, with the third corps, had been directed to advance from Metz, in order to rally the forces in his front, and had taken a position upon the Nied; a step which, perhaps, could not have been avoided, but which obviously threw a considerable portion of the French army dangerously forward, and exposed it to more than one mischance. At the same time, while the imperial guard remained in camp about Metz, a part of the sixth corps of Canrobert had been moved towards the great fortress, while the remainder continued at its post at Nancy. The conduct of Canrobert at this time was very commendable; as soon as he heard of his sovereign's disasters he speedily brought up part of his troops from Châlons, and placed himself ungrudgingly at the disposal of his junior, Bazaine, who had by that time been appointed commander-in-chief. The seventh corps, that of Douay, had been left in the place it had held far to the south, and except the division which had fought at Woerth, it was still distant from the theatre of operations. Thus the German victory at Woerth had this important effect, that for nearly three weeks it completely neutralized three out of the eight corps of which the French army consisted—MacMahon's, De Failly's, and Douay's.

About three days after the battles of Woerth and Forbach, the general position of the combatants may then be thus described:—MacMahon, with his broken right wing, towards which De Failly was inclining, was completely cut off from the main body of the French; their left and centre, hardly united, were gathering in front of and at Metz, exposed to be defeated in detail, and in part advanced on a line on which they were liable, if beaten, to serious disaster. This force, too, the principal hope of France, composed of only three intact corps, of the routed second, and of part of the sixth, numbering, perhaps, 150,000 men, with between 400 and 500 guns, was well known to be wholly unequal to the immense masses moving against it, and already victorious within the frontier. Nearly 200,000 men, from the armies of Steinmetz and Prince Frederick Charles, were on their way from the Saar to the Nied; while to the left the Crown Prince, in communication with them, was sweeping through the passes of the Vosges, and along the highways that lead into Champagne. In these circumstances we cannot be surprised that the emperor, having fortunately succeeded in rallying a respectable force on the Nied, should have fallen back without delay on Metz, and drawn under the protection of the fortress the whole remains of his left and centre. Well would it have been had the retrograde movement then been continued; but of this more presently. In the meantime, let us trace the progress of the first and second German armies.

As stated in a previous chapter, the king of Prussia, with his advisers, arrived at Mayence on 3rd August, and took command, officially, of the whole of the German armies; but before he could reach the front the important battle of Forbach had been fought and won, and the French line on the Saar irretrievably broken.

On Sunday, 7th August, the headquarters of the king were advanced to Homburg, within fifteen miles of the French frontier, and the same night Steinmetz, commanding the right of the German line, had his headquarters a little to the north of Saarbrück, while Prince Frederick Charles was at Bliescastel, a village about ten miles due east of that town. Up to this time the advanced divisions of the Prussian right had occupied Forbach, the centre had crossed the Saar and occupied Saarguemines, or, as the Germans call it, Saargemund; while the army of the Crown Prince had taken possession of Haguenau. Thus the whole line of the French frontier railway was in the hands of the Germans, from Haguenau, only twenty miles north of Strassburg, to Bening Merlbach, the station near Forbach, where this line is connected with that from Metz to Saarbrück.

While at Homburg the king of Prussia addressed the following proclamation to his army:— "Soldiers—Already a great portion of our army, engaged in pursuit of the enemy, thrown back after bloody combats, has passed the frontier. This day and to-morrow several corps d'armée will enter French territory. I expect that you will consider it a point of honour to distinguish yourselves in the enemy's country, above all by the excellence of discipline, of which, up to the present time, you have given a glorious example. We do not make war on the peaceable inhabitants of France; and the first duty of a loyal soldier is to protect private property, to preserve intact the high reputation of our army, and to prevent its being soiled by one solitary act even of want of discipline. I count on the elevated spirit which animates the army; and I rely no less on the severity and watchfulness of all its chiefs.

"WILLIAM.

"HEADQUARTERS, HOMBURG,
"8th August, 1870."

Prince Frederick Charles and General von Steinmetz addressed similar proclamations to the soldiers:—"Show, by the uprightness of your behaviour to friend and foe, that you are worthy children of Prussia. Show that you belong to an army which represents the cultivation of the century, by decent and friendly behaviour, by moderation and respect for foreign property, whether of friend or foe. Each one of you is responsible for the honour and reputation of the whole Fatherland."

The French had left Saargemund only about twelve hours before the Germans entered it. A young lieutenant of the Brunswick Hussars had orders to patrol towards the town with a couple of his men. As he approached it, to his astonishment he saw no signs of French troops; and with the audacity of youth he cantered into it, followed by his two hussars. He reined up opposite the market-place, inquiring the nearest way to the burgomaster's house, which was pointed out to him. In the meantime a crowd had collected, who began to give some indications of hostile designs. He had his revolver in his hand, when one of the peasants said, "What's the good of that? He dare not fire at us." "Daren't I?" replied the hussar, at the same time levelling his pistol and firing over the man's head, which so intimidated the townsfolk, that they instantly cheered him. He then proceeded to the burgomaster, and demanded quarters for two infantry regiments and a battery of artillery, which he expected would shortly enter the town. This granted, he sent one of his hussars back to his regiment, about five miles off, with the intelligence that the place was empty, and in two hours the Brunswick Hussars, trotting into it, proclaimed it a captured town. The lieutenant, a mere boy, named Herr von Kœnig, was for these two hours entirely at the mercy of 1000 inhabitants at the least.

The advance of all the German armies towards the Moselle could not, of course, on all points of their extended lines be equally rapid. After invading France and making good their stand in the country, their forces were disposed, as we have seen, between Forbach and Haguenau, forming a line which stretched east-south-east. The Moselle between Metz and Nancy flowing straight south and north, a portion of the troops, of course, found themselves considerably nearer the river than the rest. Their first or northernmost army, under General Steinmetz, was in closer proximity to the stream than the second, under Prince Frederick Charles; the third, under the Crown Prince, being the most distant of all, and, moreover, separated from the Moselle by the most difficult ground. As it was expected that the French would try to concentrate their forces as soon as possible, and make another stand in the favourable position on the banks of the Nied between Metz and Marsal, orders were given to the different German armies to time their advance, so as to remain in close contact with each other, and form gradually into a straight continuous line. While their whole cavalry were keeping almost in sight of the enemy, the three armies followed so closely as to prevent the French from forming again, notwithstanding that violent storms had swelled the streams and made the roads heavy. The French army had also exhausted the resources of the country, and fresh supplies had to be brought up from Germany. The king had commanded that every German soldier billeted upon a French household was to be fed by his host; but only in very few cases could the German soldier get from his French entertainer the 750 grammes of bread, 500 grammes of meat, 250 grammes of bacon, 30 grammes of coffee, 60 grammes of tobacco, and half a litre of wine, which he was authorized to demand daily. Mostly he lived upon the biscuit, bacon, beef, and coffee provided by the military authorities, and in some cases the French inhabitants themselves had to be fed by the German commissariat to prevent absolute starvation. An important help in victualling the troops was afforded by a novel description of food used in China. It consisted of the pease pudding, for centuries employed in keeping body and soul together among the Celestials; a cheap article that does not deteriorate for a length of time, and contains a large quantity of nutritious matter in a small compass. To make it more palatable the Germans improved upon the Chinese pattern by mixing smoked meat, chopped up small, with the pease. Whether boiled or cold it is equally good, and a small quantity will suffice a man for a day.

On Wednesday, August 10, the first army, forming the right of the German position, was at Les Etangs, a village on the left bank of the Nied, about nine miles east by north of Metz, and here they halted for a short time. The second army, meanwhile, were circling round towards the Moselle, south of Metz, to the chief points of passage, Pont-à-Mousson, Pagny, and Corny. On Saturday morning, the 13th, the Prussian infantry compelled a French battalion to withdraw in all haste from the first-named town, the largest on the Moselle between Nancy and Metz, and afterwards took possession of it. A proclamation was issued the moment possession was taken, promising security to the inhabitants on certain conditions:—1. All arms to be given up at the Maine within two hours, each arm labelled with the name of the owner, that it might be restored to him at some future period. It was added, that after the expiration of two hours, patrols would visit every house, when, if arms were discovered, the occupier would be treated "with all the severity of the military law. 2. No groups to be formed in the streets. 3. Shutters to be kept open, blinds drawn up. 4. The inhabitants to supply troops marching through the town with water. 5. No impediment to be offered to the advance of the troops. "Any one offering impediments of any kind," concluded the proclamation, "will be at once taken and shot." It was not thought necessary to visit the houses; and it was, indeed, improbable, in the face of such a proclamation, that any arms would be retained. Most, however, of the population capable of bearing arms had disappeared before the arrival of the Germans, and it may be presumed that they did not leave their arms behind.

A reference to a map will show, that during the week of which we have been treating, the whole German army had pivoted upon its right, wheeling as a column wheels upon a fixed point; and the centre advanced at a slower pace than the left, till the line which, on Wednesday the 10th, ran from Les Etangs, in a south-east direction, through Foligny, Faulquemont, Gros Tenquin, Fenestrange, and Saarburg, on Saturday the 13th ran from Les Etangs to Pont-à-Mousson, Frouard, and Nancy, while the headquarters of the king were fixed in rear of the right centre of the line at Herny, a station on the railway from Metz to Forbach. His Majesty had entered France by way of Saarbrück, on leaving which he addressed the following proclamation to the French people—a proclamation which was very often referred to after the capitulation of the emperor and his army at Sedan, to prove that the German ideas with regard to the war had then materially changed:—

"We, William, king of Prussia, make known the following to the inhabitants of the French territories occupied by the German armies.

"The Emperor Napoleon having made by land and by sea an attack on the German nation, which desired, and still desires, to live in peace with the French people, I have assumed the command of the German armies to repel this aggression, and I have been led by military circumstances to cross the frontiers of France. I am waging war against soldiers, not against French citizens. The latter, consequently, will continue to enjoy security for their persons and property, so long as they themselves shall not by hostile attempts against the German troops deprive me of the right of according them my protection. By special arrangements, which will be duly made known to the public, the generals commanding the different corps will determine the measures to be taken towards the communes or individuals that may place themselves in opposition to the usages of war. They will, in like manner, regulate all that concerns the requisitions which may be deemed necessary for the wants of the troops, and they will fix the rate of exchange between French and German currencies in order to facilitate the individual transactions between the troops and the inhabitants."

His Majesty, exercising the rights of war, also abolished the conscription in the French territories occupied by his armies; forbidding the inhabitants to render military service to his enemy. It was, of course, hardly to be expected that he should allow the French government to levy soldiers in the rear of his army.

His Majesty left Saarbrück on the 11th, and on the following day his headquarters were fixed at St. Avold, the walls of which were placarded with proclamations from him and General von

Alvensleben, the commandant of the town, to the effect that, Prussia being at war only with the soldiers of France, the troops were to pay for whatever they took, and that any attempt at plundering would be most severely punished. "Several of the inhabitants have assured me," said a reliable correspondent, "that not only are they well treated by the soldiers, but that they prefer Prussian to French troops, the latter being none too careful of the distinction between *meum* and *tuum*. The only difficulty I have heard of is about the Prussian money, the soldiers not understanding sous and centimes, and the inhabitants thalers and silbergroschen. In the garden of the house in which I am quartered, or, to speak more correctly, in which I have quartered myself, not a flower has been picked, not a bed trodden upon, and there are some plums and apples which must look singularly tempting to the men after a long march. I know of only one way of putting these German soldiers out of temper, and that is to hint that peace will be made before they get into Paris. This they seem to look on as quite a reflection on the army, and they resent it accordingly. At present, in spite of the wet weather and the hard fighting, the men all look well and hearty, and tramp away under their heavy kits, as if they already saw the towers of Notre Dame."

A good proof of the utter defeat of the French at the battle of Forbach was found by the Germans in the fact, that although extensive preparations had been made beforehand to defend St. Avold, they did not find it practicable to avail themselves of this advantage, but turned their troops off in another direction. Had they thrown themselves into St. Avold, they must have stopped the German advance for a day at least. The hills near the place were studded with rifle pits, and a large farmyard, with solid wall, which has absolute command of the road from St. Avold to Metz, had been converted into a little fortress, and if properly defended would have cost many lives. This surrender of a strong and well-fortified position is sufficiently accounted for by the experience of the French generals at Forbach and Saarbrück. As we know, the ground from Forbach to Saarbrück had been carefully got into order for defence. Earthworks had been thrown up in positions already strengthened by nature; everywhere arrangements had been carefully made to force the Germans to fight exposed to full fire from the French. Hence their unbounded astonishment at seeing the Germans scaling the acclivities without firing a shot or uttering a sound; and when they knew that after having reached the summit of the hills near Saarbrück, and from the deepest silence breaking out into loud hurrahs, they fired a volley and then took to the bayonet, the French doubtless thought it useless to occupy the fortified hills of St. Avold.

Considerable as the stream of the Moselle is, the German army possessed bridge-trains amply sufficient for several passages of it; and the temptation was great to surprise Bazaine by advancing both wings of their army at once, so as to unite them on his communications with Paris through Verdun, and shut him off with the emperor from the rest of France. Yet this plan, though presenting brilliant prospects, also offered great chances to a resolute adversary who might divine it in time; which would have secured to the French the cover of the fortress to which they evidently clung, and from which no direct attack, short of a siege, could possibly have forced them. It seemed easier therefore to manoeuvre them from under its shelter, and deal with them in the open field; and for this purpose, as we have seen, the bridge and road through Pont-à-Mousson, twenty miles higher up, lay conveniently placed. Accordingly, on the 14th the German army made a general movement by its left in a south-westerly direction on Pont-à-Mousson. To cover this the more effectually, General von Steinmetz, whose army was to the left of that of Prince Frederick Charles, was directed to make a demonstration against Bazaine's troops, then lying partly between him and Metz, as well as all round the face of the eastern side of the fortress. A severe action (the particulars of which are fully given in the next chapter) was the result, in which half of the seventh corps, first engaging the French right wing, and supported by successive divisions of the Prussians, forced the French from an intrenched position back to the cover of the outworks of Metz. Meanwhile, the passage of other corps went on steadily by Pont-à-Mousson, and they were distributed on the further side of the Moselle so as to prepare for an advance westward.

Leaving the German armies for a short time, we now turn to see what had been going on at the French headquarters.

When the double defeats of Forbach and Woerth became fully known there, it was felt by the emperor and by those around him, that an immediate change of leaders was among the steps urgently necessary to restore confidence to the troops, disheartened not more by the news than by the general retreat that immediately followed. Marshal Leboeuf, too hastily raised to the rank he had done nothing to earn—and who was looked upon as the principal cause of the reverses—was at once put aside; and as the emperor also desired to give up the chief command of the army, the great object was the appointment of a leader popular enough to inspire confidence, and who would not hesitate to take such a serious responsibility. Changarnier, the old and tried general of Africa, had in the meantime arrived at Metz. He came in the moment of danger to offer his sword to the monarch who had signed his imprisonment in 1848, and sent him into exile; and he brought the services of his rare experience to the *patrie en danger*. He was handsomely received by the emperor, and from that moment took a great interest in the council of war, and exerted a genial influence over its decisions.

At a meeting of the chefs-de-corps, to discuss the appointment of a new general-en-chef, the emperor presided; and after a few remarks on the reasons which had induced him to resign his command, he urged his lieutenants to put aside all feeling of ambition, in presence of the grave events which had occurred, and of the great task they had to fulfil; for himself, he was determined not to influence their decision in the least: and after those few sentences, the emperor buried silently his face in his hands, and waited, without adding a word, for the nomination of his successor to the command-in-chief of the armée du Ehin.

According to the Comte de Chapelle, the meeting was a stormy one. He says the favourites of the court and those egotistical men, the generals *de salon* of the second empire, could not entertain the idea of giving up their prospects of ambition and be commanded by Marshal Bazaine, for whom some of them had not much respect. But Changarnier's resistance overcame the petty intrigues, and Bazaine was appointed to the supreme command of the armée du Rhin, in conjunction with MacMahon, who was to take the command-in-chief of his own corps, of the corps De Failly, Felix Douay, and of the new columns in formation at Châlons.

It is difficult to see how any other choice could have been made. MacMahon had more than enough upon his hands in saving the relics of his beaten corps. Canrobert was still at Châlons, and moreover had decidedly failed in the Crimea as a commander-in-chief; the part being ill-suited to a man who, though of high courage, lacked utterly the firmness necessary to keep his subordinates in order, and his troops up to the full measure of their work. Bazaine was the only remaining marshal. He was the youngest and most active officer of that high rank, and had never during his arduous service in Mexico made a serious mistake, or let his men decline in their necessary discipline. The command, therefore, on being resigned by the emperor, seemed to fall most naturally to him; and the difficulty arising out of MacMahon's previous high services and seniority was, as we have seen, got over by leaving him as an independent commander-in-chief, subject only to the ministry at Paris.

As we shall not find a more suitable place, we may here give a few particulars of the previous career of the general thus raised to the command of the French army, and whose portrait is annexed. He was born at Versailles in 1811, of a family well known in the annals of French engineering, both military and civil. He pursued his studies with remarkable intelligence till the age of twenty, when he felt an irresistible vocation for the military career, and engaged himself as a volunteer in a regiment of the line. He had no reason to regret this engagement, for in two years (1833) he was appointed sub-lieutenant, and in this capacity was sent to Africa, where he passed a couple of years in constant activity, and distinguished himself in a high degree by his talent and bravery. In 1835 he was present at the famous combat of La Machta, and was made chevalier of the Legion of Honour for having, notwithstanding his severe wounds, ably sustained the retreat of his column. As soon as he recovered he joined the French auxiliary division in Spain, and took an active part in those campaigns against the Carlists in Catalonia which raised so highly the renown of the French Foreign Legion, composed of volunteers of all nations, but commanded by French officers. Among such discordant elements the young lieutenant not only reaped new laurels, but also succeeded in gaining the respect and affection of his comrades. On returning to Algeria in 1839 with the rank of captain, he took part in the expeditions to Morocco, Khabylia, and Sahara, and assisted in the capture of Millianah. At this date the corps of the celebrated chasseurs de Vincennes was organized; and as the most difficult tasks were thenceforth to be confided to the picked men forming the first battalion of that afterwards famous branch of the French army, Bazaine was appointed to the command of a company, and carried off the officers' prize as the best shot in a rifle contest. The next twelve years were passed in constant fighting and gradual promotion in Africa, where he rose to the rank of colonel in 1851. Three years later he embarked, as brigadier-general, in the Crimean expedition, and co-operated in all the principal undertakings during the long and glorious siege of Sebastopol. He also commanded the French portion of the division which reduced Kinburn. He was frequently mentioned with distinction in the commander-in-chief's reports; and on the 8th of September, 1855, after having been seriously wounded in the assault of Sebastopol, was appointed general of division and governor of Sebastopol, a post he occupied till the return of the French troops to their native country. Several honourable military positions were subsequently confided to him. In 1859 he crossed the Alps as commander of the third division of the first corps d'armée. At Marignan he covered himself with glory, having resisted for an entire day the constant attacks of an enemy in great force. Here he was again wounded, and had the honour of being mentioned in the order of the day by the Emperor Napoleon; but in spite of his sufferings he was found in the thickest of the melée at the decisive battle of Solferino, where he again attracted the approbation of his sovereign.

When the French expedition was despatched to Mexico, in 1862, General Bazaine received the command of the first division of infantry under General Forey. In October of the following year Forey was recalled, and Bazaine advanced to the chief command. In July, 1863, he led his army into the city of Mexico, and commenced a series of vigorous operations in order to expel President Juarez, whom he drove to the frontier of the republic, and whom he apparently believed he had expelled. This, at least, is the only assumption on which a number of executions of duly commissioned officers of the republic, who had been taken prisoners in regular war, can be explained. This return to practices worthier of a semi-savage Hispano American settlement than of the magnanimous French people was the more regrettable, inasmuch as it was afterwards made the excuse for the execution of the unhappy Maximilian, whose death was said to be a just reprisal for similar murders committed under the French occupation in his name. General Bazaine did not maintain a good understanding with the Emperor Maximilian, who at length avoided him, to follow a course dictated by a sentiment of personal honour. The tragical end of the enterprise is known. The French marched for Vera Cruz, after Bazaine had called the Mexican notables together, and told them that it was impossible to maintain the empire, and that the war against Juarez was without object and without hope. On his return his conduct was severely criticized in French journals and periodicals, but the emperor consistently protected him. As early as 1856 he had been made commander of the Legion of Honour; in 1862 he was promoted to the dignity of a grand cross of the Legion, and soon afterwards, in 1864, was presented with the baton of a field marshal. On his return home, in 1867, he first had the command of the third corps d'armée, and afterwards that of the imperial guard.

Possibly an instinctive feeling of the emperor, that it was unsafe to leave an absolutely supreme control in the hands of one of so decided a character as Bazaine, and so tempt him to play a part of his own in the coming events, may have influenced the decision, and outweighed the known evils of a divided command. Napoleon knew his great uncle's maxim, that one indifferent commander in the field is better than two good ones. Possibly he also remembered that, in the earlier Peninsular campaigns, the first Napoleon subordinated this truth to the supposed political necessity of not confiding too much in any single general; and in imitating his practice, for the like reason, he forgot the warning example of the French defeats that followed. For good or for ill, the original army of the Rhine was henceforward to be under two commanders, on whose exact co-operation its safety, in the face of superior forces, necessarily depended.

According to the official telegrams published at the time, Bazaine received the command of the four corps (second, third, fourth, and guards) at Metz, to which was soon after added the bulk of the sixth, moved up by Canrobert from Châlons, with a number of newly raised battalions, on the first cry of the emperor for reinforcements on Tuesday, August 9; but it will be seen from a defence of his conduct, published by himself, and of which we have given an abstract at the end of Chapter XII., that he evidently wished it to be inferred he was not responsible for the movements of the entire army till Sunday, August 13. Be that as it may, the French had now to resolve at once the great question whether the line of the Moselle should be held. The temptation to pivot round Metz for this purpose was great in a tactical point of view; but the danger of being outflanked and shut in by vastly superior forces, should MacMahon and De Failly, who were retreating rapidly to the west, not halt on the same line to support them, was imminent and certain, and over their forces those in command at Metz had no control. Yet the fatal course was adopted of waiting until the Germans actually mustered their strength before them, regardless of the possibility that the south part of the Moselle line would probably soon be left undefended.

On the 14th of August, after six most precious days had been wasted, Bazaine came to the conclusion that it was too serious a responsibility to attempt to hold his position unsupported. He therefore persuaded the emperor to depart for Châlons, and put three of his corps across the Moselle. But part of the third and the whole of the fourth were still on the eastern bank, and with the same reckless improvidence shown by the French staff fifty-seven years before at Leipzig, the retreat was conducted slowly over the regular bridge of the town. Nothing was done to facilitate the passage; so that it would not have been completed that day, even had not Steinmetz's attack with Manteuffel's corps to the south of the fortress delayed these rear corps still longer, and given ample time to develop the flank movement on Pont-à-Mousson, by which Von Moltke was preparing to pass the river.

Before leaving Metz the emperor issued the following proclamation:—

"In leaving you to combat the invasion I confide the defence of this great city to your patriotism. You will not allow the foreigner to possess himself of this Boulevard of France, and you will rival the army in courage and devotedness. I shall ever feel grateful for the reception given me within your walls, and I hope in happier times to return to thank you for your noble conduct.

"IMPERIAL HEADQUARTERS, METZ,
"*August* 14, 1870."

The emperor left the city at half past three on Sunday afternoon, August 14, for Longueville, near Metz, where he went to the house of Colonel Hènocque, his staff encamping on the lawn. Always well informed, the Prussians formed the project of carrying off his Majesty. Hiding themselves during the night in the little thickets round the Château Frescati and the neighbouring farms, they sent a squadron of Uhlans across the railroad, while they opened fire on the village of Moulins, situated to the left of Longueville, in order to intercept all aid. Fortunately for the emperor, the French engineers blew up the railway bridge under this fire, and the Uhlans being cut off, and finding a strong force at Longueville, surrendered. The next night the emperor passed at Gravelotte in the house of a farmer named Plaisant, and at four a.m. he got into an open chaise with the prince imperial and drove away, taking the valley the most remote from the Moselle, as the Prussian gunners were already getting in motion. It had been found necessary to protect the retreat by a strong escort, but no one except the imperial party had anything to eat this morning. Even the horses were not fed, but had managed to crop a little grass in the fields during the night. On they rode, however, the long escort winding its way along the hills which the road follows there. The composition of the escort was, first, a regiment of chasseurs d'Afrique by fours, keeping a sharp look out; next, a peloton of cent gardes; next the emperor, and his staff; another peloton of cent gardes, three imperial carriages, then four cent gardes, and the regiment of the dragoons de l'Imperatrice. The emperor passed through Conflans, breakfasted at Etain, and entered Verdun without further molestation. At this moment Bazaine was engaged in checking the armies of Prince Frederick Charles and Marshal Steinmetz. A staff officer galloped into Verdun with the news, but the emperor had just left by train for Châlons with the prince imperial, and hardly any escort. At the station he asked for a train. "Sire," said the station master, "I have nothing to offer you but a third class carriage." "I will content myself with that," replied the emperor, who took his seat as he found it, refusing a cushion from his carriage. He asked for a glass of wine, and got it in the glass he had just used at breakfast. The prince imperial, who was greatly fatigued, washed his hands and face with water from the same glass, using his handkerchief for a towel. On the morning of the 17th the emperor and his son reached Châlons.

When the war broke out it was expected that the presence of the prince imperial would enlist the sympathies of all on behalf of the imperial family, but it soon had a contrary effect. The cruelty of uselessly exposing the poor child to such unnecessary danger, hardships, and privations, was severely criticized; and the emperor was compared to one of those female beggars who carry about a half-clad infant on a cold day, to provoke the compassion of passers by. It was said, "C'est touchant, mais ce n'est pas la guerre."

After this invasion of only eight days by the German troops, France had already a third of her army scattered; her generals had abandoned Alsace and the passes of the Vosges, her emperor had been compelled to leave Metz, with the army of the enemy close to the fortifications, double the number of his own. Paris was in deep wrath at the course events had taken. Steadily and surely the dark-blue columns of the Germans had marched onwards, covering the eastern departments, and pushing their way into the heart of France. The whole army moved with the unity of a single will. Without noise, without haste, but without halting for a moment unnecessarily, it seemed bent on accomplishing a preconceived design, and proved that the plan of the campaign was settled before a hostile column had entered upon French territory, for it bore in every step of its progress the impress of a single mind. The effect was enhanced by the contrast presented by the armies of the defence. From the beginning of the war their movements were distracted, their attempts purposeless, and their efforts consequently without effect. One wing did not know the design of the other, and an object was proposed only to be abandoned as soon as anything was done towards attaining it. At Paris, too, as has been shown in the previous chapter, great mistakes had been committed. Had General Trochu been appointed dictator when the news of the first French disasters reached the capital, as he would most probably have been had the Corps Législatif contained fewer nominees of the Tuileries, or had Paris not been stricken for once with an excess of moderation, there might have been an appreciable chance for the country. As it was, the interests of the Napoleonic dynasty and those of the nation were everywhere clashing, until time, which should have been counted by seconds, was wasted by days. The single prospect for France after the fatal demoralization produced by Woerth and Forbach (demoralization which spread with almost inconceivable rapidity, till, as already stated, even in central France authority seemed paralyzed, and villagers far from the war rushed helplessly to the mountains), was to concentrate power in one strong hand; to abandon Metz to a determined garrison, with orders to perish there, but to employ 50,000 Germans while they were perishing; to withdraw the whole army of the Rhine to Châlons; to urge forward to that point every soldier in Paris, Lyons, the centre, and the south; to fill all weakened battalions with gardes mobiles, who under vigorous regimental control would be twice as efficient; to bring up every gun the trains could carry; and then to fight, on the best-known exercising ground in France, the first grand battle of the Republic. Could that policy have been carried out at once and with revolutionary energy, the penalty for slackness, disobedience, or cowardice being certain death, Bazaine might have had 300,000 efficients at Châlons, might have stopped the tide of invasion, and revived once more the spirits of the people, now sinking under the feeling that to fight for France was also to fight for the emperor. Unhappily the Chamber in the decisive moment shrank from extremities; a compromise was accepted between the dynasty and the country; and effort was almost paralyzed by the necessity of aiming at a double purpose. Had the plan here indicated been adopted, at least ten days would have been gained for the organization of new levies, who would have fought well in an entrenched position with Paris and all France behind them; for the Prussians would have found the difficulties of advance increasing with every yard, having to drag behind them a lengthening chain. The fortresses of Metz, Toul, Verdun, Thionville, Bitsche, and Phalsbourg would have taken 80,000 troops to mask or besiege; and their one railway being interrupted by the garrison of Toul, the Prussian trains and supplies must have moved slowly.

The emperor's own explanation of his conduct at this period, as given in "Campagne de 1870: des causes qui ont amené la capitulation de Sedan," which we have already referred to, is that after the battles of Woerth and Forbach he became profoundly depressed on finding all his combinations destroyed; and driven at once to abandon all thoughts of any but a defensive position, he resolved immediately to lead back his army to the camp of Châlons, where it might have gathered together the débris of Marshal MacMahon's army, Failly's corps, and that of Douay. This plan, when communicated to Paris, was at first approved by the Council of Ministers; but two days afterwards a letter from M. E. Ollivier informed the emperor that, upon mature consideration, the council had decided that it had been too hasty in sanctioning the retreat of the army upon Châlons, since the abandonment of Lorraine could not fail to produce a deplorable effect on the public mind; in consequence, he advised the emperor to renounce his project, and to this counsel he yielded!

The effective force of the army of Metz was brought up to 140,000 by the arrival of Marshal Canrobert with two divisions and the reserve, and it received orders for its concentration around Metz, in the hope that it might be able to fall upon one of the Prussian armies before they had effected their junction.

Unfortunately, as if in this campaign all the elements of success were to be denied to the French, not only was the concentration of the army retarded by the combat at Spicheren and by bad weather; but its action was paralyzed by the absolute ignorance which existed concerning the position and the strength of the hostile armies. So well did the Prussians conceal their movements behind the formidable shelter of cavalry which they deployed before them in all directions, that, notwithstanding the most persevering inquiries, it was never really known where the mass of their troops was, nor, in consequence, where the chief efforts of the French should be directed. On the 14th of August, as also on the 16th, no one imagined that the whole Prussian army had to be dealt with; no one doubted at Gravelotte that Verdun could easily be reached on the morrow. At Paris they were no better informed.

These melancholy openings of the campaign must, naturally enough, have affected public opinion in a painful manner. The emperor felt that he was held responsible for the wretched situation of the army, whilst that army was charging Marshal Leboeuf with the delays and with the insufficiency of the organization. He decided, therefore, to give the command to Marshal Bazaine, whose ability was recognized on all sides, and to suppress the functions of the post of major-general.

Whilst these events were taking place several generals implored the emperor to leave the army, pointing out that it might happen that communication with Paris would be cut off, and that then, locked up in Metz and separated from the rest of France, the head of the state would be incapacitated for conducting the affairs of the country, or of giving them proper direction, and that revolutionary agitations might arise from this situation. These considerations had an indisputable weight which did not escape the emperor, who, however, did not wish to leave the army until it had recrossed the Moselle on to the left bank. This movement, of which Marshal Bazaine fully appreciated the importance, the emperor hurried on as much as possible; but the bad weather, and the encumbrance of baggage, delayed its prompt execution. Arrived at Gravelotte, the emperor, not foreseeing a general battle, and only looking for partial engagements, which might retard the march of the army, decided to precede it to Châlons.

Leaving the contending forces in their respective positions in and around Metz until the commencement of the next chapter, we shall conclude this with a description of that city and fortress, which will serve to explain the accompanying plan, and is warranted by the exceedingly important events of the war which took place in connection with it.

The town was the capital of the French department of Moselle, and is distant 228 miles from Paris, 20 from the frontier towards Saarlouis, its German counterpart on the Saar, but 40 from the frontier at Saarbrück and Sarreguemines. It was well known to the Romans, and six of their great military roads met at the spot. They called the place, surrounded by vine-clad hills, Divodurum; but by the half German tribe known as the Mediomatrici, the name of the strong fort on the

Moselle was corrupted, about the fifth century, into Mettis, and eventually it slid easily into Metz, or Mess, as it is now pronounced. Grey old Roman walls remain here and there; near the southern outworks are fragments of an amphitheatre and naumachia (for small sham sea-fights); and a great aqueduct once stretched away southward, of which 17 gigantic arches still remain out of 168. Metz was much troubled about A.D. 70 by Vitellius, and in 452 by Attila, whose Huns sacked, burned, and destroyed everything portable, consumable, and destructible. At the death of Clovis the city became the capital of the kingdom of Austrasia, and later the capital of Lorraine. In 988 it was made a free imperial town, and became a self-supporting neutral fortress on the border of Charlemagne's old domains.

Metz played an important part in the wars between Maurice of Saxony and Charles V. The French, as allies of Maurice, marched into Lorraine in 1552, and took Toul and Verdun. The Constable Montmorency, having artfully obtained permission to pass through Metz with a small guard, quibbled about the word "small," and took advantage of it to introduce troops enough to capture the strong city. Charles almost immediately advanced to besiege Metz, to which Francisco of Lorraine, duke of Guise, had already been sent by Henry II. to direct the operations of its 66,000 inhabitants. This brave, sagacious, and ambitious prince had brought with him Conde, several princes of the blood, and many noblemen of rank, as volunteers to aid in the chivalrous defence against 100,000 Germans.

The duke found the town in a confused and helpless state. The suburbs were large, the walls in places weak, and without ramparts. The ditch was narrow, the old towers stood at too great a distance apart. He at once ordered the suburbs to be pulled down, with the monasteries or churches, not even sparing St. Arnulph, where several French kings had been interred; the holy robes and the sacred remains being, however, all removed in solemn processions. The duke and his officers laboured with their own hands in pulling down the old houses that impeded the fire from the walls. The magazines were filled with provisions and military stores, the mills in the nearest villages burnt, and all the corn and forage removed or destroyed. The young duke created such enthusiasm in the town, that the people were longing to see the enemy's banners approaching; and the moment the duke of Alva and the marquis of Marignano, Charles' generals, appeared, the inhabitants attacked the vanguard with great success. The sallies of the French were so hot and incessant, indeed, that the duke had frequently to hide the keys of the gate to prevent the young French gallants, his companions, from too rashly and frequently exposing their lives. Behind every breach made by the German cannon new works immediately sprang up. It was now October, but Charles, against the advice of his generals, determined to press the tedious siege on through the winter, in spite of the incessant rain and snow. He himself, though ill with the gout, was brought from Thionville to Metz to urge forward the batteries. Provisions now became scarce, for the French cavalry were cutting off the convoys, and disease was spreading among the Italians and Spaniards, who formed part of the besieging forces, and were suffering from the climate.

Charles, maddened at the delay, ordered a general assault; but the discouraged army, seeing the troops of the enemy eager for the combat, refused to advance, and the emperor, protesting that they were unworthy of the name of men, retired angrily to his quarters. He then tried the slower and more secure way of sapping; but the duke of Guise sunk counter-mines, and everywhere stopped his advance. After fifty-six days before the town, the emperor at last reluctantly consented to retire: 30,000 men had fallen by the enemy's steel and lead, or by the invisible sword of the pestilence. The French, when they broke out of Metz, found the imperial camp full of the dead and dying. The old Porte des Allemands on the east of the town still bears traces of the emperor's cannon shot. The city was finally secured to France by the peace of Westphalia in 1648. When Blucher passed it in 1814 he merely left a Prussian division to watch it.

Metz was not only the strongest inland fortress in France, but possessed one of the largest artillery arsenals, with a cannon foundry, and the principal school for the instruction of French military engineers and military officers. Owing to its position upon a rising ground and several islands, the whole nearly surrounded by the confluent waters of the Moselle and the Seille, which joins the Moselle just below the town, it is most favourable to military defence. It was, in fact, the centre of the permanent defence of France between the Meuse and the Rhine. In a war with Germany it was the French Mayence. As just stated, its position is one of the best on which a great stronghold could be placed—at the junction of two rivers. A fortress on a river where communications cross, not only fulfils the condition of security, but commands both banks, and gives opportunities for attacking the enemy that attempts to pass the stream. It is also more difficult to invest, from the necessity of constructing and maintaining bridges above and below it. Metz, on the west, is washed by the Moselle, which makes a bend, and then traverses the town, where it is crossed by fifteen bridges. The Seille enters the place on the south, diverging into two branches, one of which flows between the ramparts, while the other runs through the town. This abundance of water became an important element in the defence of the fortress. By closing the sluices of the Seille the waters could be raised twenty-four feet, so as to form a lake more than six miles in extent. There are nine gates to the town, and as many draw-bridges. The enceinte was planned by Vauban, and continued by Marshal Belleisle. The chief works in advance of the enceinte are the Double Couronne works of Moselle and Belle-Croix (constructed by Cormontaigne, one of the greatest masters of the art of fortification which France ever possessed), and considered his *chef d'oeuvre*.

The main works have been often increased and strengthened since his time, but his principle has not been much interfered with. Cormontaigne resided at Thionville, and reconstructed most of the fortifications in this part of France. Improving upon Vauban's system, he carried the salient point of the ravelin—that two-faced, wedge-like work, which is opposite the curtain, in front of the tenailles—much further out. By this construction it became impossible for an enemy to ascend the glacis of a bastion until he had got possession of the two collateral ravelins, owing to the fire which might be directed from these upon his approaches; thus the time necessary for conducting a siege was increased.

It will be noticed in the plan that two bridges, the Pont des Morts and Pont Tiffroy, lead from the town proper to the Place de France, in the northern suburb. Here are vast ranges of barracks, magazines, and military store-houses, with an hospital to accommodate 1500 patients. Behind these, extending to the water's edge at each end, and entirely closing this side of the town, is the twofold series of ramparts, called the Double Couronne de Moselle, built in 1728. It is an intricate arrangement of walls and ditches, in various angles more or less projecting, so placed as to cover and protect each other, and to afford the garrison ready communication between all parts of the interior, while combining their artillery to destroy the assailant outside. The fosses, or moats, can be kept full of water from the river at each end. The road to Thionville, accessible from the Pont Tiffroy, passes out through these fortifications to the open country. It was by this gate that the Emperor Napoleon, with the prince imperial and his suite, escaped from Metz on Sunday afternoon, the 14th of August, when a portion of his army was actually fighting with the Prussians about three miles away, on the other side of the city. There is another strong fort towards the farther extremity of the Ile Chambière; but the most conspicuous and important feature in the fortifications on the eastern side is the Double Couronne de Bellecroix. This complicated range of massive bulwark is even more stupendous than the one just noticed at the Thionville gates. It extends like a crest along the ridge of the hill which rises from the right bank of the river Seille, just above its confluence with the Moselle. The Bellecroix fortifications would be an almost insurmountable obstacle to any attack from the direction of the position first taken by the Prussians when they approached Metz from St. Avold, on the east side. A movement from that road to the left, in order to cross the Seille towards the railway station at the Porte Serpenoise, would be opposed by the Redoute du Paté (which is so built that it can easily be converted into an island), and other detached forts.

The defences of Metz were not, however, confined to its fortifications. It had several exceeding strong forts (many of them new) outside it, which made it a great intrenched camp. These had each sixty guns, casemates, and bomb-proof barracks, and ditches five yards deep. They stand chiefly on the summit of a high hill, which overlooks for miles the broad valley in which the city stands. Their guns could play with tremendous effect on any enemy advancing up the valley to attack the town at its feet; and, as the event of the war showed, a large beaten army was able to find ample shelter in the valley, guarded on one side by the guns of the town, and on the other by the forts. In fact, no force could get near the fortress of Metz proper while the outworks held out; and had the place been properly garrisoned and provisioned, it might have kept its ground for years.

The population of Metz, approaching 60,000; its fine bridges, public gardens, quays, and esplanade; its magnificent Gothic cathedral of the fourteenth century, with spire 373 feet high, and with splendid painted glass windows; its church of the Knights Templars, joined to its historical renown—made this ancient city an object of justifiable pride to every Frenchman.

CHAPTER XI.

BATTLES OF COURCELLES AND VIONVILLE.

IN the previous chapter we have described the concentration of the whole of the French army—except, of course, the corps of MacMahon, Douay, and part of that of De Failly—under the guns of Metz; the transference of the command-in-chief from the emperor to Marshal Bazaine; the fatal mistake of the French in delaying a retreat by Verdun on Châlons, where, as Schiller says, "Measureless spread is the table dread, for the wild grim dice of the iron game," and where only they could have hoped to effect a junction with their defeated right, and thus renew the re-organization and strength of their whole army. We have also noticed the steady and systematic advance of the Germans to the stronghold to which the French had retired for protection, and the admirable strategy displayed by Von Moltke.

On Saturday, August 13, the columns of Steinmetz had advanced to the northern verge of the fortress of Metz; a large part of the second army was within a few miles upon the east, while the remainder, under Prince Frederick Charles, had crossed the Moselle at Pont-à-Mousson, and moving northwards, was already in a position to threaten the line of the French retreat, and even reach the flanks of the French army, should it seek to march by Verdun on Châlons; or to assist in investing it if it should remain in its place. Not far from 250,000 men, with about 800 guns, had filled the country round the stronghold of Lorraine; and the much weaker force which had become bound to it was encompassed by dangers on every side.

After wasting three precious days, on Sunday, the 14th, the vanguard of the French began crossing the Moselle on the road to Verdun, and its leaders had evidently no notion that a German force was already on the way to intercept its retreat. The emperor was with the body which effected safely the passage of the river, and evacuated Metz without loss, but halted at no great distance. As we saw in the previous chapter, however, he next day moved off, and ultimately reached Châlons. But the mass of the French army did not attain the Moselle on the 14th; nearly three of its corps—that of Frossard, the third, now commanded by General Decaen instead of Bazaine, and part of that of L'Admirault—continued in the camp on the east of Metz, and did not attempt beginning their march until the afternoon. The position they occupied was a circle outside the eastern ramparts of the fortress, including the villages of Ars-Laquenexy, Borny, Colombey, Montoy, Noisseville, and Nouilly, and the three different camps extended over a space of nine kilomètres, or nearly six miles. Frossard occupied the left, protecting a deep, wide valley; on the right was the third corps; and over on the other side of the valley was L'Admirault and the part of the fourth corps which was not engaged in crossing the Moselle. As the French troops crossed from north to south here, a portion of the German army crossed from south to north higher up the river. Had the French been in a position (as they ought and might easily have been) to have harassed their enemy whilst they were crossing the river, the battles of Vionville and Gravelotte need not have been fought, and Bazaine's route through Briey would have been left open to him. But even on the morning of this day the marshal's mind was not quite made up, and there was great vacillation still evident. An order was given to one corps d'armée to march southward upon Pont-à-Mousson, where the Germans were crossing the Moselle; an hour afterwards it was recalled, and no sooner was L'Admirault well settled on the slope of St. Julien than he was ordered once again to cross the river by the Ile Chambière, and retreat to the other side of Metz. This movement was being carried out when the battle, known as that of Courcelles, was commenced by the Germans.

Before the engagement the first German army occupied the following positions:—-The first corps was at Les Etangs, on the road between Metz and Boulay, with the first division at Courcelles-Chaussy, on the road from Metz to St. Avold. The seventh corps with the thirteenth division was at Pange, with the fourteenth division at Domangeville. The eighth corps was in reserve at Varize and Brouville. The third cavalry division was on the right wing of the army at St. Barbe, and the eleventh division on the left at Frontigny. All the outposts were in feeling with the French around Metz, while the main body of the army encamped on the river Nied.

About four o'clock in the afternoon evident signs of retreat were perceived on the part of the French, and this caused the German advanced posts to make a reconnaissance, as General Steinmetz was aware of the great importance of detaining his enemy until the German flanking movement beyond the Moselle, under the direction of Prince Frederick Charles, described in the previous chapter, had been sufficiently developed. With the view, therefore, of occupying them, of covering the march of the troops crossing at Pont-à-Mousson, and of delaying the general retreating movement of the French army, the German commanders resolved on an immediate attack. Besides holding the villages above named the French army had intrenched themselves at points in their front; and although at first the engagement was little more than a skirmish, they soon showed such a determined opposition and came out in such force, that they caused General von Manteuffel, the commander of the first army corps, and General von Zastrow of the seventh, to bring the whole of their corps into action.

The vanguard of the seventh corps, and the brigade of General von der Goltz, announced at four p.m. that the first division (Von Bendheim) was advancing to the attack of General Decaen's corps, which occupied the village of Colombey, and was soon engaged in a very severe struggle, for the ground was obstinately contested; the fire of the Chassepot, which in the previous encounters had been comparatively wild and irregular, being now especially deadly from the rifle pits, in which the French lay concealed. The woods also afforded good cover. The German troops, however, by bringing up their reserves, succeeded in maintaining themselves in the position at Colombey against considerably larger forces until the arrival of the brigade of General von der Osten. General von Zastrow arrived at five p.m. to the east of the village, undertook the command, and at once ordered the entire corps to advance. The contest now became so severe, that some detachments of the troops under General Frossard were obliged to hasten to the assistance of their comrades. General Glümer then brought his division of East Saxons to the front, and about six p.m. the whole of it was under fire at Colombey, and with difficulty maintained its position against the overwhelming numbers of the French. The division of General Kameke was concentrated at Maizery at half-past six p.m. At this time six batteries were under fire, the others acting as artillery reserves, and stationed to the south of Coincy. To assist and support the division of General Glümer, at half-past six General von Zastrow ordered the brigade of General Voyna to attack the right wing of the French; and this movement was executed with such effect that they were driven out of their position, and material assistance was given to the brigade of General von der Osten to take up its ground in the wood to the north of Colombey.

One after another the Germans then succeeded in taking the pits and intrenchments near Ars-Laquenexy, Grigy, and Borny, and some other hamlets which, surrounded with hedges, presented considerable difficulties for attack. The fight, however, was most vehement and sanguinary; and as the French stood on the defensive, and only popped up out of their shelter to fire, their loss here was chiefly in killed, who were nearly all shot in the head. In one entrenchment alone 781 corpses were found—an incontestable proof of the correctness of the aim of the German sharpshooters.

The fight in this part of the field had all through been of the most severe character, and every inch of ground had been obstinately contested. From every hill and wood there burst forth a fearful roar; cannons, mitrailleuses, Chassepot, and needle-gun, all yelled out together, from both sides of the valley. One German regiment alone here lost 32 officers and 890 men, and some of the French regiments suffered almost as severely. Decaen, wounded before, had his horse killed, and in falling, crushed once more the smashed knee the general had refused to dismount for. General Castigny was also hit, and all around were huge heaps of dead.

The engagement about Borny, as described by an eye-witness who was in the very midst of the French troops there, was unusually severe, and especially disastrous to the Germans. The latter, who after their advance were protected by the natural rampart of the woods of Borny, had twice succeeded in taking a mitrailleuse from the French; and the recapture of it by the fourty-fourth French infantry was the cause of drawing out from their shelter an immense body of Germans, who precipitated themselves like an infuriated torrent on the French divisions. The imperial guard, commanded by Bourbaki, had, however, been kept in reserve; their artillery, from a strong position, began the defensive; the grenadiers advanced, and from that time till the Germans retreated, at about a quarter to nine, the contest raged here with tremendous fury—the French deriving much assistance from Fort de Queuleu, whose powerful batteries swept the flank of the enemy's columns.

Simultaneously with the advance of the seventh corps towards the French centre and right, the vanguard of the first corps, followed by the corps itself, under General von Manteuffel, proceeded along the roads from St. Avold and Les Etangs towards Metz—the first division to Montoy, and the second towards Noisseville. The Germans succeeded in placing fourteen batteries on the heights northwest of Montoy, and their concentric fire caused the French serious injury; whereas the French artillery did little damage, as nearly all the German wounds, even those of their artillery, came from the Chassepot. The German artillery would have done even more, had it not had to contend against two difficulties—the direction of the wind, which wrapped the enemy's position in thick clouds; and the sun, which shone in the face of the Germans and prevented the accurate aiming of the guns.

The conflict in this part was thus graphically described by a thoroughly reliable eye-witness (Mr. G. T. Robinson, of the Manchester Guardian) who was present on the French side:—

"The first division of L'Admirault's corps descended the hill to cross to the left bank of the river; the second division was on the move, under General Grenier, when the first sound of the enemy's approach was heard. That sound grew louder; and into the retiring forces of L'Admirault, at four o'clock, fell the first shell—the first instalment of that enormous quantity of Prussian iron we were to have presented to us. Our artillery, which was in our rear, quickly turned round, taking up a position on our left, so as to enfilade the ravine and cover the rising ground in front of Servigny. General Veron orders up the fifth battalion of chasseurs, the thirteenth and the forty-third, and takes up a position in front of, and a little higher up the slope, than the little wood of Mey. Orders are sent forward, and the troops which were retiring upon Metz are brought back at the double. Whilst these things are being done, down from the superior heights of St. Barbe came the fire of the Prussian artillery. L'Admirault pushes forward his to reply, but our fire cannot reach their guns; all we can do is to push forward, under the cover of our fire, a strong force of infantry in skirmishing order. These creep off into the vines and disappear. Down from the hill roll long lines of Prussian troops, who likewise melt away into the green vineyards and disappear also. The hill sides throw up a sudden fog of smoke, as each army blazes away at his hidden enemy. The Prussian torrent never seems to stop; it overflows the hills and fills the valleys, and its smoke gets nearer. Our men drop suddenly, too fast, and we have to retire. The wood of Mey is behind us, and to that wood, with the ancient instinct of their race, these Germans want to get. Our sixty-fourth holds well for a time, but their ammunition is expended, and they break cover and run. Now the thirteenth go to their aid, but they have 600 new recruits with them, who joined only yesterday. They run too; the deadly hail of the needle-gun is too strong for undisciplined soldiers. The Prussians, with a wild hurrah, gain the wood; then, bush by bush, tree by tree, the place is fought over, and we are driven out. The Prussians have now pushed forward their infantry, and occupy Servigny; they place their batteries on the Buzonville road, and Vernon's brigade is forced to retire under a heavy shower of shells. Their shells, too, filled our men with horror, especially the new recruits. Many had never seen such things before; and these percussion shells, which exploded where they struck, and left no time to get out of their way, created much uneasiness in the minds of all who saw them now for the first time. Indeed, such a panic did they occasion that all our reserve ammunition ran away. The horses were frightened, the men said. The horses said nothing about it; but if they had spoken they would probably have said much the same thing of the men.

The Prussians now pushed up the valley in two strong bodies, and no one seemed inclined to stop them. L'Admirault's corps on the left thought Decaen's corps on the right would do it, and between the two General Pritzelwitz pushes his men between them. I don't know if his name was then made known to L'Admirault and Decaen, but think it must have been, and their astonishment at the sound of it momentarily paralyzed them. There is no other supposition I could for a moment entertain; it must have been their astonishment at this which allowed so great an advantage to be gained so easily. After a little while General Pradier makes up his mind to face the Pritzelwitzers; and rushing into the gorge, he throws out a couple of battalions along the side of the valley in skirmishing order, and drives them back for a while. They move up a few guns and rake the valley, forcing us to retire. Then they advance under cover of their fire, and our artillery opens on to the valley. Crash comes after crash, as shell fired from the French batteries comes into the mingled mass; what with the fire of friend and foe, those French soldiers there had a very bad time of it. But the end comes. The Prussians carried that position; the north side of Lauvallier is theirs."

One of the incidents in the battle in this quarter is worthy of special mention. A part of the Germans were stationed behind a small wood, which could only be approached by a narrow lane on their left, running for about a quarter of a mile down to the main road from Metz to St. Avold. About seven o'clock, the Prussian sentinels stationed there to watch came running in to the main body, to say they saw the French skirmishers advancing up the road, and thought they could distinguish columns following them. The men of the most advanced company of the Prussians ran to occupy the lane, which was bordered by trees on both sides, and in some places by juniper bushes, so thick that even in the daytime it would be impossible to see through them. Here some 200 men awaited the French onset. Not a shot was fired till the two French columns, consisting of two regiments of the line, and a battalion of chasseurs a pied as skirmishers, had got within about 150 yards of the hedge. Then the Prussians fired, and the effect was terrible. Within 100 yards more than fifty French soldiers were immediately killed—nearly all shot through the head. One of the regiments drew back to the road, after receiving the first Prussian volley, the men falling all the way. The other tried to charge up the lane, to dislodge the Prussians; but the latter, whose supports had not yet come up, and who had little more than a company of 250 men engaged against the immensely superior forces of the French, retired to the end of the lane, where those left behind had thrown up a breastwork. From behind this they shot down the French soldiers as they advanced up the lane, and all along it the French corpses lay in groups of two and three, sometimes piled on one another, officers and men literally "in one red burial blent." Meantime, the Prussian supports had come up, and at once rushed forward to drive back the French, who had been forced to the main road, which they held for a mile. They were attacked in front and on their right flank, which was protected by a sharp hill, from the brow of which they did great execution on the advancing Prussians, who, however, in spite of a battery of field guns brought up by the French, succeeded in driving them from their position, and forced them to take shelter under the walls of the fortress.

Whilst the fighting was going on in other parts of the field, the first German cavalry division, under General von Hartmann, advanced at the extreme wing against Mercy-le-haut, and their battery took up a position facing the front. The thirty-sixth infantry regiment, belonging to the ninth corps, which formed the right wing of the second army, also proceeded to the east along the same road, and joined in the engagement.

Towards eight p.m. the French were driven back at all points under the guns of Metz; and to avoid further losses from the guns, from which they had already suffered very severely, the Germans did not pursue their victory. They therefore made few prisoners and obtained few trophies of the victory.

General von Steinmetz, as soon as it was announced that an engagement was going on, hurried up with his staff and made the requisite dispositions for the night and the following day, in order to place the army again in order of battle, but the French did not attempt any further attack; and leaving behind the first army corps and both cavalry divisions to guard the communications towards Forbach, on the following day the first army commenced marching along the right bank of the Moselle, without meeting with any hindrance either then or in crossing the river, which was effected at Corny and Ars.

The nature of the conflict, at first known as that of Pange, but which the king of Prussia afterwards ordered to be called Courcelles, prevented the display of any remarkable strategy on the part of the commanders on either side. The engagement was, in fact, emphatically a "soldiers' battle," and the success of the Germans in driving back their opponents was attained solely by hard determined fighting. The French resisted with great obstinacy; and the admission of the king of Prussia that many of their wounded were safely taken into the fortress, was a testimony that the imperialist soldiers made a good retreat, and fought a battle resembling rather a Corunna or a Busaco than a Woerth or a Forbach. In fact, the French soldiers looked forward to a renewal of the engagement and a decisive victory on the morrow.

Both sides claimed the victory. The emperor, in a despatch to Paris dated Longueville, ten p.m., said, "The French army commenced to cross over to the left bank of the Moselle this morning. Reconnoitring parties announced the presence of the Prussian vanguards. When one half of the army had crossed, the Prussians attacked in great force, and after a fight which lasted four hours they were repulsed with considerable loss. Generals L'Admirault and Decaen manoeuvred so as to bring the Prussians under the fire of the forts, causing them thereby considerable loss."

At first the French reports of the German losses were absurdly exaggerated; they were set down at from 16,000 to 18,000, whilst they had not lost more than 1000! Ranks of men, it was also said, were mown down with the regularity of grass under a mower's scythe, and living men were found under the dead. "All this was the work of the French mitrailleuse!"

On the other hand, the king of Prussia telegraphed to the queen from Herny on Monday morning, that a "victorious battle" had taken place before Metz, and that he was about to proceed immediately to the battle-field. In the evening he sent the following account of the affair:—"I returned from the field of battle at Metz at three o'clock to day. The advanced guard of the seventh army corps attacked the retreating enemy at about five o'clock yesterday evening. The latter made a stand, and was gradually reinforced by the troops from the fortress. The thirteenth division and a part of the fourteenth supported the advanced guard, as also parts of the first army corps. A very bloody fight ensued along the whole line, and the enemy was thrown back at all points. The pursuit was continued up to the glacis of the outworks. The nearness of the fortress allowed the enemy in many instances to secure his wounded. After our wounded had been secured, the troops marched to their old bivouacs at dawn. The troops have all fought with incredible and admirable energy, and also with enthusiasm. I have seen many, and have thanked them heartily. The rejoicing is really affecting."

The French losses were estimated by their opponents at 4000, and the Germans admitted their own to be exceedingly heavy. As in the previous actions, some particular regiments suffered very severely. The forty-eighth (Rhinelanders) lost thirty-two officers and 891 rank and file, or about one-third its complement. A rifle battalion in the same locality was by the enemy's fire deprived of nine of its officers and 270 rank and file, or a third of the officers and a fourth of the men.

The regiments most closely engaged on the French side were the sixty-ninth, ninetieth, forty-fourth, sixtieth, eightieth, thirty-third, fifty-fourth, sixty-fifth, and eighty-fifth of the line, the eleventh and fifteenth foot chasseurs, and the eighth, ninth, and tenth batteries of the first regiment of artillery. Those which suffered most were the forty-fourth and ninetieth line, and fifteenth foot chasseurs. The forty-fourth, especially, was greatly shattered; while the eighty-fifth, though in the thickest of the action, lost but thirty-five men killed and wounded. Loud complaints were made by the Prussians of the want of care for the wounded shown by the French, who after the fight sent not a single surgeon from Metz to see even those of their own wounded left on the field.

Although the German loss had been so considerable, the result of the action completely justified it, as they had gained their object in delaying the retreat of the French until Prince Frederick Charles had time to complete his turning movement with fatal effect. Had the action not been fought, a considerable portion of the French army would have been on its way to Verdun. It is not very easy to understand why the French should have stood to fight when they might have fallen back within the lines of Metz, as they were forced to do ultimately, and as they actually did after losing 4000 men. They had nothing to gain by fighting. Had they maintained their ground and beaten the Germans, they would still have been under the necessity of retreat, and must have withdrawn from the battle-field. No victory could have rendered it other than imperative on them to leave Metz and cross the Moselle. Their heavy loss was therefore so much strength thrown away; for although, the Germans suffered as much, they could far better spare the men.

During the 14th, 15th, and 16th of August, the whole of the second German army, together with the seventh and eighth corps of the first, had successively crossed the Moselle, leaving only the first corps, with the third cavalry division, on the right bank, in the position near where the action of the 14th had been fought. The ninth corps, which had manoeuvred on the left of the first and seventh corps on that day, covered this movement on the south side of Metz, where the railways to Saarbrück and Nancy debouch from the fortress.

The whole of that portion of the first German army which crossed the Moselle on the 15th had, of course, done so south of Metz. To have crossed on the north, whilst the second army was on the other side, would have given the French a coveted chance of striking right and left at the divided portions—a chance that may possibly have counted for something in the fatal delay of the French on this day, which will be more particularly alluded to immediately. Between Metz and Nancy, therefore, where the country was wholly in German hands, must the point of crossing be sought. Pont-à-Mousson, which was a day's march from the German camps, with nearly a day's march back again to the French line of retreat, was too far off, and was therefore not employed. But between Pont-à-Mousson and the fortress there were two passages across the river. Half-a-dozen miles distant, the viaduct at Ars carries to the right bank the railway from Paris and Nancy by Frouard, which hitherto runs down the left bank; while near the village of Corny, eight or nine miles from Metz, a departmental road strikes off from the highway between that place and Nancy, passing over a bridge (which the French had neglected to destroy) to the left bank, where it continued to run northwestward, ascending the heights that border the river, until at Mars-la-Tour it abuts upon the main route from Metz to Verdun.

On Monday the 15th, the German generals pressed forward the march of the columns of both their first and second armies in this north-westerly direction towards the road to Verdun, and seized upon the wooded valleys to mask at once their numbers and their movements. It appears, however, from despatches of the king of Prussia about this time, that complete success was thought still doubtful, and the escape of the French not yet impossible. At Gravelotte, six or seven miles west of Metz, the road to Verdun, some thirty-five miles distant, divides; one branch (one of those straight highways, fringed with rows of tall poplars, familiar to every traveller in France) tending a little to the southward, runs through Rezonville (nine miles from Metz), Vionville(twelve miles), Mars-la-Tour (fifteen miles), and Manheulles; the other, bending slightly northward, passes by Doncourt, Conflans, and Etain. The two roads are never more than eight or ten miles apart; at Vionville they are about six, at Rezonville, at most three, miles asunder.

Meantime Bazaine, who thenceforward must be held solely accountable for what happened—even supposing him to have been influenced by the advice of the emperor in not attempting his retreat earlier—had defiled with the bulk of his army through Metz, which was now left to its garrison under General Coffinières, and crossed to the left bank of the Moselle. He had also sent forward a part of the baggage and other impedimenta of his troops, and rejoining his vanguard, had advanced his outposts to Mars-la-Tour and Doncourt, on the two lines of road described, leading respectively to Verdun and Etain, his main force stretching towards Metz backwards. As he ought to have known that the Germans were converging towards him and making for his only line of retreat, this march seems to fall short of what it ought to have been; and his proceedings have therefore been very generally censured, as showing that want of decision and promptitude which characterized all the French movements in the early part of the campaign.

In fact, circumstances which came to light after the first accounts of the French movements on this and the next day were made known, render the conduct of their generals more extraordinary than ever. It seems that, even as early as the morning of the 15th, the cavalry division of Legrand had been pushed on as an *avant garde* so far as Mars-la-Tour, and that it was there arrested by a strong column of German cavalry who held the height. Forming in charging order to force his way through the opposing ranks, Legrand saw the German cavalry open, wheel to the right and left, and a battery of four-pounders belched out a murderous fire against him. To charge would have been useless, and Legrand therefore retired. This demonstration checked the advance, and Legrand had to wait until the rest of the army approached, or, at any rate, until valid supports arrived. It was, however, evident thus early that the enemy's onward march had not been seriously arrested by the battle of the 14th, and that only a portion of their forces had then been engaged. Whilst the French were fighting one division of the army there, the Germans had been racing the other divisions here, and they had so far won. On the same day the maire of Gorze sent word to Frossard that the country to the south of Metz was being filled with German troops, and early the next morning he went himself, but no notice whatever was taken of him. "I know all you have to tell me," said the general, "and you know nothing about the enemy's forces?" The maire went back a little way to Gorze, only to find that the Germans had occupied his country to the verge of the wood in front of Frossard's corps; but the Germans would not, of course, permit him to return again to the French general.

The French front was thus being gradually hemmed in, whilst their rear was yet dragging its enormous length slowly out of Metz. All day and night of the 15th, and all the morning of the 16th, there filed out from the city a thickly-packed line of baggage waggons and auxiliary carts. So certain, it seems, did Bazaine feel that his march to Châlons would be unimpeded, that nothing was left in Metz, and consequently never scarcely was any army accompanied by anything like such a collection of impedimenta. They blocked up the roads in all directions. Artillery could not get forward. Troops had to leave the highway and flounder through the fields and by-ways, cavalry took to steeple-chasing, and everbody swore at everybody, especially at the immovable, stolid, stupid, hindering body of auxiliaries. These men, picked up anyhow, anywhere, and under no known direction, were always clubbing themselves and their carts at a corner, or getting into a hopelessly inextricable confusion, and neither threats, prayers, nor blows could induce them to be anything but hindrances.

If, instead of having thus allowed himself to become encumbered with these impediments, with their inevitable confusion and delay, Bazaine had made the necessary arrangements for a determined and rapid advance, there can be little doubt that on the 15th the road to Verdun was still open, at least to an army of the strength of his; the German generals feared that he might be in time to retreat; and it is quite probable that if he had advanced with more celerity on that momentous day, and had massed his divisions closely, he might have succeeded in breaking through the toils which his vigilant antagonists were winding round him. It seems, however, that he was not fully aware of the peril which was becoming imminent; for on the night of the 15th, or the next morning, he despatched a message that he would be "with all his army at Etain on the 16th." On the strength of this despatch it was officially announced in Paris that he had actually arrived there. Had he succeeded so far he would, of course, have got beyond the immediate reach of his enemy; whereas we know the night found him not a dozen miles on his way.

The loss of this day, however, led to the most disastrous consequences to the French, for on the following morning (August 16) about nine o'clock, Bazaine was attacked on the lower of the two roads we have mentioned, by the cavalry of the third German corps (Brandenburgers), which had arrived on the left flank of the French, and broke out upon them from the woods at Vionville. It may be remembered that it was this corps which, under Alvensleben, came so opportunely upon the ground to Göben's support at Forbach. These horsemen, with that stubborn daring which characterized the operations of the Germans whenever a great stake was to be won, fell on the enemy, and succeeded in stopping him until their infantry supports came up, and rendered the fight somewhat more equal. It is indeed said, that the German troops at first mistook those before them for the rear of the hostile army, which they supposed to be in lull inarch westward, and for that reason they attacked at once; but the fight had not lasted long before they became aware of their error, and that they had to deal, not with the lingering remnant, but with the main body of their enemy. Fortunately for them, perhaps, the leading column of the French attacked chanced to be a part of the routed corps of Frossard, demoralized by the effects of its defeat at Forbach; and panic-stricken by the German onslaught, it fell into confusion in attempting to deploy, and made only a feeble resistance. This was doubtless partly due to the fact that, as at Wissembourg and Forbach, the French were again taken completely by surprise. Frossard, as we know, would take no notice of the statement of the maire of Gorze, that the Germans were rapidly advancing, and not one of his officers knew of the vicinity of the enemy until their attack actually commenced! This is the more extraordinary, as General Forton was camped on the rounded edge of the hill, looking out on the valley which creeps up from Gorze. Both sides of the hill he occupied form watersheds, the one towards Trouville, and the other towards Rezonville. It was thus the very place for a keen look-out, and yet the general knew nothing of the Germans' whereabouts. Indeed, so little did he think about them, that when the attack began his men were in their camp, without a single thing packed up, and he himself was comfortably sitting down to breakfast. The colonel of the fourth chasseurs had just been to him, and asked for orders, but the general had none to give. "It is evident," said he, "that your regiment won't be wanted to-day." The intendant-en-chef even sent a couple of commissariat agents to Trouville, not two miles away, to make a requisition for cattle, not knowing that Trouville had been in the German hands all night, so ignorant was everybody of that which they ought to have known. Before Frossard's men were on the move, before he had finished his breakfast, and before these commissariat agents could set out for Trouville, the German attack commenced, and created the wildest surprise. So unprepared was every one, in fact, that all General Bataille's artillery horses were at the time away at a watering place.

Had another corps than Frossard's led the van, the French might possibly have shaken off the obstinate Brandenburgers, and pushed on towards the Meuse, showing, of course, a powerful and resolute resistance to their pursuers. But it was not so to be. The cavalry, striking the French fiercely in flank, threw them in a short time into complete disorder, which spread to the next column, as it was advancing to the aid of the one in front; but, unable to clear the road, it fell back baffled and disconcerted. Bazaine was thus forced to stop and deploy Frossard's corps, and by degrees to bring into line, to the right and left, the corps of Decaen, L'Admirault, Canrobert, and the imperial guard.

For nearly four hours the daring horsemen who had commenced the action, assisted, after the lapse of about an hour, by a brigade of infantry and some small batteries, kept the whole French force in check, but suffered very severely in doing so. Ultimately, however, the nearest German divisions (the third of the tenth corps, and late in the evening the division of the ninth corps) appeared on the scene, and the action now developed into a very severe battle, extending over several miles of broken country, from Mars-la-Tour to Rezonville. At first the German line looked northward, but as the corps successively took ground to the left they at length formed a line looking eastwards, the left extremity of which reached to the northern of Bazaine's two lines of retreat—that by the road to Etain. Thus, in exactly a fortnight from the celebrated affair at Saarbrück, the German second army was fighting with its front facing the Rhine, whilst Bazaine's front was turned towards Paris—a strategical result which may be not unfairly held as eclipsing Napoleon's proceeding with Mack at Ulm in 1805.

The severest part of the struggle was on an undulating plateau near Gorze, a town with 1500 inhabitants, situated about eight miles southwest of Metz, on a small stream running into the Moselle at Noveant les Près. It is about four miles south from Rezonville and six from Gravelotte. The first two miles from Gorze to these places are covered with dense woods, hanging over deep valleys, in some places almost like ravines, and apparently unassailable. On emerging from these woods is the undulating plateau already described, which extends to the Verdun road about one mile and a half, and is about three miles in length. On this plateau the French had taken up a most formidable position, and it was only by resolute bravery that the Germans could obtain possession of it. On the French right the ground rises gently, and this was the key of their position, as the artillery, which could maintain itself there, swept the whole field. More towards the centre are two small valleys, one of which, from its depth, was most useful to the Germans in advancing their troops. In the centre of the field is the road from Gorze to Rezonville and Gravelotte, joining the main road to Verdun, between the two villages. From the woods to Rezonville, on the Verdun road, there was no cover, except one cottage, midway on the Gorze road. The action here was sustained on the German side by the infantry of the third corps. When it arrived, under General von Alvensleben, it came up from the south-east, through the defiles of Gorze, with its advance, composed of the eleventh regiment, concealed by the Bois des Ognons, and it was thus enabled to attack the enemy on his left flank. The divisions under General Frossard and L'Admirault, which now formed about the centre of the French army, at once changed front, resting their base upon Rezonville, and immediately advanced to take possession of the wood at the back of the plateau of which we have spoken, but that was now held by the Germans. The mistake was irreparable, so the artillery of the imperial guard opened a tremendous fire of shrapnell and shell upon the wood. The eleventh German regiment were the first to emerge from it and advance to the attack, whilst the thirty-fifth, the "fighting fortieth" (which, it will be remembered, was engaged at Saarbrück and suffered severely at Forbach), and the seventy-second, advanced through the wood to the left. All these regiments suffered greatly from the French shells, which now literally lit up the wood. No sooner did the right battalion of the eleventh emerge and deploy, than the French opened fire at 700 yards, and fearfully effective was the discharge, which caused the loss of their colonel and five officers, besides a considerable number of men. They then retired into the wood until the whole line could advance together, the French shells meanwhile inflicting fearful loss upon them, although under a screen of foliage. Whenever the German advance appeared the French troops opened fire, the assailants falling literally in heaps; but "*Immer vorwärts!*" was the cry, and, under a storm of shot and shell, the gallant fifth division, led by the troops above-mentioned, moved on to meet the foe. For fully an hour they fired at each other from a distance of fifty paces, the French, who had not until now suffered much, losing many men. The first line of their troops then gradually retired, and three regiments of the garde imperiale stood the brunt of the German advance almost, for the moment, alone in their glory. Here the German line was strengthened, and at twenty to thirty paces the fire was fearful, so much so that the French guard had to fall back. Behind the German position were the woods they had gained, and in front of them the ground rose slightly, for a long distance, along the sides of the road leading to Rezonville.

About one p.m., when the whole finally emerged from the wood, General Stulpuagel rode round to the heights on their left to observe the position of the enemy. After a few minutes' consultation, the eleventh regiment was advanced along the road on the French centre, having for their object the lone cottage on the road already spoken of, and in which the French mitrailleurs were posted. This, however, was unknown to the Germans when the order to advance was given. Simultaneously, the fortieth, sixty-seventh, sixty-ninth, thirty-fifth, and seventy-second were ordered to advance on the fortified heights on the French right centre. This was the key of their position; hence the number of men (15,000), sent against it at once. The French, knowing how vitally important it was to keep possession of the hill on the right, as soon as their troops began to fall back from the woods, threw up a hastily made earthwork to shelter their infantry lying down. Behind them again were the sixty-second regiment of the line, with several batteries of artillery firing over their heads. The Prussians came up the slope, but were several times repulsed; and it was not till after three hours' fighting that they drove the French from the heights, and succeeded in bringing up their own artillery. As battery after battery of Krupp guns was moved up the heights, the gunners using their spurs and whips freely, the French were partially outflanked; and it became evident that, however bravely they might fight (and the Germans allow that they fought splendidly), they must ultimately give way. Their batteries, driven from their first position, retired to the hill dividing the two valleys on their right, and a regular artillery duel took place between them and the Prussian batteries on their recently conquered hill; the short distance, only about 500 yards, insuring frightfully "good practice." The hills were strewn with the *débris* of men, gun-carriages, limbers, and horses (the latter in greatest number, many of them literally blown to pieces); and the ground was ploughed with shells. After two hours' cannonade the French guns retired to the heights over the second valley, where another engagement with the German batteries took place, as the latter of course galloped to the French position as soon as they were driven from it. The French then fell back to another rise behind, and maintained themselves there with great loss till eight p.m., when they retired under cover of the dark. In their retreat there had not been the least appearance of rout or confusion; on the contrary, they retired steadily and in perfect order, fighting every inch of the way.

In the meantime charge after charge was made up the Gorze road by the Germans on the lone cottage, and the half battery of mitrailleuses in it, which were admirably served, and did frightful execution, as the ground was perfectly open. They were also supported by a regiment of the grenadiers of the imperial guard, and the twenty-first of the line. The eleventh German regiment, which was the first to charge the French, went into action over 2000 strong (it had lost heavily at Spicheren), and in the evening only 200 men answered to their names! But the house was at last carried, as more and more German troops were brought up by the road from the wood.

In spite, however, of the greatest bravery, the Germans were unable to drive back the French until their artillery gained the hill on their right. The precision of the fire of the French artillery at this point then told with proportionate effect on the advancing columns, and it was only by the pushing on of regiment after regiment, regardless of loss, and with a view to victory at any cost, that the French were driven back fighting, and with heavy loss to themselves.

Although the most important part of the battle was fought on this plateau to the north of Gorze, there had also been a most severe and bloody struggle a little further west, in the vicinity of the villages of Vionville and Mars-la-Tour; after the former of which the engagement was officially named by the king of Prussia. Near these villages the action had begun by the attack of the German cavalry of the third corps, supported shortly afterwards by a brigade of infantry and a half dozen batteries. At the commencement the Germans were opposed to a force which certainly quadrupled theirs. They advanced in the shape of a half moon. The French retired towards their left rear, holding the village of Vionville with great obstinacy, covered by artillery on the heights. This was in turn answered by the Germans, and the French were then observed to retire. At eleven o'clock the first brigade of German infantry, under the command of General Lehman, came into action, advancing in echelon of regiments under the most galling fire of mitrailleuses—three on the right and five battalions in the same formation on their left rear. The whole force then brought its left forward, and advanced on the enemy.

The infantry were all engaged, both on right and left, when L'Admirault hurled the chasseurs d'Afrique at a battery which, from the nature of the ground, his artillery could not reply to. A strong force of riflemen supported the enemy's artillery; and though the chasseurs at length, after severe loss, carried the position, they did not know how to spike the breech-loading guns. Before they could find out, a Prussian hussar regiment dashed into them. The heavy lancers of the French guard next charged these hussars in flank, and after them pressed the third dragoons (the empress' regiment). A dreadfully confused struggle now ensued. The Prussians pushed forward regiment after regiment, and so did the French. When they at last emerged, the valley was thickly strewn with men and horses. The only trophies captured by the French, a standard and two guns, were carried off during this *melée*.

From the beginning, however, it was apparent that the German force here was too small to cope with that before them, and it became a matter of life and death to bring up infantry. One corps d'armée which had been expected failed to arrive, and was anxiously looked for.

Up to this time, the soldiers' opinion was, that throughout the day the fire on the part of the French had been fearful, that they had never on any occasion stood their ground better. In consequence, the Germans suffered grievously from the first. Gradually their numbers were reduced; till at last, as we have seen, the French could venture to attack their guns, and although this attack had been warded off, it was noticed that the French were again massing their columns for another. It was nearly three o'clock in the afternoon, and they had been under fire from ten in the morning. What was to be done? In this critical emergency there seemed to be nothing left but to send the remaining cavalry against the hostile battalions. Experience in the early part of the day had indeed proved that, to let cavalry charge infantry at a distance which exposed them to several rounds of fire, would be to sacrifice vast numbers without, perhaps, producing any adequate advantage. But necessity knows no law. The attack was ordered and executed. Two regiments of dragoon guards and one of cuirassiers, the whole forming a column of 1900, rode against the enemy—a thundering block of steel. Decimated long before they could flash their swords, their shattered remnants sufficed to cut down or disperse whole battalions. Then, attacked in their turn by cuirassiers, and immediately rescued by their own swift hussars, they again cut a path for themselves into the enemy's ranks, and actually succeeded in preventing his contemplated assault.

The cuirassier regiment which took part in this brilliant cavalry charge—worthy of the best deeds of Seidletz—was the Halberstadt, more generally known as the Bismarck cuirassiers, Count von Bismarck being *à la suite* of the regiment, and wearing the uniform, though the chief is the duke of Saxe-Coburg Gotha. The major of the regiment, Count Schmettow, in a graphic description of the engagement, which he wrote soon after the battle, said, "I quite agree that a commander would be inexcusable in leading his troops into such a mess unless there were the most urgent reasons. But such was the case in the present instance. The chief of the staff of the third corps d'armée came to our brigadier, Von Bredow, whom we have on every occasion been accustomed to see in the thick of it, and said, 'General, in concert with General von Rheinbaben, commander of the cavalry division, the commander-general has decided that you must break through at the wood, and you are still standing quietly here!' General von Bredow replied, 'Am I to understand that cavalry is to break through infantry and artillery here by the wood?' 'Certainly,' was the answer, 'we have already taken the hamlet, but cannot reach the wood, so the issue of the battle depends upon your clearing away everything along the forest. You must attack, and with the utmost energy.' So you see we had got to do it. We formed two divisions, the cuirassier regiment on the left wing along the edge of the wood, the dragoon regiment on the right wing, and one hundred paces further back. Our brave general, with his staff of four officers, three of which he lost, was nearly on a line with the cuirassiers. Before the French battery had discharged its third gun we were masters of it. The honour of challenging the French commander I could not leave to another, and I rather think I found him. It was clear to me that in this death-ride the object was not to bring home trophies, but to strike down everything between the wood and the road. At the battery all were put to the sword, and then we went in tearing course at an infantry column, which was ridden over and cut down. Its remnants, however, sent a good many shots after us. At this moment the dragoons were close on our heels. A second battery was attacked, and all who did not run were put to the sword. Then, as many as were left of us made for a second infantry column. Just before reaching it two squadrons of French cuirassiers wheeled from a woody hollow into the gaps of our little handful, and after the last infantry column had been ridden down we wheeled to the right and rushed back. By this time we were pell-mell with the French horse. Before the battery I received two shots, which went through my helmet, without, however, touching me. The adjutant, hit by two bullets, fell from his horse; one trumpeter was shot down, the horse of the other wounded. I was just speaking with Captain Heister when he also fell. Lieutenant Campbell was for a while by my side until, in the attempt to tear away from the French cuirassiers the standard he had seized with his left hand, he was fearfully maltreated. Some one helped him to cut his way out. I shall never forget my ordering the first trumpeter I found, nearly on the same spot where we set out on our ride of nearly a quarter of a German mile, to blow the regimental signal. The trumpet had been bored through by shots, and a sound came out that pierced me to the quick. At my call three sections out of the eleven (three had been detached) assembled. A gloomy bivouac followed, as little more than a fourth of the regiment had responded to the call."

The other regiments also suffered terribly; but the attack was so far successful that it gave time for the tenth German corps to come up in support of the gallant fellows of the third, and for the capture of two French eagles. It was even superior to the famous English charge of Balaklava, inasmuch as it served the highest military purpose—the winning of the battle; superior also to the French heavy cavalry charge at Woerth, as it was done with a chance of success. The French at Woerth threw away their cuirassiers, whilst the Prussians in this battle saved a corps d'armée by the heroic self-sacrifice of cavalry regiments; and although it had cost the lives of so many hundreds of brave men, the loss in a military sense was as nothing to the advantage.

Some time before this charge, Prince Frederick Charles appeared on the battlefield and assumed the command. Eager to share the dangers, and if possible, the laurels of his troops, he had ridden the eighteen miles from Pont-à-Mousson in an hour. He was just giving orders to his cousin, Duke Wilhelm of Mecklenburg, who led the cavalry charge, when the long-expected succour at last appeared. It was the head of the tenth (Hanover) corps d'armée, under General von Voigt Rhetz, which, after a forced march on the plateau rising from the valley of the river, fell upon the enemy's right flank, and the fight now extended lengthways to Mars-la-Tour, a hamlet three miles beyond Vionville upon the same main road. But although the Hanoverians advanced with a gallantry worthy of the military renown of their race, and were commanded by a most able general, the battle remained stationary for two more hours—a sort of duel going on between the combatants which, though at some distance, was near enough to have fearful results. At last the French again retired, but scarcely a quarter of a mile, where they remained to the close of the battle. Late in the evening the German reserve cavalry were ordered to charge the infantry. This they did with loud hurrahs, but sustained great loss from the murderous fire poured into them. As in all other parts of the field, the fighting at Mars-la-Tour had been of a very obstinate character. This village was held by the fourth regiment of the line, part of Canrobert's corps; and six times did the Germans advance from the wood in front of this position, and as many times retire, whilst of the fourth French hundreds of men and most of its officers were either killed or wounded. The imperial guard under Bourbaki arrived about three o'clock, and their additional weight bore back the Prussian left, so that they retired behind Mars-la-Tour, seeking again the friendly shelter of the woods, and at the close of the fray at this point neither side could be said to have gained ground.

During the greater part of the day the French had considerably outnumbered their opponents, having at least 180,000 men engaged, whilst the Germans had only 75,000 altogether under fire, and not more than 40,000 for a long time. Bazaine does not appear to have thoroughly comprehended the enemy's tactics, or perceived the extent of his own danger; and he should have cut his way through at any sacrifice, on this the last day on which he could have done so. He was fighting not only for the very existence of his army as an active field force, but also for the safety of the capital.

Both sides claimed the victory. In his despatch to Paris on the following morning, Marshal Bazaine said that the enemy had been repulsed, and the French had passed the night in the positions they had conquered, but he should delay his further movements a few hours, in order to largely increase his ammunition. In another despatch he said they had everywhere maintained their position; had inflicted considerable loss on the enemy; and at eight o'clock in the evening they had been repulsed along the whole line. Their own loss had, however, been very serious.

The German accounts were as follow:—Ponta-Mousson, August 17 (7.10 p.m.).—Yesterday, Lieutenant-general von Alvensleben advanced with his army corps westwards of Metz, on the road of the enemy's retreat towards Verdun. A bloody fight took place between the divisions of Generals Decaen, L'Admirault, Frossard, Canrobert, and the imperial guard and the third and tenth corps, successively supported by portions of the ninth corps. Notwithstanding the great superiority of the enemy, they were driven back to Metz, after a hot fight lasting twelve hours. The loss of infantry, cavalry, and artillery on both sides is very considerable. On our side Generals von Doering and Von Wedel have been killed, and Generals von Rauch and Von Groeben wounded. His majesty the king greeted the troops to-day on the field of battle, upon the glorious manner in which they had retained possession of the ground."

"Marshal Bazaine, while retreating from Metz to Verdun, was attacked at nine a.m. on the 16th by the fifth Brandenburg division (the same which was victorious in the battle of Saarbrück), and was stopped on his march. Our troops showed heroic courage, being opposed by four French corps d'armée, including the imperial guard, who fought well, and were ably led. Our troops were only reinforced after six hours' fighting, by the arrival of the tenth corps d'armée. The losses on both sides are considerable, but our success is complete, as the French have been prevented from continuing their movement of retreat, and have been driven back to Metz. They have lost 2000 prisoners, two eagles, and seven cannon."

The statement of the French commander, that his troops had everywhere maintained their positions, was certainly not in accordance with fact; for on that night the largest portion of them had fallen back to Gravelotte, having yielded several miles of the road by which he had marched on the 15th. It was no doubt true that the French inflicted more loss on the Germans than they sustained themselves, as the German commanders were obliged to hurl forward their men as rapidly as they could bring them up; but, measured by their strategical results, the operations of the day were unquestionably most disastrous to the French, although they did not at the time see the whole truth, and undoubtedly believed they had achieved a certain success. This was especially the case with the sixth (Canrobert's) corps, at Mars-la-Tour, where, as we know, there was some ground for the belief. On the following day one of his aides-de-camp wrote a letter to a friend in Paris, in which he said the contest had been horribly obstinate on both sides, but that the French had carried off all the honours of the day in spite of their great losses, and that the Germans were routed.

In fact, however, the real advantage had all been on the other side; for notwithstanding their fearful loss the German commanders had attained their object, and Bazaine's retreat westward had been effectually stopped. At night-fall the south road from Metz to Verdun had been occupied and retained, and their extreme left had also reached to within a short distance of the northern road which the French general had intended to use; so that there now lay between him and the Meuse an army strong in number, and stronger still in courage, discipline, and the superiority which consciousness of victory bestows.

As already stated, the losses on both sides were appalling. The Germans admitted no less than 17,000 being killed, wounded, and missing; and the French must have lost at least from 10,000 to 15,000 men, including a large number of the imperial guard. Four German generals were killed or wounded; on the French side Generals Frossard and Bataille were injured; and at one moment an audacious irruption of the hostile cavalry (uhlans), into the French lines nearly resulted in the capture of Marshal Bazaine himself, and led to the destruction of twenty men of his escort. On the German side the best blood of the country was spilt like water. Within a few moments, by the unexpected unmasking of the mitrailleuse battery, Count Westarp, Count Wesdelen, Baron Kleist, Henry VII., prince of Reuss, Baron Grimm, Baron Witzleben, and many other noblemen of high rank and position were killed; and the battle, altogether, cost that country twice as many men as that of Königgrätz. Some regiments especially suffered very terribly. The twelfth infantry lost 61 officers of the 69 it had, and 1500 rank and file of the 3000 forming its full complement. The forty-seventh, almost equally unfortunate, had 47 officers and 1400 men removed from the ranks; the sixty-fourth, 41 officers and 1000 men; the seventy-second, about 30 officers, 13 of whom were killed, and 1000 men. Gloomiest of all, however, was the doom of the eleventh, which lost 1800 men and nearly all its officers. Of the dragoon guards nearly one-half the rank and file, and more than a proportionate number of officers, were either killed or wounded. The announcements of officers' deaths in the newspapers filled whole columns, and fathers, brothers, and brides, left all parts of Germany to fetch the corpses of their beloved ones. The Germans had, however, determined to succeed at any cost, and they stood firmly and toughly to be shot down until help arrived, and the tremendous slaughter inflicted on them at some points by the French fusillade completely failed to shake their determination.

The king of Prussia, on the night of the battle, slept on the field among his troops, and was very well pleased to get a plate of rice and soup from a neighbouring camp-kettle, after a long day on horseback, and at the age of seventy-three!

The Germans had now (for a time at least) frustrated the retreat of the French, by forcing them from their forward positions on the Verdun and Etain roads, and, having closed on their flanks and front, were already upon the principal lines by which they could make good their way to Châlons. It therefore became absolutely necessary for the French general to face the question—

What if the enemy, whose united strength was largely superior to his own, should plant himself firmly on these avenues, should oppose an invincible barrier to him, and hemming his army in upon Metz, should completely sever their communications, and lock them up imprisoned in the fortress? Marshal Bazaine, therefore, like a brave soldier, resolved, to the best of his judgment, to make the most of the situation; and having managed to persuade his lieutenants that they had been victorious on the 16th, and that the army had only fallen back "in order to obtain ammunition," set himself to oppose his enemy with a vigour he had not before displayed. If on the 15th he was remiss, and on the 16th did not display the fierce determination which the exigency required from a great commander, now, when the peril was becoming manifest, he strenuously set himself to avert it. He still had 160,000 men, after making all allowances for sick and losses; his first care was to choose a strong position, where he could offer a vigorous resistance, retain his hold on his lines of retreat, and whence, if victorious, he could break forth and make good his intended movement to Châlons. Such a position was found in the range of uplands which, intersected at points by ravines, with brooks and difficult ground in front, and belts of wood in the near distance, extends from the village of Gravelotte to the north-east to St. Privat-la-Montagne, beyond the road that runs from Metz to the frontier. The 17th of August Bazaine spent in stationing his troops along this line, and in collecting every means of defence which could increase its natural strength; and his arrangements certainly gave proof of the tactical skill for which he is renowned. Their old position of the 16th, from Rezonville to the Moselle, was still occupied; but the right, now thrown back at rather a sharp angle, extended from Rezonville by St. Marcel (on the north Verdun road, three miles from Gravelotte, and eight from Metz) and Verneville to St. Privat (on the road from Metz to Briey, eight miles from Metz). Rezonville, at the angle, thus formed the centre. St. Privat formed the extreme right, on a commanding hill whose steep slopes were perfectly bare of cover, and its natural strength was enhanced by all the resources of engineering art. The left, occupying Gravelotte, at the junction of the roads from Verdun and Etain, and thence prolonged by the high road to Metz, held a range of heights, with a wood beneath, which commanded all the neighbouring approaches. Protected in front by fines of intrenchment, with rifle pits and a formidable artillery, and resting on the fort of St. Quentin in the rear, it might be considered well-nigh impregnable. The French centre, though not so strong, had also the advantage of rising ground, with numerous obstacles along the front; it likewise had been fully intrenched. Bazaine posted about 140,000 men along this formidable defensive line, clinging to Gravelotte with his best troops, and leaving about 20,000 as a reserve near Metz.

These dispositions of the French commander, viewed simply as defensive, displayed real ability and skill; but the result was to illustrate the truth of the saying of the first Napoleon, that a defensive position is always defective if it does not afford facilities for offence, since it enables your enemy at his leisure to search out the weak points in your armour. The French could only resist passively along the whole extent of their front; they had no means of attacking in return, and ranges of woods beyond their reach, which stretched before a great part of their centre and right, gave a daring adversary a vantage-ground to turn their position at the weakest end. In justification of Bazaine, it ought perhaps to be remembered, that he commanded soldiers who from the beginning of the campaign, before he assumed the command, had known nothing of victory, and who also believed that they were ever immensely outnumbered; though even then, as at Vionville, it was not true. He might naturally expect that such would be the case in the great trial of strength which was now impending, and may therefore have felt that his present duty was simply self-preservation, as far as possible, leaving future contingencies to be met in the best way he could, according to circumstances.

It was considered by the Germans that the flank march by the north road, or by making a wide *détour* further north, might still be possible to the French. Although such a retreat exposed them to great dangers, it appeared probable that they would undertake it, as the only mode of escape from a highly unfavourable position, in which the army would be cut off from Paris, and all its means of assistance. On the German side, the 17th was therefore turned to account in bringing forward for a final struggle the necessary corps, part of whom had already crossed the Moselle, while part had in the night thrown various bridges over it above Metz. At the same time the enemy's movements were carefully watched by the cavalry. His Majesty the king remained on the spot until, from the advanced hour of the day, further watch was unnecessary.

Count von Moltke could not have foreseen the perfect success of the action of the 16th, at the time he ordered his great flank movement with the view of intercepting the French retreat; and it was therefore necessary to push forward some of the corps which crossed the Moselle at Pont-à-Mousson and Dieulouart, to a great distance west of the river, in order to be prepared to catch up the left flank of the French army, in case it should succeed in effecting its retreat by the north road. On the 17th, and up to mid-day on the 18th, it was not known at the German headquarters whether Bazaine might not have succeeded in gaining this road, through the hilly country north of Moulins and Gravelotte. All these corps d'armée had therefore to march northward on the 17th from their respective positions towards the southern road, and parallel with the river; and others which had crossed at Dieulouart, Pagny, and Corny had to march to the north-west. In directing the troops, it had equally to be considered that the enemy might try to escape by the north road, and, perceiving the great difficulty of this, might prefer to accept battle immediately before Metz, with his back turned towards Germany.

This night, or early the following morning, the Germans had thus succeeded in bringing into line the second, seventh, eighth, ninth, and twelfth corps, with the guards and artillery of the third corps; so that, including the third and tenth corps already in position, the king concentrated for the inevitable attack eight corps d'armée with the artillery of the first corps. The first corps, as we know, was left under Von Manteuffel, on the east side of the Moselle. The French, on the other hand, had not of course been able to increase their strength by a single regiment, for all their reserves lay far away at Châlons, and behind the fortifications of Paris.

Thus Wednesday, August 17, was passed in the awful hush between two mighty conflicts, while the dead lay sweltering in the sun, or were laid in yawning pits; and the wounded were by thousands bleeding out their lives on the field, whence it would have needed ten times the available staff to have removed and properly attended to them.

An eye-witness of the scene in the morning of this day, said it was beyond all description. Every two or three yards on the road from Gorze to the battle-field, by which most of the Germans had advanced, might be seen either one who had died of his wounds in the night, or some poor wretch waiting for the stretcher and surgeon's knife. Blood was literally running down the hill to the town. Now and then might be passed six or seven wounded lying side by side, attended by doctors and nuns—improvised out-door hospitals, for every house in Gorze was full. There was at that moment in and around the town 18,000 French and German wounded, and as its population was only 1500, it may be imagined what sort of accommodation these unfortunates had. At the Château St. Catherine, one mile on the other side of the town, belonging to an old chevalier of the Legion of Honour, there were 1500 French and German soldiers and officers in different states of mutilation. Great indignation was felt by the Germans, that the French did not send out any doctors to take charge of their wounded after the battle.

Before proceeding to describe the great battle of the 18th, it may be proper to notice two other movements which might have been made by Bazaine after the battle on the 16th, and for not adopting which he has been blamed by some military critics. In the first place, it is said by some—amongst others, by the writer who so ably sketched the progress of the war week by week in the *Saturday Review*, and to whom we would here express our indebtedness—he ought to have resumed offensive operations early on the morning of the 17th. Of the troops under his command a very large proportion had not been seriously engaged the day before. They had suffered nothing of the depression of defeat, and, although strategically outmanoeuvred, officers and men at that moment undoubtedly regarded the day's proceedings as successful, and would have been in good spirits to recommence the engagement. The Germans could certainly not have brought more than half their army at most into action before late in the next day. Their total strength in the district was a paper force of 330,000 men, reduced by casualties, and the actual necessity of leaving one corps on their communications eastward of Metz, to 220,000. Bazaine might therefore have resumed the offensive early on the 17th with a preponderance of force on his side all the early part of the day, and with the impetus derived from a supposed success already won (that element of good fighting so peculiarly essential to the French soldier), to impel his men to their utmost efforts. Possibly, perhaps even probably, he might have attacked only to be severely beaten. But it is clear that he could not have suffered much more at the time, nor more at all in the end, than he did by adopting the determination of falling back to fight a wholly defensive action within reach of the works of Metz, and in what he judged a safer position, from its own natural strength and its proximity to the works, for receiving the enemy. Two most material consequences followed. The veil at once fell from the eyes of his men, who found themselves henceforth half imprisoned, struggling for liberty instead of striking for victory; and, besides, every mile that he retired made easier the task which devolved on Von Moltke of following up the retreat, and wheeling the whole second army to the right, corps by corps, to front the enemy completely. The marches of the guards and Saxons, for instance, who formed his extreme left, were diminished one half by this move of his adversary, and the next day saw the whole German army with its face towards the east, and its back to the enemy's communications, in a manner that would have been wholly impossible had Bazaine retained a more advanced position.

Other critics think Bazaine missed a great opportunity, on the night of the 17th and the morning of the 18ch, in not retreating with a large portion of his forces through Metz, and endeavouring to entice the Germans back over the Moselle, and defeat them in detail. The data on which they base their conclusions are, that the distance from Metz to his different divisions varied from one to eight miles. On the night of the 17th the king's army had all passed to the western side of the Moselle, taking along with it even the artillery of Manteuffel's (first) corps, which was left alone on the eastern bank to observe Metz, and to protect the German communications. Here, then, was a rare opportunity. To reach and overwhelm Manteuffel, Bazaine's troops could march by the diameter, through the town and over the bridges of Metz, while, to sustain him, the German troops must move round the circumference, their most available bridges being at a distance of nearly ten miles from the town. For this purpose the French divisions of the right wing, extending from Rezonville to St. Privat, should have been withdrawn in succession from the right, before dawn on the 18th; the line of outposts being left to face the enemy to the last moment. The turning movement of the Germans by St. Privat was not completed until past three in the afternoon of the 18th, and the whole country being thickly wooded, the withdrawal of the French could not have been discovered at the earliest before noon, when the first attack was made on them at Verneville by the ninth corps. This, to say nothing of the advantage in distance, would have given them a start, in time alone, of eight hours, which ought to have sufficed for the discomfiture of Manteuffel east of Metz. Owing to the position of the bridges, the German divisions nearest to the river would have had to march at least twelve miles to succour Manteuffel, and the sound of the French guns would have given the first intimation of the necessity. Had they come to his support one after another, they might have been beaten in detail; and any attempt of the German corps, which had reached the Briey and North Verdun roads, to follow the French into the fortress, would have been obviously hopeless, and just what Bazaine ought to have desired. The operation was safe and easy, and if properly conducted, must have succeeded. Even though the result physically might not have been great, the moral effect of such a success would have been of incalculable advantage to the army and to the nation. "All military science," say the critics who take this view of the case, "is useless, if the possession of a secure central situation—between the two parts of a superior hostile army, separated from each other by obstacles or by distance—is to confer no advantage to remedy the disproportion of numbers." The marshal's own explanation of his conduct at this time is given at the   conclusion   of   the   next   chapter.

CHAPTER XII.

Extraordinary Conduct of their Generals—A Regiment shot down without being able to fire a shot in return—Shelling an Ambulance—Fearful Scene—A Regiment with only 68 men left out of 1100!—Disgraceful Panic whilst retreating—Scene on the Road—Inactivity of the French Guard—Valour of the Germans—State of the French Troops—Uselessness of the Engagement on the part of the French—General Order of Marshal Bazaine—His own Explanation of his Conduct from the time he assumed the Command to his being shut up in Metz—Construction of a Railway by the Germans—Instance of the Wonderful Foresight manifested by them.

THE BATTLE OF GRAVELOTTE.

On the morning of the 18th the first and second German armies stood thus: first corps and third cavalry division at Pange, on the right bank; seventh corps at Ars-sur-Moselle and Vaux; eighth and ninth corps and first cavalry division at Gorze. The task allotted to this portion of the first army was to prevent the enemy from debouching by Moulins les Metz, whilst the second army was performing a movement intended, first, to prevent the French from retreating by the north road to Etain, and secondly, to assist an attack on their left at Gravelotte, should it be ascertained that they were not attempting to continue their retreat. The position they had taken up at this village was so strong, that it was seen it would be exceedingly difficult to carry it; and it was therefore resolved to move a large part of the vast force now at the disposal of the German commanders across the front of Bazaine's army, to assail and turn his right wing, while the left was simultaneously attacked, in the hope that through the pressure thus brought on it, the whole French line would gradually give way, and be driven under the guns of Metz, there to be isolated and completely cut off. For this purpose, not less than five corps were to execute the great turning movement, while three occupied the French left. The strength of the Germans would, it was considered, render the march across the front of Bazaine less dangerous than it appeared, while the intervening lines of wood would cover the movement in a great degree, and prevent a serious attack by the French. The leading corps of the second army were thus to form an *échelon* from the left wing forwards: the twelfth corps advancing from Mars-la-Tour on Jouaville; the guards to the east of Mars-la-Tour by Bruville on Doncourt-en Jarnisy, and still farther to the east between Vionville and Rezonville; and the ninth corps by St. Marcel to Cautre Ferme: in fact, as already stated, they started from the south road to gain the end points just named on the north road, that in the first instance they might possibly come on the flank of the French army filing off towards Etain by the same way. Large bodies of Prussian and Saxon cavalry preceded these columns, which were followed by a second line consisting of the tenth and third corps, with the second corps, the last of which marched from Pont-à-Mousson by Buxières at two o'clock in the morning, as a last reserve. At half-past ten it was evident that Bazaine's force had not left the environs of Metz; and the corps forming the *échelon* received orders to turn to the right, the ninth corps from Cautre Ferme by Verneville and Amanvillers, the guards and the twelfth corps from Doncourt-en-Jarnisy, on St. Privat la Montagne and Ste. Marie-aux-Chênes, with the view of bringing them out on the high road leading from Metz to Briey, and shutting up Bazaine in Metz.

Non-professional readers can hardly comprehend sufficiently the merits of an operation of this magnitude. Upwards of 200,000 infantry and cavalry, with an immense force of artillery, were directed with such precision against a line about eight English miles in length, that not one single opening was left to the enemy to effect a breach in the German line. The credit of conceiving such a manoeuvre is due to Count von Moltke, but the rapid and precise working out of the details reflects the greatest credit on Prince Frederick Charles and his staff officers.

The position of the different French corps at this time was as follows:—Canrobert, with the sixth, was camped on the high lands of St. Privat; L'Admirault and the fourth, between St. Privat and Amanvillers, forming, with Frossard and the second, the centre of the position; whilst Leboeuf and the third extended down towards Gravelotte. Marshal Bazaine and the imperial guard occupied Châtel, perched on the edge of the river which separates that high table-land from St. Quentin.

The Germans hoped at one time to have been able to do even more than shut up the French in Metz. It had been decided that if they were found intrenched on the Etain road, only a slight attack should at first be made on their right, hoping thus to tempt Bazaine from the strong position he occupied near Gravelotte. In that case the Germans could immediately have thrown between him and the forts of St. Quentin and Plappeville, and the town of Metz, the whole of their seventh army corps, which had been brought up from Gorze on the previous night through the Bois des Ognons, and now lay concealed by it on their extreme right. They would thus have had troops enough to surround Bazaine and his army. If they could not cut him off from this position on his left, their course then was to attack him there at any risk, and drive him into Metz. Had Bazaine fallen into the trap thus set for him when a feeble attack was made at the commencement of the battle by the German left, and abandoned the strong position on his left in the belief that the enemy were not in great force, the subsequent disaster at Sedan was not more complete than his would then have been.

The ninth German corps was the first to engage, about mid-day, some advanced detachments of the enemy at Verneville, a hamlet in the centre of the French position. From the German batteries at this point to Leboeuf's position in front of Amanvillers, runs a long ridge of land, and on this was a small farm called Montigny la Grange. It was there that the first shells fell, and soon after the artillery thundered out on both sides all along the line to St Privat. Taking advantage of the two woods of Dosenillions and De la Cusse, the Germans pushed forward enormous masses of men, not only with the view of supporting the attack here, but of assisting in that which they knew would soon be made from Ste. Marie-aux-Chênes on the strong French position at St. Privat.

Meantime the Prussian guards, followed by the twelfth corps, continued their north-easterly march towards this point. When they reached St. Privat, which was not till half-past three, they wheeled up to the right for the attack; the twelfth corps in the rear doing the same, and prolonging the line towards the left. The third and tenth corps, at first held in reserve, filled the gap between the ninth corps (engaged at Verneville) and Vionville. Thus gradually the French right and right centre, from Amanvillers to Roncourt, was beset by a vast host of assailants, who, issuing from the woods and swarming up the heights, endeavoured to seize the road to Verdun and to break through or outflank the enemy's line. The resistance, however, was fierce and obstinate; every point of defence was hotly contested; and it was not until the evening that St. Privat was stormed by the Prussian guards, and a lodgment effected there in the French position.

The storming of this village, the extreme right of the French, and after which the battle is generally called by them, was exceedingly sanguinary, and the loss amongst the Prussian guards was fearful. The village stands on a steep and lofty cliff, which commands the ground for many miles round. It had many stone buildings of considerable height, which offered great facilities for defensive purposes; and both its position and the houses had been turned to excellent account by the French. In fact, the earthworks they had thrown up, and the heaps of manure and trenches that existed, gave them almost the advantages of a regular fortress. They also felt all the more secure, as the ground around is perfectly bare; and as the attacking party, as soon as it could be descried in the distance, would be unavoidably exposed to the full effect of their guns, they thought they had done enough, and might confidently await coming events.

The German artillery, consisting at first of nine, and afterwards eleven batteries, under the command of General Prince Hohenlohe, began the attack. Towards four o'clock, that is, after an incessant cannonade of three hours, the enemy's guns were silenced by these batteries, and the infantry were then ordered to advance. It was essential to come to close quarters before dark, as the enemy might otherwise effect his retreat without very serious losses, and force another battle upon the Germans the day after. At five o'clock, therefore, the brigade which formed the first line of the assaulting party left a ravine in which it had sought shelter, and marched against the village. As soon as they were observed a most destructive fire was opened upon them. After a few minutes numbers of them were lying on the ground, and the nearer they proceeded the greater the losses they sustained. Nor had they even the satisfaction of retaliating upon their adversaries, who, stationed behind houses and walls, or crouching in ditches, were perfectly invisible to the advancing troops, and could not be fired at with any effect. All the generals and staff-officers were mounted in front of the attacking party, and after a short time were either shot or had their horses killed under them. The enemy's fire was like a hailstorm, extending over a distance of at least 1500 paces in front of the hills. The noise it made completely drowned the German commands, and the smoke rendered it impossible for their men to handle their weapons with the remotest chance of success. Yet the guards did not hesitate for a moment. On they went, strewing the ground with their dead and wounded, determined to conquer or to fall. Long before they had reached the enemy their losses had, however, been so tremendous, that the prince of Würtemburg, their commander, gave orders to halt until the Saxons had made some impression on the right wing of the hostile position. This and another engagement of artillery, who were again sent to the front and resumed operations against the solid masonry of the village, delayed the progress of the advancing troops for some time. At last the village took fire, and they had some hopes of being able to penetrate through the shower of missiles which were still falling as fast and thick as ever. At half-past six they resumed the charge. The French, though their flank had been now turned by the Saxons, still fought with desperate valour, and defended every single house in the place. Within fifteen minutes, however, the Germans dislodged them entirely, when their ranks suddenly broke, and the mass, which had made so long and obstinate a resistance, at once retreated towards Metz.

The cost of victory, however, in this part of the field as well as at Gravelotte, necessarily damped the joy of the Germans. Nearly all the officers in the brigade which first advanced were either killed or wounded. The rank and file likewise presented a frightful quota of casualties.

Every one lamented the death of a relation, a friend, or an acquaintance. They passed the night on the battle-field, many of them sleeping in the tents which the enemy had left behind him. Abundant luxuries and comforts were discovered in those of the officers. Beds and chairs, rockers, curtains, and carpets adorned the temporary abodes of these refined gentlemen; nor was there any lack even of perfumery and looking-glasses. What a contrast to the Germans, who had been sleeping on the bare ground, their generals lying down with the rest whenever they could not find shelter in a village! A German officer who was present said, "When we looked at the French tents, and the numerous *impedimenta* contained in them, we quite understood why they cannot march so rapidly as we do. But, to give them their due, they fought well while under cover. As long as they kept behind walls, their conduct *etait tout ce qui peut être desiré*. As to assuming the offensive, they never thought of it. They are brave soldiers, and slaughtered us in the most terrific style; yet there is no denying that they have lost the *élan* that formerly distinguished them, and place greater confidence in a ditch and a long-range gun than in anything else."

Another brigade, which attacked the village to the left of that whose movements we have just described, had to adopt the manoeuvre of advancing at a double and then lying down some half dozen times, leaving an enormous number of dead and wounded in their rear as they advanced, until at last they gained the road, which was some 400 or 600 yards from the village; they then sought cover in the ditches, and only showed the points of their helmets. Their leader and several officers had already been wounded and withdrawn to the rear. When they had sheltered themselves in the ditches they poured forth volley after volley, until they had expended fifty cartridges, and then came the order to storm the village. The men, springing up, formed in the middle of the road and advanced at the charge; but the enemy's fire became so deadly that they were driven back to the ditches again. At this important moment artillery, which had hitherto been unable to advance owing to the inequality and roughness of the ground, appeared in the rear and opened fire. The first shot demolished a wall which had served as a cover for more than 100 of the enemy's men, who were now exposed to the fire of German musketry. A second shot struck the roof of a stable, smashing the tiles and setting it in flames, which caused a whole division of the enemy to make a speedy exit. The German artillery kept up their fire, demolishing walls and burning houses and stables, until at last nearly every building was destroyed. Meantime, the brigade advanced to the principal entrance of the town. With their bayonets, and the butt-ends of their muskets, they broke open the barred doors and windows of the first house; and on their entrance fifty of the enemy, finding all hope of retreat cut off, surrendered themselves into their hands. From each stable, cellar, and corner issued the French, and the combat was renewed with the fiercest obstinacy. The arrival of the Augusta regiment and the artillery upon their right, and the second regiment of the guard and the fusiliers upon their left, enabled them to drive the enemy completely out of the village and capture a large number of prisoners. The French had, however, here made a very stout resistance. When the Germans were all collected in this place, a division of the enemy's artillery took up a position in a neighbouring village and poured volleys of grape amongst them; but they were soon silenced by the advancing troops of the Saxon corps d'armée.

In these encounters the guards lost exactly half their number, and more than that proportion of officers. Amongst the latter was Prince Salm, who accompanied the Archduke Maximilian to Mexico, and so narrowly escaped sharing his fate. On his right arm being shattered by a shot, he picked up his fallen sword with the left and continued the attack. Another shot in the arm he disregarded, until he was mortally struck in the chest. "Have we conquered?" he asked a clergyman who stood by his couch. "Yes." "Then all is well; comfort my wife," were his last words. The Queen Augusta regiment, to which he belonged, had on this day 28 officers and 900 rank and file struck off its muster-roll.

By the side of the guards, between Verneville and St. Privat, fought a battalion of rifles, which also left more than half its men on the ground.

The following extract from a letter, written by one of its officers immediately after the battle, gives a good description of the scene:—

"After a march of thirty miles we reached the village of Mars-la-Tour, where the guards met. We slept in the cottages and mustered at four o'clock in the morning. At five o'clock we left, but proceeded slowly, our rear being some distance behind. At a quarter to eight we were in our allotted position. Colonel Knappe had just given us the *ordre de bataille* when the news arrived the enemy had drawn off. But it was a false report. We lay down on the ground, and at half-past twelve were ordered to form columns of attack and proceed to the front. Marching forward, we soon heard the thunder of the guns and the harsh grating of the mitrailleuse. Presently the needle guns join in on our right, and the military orchestra, which we have listened to so many times before, was again complete. The ninth corps d'armée was engaged at Verneville. When the guards attack and the Saxons outflank the enemy's left, he will not be long in giving way. So we are led to think; but man proposes and God disposes.

"Towards one o'clock we saw the battle before us. The artillery of the guards and the Saxons were already engaged. Close to us we had the first division of the guards, concealed by an undulation of the ground; to our left the Saxons were struggling manfully. We watched the shells of our artillery as they burst with remarkable precision among the tirailleurs of the enemy. Queen Augusta's regiment was the first ordered to support the Saxons; the turn of a battalion of the 'Emperor Alexander' came next. The Saxons were evidently gaining ground in their flank movement, and all went well. I must say we began to be disgusted with playing the part of spectators. At last we moved to support the Hessians on our right. We stopped again in a slight hollow, until at last there came the command, 'Rifles to the front!' Now we are in for it in right earnest. It is a quarter to five, and as we begin to advance we get a taste of Chassepot balls.

" ' Second company to the right; first to the left.' As we are turning a copse we are suddenly in the thick of it. Into the copse then, and along its outskirts. The fire is heavy, but as yet the balls fall short of us. At first we are at a loss to make out whence they come. Can it be that we are fired at from the heights in front, at a distance of at least 1800 paces? As we proceed our doubts are set at rest. We have the enemy really before us, and in a few minutes begin to suffer very perceptibly. Forward! forward! Spreading out in thin lines, we are running on while our breath lasts. But we are exhausted even before we can see the enemy, so great is the distance, and so steadily ascending the long-stretching slope we have to go over. Stop! We are still at 1000 paces from the French, and must take breath before we proceed. Not a shot is fired. Now on again a few hundred paces, right into a potato-field. Stop again, fire a few shots, and now at them at a run.

"At last we succeeded in getting near enough to see the heads of the French popping out of their ditches. As usual, they were in rifle pits on the slope and top of the hill. By this time very many of us had fallen, and we halted, on wholly unprotected ground, to exchange some rounds with the enemy. Captain Baron von Arnim was shot in the foot, but remained sitting in our midst to direct the movements of the company. He soon got another ball in his breast, when he had to give it up. Finding we could not do much execution, we betook ourselves to our feet again, and ran to within 500 paces of the enemy. Now at last we had a fling at them. I measured the distance myself, took a dead man's rifle, and popped away as fast and as well as I could. At this juncture Major von Fabeck was shot, Captain von Hagen was shot, four men next to me were shot. We were in skirmishing order, and beginning to melt away like wax. In front stood the French, concealed in excavations up to their very eyes; behind us, for a distance of 800 paces, the ground was strewn with dead and wounded. If we had been strong enough we should have tried to cross bayonets, but our numbers had already been so very much reduced that we could not think of making the attempt. Indeed, had the French assumed the offensive they must have taken or killed every man of us. But according to their practice they kept in their ditches, and were quite satisfied with slaughtering us at a distance. The thing became perfectly unendurable, and there arose a low murmur in our lines that we had better fly at them at any expense, and knock down as many as we could while there were any of us left to do it. At this moment Captain von Berger, the adjutant of our brigadier, came up at a gallop, shouting from a distance, and ordering us to remain where we were if we would escape being taken prisoners. So we just stood our ground until troops were perceived coming to our support in the distance, when we all advanced again, and at 300 paces once more opened a murderous fire. All through my men were very calm and self-possessed. Under the circumstances they could not but know that the greater part, and perhaps all of them, had got to die. Yet they were as tranquil as the few of their officers still remaining, and looked with perfect equanimity upon the French relieving again and again their tirailleurs in the ditches. We were now near enough to see that they had four rows of rifle-pits, the one over the other. The fire was terrific, and Königgrätz in comparison to it mere child's play. By and by our cartridges got exhausted, and we had to empty the pouches of the dead and wounded. As many of the latter as had a spark of life left did all they could to assist us in this. But everything has an end, and so had our ammunition. I had given orders that every man was to reserve two cartridges in case the French took the offensive; and with these two cartridges in our possession we confronted the enemy even after we had ceased to fire. After a little while, which seemed to us terribly long, our supports came up. They were skirmishers of Queen Elizabeth's regiment; and the moment they joined us I heard their captain give the command in my rear,

'Charge with the bayonet!' I was lying on the ground with a shot in my left arm and shoulder-blade; but as I heard those glorious sounds I jumped up, and halloaing to my men, fiercely repeated the word of command, 'Charge with the bayonet!' But, alas! there were only three men left to respond to my call. With the exception of a few who had joined another company, the whole of my men were down. I do not know whether the three survivors took part in the attack. As for myself, I could not do it, and sat down on the ground. The moment the Elizabeth regiment charged, the French jumped out of their ditches and ran away. An enormous quick fire was opened upon them, and, as I can assure you, to some purpose.

"The French were driven from their whole position. The villages around were on fire, and the shooting continued here and there. We had been opposed to the guards, who were the last to retreat. All the officers of the battalion are either dead or wounded; and of the 1000 men with whom we went into battle, only 400 are left."

The battalion which met with this melancholy fate was one of the finest in the Prussian army. The men were crack shots, and the officers belonged to the best Berlin society.

In addition to their victory at St. Privat the Germans were also ultimately successful in their attacks on Verneville, although determined resistance was offered, and the village was set on fire during the struggle. Advancing steadily from the ground they had so hardly won and maintained, they pushed back the French out of the village of Rezonville, which was more shattered than any other on the battle-field, and was the scene of a rather critical episode in the struggle. In a large building at the northern extremity of the village, which had at the side, level with the road, a large oblong walled garden, the Prussian ambulance established their hospital, and its rooms were quickly filled. Suddenly the tide of battle was heard rolling back towards it. A hurried message was quietly delivered to the surgeon-in-chief, that the French were storming the village at the other end. He hastened into the garden to inquire as to the fact. Louder and nearer grew the musketry firing; the garden wall was breached with cannon shots. A throng of fugitives rushed up the road confusedly, horses broke loose, waggons, and a troop of cavalry whirled past in wild disorder. The surgeon summoned his colleagues into the garden, and after a hurried consultation they resolved to remain at their posts and abide the issues. Hardly was this decision formed before thundering hurrahs were heard, and advancing columns of fresh troops were seen descending the slope. The fugitives were headed; officers galloped to and fro, calling out the numbers of the broken regiments, which rallied, and once more the tide of war ebbed back. It had been a momentary, but while it lasted a wild panic, arising from the horses in some ammunition waggons taking fright and dashing madly through the lines of the advancing regiments.

Whilst this fighting had been taking place on the French right and right centre, the German seventh and eighth corps had made a tremendous attack on the strong position occupied by the French left, near Gravelotte, from which village the whole action was afterwards named by the king of Prussia.

Soon after the first attack on the French centre had commenced at Verneville, it was evident that Bazaine was not to be drawn away from Gravelotte, but was quite aware of the disagreeable proximity to his left flank of the seventh German army corps. Suddenly therefore, seven or eight four and six pounder field-guns, which had been protected on the Vionville road by earthworks, began to rain shells into the Bois des Ognons, where the Germans were concealed. General von Göben, who commanded here, perceiving that the French general was not to be out-manoeuvred this time, as the Germans had hoped, gave the order for a general attack. Some forty or fifty guns were set in motion for different places, and in five minutes were in positions to the right and left of the Bois des Ognons, and pouring a destructive fire of shells into Moscow, Malmaison, and St. Hubert. An hour after the first shot was fired the action had become general here, and the outskirts of the village of Gravelotte were soon won; but the slopes beyond proved the scene of one of the most murderous contests recorded in the annals of war, and were at last carried by direct assault at an expenditure of life not before reached even in these days of improved weapons.

The French position on these heights was very formidable, as it was only approachable from the front by a steep hill, reached by a winding road, a mile in length, from the village of Gravelotte to the French batteries. On the French right centre here was a wood, which was filled with their skirmishers. In this wood, half-way down the hill and to the right of the road leading from Gravelotte, was a farm-house, named La Villette, which was one of the chief French defences. It commanded the road up the hill, which for nearly every yard of the way from Gravelotte runs in a deep cutting, open only in places on one side, and thus the house afforded a very favourable point-de-mire for the marksmen. On the German left was another large farm-house, named Malmaison.

The French had strengthened themselves by a succession of entrenchments, and had also thrown up small works to protect their guns. The walls of the gardens and the houses near their position, were also made as defensible as possible, and had been lined with tirailleurs, who could pour an incessant cross fire upon troops advancing up the road from Gravelotte. The situation had been taken up with extreme judgment, as from it almost every movement the Prussian troops made was distinctly visible, even to the shifting of the position of a single man, which accounts for the fearful slaughter the French were able to inflict. The top of the plateau was commanded by powerful artillery, with an ample sprinkling of mitrailleuses, and all the Germans could see of their enemies was the tops of their kepis. Behind the Germans lay the bloody battle-field of Gorze, fought two days previously, the dead still unburied, and some of the wounded still uncared for, the French having left theirs to the tender mercies of strangers. The sun struck fiercely upon the plateau, and the stench from the putrefying bodies was almost insupportable.

The chief occupation of the Germans at first was the shelling of the woods to the left of Gravelotte, which were filled with French skirmishers, and the road leading to Verdun, which, running along the brow of the hill, commanded Gravelotte, and was occupied by a couple of French batteries, that sent shrapnel and case shot among the German battery of horse artillery, on the right of Gravelotte, with wonderful precision. After some two hours' shelling the French fire grew slacker, and at 1.40 p.m. the German batteries advanced, and took up fresh positions 500 yards closer to the French guns, which, as they advanced, shelled them persistently, knocking the ammunition waggons to pieces. When, however, they had once got forward, they soon compelled the two French batteries on the road to retreat, and shortly after two o'clock cleared it. But in withdrawing their batteries of field artillery, the French had left a battery of eight mitrailleuses for the benefit of the troops as they came to close quarters. Each of these mitrailleuses was placed behind a small epaulement, which protected them in a great measure from the fire of the German skirmishers, and they were shortly destined to cause fearful havoc in the German ranks.

The cavalry now moved forward and massed near Gravelotte, and the infantry began to advance rapidly on the right; but in the meantime the French held good on the left, and so tremendously shelled the farm-house of Malmaison, on the hill to the left of Gravelotte, filled by German sharpshooters, as to set the place on fire, soon rendering both the house and garden untenable; when the Germans retired to the left, and took up a fresh position in the distance till their batteries could silence those of the French.

At 2.20, therefore, their artillery was pushed forward to the left of Gravelotte, and opened on the Verdun road, but even so late as half-past two the French continued to throw shells at the farmhouse of Malmaison. The Germans, however, paid little heed to this, but gradually got up their cavalry on each side of the road. As the uhlans and cuirassiers wheeled to the right on their way to the front, the batteries of the imperial guard threw some shells among them in a style which even their enemies admired. The cavalry and two regiments of cuirassiers, two of uhlans, and two of hussars, pressed forward all along the line, although they were not actually sent into action for some time.

The French now made a desperate effort to hold on to the last bit of the Verdun road, between Rezonville and Gravelotte. It was, however, unavailing, for every man in their ranks had two to cope with, and their line at this point was already beginning to waver. It was soon plain that the French right here was withdrawing to a new position, which was swiftly taken up, under protection of a continuous blaze of their artillery from heights beyond the village. The movement was made in good order, and the position reached was one that nine out of ten military men would have regarded as normally impregnable.

The Germans having succeeded in compelling the French right at this point to shift its position, concentrated their efforts entirely on La Villette, their central position in this part of the field. And now commenced what may be called a massacre of the German troops, for regiment after regiment went up the fatal slope, and was compelled to retire, always with heavy loss. A fierce fire of artillery from 120 pieces was kept up all along the German line on the French works, and after about half an hour's shelling the thirty-third Prussian regiment dashed up the hill. When they were half-way up the mitrailleuses opened on them, and did terrible execution at close quarters. The men, however, pressed on, and though they were literally falling by hundreds, they actually got into the works, and a half battery of four-pounders, which had followed them, got more than half-way up the hill. But the French ran their mitrailleuses 400 yards farther back before they could be caught, and from them and their guns, which had been drawn back a couple of hours before, opened so deadly a fire that the thirty-third was compelled to retire down the hill. Then the French mitrailleuses were dragged forward again, and sent a terrible fire into the retreating infantry. The half battery endeavoured to return their fire, but it was silenced, and all the horses being either killed or wounded, the guns had to be left on the hill-side. Of course their breech-pieces were withdrawn, so that they were useless to the French, who, besides, did not dare to take them, the German tirailleur fire being far too severe. Then the Prussians, according to their system of sacrificing masses of men to gain their purpose, made an attempt to charge the hill with cavalry, and the cuirassiers and uhlans dashed up at the batteries; but men and horses rolled over in the hollow road, and they were in turn compelled to retire. Then another infantry regiment, the sixty-seventh of the line, tried the attack in skirmishing order instead of in column. Their men crept from bush to bush and from rock to rock, taking advantage of the slightest inequality of ground to shelter themselves, but were unable to accomplish their object. Another attack was then made up the road, covered by a tremendous artillery fire; but though the men again got to the French works, they were again shot down in such numbers that they could not hold their ground. In fact, no living being could exist on the road. The men who had only seen the mitrailleuses fire at a distance despised them, and now rushing on them recklessly, were frightfully butchered. These murderous instruments, each behind its separate earthwork, were so placed that it was next to impossible for the German artillery to reach them, as they were a little lower than the road, and just sweeping it, which not only served to protect them from the enemies' shells, but prevented the gunners from firing at too great distances, for the mitrailleuses were placed so low down that they could only reach the Germans either on the road itself or on the last 200 yards up the slope. Never did troops go into action more bravely than the Germans on this occasion; and when, more or less severely wounded, they returned from the fatal heights, many of them made a joke of their wounds, and said the position was sure to be taken in the end. From three until half-past four there was one continuous fusillade: first the rattle of the Chassepots; then the reports of the needle-guns of the German tirailleurs crawling up the hill; and lastly, the sullen roar of the mitrailleuses as regiment after regiment rushed forward or returned always in good order, but often with the loss of half their number on the hill above. Under the circumstances, it was wonderful to see the coolness of both officers and men. More than one of the former, as soon as their wounds were bound up, returned to their charge as if nothing had happened. But all the while the house of La Villette and the sharpshooters on the hill continued their fire. In addition to their infantry, the Germans also again and again brought forward regiments of cavalry to the scene of contest; but the slaughter, especially from the mitrailleuse, was still so great that they were killed in large numbers, and were for a time unable to make any more impression on the enemy than the infantry had done.

After a time, however, the Germans got two guns to the angle that the Verdun road makes with itself; but the infantry had not yet come up to that point; and so fearful a fire was rained upon these two pieces that General Steinmetz deemed it proper to issue an order to bring them back. On riding up to execute this order, Hauptmann von Schmelling found but one surviving officer and three men with the two cannon, one of which was destroyed. There were still sufficient horses to bring the other out of action, or to a place nearer supports; but the young officer in charge, proud of his foremost position, heedless of the danger, and vexed at having to retire from lack of proper support, replied from the midst of his dying comrades, "Tell General Steinmetz where guns have advanced, there can also infantry. Let him send supports to me; I will not retire to them; rather will I die on my gun-carriage, and rest here with my comrades." He was as good as his word; he did not retire from his position until he had expended his last shot, and brought his gun, which he had worked with the assistance of three men, safely out of action; for the infantry did not come forward here until much later.

From the severe fighting at St. Privat and Gravelotte—the extreme right and left of the French position—about half-past four it seemed not altogether impossible that the French might regain possession of the very central Verdun road for which the armies were struggling; and accordingly the Germans brought up a large body of fresh troops, and placed them along the road out of immediate danger, but ready to fall upon the French centre had it defeated those with which it was contending. The French thus seeing themselves hopelessly out numbered, the struggle at that part became very weak on their side, but it was carried on with redoubled fury on their left.

At a quarter past five the king rode slowly along the Gravelotte road, scanning with grave and serious eye the scene of havoc around him. Count von Bismarck was intent only on the battle, and could not conceal his excitement and anxiety. At half-past five there was a partial cessation in the firing. The Germans got a battery (the third) in position just to the right of the Gravelotte road, and about 1500 yards from the French post. They then commenced shelling the farm-house of La Villette, from inside which and from its garden such a destructive fire had come. At twenty-five minutes to seven the firing had again greatly slackened, and was confined to the skirmishers on either side. The Germans then brought up reserve ammunition, of which nearly all their batteries were short, preparatory to another attack before dark. Just after this, however, the French began to fire with new life along their whole line, and attacked with such suddenness and brilliancy as to cause a panic in the German ranks. Advancing from the rifle pits to which they had retired, they took possession of their original position; and according to the testimony of the Hon. C. A. Winn, who was present, had the French cavalry at that moment charged down the hill nothing could have resisted them, for the German soldiers, surprised and startled by the suddenness of the attack, instinctively ran like hares. (See "What I saw of the War at Spicheren, Gorze, and Gravelotte," by the Hon. C. A. Winn.).

"Any one coming up at that particular moment would have been under the impression that the Prussians had been completely routed. Such a stampede I never saw before, and I should think few military men had. Artillery, foot-soldiers, baggage-waggons, ambulances, every species of troop conceivable, in our immediate neighbourhood were rushing pell-mell to the rear. The words, ' the French cavalry are coming,' were on every Prussian's lips, except the officers, who shouted themselves hoarse with summoning the flying soldiers to ' halt.' All this had happened in an incredibly short space of time. I was standing at the door watching it all, and wondering when the French cavalry would come, and when they would begin to shell the village. Soon I heard, faintly in the distance to the rear, the national anthem, and I knew that the king in person was rallying his troops. On looking through my glass I found to my surprise that the French were not advancing from their original position of this morning, which they had just re-occupied.

"It has ever been a mystery to the German officers present at this stampede, why the French did not follow up their advance by charging the village of Gravelotte with cavalry. They must have taken many prisoners and guns, and might have gained the position a step further on the Verdun road. To show how convinced every one was that at this point the battle had been lost, while I was away a major of the Prussian army who was shot through the leg and unable to stand, implored my companion not to leave him alone, but to help him off somehow, as he would rather endure any pain that dragging his broken limb after him might entail than be made prisoner by the French. Anybody that knows the Prussian character, will know that it takes a good deal to make one of those officers work himself into a state bordering on excitement."

His Majesty, who displayed wonderful vigour in the rallying of his troops, had arrived from Rezonville, and had temporarily placed General von Steinmetz, who had hurried up, in command of the second army corps, giving him permission to draw supports from it should he need them. This corps had been marching since two a.m. and had not yet been before the enemy. Under the eyes of General von Steinmetz, who had ridden into the defile with his staff, within rifle range, these brave troops, with loud hurrahs, drums beating, and bugles blowing the advance, rushed up the dark woody ravine to deploy on the other side, and hurl themselves upon the foe.

About a hundred yards from the centre of the village of Gravelotte, on one of the Verdun roads, stands a farm-house, with inclosures, in a line directly facing that upon the higher ground, with a ravine between, called Moscow. This, named Mogador, is much larger. On the 16th it had served as the chief hospital of the French, and was filled. In their retreat from Gravelotte backwards towards Moscow, the wounded were got out. It was here that, in the large, slightly hollow-backed meadow between Mogador and the main Gravelotte road, King William and his staff gathered, to witness this final and crowning achievement of the day, the storming of the position occupied by the French, who were now chiefly posted on the crest of the plateau, upon which stood the farm-houses with their high walled inclosures—Leipsic, Moscow, and St. Hubert. Here were massed powerful batteries, protected by entrenchments, and a number of mitrailleuses. From Gravelotte to the bottom of the hollow the road for 700 yards runs somewhat steeply down and straight as a line; it rises again to the crest at a slant, and nearly midway, upon the roadside slope, stands St. Hubert, effectually commanding its approach. The attack, which fell chiefly to the seventy-second regiment, who charged up the slope, followed by a regiment of hussars, was preluded by a fierce artillery duel on both sides, in which Mogador and Moscow were both fired and reduced to bare walls. This was the moment of which the king speaks in his despatch, "The historic grenades of Königgrätz were not wanting;" the positions, within near range and point blank opposite each other, were perilous, and General von Roon did right to insist upon the king's withdrawal. Slowly, and at fearful sacrifice, St. Hubert was at last carried, but further progress was long arrested, and the struggle relapsed into a fresh cannonading! Though the German guns enfiladed part of the enemy's position, hardly any ground was really won, and the resistance was still as heroic as the attack. But in the interval, the great turning movement of the morning had produced its effect; the right of the French had been outflanked and their centre slowly compelled to give way; and the line of fire which gradually receded from Verneville, Amanvillers, Jaumont, and St. Privat, warned the brave defenders here on the left that the time for a retreat had come. They fell back sullenly, fighting to the last, and protected by the mitrailleuse; but the Germans now gained the blood-stained slopes over Gravelotte, and the whole French army yielding the position, retired under the cover of Metz. The battle did not terminate till it was quite dark, and for some time the direction of the troops could only be traced by the fiery paths of their bombs or the long tongue of fire darting from their cannon's mouth.

A number of the citizens of Metz who had come in carriages to see the fight, and were stationed on the road just below the crest, were captured by the Prussians and treated as prisoners.

After witnessing this last attack on the French position, the king of Prussia and his staff rode back to Rezonville, where a watch-fire was lit, and where, failing a stool, his Majesty sat upon a saddle raised upon some logs. At his side were Prince Charles, the Grand-duke of Weimar, the Hereditary Grand-duke of Mecklenburg, Count von Bismarck, and General von Roon. Roon had taken off his helmet, and, contrary to his custom, was wearing a field cap. The king had his helmet on. All were very silent, expecting that about this time the decisive tidings must arrive. Presently Moltke, much heated, rode up to the king:—"Your Majesty, we have conquered. The enemy is driven from all his positions." A vigorous hurrah from the bystanders was the response, and by the firelight Bismarck took down from his sovereign's dictation the following telegram, announcing the victory to the queen:—

"BIVOUAC NEAR REZONVILLE,
"*August* 18, 9 p.m.

"The French army, occupying a very strong position to the west of Metz, was to-day attacked under my leadership, and after nine hours' fighting was completely defeated, cut off from its communications with Paris, and driven back towards Metz.

"WILLIAM.

This extraordinary historical scene was sketched on the spot by Fritz Schulz, a painter in the royal suite, and from the sketch a painting was afterwards executed by the king's commands. The telegram despatched, refreshments were thought of; a sutler standing not far off was called up, and the party filled their flasks. The king drank out of a broken tulip-glass, while Bismarck complacently munched a large piece of ammunition bread. His Majesty did not leave the field, as he was desirous to ascertain by the break of day on the 19th whether the French had actually withdrawn into the fortress. Everything was therefore at once got ready for him and his attendants to bivouac on the spot, but in the distance a solitary farm-house was discovered standing, though terribly devastated. Yielding to the advice of his staff, who insisted on the necessity of his having a night's rest, in view of the possible renewal of the fight the next day, his Majesty withdrew for a few hours to a small room of this farmstead, while the generals put up with such accommodation as they could find in the stables.

According to another account, some cutlets were with difficulty obtained for the king; and Count von Bismarck, after eating some unboiled eggs, went with his attendants to seek a lodging. Several houses at which he made inquiries were full of wounded. At one house where he received the same answer, he asked whether there was not some straw "up there," pointing to a gloomy window on the first floor; but that, too, he was assured was full of wounded. He insisted, however, on seeing the room, and discovered two empty beds, on one of which he threw himself, while the Grand-duke of Mecklenburg appropriated the other, and the American General Sheridan made himself comfortable on the floor.

His Majesty remained all the following morning on the battle-field, receiving despatches from all quarters, and afterwards sent the annexed letter to her Majesty:—

"REZONVILLE, *August* 19.

"Yesterday was a day of renewed victory, the consequences of which cannot yet be estimated. In the early morning of yesterday the twelfth corps, the corps of the guard, and the ninth corps proceeded towards the northern road of Metz-Verdun as far as St. Marcel and Doncourt, and were followed by the third and the tenth corps, while the seventh and the eighth corps, and subsequently also the second, halted at Rezonville, facing Metz. When the first-named corps wheeled towards the right, in a very wooded terrain, towards Verneville and St. Privat, the last-mentioned corps began their attack upon Gravelotte, but not vehemently, in order to await the corps engaged in the great flank movement against the strong position of Amanvillers as far as to the road of Metz. The corps effecting this wide flanking march only entered into the fight at four o'clock, co-operating with the pivot corps, which had been engaged in the action since twelve o'clock. The enemy opposed us in the forests with violent resistance, so that we only slowly gained ground. St. Privat was taken by the corps of the guard, Verneville by the ninth corps; the twelfth corps and artillery of the third corps now joined in the contest. Gravelotte was taken by troops of the seventh and eighth corps, and the forests were scoured on both sides with great loss. In order to attack once more the hostile troops, forced back by the outflanking movement, an advance was made at dusk across the Gravelotte. This was met by such tremendous firing from the parallel ranges of rifle-pits and from the artillery that the second corps, just arriving, was obliged to charge the enemy at the point of the bayonet, and by this means it conquered and maintained the strong position. It was half-past eight when on all sides the firing gradually subsided. At the last advance the shells—of Königgrätz memory—were not wanting, at least where I was standing. This time I was removed from their range by the minister Von Roon. All the troops I met cheered me with enthusiastic hurrahs. They performed miracles of bravery against an equally brave enemy, who defended every step, and often undertook offensive attacks, which were repulsed each time. What fate is in store for the enemy, who is now pent up in the entrenched and very strong camp of the fortress of Metz, is beyond present calculations. I shrink from inquiring after the casualties and names, for by far too many acquaintances are mentioned, often without just grounds. Your regiment is said to have fought splendidly. Waldersee is wounded seriously, but not mortally, as I am told. I had intended to bivouac here, but after some hours I found a room, where I rested on the royal ambulance, which was brought here, and as I have not taken with me anything of my equipment from Pont-à-Mousson, I have remained in my clothing these thirty hours. I thank God that he granted us the victory.

"WILLIAM."

The German official report of the battle was much more elaborate than this letter, but in consequence, we suppose, of the great area over which the conflict extended, it fails, as do nearly all the popular accounts of the action, to give anything like an adequate idea of the fearful nature of the struggle at St. Privat; and from reading it one might almost imagine that scarcely anything of importance took place elsewhere than in the neighbourhood of Gravelotte.

The report states that, at the commencement of the day, the first army (that of General Steinmetz) kept in concealment, and allowed the second army (Prince Frederick Charles's) to carry out its movement towards Verneville and St. Marie-aux-Chênes. When, however, towards noon, cannonading was heard from Verneville, and reports came in that the head of the ninth army corps had already reached that place, and was engaged with the enemy, the first army received orders to advance. The seventh army corps brought up strong batteries to the south and east of Gravelotte, who advanced with the greatest precision under an effective fire from the enemy's artillery. The infantry of the corps remained—until a later occasion should arise for them to be employed—in a covered position in the wooded valley separating Gravelotte from the heights of Point du Jour. Only the brigade of General von der Goltz, which was in position at Ars-sur-Moselle to secure the valley of the Moselle, had already been engaged. They captured the village of Vaux, in the valley of the Moselle, and afterwards stormed the heights of Jussy, the possession of which they maintained. Simultaneously with the seventh army corps, the eighth army corps advanced from Rezonville against the Bois de Genivaux, and attacked the enemy. The eighth corps at once opened a powerful battery from its front on to the road from Vancour-en-Jarnisy, whilst the first cavalry division at once took up a covered position in the rear, and the infantry advanced to attack the Bois de Genivaux in front, which was occupied by the enemy. Here also the enemy's artillery was quickly silenced, while the infantry met with a most obstinate resistance in the Bois de Genivaux. A close and bloody fight raged here for hours. Owing to the density and impenetrability of the wood, the combating parties were completely intermingled, and at certain parts of the Prussian lines so obstinate a resistance was encountered, that they were only able to press slowly forward; whilst in other parts they reached the eastern skirt of the wood, and, even breaking through it, advanced to attack the opposite heights and farm-houses of St. Hubert. The latter were at last taken by slow degrees, after repeated attacks, and held, whilst all attempts to proceed further to the ridge of the heights were baffled by the strongly occupied rifle pits. The infantry encounter came to a standstill, the artillery of the enemy being almost silent, and our guns not having any effective object to be achieved by firing.

It being imagined that the enemy was now about to withdraw, two batteries of mounted artillery and a regiment of cavalry were ordered to pursue; but it soon became apparent that the French had only sought cover from the artillery fire of the Prussians, and the pursuers were very hotly received. They maintained their position, however, and fought against serious odds until relieved late in the evening by the cavalry reserve. More than half of the men and horses were killed. The conclusion of the battle is thus described by the official writer:—"From the left wing the heavy roll of infantry rifles, mixed with the thunder of cannon, was heard between Verneville and Amanvillers, which had been eagerly awaited. Apparently the sound came nearer—a favourable sign of the approach of the army of Prince Frederick Charles. Our infantry maintained the battle more tenaciously than ever, the appearance of the second army promising to bring up support, and the brave artillery, despite their severe losses, served their guns as if on the parade ground. The French continued their fire the whole day, especially from the rifle-pits, with their Chassepot rifles, at a range of 2000 paces, whereby the position was continually held in insecurity, and occasioned considerable loss. The French were in a desperate situation, surrounded on all sides, and nothing remained for them but to retreat into the fortress of Metz, into which their army was forced to disappear. About seven p.m. they made one desperate attempt to break through by Gravelotte from Metz to Paris. Thick clouds of skirmishers, one behind the other, uttering loud shouts, and keeping up a continual volley, rushed forward from behind the heights against the wood in the ravine. Our weak decimated infantry squads were nearly all dispersed, and the danger was great that this attack, made apparently in force, would be successful against our exhausted troops. But our brave artillery opened upon them over the heads of our infantry so effectively, that the attack was repulsed by the combined action with the infantry, which once more made a stand. Material and decisive support was, however, at hand. His Majesty the king Lad arrived during the battle from Rezonville, in the northern direction towards Gravelotte, and had temporarily placed General von Steinmetz, who had hurried up, in command of the second army corps, giving him permission to draw support from this corps should he need it. This second (Pomeranian) army corps, which had not yet been before the enemy, hastened up in quick step, inspired by lust of battle, and at nightfall decided the conflict. The discharges from the guns shone out brightly in the dark night; but the line of fire grew more and more distant, and although many a brave man sacrificed his life, and the losses were fearfully large, yet the slope and the hostile heights were ours. So ended the battle of the 18th of August. On the following morning the enemy had evacuated the heights, and withdrawn within the fortifications of Metz. The battle-field is strewn with corpses and wounded men. The victory was dearly won, but it was brilliant and decisive, as the enemy is now shut up in his fortress."

Such then was the desperate battle of the 18th of August, as nobly contested as any ever fought, and unquestionably the crudest conflict waged in this generation. The French, brought to bay, never—not even at Waterloo nor at Borodino—fought more splendidly. They are not usually supposed to excel in defence, but they held the hill above Gravelotte in a way that the troops who kept the heights of Inkermann would have been proud of, and their bravery and skill won admiration even from their enemies. That after so much fighting on the previous Sunday and Tuesday, under the most discouraging conditions, they should on this day have so well resisted the attack of greatly superior numbers for nine hours, reflected infinite credit upon their courage and resolution; and never, in fact, even in its most triumphant campaigns, did their army win more real glory than in this disastrous attempt to retreat from Metz. They are said to have lost 19,000 men; and the sudden wail which broke out from Germany attested the fearful gaps which were made in her army. There can be little doubt that, near Gravelotte, the assailants suffered in the proportion of nearly three to one compared with the defenders (the Hon. A. Winn, indeed, estimates that the Germans there lost as many thousands as the French did hundreds); nor is it improbable that the Germans were weakened by more than 25,000 soldiers. Amongst the wounded were two sons of Count von Bismarck, and a son of General von Roon, the Prussian minister of War. The fearful loss on the side of the Germans proves the energy of the French resistance, and does credit to the tactical power of Bazaine, who, with an army inferior in numbers, and already shaken by serious reverses, contrived to strike his adversaries with such terrible effect. The dispositions of the marshal, however, were, as we have seen, entirely defensive; and though this may have been unavoidable, the inability of the French to assail the Germans as they were making the turning movement, exposed them ultimately to defeat. The long march round on the French right, though fully justified by the event, and owing to the peculiarities of the ground much less hazardous than it might have been, was, nevertheless, not without peril to the Germans; for experience has shown what may be done under such circumstances by great generals, who have the means of attacking during an outflanking movement.

During the terrible hours of the assault, the Prussians were so many live targets to be shot at by the French; while they were to the Prussians an intangible enemy, whose existence was known less by the eye than the ear. To march against their position would, it was clear, be certain death to a large proportion of the attacking forces; yet march they repeatedly did, until at last their efforts were crowned with dearly-bought success. At Gravelotte, as at Woerth, victory was ultimately insured by a flank attack assisting the charge in front; but in both instances the ground from which the flank attack proceeded had to be first wrenched from the enemy, and only after a fearful contest. Looking, however, at the operations as a whole, although Bazaine fought a good battle and the losses of his foe were immense, the German commanders had fully succeeded in their grand if somewhat hazardous strategy. The French, driven completely into Metz, had been forced off their line of retreat; their enemy encompassed them on every side, and occupied their communications with Châlons; the roads to Verdun and Etain had been lost; and nothing but a decisive victory over an adversary immensely superior in strength could extricate them from their position. Bazaine's army, including the flower of the French troops, was altogether isolated and cut off from the other forces of France; imprisoned within the fortress, it had no prospect but to force its way through at great odds, or to surrender; and well would it have been if it had not attracted a relieving army to its assistance; which, in a vain attempt at rescue, as we shall see in the next two chapters, became involved in its defeat and ruin.

The battles of Tuesday and Thursday had the same object and the same general result; first, to make it impossible for the French army to continue its retreat towards a point where it might have effected its junction with the other military forces of France; and, secondly, to cut it off from communication with the government of the country, on which it depended for orders, money, reinforcements, and succour of all kinds. The difference between the battles was that, whereas on Tuesday night Marshal Bazaine's army, although temporarily and seriously disabled, was at least in a condition to fight again, by Thursday night it was completely defeated and rendered to a great extent useless.

The scene in Gravelotte and the villages around, after the battles of both the 16th and 18th, was awful. After eight days, in spite of every exertion, corpses still lay on the field; and after three days, wounded were still found who had not been attended to. The desperately wounded lay on straw, littered down on the floors of the deserted houses and out-buildings. The devoted nurses, male and female, who attended them dressed them three or four times a day, stooping over them in the most painful positions, for there were no seats, and to kneel upon the floors, drenched with blood and other secretions, was impossible. To clean the floors there were no brooms, no cloths, nor was there soap or water even to wash the sufferers. When darkness, too, came on, there were no candles nor matches; and the brave men, French and German, who had given their best blood for their country, were left to die in the dark.

We have thus reached the end of a week of battles; a week, perhaps, in which more men fell by the hands of their brother men than in any similar period since war was known on the earth; and it is, we believe, no exaggeration to say, that in the fortnight which elapsed between Thursday, August 4, when the Crown Prince fought the battle of Wissembourg, and the evening of Thursday, the 18th, when his father won the battle of Gravelotte, 100,000 men had fallen on the field.

Disheartened as his men now were by finding that their chief had counted their supposed victory of the 16th a disadvantage, and by their subsequent decided defeat in the position he had selected for this battle, it is extremely doubtful whether an instant march northwards from Metz (which the French commander was afterwards blamed by some for not having attempted) would have been of any service to them. It is true that the Saxon cavalry were the only bar in his way to Thionville early on the 19th; but to have started thither along the flank of the victorious Prussian general must have brought Bazaine between a now practically superior force and the Belgian frontier, and by this it is probable enough he would have anticipated with his army the disaster of Sedan. But German critics of a high class believe that, had he marched due south, starting from the works above Metz on the Moselle, he would for the time have got clear of their army, which had suffered so heavily on that flank just before dark, that it could not have been fit to move early. On the other hand, it is clear he would have met the fourth corps returning from its movement toward Toul, and fresh for action, as it lay just in his way on the left bank, while the first was similarly detached on the right; and it could only have been by promptly overwhelming one of these, before his rear was severely attacked, and driving it so clean out of his way as not to allow it to fall back for support on the Crown Prince's army, that he could have carried the bulk of his troops away. The propriety of encountering this risk may have been somewhat doubtful, even supposing he had his troops sufficiently in hand; but a general of higher order would doubtless not have tamely allowed himself to be shut in, when the German army, in forming its line, had thus left an opening on its flank by which to escape. More than this, it is very possible that in doing so such a general would have dealt the first army, or right of Von

Moltke's line, such a counter-stroke as would have more than atoned for the defeat of the day before, which, after all, the victors paid for heavily.

Instead of this, Bazaine sank into a state of perfect quiescence for eight days, which gave to the Germans invaluable time and opportunity of counter-intrenching their army so strongly as not only to make egress from Metz difficult, but, as we shall see, to enable the three corps forming their new fourth army to be withdrawn to occupy the line of the Meuse, and completely bar the rash attempt which MacMahon made to relieve his brother marshal.

The foregoing description of the battle has been compiled chiefly from the best accounts of it as it appeared to reliable observers on the German side; but it cannot fail to be interesting if we give the views and opinions of an able and thoroughly trustworthy witness who was present with the French, Mr. G. T. Robinson, the special correspondent of the *Manchester Guardian*, and author of the "Fall of Metz." As at the preceding battles of Courcelles and Vionville, he was again on this occasion the only English writer present on the French side, and witnessed the battle in the neighbourhood of Verneville and St. Privat. He considers that the whole proceedings of the Germans on this day involved a loss of life on both sides as unnecessary as it was fearful; and believes they could have attained their object of hemming in the French without it, as it was almost impossible for the latter to act on the offensive. He says, that as the Germans poured on their men the French batteries of mitrailleuses established on the heights mowed them down at 1200 to 1400 yards distance in long black rows. There was no science in their (the German) attack, it was simply brute force and stupidity combined; the more the French killed, the more there seemed to be to kill. After a time they knew it would be physically impossible for them to keep on killing them, as both their men and ammunition would be exhausted; so on they kept pouring fresh troops after fresh troops in murderous wantonness. To crush by force of numbers seemed the only idea. "There was no attempt to outflank us, which might so easily have been done, as their line was longer than ours, and we could not advance, they holding the roads in check. If they had worked up the Orne they would have compelled us to retire with hardly firing a shot. As it was, we were simply beaten, not by tactics, but because we could not butcher any more. At last our ammunition failed us, and then the generals lost their heads. Regiments were ordered into impossible places, overlapping each other in the clumsiest fashion, simply placed where they could be the most conveniently killed, and then forgotten; no supplies of ammunition were brought up, and Canrobert's corps was absolutely pushing back the enemy from his position on our right, really bending him back, when the last round his artillery had was fired. At the same time the sixty-seventh stood for three hours right in front of a wood, being leisurely shot down by the Prussians without a single cartouch to fire; not a single non-commissioned officer came away from that wood; and two-thirds of the regiment remained with them. An ambulance was pitched at a place appointed by Frossard, who in half an hour afterwards had so far forgotten where it was that he ordered some artillery immediately in front of it. Of course, the Prussian fire comes plunging into this to silence it, and over it into our ambulance, to silence many there. Bursting in the midst of the poor maimed, wounded, and amputated men, come the shells, and the horrors of war are intensified to a pitch beyond the power of the most devilish imagination to surpass. Here are poor men killed over and over again, that is, they go through the horrors of death many times; and what with their generals and what with their doctors, it's a wonder there are any left. Certainly glory is very beautiful when it is encountered in a shelled ambulance; and one is rather puzzled to define what is murder, or what not.

"A regiment of the fourth corps was also placed in position with a muster-roll of 1100, and came out 68! It was very fortunate for human nature that King William had not the power of the Jewish commander, for had that day's sun been stayed, scarcely a Frenchman there would have lived, and the slaughter of their enemies would have been even greater than it was. Truly, indeed, the soldiers say, in speaking of that day, 'It was not war, it was a massacre.' All the ammunition being expended, we had nothing to do but to withdraw; and now commenced a scene of most disgraceful confusion. Seeing the forces retire, and perhaps being rather more than usually sworn at, those wretched auxiliaries took fright, and a regular stampede occurred amongst them; their terror threw them into an even greater confusion than usual. They rendered the road utterly impassable. Waggon after waggon was emptied, and huge piles of provisions were set fire to. Sugar, coffee, biscuit, fodder, private baggage, anything and everything, was heaped together, and more than 100,000 francs worth of provisions were there and then destroyed, under the pretext of preventing them falling into the hands of the enemy. All along the road from the village of Gravelotte, from which our left was rapidly retreating under a heavy fire from the Prussian advancing forces, the ditches were choked with huge boxes of biscuit, bearing the familiar English record of their weight, and the inscription, 'Navy Biscuits,' in most stumpy British characters. Broken open by their fall, they scattered their contents all over the road, and were ground into the dust by the wheels of the waggons. Whole cart-loads of sugar lay on the roadside; the soldiers filled their sacks with, or shouldered great loaves of it, and sold them in Metz for a few glasses of wine or spirits; everything that could be destroyed was, and the vehicles rolled empty down the hill in one mad panic. A quartermaster in French uniform galloped by. 'Fly, fly for your lives!' he cried, and he fled. It was of course afterwards said that he was a Prussian spy in disguise; such things always were said, all these things were done by Prussian spies, who acted the character they assumed to a marvel, and were always on the spot at the right time—clever fellows. The Prussian batteries had now crept round to St. Privat, following our retiring silent artillery, silent from want of ammunition, and began to rake our lines. The noise of the panic in the rear reached the soldiers; it spread like wildfire, whatever that may be, it seized hold upon them at once; encampments were abandoned, arms were flung away, knapsacks, great-coats, everything which could encumber flight was cast aside; *sauve qui peut* was the order of the day; and if that quartermaster had been a spy, he would have ridden forward to the Prussians, and Bazaine's army would have been annihilated. Fortunately the enemy did not know of it; he did not follow up the retreating rabble; indeed, I have heard that something similar occurred on his side, too, but as I only heard of it from some prisoners, I do not know if it is true. Night kindly and charitably covered us and our disgrace. Some of our men held the quarries of Amanvillers, and kept up a semblance of a resistance. Canrobert's silent artillery held bravely in the rear, and probably the Prussians feared a feint; but the major part of the army rushed away down into the ravine, and never stopped until it found itself, panting and exhausted, safely under cover of St. Quentin and Plappeville. Some few troops remained on the ground all night in front of Amanvillers. Pradier's division of L'Admirault's corps held their ground till seven in the morning of the 19th, having been twenty-one consecutive hours under arms and without food. On our left the second battalion of the eightieth held the little inn of St. Hubert until three p.m., checking the advance of the Prussians until their shells set fire to the place, and only allowed eighty-six of our men to come away. As for the guard, they did nothing; they stayed at Chatel St. Germain, perfectly safe, and Marshal Bazaine stayed with them. He had had enough of erratic charges on the 16th, when he was so nearly being taken prisoner, and did not want to see any more uhlans, so he kept at a very safe distance. One shell, it is true, did reach the quarters of the guards, so they claim to have been under fire that day; their list of killed, wounded, and missing amounted to one!

"Thus terminated that murderous, needless day of St. Privat, or, as the Prussians call it, Gravelotte; a day nothing could have converted into a useful victory for the French, and one which was only made into a Prussian one by wholesale slaughter. Very bravely fought their soldiers; they marched to certain death with heroic coolness; right up the slope they came, only to die the faster the nearer they approached; up to within two hundred yards some made their way, and there they rested for ever; nor was it until our ammunition failed us, and our men were physically exhausted, that one ever reached our lines. Incessant marching, three days' fighting, without food, without rest, and without ammunition, our men gave way, overcome more by these things than even by the number of their foes without. It was their foes within which conquered them; and many a man lay down and died there without a wound, slain solely by too much fatigue and too little food. For three days some of them had eaten nothing but unripe grapes, and so, of course, they died. What our losses were we never knew; but these two days' fighting at Rezonville and here must have cost us at least 30,000 men, and this day's fighting must have been trebly murderous to the Prussians, and for what? Not a single thing was gained by all that slaughter. The untenable and useless position was abandoned, and what was left of the army now retired upon Metz, where it might just as well have taken up its quarters after the 16th, if, as the marshal demonstrated by his taking up so defensive a position, it found itself too ill provided and too ill provisioned to proceed. On the 20th came out this order of the day, a collective sort of ' order,' embracing all the fighting of this bloody week:—

" 'GENERAL ORDER.

" ' Officers, non-commissioned officers, andsoldiers of the army of the Rhine,—You have fought three glorious battles, in which the enemy has suffered grievous losses, and has left in our hands a standard, some cannons, and 700 prisoners. The country applauds your success.

" ' The emperor delegates me to congratulate you, and to assure you of his gratitude. He will reward those amongst you who have had the good fortune to distinguish themselves.

" ' The struggle is but commencing; it will be long and furious; for who is there amongst us who would not shed his last drop of blood to free his native soil?

" ' Let each one of us, inspired with the love of our dear country, redouble his courage in the field, and bear with resignation fatigues and privations.

" ' Soldiers,—Never forget the motto inscribed on your eagles, *Valour and discipline*, and victory is certain, for all France is rising behind you.

" ' At the Grand Quartier-Général of Ban St. Martin, 20th August, 1870.

" ' The Marshal of France, Commander-in-Chief,

     " ' (Signed.)   BAZAINE.'

"Three large battles, and only that! One standard, 'some,' that is to say, two, cannons, and 700 prisoners. We knew we lost two eagles, and a good many more than two cannons, and I hope many more than 700 prisoners. I say hope, for if not our list of dead and wounded must be great indeed. The country applauds, and the emperor is grateful; verily the survivors have indeed their reward, but I cannot help feeling that the dead have been needlessly sacrificed. At the same time that the marshal's 'order of the day' appeared, came out also an official communication from the quartier-général. It, of course, endeavoured to palliate these repeated disasters, and congratulated everybody that for two days the army had not been harassed by the enemy, and that they have been quietly allowed to take up those positions round Metz appointed for them by the marshal. But as these positions were behind the forts, it struck all who thought upon the subject, that the cause for congratulation was not much; the enemy, we thought, might congratulate himself more on the fact that he was allowed to take up his position on the other side of them equally quietly. 'It is unfortunately true,' says this correspondence, 'that certain regiments had not received a sufficient quantity of ammunition, and that at certain points we have to deplore the existence of momentary panics, which in some degree compromised the issue of the day, and of which the ill effect was felt in the town, giving a certain feeling of faint-heartedness, soon, however, overcome. These are only accidental occurrences, and we can truly say that the enemy's plan of the 18th has not succeeded.' As, however, Bazaine's army was now completely cut off from all the rest of France, and as our communications were entirely stopped, none but the very sanguine amongst us felt much satisfaction at the thought that whatever other plans the enemy might have had, he had succeeded thus far, and a faint shadow of the coming events began to envelop us. MacMahon was our hope, and we relied on him much more than on Marshal Bazaine, possibly because we knew so much less of him. We were told that he was coming from Châlons to our help; so we waited for the good time and MacMahon coming together, and unfortunately neither came so far as Metz."

Under the title of "A Brief Report of the Operations of the Army of the Rhine, from the 13th August to the 29th of October, 1870," Marshal Bazaine, after the capitulation of Metz, published a justification of his conduct in relation to the events described in this and the preceding chapters. He practically disclaims any share in all that went on up to the 13th of August, the day on which he officially took the command. The decree appointing him, and at the same time abolishing the functions of Leboeuf as major-general to the emperor, was only dated on the 12th; and by his utter silence as to all previous transactions, Bazaine would clearly wish it to be understood that he had nothing to do with the command until the official transfer was made. This may be, of course. On the other hand, we have on record the semi-official telegrams from Metz of the 9th, stating distinctly that "Marshal Bazaine is charged with the direction of the operations," closely followed by "official" telegrams of the same date, not signed, but accepted as coming from the emperor himself, and calling the whole force round Metz "the army of Marshal Bazaine." In the emperor's pamphlet, to which we have already more than once referred, there is great obscurity as regards this particular episode. The secret history of the unhappy and fatal delay of the six days is not yet known, and Napoleon cannot be absolved from having had to do with it. But neither can the marshal be exempt if, as the telegrams led the world to believe, he was already named commander-in-chief of the whole army. The crisis required that rare quality of moral courage which would have insisted on receiving full and immediate power corresponding to the responsibility to be imposed on him. This quality was not displayed, and hence we have the strange fact of an emperor and commander both suffering in reputation for the loss of precious time, and neither able to acquit himself of share in the blame. From the 13th Bazaine first admits his unfettered leadership, as indeed it was then officially his; and in his pamphlet is the fatal admission that the paucity of the bridges kept his last two corps, Decaen's and L Admirault's, from concentrating on the left bank, before marching off, until the 16th came, and with it the battle of Mars-la-Tour. It is noteworthy that the latter of these corps is stated to have "almost completed its passage over the stream "on the morning of the 14th, and to have been brought back voluntarily in order to support the other, the third, against the assault which Steinmetz's troops suddenly made. The object of the Germans is distinctly said to have been, as indeed it unquestionably was, to delay the passage of the French, who, however, had on that side only to withdraw within the works, instead of accepting Steinmetz's challenge, in order to be perfectly safe. In place of doing this, the French staff played into their enemy's hands by bringing part of L'Admirault's corps across to join in the fight; and for this, as no excuse whatever is offered by Bazaine in his defence, we may presume there is none, save that they did not then discern what he saw very clearly afterwards. So the rest of the 14th was thrown away in a useless combat, and the 15th and morning of the 16th were consumed in attempting to repair the mistake by re-crossing the fourth corps to the west bank, and after it bringing over the third. Meanwhile, though the safety of the whole army was already known to be imperilled by the slowness of its movements, "the bridges were insufficient in number," simply because the marshal and his engineers had neglected to prepare additional means for the coming emergency. Then follows the next episode of this history of disasters. Bazaine, having fought the indecisive action of Mars-la-Tour, and, as he says fairly enough, "kept the enemy in check for the moment," found himself ill-provisioned as to rations, and particularly short of cartridges for his artillery and infantry. It is true that the intendance had put several millions of the latter (five-sixths, in fact, of the whole reserve) where the responsible officer was unaware of their existence; and the marshal is not to be blamed for this fatal error of centralization which, with others of a similar kind, helped so much to destroy the army it was designed to serve. We must take his view, therefore, as formed according to the circumstances reported at the time. But even allowing that these were alarming, his putting his advancing army suddenly on the defensive by the retreat which he determined on, led to such fatal results that it seems to stand self-condemned. It was done, as he informs us, to get rid of the wounded, to obtain supplies for a march, and to avoid further immediate action which should impede the hoped-for retreat. It ended in the army being shut in with its wounded, the march being wholly stopped, and the battle of Gravelotte being fought and lost on the very next day. The marshal pleads also want of water in his previous position; but the well-known surprise and reluctance manifested by his army at the order to fall back sufficiently refute his plea. He takes especial pains at this point to contradict those who say that he should have continued the action at once, instead of falling back on the St. Privat position. But the two causes stated as making this impracticable form perhaps the most unsatisfactory part of the defence. They are that the Prussians "had sent forces to occupy the position of Fresnes, before Verdun," and that the French had not only been hotly engaged, but were obliged to wait for the fractions of their army left behind, "especially the grand reserve park which was at Toul!" The Prussians had, in truth, had quite enough to do to hold their own on the day of Mars-la-Tour without making detachments to their rear to take up fresh positions; and as their whole army was now pressing on across the line between Bazaine's forces and Toul, and had on the 17th its back to the latter place, with one corps echeloned towards it, he might just as well have waited for the runaways of MacMahon who had got shut into Strassburg, as for the reserve park he speaks of. Had he risked an action, he adds, "the army might have experienced a severe check, affecting disastrously its further operations." Possibly it might, but the check could certainly not have been more serious than the defeat of Gravelotte, nor the consequences more disastrous than being shut up in the position in which he found himself in and around Metz. Even if Bazaine could not make up his mind to assume the offensive at daylight on the 17th, before the Germans received more succour, in the opinion of many military critics it was still open to him to have sent back such of his trains as were near Metz, and, masking the movement with a part of the troops which still faced the enemy about Vionville and Mars-la-Tour, to have filed the rest of his army behind it on the northern road, which had not then been reached by the Germans, and so have pushed on towards Verdun by Briey. The Germans, we know, believed that such a movement would be attempted, and immediately they had observed it there would doubtless have been a pursuit; but a short start, carried out with activity, might have carried Bazaine to Verdun, and the line of the Meuse once gained, he should hardly have allowed himself to be intercepted in attempting to join MacMahon, who could have moved to meet him. To have accomplished such a flank movement, from the front of a resolute enemy, would unquestionably have been no slight task, and could not have been attempted successfully unless decided on promptly and carried out energetically; and it must be admitted that promptitude and energy seem to have been qualities sadly wanting amongst the French staff at this time. It is necessary, however, in order to obtain a complete understanding of the whole campaign, to show that there was not strictly, at this crisis of the war, an absolute necessity for choosing between renewing the bloody attacks of the 16th and falling back and fighting defensively before Metz; but that the means of escaping, without the risk of a general action, were still at hand, had the French commander had the quickness and resolution to have availed himself of them.

As the sequel of the battle of Gravelotte (called by the Marshal, from the central village of his position, the Defence of the Amanvillers Lines), he says that the French army on the following morning took up its position among the detached forts round Metz, and from that day (it should rather have been said, from after the preceding battle of the 16th), remained on the defensive. No word is said as to the possibilities which the Germans have noted that, instead of retreating finally to this shelter, the marshal should at least have attempted to debouch at once by one of his flanks, before they had time thoroughly to inclose him. The marshal points out exactly enough what was then the chief desire of his enemies, and how real were their fears of its frustration, when he says in his next sentence, "they lost not an instant in completing our investment by destroying the bridges over the Orne (a small stream which flows into the Moselle north of Metz) and breaking up the railroad to Thionville on the other side." In excuse for his inaction at this crisis of the fate of his army, he alleges the necessity of giving it some repose, and refilling the diminished cadres of officers. No one has ever pretended that the German losses were less than his own, and their activity, which he confesses, is a sufficient refutation of this so-called necessity.

As the fortress of Metz interrupted the railway from Saarbrück, through Pont-a-Mousson to Paris, and by Nancy to Strassburg, General Von Moltke, as early as the 20th of August, directed the construction of a railway fourteen miles long from Metz, to unite the Metz and Saarbrück with the Metz and Paris line. Herr Weisshaupt undertook its construction; skilful civil and military engineers were placed at his disposal, many of the neighbouring peasantry and 3000 unemployed miners from the Saarbrück collieries were set to work, and amid the thunder of cannon the undertaking was commenced. The railway leads from Pont-à-Mousson to Remilly, on the Saarbrück and Metz line; and it was prosecuted night and day so actively, that in spite of the partially very difficult country it had to pass through, it was opened in a few weeks, and then Metz caused no obstruction to the German communications. By means of it, too, supplies and *matériel* could easily be conveyed to any part of the siege works that might be desired. As a proof of the marvellous foresight of the Prussians in everything connected with the war, it has been stated on apparently good authority that the survey of the line was made three years before, immediately after the settlement of the Luxemburg question, which the Prussians as well as the French understood was not a settlement of the general question. The survey, it is said, was made by a Prussian engineer who took employment, in 1867, at some ironworks near Metz, and employed his leisure in surveying the country.

CHAPTER. XIII.

Arrival of MacMahon at Châlons on August 16—Description of the Camp and of MacMahon's Fugitives—Arrival of Reinforcements and Re-organization of the French Troops—Progress of the Third German Army, under the Crown Prince—Capture of Marsal— Unsuccessful Attempt to take Toul—General Sketch of the Advance of the Germans— Behaviour of the Troops and Feeling on the part of the French—Full Explanation of the German System of "Requisitions"—Proclamation of the Crown Prince to the Inhabitants of Nancy—The Courses open to MacMahon—His Intention to retreat to Paris is objected to by the Government, and he is compelled to undertake the Desperate Task of attempting to relieve Bazaine—Statements of the Emperor on the Subject—Critical Examination of the Peril of the Proposed Undertaking—Breaking up of the Camp at Châlons—The Composition of the French Army—MacMahon delayed at Rheims—His Plans for the Future—Insubordination on the part of the French Troops and want of Confidence in their Officers—A Fourth Army formed by the Germans to operate against MacMahon—Wonderful Promptitude displayed by it—The Crown Prince joined by his Father—Alteration of their Plans on hearing of MacMahon's Movement—Extraordinary Marching on the part of the Germans—General Positions of the French and German Armies on August 27—Cavalry Encounter at Buzancy— MacMahon seeing the hopelessness of his Enterprise resolves to retreat, but is again over-ruled by the Government at Paris—Capture of Vrizy by the Germans—The Battles of Beaumont and Carignan on August 30—The French at Beaumont again taken completely by surprise—Stout Resistance on their part, but they are ultimately compelled to retreat—The fighting in the town of Beaumont—Description of the Engagement and of the State of the French Troops by a French Officer—The Battle at Carignan—Skill and Decision displayed by MacMahon, but he is obliged to retreat for fear of being outflanked—The last Proclamation ever issued by the Emperor to the French Army—The Positions of the Contending Forces on the following morning—The best course open to MacMahon is not taken—Description of the Position taken up by him near Sedan—Operations of the Germans on the 31st with the view of encircling their Enemy—Desperate Position of the French at Nightfall.

THE events of the war require that we now return to the south and south-east, and follow the movements of the French corps which had formed the right of their army at the commencement of hostilities, and of the third German army under the Crown Prince.

In Chapter X. we have detailed the disgraceful flight of MacMahon's forces after the battle of Woerth, and the retreat of that general from Saverne to Nancy, where he arrived on August 12, and where he effected a junction with a small portion of the sixth corps (Canrobert's) which had been left there, the remainder having previously joined Bazaine at Metz, from Châlons. Retreating with this force, he, on the 16th, reached Châlons, at the junction of the roads leading directly from the Vosges, and covering the approaches to Paris; this being evidently the position on which the remainder of the French army, falling back from the frontier, would concentrate.

At Mourmelon, about twenty miles to the north, was a large permanent camp, which had been long used for military manoeuvres in time of peace, and where the reserve forces of the empire were collected in order to be organized into a second army, consisting of the marine infantry and other troops withdrawn from the naval expedition fitted out at Cherbourg and Brest, and intended to have operated in Northern Prussia, with the garde mobile, recruits, volunteers, and the few regiments or battalions of the line which had been left in different parts of the country. The composition and organization of this force was, however, very unsatisfactory. The garde mobile, whom the government had been afraid to arm properly in time of peace, were then only beginning to learn the use of their rifles; and as many of them were persons of means, and were continually treating their less wealthy brethren in arms, the camp presented a scene very different from what might have been expected, considering the serious position in which the country was placed, and which boded ill for the future. A day or two before the arrival of MacMahon, an eye-witness said that, short of battles, the place presented a spectacle which he hoped neither this century, nor any other, would ever witness again. There was not a minute's silence. Troops were coming in, troops going out; caissons rumbling along the street; carts, cannons, donkeys, horses, men, drays, ambulances, wounded men and straining runaways (in great number)—all pervaded by the din of singing and shouting in every direction. "Well, notwithstanding all these signs, which denote assuredly the throes of a nation dangerously struck, the place is full of Paris prostitutes, and the *cafés chantants* here never made such a harvest before. Although in three days the floods of a routed army may sweep over this very place, closely followed by the hordes of an infuriated enemy, although every man in France feels this now, and has put aside his *jactance*, dissipation is just as great, and amusement as eagerly sought after as ever. The streets are thronged with people; and numbers of men in blouses, who seem to have it all their own way, mingle with soldiers of every possible corps and arm, all half, if not quite, drunk, and render circulation anything but pleasant. The mob, in fact, are thoroughly in the ascendant, and shout, sing, drink, smoke, and swagger about as they like. As I write parties of mobiles are passing under my window, and one of the group shouts 'Vive l'Empereur!' to which the others all answer by an exclamation of disgust and contempt. This kind of chorus I have heard several times to-day. It is just on the cards that by staying here I shall see a spectacle dreamt of nowhere excepting in the Apocalypse, under the name of the Battle of Armageddon; for if the French should lose the next battle this would be the scene of the final slaughter; I will not say battle, for one it would not be."

The following order of the day was read at the camp on Monday, 15th August, the anniversary of the Fête Napoleon:—

"Gardes Mobiles,—The 15th of August is, under ordinary circumstances, a day of rejoicing in France. But it would be out of the question for you, or any one whose heart pulsates within him, to keep a holiday so long as the land is desecrated by an invader's foot. You are about to receive arms. Learn quickly how to use them, in order to go forth and avenge your brothers, whose blood flowed at Forbach and Reichshoffen. They fell as brave men should fall, before the enemy. Let their last cry uttered when about to die be also yours, Long live France! Death to the Prussians!"

The omission of Vive l'Empereur! in this production was remarkable; but already amongst nearly all, except the soldiers, the feeling began to be openly expressed that they would have no more of him—"*Nous n'en voulons plus.*"

MacMahon, as already stated, reached the camp on Tuesday, August 16, bringing with him at the most 15,000 disheartened men—the relics of the 55,000 whom he had ranged in battle-order at Woerth; three-fourths of whom, instead of one-fourth, might have been preserved to his standards but for the shameful loosening of the bonds of discipline which defeat and retreat had induced. As the soldiers reached the camp, they presented a strange medley of all arms and regiments, with out arms, without cartridges, without knapsacks the cavalry had no horses, the gunners no guns a motley demoralized crew, whom it would take a long time to form into battalions, squadrons, and batteries. The work of re-organization—resurrection one officer called it—was, however, at once commenced, and within a few days the French marshal received further reinforcements, including the twelfth corps, under General Lebrun, which had been hastily put together, the administration of Count Palikao at Paris having strained every nerve to repair the French disasters. But the forces now under MacMahon were of very inferior quality compared with the well-trained legions he had commanded in the Vosges, although they contained the elements out of which a good army might have been formed had there been time for the purpose.

Meanwhile the seventh corps, that of General Douay, the only one in the first French line which as yet remained intact, had been hurried from Belfort to Châlons via Paris, and two divisions of De Failly's fifth corps had arrived from Bitsche. Terrified at the disasters of the 6th, De Failly, by a forced march from Fenetrange and Nancy, escaped along the west of the Vosges, between the hostile armies on either side. It is due to him to say that this movement was well executed; and though it is not improbable that the fortifications of Bitsche, which checked a detachment of the Crown Prince, contributed to his safety, his retreat appears to have been rapid and judicious. By the 20th of August Marshal MacMahon, who had been rejoined by the emperor from Metz (whose body-guard from that place was incorporated with the army), had concentrated in the great camp at Châlons from 130,000 to 150,000 men, with above 500 guns; but this force, however imposing in numbers, was from its composition unsafe and feeble as an instrument of war, more especially for offensive operations.

While the right wing of the French army had in this manner avoided destruction, and was being recruited on every side, though separated from the centre and left at Metz, the triumphant forces of the Crown Prince had followed it through the passes of the Vosges; and in Chapter X. we have traced their progress to August 14, when a part of them had effected a junction with those of the army of Prince Frederick Charles at Pont-à-Monsson, between Metz and Nancy. On the 15th the small fort of Marsal, after having been bombarded for a short time, capitulated to the Bavarian army corps under the Crown Prince. It is five miles east-south-east of Château Salins, on the road from Dieuze to Vic and Nancy. It had been passed several days before, but its fall gave the Germans better command of the road, besides the war material of the place, and forty cannon.

An attempt to capture Toul, a fortified town with 8000 inhabitants, and a station on the direct railway to Paris, was less successful. The garrison, consisting of garde mobile, two battalions of regulars and artillery, had a battery on St. Michel, which commands the town, and covered their front with earthworks. The officer in command of the artillery, M. Barbe, did all he could for defence. The attack was made by two columns of Prussian and Bavarian troops, who hoped to storm the works and take the place by surprise; but the French, quite prepared, received the onslaught with firmness, and a deadly fire from their guns in position and from musketry inside the works. The attack failed, and the German loss in that and in a subsequent one, which also failed, was about 300 killed and 700 wounded. As nothing short of a regular siege could reduce the place, which was not worth the sacrificing of more lives in attempts to carry it by main force, a small corps was left to mask it. As will be seen in Chapter XVIII., it held out gallantly a very considerable time, affording another instance of the inconvenience caused to an enemy, and of the advantage rendered to the country invaded, by even feebly-fortified places against which only field artillery can be brought.

The Crown Prince's headquarters were established at Nancy several days; for so long as there seemed a chance that the French might get away from Metz—that the desperate efforts of their guard might turn the scale against the skill and spirit of the Germans—it was necessary to hold the third army in readiness to march northward. While, therefore, the battles were raging near that fortress, on the 14th, 16th, and 18th, this army lay in the country about Nancy and Luneville, half expecting to be ordered up in support of the other German forces. When the news of the defeat of the French by Steinmetz and Prince Frederick Charles arrived, there was, of course, no further occasion to hesitate about invading central France, and the third army was free to continue its inarch. It received considerable reinforcements from Metz, and having turned the fortress of Toul both to the north and south, advanced rapidly on the Marne. The general scene at this time was thus vividly pourtrayed by one of the many very able correspondents sent to the war by the *Daily News:*—"The roads are crowded with trains of ammunition waggons, with stores of provisions, and with masses of infantry. Woe to the luckless wayside villages; woe to the farmers who have crops in wayside fields; there is no danger to life or limb among the peaceable inhabitants, but there is danger of being fairly eaten out of house and home. There is an unavoidable trampling down of crops in the fields where the soldiers pass, and there is such a demand for means of transport as leaves little chance to the farmer of keeping his horses for himself. He gets a receipt of some sort in most cases. But no amount of paper security will comfort the average French farmer in the present crisis. Poor man! It is such an unexpected blow. 'Why does the emperor make war,' I have heard a dozen sad-looking men in blouses exclaim, 'if he knows not how to make it?' A plebiscite in the occupied districts at this moment would need no foreign pressure to be flooded with 'nons.'

"There is a straight and rapid march westward of the third army, supported by other troops all full of confidence, flushed with victory, and splendidly organized. Three or four columns are marching abreast on some of the roads; two go by the road itself, and in some cases two more move through the fields to right and left, or at least one other column makes a way which is a little out of order serve the purpose of the moment. Great are the blocks and crushes, tremendous the swearing at critical corners. But, on the whole, it is remarkable how well these columns are directed; how carefully they choose their routes through the invaded provinces. Wheels are rumbling, and whips are cracking along many a road. The columns are halted to rest in some places, and there may be seen the bright bivouac fire twinkling in the fields, or long lines of horses standing silently at supper Though many columns are halted others are moving on. The road is still alive with military preparation. Do not fancy the pomp and circumstance of war as attending the march of the columns of supply. It is a pretty sight to see the lancers or dragoons who lead the invasion trotting over hill and dale, with every nerve strained to detect a possible foe. There is an impressive force about the advance of the dusty and tired infantry—the murmur of many voices, and tramp of many feet passing forward like a storm sighing in the woods. Even the weight and slowness of the guns has its own peculiar dignity. They are deadly weapons in charge of determined fighting men. But the innumerable columns of supply, the baggage and ammunition, the food and provender, are very prosaic, though very necessary. There are miles of hay waggons—a good omen for cavalry horses. Further on are other miles of bread waggons, of bacon and beef waggons. Horned cattle are led along by the score to become beef in due time; clothes and equipments, medicines, and blankets, are brought rumbling on into France. If the people were astonished at the earlier stages of the journey, they are now simply bewildered beyond all power of recovery. An avalanche has fallen upon them. One cannot see it for oneself, but the sight of the advancing host, as a wayside village sees it, from first to last, must be something to remember. The people will tell in a dreamy way how they heard that the Prussians were coming. There was news of them four, five, six days ago, as the case may be. Yes, *ma foi*, they heard that they were coming, but did not believe it. Then there was a party of lancers seen upon the road. The people wondered what would happen. Monsieur le cure told them that in modern wars they did not kill those who remained quiet, so their confidence was enough to keep them at home. The village shop was shut, and everybody closed his door and peeped from the window. Now the lancers rode into the street, and a few came forward to the principal house— the hotel de ville, if the place ranked as a 'bourg,' or small town. The soldiers asked for food and drink, said they would do no harm if they were not molested, and presently got off their horses. With details very slightly varying I have heard of this first entry in several places, and have heard how infantry soon began to come: one regiment—two, three, a dozen regiments. The bread was eaten, the wine was drunk, and the people were well nigh ruined by feeding their guests. Were they bad fellows in their way? A delicate question this, and one to which a stranger can expect but a guarded answer. What sort of fellows were they, these invading soldiers? 'Oh, not very bad, if only they had not such dreadful appetites, and if they could make themselves understood.' It is hard to be shaken and growled at in La Belle France itself for not speaking the language of the German Fatherland. It is harder still to have a slip of paper, negotiable, Heaven knows when, instead of a good cart-horse or fat bullock. I have, however, heard no complaint of personal violence, and the women do not seem at all afraid of the rough, loud-voiced fellows who swarm around them. The fact is, that if we start with a notion of war founded on what the armies of the French Republic did to their enemies in 1795—96, this German invasion of France in 1870 will seem very civilized and merciful. If, on the contrary, we take our stand on the rights of private property and the highest English ideal of a 'ready-money commissariat,' there will seem to be something harsh and oppressive in the quartering of troops on the villagers. All foreigners have this notion, that troops should be quartered on the conquered people, who find their visitors in food. The luckless village which lies near the road is eaten up by thousands of unwelcome guests, and the more remote village escapes with a trifling loss. This is a bitter time for the conquered French, and many individuals—farmers, horse-dealers, and wayside cottagers—suffer grievous loss."

And here it may be well to explain more fully the German system of requisitions. It was this:— Every town or village occupied by German troops had to furnish a certain quantity of provisions for the use of the soldiers and supplies for their cavalry, to be paid for by cheques, which were to be honoured at the end of the war by the vanquished. If Germany won France was to pay; if France, Germany was to pay her own cheques and any the French might draw on German ground. The superior officers alone could make requisitions, and if people were uncivil or obstinate, they were treated to a few of the smaller horrors of war.

In the interesting little work, "From Sedan to Saarbrück," by an artillery officer, the writer, who is certainly very impartial in his statements, says, "One point which we took the greatest pains to clear up, was the oft-asserted and contradicted integrity of the Prussians, in paying for all they took by means of bonds. These, which might more properly be called receipts, were invariably given for every franc's worth exacted; but our suspicions were first aroused by finding that their recipients looked upon them as so much waste paper, and considered themselves robbed. Hence the continual phrase, '*Ils nous ont pillé partout.*' On this doubt, then, the whole question hinged; and in order to remove it we were persevering in addressing our inquiries to every grade of authority, high and low. It would not perhaps be quite fair to mention their names, but in many cases their status was such as to preclude the possibility of inaccurate information. Our questions usually took the following form:—

" ' As for these bonds, do you look upon them as redeemable at Berlin at the end of the war?' (With a laugh.) 'Certainly not. Our own national pecuniary losses will be heavy enough as it is, without our burdening ourselves with our enemy's debts.'

' But you will probably obtain an indemnity from the French at the end of the war. Will not this be calculated on a scale which may enable you to redeem these bonds?' 'Ah, no! We shall want all the money we can get to pay our own bill.'

" ' Well, then, you will at least make it one of the conditions of peace that the French government shall take up and honour them?' 'I think you misunderstand the whole matter. When these bonds are once signed and delivered, we entirely wash our hands of them; we ignore them completely, and recognise no claim founded on them.'

" ' Then what is the good of issuing them?' (*With a shrug.*) 'Well, it is more orderly. Besides, when peace is concluded, the French will perhaps make some national efforts to relieve the poverty of the districts in which requisitions were made, by calling for the assistance of those departments which have not suffered. In such a case our bonds will enable the maires, sous-prêfets, and prêfets to distribute their funds equitably.'

"This, then, the Prussians call paying for all they take; and the world praises their honesty. There seems to be an unusual amount of balderdash talked on subjects connected with the war. Possibly they may have little choice in the course they have pursued; but it is, we think, indisputable that these French peasants are as completely stripped of their possessions as were the Hamburgers under the rule of Davoust; only, in the present instance, the process is carried on in a more civil way. The medium of communication is the maire. On him the Prussian commandant issues the requisitions for forage, provisions, billets, carts, horses, rations, &c.; and the former distributes the burden as evenly as possible. All that comes under the head of ' luxuries ' is supposed to be paid for; though even in this respect the rule does not seem to be very clear. For instance, we noticed at Conflans that, instead of the everlasting, big, hanging pipe, every soldier was puffing away at a cigar. On inquiry, the Prussian officer told us that they had that day obtained (? obtained) an unexpected supply from the neighbourhood of 6000 cigars; which, distributed among 250, gave 24 cigars per man.

"There is also apparently great laxity in conniving at the private soldiers helping themselves, provided there is no theft of money. They laughingly told us that their men were very sharp in discovering the hidden treasures of best wine. One woman came to complain of forcible abstraction of wheat for the horses by some men billeted on her:—

" 'Did they rob you of any money?' inquired the commandant. 'No, monsieur; but ——.'

" ' Then,' interrupted the other, 'I cannot redress your complaint. Our horses must be fed; and if we cannot obtain oats, we must take wheat.' "

During the stay of the Crown Prince at Nancy, some of the inhabitants were prevailed on to assist in restoring the railway which was to join his own main communication; and on hearing of it he issued the following proclamation:—

"Germany is making war against the emperor of the French, not against the French. The population has no reason to fear that any hostile measures will be used towards it. I am exerting myself to restore to the nation, and to the people of Nancy in particular, the means of communication which the French army has destroyed, and I hope that industry and commerce will soon resume their usual way, and functionaries of every class continue at their work. I only require for the support of the army the surplus of provisions over what is necessary for the French people. The peaceful part of the nation, and Nancy in particular, may count upon the utmost consideration."

By the 20th of August the Crown Prince's columns had not advanced far beyond Nancy, though his uhlans had reached St Dizier and Vitry. It will be remembered that from his arrival at the camp of Châlons on the 16th to this date (August 20), MacMahon had been busily engaged in endeavouring to re-organize his troops, and had just been joined by De Failly. When he became aware that Bazaine had been prevented from making his intended movement on Châlons, and that the Crown Prince had resumed his westward march, several alternatives must have presented themselves to the French general for choice: (1) He might fall back on Paris for the purpose of assuring its successful defence, if besieged, or if fighting outside, with it still behind him to receive his army in case of defeat; (2) he might retreat northwards by Rheims, Soissons, and Compiegne, constantly threatening the right flank of the German advance on the capital, but never allowing himself to be drawn into any serious engagement; (3) he might, on the other hand, draw off to a flanking position on the south, having Lyons in the rear with the new levies there in course of formation: in either of these cases he could have kept an untouched district behind him from which to feed his army, and at the same time threaten the communications by which the Germans must needs supply theirs; (4) if, instead of either of these safe courses, he decided to attempt the relief of his beleaguered comrade at Metz, he could either proceed first to the southward and then to the north-east according to circumstances, and if the enemy came on him on the way he would have two-thirds of France on which to fall back; or he could break up suddenly and as secretly as possible from Châlons, and by forced marches hope perhaps to elude both the Crown Prince and any other force that might be sent to intercept him; in which case he might fall on the rear of the investing force at Metz, and having, in combination with Bazaine's army, defeated it, then with an united army of 250,000 men, encouraged by victory, and with France in good heart, oblige the Germans to begin the game again almost from the commencement.

According to a letter published by him after the disaster at Sedan, the first course—to fall back on Paris—was that which MacMahon intended to adopt; but by order of the minister of war, Comte de Palikao, and the Committee of Defence at Paris, he was compelled to attempt the last, and enter on an undertaking fated to prove most disastrous to the arms of France. "This," he says in his letter, "is what infallibly happens when people take upon them to direct the movements of distant armies from the closet. In these circumstances one can draw up a general plan, but one cannot descend to details; and this is what Comte de Palikao forgot."

The marshal's statement is fully borne out by the emperor, who says that, as soon as he reached the camp at Châlons from Metz, he found there the duke of Magenta (Marshal MacMahon) and General Trochu; the latter had been nominated by the minister of war commander of the troops at the camp. These two general officers were summoned by the emperor to a council, at which were present Prince Napoleon, General Schmitz (General Trochu's chief staff officer), and General Berthaut, the commander of the national garde mobile. It was decided that the emperor should nominate General Trochu to the command of the army in Paris; that the troops collected at Châlons should be directed towards the capital, under the orders of Marshal MacMahon; that the national garde mobile should go to the camp of St. Maur, at Vincennes; and that the emperor should go to Paris, where his duties called him.

The following draught of a proclamation to be issued by Marshal MacMahon was also agreed to:—

"IMPERIAL HEADQUARTERS, .　　　.　　　.　　　1870.

"Soldiers,—The emperor has confided to me the command of all the forces which, with the army at Châlons, are about to assemble round the capital. My most ardent desire would have been to go to the help of Marshal Bazaine, but after close examination I am convinced this enterprise is impossible under present circumstances. We could not reach Metz for several days, and before that time Marshal Bazaine will have broken through the obstacles which detain him. Our direct march upon Metz would only . . . . During our march towards the east, Paris would be uncovered, and a large Prussian army might arrive under the walls. After the reverses Prussia suffered under the first empire she has formed a military organization enabling her to rapidly arm her people, and within a few days place her entire population under arms. Prussia has, therefore, a considerable force at her disposal; the fortifications of Paris will stop the flood of the enemy, and give us time to organize the military forces of the country; the national ardour is immense, and I am convinced that with perseverance we shall conquer the enemy and drive him from our territory."

The emperor says that when the decision of this council of war was made known to the government in Paris, it excited an animated opposition. "Paris," it was said, "is in a perfect state of defence; its garrison is numerous. The army of Châlons ought to be employed in breaking the blockade of Metz; the national garde mobile would endanger the tranquillity of the capital; the character of General Trochu inspires no confidence; in fact, the return of the emperor to Paris would be very ill interpreted by public opinion." Nevertheless, it was decided to carry out the orders of the emperor, whilst the propriety of succouring Bazaine was still insisted upon. But Marshal MacMahon informed the minister of war that the march towards Metz would be one of the greatest imprudence. He pointed out all the dangers of such a movement in the then position of the German armies, and declared his unwillingness to expose troops, still imperfectly organized, in making an extremely perilous flank march in the face of an enemy very superior in point of numbers; but he announced his intention to make his way towards Rheims, whence he could proceed either to Soissons or to Paris. "It is only," said he, "under the walls of the capital that my army, when rested and reconstituted, will be able to offer the enemy any serious resistance." "But," says the emperor, "the language of reason was not understood in Paris; it was wished, at all hazards, to give public opinion the empty hope that Marshal Bazaine would still be succoured; and Marshal MacMahon received from the council of ministers, to which had been joined the privy council and the presidents of the two Chambers, a most pressing injunction to march towards Metz. The government had taught Paris to expect the junction of the two marshals, and he was assured by them that every facility should be given him to carry out their wishes by sending him stores and more men."

Marshal MacMahon, a man, above all things, of duty, obeyed, and resolved to take the chance placed before him. Anything which resembled a sacrifice for the public good recommended itself to him; and he was flattered by the idea that, by attracting towards himself all the forces of the enemy, he was for the moment delivering the capital, and giving it time to finish its means of defence. As to the emperor, he says he made no opposition. "It could not enter into his views to oppose the advice of the government and of the empress regent, who had shown so much intelligence and energy in the midst of the greatest difficulties; although he perceived that his own influence was being completely nullified, since he was acting neither as head of the government nor head of the army. He decided to follow, in person, the movements of the army, fully sensible, however, that if he met with success all the merit would in justice be ascribed to the commander-in-chief; and that in case of a reverse, its responsibility would fall upon the head of the state."

But by what route, and with what means, was the operation to be accomplished? It was certainly known in the French capital that the Crown Prince was marching on Châlons in too great strength to be attacked; it was probably known that powerful corps were being moved from Metz to his aid; and it might be assumed that the other German armies were in possession of the main roads which led by Etain and Verdun to Châlons. An advance, therefore, by the direct routes to the Lorraine fortress was not to be thought of; such a movement could only lead to a battle against very superior forces, and the object was to unite with Bazaine and avoid an engagement with any part of the enemy except that besieging Metz. It seemed to the French leaders, the best way of accomplishing their purpose would be to advance northwards on the railway line from Rheims to Bethel, thence push on rapidly by forced marches through the Argonne hills and across the Meuse, reach Montmèdy and Longuyon, and descending from Thionville on Metz, and taking the beleaguering force in reverse, thus relieve the defenders of the fortress. This plan, undoubtedly, was not free from danger, for the march from Bethel to Montmèdy and Thionville would be long, and through a difficult country, in which the enemy might be able to gain and fall on the army's flank, when a vigorous attack might not only baffle the whole operation, but expose the French to serious defeat. But until Bethel was attained the movement would be necessarily masked; it was not likely that the Crown Prince would be in a position to arrest it; any German divisions upon his right would be insufficient by themselves to stop it; and Thionville once passed, Bazaine would co-operate with the relieving force, and engage the armies around Metz. Besides, was it to be assumed that the Crown Prince and the corps on his right, supposed to be on their way to Paris, would turn northwards to attack MacMahon? If they did, could they reach him in time? And was it not probable that they would advance at once to Châlons, would pause, hesitate, and do nothing, until it was too late to prevent the movement? Great risk there might be, but the plan if successful would justify and compensate it; for could the two French armies reunite at Metz, not only would Bazaine be set free, but the German armies there endangered, and the Crown Prince, advanced into the heart of France, would be exposed to serious disaster. It would then be the turn of the German commanders to be isolated and divided from each other; and what might not be hoped from the soldiers of France, burning to avenge unexpected defeats?

Such was the operation planned at Paris, and such, it is said, were the reasons for it. It is unfair to judge of strategy by the event; but in this instance it may be safely said that the scheme was at least hazardous. It is true that, at the time, the Crown Prince was many miles distant on the great road from Nancy to Châlons; and the result showed that if MacMahon's army had marched with even tolerable speed, the Crown Prince, though he moved northwards, would not have succeeded in reaching the French, at least until after they had crossed the Meuse. It is true, also, that the German corps detached from Metz to the Crown Prince's right, might have been unable, on the supposition that they alone were to assail MacMahon, to drive back the French; and, undoubtedly, the presence of Bazaine at Metz would necessarily detain a very large part of the first and second German armies on the spot, and prevent them from turning against another enemy. Nor can it be disputed that, could it have been accomplished, the French scheme was extremely promising—nay, that, as some admirers boasted, it might have been attended with as mighty results as the march from the Douro upon Vittoria. But in war, as in everything else, means must be proportioned to ends. Let it be conceded that up to Rethel the intended movement would not be understood; that the Crown Prince would be unable to stop it until the Argonnes and the Meuse had been passed; that the corps on his right could not alone defeat it, and that Prince Frederick Charles and General Steinmetz would not be strong enough to turn on MacMahon in force—the operation, nevertheless, was very daring. The French army, in advancing from Rethel by Montmèdy upon Metz, must have moved along an extensive arc of which the enemy held at all points, and in very superior strength, the chord; and, once checked, it must have been exposed to the most tremendous defeats. It was almost inevitable that it would be reached by the German corps on the Crown Prince's right, as it approached the region of the Argonnes and the Meuse, for these were already not far from that line; and if this were done, and time were gained for the Crown Prince's army to come up with it, a disastrous reverse was to be expected. Nay, more, supposing these perils were escaped, and that MacMahon made good his way to Montmèdy, there was nothing to prevent the Crown Prince from turning backward, and, having attained Metz, from effecting his junction with the other German armies and beating his enemy as he advanced by Thionville. In fact, the manoeuvre was an immense and most dangerous flank march by a disorganized and raw army, within certain range of a formidable adversary in possession of all the interior lines, and, when at all united, of overwhelming strength. Local circumstances, too, not only rendered this march especially liable to failure, but exposed Mac Mahon, if beaten, to ruin. His path lay across the Argonnes and the Meuse by indifferent roads and an intricate country, and the Meuse once crossed, he would be close to the frontier along the whole way from Montmèdy to Thionville. He was, therefore, going upon an enterprise in which he would probably be caught in flank, and brought to bay by superior numbers; and once defeated, he would most likely be cut off from the chance of retreat, or forced into the territory of Belgium, where his soldiers would be obliged to lay down their arms. As for the notion that the Crown Prince would go on to Paris, and would not turn round when he had ascertained the direction of the French marshal's movement, it is strange it could ever have been seriously entertained by those who had learnt by experience how the Prussian troops can march.

This was the operation to save France, and to annihilate the vain-glorious German princes, which paper strategists in Paris compared to the Alpine march that led to Marengo. Its designers may have had in mind the celebrated movement of Napoleon I. in 1814, when, leaving the allies to advance on Paris, he fell back towards his frontier fortresses to draw in their garrisons to his diminished army. But there was much difference between the two cases. Napoleon, when he retreated on St. Dizier, was not sufficiently strong to cover Paris, then, it must be remembered, wholly unfortified; he had reason to believe that the timid Schwartzenberg would pause and halt when the dreaded emperor was known to be threatening his rear; above all, he ran no risk of being destroyed on his way into Lorraine, and when he reached Metz he was absolutely certain to be rejoined by a considerable force which, after the glories of Montmirail, might at least have prolonged a doubtful contest. His movement, therefore, was compelled by his needs; in a military point of view it had a prospect of success; it did not place his army in danger; and had the allies been as feeble as of old, or had Paris held out for a single week, momentous consequences might have ensued. But MacMahon had more than sufficient means to defend Paris, now well fortified; his army was exactly in the condition for being so employed. The French government ought to have counted that the Crown Prince, as a matter of course, would turn on him as he marched northwards; especially ought they to have seen—and this is the distinctive point—his advance to Metz along the Belgian frontier would inevitably expose him to danger, and very probably lead to a catastrophe; and as the enterprise on which they ordered him was not dictated by any exigency, it was precisely that which should not have been attempted. It had hardly a reasonable chance of success, and it might involve France in a tremendous calamity; for it abandoned all direct communications with Paris to the mercy of the enemy, it drew the last available forces of France away from the centre towards the periphery, and placed them intentionally farther away from the centre than the enemy was already. Such a move might have been excusable, had it been undertaken with largely superior numbers; but here it was undertaken with numbers hopelessly inferior, and in the face of almost certain defeat. And what would that defeat bring? Wherever it occurred it would push the remnants of the beaten army away from Paris towards the northern frontier, where they might, as we have shown, either be driven upon neutral ground or forced to capitulate. MacMahon, in fact, by undertaking the move, deliberately placed his army in the same position in which Napoleon's flank march round the southern end of the Thuringian forest in 1806 placed the Prussian army at Jena. A force numerically and morally weaker was deliberately placed in a position where, after a defeat, its only line of retreat was through a narrow strip of country leading towards neutral territory or the sea. Napoleon forced the Prussians to capitulate by reaching Stettin before them. In the most favourable case, MacMahon's troops could hardly have done more than escape to the northern fortresses, Valenciennes, Lille, &c., where they would have been quite harmless, and France would at once have been completely at the mercy of the invader. Even without his explanation and that of the emperor on the subject, it could hardly have been believed that a commander of great experience and proved ability was the author of this scheme; but the pressure put upon him does not relieve him from the responsibility of so fatal a step. In his position he ought to have refused to lead his troops into peril so evident.

On Sunday, August 21, he broke up suddenly from the camp at Châlons, burning everything in it that could be of the least use to the enemy; and fell back with his forces to Courcelles, a few miles from Rheims. It was here that Count Palikao transmitted to him his final and pressing orders to effect a junction with Bazaine, and on the following day his army commenced its fatal march northwards. Its aspect and movements ought to have warned a prudent commander that it was unfit to undertake a perilous enterprise, in which celerity was indispensable to give a chance of success. The guns were ill-horsed and ill-mounted, the trains insufficient and out of order, the cavalry inferior and too few in number; and the infantry, made up of a medley of regiments, of raw levies, and of disheartened soldiers, was wanting in the real elements of power. The emperor's own description of the force was, that the first corps, formed principally out of regiments from Africa, that had given proof at Woerth of a heroic bravery which only the crushing numerical superiority of the enemy had forced to succumb, were still strongly impressed by that defeat and by the tremendous effects of the German artillery. They came away from the field of battle with dissatisfied and mutinous feelings, which the retreat upon Châlons, long and incessant marches, and physical privations, had still further aggravated. Marshal MacMahon did not shut his eyes to this, and considered that, before leading them again under fire, they needed repose and time to strengthen themselves after their defeat. These were the oldest of the French veterans. The renown which rightfully belonged to them as the soldiers of Africa, they had amply justified. The effect which their discouragement might have on the rest of the army was, therefore, doubly to be feared. Already, indeed, was the fifth corps specially feeling that effect. Exhausted, like the other, by forced marches from Bitsche across the Vosges, by Neufchateau and the Haute Marne, to the camp at Châlons, and having lost without a fight a portion of its equipments and almost all its luggage, this corps had an appearance of disorganization sufficient to inspire the most lively anxiety. The seventh corps, whose tardy organization was scarcely finished, had not encountered the same trials as the two foregoing; but in consequence of the long march from the rear, from Belfort, through Paris, to the camp of Châlons, it did not show such solidity as might have been desired. As to the twelfth corps, of very recent formation, it comprised elements of different degrees of value: the first division was composed of new regiments, upon which there was reason to depend; the second, of four marching regiments formed out of fourth battalions, with incomplete staff, and of soldiers who had never fired a gun; and, lastly, the third division was composed of four regiments of marines, which bore themselves bravely at Sedan, but which, little accustomed to long marches, dotted the roads with stragglers. Such were the troops upon whom was to be imposed a most difficult and dangerous campaign.

It was not until the afternoon of August 23 that MacMahon's army passed through Rheims. Anxious, and knowing that everything depended on speed, he addressed some columns as they toiled onwards, reminding them that French soldiers had marched thirty miles a day under the sun of Africa. The difference, however, was great between raids made by a few light regiments and the advance of a raw unwieldy mass; and though the marshal endeavoured to hurry them forward, he was confronted with almost insurmountable obstacles. Scarcely had the army made a march towards establishing itself at Bethniville, on the Suippe, when commissariat difficulties obliged him to re-approach the line of the railway. He made a movement on his left, and reached Rethel on the 24th, in order to obtain for his troops several days' subsistence. This distribution occupied the whole of the 25th.

From the commencement of the war to this time the Prince Imperial had accompanied his father; but in view of the exceptional dangers which were now threatening, Marshal MacMahon and the emperor both insisted that he should be removed from the theatre of war. He therefore set out for Mézières, and thence entered Belgium, where he was soon to learn the news of the capitulation of Sedan.

As the direction of the French movement could not now be concealed, at this point MacMahon made arrangements for marching with all possible rapidity. It may be doubted, however, whether Napoleon himself, at the head of the grand army, could have made the haste which the marshal designed with his raw and partly demoralized troops. He divided his forces into three parts, and having despatched about 20,000 men by the railway line from Rethel to Mézières, where they were to join an auxiliary corps coming up from Paris under General Vinoy, and to close on his rear when he had passed the Meuse—he advanced in two great columns by the parallel routes which lead through the Lower Argonnes, a hilly and thickly wooded district watered by the Meuse. In these dispositions there is nothing to blame: the fatal enterprise had been entered on, and we may believe that the marshal endeavoured to hasten forward as quickly as possible. He doubtless hoped to pass round the right flank of any force moving in the direction of Paris from Metz, and had gained, as he supposed, such a start on the Crown Prince as would enable him to evade pursuit by the latter, should he turn northwards after him. His right was at first directed on Montmèdy, an important station on the French line of railroad which runs along the Belgian frontier, and connects the fortresses of Mézières and Sedan with Longwy and Thionville, where it strikes the Moselle. His left went more westward towards Sedan; and though thus obliged to divide his columns for the sake of speed, he doubtless hoped, on reaching the railroad, to use it for the purposes of supply and concentration (it had, however, been cut by the Germans on the 25th), and to push on to the Moselle with, if not the whole, at least so much of his force as might enable him to make a powerful effort on the rear of the Prussians watching Bazaine. But to do this it was necessary to march first to the northeast, and finally a day more to the south, before he could come within such a distance of Metz as would enable him to signal to Bazaine; so that he was, in fact, attempting to get round three sides of an irregular quadrangle, within which were gathered, a week before, the eight Prussian corps which had fought the battle of Gravelotte.

It would have been scarcely possible to do this with the best troops in the world. As matters were, his army was altogether unequal to forced inarches, and moved at this critical moment with the sluggishness inherent in its defective organization. Encumbered with stragglers, badly pioneered, and checked by hindrances of every kind, it made hardly ten miles a day; and it was the 27th of August before its right column, still far from the Meuse, passed through Vouziers, and the left reached Le Chêne.

The defective composition of the army was shown not only in the slow progress it made, but in the want of discipline, and in a spirit of lawlessness and even mutiny, which augured very ill for the future. Before the departure from Châlons some of the stragglers commenced pillaging their own army, and selling the articles for a trifle. For more than two hours the railway station was pillaged by three or four hundred men from the corps of General de Failly, many of them belonging to the artillery. They broke or opened 150 goods, waggons, and threw out on the line, at the risk of accidents, barrels of wine and gunpowder, cartridges, shot, shell, biscuits, bales of clothing, coffee, salt meats, and other provisions. These they sold to hucksters who waited outside. Officers' trunks were also forced and plundered, and amongst the articles sold was part even of the emperor's baggage. His sheets went for four sous each; loaves of sugar brought only fifty centimes, and bales of coffee a franc. The railway servants attacked the plunderers with sticks, but were in return pelted with cartridges. The whole scene was described as being more heartrending to a soldier than a battle-field. Great excesses, of a somewhat similar character, were also committed at Rheims; and worst of all, scarcely any notice could be taken of such disgraceful conduct.

On the other hand, it must be admitted that the army altogether doubted the ability of its chiefs, became weary of their orders and counter-orders, and exasperated by the obvious want of a comprehensible plan. It fretted with impatience, and wore itself out by marches without advance. The weather was bad, and the distribution of food rare and insufficient. Nor was it ever known, for want of scouts, whether the enemy was marching away, or coming near. The headquarters on the 25th August were fixed at Bethel, and on the 27th they were at Chêne, evidently in hesitation. The want of a good and numerous cavalry became every hour more apparent.

In a note-book found on an officer of De Failly's corps who was killed at Sedan, under the date of August 26, it was said:—"There is no distribution of rations; we have, however, reserve biscuits to last us to the 28th. . . August 27. Awakened at three a.m. An order from the commander-in-chief that we are to march against the enemy. The positions each division has to take are distinctly indicated by the names of the villages. We start in the same order as yesterday; but the whole day is spent in marches and countermarches, very trying, and, as we learn afterwards, quite unnecessary. Our general of division (Guyot de Lespart), not conforming to orders, wandered à l'aventure, with no other result than that of exhausting and greatly discontenting his troops. Both men and horses are quite worn out by marching over tilled ground, softened for several days by almost incessant rain. In a village we pass through the inhabitants give all the bread and other food they have to our soldiers, some of whom were absolutely begging for it. On our arrival at Bois-les-Dames we see on all sides uhlan videttes, against which we are forced to send out riflemen. The uhlans go to and fro, in full gallop, over the very places on which we intended to take up our bivouac."

Leaving MacMahon for a short time, we must now turn again to the Germans. From the moment when the battle of Gravelotte had shut up Bazaine in Metz, MacMahon's army was the next object kept in view, not only by that of the Crown Prince, but by all other troops which could be spared from before Metz. Within two days of the battle of the 18th, a great force of landwehr had reached the fortress to fill up the losses in the late engagements, and a considerable part of the regular troops was thus set free for new operations. A fresh army was placed under the command of the Crown Prince of Saxony, and detached from Metz about the 19th of August, to co-operate with the Crown Prince of Prussia, and join his right wing on his way to Châlons. It was composed of the Prussian guards, of the twelfth Saxon corps, and of the fourth German corps (the latter had not taken part in the battles at Metz), altogether about 70,000 or 80,000 men in the highest state of efficiency; and it was advanced beyond Verdun upon the Meuse with the view of ultimately attaining Châlons by the line of Clermont and Ste. Menehould.

The Saxon corps under Prince George, with which went the Crown Prince of Saxony's headquarters, did not receive orders to move westward from before Metz as part of the fourth army until the 22nd. At the close of the fourth day's march the headquarters were at Jubecourt, six miles from Clermont, in the centre of the Southern Argonnes, and nearly fifty miles in a direct line from the position quitted before Metz. During these four days the fourth army had marched almost wholly on cross-roads, made the passage of the Meuse, and lost some time as well as some lives in a rash attempt upon Verdun, where finding their first attack repulsed, they did not choose to waste time in minor operations.

The position of this fourth army, owing to the promptitude it had displayed, fully answered the masterly design of General von Moltke, since it was ready to move on towards Paris on lines parallel to those followed by the Crown Prince, whose main body was at Bar-le-Duc, two days' march to the south. Thus any position to oppose him taken up by MacMahon would have been imperilled by this fourth army. If he fought at Châlons he could be opposed by both armies, and, if defeated, pushed back to Paris; and if he retired on Paris without fighting, the two crown princes, moving side by side, would follow him with overwhelming forces. On the other hand, should he make, as he did make, the desperate attempt to slip past them, a two days' march northward would plant the fourth army directly in his way, and close the defiles of the Northern Argonnes until the third army came in on his flank.

Meanwhile the king, with a small escort, had set off to join the Crown Prince, his son, by Ponta-Mousson and Commercy. The weather about this time was unusually inclement for the season—being very cold, and heavy rain falling almost incessantly. This caused the Germans much suffering, as they never carry tents. Some of them had slept for three weeks on the wet ground, in potato fields, or under hedges. They had no blankets—nothing but their cloaks, and up till then, some straw. From the scarcity of forage, however, they were now denied even that luxury.

On the morning of the 26th of August the king and the Crown Prince had their headquarters at Bar-le-Duc, still at a considerable distance from Châlons. The mass of the third German army was before Bar-le-Duc, and to Ligny backwards, though its cavalry filled the whole of the adjoining region, and had even advanced beyond Châlons and taken possession of the town. This feat was performed by five Prussian dragoons and one officer. One of the privates rode into the town smoking his pipe with imperturbable coolness. The French General de Brehault, who had been quartered there with a small force of cavalry, had just previously withdrawn, doubtless in pursuance of orders. The mayor issued a proclamation, telling the citizens that, as they had no means of even checking the enemy's advance, they should keep quiet.

The presence of the king of Prussia at Bar-le-Duc, even if a single Prussian soldier had not made a mile's march beyond, was highly significant. It meant that, without firing a shot, the French armies had abandoned the line of the Meuse and the Argonne, just as they abandoned the line of the Moselle when they allowed the Crown Prince to occupy Nancy. Thus another of the natural defences of France had fallen without a blow, and the invaders of 1870 had already advanced farther than those of 1792 ever reached—farther than those of 1814 had attained before the great Napoleon had dealt some thundering strokes against their converging hosts.

The German commanders thought that MacMahon was awaiting them near the great camp of Châlons, or that he would fall back on Paris; and did not credit the rumour, already floating on the 25th, that he had gone north. But next day the report was confirmed, and the Prussian staff, in common with the rest of the world, understood what was meant by the premature declaration of Count Palikao in Paris, that a grand scheme had been formed by which the two French armies were to co-operate. Had the general conception been in any degree carried into effect, of drawing the Prussians near to Paris, and letting them pass by the army of MacMahon, so that he might fall straight on the rear of that before Metz, there would have been some excuse for this boast. As it was, it only had the effect of arousing the vigilance of the Germans.

We have said that on the 26th the rumour of MacMahon's northward movement was confirmed, by the capture of letters by the Prussian cavalry, and that on the morning of this day the German headquarters were advanced in the direction of Paris as far as the fine town of Bar-le-Duc. The road from Ligny to this place inclines to the north-west, so that the movement brought the Germans indirectly somewhat nearer Sedan, and it opened to them the best of the cross-roads which lead through the Argonnes district towards the passages of the Meuse near that town. The headquarters were but seventy miles due south of it that evening; and though MacMahon had broken up from Rheims, about the same distance to the south-west, four days before, he had made so little progress, that he was still to the west of the line on which the Germans would move when they marched northward, which on this very morning they were ordered to do. At night the headquarters of the king were at Clermont-en-Argonne, twenty-three or twenty-four miles distant.

Never, in fact, were plans better laid than those of the Crown Prince and the chief of his staff, General Blumenthal. Some days before, when it was thought possible, but scarcely probable, that MacMahon might attempt the movement he made, the whole manoeuvre of doubling up the French line by swinging round upon it, "left shoulders forward," was discussed at the prince's headquarters. It was calculated that, by a very rapid march, the fifth and eleventh Prussian corps, the Bavarians, and Würtemburgers, might effect such a concentration as would baffle the French should they attempt the relief of Metz. The sixth corps was scarcely able to get up in time, by any efforts, that is, to swing round in its wide circle to the westward; but it would be ready to guard the left flank of the Germans, and to act as a support to the Würtemburgers in case of need. Here was the trap ready laid. Here was a repetition of the shutting in of a French force northward of the main road such as had been effected at Metz. But this time it was even more serious for those who might be so shut in. The Belgian frontier was the rock ahead in case of defeat. Had the French been strong enough to have a well-appointed corps of observation, say 80,000 men, to the southward of Vitry, this wheeling round of the Prussians could hardly have been risked. But the Crown Prince disregarded the slight danger of an attack upon his rear by ill-organized militia, and with the sixth corps covering his left, more from necessity than choice, closed upon MacMahon.

On the 27th it was openly boasted of in Paris that MacMahon had gained at least forty-eight hours' start of the Crown Prince, and his coming success was firmly counted on by the imperialist cabinet, whereas, in reality, the whole scheme was foiled beforehand by Von Moltke's and General Blumenthal's prompt combination. The French government had overlooked the fact, that the corps forming the fourth army, numbering at this time on the lowest estimate 70,000 men, were immediately in his way. Moltke had directed them on the Argonnes between Verdun and Sedan. He knew that, owing to increased cultivation and improved roads, this historic district, which had once starved and ruined a Prussian force, might be as easily traversed by an army as any ordinary part of France. He was not afraid, therefore, of a repetition of the failure of 1792, and was only anxious that an opening should be left by which either MacMahon's or any other important body of troops should be left behind in the combined movement towards Paris.

As soon as the northward movement of the Crown Prince was decided on, intelligence was despatched to the fourth army, who were ordered to stay the enemy on the Meuse passages at all costs. On the 27th the Saxon corps was accordingly lining the river about Dun and Stenay, prepared to stop the passages, but their services were rendered unnecessary by the slowness of their enemy's movements.

MacMahon left Rheims on the 23rd, only a few hours later than the prince of Saxony quitted Metz. Mouzon, the point on the Meuse which he chiefly aimed at, is the same distance from the one starting point as the other. Yet five days afterwards the main body of the French were about Vouziers, scarcely half-way to that passage; whilst the Saxons had first gone past it on their way to Paris, then halted, and moved northward to the points on the Meuse next above it, making two sides of a large triangle, the French not having yet gone over half of the third side of one of similar extent. If in fighting, in the boldness of their cavalry, the activity of their staff, the cool firing of their infantry, and the skilful tactical use of their guns, the superiority of the Germans to their antagonists had been already proved; it only required the contrast now presented between the movements of the two armies to show, that in no point had the difference of training and moral feeling told more in favour of the invaders than in that of the marching, on which the elder Napoleon so often relied for his advantage over these very Germans. Quickness of movement, as in his earlier campaigns, and hardly less in those of the Confederate General Lee, has often made up for inferior numbers. But when combined with numerical majority, it leaves no chance to the weaker party.

The causes of the slowness of the French march towards Sedan have already been explained. The Germans, on the other hand, both those of the Crown Prince's army, who had accomplished the toilsome passage of the Vosges and the long direct movement to the valley of the Marne, and those under the prince of Saxony, who had just taken a share in the tremendous fight at Gravelotte marched with a speed, order, and endurance indicative at once of physical energy and high spirits and discipline. This will appear the more surprising to those who have not noticed the bodily activity of the heavy-looking youth of Germany, when it is remembered that more than a third of the infantry, *i.e.*, the two last years' recruits of the peace strength of the battalions, and nearly the whole of the *einjährige* volunteers who were suddenly called by the war to that real service which few of them were designed to share, were under twenty-two years of age, and had probably not reached the full limits of their muscular power. Whatever might be the respective merits of the Zundnadelgewehr and the Chassepot, there is no doubt that this dogged perseverance of the Germans in marching, and their utter indifference to fatigue, had in this instance done more than their steady fusillade to win success for their cause.

We have now shown the movements of the contending forces in the eventful period from the 20th to the 27th of August, but that with a map the reader may understand more clearly the important events which immediately followed, it may be as well to recapitulate very briefly their respective positions at this time. The new scene of hostilities to which the operations of the belligerents had so suddenly been transferred, may be described as an equilateral triangle, whose sides are about sixty miles long, and whose angles are marked by Rheims and Verdun at the base, and by a spot just within Belgian territory not far from Bouillon at the apex. The sides are formed by the road and railway from Verdun by Ste. Menehould and Suippes, to Rheims, on the south; the road and railway from Rheims, by Bethel, to Mézières, on the west; and the course of the Meuse from Verdun, by Dun and Stenay, to Sedan, on the east. From Suippes a road runs northward to Attigny and Mézières; and from Ste. Menehould another road runs parallel by Monthois as far as Vouziers, where it diverges on the left to Bethel, and on the right to Le Chêne and Sedan. These routes are crossed by only one main road, leading from Bethel to Vouziers; but there it sends off branches to Stenay and Montmèdy by Le Chêne on the north and Buzancy on the south, and to Verdun by Grand Prè and Varennes; the two lower roads diverging at La Croix aux Bois, a few miles east of Vouziers. When Marshal MacMahon quitted Rheims on the 23rd he marched north-eastward to Rethel, and thence eastward to Vouziers, pursuing his way towards the Meuse both by the routes of Le Chêne and of Buzancy, which form a loop, and meet again at Laneuville-sur-Meuse, just opposite Stenay, and some twelve miles from Montmèdy. Thus his main columns might have been expected to strike the Meuse about midway on the eastern side of our triangle, with subsidiary columns directed along the country roads that lead from the eastern side of the Argonne forest to Mouzon on the north, and to Dun on the south of Stenay, all three places commanding the passage of the river.

Of the triangle we have described, two sides—the base and the eastern—were now occupied by the German troops, while the French, engaged far from their base on the western side, were several days' march farther from the capital than the invaders. The army of the Crown Prince, turning to its right from the roads direct to Paris, was now pouring into the triangle, and MacMahon in reality possessed but a very small portion of it towards the north and east. Every hour, too, that he failed to force his way across the Meuse to join Bazaine, saw him more narrowly hemmed in between the Germans advancing from the south and those holding him in check in the east. By this time, according to reasonable calculations, he should have been close to the Meuse; and, as a glance at the map will prove, he ought thus, on the line between Bethel and the river, to have escaped the third German army, about two marches still to the southward. This, however, does not place the strategy of the French in a very favourable degree; for before MacMahon could have reached Metz by Montmèdy and Thionville, he could not miss being intercepted by the Crown Prince of Saxony, or even by the Crown Prince of Prussia, and placed in a very critical position. He was still about twenty-five miles from the Meuse, with a somewhat intricate country between; and as he was altogether late, and must have expected that the German armies would endeavour to fall upon his flank, he ought to have spared no effort to advance speedily. Yet, between the 27th and the morning of the 29th, the right column of the French army had only its outposts at Buzancy, while the left, though its outposts touched Stenay, was only at Stonne and Beaumont, both columns spreading a long way backward; in other words, they were still a march from the Meuse, which they ought to have passed three days before, and their rearward divisions were yet distant. The German armies, from the 26th to the 29th, made astonishing exertions to close on MacMahon as he crossed towards the Meuse, and success was already within their grasp. The force of the Crown Prince of Saxony, in two columns, had reached the Meuse at Dun on the 27th, and was thus in a position to arrest and retard the vanguard of the French whenever it attempted to cross the river. Meanwhile the army of the Crown Prince of Prussia, hastening forward by Varennes and Grand Prè, and to the left by Senuc and Suippe, had arrived close to the line of march of MacMahon's right column, and by the evening of the 28th had occupied it about Vouziers. A step farther, and this immense army would be upon the positions of the luckless French, who, assailed in flank and rear by superior numbers, could not fail to be involved in terrible disaster.

We are, however, slightly anticipating the course of events, for as early as Saturday, the 27th, the opposing forces came into collision at Buzancy, on the southern road by which the French were marching from Vouziers to Stenay. It was, however, only a sharp and brilliant cavalry combat between four squadrons of the third Saxon regiment, one squadron of the eighteenth uhlans, and a Saxon battery, on the one side, and six French squadrons, detached from De Failly's corps to cover the cross roads, on the other. The victory was with the Germans, who completely cut up the twelfth regiment of French chasseurs and took its commanding officer prisoner. It was now evident that the whole French army was very near, and every exertion was made by the Germans to close with it. On this day, too, MacMahon, observing that the enemy so completely surrounded him, felt more than ever satisfied that it would be impossible to carry out the plan which had been prescribed to him at Paris; and to save, if possible, the sole army which France had at her disposal, he accordingly resolved to turn back in a westerly direction. He immediately gave orders to this effect, and sent the following despatch to the superior commandant at Sedan:—

"LE CHÊNE, *August* 27, 3.25 P.M.

"I beg you to employ all possible means for forwarding the following despatch to Marshal Bazaine:—

"*Marshal MacMahon, at Le Chêne, to Marshal Bazaine.*

"Marshal MacMahon warns Marshal Bazaine that the Crown Prince's arrival at Châlons forces him to carry out his retreat on the 29th on Mézières, and thence to the west, unless he hears that Marshal Bazaine's retreating movement has commenced."

The same evening he sent the annexed telegram to the Count Palikao, at Paris, in which it will be seen he predicts almost the very fate which was so soon to overtake his army:—

"LE CHÊNE, 27th of *August*, 8.30 P.M.

"The first and second armies, more than 200,000 men, blockade Metz, chiefly on the left bank. A force, estimated at 50,000 men, is established on the right bank of the Meuse, to obstruct my march on Metz. Intelligence received announces that the Crown Prince of Prussia's army is moving to-day on the Ardennes with 50,000 men. It must be already at Ardeuil. I am at Le Chêne with rather more than 100,000 men. Since the 9th I have no news of Bazaine; if I attempt to meet him I should be attacked in the front by a part of the first and second armies, which, favoured by the woods, can deal with a force superior to mine, and at the same time attacked by the Crown Prince of Prussia's army, cutting off all line of retreat. I approach Mézières to-morrow, whence I shall continue my retreat, according to events, towards the west."

In reply to this, the government sent a telegram to the emperor at eleven o'clock the same night, telling him that if they abandoned Bazaine there would certainly be a revolution in Paris, and they would themselves be attacked by all the enemy's forces. "Paris," continued Count Palikao, "will protect itself against the external attack. The fortifications are completed. It seems to me urgent that you should rapidly reach Bazaine. It is not the Crown Prince of Prussia who is at Châlons, but one of the princes, the king of Prussia's brothers, with an advanced guard and considerable cavalry forces. I have telegraphed to you this morning two pieces of information which indicate that the Crown Prince of Prussia, feeling the danger to which your flank march exposes his army and the army which blockades Bazaine, has changed his course and marches towards the north. You have at least thirty-six hours' start of him, perhaps forty-eight hours. You have before you only a part of the forces which blockade Metz, and which, seeing you withdraw from Châlons to Rheims, had extended themselves towards the Argonne. Your movement on Rheims had deceived them. Like the Crown Prince of Prussia, everybody here has felt the necessity of extricating Bazaine, and the anxiety with which you are followed is extreme."

The emperor admits that he could unquestionably have set this order aside, but "he was resolved not to oppose the decision of the regency, and had resigned himself to submit to the consequences of the fatality which attached itself to all the resolutions of the government." As for MacMahon, he again bowed to the decision intimated to him from Paris, and once more turned towards Metz.

These orders and counter-orders naturally occasioned further delay, and the French headquarters had reached no further than Stonne on the 28th. The intention of MacMahon was to reach Stenay, and thence Montmèdy, but, as has been seen, the Germans were in strength in the first of these towns two days before. The mistake, too, which had been committed in the first part of the campaign was again repeated; for the different French corps, isolated from each other, as we shall see, were attacked separately, and easily defeated.

On August 28, Vouziers, an important crossing of roads in the Argonnes, was in possession of the Germans, two of whose squadrons charged and took Vrizy, a village situated between Vouziers and Attigny, which was occupied by infantry. The defending force, including two officers of MacMahon's staff, were taken prisoners; a feat of which there is but one previous example in modern history, the taking of Dembe Wielkie by Polish cavalry from Russian cavalry and infantry, in 1831.

On Monday, August 29, De Failly occupied the country between Beaumont and Stonne, on the left bank of the Meuse; while the main body of the French army, under MacMahon in person, had crossed the river, and were encamped on the right bank at Vaux, between Mouzon and Carignan, and on the morning of the 30th the emperor telegraphed to Paris that a brilliant victory might be expected. MacMahon's position was in a sharp wedge of country formed by the confluence of the rivers Meuse and Chiers, and it was his intention to advance towards Montmèdy. The other part of his army was close to the river on its left bank.

The troops opposed to MacMahon's force consisted of both the third and fourth German armies, the former commanded by the Crown Prince and the king of Prussia, and the latter by the Crown Prince of Saxony. It may, perhaps, be useful if we here recall to mind the corps of which these armies were composed. The third army comprised the fifth corps, from Posen; the sixth, from Silesia; and the eleventh, from Hesse and Nassau; and the first and second corps of the king of Bavaria's army, with the Würtemburg division. The first Bavarian corps was commanded by General von der Tann. The army of Prince Albert of Saxony was formed by taking three corps, each of about 30,000 men, from the second German army, that of Prince Frederick Charles, which had been found larger than was required at Metz. These corps were:—(1.) The Prussian guards, under Prince Augustus of Würtemburg; (2.) the fourth, composed of men from the Saxon provinces of Prussia, and the Saxon duchies of Weimar, Coburg-Gotha, Altenburg, and Meiningen, under General von Alvensleben; and (3.) the twelfth, which consisted of subjects of the kingdom of Saxony, led by their Crown Prince. The last was the corps which fought under that leader against the army of Prussia in July, 1866, at Gitschin and Königgrätz, in Bohemia. Of the whole German force assembled on the Meuse, it will thus be seen that two Bavarian and one Saxon army corps, numbering scarcely less than 90,000 men in all, were not soldiers of the kingdom of Prussia, but served the other German states, which, having vainly opposed her in 1866, were now allied with her.

The two Bavarian corps of the third army were sent to join the twelfth corps of the fourth; these together marched up the left bank of the Meuse, while the guards and fourth corps of the fourth army marched up the right bank. The fifth and eleventh corps of the third army were on August 29 at Stonne, seven miles west of Beaumont; while the twelfth corps of the fourth army, joined with the first Bavarians, and having the second Bavarians advancing in their rear, were close to Beaumont.

BATTLE OF BEAUMONT.

Bearing in mind that the design of MacMahon was to move southward up the course of the river, but still if possible to keep possession of both its banks until he should arrive opposite Montmèdy, it will at once be perceived that an immediate collision was inevitable. Accordingly, the battle—or rather series of battles, for the fighting extended over three days—which was to decide whether or not he would reach Metz and liberate Bazaine, began in earnest a little before noon on Tuesday, August 30.

The French had been so careless in their movements that they were taken completely by surprise, especially on the left bank of the river near Beaumont. Here they were close to the very ground on which the right of the third German army was to unite with the left of the fourth. Had they been at all vigilant in their outlook towards the south, and strongly guarded the cross roads leading thence upon their right, their adversaries would hardly have dared to effect the junction of the third and fourth armies by a single road close to ground held by De Failly's corps, and that afternoon at least might have been gained to MacMahon. The affairs at Buzancy and Vouziers on the preceding days should have roused a spirit of watchfulness in the most careless staff officer; but so confident was General Guyot, who commanded this division, that the Germans were not near him, that he omitted even the most ordinary precaution of placing outposts and sending out scouts in the woods immediately in his front. The first division of Von der Tann's Bavarians, admirably led by General Stefan, advanced along the road that runs directly north from Buzancy to Raucourt, passing through the village of La Besace, which is about three miles distant from the latter place. About half-a-mile on the Buzancy side of La Besace is a branch road leading to the right, and almost at right angles with the town of Beaumont, about three miles to the eastward. General Guyot's division was encamped on both sides of this road; and the Bavarians, learning from their scouts that the enemy was so near, made all their dispositions under cover of the woods. The French, simultaneously attacked with artillery from the heights behind the wood, and with infantry from the wood itself, were, as we have said, completely surprised; but yet they made a stout resistance, for after the fight the road was found lined on both sides with bodies— the Bavarians, for the most part, lying on the side nearest Buzancy, the French on that nearest Raucourt. When the Germans had driven them from the road, the French retreated—some in the direction of Raucourt, and some (the greater part) towards Beaumont itself. They were pursued in both directions; those who had gone towards Beaumont were followed into the place, which was at the same time attacked along another fine of road leading to the same point, and, after a very severe struggle, occupied by the Germans. The French made a desperate stand at the entrance to the town, firing from windows and from behind walls, and taking advantage of every possible kind of cover. After retiring into the market-place they renewed the contest, inflicting heavy losses on their opponents. Ultimately, however, the Germans drove them out of the town, and pushed them past La Besace towards Raucourt. The whole country between these places is a succession of hills and dales. Here and there the hills are very high, and in many parts thickly wooded; whilst the dales form deep valleys. This is the general character of the district for miles around, in every direction; and it was, therefore, open to the weaker side either to defend itself on the heights, to seek the shelter of the woods, or to endeavour to march unobserved along the fines of the valleys. To prevent the complete success of either of these courses, orders were given to the Bavarian cavalry to observe the woods; the infantry went down into the valleys, and up the hills on the other side; and the artillery threw their shells over the heads of their infantry into the dales beyond.

The advance of the first Bavarians in the centre of the line had the effect of turning the French right rear, which had taken up a strong position at Stonne, and had withstood, with apparent firmness, up to that time the advance of the Crown Prince of Prussia's left columns, the fifth and eleventh corps. The fourth and twelfth Saxon corps, belonging to the fourth army, co-operated with the Bavarians on their right, nearer the Meuse; and aided in driving the French from Beaumont, on to the passage at Mouzon, whither De Failly now pressed to put the river between himself and his enemies. He succeeded in crossing by the bridge at Mouzon, and effected a junction with MacMahon on the other side. In the evening, after a short cannonade against the fourth Prussian corps and the Bavarians, the French retreated from Mouzon in the direction of Sedan; and the Germans then gave up the pursuit, but not before they had captured twelve pieces of cannon, six mitrailleuses, and several thousand prisoners.

The following extract from the diary of an officer of the chasseurs de Vincennes, who was fatally wounded at Sedan, presents a striking picture of the causes that led to this great disaster, and the state of the army near him, as well as of the retreat itself:—

"August 30.—We arrive at Beaumont, a hilly and woody country, at four a.m. The men were utterly exhausted by the march, by hunger, and above all by want of sleep. There is no possibility of bringing order into the ranks. The presence of the generals was indispensable, but none of them were to be seen on the spot, and the soldiers fall down asleep, without guard, without a single sentry. The sight was most lamentable; but the enemy being supposed to be still in his old position, and the desire for rest being invincible, every, one brings his thoughts to silence as best he can. At nine or ten a.m. the men begin to wake up. A distribution of bread is going on. Six or eight loaves are given to each company, and 150 men must be content with them. This is all they have to restore their strength after endless marching, with only a few hours' sleep. But scarcely has the bread been swallowed, when a lively fusillade begins from the neighbouring wood, some 400 mètres distant. A couple of minutes pass in consideration as to what it can mean, when several shells, falling into the very heart of the camp, leave no more doubt about the matter. The whole camp seizes its arms in disorderly fashion; the officers do their best to give some kind of organization to the first movements; the artillery is soon at work, and the battle begins. But a tremendous panic arises in the village, crowded with unarmed soldiers, who were gone from the camp in search of provisions. A frantic rush begins in the direction of Mouzon; and the flying mass would naturally have drawn with it a part of the troops already in line on this side of the village, if the officers had not intervened, pistols in hand. The generals, just as much surprised as the troops, presently come to their senses. They take the command; the retreat is gradually organized, and on reaching rather elevated ground we come out from under the intolerable fire. The cannonading begins to be less intense; and a discussion arises between General de Failly and his *chef d'état major*, General Besson, with reference to the advisability of changing our position. The latter uses very strong language in support of his opinions, but the position remains the same. Ten minutes after this discussion the Germans appear on our left flank, and open fire on us at a distance of 1000 mètres. Such is the morale of our troops now, that at the very first shot from this side infantry and artillery break front and begin to ran away—the former into the wood, the latter into the plain close to it, leaving several guns in the impracticable part of the ground. However, the batteries soon regain another hill, open fire, and begin to protect a little the retreat of the infantry, which takes the direction of Mouzon. It is six o'clock, and we see on the height the seventh corps appearing on the left flank of the Prussians, while a part of the twelfth corps was found by us in the plain to which we were rushing. These two corps now take our place in the struggle with the enemy. The enemy had, however, already established his batteries, some fifty guns strong, on the same hill where a few moments ago our artillery stood. These batteries send death into all the lines of the newly arrived forces, and compel them to retreat. The seventh corps retires to the position whence it came to our aid, while the twelfth takes the direction of the bridge of Mouzon, the cavalry and artillery having, happily enough, found a ford in the river, so that the bridge is mainly left for the use of the infantry. But still what confusion prevails! What a lamentable spectacle! It is the last rout of the day; and it is the more painful for our corps because we witness it in the mere capacity of onlookers. Soon in the background of the sad picture rises to heaven a large black cloud of smoke. The fire has commenced which must level to the ground the unhappy village of Mouzon. We see war now in all its cruel reality. Such was the day of the 30th, which will never be forgotten by me, and the result of which must be a sufficient punishment for the general with whom rests the responsibility of the disaster. But what is our corps to do now? Is it to camp on its position, or to move? If it is to move, in what direction? The generals decide that they will start at once, and the soldiers are to march again all night. Thus, after several days' fatigue, we have two consecutive nights of marching, with a day's desperate fighting between, and with no other refreshment than the bread distributed at Beaumont. We are retiring in the direction of Sedan. Fearful and miserable night! Our men fall asleep by the side of the road, and to awaken them is impossible. Towards two a.m., amid the obscurity of a dark night, we meet on the junction of two roads the first and the twelfth corps. They left their positions at midnight, and are also marching towards Sedan. Here disorder reaches its climax. Men, horses, and ammunition waggons are almost heaped upon one another in dreadful confusion. No possibility of moving, no possibility of seeing anything; and, notwithstanding this, almost dead silence reigns over this enormous incoherent mass. A terrible silence it was, at which one shudders to think. Malediction upon those who are responsible for all this!"

BATTLE OF CARIGNAN.

On the right bank of the Meuse another contest, far more bloody and resolute, had been going on at the same time as the action between the Bavarians and De Failly's corps on the opposite side. Here the main body of the French army, under Marshal MacMahon, moved gaily forward in the morning from its camp at Vaux, between Mouzon and Carignan, hoping to reach Montmèdy, about twelve miles distant, the same day. Their left wing was, however, surprised on the march between Carignan and Stenay, by the cavalry of the Prussian guards, aided by their horse artillery, and before they could effectually resist the unexpected onset, they were forced to retire on the heights where they had encamped on the previous night. In this emergency MacMahon displayed great skill and decision. The return to Vaux was effected in good order; and the marshal then rallied the whole of his army, keeping the Germans on the other side of the Meuse in check, meantime, by a deceptive show of force on the river banks. The heights of Vaux were obstinately defended by the French, who in this separate affair considerably outnumbered their opponents. Indeed, in the middle of the day, they gained some advantages, and in all probability would have been able to hold their own independently; but they were compelled to retreat by the threatening of their flank and rear, for they heard the thunder of the guns on the other side approach nearer and nearer to Mouzon, as the converging forces of Von der Tann and the Prussians of the fourth army drove De Failly pell-mell towards the bridge at that place. As night came on, the French retired through Carignan, two miles from Vaux on the road to Sedan; and thus the issue of the battles on both banks of the river was the same, though the last hours of the combat near Carignan were desperate in the extreme, and there was great slaughter on both sides. The French cavalry, cuirassiers, and chasseurs, suffered considerably. At five o'clock the emperor and his staff were at Carignan; and the cannonade, which had been considerably increasing for two hours, was at its height. About an hour later the emperor left for Sedan, and the artillery fire entirely ceased soon after eight o'clock. A firm belief in a success had been entertained all the afternoon in the little town of Carignan. The presence since the evening before of the fine army of Marshal MacMahon, the arrival of the emperor, the officers of his household looking out for night accommodation, and the encampment of the troops at Vaux, had all combined to inspire the inhabitants with confidence; so that, notwithstanding the engagement was so near, no anxiety was felt, and a victory was looked for as a matter of course. But when in the evening the emperor, who had made arrangements to sleep at Carignan, was seen leaving the town suddenly, followed by the couriers and suite, and the cannonade was heard approaching nearer and nearer, a complete panic seized the population. Masses of soldiers now arrived, and the people began to flee in every direction, though the Prussians did not enter the town till next morning. The emperor arrived at Sedan during the night of Tuesday. Nothing would have been easier for him than to have gone on to Mézières, and thus have secured his personal safety. The proposition to do so was made to him; but he rejected it, desirous not to separate himself from the army, and determined to share its fate, whatever it might be. On the morning of the 31st the following proclamation was issued to the troops:—

"Soldiers!—The opening events of the war not having been fortunate, I determined to set aside all personal considerations, and give the command of our armies to the marshals more particularly indicated by public opinion.

"Up to the present time success has not crowned your efforts; nevertheless, I learn that the army of Marshal Bazaine has re-formed under the walls of Metz, and that of Marshal MacMahon met yesterday only a slight reverse. There is, then, no reason to be discouraged. We have prevented the enemy from penetrating to the capital, and all France is rising to drive back her invaders. Under these serious circumstances—the empress worthily representing me in Paris—I have preferred the role of soldier to that of sovereign. No effort shall be spared by me to save our country. It still contains, thank God! men of courage; and, if there are cowards, the military law and public contempt will mete out justice to them.

"Soldiers, be worthy of your old reputation! God will not abandon our country if all do their duty.

"Given at the Imperial Headquarters, at Sedan, August 31, 1870.

"NAPOLEON."

This proclamation, which there was barely time to distribute, was the last appeal which the emperor addressed to his soldiers.

In judging of MacMahon's conduct on this occasion, it should always be remembered that he had to fight at a grievous disadvantage, from being compelled to cover the retreat of De Failly; and that, notwithstanding this, he succeeded in keeping his enemy in check for some time, a gleam of his well-known tactical skill being observable in the manner in which he masked his retiring movement, so disposing his forces that the commander of the fifth German corps reported to the Crown Prince of Prussia that he was in the presence of at least three complete divisions of the enemy, and was not strong enough to attack! Yet at that moment MacMahon was withdrawing his troops rapidly across the Meuse to the neighbourhood of Sedan; and had he not so skilfully hid his movements by the disposition of his artillery and mitrailleuses, and so deceived his assailants, his whole army must then have been utterly routed.

Thus ended the fatal 30th of August. The vanquished troops lost twenty guns, including several mitrailleuses, an encampment, and about 7000 prisoners, besides a large amount of warlike material. The substantial success of the victors consisted in thwarting the attempt of MacMahon to move upon Metz, and in forcing the French back upon a small fortress only seven or eight miles from the neutral frontier of Belgium. Well might the Prussian official report of the affair state, that "after this engagement it became probable that the French army of the north was fast approaching a final catastrophe!"

The Germans were now in line from Stonne across the Meuse, near Mouzon, to Carignan. The greater part of their army remained on the left bank, but the forces of the Crown Prince of Saxony, having crossed the river, advanced beyond Mouzon in the direction of Carignan and Sedan. Early in the night and at daybreak the French corps which had been routed at Mouzon fell back along the right bank of the Meuse in a state of panic and demoralization, throwing their arms and accoutrements into the stream; and were stopped only when they had passed the Chiers, a deep narrow river which, flowing to the north-west, falls into the Meuse near Remilly, about three miles above Sedan. They crossed this stream by the bridge at Douzy, four or five miles from Sedan. At the same time the other French corps which had retreated before the Crown Prince of Saxony, retired from Carignan behind the Chiers, and effected a junction with their defeated comrades. The two corps commanded by Ducrot and Lebrun, who were to the eastward on the 30th, being the nearest, came in first; Douay's and De Failly's following them, and approaching Sedan by all the roads from the south. The whole army then took up its position about a mile and a half from Sedan, on the strong heights above Bazeilles, covering the approach to that fortress.

Such were the positions of the contending hosts on the morning of Wednesday, the 31st August; and MacMahon had now to make up his mind speedily to some decisive course. To force his way onwards with troops demoralized by their rapid retreat, and by the defeat which had cost them thousands of prisoners and many guns, was not now to be thought of. The Germans, indeed, held Mouzon and Carignan, the two points through which he had attempted to pass eastward, and so completely barred the road to Montmèdy. There remained, therefore, only three courses—either to attack the enemy before he could further concentrate; to attempt to slip from him by a rapid flank march on Mézières; or to continue solely on the defensive. The first would have been the natural course, had mutual confidence existed between the marshal and his army. It would have been in keeping with the old reputation and tactics of the French service; and if conducted with skill, there seemed in theory no reason why a bold attack should not have severed the extended line held by the enemy, and crushed the portion assailed. MacMahon's army was concentrated behind the Chiers; the Crown Prince of Saxony was alone before him; and the Crown Prince of Prussia was on the left bank of the Meuse, at some distance, and with the river between them. The French general had about 100,000 men. Breaking out with these he might have fallen on the Crown Prince of Saxony, who had not more than 70,000 or 80,000, and endeavoured to crush him and extricate himself before the Crown Prince of Prussia could have crossed the Meuse, and overwhelmed him with superior numbers. But MacMahon was an old enough soldier to know thoroughly the truth of the maxim, that in war "the moral force is to the physical as three to one," and to feel that his troops wanted the discipline, energy, and heartiness necessary for any such sudden combination. He should, therefore, have instantly despatched Ducrot or Lebrun to seize and guard the passages of the Meuse below Sedan, and, sacrificing perhaps a single corps to this duty, have filed the rest of the army at once behind Sedan on Mézières, by the roads on the north side of the river. Instead of this the marshal, feeling that the French army was not equal to a great offensive movement, took up a position strictly defensive. He certainly was not aware that the whole army of the Crown Prince of Prussia was close to his right flank, though on the other side of the Meuse. He had therefore some reason to hope that, by compelling the army of the Crown Prince of Saxony immediately in his front, and the only one, as he thought, that was then near him, to attack his troops while they occupied a strong position, he might yet be able to defeat the enemy, and retrieve his late disaster. Subsequent events proved that he really took the most fatal course of all; for he was obliged to stand his ground against immensely superior numbers, round a mere nominal fortress, not large enough to shelter his troops if beaten, nor powerful enough in armament to affect the fortune of the battle, and commanded in every direction by hills within the range of modern field guns. Yet the position he took, though essentially faulty in these and other respects, and not as well occupied as it might have been, had, nevertheless, certain strong natural advantages, and in his forlorn situation was the best he could have chosen. Behind the Chiers, and in the angle formed between that stream and the course of the Meuse, a series of heights intersected by ravines, with hills and intricate ground between, stretch from Givonne on the Belgian frontier, to Sedan on the Meuse; and, with the villages of Balan and Bazeilles in front, on the main road from Sedan to Carignan, make, with the Chiers, like a fosse, before them, a succession of formidable lines of defence to an enemy advancing directly against them. Givonne, resting on masses of forest which spread densely across into Belgium, affords a good position to an army's wing, which could not there be easily outflanked; and Sedan, on the other side, presents advantages 'in many respects as a defensive point to another wing. The town is on the right bank of the Meuse, with a small suburb on the left; and in passing it the river forms a huge loop, flowing to the north-west, and returning in a southerly direction, opposing a kind of double barrier to an enemy assailing it from that quarter. Behind Sedan, and on its side of the loop, the eminences near Floing and La Garenne, crowned with woods and villages, command the river, and in case of an attempt to force it, could be stoutly defended against an attack to the rear of the town.

Whilst MacMahon rested on the 31st, and strove to strengthen the open hills to the west of Sedan with fieldworks, the combined armies of the two crown princes extended right and left to inclose his position. Their numbers, including the sixth corps, which was still behind, just doubled his; and the moral superiority they had gained enabled them to dispense with large reserves, and to extend on a wide curve, twelve miles long, outside of and parallel to the enemy's position. The third German army executed the following movements on the 31st. The first Bavarian corps marched by Raucourt to Remilly. The eleventh Prussians proceeded from Stonne to Chemery and Cheveuge, with orders to stop on the left bank of the Meuse, and encamp opposite Donchery, a little town on the other side of the river. The fifth Prussian corps followed the eleventh, and the second Bavarians the first. The Würtemburgers likewise moved on to the Meuse by way of Vendresse and Boutencourt. The routes prescribed to the different portions of this army thus converged on Sedan, while the Prussian guards of the fourth army, after occupying Carignan in the morning, pressed forward to Douzy; the object being to surround the enemy, and compel him either to surrender, or to retreat beyond the Belgian frontier. As the latter contingency was considered very possible, it was provided by the order of the day, that in the event of the French not being immediately disarmed on the other side of the border, the German troops were to follow them into Belgium without delay. The second Bavarian corps and the Würtemburgers had no difficulty in carrying out their orders; but the fifth Prussian corps, which went by Chemery, and there defiled past the commander-in-chief, did not reach its allotted position till a late hour in the evening.

This day (Wednesday, the 31st) passed without any very important encounter, though a heavy cannonade was kept up at some points. At Remilly the first Bavarians fell in with the French troops; and, making a rash attack on Bazeilles, were driven back by Lebrun's corps with considerable loss. During this engagement, four or five batteries of the Prussian guns were sedulously employed in shelling the village, a suburb of Sedan, surrounded by gardens and trees, amidst which were a fine chateau and several handsome residences. The ill-fated village was set on fire in half-a-dozen places, and at one time burned so furiously all over that the French could not occupy it; and though the Bavarians seized it for a short period, they, too, were forced to retire. Fighting also commenced early in the morning, as the French were crossing the plain of Douzy; and for three hours this engagement extended over nearly four miles of country, between Douzy, Armigny, and Brevilly, about five miles from Carignan, in the direction of Sedan. Here also the French drove back the enemy, and ultimately occupied the heights whence, an hour before, the German artillery had made fearful havoc in their ranks. In the afternoon another attack by the Saxons on the left of MacMahon's position was likewise repulsed; and these partial successes so raised the hopes of the emperor, that he telegraphed to Paris that "all was going on well, and that a brilliant victory might be expected!" But that negligence which throughout the campaign had marked the conduct of the French officers, again caused their defeat. Not only had they omitted to destroy the bridge over the Chiers, as they fell back after their reverses on the 30th; but even now the cavalry which should have watched the passage of the river, were more than a mile away, so that the Germans were enabled gradually to cross unopposed; and turning the left of MacMahon's army, compelled the victorious right and centre to retreat. Thus the Germans recovered the advantage they had lost, and ere the night had fallen they had swung round their right to the north of Sedan, and neared the villages of La Chapelle and Givonne, which command the high road to Bouillon, twelve miles off, in Belgian territory, on the slopes of the Ardenne forest. The general object sought was, therefore, all but attained that day, and was fully accomplished early on the morrow, when the French army in Sedan was completely shut off from all the avenues by which it might have escaped; and nothing remained but the alternative of capitulation, or a resolute attempt to cut a way out through the forces of an enemy superior in numbers, and flushed with victory. In fact, MacMahon's position was much worse even than that of Bazaine at Gravelotte, on the 18th of August, a short fortnight before. Bazaine had in his rear a first-class fortress, with an entrenched camp, and more than two months' supply of provisions; while Sedan, a neglected second or third rate place of 15,000 inhabitants, had scarcely three day's food for MacMahon's army within its walls. So completely had the German troops got their prey in their power, that Von Moltke had been able to dispense with reserves, and throw his whole force, one corps alone excepted, in a vast circle round the French position, a tactical movement fully justified by the event, but which, against any but ill-led and very disheartened troops, might have been the ruin of the assailants.

CHAPTER XIV.

THE BATTLE OF SEDAN.

A LARGE army driven into a corner does not easily succumb. It took three desperate battles to teach Bazaine's troops that they were shut in before Metz; nor did the engagements of Beaumont and Carignan suffice to induce those of MacMahon to confess that they were hopelessly defeated. A fresh battle—the greatest and most bloody of all the series—had to be fought around Sedan before the French soldiers fully realized the disastrous position into which they had been driven. The situation in which MacMahon was placed was singularly curious. The fortresses of Mézières, Sedan, and Montmèdy were constructed to meet an invasion of France from the Belgian territory. A French army facing the north and resting on these fortresses, must have been the state of affairs anticipated when they were built. Yet now, at this very spot, was a French force with its rear to Belgium, standing an attack from an enemy operating from the interior of France. *L'homme propose, mais Dieu dispose.* Never surely were human plans more completely frustrated.

It was originally intended by the Germans to put off the decisive blow till the 2nd of September, to give a day's rest to the Saxon army, which had undergone considerable fatigue in their forced marches and fighting on the 30th and 31st of August. But between five and six o'clock in the evening of the 31st, as the king passed Chemery on his way to his headquarters at Vendresse, he held a consultation with the Crown Prince and Generals von Moltke and Blumenthal, when it was determined that the attack on Sedan, and the French lines between the Meuse and the Ardennes, should be undertaken on the ensuing day.

The plan of the battle-field which accompanies this chapter will make the situation of the opposing forces so clear to every reader, that it is only necessary here to point out, very briefly, the leading features of the country.

Sedan, a manufacturing town containing about 15,000 inhabitants, chiefly engaged in the woollen trade, is situated at one of the finest points of the valley of the Meuse, which runs close under the walls of the town. It is built in a hollow, commanded by heights about a mile off, which are crowned with forests and rise in terraces on either side of the river. On the right bank is a narrow strip of meadow-land by the waterside, which by a temporary overflow of the Meuse was converted into a broad sheet of water resembling a lake, artificially contrived to strengthen the military defences, and spreading a couple of miles on the south side of the town. On the same bank of the river, and a little to the left of Sedan, is an open plain, with the town of Donchery pleasantly situated in its centre. This plain is traversed by a slight elevation. To the right of it the Meuse makes an extraordinary bend or loop, inclosing a strip of land two miles and a half in length. In this peninsula, which is for the most part bare, lie the hamlets and mansions of Glaire, Villette, and Iges. Between Iges and Sedan, on the right bank of the river, is the village of Floing; and, further to the right, Illy and Givonne. The main road between Donchery and Sedan proceeds from a bridge at Donchery, and touches the village of Frénois. To the south-east are, or rather were, the large suburban villages of Balan and Bazeilles. Balan, the nearest to the city, indeed just outside the walls, is close to the sheet of water formed by the overflowing Meuse; and about a mile and a half further to the south, on the Carignan and Montmèdy high road, was the unhappy village, or small town, of Bazeilles, the birthplace of Marshal Turenne, and the scene of a battle in 1641 during the civil wars in France. Douzy, where the guards crossed the Chiers, is on the extreme right. Sedan is a fortress of the second class, the approaches to which are not, as at Metz and other places, defended by works and advanced forts. At this time, too, the supply of ammunition in the town was very deficient, and the armament altogether incomplete. Undoubtedly, in the time of the old field and siege guns, it was a strong fortress; but notwithstanding its walls, its gates, its fosses, and its series of earthworks studded with guns of position, it is now to all intents an open town to modern artillery occupying the heights around. The fortifications are high, but these hills are still higher; so that, from the moment the German artillery possessed itself of them, Sedan was as good as taken. It is generally admitted that when the capitulation took place, successful resistance was impossible, and that to have prolonged the struggle would have been to insure the destruction of the town with all its inhabitants.

On the evening of Wednesday, the 31st of August, the German armies had reached their prescribed positions, and before dawn on Thursday the commanders reported that on each side everything was complete. The troops on the left stood ready to cross the Meuse; those on the right, under the Crown Prince of Saxony, were waiting for orders to assume the offensive; and from one end of the position to the other they were able to close in on Sedan at the shortest notice. On the Meuse, opposite Bazeilles and Balan, the first and second Bavarians formed the right wing of the Crown Prince of Prussia's army; next them was that of the Crown Prince of Saxony, the fourth and twelfth corps, facing towards Moncelle, Daigny, and Villers Cernay, while the guards were marching towards La Chapelle. To the west of Sedan was the Crown Prince of Prussia's fifth and eleventh corps, the former moving towards Fleigneux, the latter to St. Menges and Floing. The loop formed by the Meuse rendering escape in that direction impossible, no troops were posted between St. Menges and Donchery; but at Dom-le-Mesnil, a little to the left of Donchery, the Würtemburgers were stationed, who not only covered the rear against sallies from Mézières, but watched the road against any attempt of the French to break through in that direction. As MacMahon's right was, however, completely outflanked by the fifth and eleventh corps, none of his troops appeared in that quarter. Towards the close of the battle, the Würtemburg artillery was brought up to take part in the bombardment which was to reduce the enemy to terms; but it only arrived in time to learn that further proceedings had been stayed by a flag of truce. Count Stolberg's second, and the fourth and sixth cavalry divisions under Prince Albrecht, were at different points in the plain of Donchery, covering and connecting the German right wing.

Before night closed in on Wednesday, MacMahon, who, allowing for the losses of the previous two days, had little more than 100,000 men and about 440 guns, must at last have realized the extent of his peril. The prince of Saxony, with his whole army, was in his front, beyond the Chiers; and to his right, on the other bank of the Mouse, were the forces of the Crown Prince of Prussia. Had his soldiers only been able to hold their ground, he occupied a naturally strong position on the outer line of the heights around Sedan, and he made the best possible arrangements with the forces at his disposal; though it is certain he only expected an attack in front and on his right flank, for he could not foresee in what other direction than on the right the Crown Prince of Prussia was to operate against him. The right and front of the French position was intrusted to the corps commanded by Generals Ducrot and Lebrun; the left was defended by Generals Wimpffen and Douay. The seventh corps (Douay's) occupied the ground from Floing and St. Menges to Illy and Fleigneux, on the north of Sedan; the fifth (Wimpffen's, formerly De Failly's) was posted partly in the town and partly on the heights which command the gully of Givonne; the first (Ducrot's, formerly commanded by MacMahon himself) stretched from Petite Moncelle to Givonne; and the twelfth (Lebrun's) occupied Bazeilles in force and also held La Moncelle, about a mile higher up. The French army was thus formed in a semicircle round Sedan, the two wings leaning on the Meuse. The left, which rested on Givonne and the adjoining forest, was composed of the feeblest troops, as it was considered that, from the obstacles in the way and its being in the neighbourhood of a neutral frontier, it could not be turned. The French line extended thence along the ranges of heights which trend back to Sedan; the right occupied Bazeilles and Balan, and MacMahon stationed in considerable force his best divisions in these prominent positions, in order to hold the main road to Carignan, and to give strength to his projecting front. The defensible positions along the line from Givonne to Sedan were made the most of; guns, with masses of infantry, crowned the eminences or commanded the wooded valleys between; and at some points entrenchments were thrown up to baffle any hostile attack. The right of the French was protected in part by the course of the Meuse, in part by the western edge of the town, and in part by the artificial inundation of the river over the meadow land before described; and beyond Sedan on the other side the plateaux and ridges of Floing and La Garenne were occupied by large bodies of troops, though a dangerous attack at this point was not thought probable. The Chiers, from Douzy to Remilly, flowed directly across the French front, and opposed a natural barrier to the Crown Prince of Saxony. In this situation, covered by two rivers and behind obstacles of every kind, MacMahon awaited the German attack. The position of the French, though strong at some points, and formidable in its natural defences, was open to the fatal objection that everything depended upon their making a successful stand; if defeated at any point, no loophole was left for a safe retreat. Their projecting front was liable to a cross fire; once driven in, defeat would be inevitable; and while their wings would find it difficult to move, the turning of either would imperil both, and cause the whole mass to recoil inwards, where it would be involved in utter confusion. Sedan, on which, in that case, they would inevitably crowd for protection, was exposed to the fire of field guns from the heights of the valley of the Meuse; and if the slopes to the rear of the town were taken, it would be literally crushed by the weight of artillery.

The German commanders were not slow to perceive the advantages within their grasp; and, as we have already seen, on the 31st August they formed the plan of enveloping the French army, hemming it in upon Sedan, and cutting it off from the one chance which despair alone might prompt it to attempt, that of retreating across the Belgian frontier. They had about 220,000 men, and from 600 to 700 guns; with this immense superiority of force, and the ascendancy obtained by unbroken success, they were justified in determining on operations which, against a stronger and more confident foe, would have been attended with no little danger. The Crown Prince of Saxony was to attack and turn the extreme left of the French, assailing their front at the same time; this done, he was to send a force right round in their rear, which, meeting a detachment from the third German army, was to close completely upon them. Meanwhile the Crown Prince of Prussia was, with the Bavarian corps, to attack MacMahon's right at the projecting points of Bazeilles and Balan, effecting a junction with his colleague; he was also to overwhelm the French right wing as it was thrown backward behind Sedan, and to the north his troops were to meet those of the Crown Prince of Saxony and complete the hemming in of the enemy. Altogether, about 170,000 men, with nearly 600 guns, were to be engaged in the shock of battle; the remainder were to close round on the French, or watch the roads against any attempt to break through.

Such was the plan of the German commanders; and considering the strength of the opposing hosts, and the great results looked for from it, it was alike daring and admirable. Though not without risk, it was less hazardous than that which had issued in Bazaine being driven back into Metz; while, on the other hand, its success would insure the annihilation of MacMahon's army.

The night of the 31st was bright, and the horizon showed like a huge red vault, as, far on either bank of the Meuse, innumerable watch-fires marked the bivouacs of the armies awaiting the fight of the morrow. About one a.m. on September 1 the Crown Prince of Saxony received orders to advance, with a view to opening fire at five o'clock. The Crown Prince of Prussia left his headquarters at Chemery at four a.m.; and, with General Blumenthal and his staff, took up his position on an eminence overlooking the valley of the Meuse, near the town of Donchery, in front of a small newly built mansion called Château Donchery. From this point the whole of the German army could be surveyed, and the progress of the battle observed in all directions. Three hours later, the king of Prussia, with Count von Bismarck, General von Moltke, General von Roon, the Prussian minister of War, and a numerous staff (including Generals Sheridan and Forsyth, belonging to the army of the United States of America), arrived, and watched the movements of the troops from a high hill near Frénois, about a mile to the right of the Crown Prince, and three miles from Sedan. This spot commanded an excellent bird's eye view of the country round, including the hills on the king's left hand, to the west and north of the fortress, and the long bend of the Meuse; while he could look down on his right, over the southern suburbs, to Bazeilles, and towards the Saxon corps. Between the position which he occupied and Sedan is a lower ridge, with a wide gently-sloping valley intervening; and beneath the shelter of this ridge (for it was scarcely within range of the French batteries) masses of Prussian troops of all arms were drawn up in readiness for a forward attack, or for detachment to any threatened or critical point. These splendid slopes, interspersed with thickets, and unbroken by hedges, banks, ditches, or any other obstacle, offered great facilities for rapid movement, to which in some measure, no doubt, was due the success of the battle. To this the field telegraph, a method of communication neglected by the French, also contributed.

At daybreak part of the army of the Crown Prince of Prussia crossed the Meuse at Donchery by means of two pontoon bridges, under cover of the morning fog and of a thick wood close to the river's bank. The advanced guard of the Crown Prince of Saxony also took advantage of the fog to cross the Chiers a little after five o'clock; while the Bavarians, who had previously passed the Meuse, came into line with his left wing, and made preparations to attack Bazeilles. With the negligence which throughout the campaign too often disgraced the French staff, the bridges over the Chiers had not been broken; and the first fine of MacMahon's defences was carried without loss, the French cavalry outposts not even attempting resistance. At half-past seven the sun broke out, clearing away the dense fog which covered the valleys and the hills; and as the day advanced it became hot and sultry. Between five and six o'clock, simultaneously the Crown Prince of Saxony's columns were directed upon Givonne in order to turn the French left, and against the heights which protected then: left centre; while the Bavarians pressed forwards to storm Bazeilles, and force their front inwards towards Sedan. At the sight of the enemy the inefficient troops which held the important point of Givonne began to give way; and after a brief but decisive combat the French left wing was turned and driven in, crowds of fugitives hurrying into the woods, while others fell in on the now pressed centre.

About ten o'clock the victorious Saxons were pressing forwards from Givonne towards Illy and St. Menges, to the extreme left of the French army, in order to effect the junction with the Crown Prince of Prussia which led to such important results; and meeting with no opposition, they easily accomplished their object. At the same time the German left wing prepared to turn the other flank of their enemy. The eleventh corps proceeded along the slight elevation in the midst of the plain by Donchery; the fifth marched straight on to get to the rear. According to the plan of the battle, these corps were to meet the right wing, and, by surrounding the enemy, to cut off his retreat towards the Ardennes. The Würtemburgers and the cavalry division, subsequently sent to their support, were to protect the plain in case the French should push forward in this direction; which, however, from the difficulty they must have found in crossing the Meuse, was not very probable, as they had themselves destroyed the railway bridge between Donchery and Sedan. MacMahon seems to have thought that on this side his line was not exposed to serious danger, and that his breaking down the railway bridge was a sufficient protection. As we have seen, however, the Crown Prince of Prussia crossed over his pontoon bridge unperceived by the French, and the fog enabled him to crown with batteries the crest of the hills which overlook

Floing and the surrounding country. At a quarter past nine the eleventh corps had so far turned the French flank as to come close upon them. Then the German troops, under the protection of their guns, attacked in force the astonished enemy, who, caught in their rear, could do nothing save in the way of defending the positions they still held. Their main defensive point on the north side of Sedan was at Floing, on the east of the long loop of the Meuse. Here they had entrenched themselves upon the crown of a hill just above the village; and as this spot was the keystone of MacMahon's left, it was most hotly contested. On it were placed six mitrailleuses, which completely commanded the valley in front, so that, as the Germans advanced to the attack, whole masses, numbering perhaps 200 men, were swept away by a single discharge. In this instance the destructive effects of the mitrailleuse were confessedly greater than could have been produced by common shell. Nothing, indeed, could withstand a fire so murderous, and the Prussians fell back in confusion. Almost exactly opposite the French, however, at a distance of about three quarters of a mile, was a conical hill, named the Mamelon d'Atoi, which had been left undefended, an omission for which MacMahon has been severely criticized. But it would seem he had only a choice of evils. To defend the hill as an isolated post would have been useless, and to extend his line so as to embrace it within his general position would have dangerously weakened his front. The Germans at once seized upon this height, and to use the words of an English artillery officer on viewing the scene shortly afterwards, "with a judgment amounting to genius" twelve field guns were immediately posted on it in such a position that, while they themselves were in great measure protected from fire on the reverse brow of the hill, the French were forced to choose between the alternative of being made a target of by the direct fire in their front, or of seeking shelter from it by retiring over the crest, there to be enfiladed from their right. It is not too much to say that the successful attack on the Floing ridge, and consequently the decisive results of the battle, were in no small degree due to the effective fire from these two batteries. The Germans now plied their artillery fast and furiously on the opposite hill, and quickly silenced the enemy's guns. At ten minutes past twelve the French infantry, no longer supported by their artillery, were compelled to retire from their position at Floing, which was at once seized by the Prussian infantry. At twenty-five minutes past twelve were to be seen clouds of retreating French infantry on the hill between Floing and Sedan, and a Prussian battery in front of St. Menges making good practice with percussion shell among the retreating ranks. The whole hill for a quarter of an hour was literally covered with "Frenchmen running rapidly." "Less than half an hour after, at fifty minutes past twelve," says the special correspondent of the *Pall Mall Gazette*, who was viewing the battle from the hill occupied by the king and Count von Bismarck, "General von Roon called our attention to another French column in full retreat to the right of Sedan, on the road leading from Bazeilles to La Garenne wood. They never halted until they got to a small red-roofed house on the outskirts of Sedan itself. Almost at the same moment General Sheridan, who was using my opera-glass, called my attention to a third French column moving up a broad grass road through La Garenne wood immediately above Sedan, doubtless to support the troops defending the important Bazeilles ravine to the north-east of the town. At fifty-five minutes past twelve the French batteries on the edge of the wood of La Garenne and above it opened a vigorous fire on the advancing Prussian columns, whose evident intention it was to storm the hill north-west of La Garenne, and so gain the key of the position on that side. At five minutes past one yet another French battery near the wood opened on the Prussian columns, which were compelled to keep shifting their ground till ready for their final rush at the hill, in order to avoid offering so good a mark to the French shells. Shortly after we saw the first Prussian skirmishers on the crest of the La Garenne hill above Torcy. They did not seem in strength, and General Sheridan, standing beside me, exclaimed, 'Ah! they are too weak; they can never hold that position against all those French.' The general's prophecy soon proved correct, for the French advancing at least six to one, the Prussians were forced to retire down the hill to seek reinforcements from the columns which were hurrying to their support. In five minutes they came back again, this time in greater force, but still terribly inferior to the huge French columns. 'Good heavens! the French cuirassiers are going to charge them,' said General Sheridan: and sure enough the regiment of cuirassiers, their helmets and breastplates flashing in the September sun, formed up in sections of squadrons, and dashed down on the Prussian scattered skirmishers. Without deigning to form line—squares are never used by the Prussians—the infantry received the cuirassiers with a most tremendous 'schnellfeuer' (quick fire) at about 108 yards, loading and firing as fast as possible into the dense squadrons. Over went men and horses by hundreds, and the regiment was compelled to retire much faster, it seemed to me, than it came. The moment the cuirassiers turned bridle, the plucky Prussians actually dashed in hot pursuit after them at the double. Such a thing has not often been recorded in the annals of war. The French infantry then came forward in turn and attacked the Prussians, who waited quietly under a most rapid fire of Chassepots until their enemies got within about 100 yards, when they gave them such a dose of lead that the infantry soon followed the cavalry to the 'place from which they came'—that is, behind a ridge some 600 yards on the way to Sedan, where the tirailleurs could not hit them. The great object of the Prussians was gained, as they were not dispossessed of the crest of the hill, and it was fair betting that they would do all that in them lay to get some artillery up to help them before Napoleon III. was much nearer his deposition. 'There will be a fight for that crest,' says Sheridan, peering through his field-glass at the hill, which was not three miles from where he stood, with the full fire on it from behind us. At half-past one the French cavalry—this time I fancy a regiment of the carabineers—made another attempt to dislodge the Prussians, who were being reinforced every minute. But they met with the same fate as their brethren in the iron jackets, and were sent with heavy loss to the right about, the Prussians taking advantage of their flight to advance their line a couple of hundred yards nearer the French infantry. Suddenly they split into two bodies, leaving a break of 100 yards in their line. We were not long in seeing the object of this movement, for the little white puffs from the crest behind the skirmishers, followed by a commotion in the dense French masses, show us that 'ces diables de Prussiens' have contrived, heaven only knows how, to get a couple of four-pounders up the steep ground, and have opened on the French. Something must have at this point been very wrong with the French infantry, for instead of attacking the Prussians, whom they still outnumbered by at least two to one, they remained in columns on the hill, seeing their only hope of retrieving the day vanishing from before their eyes without stirring. The cavalry then tried to do a little Balaklava business, but without the success of the immortal 'six hundred.' We took the guns in the Balaklava valley. Down came the cuirassiers once more, this time riding straight for the two field-pieces. But before they had got within 200 yards of the guns, the Prussians formed line as if on parade, and, waiting till they were within fifty yards, gave them a volley which seemed to us to destroy almost the whole of the leading squadron, and so actually blocked up the way to the guns for the next ones following. After this last charge—which was as complete a failure, although most gallantly conceived and executed, as the two preceding ones—the infantry fell back rapidly towards Sedan, and in an instant the whole hill was covered by swarms of Prussian tirailleurs, who appeared to rise from the ground. After the last desperate charge of the French cavalry, General Sheridan remarked to me, 'I never saw anything so reckless, so utterly foolish, as that last charge—it was sheer murder!' The Prussians, after the French infantry fell back, advanced rapidly, so much so that the retreating squadrons of French cavalry turned suddenly round, and charged desperately once again. But it was all of no use. The days of breaking squares or even lines are over, and the 'thin blue line' soon stopped the Gallic onset. It was most extraordinary that the French had neither artillery nor mitrailleurs, especially these latter, on the hill to support the infantry. The position was a most important one, and certainly worth straining every nerve to defend. One thing was clear enough—that the French infantry, after once meeting the Prussians, declined to try conclusions with them again, and that the cavalry were trying to encourage them by their example. About two, more Prussian regiments came over the long-disputed hill between Torcy and Sedan, to reinforce the regiments already established there."

Another better known and most able special correspondent, Dr. Russell, of the *Times*, in a vivid description of the fearful nature of the struggle in this part of the field, said, "the Prussians coming up from Floing were invisible to me. Never can I forget the sort of agony with which I witnessed those who first came out on the plateau raising their heads and looking around for an enemy, while, hidden from view, a thick blue band of French infantry was awaiting them, and a brigade of cavalry was ready on their flank below. I did not know that Floing was filled with advancing columns. There was but a wide, extending, loose array of skirmishers, like a flock of rooks, on the plateau. Now the men in front began to fire at the heads over the bank lined by the French. This drew such a flash of musketry as tumbled over some and staggered the others; but their comrades came scrambling up from the rear, when suddenly the first block of horse in the hollow shook itself up, and the line, in beautiful order, rushed up the slope. The onset was not to be withstood. The Prussians were caught *en flagrant d'élit*. Those nearest the ridge slipped over into the declivitous ground; those in advance, running in vain, were swept away. But the impetuosity of the charge could not be stayed. Men and horses came tumbling down into the road, where they were disposed of by the Prussians in the gardens, while the troopers on the left of the line, who swept down the lane in a cloud of dust, were almost exterminated by the infantry in the village. There was also a regular cavalry encounter, I fancy, in the plains below, but I cannot tell at what time; the cuirassiers, trying to cut their way out, were destroyed, and a charge of two Prussian squadrons, which did not quite equal expectations, occurred. The feat of those unfortunate cavaliers only cleared the plateau for a little time. In a few minutes up came the spiked helmets again over the French *épaulement*, crossing their sabred comrades, and, therefore, all alive to the danger of cavalry. They advanced in closer order, but still skirmishing, and one long, black parallelogram was maintained to rally on. As the skirmishers got to the ridge they began to fire, but the French in the second line of *épaulement* soon drove them back by a rattling fusillade. The French rushed out of the *épaulement* in pursuit, still firing. At the same moment a splendid charge was executed on the Prussians, before which the skirmishers rallied, on what seemed to me to be still a long parallelogram. They did not form square. Some Prussians too far on were sabred. The troopers, brilliantly led, went right onwards in a cloud of dust; but when they were within a couple of hundred yards of the Prussians, one simultaneous volley burst out of the black front and flank, which enveloped all in smoke. They were steady soldiers who pulled trigger there. Down came horse and man; the array was utterly ruined. There was left in front of that deadly infantry but a heap of white and grey horses—a terrace of dead and dying and dismounted men and flying troopers, who tumbled at every instant. More total dissipation of a bright pageantry could not be. There was another such scene yet to come. I could scarce keep the field-glass to my eyes as the second and last body of cavalry—which was composed of light horse also—came thundering up out of the hollow. They were not so bold as the men on the white horses, who fell, many of them at the very line of bayonets. The horses of these swerved as they came upon the ground covered with carcases, and their line was broken; but the squadron leaders rode straight to death. Once again the curling smoke spurted out from the Prussian front, and to the rear and right and left flew the survivors of the squadrons. The brown field was flecked with spots of many colours, and, trampling on the remains of that mass of strength and courage of man and horse, the Prussians, to whom supports were fast hastening up right and left and rear, pressed on towards the inner *épaulement*, and became engaged with the French infantry, who maintained for some time a steady rolling fire in reply to the volleys of the Prussians. To me the French force seemed there very much superior in number. But they had lost courage, and what was left of it was soon dissipated by the advance of a Prussian battery, which galloped up to the right flank of their infantry, and opened a very rapid fire, to which there was no French battery to reply. The French left the *épaulement*, and made for a belt of wood, dropping fast as they retreated, but facing round and firing still. In a few moments more the plateau was swarming with the battalions of the eleventh corps, and the struggle there was over. Only for a minute, however, because from the flanks of the wood came out a line of French infantry. The musketry fire was renewed; but it was evident the Prussians were not to be gainsaid. Their advance was only checked that they might let their artillery play while their columns assisted it by incessant volleys. A fierce onslaught by the French, made after they had retired behind the wood, only added to their losses. The Crown Prince's army, notwithstanding the cavalry success at the outset, had by three o'clock won the key of the position of the French with comparatively small loss."

In the meantime the fifth German corps had performed the long distance to the extreme heights, and after a sharp encounter succeeded in driving back the detachments making for the

Ardennes; only a few scattered bodies of infantry, about 12,000 men altogether, having succeeded in effecting their retreat across the Belgian frontier, about six miles off, and where they laid down their arms. Affairs had, in fact, assumed a very favourable aspect for the Germans; and the Saxons, who had designedly reserved their strength, pressed forwards with an overpowering force. As early as midday, from the fire of the Prussian batteries on the right and left wings, so rapidly closing in on each side, it was evident the enemy would soon be completely surrounded. "It was a grand sight," says the German official report of the battle, "to watch the sure and irresistible advance of the guards, marching on, on the left wing, partly behind and partly by the side of the twelfth corps d'armée." Since a quarter-past ten the guards, preceded by their artillery, had been pushing towards the woods to the north of Sedan. The advancing smoke of their guns showed how fast they were gaining ground; and when, from the line of fire passing beyond Givonne, the Crown Prince of Prussia learned the defeat of the French left, and the progress which his Saxon colleague had made, he could spare more than enough of men to hem the enemy in on all sides, and render the flight of the French impossible. Their line receded from point to point, and at last breaking into a confused mass, was driven headlong into the town by the weight of a crushing artillery. "Soldiers of all corps were crushing against each other in the struggle to get inside the town. Dismounted cavalry were climbing over the ramparts, cuirassiers were jumping, horses and all, into the moats, the horses breaking their legs and ribs. Guns, with their heavy carriages and powerful horses, forced their way into the throngs, maiming and crushing the fugitives on foot. To add to the confusion and terror, the Prussian shells began to fall into the midst of the struggling masses. On the ramparts were the national guard, manning the guns, and striving to reply to the Prussian batteries. It was a scene of indescribable horror."

Meanwhile a struggle of a different kind, worthy of their martial renown, was raging along the French front, where the fortunes of the day long hung in the balance. The hill ranges were fiercely disputed; every slope was the scene of a stern encounter; and though the French line receded gradually before the crushing effects of the enemy's guns, the fight was gallantly contested. The Prussians began firing before five o'clock, first against the French right and centre, from Balan and Bazeilles to Moncelle, which were the scene of the most terrible conflicts of the day. To these points the French, conscious of their vital importance, clung with desperate tenacity; and though the Bavarians advanced with resolute bravery, supported by batteries able to pour in a destructive cross-fire, they were at first steadily repulsed, and the resistance was long-sustained and heroic. The slope before Bazeilles was covered with their killed and wounded; but in spite of the destructive fire from the French mitrailleuses, the Bavarians stormed the bridge leading into the town, where, as early as six o'clock, they obtained a footing from which they could not be dislodged.

The solidly-built, compact town, with its wide communications, presented rare capabilities of defence, and a stubborn resistance was made at every step, until the contest became one of almost unparalleled fury. The French, evidently determined not to surrender, surpassed their former deeds of valour; while the German obstinacy and perseverance appeared equally decided.

The splendid courage of the French troops was, unfortunately, of no avail, and they were gradually driven back in the direction of Sedan, though at a late hour in the afternoon the murderous contest was still doubtful.

At five o'clock in the morning MacMahon proceeded to the advanced posts near Bazeilles, to reconnoitre the positions, and sent to inform the emperor, who mounted horse soon afterwards, and rode to the field of battle. While apparently almost seeking death the gallant marshal was struck on the hip by a piece of bombshell which exploded near him, killing his horse; and he fell, severely wounded, into a deep trench by the side of the road near Bazeilles. He was immediately placed in an ambulance waggon, and carried back into the town. The command was then taken by General Wimpffen, who had arrived from Algeria only two days before, and had been ordered at once by the Parisian ministry to supersede De Failly, who, as has been shown in the previous chapter, by allowing himself to be surprised on Tuesday at Beaumont, opened the door to the three days' flood of disasters. This change of generals at the commencement of the action was unfortunate; for while the army had unbounded confidence in the bravery and skill of MacMahon, his successor was comparatively unknown to them; and he, on the other hand, knew nothing of the marshal's plans, or even the disposition of the corps on the plateaux above Sedan. Indeed, it is said that MacMahon felt this so strongly, that he at once gave his instructions to General Ducrot, whom he knew well, and would no doubt have preferred as his successor; but when Wimpffen came and asserted his right, as the senior, to the chief command, he obtained it as a matter of course. The consequence, however, was that in many parts of the field in reality nobody commanded, and divisions and regiments were left to fight their own battle.

In their repeated attacks upon Bazeilles and Balan the Bavarians suffered enormously. After they had crossed the Meuse by their pontoons and by the railway bridge, they could receive but little protection from their own artillery on the heights; and they were exposed to a fire of infantry in the houses, and to the guns of the works, as well as the musketry from the parapets. In the strenuous attempts of the French to repulse them, the marines from Cherbourg particularly distinguished themselves; and three divisions of Bavarians, who began to fight at four o'clock in the morning, sustained three distinct onslaughts from the town, and from the troops under the walls. At one time it appeared as though the Germans must be overpowered; but a partial success at this point would scarcely have secured the French army from its ultimate fate.

The following interesting description of the fighting at this point is taken from a letter published a few days afterwards, by "an English M.P." (Mr. Winterbotham, the member for Stroud), who was present with the German army as a member of an ambulance corps:—"We were about the middle of a valley some three miles long, stretching from Remilly on the south-east to Torcy on the northwest. Through it flowed the Meuse, as broad on our right as the Thames above Teddington. Between the road and the river on our left ran the rail, which, just at this spot, turns sharply across the river by an iron bridge into the town of Bazeilles, which stood a little back from the river, immediately in our front, on the opposite side of the valley. Close behind us, and forming the south-west side of the valley, was a range of hills, the tops and sides of which, forming the north-east side of the valley, were covered with woods, not one continuous wood, but patches of twenty or thirty acres, with sloping glades of grass between. It was on these open slopes that I found, after the battle, most traces of German losses. They must have suffered severely in driving the French from the woods, which were well lined with mitrailleuses. The artillery and troops crossed the river on the south-east side of Bazeilles by a pontoon bridge they had constructed in the night. The town of Bazeilles had already been seized by the Bavarians, though with great loss, before six o'clock in the morning; and two hours afterwards artillery, followed by infantry, were mounting the ridge beyond, on the right of the valley or gully running up from Bazeilles to Givonne. At the top of this ridge, about midday, I first saw the Saxons. Both Saxons and Bavarians kept up a heavy fire of artillery from this spot over the gully against the French, who were in front of us on the opposite ridge. When the French were driven from this, we crossed the gully, occupied their position, and began again at the next ridge. This was wooded, and the French clung to it till between two and three o'clock in the afternoon, when we saw them making off fast down the hill towards the river; in fact, to the village of Balan, which lay between Bazeilles and Sedan, at the foot of the ridge. In crossing the gully between Bazeilles and Givonne from ridge to ridge, and retreating up the valley from Bazeilles, the French fought well, and clung to every house and bit of wood; yet the Bavarians were so close upon them that some of them were cut off and left in Bazeilles. Here they remained concealed in the houses while the Bavarians passed through. It was only about eleven o'clock, when I happened to be in the town, that they were discovered. Bazeilles was then on fire in several places; and the flames had reached a large house at the corner of two streets in the centre of the town. Suddenly, from the windows of this house, was opened upon us a sharp fire, and the men of the small Bavarian force then in the place began to fall fast. The little garrison in the house refused to surrender. The Bavarians fired in vain, and straw was then heaped against the doors and lighted, but the wind blew the flames steadily back, leaving the front of the house untouched; and from the cellars and the ground floor on that side the French still kept up their fire. At last their officer fell, mortally wounded, from the window. He was picked up and brought in by our men, and soon afterwards the remnant of the little force surrendered. There were 200 men of the marines in that house. Their gallant young commander would not hear of a surrender, and only forty came out at last unhurt. In other houses smaller bands were found. Some of the inhabitants, not soldiers, and even women, fired on the Bavarians. *I saw them taken with arms in their hands;* and I was assured they would be hanged the next day. Returning to the Bavarian batteries on the ridge west of the gully, I saw the Bavarian infantry twice advance below me to seize Balan, and twice repulsed. The third time they did not return; and I concluded that the village, which was hidden in trees, was won.

"Taking advantage of a lull in the firing about three o'clock, I went forward over the open ground in front towards the woods, which I thought the French had left. In a little hollow over which the Bavarians had twice passed, by a willow tree (the only sign of vegetation around), I found some eight or ten wounded men—five French, the rest Germans. With my little stock of bandages and my flask I did what I could for the poor fellows, but before I could return the firing recommenced. The bullets and balls whistled and hummed over me and around me, and patted or thudded the ground close to my feet. I crept under the slender shelter of the willow stump, and sat down among my wounded friends. I thought that half-hour would never end. The wounded Frenchmen groaned dreadfully. The Germans, though equally badly wounded, were more quiet and less complaining. This I found, too, in the hospitals. I think the French are more tenderly made. It was heart-rending to see so much misery I could do so little to relieve. I laid this one on his back, with his knapsack for a pillow, turned that one on his side, covered another's head with a cloth to shelter it from the burning sun, put a bit of shirt on this man's wound, unbuttoned the throttling coat of the fifth, took off the boot from the wounded foot of another, gave all a little cognac, and then sat down and talked with them. How grateful they were! How polite, in the midst of all his sufferings, was one poor French soldier! and, most touching of all, how kindly helpful the poor fellows were to one another, French and German alike! 'But, monsieur,' asked one poor Frenchman, ' are the Prussians Christians?' 'Certainly,' said I. I knew he was thinking of those heathen Turcos of his. 'Then,' said my poor friend, breathing heavily (he was badly wounded in the chest), 'why do we kill one another?' I interpreted our conversation to his German neighbours, and, the fire having slackened, I left them to seek the bearers to carry them off. The one question each asked was, 'Tell me, tell me, shall I die?' I am not a doctor, so I took refuge in a hope for each; but how some lived a minute I cannot tell. One poor fellow, a Bavarian, had been struck down by a bullet just between the eyes, leaving a clean hole as large as a fourpenny piece. He was lying on his back, yet I saw him raise himself deliberately on his elbow, and heard him distinctly ask me for water. I gave it him. He drank it, said 'Thank you, thank you,' and lay down again. In the evening, when the firing had again ceased, I brought back bearers with stretchers, and carried off all my poor friends to the field hospital."

The alleged participation of the inhabitants in the obstinate defence at Bazeilles, led to one of the most horrible incidents of the war. On the previous day (the 31st of August), the houses bordering on the Meuse were fired by missiles from the Bavarian artillery, on account of their serving as a protection to the French defending the passage of the river. This was a simple strategic necessity; and a number of people who had taken refuge in their cellars were undoubtedly buried in the ruins. The shells thrown into the place on Thursday, September 1, also raised a conflagration here and there; but so enraged were the Germans at the conduct of the inhabitants that orders were given to raze the whole town to the ground; and in the evening, after the battle, the Bavarian troops returned and destroyed what remained of it, by firing masses of straw in each separate house. They did their work so effectually as to make Bazeilles as complete a ruin as Pompeii: indeed, there are houses at Pompeii in a better state of preservation than any left here, for not a roof nor a floor remained to any one of them. An English artillery officer, who visited the spot three weeks afterwards, and gave his experience in an interesting work entitled, "From Sedan to Saarbrück," declared that the ruins were then still smoking! The same gentleman adds, that a woman who lived in the place confessed that the Germans sought for and removed the helpless before applying the torch, and proceeds:—Bazeilles was something more than a prosperous village; it must have been a flourishing town emerging into importance, with substantial stone houses, numerous wide streets, hotels, churches, many factories, and several large public buildings. Now, only enough remains to show what they once were. Not a house is left standing—scarcely one stone upon another. All around is a mass of ruins. Long rows of cleft wall, ready to totter over with a breath, show the outline of the streets; piles of fallen masonry block up the road; masses of rubble, house fittings, and splintered furniture, perplex the eye. Shot and shell manifestly did their work here, as elsewhere; but the charred skeleton walls standing in ghastly isolation show that fire was the chief element by which such destruction was wrought. Here are exhibited in all their frightful reality the murderous results of wanton cruelty; though which side was most to blame for these horrors it is difficult to determine. Indeed, the accounts of the events which preceded this terrible retaliation are so varied and conflicting, that it is almost impossible for an impartial writer to arrive at the real truth; but there can be little doubt that, after the place had surrendered, many of the attacking l'orce were shot down in the streets, from the houses, by men not in uniform, and even by women. Some of the former, perhaps, were francs-tireurs; but many were believed to be ordinary working men. Thereupon the Bavarians broke into the houses, made prisoners of the inhabitants found with arms in their hands; and, some hours later, burned the town and shot their captives. The number so executed is admitted by the Germans themselves to have been at least forty. One old woman was seen to shoot three Bavarian officers in succession, with a pistol fired from a window. Again, two officers of one of the Bavarian regiments that first entered the town and recaptured it after a repulse, asserted positively that, upon this second entry, their troops missed the wounded they had left helpless in the streets, and presently discovered their bodies half consumed in some of the burning houses, to which they must have been dragged or carried a considerable distance. A wounded Bavarian officer also declared that the inhabitants poured hot oil over him as he lay helpless in one of the streets! These statements tend to show that the severity of the German troops was not unprovoked; and therefore we can hardly wonder at the excesses by which the rough soldiery (who believed most implicitly that these atrocities had been committed) avenged their hapless comrades.

M. Hermann Voget, writing to a German newspaper, states that he was in Bazeilles from one o'clock in the morning till five in the evening, and was himself a witness of the brutal misdeeds which led to the destruction of that ill-fated place. The following extract from his letter gives a most thrilling picture of the scene from a German point of view:—"Suddenly, what a tumult, what a wild clamour! What an unusual rushing sound! It was the bullets striking on the stones. In reality, not forty paces in front of us, at the entrance to the street, raged the fight. The Bavarians were being hurled back by the French. A wild scream of jubilee filled up the brief intervals between the crackling musketry fire. It came from the inhabitants, who took part in the fight, and exultingly celebrated the victory of their troops. But their joy was premature. It was but a few minutes, and our people drove them back. It was the last time that the enemy had any success at this point. I hurried into the streets to see how the battle ended. I took post behind a garden wall: some holes in it which had visibly served as firing apertures afforded me a prospect of a large, strongly-built house, round which for many hours the fight had raged. It looked towards two streets, and from the windows on both sides a continuous firing had been kept up. Many

Bavarians had already fallen victims to this fire. The house seemed an enchantment against which the bravery of our soldiers would melt. The pointing of artillery against it was impossible, owing to its situation, and a general bombardment of the hamlet was forbidden by the many wounded who lay in its streets and houses. To destroy the enemy's wall of defence nothing remained but the invocation of flames. Some pioneers, at great peril, made a circuit, burst in the back of the house, and flung firebrands into the breach. The flames bursting forth compelled the French to abandon their position; they retreated through the garden. The Bavarians stormed after them through the blazing house; but they were, as I was later informed, too hasty in pursuit, and in consequence, as they rushed pell-mell through the garden, encountered the enemy's reserves, who, so far, had taken no part in the fight. Now again, for our people, was the moment come for a retreat. But this was now well-nigh become an impossibility. The fire had in the interim made such progress that the house they had rushed through was no longer passable. Two standards were for some time in danger of falling into the enemy's hands. A quick, cool, sharply maintained fire, which teased the pursuing foe, enabled, during their confusion, the standard-bearers to make a rapid escape over a wall not too high, but many officers who had advanced too far in the attack were cut off and made prisoners.

"While this struggle was going on behind the houses I walked up the street. Frightful was the wretchedness I saw there. I was the first person to appear after the storm of battle had passed further away. Dead and wounded lay piled indiscriminately together. Hundreds of dying eyes looked at me imploringly. I was seized with shuddering. I sought to go away. Too terrible was the scene, and yet what was it compared with the barbarity which I had directly afterwards to witness! A wild cry, more like that of an animal than of a human being, rang in my ears. I looked towards the place whence the sound came, and saw a peasant dragging a wounded Bavarian, who was lying on the ground, towards a burning house. A woman was so far aiding that she continued kicking the poor creature in the side with her heavy shoes. The heart-rending cry of the wretched man had drawn three of his comrades to the spot. 'Shoot her down; no, hang her.' Two shots rang out, the peasant dropped. The Megaera laughed, and before the soldiers had gone three steps forward, she stood once more beside her victim. The woman must be mad. One blow cleft her skull. 'Hang her up; into the fire with the brute.' While the troops gave vent to their evidently outraged feelings, I stooped down to the ill-used soldier. He was dead. His last breath had passed with his cry for help. He was a fine, powerful young fellow. Well was it for his loved ones that they had not heard the last cry of agony of their son or their brother. I shall never forget his cry. It will haunt me while I live. I had but just quitted this scene of cruelty, when a new horror encountered me. From a house close behind me came the reports in quick succession of two shots. I turned, and saw a krankentrager, in the exercise of his duty, fall convulsively to the ground. The wounded man he was carrying rolled with him in the dust. From that house proceeded the shots; five, six Bavarians force a way in, the door breaks tinder the blows of their butt-ends. But the soldiers stand as if stunned. On the threshold appears, armed with a double-barrelled gun, a tall woman; she may be fifty years old, for dishevelled gray hairs fall around a fine—yes, a noble face. As she regards the soldiers her features are distorted, she laughs wildly;

the laugh of this woman is a fearful thing. *Vous êtes une bête*, calls out a doctor hurrying by. Her laugh is silenced, a torrent of tears gushes down her face, she exclaims softly, but in tones of heartrending pain—'*Non, je suis épouse, je suis mère! Vous avez assassiné mon mari; vous avez assassiné mes deux fils. Tuez moi aussi! Je vous en remercierai. Si vous ne me tuez pas, c'est moi qui vous tuerai.*' With the last words the old wrath returns. She again raises the gun. The soldiers have not understood her. They seek to avenge their comrade and to protect themselves. The doctor stands shuddering, like myself. Before we can say a word the unhappy woman falls, struck by two bullets in the breast. 'Let her die in quiet,' calls out the doctor to the men, who seem not yet to have satisfied their revenge; ' she has lost her husband and her two sons.' That makes an impression on the soldiers, and they silently turn away. I turn back with the doctor. We stoop down to the poor woman. Her wounds are fatal. She regards us wildly. I take her hand, and involuntarily my lips utter '*pauvre femme.*' The words seemed to have pleased her, she feels they come from the heart. Her eyes grew dim; and as she clasped my hand firmly her bosom heaves a last sigh. I was most deeply moved, and in silence I traversed the burning hamlet, scarcely noticing that the flames were ever extending farther. New tidings of horror arrived. The flames menaced a French hospital established in a mansion. To extinguish the fire was impossible. Our force were to proceed to the rescue of the wounded from the flames. Wounded krankentragers appeared, and complained that they were being fired upon from the houses. These complaints were renewed at short intervals, and directions had to be given to search the houses to eject the parties firing. It was a perilous undertaking, costing many a soldier his life, and though more than fifty men and women were made prisoners, though more than twenty who resisted were shot on the spot, the firing from the houses did not cease. Persistently were the krankentragers aimed at, and on all sides was the destruction of the hamlet demanded. Not until fifty of our people had been struck was the order given to fire every house from which shots proceeded. It was punctually fulfilled. The soldiers, heated by the fight, and angered at the concealed firing upon them, made short work wherever resistance was shown. The inhabitants—who had been reduced to beggary, and had each lost one, if not more, of their relatives—had but one feeling, that of revenge. Like that unhappy mother whose end I have narrated, they had no fears for the bullets of their enemy, but welcomed the destroying lead, if first they had slain one of the hated '*chiens Allemands.*' "

We gladly leave the scene of desolation and horror, to resume our account of the general progress of the battle. It has been seen that, during the whole of the forenoon, the German left was sweeping on from the west to the north of Sedan, whilst the guards, forming the right of the Crown Prince of Saxony's forces, had advanced in a north-westerly direction on the road to Bouillon. Shortly before two o'clock the two armies united near Fleigneux, and from that time the day was completely lost to the French; for all around Sedan, from Donchery on the west, to Givonne on the north, to Douzy on the east, to Remilly and Cheveuge on the south, they were encompassed by a cordon of enemies, in at least two-fold strength, and occupying commanding positions on the heights. The junction of the two armies was witnessed, amidst intense excitement, by the king of Prussia and his staff, who were stationed on the hill near Cheveuge.

Here and there villages and hamlets were still burning, and the roar of cannon had not ceased; for, almost at the gates of the fortress, the remainder of the French army was yet fighting. But unable to unite, their corps could no longer offer a combined defence, so that only small detachments were continuing the struggle in isolated localities. As the French fell back, step by step, the fire of the German guns, superior from the first and gradually converging, became more deadly; and at last their disordered and despairing columns were absolutely thrust down into the bottom of the funnel represented by Sedan. Then, indeed, all hopes of escape, of successful resistance, or even of honourable death, had to be abandoned. The engagement had, in fact, become a mere battue, and the army lay as it were prostrate at the mercy of the victors, who, crowding their guns on the closely surrounding hill-tops, whence they could peer into the town, seemed to menace both it and its defenders with annihilation. So desperate was their position that an officer of the British artillery, who subsequently visited the spot, declares that his original surprise at the capitulation of the French, and wonder at their not having attempted at all hazards to cut their way out of the trap, was changed into amazement that, on awakening on the morning of the 1st of September, and finding themselves in such a fearful predicament, they could have summoned resolution to fight at all; for from the moment the first shot was fired the result must have been all but a foregone conclusion.

About four o'clock General Wimpffen, reluctantly abandoning all hope of further resistance, sent a letter to the French emperor, proposing that he should place himself in the middle of a column of men, who would "deem it an honour" to cut a passage for him through the enemy in the direction of Carignan. The following is a copy of this now historical document:—

"Sire,—Je me décide à forcer la ligne qui se trouve devant le Gl. Lebrun et le Gl. Ducrot plutôt que d'être prisonnier dans la place de Sedan.

"Que votre Majesté vienne se mettre au milieu de ses troupes, qui tiendront à honneur de lui ouvrir un passage.

"DE WIMPFFEN.

"4hr., *1st Sepre.*"

Napoleon, aware of the impossibility of leaving the place on horseback, replied that he could not rejoin the general (one of the officers who came with the proposal was himself unable to get back to General Wimpffen); that, moreover, he could not consent to save himself by the sacrifice of a great number of his soldiers; and that he was determined to share the fate of the army.

About this time a rumour spread among the soldiers that Bazaine had arrived, and immediately enthusiasm and hope took the place of despair. It is quite probable that the approach of this general may really have been believed by Wimpffen, for, as we shall see at the conclusion of this chapter, his breaking out from Metz and assisting MacMahon was to have formed part of the general operations of the day. The French commander, therefore, collected about two thousand of his troops, who rushed forward to the gate of Balan with a valour and determination which nothing could withstand, and in a few minutes they were complete masters of the village. But they quickly discovered that they had been deceived; and, not being supported by their comrades, the gallant band was once more compelled to retire before the renewed attacks of the Germans, who returned in overwhelming numbers.

Meanwhile, among the troops surrounding the town there had been a general rout, and the army had been beaten back into Sedan, a shapeless, hopeless horde of mutinous and starving men. All the efforts of the officers to rally them were fruitless, and the belief was general throughout the ranks that they were betrayed. Several generals went to the emperor and announced that further resistance was impossible. Their soldiers, after having sustained an unequal fight for nearly twelve hours, almost without food, were so weakened by fatigue and hunger that they were easily driven back against the walls and thrown into the ditches, where they were decimated by the enemy's fire. As they fled into the town they crowded against each other in the streets in utter confusion. While thus choked with the *débris* of all the corps, Sedan was bombarded on all sides, and the Prussian shells, falling amongst the struggling mass, carried death at every stroke. Many of the officers and men were killed in the streets, amongst the former being two generals. Live shells were poured into the town, and set fire to a large straw shed, from which a column of dense black smoke rose immediately to the sky. The emperor was painfully reminded of the imminent danger of his position, by several shells which burst on the roof and in the court of the sub-prefecture. Others set many private houses on fire, and struck the wounded who had been carried into them. The great barracks, converted into an hospital, upon the top of which floated the red-cross flag, were not spared; and men and horses, huddled up in the court-yard, were continually hit. The emperor then endeavoured to make known to General Wimpffen the advisability of asking for an armistice, since every moment of delay only increased the number of victims. Not receiving any tidings of the general, and seeing such a useless waste of life, and the situation so hopeless, he ordered the white flag to be hoisted upon the citadel. At the time it was fixed upon the ramparts Napoleon sat in the court-yard of the prefecture, his staff standing apart. His face was buried in his hands, and he appeared completely overwhelmed by the catastrophe. Owing to the severe disease from which he suffered he was compelled to dismount several times during the battle, and to great physical exhaustion moral prostration was now added.

The signal of surrender was for some little time unnoticed by the Prussians, and a lancer's flag was waved from the battlements, while a trumpet sounded; but in that infernal din and turmoil neither the sight nor the sound attracted the notice of the besiegers, so that it was only when the gates were opened that they saw the first indication of their stupendous victory. The news spread rapidly; and about five o'clock the cannonade, which was gradually suspended along the whole line, entirely ceased. The Crown Prince of Prussia sent the message, "Complete victory," to headquarters; and immediately after, with the duke of Coburg, the other princes, and his orderly officers, he proceeded to join the king.

A French colonel, escorted by two uhlans—one of whom carried a white duster on a faggot stick as a flag of truce—rode out from Sedan to the hill of Cheveuge, to ask the king of Prussia for terms of capitulation; but after a brief consultation between his Majesty and General von Moltke, he was told that, in a matter so important as the surrender of at least 80,000 men and an important fortress, it was necessary to send an officer of high rank. "You are, therefore, to return to Sedan, and to tell the governor of the town to report himself immediately to the king of Prussia. If he does not arrive in an hour our guns will open fire again. You may tell the commandant that it is useless trying to obtain other terms than unconditional surrender." The *parlementaire* rode sorrowfully back with that message.

Up to this time the Germans had no idea that the French emperor was shut up in Sedan; but now among the king's staff there arose a sudden cry, "Der Kaiser 1st da!" (The emperor is there!), which was followed by a loud hurrah. About half-past six General Reilly (who was personally known to the king of Prussia, having been appointed to attend him when he visited Napoleon at Compiègne), accompanied by the Prussian Lieutenant-colonel von Brousart, the officer intrusted with the negotiations on the part of the Germans, brought from the emperor of the French to the king an autograph letter, containing these few words:—

"Monsieur mon frère,—N'ayant pas pu mourir au milieu de mes troupes, il ne me reste qu'à remettre mon épée entre les mains de votre Majesté. Je suis, de votre Majesté le bon frère,"

"NAPOLEON."

[TRANSLATION.]

"Sire, my brother,—Not having been able to die in the midst of my troops, it only remains for me to resign my sword into the hands of your Majesty. I am, your Majesty's good brother,"

"NAPOLEON."

On receipt of this letter there was a short consultation between the king, the Crown Prince, Count von Bismarck, Von Moltke, and Von Roon, after which the king sat down, and with a chair for his table wrote the following reply:—

"Monsieur mon frère,—En regrettant les circonstances dans lesquelles nous nous rencontrons, j'accepte l'épée de votre Majesté, et je vous prie de bien vouloir nommer un de vos officiers munis de vos pleins pouvoirs pour traiter de la capitulation de l'armée qui est si bravement battue sous vos ordres. De mon côté j'ai désignée le Général Moltke à cet effet. Je suis de votre Majesté le bon frère,"

"GUILLAUME.

"Devant Sedan, *le Sept.* 1, 1870."

[TRANSLATION.]

"Sire, my brother,—Regretting the circumstances under which we meet, I accept the sword of your Majesty, and I pray you to name one of your officers provided with full powers to treat for the capitulation of the army which has so bravely fought under your command. On my side, I have named General Moltke for this purpose. I am, your Majesty's good brother,"

"WILLIAM.

"Before Sedan, *Sept.* 1, 1870."

When the king had written this letter, he himself handed it to General Reilly, who stood bareheaded to receive it, the Italian and Crimean medals glittering on his breast in the last rays of the setting sun; and again escorted by the uhlans, he at 7'40 left for the beleaguered town.

When General Wimpffen found that, unknown to him, the white flag had been hoisted on the citadel by the emperor's orders, and that *parlementaires* were being received at the imperial quarters, he proceeded thither and protested very warmly that these acts properly belonged only to himself as commander-in-chief. Refusing to carry on the negotiations, he then proceeded to his quarters, and sent in his resignation. The emperor refused to accept it, and wrote him the following letter:

"General,—You cannot be allowed to resign while it is possible to save the army by an honourable capitulation. You have done your duty all day. Do it still. You are doing a service to the country. The king of Prussia has accepted an armistice, and I am awaiting his proposals. Believe in my friendship.

"NAPOLEON."

General Wimpffen now seeing no hope of escaping from the enemy's grasp, submitted to the inevitable.

General Reilly, who had taken the emperor's letter to the king of Prussia, also carried General Wimpffen's proposal for a capitulation of the army. In answer to this, General von Moltke, at the king's desire, sent word that the only terms that could be allowed were the absolute and unconditional surrender of the whole force, with guns, horses, and *matériel*. General Wimpffen at first declared that he would die sooner than sign terms so disgraceful, for even then he could scarcely believe that his situation was so desperate. Arriving, as we have said, only two days before from Algeria, he found on his hands an army already beaten, and now his name would go down linked to a humiliating capitulation for all time! Being informed that, in the event of the proposals not being accepted, hostilities would be resumed on the following morning, he went himself to the Prussian headquarters at Donchery, and endeavoured to obtain more favourable conditions; but although the negotiations were continued far into the night, Von Moltke was inexorable. The French general was told that he might hold out if he preferred the destruction of his army; but to show him that such must inevitably be the issue, maps were produced, and the position and force of the corps of the German army and of its batteries indicated. "Your force," said Von Moltke to him, "does not number more than 80,000 men; we have 230,000, who completely surround you. Our artillery is everywhere in position, and can destroy Sedan in two hours. Your troops can only go out by the gates, and cannot possibly form before them. You have provisions for only one day, and scarcely any more ammunition. In such a case the prolongation of your defence would be only a useless massacre, the responsibility of which must rest upon those who will not prevent it."

The discussion ended without any definite decision, and General Wimpffen returned to Sedan. Meanwhile, night had closed on the woeful spectacle, and while the Germans rested on the positions they had won, the French lay meshed, as it were, in a deadly coil—a ruined and helpless army, within the grasp of its mighty conquerors. The victorious soldiers everywhere evinced the greatest eagerness to learn the details of the action. It was obvious they had comprehended the importance of the day, and were proud of having contributed to a success seldom equalled in the annals of history. The Crown Prince of Prussia returned to his headquarters at nine o'clock, when his men vied with each other in giving him a festal reception. The main street of the village was illuminated, and the soldiers who lined the way, in default of better materials, held small ends of tallow candles in their hands. Loud hurrahs welcomed the arrival of his royal highness; and the bands played, first, the German national anthem, and then the Dead March, in honour of the fallen.

The Crown Prince of Saxony's division made 11,000 prisoners during the day, and also captured twenty-five guns, seven mitrailleuses, two flags, and one eagle. The fifth and eleventh corps of the Crown Prince of Prussia's army also took more than 10,000 men, and adding to these those taken by the Bavarian troops, a total of about 25,000 men fell into the hands of the victors during the battle alone.

With regard to the killed and wounded, so terrible was the German artillery fire, so completely were whole French divisions taken in flank, in rear, and all round the compass, as their enemies closed upon them, that it is pretty safe to fix the French loss at about twice that of the Germans, or even two and a half times, and this would make it from 18,000 to 24,000 men. The splendid cavalry regiments were literally annihilated, and the ground for miles was strewn with corpses, where the Prussian shells had burst among the helpless masses.

The scene on the battle-field was unusually terrible. An eye-witness not unaccustomed to such sights said, "No human eye ever rested on such revolting objects as were presented by the battle-fields around Sedan. Let them fancy masses of coloured rags glued together with blood and brains, and pinned into strange shapes by fragments of bones. Let them conceive men's bodies without heads, legs without bodies, heaps of human entrails attached to red and blue cloth, and disembowelled corpses in uniform, bodies lying about in all attitudes, with skulls shattered, faces blown off, hips smashed, bones, flesh, and gay clothing all pounded together as if brayed in a mortar, extending for miles, not very thick in any one place, but recurring perpetually for weary hours—and then they cannot, with the most vivid imagination, come up to the sickening reality of that butchery. No nightmare could be so frightful. Several times I came on spots where there were two horses lying dead together in harness, killed by the same fragment. Several times I saw four, five, and six men, four, five, and six horses, all killed by the explosion of one projectile; and in one place there lay no less than eight French soldiers who must have been struck down by the bursting of a shell over a company, for they lay all round in a circle with their feet inwards, each shattered in the head or chest by a piece of shell, and no other dead being within a hundred yards of them. A curious, and to me unaccountable phenomenon, was the blackness of most of the faces of the dead. Decomposition had not set in, for they were killed only the day before. Another circumstance which struck me was the expression of agony on many faces. Death by the bayonet is agonizing, and those who die by steel, open-eyed and open-mouthed, have an expression of pain on the features, with protruding tongue. A musket ball wound, which is at once fatal, does not seem to cause much pain, and the features are composed and quiet, sometimes with a sweet smile on the lips. But the prevailing expression on this field of the faces which were not mutilated, was one of terror and of agony unutterable. There must have been a hell of torture raging within that semicircle in which the earth was torn asunder from all sides with a real tempest of iron hissing, and screeching, and bursting into the heavy masses at the hands of an unseen enemy."

The losses on the German side were comparatively small; in fact, for the first time since the war began they were enabled to announce them as moderate. The Bavarians suffered more than any other of the German troops, and 1800 of them were buried in one field at Balan—a proof, if any were needed, of the severe fighting around Bazeilles.

Amongst the killed on their side was a gallant Englishman, whose death caused the deepest general regret. We allude to Lieutenant-colonel Pemberton, who was acting as correspondent for the Times. In the evening he was riding by the side of H.R.H. Prince George of Saxony, who commanded the twelfth army corps. Towards the close of the battle they observed a column of French soldiers making signs with handkerchiefs. They rode towards them, thinking they had surrendered, when they were at once fired upon, and Colonel Pemberton fell. The bullet entered his temple, and death was instantaneous.

The night of Thursday was indeed a very sad one for the French army and its chiefs, completely defeated, fatigued, and dispirited as they were by three days' continued fighting. The fact, too, that almost the only provisions in Sedan were the horses shot in the battle added to their misery. "Even before the battle," said a resident in the town, "our men had lost all heart, and never anticipated success. After it, I saw broken masses of French troops rushing about the streets, breaking their Chassepots, setting their officers at defiance, and even shooting at them." "Hell," it has been said, "was let loose in Sedan;" the bonds of discipline were utterly broken, and the despairing officers had lost all power over an infuriated and mutinous soldiery.

The morning of the next day (Friday, 2nd September) revealed to the French the serried masses of their victorious enemies; and the smoking ruins of Bazeilles and Balan, destroyed by shells and fire the day before, gave fearful presage of the fate of Sedan, should it attempt to hold out against the artillery ready to open upon it. To make assurance doubly sure, and to show that the gros bataillons were on the side of the Germans, a great display of force was made all round the town, whose entire circuit was covered with the Prussian hosts; even the Würtemburgers having been ordered up from the direction of Mézières. The hill tops were black with troops, and all along them clustered the batteries in position. Then it was that the French commanders became thoroughly convinced their hour was come. When General Wimpffen assembled a council of war, it was mournfully admitted that the impending doom could not be averted, and that it was necessary to submit to whatever terms the victors thought fit to impose. Of about thirty-two general officers present, there were only two dissentient voices.

To have gone on fighting would have been madness, for the German troops held every approach to the town, and the French troops, shattered and discouraged, could not have hoped to cut their way through. They were reduced to so small a circle of outworks that, whilst they attacked one German corps, they might have been cannonaded in rear by most of the others. In a word, their condition was desperate.

General Wimpffen accordingly again repaired to the German headquarters, where the negotiations were continued for several hours, and it was past eleven o'clock before some modifications which he urged as to the officers' side arms and parole were agreed to. The following is a copy of the formal act of capitulation, which was signed towards noon in the chateau of Bellevue, near Frénois:—

"Between the undersigned the chief of the staff of King William, commander-in-chief of the German armies, and the general-commandant of the French army, both being provided with full powers from their majesties King William and the Emperor Napoleon, the following convention has been concluded:—

"Article 1. The French army placed under the orders of General Wimpffen, finding itself actually surrounded by superior forces round Sedan, are prisoners of war.

"Article 2. Seeing the brave defence of this French army, exemption is made in respect of all the generals and officers, and also of the superior *employés* having the rank of officers, who pledge their word of honour in writing not to bear arms against Germany, nor to act in any manner against its interests, until the close of the present war. The officers and *employés* who accept these conditions will retain their arms and personal effects.

"Article 3. All arms, as well as the *matériel* of the army, consisting of flags, eagles, cannon, horses, ammunition, &c., shall be immediately delivered at Sedan to a military commission appointed by the general-in-chief, in order to be forthwith handed over to German commissaries.

"Article 4. The town and fortified works of Sedan shall be given up in their present condition at latest on the evening of the 2nd of September, and be subject to the disposition of his Majesty King William.

"Article 5. Those officers who shall not have accepted the engagement set forth in Article 2, together with the disarmed troops, shall be marched out, ranged according to their regiments or corps, in military order. This proceeding will commence on the 2nd of September, and will terminate on September 3. These detachments will be marched to the districts bordering upon the Meuse, near Iges, to be handed over to German commissaries by their officers, who will then resign their commands to their sub-officers. The chief surgeons, without exception, will remain behind to attend to the wounded.

VON MOLTKE.
"WIMPFFEN.

"FRÉNOIS, *Sept.* 2, 1870."

The detention of the Emperor Napoleon in Germany was understood to be a part of the stipulations. The king of Prussia received a copy of the capitulation soon after twelve o'clock, on the very spot whence the Crown Prince had watched the movements of his army on the previous day; and after reading it aloud to the princes and staff who surrounded him, he addressed them as follows:—"Gentlemen, you now know what a great historical event has happened. I am indebted for this to the distinguished feats of the allied armies, to whom I feel bound on this occasion to express my kingly thanks; the more so as these great successes are calculated to rivet more closely the bond which unites the provinces of the North German Confederation and my other allies, whose numerous princely representatives I see assembled round me. We may thus hope for a happy future. Our task, however, is not completed with what has occurred under our eyes, for we do not know how the rest of France will accept and estimate it. We must, therefore, remain ready to fight; but, meanwhile, I present my thanks to every one who has contributed a leaf to the laurel crown of fame of our Fatherland." In speaking these last words, the king rested his eye especially on Prince Leopold of Bavaria and Prince William of Würtemburg, to whom he afterwards extended his hand. His Majesty then sent the following despatch to the queen:—

"BEFORE SEDAN, *Sept.* 2.

"A capitulation, whereby the whole army at Sedan are prisoners of war, has just been concluded with General Wimpffen, who was in command instead of the wounded Marshal MacMahon. The emperor only surrendered himself to me, as he himself has no command, and left everything to the regency in Paris. His place of residence I shall appoint after I have had an interview with him at a rendezvous, which will immediately take place. What a course events have assumed by God's guidance!"

General Wimpffen performed the painful duty of announcing the capitulation to the French troops, by at once issuing the following proclamation:—

"Soldiers!—Yesterday you fought against very superior forces. From daybreak until nightfall you resisted the enemy with the utmost valour, and expended almost your last cartridge. Exhausted by the struggle, you were unable to respond to the appeal made to you by your generals and your officers to attempt to gain the road to Montmèdy and to rejoin Marshal Bazaine. Two thousand men only were able to rally in order to make a supreme effort. They were compelled to stop at the village of Balan, and to return to Sedan, where your general announced with deep sorrow there existed neither provisions nor ammunition. The defence of the place was impossible, its position rendering it incapable of offering resistance to the numerous and powerful artillery of the enemy. The army collected within the walls of the town being unable either to leave it or defend it, and means of subsistence for the inhabitants and the troops being wanting, I have been compelled to adopt the sad resolution of treating with the enemy. Having proceeded yesterday to the Prussian headquarters with full powers from the emperor, I could not at first resign myself to accept the clauses which were imposed. It was only this morning, when threatened by a bombardment to which we had no means of replying, that I determined to make further efforts, and I have obtained conditions which relieve you as far as possible from the humiliating formalities which the usages of war usually exact under such circumstances. Nothing now remains for us, officers and soldiers, except to accept with resignation the consequences of necessities against which an army could not struggle—want of provisions and deficiency of ammunition. I have at least the consolation of having avoided a useless massacre, and of preserving to the country soldiers who are capable at some future time of rendering good and brilliant service.

"The General Commanding-in-chief,

"DE WIMPFFEN"

As the news of the capitulation spread, curses both loud and deep, with fierce cries of treachery and revenge, broke forth from the armed crowds. The French colonels burned the flags and eagles of their regiments; some of the soldiers threatened to turn their arms against their own officers; others threw their guns, their swords, ammunition, &c., into the Meuse, and broke up everything, that it might not come into the hands of the enemy. The impotent fury of despair, however, was vain; the French army, broken into defenceless masses, was huddled into camps where a few guns and regiments sufficed to control it; and the passion of the soldiery only provoked comments from the stern Germans on their want of discipline. Yet there were nobler spirits who, in their misfortune, showed themselves worthy of the French name.

Though this memorable capitulation was the eighteenth that had occurred in Europe since 1700, it was the only one which included a sovereign, and it was also by far the most important in point of numbers. Besides the 25,000 soldiers taken in the battle, 84,450 became prisoners of war by the surrender, and 14,000 French wounded were found in and around Sedan. More than 500 guns, including 70 mitrailleuses, 330 field and 150 fortress guns, 10,000 horses, 100,000 Chassepots, 80,000 cwts. of gunpowder, and large quantities of other war *matériel*, also fell into the hands of the victors. When parked, the artillery alone covered several acres. Among the prisoners were an emperor and a marshal of France, 39 generals, 230 staff and 2095 other officers, nearly all of whom chose to accompany the soldiers into captivity, rather than be liberated on parole. The remainder of the army, about 14,500 men, with 12,000 horses, cannons, and gun carriages, succeeded in reaching the neutral territory of Belgium. MacMahon's army of 150,000 men had thus, within three days, ceased to exist, almost every man being either killed, wounded, or taken prisoner; for even those who escaped to Belgium were immediately disarmed and confined in the fortresses of that country.

The vast body of captives having been stationed on the peninsula formed by the Meuse between Iges and Villette, the Prussians took possession of Sedan, and made requisitions, but did not attempt to pillage the town. General von Moltke issued an order that the prisoners were to be victualled from provisions which, in accordance with the promise of General Wimpffen, their late commander-in-chief, would be sent from Mézières by rail to Donchery; but at first they were compelled to endure the most severe privations, though probably this was unavoidable. Within a few days they were sent off to Germany, partly by Stenay, Etain, Gorze, and Remilly, and partly by Buzancy, Clermont, St. Michiel, and Pont-à-Mousson. The horses taken were immediately portioned out among the various German forces.

The history of the capitulation is given at length in Count von Bismarck's official report to the king—a document so full of historical and general interest that we reprint it entire:—

"DONCHERY, *September* 2.

"After I had repaired hither last evening by your Majesty's command, in order to take part in the negotiations as to the capitulation, they were interrupted till about one a.m. by the granting of time for consideration. This General Wimpffen begged for after General von Moltke had firmly declared that no condition other than a laying down of arms would be approved, and that the bombardment would be resumed at nine a.m. if the capitulation were not previously concluded. Early this morning, towards ten o'clock, General Reilly was announced to me, and he informed me that the emperor wished to see me, and was already on his way from Sedan. The general immediately turned back in order to tell his Majesty that I was following him, and shortly afterwards, half-way between here and Sedan, in the vicinity of Frénois, I found myself opposite the emperor. His Majesty was in an open carriage with three superior officers, and with a like number on horseback close by. Among the latter, Generals Castelnau, Keilly, Moskowa, who appeared wounded in the foot, and Vaubert, were personally known to me. Arrived at the carriage, I dismounted, stepped up immediately to the emperor's side, and asked his Majesty's commands. The emperor expressed a wish to see your Majesty, apparently thinking that your Majesty was at Donchery. After I had replied that your Majesty's headquarters were at the moment three German (about fourteen English) miles distant, at Vendresse, the emperor asked whether any place had been fixed in the locality whither he might repair, and, in fine, what my opinion was on the matter. I replied that I had come here when it was quite dark, the country being unknown to me, and placed at his disposal the house occupied by me at Donchery, which I would at once vacate. The emperor accepted this, and proceeded towards Donchery, but halted about 100 paces from the Meuse bridge leading into the town, before a working man's house standing by itself, and asked whether he could not dismount there. I sent Count Bismarck Bohlen, who, in the interim, had followed me, to inspect the house, and after he had announced that its internal accommodation was very poor and narrow, but that it was free from wounded, the emperor dismounted and directed me to follow him inside. Here, in a very small room, containing one table and two chairs, I had about an hour's conversation with the emperor. His Majesty was extremely anxious to obtain more favourable terms of capitulation for the army. I declined to discuss this matter with his Majesty, when so purely military a question was pending between General von Moltke and General "Wimpffen. On the other hand, I asked emperor whether his Majesty was inclined to the negotiate for peace. The emperor replied that, as a prisoner, he was not now in a position to do so; and on my further question by whom, in his view, the executive authority of France was at present represented, his Majesty referred me to the government at Paris. He declared that, as he had given full powers to the regency, with it alone could negotiations for peace be conducted; that he merely delivered his own person into the hands of the king, claiming nothing for himself, but appealing to his generosity for the army and for France. After the clearing up of this point, which from the emperor's letter of yesterday to your Majesty could not be certainly judged of, I perceived, and did not conceal this from the emperor, that the situation, to-day as yesterday, offered no other practical question than the military one; and I signified the necessity which therefore rested on us of obtaining before all things, through the capitulation of Sedan, a material pledge for the stability of the military results already achieved. I had already, yesterday evening, considered the question on all sides with General von Moltke, whether it would be possible, without prejudice to German interests, to offer more favourable conditions than those laid down, in deference to the military feeling of honour of an army which had fought well. After due consideration we had felt ourselves obliged to settle this question in the negative. When, therefore, General von Moltke, who meanwhile had come from the town, went to your Majesty for the purpose of laying before you the emperor's wishes, this was not, as your Majesty knows, with the intention of supporting them.

"The emperor then went out into the open air, and invited me to sit by him before the door of the house. His Majesty submitted to me the question whether it was not practicable to allow the French army to cross the Belgian frontier, in order that they might be disarmed and ' interned.' I had already, the previous evening, conversed on this eventuality with General von Moltke. As regarded the political situation, I on my side did not take the initiative, nor did the emperor, except that he deplored the misfortune of war, and affirmed that he himself had not desired war, but had been forced into it by the pressure of public opinion in France.

"Through inquiries in the place, and especially through a search by officers of the general staff, it had, meantime, between nine and ten o'clock, been ascertained that the chateau of Bellevue, near Frénois, was suited to the reception of the emperor, and, moreover, was not occupied by wounded. I mentioned this to his Majesty, fixing Frénois as the place which I should propose to your Majesty for the interview; and accordingly put it to the emperor whether his Majesty would wish to proceed thither at once, as to remain within the small working man's cottage was inconvenient, and the emperor would possibly require some rest. His Majesty gladly acquiesced, and I accompanied the emperor—a guard of honour of your Majesty's body cuirassier regiment preceding him—to the chateau of Bellevue, where in the interim the emperor's additional suite and equipages, the arrival of which out of the town had till then appeared uncertain, had come from Sedan. General Wimpffen also arrived, with whom, in expectation of the return of General von Moltke, the discussion of the capitulation negotiations, broken off yesterday, was renewed by General Podbielsky, in the presence of Lieutenant-colonel Verdy and General Wimpffen's chief of the staff, both which officers drew up the protocol. I only took part in them by sketching the legal and political situation according to the explanations given me by the emperor himself. From Count Nostis, commissioned by General von Moltke, I received the announcement that your Majesty would see the emperor only after the conclusion of the capitulation, an intimation on which the hope on the other side of obtaining other conditions than those laid down was given up. I rode off upon this with the intention of informing your Majesty of the position of affairs towards Donchery, but on the way I met General von Moltke with the text of the capitulation approved by your Majesty; and this, after we went with him to Frénois, was then accepted and signed without dispute. The conduct of General Wimpffen, as also that of the other French generals the previous night, was very becoming. That brave officer could not refrain from expressing to me his great pain at being called on, forty-eight hours after his arrival from Africa, and half a day after taking the command, to subscribe his name to a capitulation so deplorable for the French nation. Want of provisions and munitions, however, and the absolute impossibility of any further defence, imposed on him as a general the duty of restraining his personal feelings, as further bloodshed could not alter the situation. The concession of the release of the officers on their word of honour was accepted with warm thanks, as an expression of your Majesty's intention not to overstep the limits which our political and military interests made necessary with regard to the feelings of an army which had fought bravely. To this sentiment General Wimpffen afterwards gave expression in a letter, in which he thanked General von Moltke for the very considerate manner in which the negotiations were on his side conducted.

"(Signed.)   BISMARCK."

As an instance of the scrupulous respect paid to the fallen emperor, it is related that the Prussian minister of state uncovered his head, and stood, hat in hand, while Napoleon alighted from his carriage. On the latter requesting him to put it on, the count replied, "Sire, I receive your Majesty as I would my own royal master."

When all had been arranged the two sovereigns met in the chateau of Bellevue—a pretty, new country house, built in imitation of an old chateau, and provided with glass conservatories at the angles, which stands on a wooded knoll sloping down towards the Meuse at Frénois, a short way outside Sedan, and separated from it by the river. The house well deserves its name, for it commands a lovely and extensive prospect. About two o'clock on Friday afternoon the king of Prussia, with his body guard and an escort of cuirassiers, attended by the Crown Prince and a staff of general officers, proceeded to this chateau, which was charmingly furnished. The emperor, who came with his personal followers and staff in charge of a strong cavalry escort, which was ranged on the other side of the avenue leading to the mansion, facing the cuirassiers, had been for some time awaiting his Majesty's arrival. Napoleon received the victor of Sedan at the foot of the steps leading to the house. When the king approached he took off his military cap and made a deep and respectful bow. Both then retired into the glass house, off one of the saloons on the drawing-room floor, where they could be seen by the staff outside engaged in earnest conversation. From the windows of the little room in which they met, Sedan itself, the heights where the armies were still encamped, and the large masses of troops which occupied them, were all visible. During the meeting Napoleon was informed that the palace of Wilhelmshöhe, near Cassel (a favourite summer residence of his uncle, King Jerome), was to be the place of his abode during his captivity in Germany. An account of this interview, understood to emanate from the French emperor himself, says:—"At this conference the king showed the lofty feelings which animated him, by exhibiting to the emperor all the consideration which his misfortunes demanded, and the emperor preserved an attitude of the utmost dignity. General Wimpffen, who had told the emperor that the army counted upon his intervention with the king of Prussia for better conditions, was informed of the fruitlessness of his efforts." After this meeting, which lasted about half an hour, the emperor had a few minutes' conversation with the Crown Prince, during which he was much agitated when alluding to the kind and courteous manner in which he had been received. His great anxiety seemed to be not to be exhibited as a prisoner to his own soldiers. Wishing to escape one humiliation, however, he was exposed to another, for when his course was altered to avoid Sedan, he had to pass through the lines of the Prussian army.

The easiest route to his destination was through Belgium; and the permission of that government having been readily granted, his departure took place at nine o'clock on Saturday morning, amid a terrible storm. The city of Sedan had been occupied by the Prussians on the previous day, and all the French soldiers disarmed and put under guard as prisoners of war; but the emperor, instead of re-entering the town, was permitted to stay on Friday night in the chateau or villa at Frénois, from which he started in a close carriage with four horses and two postillions for the Belgian town of Bouillon, on his way to Germany. The carriage was escorted by a troop of Black Hussars, some riding before and some behind it. An open carriage, with several French and German officers appointed to wait on his Majesty; a dozen other carriages, in which were his personal attendants and domestic servants; and a number of fine saddle-horses belonging to him, formed part of the procession. The emperor himself, who wore the kepi and undress uniform of a lieutenant-general, with the star of the Legion of Honour, but without his sword, looked pale and worn, yet quite self-possessed. Beside him in the carriage sat the prince de la Moskowa, a son of Marshal Ney. Among his attendants were General Castelnau, one of his aides-de-camp, Generals Reilly and Vaubert, and twenty other French officers. All the carriages bore the imperial escutcheon, and were drawn by horses from the imperial stables. There was a crowd of curious spectators, who, however, gave no outward sign of their feelings. On entering Belgian territory the escort was changed for one of Belgian chasseurs. His Majesty passed Saturday night at the Hotel des Postes, at Bouillon, where he dined with thirty guests. On Sunday he went on by railway to Liege and Venders, and proceeded next day to the palace of Wilhelmshöhe.

Some days before the battle of Sedan the Prince Imperial had been sent into Belgium for safety. On his journey to Germany the emperor received a telegram announcing the safe arrival of his son at Maubeuge.

After his interview with the emperor the king of Prussia addressed the following telegram to the queen:—

"September 2.

"What a thrilling moment that of my meeting with Napoleon! He was cast down, but dignified in his bearing and resigned. I gave him Wilhelmshöhe, near Cassel, as the place where he will stay. Our meeting took place in a small castle in front of the western glacis of Sedan. From there I rode through the ranks of our army round Sedan. The reception by the troops—thou mayst imagine it—indescribable! I finished my five hours' ride at nightfall at half-past seven, but only arrived back here at one a.m. May God aid us further."

Later in the day the king wrote her Majesty the accompanying letter:—

"VENDRESSE, South of Sedan, *Sept.* 3.

"You will have learnt through my telegrams the whole extent of the great historical event which has just taken place. It is like a dream, even when one has seen it unrol itself hour by hour; but when I consider that after one great successful war I could not expect anything more glorious during my reign, and that I now see this act follow destined to be famous in the history of the world, I bow before God, who alone has chosen my army and allies to carry it into execution, and has chosen as as the instruments of his will. It is only in this sense that I can conceive this work, and in all humility praise God's guidance and grace. I will now give you a picture of the battle and its results in a compressed form. On the evening of the 31st and the morning of the 1st, the army had reached its appointed position round Sedan. The Bavarians held the left wing near Bazeilles, on the Meuse; next them the Saxons, towards Moncelle and Daigny; the guards still marching on towards Givonne, the fifth and eleventh corps towards St. Menges and Fleigneux. As the Meuse here makes a sharp bend, no corps had been posted from St. Menges to Donchery, but at the latter place there were Würtemburgers who covered the rear against sallies from Mézières. Count Stolberg's cavalry division was in the plain of Donchery as right wing; the rest of the Bavarians were in the front towards Sedan. Notwithstanding a thick fog, the battle began at Bazeilles early in the morning, and a sharp action developed itself by degrees, in which it was necessary to take house by house. It lasted nearly all day, and Scholar's Erfurt division (reserve fourth corps) was obliged to assist. It was eight o'clock, when I reached the front before Sedan, that the great battle commenced. A hot artillery action now began at all points. It lasted for hours, and during it we gradually gained ground. As the above-named villages were taken, very deep and wooded ravines made the advance of the infantry more difficult, and favoured the defence. The villages of Selg and Floing were taken, and the fiery circle drew gradually closer round Sedan. It was a grand sight from our position on a commanding height behind the above-mentioned battery when we looked to the front beyond St. Torcy. The violent resistance by the enemy began to slacken by degrees, which we could see by the broken battalions that were hurriedly retreating from the woods and villages. The cavalry endeavoured to attack several battalions of our fifth corps, and the latter behaved admirably. The cavalry galloped through the interval between the battalions, and then returned the same way. This was repeated three times, so that the ground was covered with corpses and horses, all of which we could see very well from our position. I have not been able to learn the number of this brave regiment, as the retreat of the enemy was in many places a flight. The infantry, cavalry, and artillery rushed in a crowd into the town and its immediate environs, but no sign was given that the enemy contemplated extricating himself from his desperate situation by capitulation. No other course was left than to bombard the town with the heavy battery. In twenty minutes the town was burning in several places, which, with the numerous burning villages over the whole field, produced a terrible impression. I accordingly ordered the firing to cease, and sent Lieutenant-colonel von Broussart with a flag of truce, to demand the capitulation of the army and the fortress. He was met by a Bavarian officer, who reported to me that a French *parlementaire* had announced himself at the gate. Colonel von Broussart was admitted, and on his asking for the commander-in-chief, he was unexpectedly introduced into the presence of the emperor, who wished to give him a letter for myself. When the emperor asked what his message was, and received the answer, "To demand the surrender of the army and fortress," he replied that on this subject he must apply to General de Wimpffen, who had undertaken the command, in the place of the wounded General MacMahon, and that he would now send his adjutant-general, Reilly, with a letter to myself. It was seven o'clock when Reilly and Broussart came to me, the latter a little in advance; and it was first through him that I learned with certainty the presence of the emperor. You may imagine the impression which this made upon all of us, but particularly on myself. Reilly sprung from his horse and gave me the letter of the emperor, adding that he had no other orders. Before I opened the letter I said to him, "But I demand, as the first condition, that the army lay down its arms." The letter began thus:—"N'ayant pas pu mourir à la tête de mes troupes, je dépose mon epée à votre Majesté," leaving all the rest to me. My answer was that I deplored the manner of our meeting, and begged that a plenipotentiary might be sent with whom we might conclude the capitulation. After I had given the letter to General Reilly, I spoke a few words with him as an old acquaintance, and so this act ended. I gave Moltke powers to negotiate, and directed Bismarck to remain behind in case political questions should arise. I then rode to my carriage and drove here, greeted everywhere along the road with the loud hurrahs of the trains that were marching up and singing the national hymn. It was deeply touching. Candles were lighted everywhere, so that we were driven through an improvised illumination. I arrived here at eleven o'clock, and drank with those about me to the prosperity of an army which had accomplished such feats. As on the morning of the 2nd I had received no news from Moltke respecting negotiations for the capitulation, which were to take place in Donchery, I drove to the battle-field, according to agreement, at eight o'clock, and met Moltke, who was coming to obtain my consent to the proposed capitulation. He told me at the same time that the emperor had left Sedan at five o'clock in the morning and had come to Donchery, as he wished to speak with me. There was a chateau and park in the neighbourhood, and I chose that place for our meeting. At ten o'clock I reached the height before Sedan. Moltke and Bismarck appeared at twelve o'clock, with the capitulation duly signed. At one o'clock I started again with Fritz, the Crown Prince, and escorted by the cavalry and the staff; I alighted before the chateau, where the emperor came to meet me. The visit lasted a quarter of an hour. "We were both much moved at seeing each other again under such circumstances. What my feelings were—I had seen Napoleon only three years before at the summit of his power—is more than I can describe. After this meeting, from half past two to half past seven o'clock, I rode past the whole army before Sedan. The reception given me by the troops, the meeting with the guards, now decimated—all these are things which I cannot describe to-day. I was much touched by so many proofs of love and devotion. Now, farewell. A heart deeply moved at the conclusion of such a letter.

"WILLIAM."

An anecdote in connection with this letter, derived from a very good source, deserves to be recorded. It illustrates the kindly nature of the man whom the duties of his exalted position compelled to give the word of command in so many sanguinary battles. When the Feldjäger officer who was to carry it to Berlin entered the royal apartment, the king was just sealing the letter. On seeing the officer his Majesty suspended his occupation, and, turning to him, said:— "Before giving you this packet I must tell you one thing. You will yourself place it in her Majesty's hands, and you will take care to tell her Majesty, even before she breaks the seal, that this time, at least, our losses are moderate in comparison to the result."

At the military banquet given by the king of Prussia to his principal officers, on the brief rest-day which followed this "crowning mercy," champagne was served in honour of the great occasion (*vin ordinaire* only, say the German chroniclers of the campaign, having previously appeared at the royal table); and his Majesty proposed a toast in the following terms:—"We must to-day, in gratitude, drink to the health of my brave army. *You*, war minister Von Roon, have sharpened our sword; *you*, General von Moltke, have guided it; and *you*, Count von Bismarck, by your direction of the national policy for years, have brought Prussia to her present pitch of elevation. Let us then drink to the health of the army, of the three I have named in connection with that toast, and of every one present who has contributed, according to his power, to the results now accomplished."

Such is the history of the memorable battle and capitulation of Sedan—the darkest spot in the checquered military annals of France, and unquestionably the most remarkable military event since the retreat from Moscow. Neither Crecy, nor Agincourt, nor Pavia, nor St. Quentin, nor Blenheim, nor Waterloo, was so calamitous; modern history seeks in vain for a parallel to the dire catastrophe, for no modern European nation had ever received so crushing a blow. Since Pavia no French monarch had been taken in siege or battle. This untoward consummation was the natural result of the fatal strategy which had led the French to the frontier of Belgium, with an army wanting in every element of military power; while their enemies, twice as strong and efficient, were in a position to overtake and crush them by overwhelming numbers. Doubtless, the tardiness of MacMahon's movements, the want of discipline of his troops, and the faults of his lieutenants, contributed largely to the unhappy result; but the original error was in the design of a march from Rheims by Montmèdy on Metz, while the Germans held all the shorter lines—a march all but certain, with such an army as MacMahon's, to end in disaster. The marshal also made a grave mistake on the 31st of August, when he took no means to prevent his being shut into Sedan by superior forces, and did not discover this danger until he was in the presence of the enemy that surrounded him on the morning of the 1st of September, when, after being wounded, he thought of a retreat on Mézières. Had an order to that effect been issued twenty hours earlier, it would almost certainly have saved the bulk of his army. But after the battle had begun it was far too late to try this movement, which he ought to have attempted the day before, the instant he had brought his troops back to Sedan after their defeat on the 30th. Then the Prussian left was many miles away from the Meuse; and it took the fifth corps and the Würtemburg division the whole of the 31st to reach their assigned points of passage. Certainly, on the afternoon at least of that day, it was in MacMahon's power to make a swift and compact movement in retreat towards Mézières; and it is hardly too much to assert that a determined resolve to avoid another general action by instantly falling back on the fortresses in the north-east of France, and the sacrifice of a corps at Sedan and Mézières to gain a day or two's march, might have saved from a humiliating fate the greater part of the soldiers who were surrendered. At Mézières MacMahon would have been joined by General Vinoy's corps, which was marching up to his aid; and although even then the Prussians could easily have cut him off from Paris, if they failed to intercept him before he gained the shelter of the nest of fortresses about Valenciennes, yet the task of besieging the capital under those circumstances would have been difficult and dangerous, if not impossible.

In reply to this view of the case it has been said, that a movement in the direction we have indicated, with the Crown Prince's army hanging on his flank, would have led to MacMahon's being destroyed before he could reach the shelter of the nest of fortresses beyond Mézières, which at a later period covered Faidherbe's operations. Very probably, if we may judge from the marked inferiority of the French in marching no less than in fighting, destruction would have been the end of such an attempt. But it is quite clear that there would have been hopes of saving some part ol the army by sacrificing the rearmost corps; whilst the fatal resolution of taking up a simply defensive attitude round Sedan was the short way to such complete ruin and disgrace, as no French commander had ever met before, since Dupont lost his head and surrendered to a mob of Spaniards at Baylen. Other critics have denounced the timidity which induced the French to withdraw the part of their army which had got beyond the Meuse on the 30th, only to fall back before the German cavalry. Ducrot's corps, which had reached Carignan, might, it is said, have been pushed on to advance separately to the succour of Bazaine. But to this criticism little serious importance need be attached, since a single corps could hardly have produced an appreciable effect on the vast operations near Metz; and isolated between the German armies, it would almost infallibly have been cut off without accomplishing any object worth the risk of separation.

As stated in the preceding chapter, it subsequently became known from official documents that this celebrated flank march of the French army was only undertaken in obedience to express orders from the ministry in Paris, which of course, to a great extent, absolves MacMahon from blame. Still it should never have been commenced; and if anything could add to the conclusive proofs of the folly of taking such a step, it is the consideration that Marshal Bazaine was not then in want of immediate relief; that MacMahon's army was the main hope of France; that it was instantly required to protect the capital; and that if it had (alien back on Paris, as it could easily have done, the subsequent situation might have been wholly different from what it was. The manner in which the German commanders availed themselves of their antagonist's mistakes was admirable, for the annihilation of MacMahon's army was due quite as much to the promptness with which these were turned to account by General von Moltke, as to the fatuity which led to their being committed. An impartial historian cannot fail to notice the prescience with which the army of the Crown Prince of Saxony was moved in order to aid the Crown Prince of Prussia; the readiness with which it was marched towards the Meuse; and the energy with which the two German armies were, without the delay of more than a few hours, turned northwards to stop and destroy MacMahon. These are truly great illustrations of the art of war; nor are the final operations less instructive, by which the whole French army, brought to bay at Sedan, was cut off from the possibility of retreat, and compelled to surrender. The Prussian staff were better acquainted with the difficulties of MacMahon's situation than he was himself. At least four days previous to his selecting that position, General Blumenthal, putting his finger on the map, said, "MacMahon is quite lost. There he must stand and fight, and there he must be beaten without a chance of escape. They are quite lost. I wonder what they can mean." In proof of their utter helplessness, it is stated that some time afterwards an English military man remarked to some Prussian staff officers, that the surrender at Sedan of so large an army had struck him as rather inglorious; and asked them whether in the circumstances of the country and the capital, the army ought not rather to have cut its way out at the expense of half its numbers. They answered that the surrender was not inglorious, for there was no other resource left. "They ought not to have got into such a position; but once there, there was no getting out of it." The ability of the German chiefs was ably seconded by their troops, who in their operations gave proof of power, vigour, and celerity of movement, not easily matched in military annals.

From our previous description it will have been noticed that the leading feature of the battle of Sedan was a prolonged artillery duel at comparatively long ringes, followed up by desperate charges of infantry. There was hardly any manoeuvring during the day. The whole German army formed a vast semicircle, with the horns of the crescent pointing to the Belgian frontier, and slowly approaching one another. When these horns met to the north of Sedan, the great mass of the French army was forced steadily back upon the town: then the German circle grew ever smaller, until at length its circumference was, at some points, inside the outworks of Sedan itself. The strength of the French position—on an inner line of heights on either side of the fortress—counterbalanced the disparity in numbers so long as they maintained their ground. But when they gave way, however slightly, and allowed the hostile crescent to contract, they became necessarily exposed to a converging fire, from which it was impossible to escape unless by thrusting back one or other of the inclosing armies: and as this was hopeless, the French were compelled to remain on the defensive throughout.

On two occasions during the day the French emperor providentially escaped being instantly killed. In the confusion which ensued upon the irruption of the panic-striken French into Sedan, when riding slowly through a wide street swept by the German artillery, and choked by the disordered soldiery, he paused for a moment to address a question to a colonel of his staff. At that instant a shell exploded a few feet in front of him, leaving him unharmed, though to all around his escape appeared miraculous. An eyewitness affirms that the emperor continued on his way without manifesting the slightest emotion, and greeted by the hearty *vivats* of the troops. Later, while sitting at a window, inditing his celebrated letter to the king of Prussia, a shell struck the wall just outside, and burst only a few feet from his chair, again leaving him unscathed and unmoved.

GREAT SORTIE FROM METZ.

During the movements before the battle of Sedan, communications—it is believed through a subterranean telegraph to Mézières—had been maintained between Marshals Bazaine and MacMahon, and a sortie was prepared by the former on August 26, eight days after the Germans had succeeded in imprisoning his army in Metz, had intrenched themselves in every direction, and had organized a telegraphic communication all round the city, by means of which 8000 men could be collected at any one spot in fifteen minutes, and 22,000 men in twenty-eight minutes;

and the weak German force on the eastern side could be enabled to hold its own until the arrival, at the end of five and six hours respectively, of two additional corps from the western side, passing over pontoon bridges at Argancy and Hanconcourt. Bazaine's sortie was to have been made on this eastern side, along the right bank of the Moselle, and three corps were moved for the purpose; but it was abandoned in consequence of a torrent of rain coming on.

Nothing further was attempted till the 30th, when advices dated from Rheims were received by Bazaine from the emperor, stating that an attempt would be made to relieve the imprisoned force. It was therefore determined that a sortie on a large scale should be attempted on the following day; it was again to be made due eastwards at first, and if successful there the French hoped to be able to obtain possession of the roads leading down the right bank of the Moselle on Thionville, and render that fortress accessible without having to cross the Orne. The engagement which ensued was rather on an extensive scale.

By far the best description of the sortie yet published is that of Mr. G. T. Robinson, the special correspondent of the *Manchester Guardian*, who was shut up with the French army in Metz during the whole of the siege, and to whose interesting work on the "Fall of Metz "we have been more than once indebted. He says that when, on the evening of the 30th, the soldiers heard of the attempt proposed for the morrow, they were full of glee, though somewhat in doubt. A similar report was circulated on the 26th of August, and although the weather was then miserable, and the roads almost impassable, the attempt had begun. The troops came down from Plappeville, and the Ban St. Martin emptied. Round from Montigny came long lines of troops, and they marched all the way up the hill of St. Julien, and then they marched down again, after displaying themselves to the enemy, and doing nothing more. This time, however, the weather was fine. The hot sun had dried up the roads, and before daybreak the troops commenced their march. It was three o'clock in the morning when they began to move. They passed over temporary bridges to the Ile Chambière, rejoining behind the fort Bellecroix the various corps which had come from the other camps. Here, however, their first misgiving awaited them. They were in hopes it was going to be an attempt to make a real *trouée*—a serious intention to cut a way through the wall of Prussians which day by day kept growing thicker around them. But here was the baggage, which was evidently not going. The tents were not packed, and the army was not in the order for a long march. Still they had faith.

Before describing the attack on the Prussian lines we may take a bird's-eye view of the position as seen from Metz, in which a glance at the plan of the battle of Courcelles, given in Chapter XI., will greatly assist the reader. To the east was the high hill of St. Julien, up the western side of which winds the little village of that name, and whose summit was capped by the long horizontal lines of its as yet unfinished fort. From this point runs out the long straight crest of a continued hill, descending somewhat at first, and then gradually rising again until it reaches a culminating point, crowned by the lofty steeple of a church. That steeple marks St. Barbe. Having an elevation of some 90 feet above even the fort-crowned hill of St. Julien, and rising some 400 feet above the flat plain of the Moselle, the importance of the situation was evident. Marvellous, indeed, was it that such a hill should have been left unguarded; but the enemy was quietly allowed to take possession of it, and thenceforth it was one of the watch-dogs of Metz. On the sloping ground which gently falls to the south of this long-crested hill are the villages of Servigny, Nouilly, and Mey, whilst placed on the little stream which cuts its quiet way at the bottom of the valley are the villages of Valliers and Vautoux, and on the opposite side of the stream, on a very gently ascending slope, are those of Noisseville and Montoy. On the northern slope, which runs down to the Moselle, rapidly, indeed almost declivitously, at St. Julien, but flattening as the valley widens, are the villages of Vremy, Failly, Charly, and Chiculles, almost all of which played their part in this two days' tragedy. Roughly speaking, the area of the battle-field was that of a scalene triangle, whose apex was at St. Julien, and whose base extended from Vremy to Montoy; its longest side being about six miles in length, whilst its base was about five miles. That was the area of the main portion of the fight. Detached skirmishing of course extended its dimensions very considerably; but the chief interest lay within these bounds. The importance of the position of St. Barbe was immediately recognized by the Germans, and the place, strong by nature, was strengthened by art. Epaulements were thrown up along the hill sides. Redoubts were erected wherever any jutting spur of higher ground projected into either of the two valleys which it dominated; and whoever held St. Barbe held possession of the road to Sarrelouis on the one side, and the lower hills, which yet were high enough to guard the valley of the Moselle, on the other. It has been necessary to be somewhat discursive on this point at first, in order to render more intelligible the description of a battle cut by the formation of the ground into two distinct parts, and extending over two days.

Although it was early morning when the march began, it was nearly four o'clock in the afternoon before the first shot was fired. On the left was the corps of Marshal Canrobert, in the centre was that of Leboeuf, and on the right that of Frossard. There appears to have been some want of preconcerted plan amongst them, something which could not be settled without a long and serious delay; for the French forces rested nearly twelve hours on the slope of St. Jullen without doing anything; resting, too, right in full view of the enemy, who had thus ample time to bring up his reinforcements to the point so deliberately threatened. Marshal Bazaine stopped in the Château Gromont. At last the troops received orders to move, and on went the dragoons, with their glistening helmets. General de Clerembault led them off the first, that they might guard the French extreme right against any surprise. The Moselle did this duty for them on the left. There are a few short words yet to be spoken to the Marshals. Canrobert, the echo of Bazaine, gives his last orders as the clock strikes four, and all are on the march. Straight out from the fort St. Julien, towards the village of Chiculles, runs the road for Buzonville. That is the line of Marshal Canrobert; he has to guard it, and all the land lying between it and the river, and as much of the rising ground up to the crest of the long-ridged hill as he can manage. Along the crest goes Marshal Leboeuf, this day taking the place before occupied by Bazaine, and leading on that third corps d'armée which the commander-in-chief led when the war began. He has to march along the crest of the hill straight on to St. Barbe, if he can, co-operating with Canrobert on his left, and touching with his right the second corps of Frossard. Between Marshals Canrobert and Leboeuf marches the division of General L'Admirault, whilst the aged General Changarnier occupies a corresponding position between Marshal Leboeuf and Frossard. Thus they diverge; and the worst of it is they do diverge. Canrobert pushes forward with the intention of reaching Malroy, and cutting the enemy's communication by the river. Vany and Chiculles are attacked by the tenth and fourth regiments of the line, with the desire to turn the enemy back upon himself, and drive him into the river. L'Admirault's corps marched right up to the village of Servigny, where, for some unknown reason, it waits for two hours under a heavy shower of shells. At last the charge is sounded. At the village they go. There is what is very rare now-a-days; there is hand to hand work, and bayonet crosses bayonet at every corner. Each house is a fortress, but it must be carried. The French long 24-pounders of St. Julien silence a Prussian battery at Gras which troubles them, and Servigny is once more French. Two hours it took to take it, and two hours under such circumstances were very long. During this long struggle here the villages of Chiculles and Vany were carried, and Canrobert's corps almost touched the walls of Failly. The twelfth line are pushed forward in open order on Charly, and its sharpshooters creep under cover of the rolling broken ground up to within three hundred yards of a Prussian battery there. For two hours and a half do they pepper at it, until at last it is compelled to retire behind the wood which backs up the little village.

If Canrobert would only now make a dash at Malroy it could be carried from the right, as this battery covers the road; but the opportunity is not seized, and it never occurs again. Meanwhile the extreme right of our forces has pushed its cavalry on to Coincy, arresting the progress of the Prussians, who, called by the heavy firing, came up from Remilly and Courcelles at the gallop. The dragoons dismount and hold the village, the Prussians file off.

Montauban pushes up the first division of the third corps to Montoy, and forces his way right up to Flanville, where, touching the line of attack assigned to Frossard, he finds himself hardly strong enough for the work, and sends to the commander of the second corps for assistance. None comes; Frossard wants to be well taken care of, and for an hour and a half Montauban holds unsupported this post, till at last, poor fellow, he falls. At length up comes General Magnan with his division (second corps), and taking charge of his own and that of Montauban, launches forth the sixty-second and eighteenth battalions of the chasseurs-à-pied and the fifty-first of the line. At the village they go, the sixty-second leading, with drums and trumpets playing. On come the fifty-first; "*à la baionnette*" they shout, and plunge into the village, whilst the eighteenth deploys to the right, and covers the road to Retonfay, along which the Prussians retreat, with a line of fire and dead men. It was a brilliant bit of work, but it cost dear, and the sixty-second left 13 officers and 400 men on that little bit of road which leads on to Flanville. In the centre Nouilly has been carried by the ninety-fifth and the thirty-second of the line, under Leboeuf; at least by what is left of these two regiments. They have both suffered heavily in this war, and the thirty-second has lost more than 1000 rank and file and 45 officers since it came to Metz. Nouilly carried, they push impetuously forward, and serve Noisseville the same; and as the last sun in August sets the whole line is ours. Charly, Failly, Servigny, Noisseville, Flanville, Coincy, are all carried.

But, alas, night comes on, and those ten hours which were wasted in the morning are sadly wanted now. Advance in the dark without more strength they could not. They did not know where the enemy was; but they knew the French position only too well, and they kept up an almost continual fire upon them. But, worst of all, Canrobert has not pushed on far enough, and the bridges of Malroy are yet in the hands of the Prussians, who keep pouring fresh troops into the threatened position. These in their turn come down upon the French, and between ten and eleven at night they are attacked in considerable force on the villages of Noisseville and Servigny. But the Germans did not venture in, and the French did not venture out; so the firing served more to check the advance of either foe than any other purpose. This was the position of things when the fighting ceased. The French were hopeful that during the night fresh forces would be brought up, and that the morrow would prove a grand day in their history. Not a single soldier, however, was brought up, nor was aught done to strengthen their weak points, whilst the enemy had all the night been making preparations for the day's hard work. By the bridges Canrobert should have taken, and by the road Frossard should have cut—from Ars-Laquenexy and Courcelles, from Remilly and Corny—did the Germans bring up fresh men, while the French, with all the imperial guard behind them, and numerous troops in Metz, moved not one man nor brought forward a single gun!

The action recommenced between five and six o'clock in the morning, the French centre being then the chief point of attack. The village of Noisseville was soon a vortex of fire, and for a time the whistling sound of the shells in the air was as continuous and as loud as that of a locomotive blowing off steam. The French, seeing they were outnumbered, and that they would not be able to hold the village much longer, brought a battery of mitrailleuses up the hill, to give the enemy as warm a reception as possible. The village was now on fire in several places, and many poor wounded fellows made their way to the rear. Meanwhile not a fresh soldier was brought up. The poor fellows who fought all the previous afternoon, and partly through the night, had now to bear the brunt again. They can stand it no longer, and, borne back by numbers, they retire. Now begins the horrible grind of the mitrailleuses. Gr-r-r-rutt it goes as the Germans rush forward, and the column wavers and spreads, leaving a large black patch on the ground. Gr-r-r-rutt, gr-r-r-rutt from each, and the first advance is silenced for ever. But it is the French turn to suffer now, and shell after shell comes right amongst them, making their position much too hot for them. Some of their horses are knocked over, but as yet none of their men are hit. The shells, however, fall too thickly to be endured, and once more Noisseville was German.

Finding the Prussian fire becoming too warm, and that the French were being pushed back in the centre, Mr. Robinson says he went over to the most extreme right, hoping that by closing in upon the enemy there the French might even yet outflank them, and change the fortune of the day by creating a diversion in their rear. Crouching down on the ground he found a regiment of chasseurs-a-pied, ready to spring up in a moment if necessary. "They don't wait long, for the order comes to deploy in skirmishing order and advance. Hurrah! we are going forward; we shall win yet. Up comes, at a swinging pace, the twenty-fifth, and we rush together for the big villa with the large grounds there. Hurrah! we are first; its wall shelters us and the game begins. Battle all along the line goes the musketry; pop, pop, from the vineyards on our left goes the sharpshooters' quiet fire. There is a Prussian battery right in front of us, but we drive the men away from the guns. We are rushing forward, when all at once sounds the retreat. Good Heaven! what has happened? We had almost snatched the victory. One's heart almost stops suddenly still.

"The troops obey the sound, and sulkily retire. As we turn to come back we see an isolated patch of French soldiers out on the hill in front of us. Who they are, or what they do there, no one knows. It turns out to be a portion of the second corps, which, touching on the right of the third, had been forgotten both by the marshal and the general. Once it indeed was remembered, and two counter-orders reached it at the same moment, and they did not know which to obey, so they send back for *written* instructions, which never came. They remained in front of Flanville, having the honour of being the last men to retire from this useless slaughter, only reaching our lines fully an hour after every other man was within them. The Prussians advance, they establish themselves at their guns, and shell us horribly. All around us the shells drop, and I am suddenly awakened to the fact that I am between the two fires, and in comfortable killing distance from both of them. Action follows reflection rapidly, and I execute a strategic movement to the rear worthy of a French general. It was a retreat all along our line. Slowly we returned down the hill, and very sadly too. We established battery after battery; but we had given up the heights to the Prussians, and their fire was longer than ours. No sooner were we in position than their shells came plunging into us, and we had to draw back again. It was thus, little by little, that we returned towards Metz, and by mid-day we had lost all we took the night before. There, as we climbed the hill again, we came in sight of all those reserves massed on Saint Julien. There, too, we saw the grim old grey-towered chateau of Gromont, from which the marshal saw the fight. 'Beaten again from want of a general,' exclaims each one; and a good many fists are shaken towards Gromont.

"Thus sadly ended our last hopeful day at Metz. Never again had we any confidence in the military qualities of the commander-in-chief. We saw a movement commenced at daybreak, suspended until evening in view of the enemy. We saw a force sent out with divided councils. We saw the movement arrested when a night's march could have carried the position. We saw a force, weakened by a fair day's work and a long night's watch, left unsuccoured. We saw our victory snatched from us when, in spite of these disadvantages, we had almost grasped it: and the shock was too rude."

The Hon. C. A. Winn, who witnessed the engagement from the German side, corroborates the statements of Mr. Robinson in all main particulars, and says there is no doubt that as far as regarded increasing their lines, and progressing towards freedom, the French on the 31st gained all the ground they could have expected in the time they had to do it in; and when darkness made artillery useless, and the firing ceased, they found themselves in a fine position for carrying the main points of St. Barbe and Malroy by night assault. He has not the slightest doubt that Bazaine, but for his inaction, would have found himself and the greater part of his troops beyond the Prussian lines in the morning. He does not, however, believe that any advantage would have accrued to him; as once out in the open country with no baggage, in a famished district, his entire army would have soon fallen an easy prey to the combined Prussian corps, long before he could have reached Thionville.

END OF VOL. I.

Made in the USA
Lexington, KY
29 January 2017